Milena Minkova and Terence Tunberg

TEACHER'S MANUAL

LEVEL 1

Second Edition

LATIN FOR THE NEW MILLENNIUM
Series Information

LEVEL ONE

Student Text, Second Edition

Student Workbook, Second Edition

College Exercise Book, Levels 1 and 2

Teacher's Manual, Second Edition

Teacher's Manual for Student Workbook, Second Edition

ENRICHMENT TEXTS

From Romulus to Romulus Augustulus:
Roman History for the New Millennium

The Original Dysfunctional Family:
Basic Classical Mythology for the New Millennium

LEVEL TWO

Student Text, Second Edition

Student Workbook, Second Edition

Teacher's Manual, Second Edition

Teacher's Manual for Student Workbook, Second Edition

ENRICHMENT TEXTS

From Rome to Reformation:
Early European History for the New Millennium

The Clay-footed SuperHeroes:
Mythology Tales for the New Millennium

LEVEL THREE

Student Text

Teacher's Manual

ENRICHMENT TEXTS

Latin 3: Select Latin Enrichment Readings

ELECTRONIC RESOURCES

www.lnm.bolchazy.com

www.bolchazy.com/ebooks.aspx

Quia Question Bank

LATIN FOR THE NEW MILLENNIUM

Milena Minkova and Terence Tunberg

TEACHER'S MANUAL

Second Edition **LEVEL 1**

Bolchazy-Carducci Publishers, Inc.
Mundelein, Illinois USA

Series Editor: LeaAnn A. Osburn

SECOND EDITION
Volume Editor: Donald E. Sprague
Contributing Editors: Laurel Draper, Karen Lee Singh

FIRST EDITION
Volume Editors: Elisa C. Denja, LeaAnn A. Osburn
Contributing Editors: Laurie Haight Keenan, Karen Lee Singh, Donald E. Sprague, Rose Williams
Proofreader: Gary Varney
Cover Design & Typography: Adam Phillip Velez
Cover Illustration: Roman Forum © Bettmann/CORBIS

Latin for the New Millennium
Teacher's Manual, Level 1
Second Edition

Milena Minkova and Terence Tunberg

©2017 Bolchazy-Carducci Publishers, Inc.
All rights reserved
First edition published 2008

Bolchazy-Carducci Publishers, Inc.
1570 Baskin Road
Mundelein, Illinois 60060
www.bolchazy.com

Printed in the United States of America
2017
by United Graphics

ISBN 978-0-86516-809-1

CONTENTS

LIST OF ABBREVIATIONS vii

PREFACE ix

RESOURCE LIST xiii

INTRODUCTION 1

CHAPTER 1 11

CHAPTER 2 27

CHAPTER 3 43

REVIEW 1: CHAPTERS 1–3 59

CHAPTER 4 73

CHAPTER 5 87

CHAPTER 6 101

REVIEW 2: CHAPTERS 4–6 117

CHAPTER 7 135

CHAPTER 8 151

CHAPTER 9 167

REVIEW 3: CHAPTERS 7–9 187

CHAPTER 10 201

CHAPTER 11 221

CHAPTER 12 237

REVIEW 4: CHAPTERS 10–12 255

CHAPTER 13 269

CHAPTER 14 287

CHAPTER 15 303

REVIEW 5: CHAPTERS 13–15 319

CHAPTER 16 335

CHAPTER 17 353

CHAPTER 18 371

REVIEW 6: CHAPTERS 16–18 389

CHAPTER 19 407

CHAPTER 20 431

CHAPTER 21 449

REVIEW 7: CHAPTERS 19–21 467

ABBREVIATIONS

AF
Anglo-French

CL
Classical Latin

CPO
Classroom Presentation Options (e.g., black/green/white/smart board, overhead or LCD projector, PowerPoint® presentation, etc.)

LL
Late Latin

ME
Middle English

ML
Middle Latin

ODF
Original Dysfunctional Family (classical mythology enrichment text)

OE
Old English

OED
Online Etymology Dictionary

OF
Old French

OLD
Oxford Latin Dictionary

RRA
From Romulus to Romulus Augustulus (Roman history enrichment text)

SE
Student Edition

PREFACE

Latin for the New Millennium is designed as a comprehensive introduction not only to the Latin language and how it works but also to the Roman world, the cultural milieu in which the language flourished. The language and cultural elements are seamlessly woven together in the course of each chapter and then again examined in the review following every three chapters.

CHAPTER AND COURSE COMPONENTS

METHODOLOGICAL APPROACH

In writing *Latin for the New Millennium*, we have aimed at combining the best elements in the various methodologies for teaching Latin that have been commonly available until now. Modern methods of teaching Latin have been divided between two approaches: (1) the analytical or deductive method according to which students must learn rules and paradigms, and then reinforce the knowledge of these abstract principles by practice with texts and exercises; (2) the inductive or reading method that enables the student to read a text and to become aware of linguistic features (or rules) from the reading and study of the text. In *Latin for the New Millennium* we hope to have combined the advantages of each. In other words, we have striven to provide a path to a thorough and systematic knowledge of the structure of the language, the main advantage of the analytical method, together with a great deal of reading and activities related to reading that lead to a more intuitive grasp of the idiomatic qualities of the language, the main advantage of the reading method.

The layout of each chapter is the key to this combination, since the student begins each chapter with an extensive reading, and these initial passages contain, in a context understandable through induction and annotations, instances of every new element to be explored further in the same chapter. In the body of each chapter, after the introductory reading, these new elements are explained in a more analytic way, yet the explanations always refer the learner back to the reading—in ways that invite comparison with the initial passage.

CHAPTER READINGS

The principal readings in each chapter consist of passages adapted (to the level of knowledge presupposed for each chapter) from some of the most significant works of Latin literature. The introductions to each passage give considerable information about the cultural context in which each author wrote, and about the development of the Latin literary tradition. The order of the chapter readings is chronological. In Level 1, students begin with readings from Plautus and Terence and proceed through the centuries to the writings of Ammianus, Augustine, and Boethius. By completing the entire course contained in *Latin for the New Millennium*, students will gain an understanding of the entire patrimony of Latin and its effect on our culture. While Level 1 of *Latin for the New Millennium* focuses on the classic texts in Latin written by such great Roman authors as Vergil, Catullus, Cicero, and Ovid, Level 2 of the series centers on the huge and fundamental heritage of works written in Latin during the medieval, Renaissance, and early modern periods—a linguistic heritage that gave us our basic vocabulary in the national languages for telling time, medicine, the natural sciences, and the academic world. The cultural information that is found in these readings and their introductions is bolstered in both levels by the Review Exercises and supplementary material pertaining to mythology, Roman history, and important Latin sayings.

ORAL LATIN AND LATIN CONVERSATION

A person who gains an active facility in any language, in addition to a reading ability, is, in our view, more likely to progress quickly to a deep understanding of the language and the works written in it. Our experience indicates that a student who learns by using a language will probably not need to be reminded about forms and grammatical rules as often as a learner who lacks active practice. Therefore, in every chapter of *Latin for the New Millennium*, we have included a set of exercises that concentrate on an oral exchange between instructor and students. The oral exercises in *Latin for the New Millennium* can be completed without any extempore speaking ability on the part of the teacher. This is possible because the oral exercises are found only in the teacher's manual. Here not only are all the answers supplied, but every question is written out in full for the teacher, along with detailed instructions for each step of the exercise. The teacher needs only to follow the instructions and read each question aloud. The response must come from the learner.

GRAMMAR

Grammar is also a great help for acquiring a sophisticated understanding of any language, and especially a language like Latin, which is primarily studied today by people whose main goal is to read works of literature written in the original Latin language, works which were designed from the start for a cultivated audience. While we believe in the value of the reading method, and we know how active usage of a language can vastly improve and accelerate a student's learning of that language, we also recognize the utility of grammar. Therefore, while each chapter is rich in exercises and activities, we have taken care to provide explanations of all the grammar relevant to each chapter. The student who uses *Latin for the New Millennium* learns by actively using Latin, but is also asked to understand the structure of the language and apply that understanding in the exercises.

OTHER CHAPTER ELEMENTS

- ***Memorābile Dictū*** Each chapter features a famous saying, labeled ***Memorābile Dictū***, a Latin phrase that is so well known that it has became a proverb in many languages. Learning each famous saying will increase a student's understanding not just of Latin, but also of English. These sayings invite discussion of their meaning and how they relate to the modern world and students' experiences. As students' facility in Latin grows, this discussion could be conducted in Latin.

- **Reading Vocabulary** All the new vocabulary in the reading passage at the beginning of each chapter is explained by copious notes. Students need not be required to learn the vocabulary that faces the reading passage. A unique feature of the **Reading Vocabulary** is that not all the verbs show in print their pronoun subject. For example, if the sentence in the reading is "*Cicero Terentiam videt,*" *videt* in the **Reading Vocabulary** would have as its definition "sees" rather than "he sees." This has been done to avoid the common beginner's mistake of translating the sentence as "Cicero he sees Terentia." On the other hand, if the sentence were to read "*Terentiam videt,*" *videt* would be defined "he sees." This unique feature gradually disappears as students learn more about verbs and become more accustomed to reading Latin.

- **Vocabulary to Learn and Derivatives Exercises** Some (but not all) of these new words are repeated in the **Vocabulary to Learn** for each chapter and students should be directed to learn these. The traditional form of writing vocabulary words is followed in the **Vocabulary to Learn**: principal parts are listed from the second chapter on and nouns show the nominative and genitive singular and gender from the start. The **Vocabulary to Learn** is followed by **Derivative Exercises**. Students who carefully learn all of the **Vocabulary to Learn** will quickly acquire a vocabulary based on words most commonly encountered in classical literary texts, and in the **Derivative Exercises** they will be exposed to English words based on Latin and thus bolster their vocabulary in English. Each chapter concludes with a list of words derived from the Latin words in the chapter's **Vocabulary to Learn**. The student text presents the list grouped like the vocabulary list by part of speech. The teacher's manual provides notes on the derivatives. Teachers are encouraged to use this material for their presentations on the derivatives. Each chapter of the student workbook for *LNM* 1 includes an exercise that tests the English derivatives presented in that chapter. In addition, the teacher's manual contains background notes for Latin words in the chapter reading that are not words that students must learn. Teachers may draw on these notes as appropriate for a given class.

DIALOGUES ON DAILY LIFE

In the latter part of each chapter of Level 1, readers will find a dialogue labeled **Talking** in which a group of modern students are the participants. The same group of students is featured in every chapter, and they encounter many of the typical situations that young people experience in modern daily life. All the necessary vocabulary is explained, so the users of *Latin for the New Millennium*, if they so wish, may conduct simple Latin conversations like those in the model dialogues. These dialogues have been designed for the benefit of those teachers who are especially interested in making use of the oral element of language learning in their classes, and who want to introduce a colloquial element to the Latin their students learn. This colloquial element can become a bridge between the lives of modern students and the thoughts of the ancient, medieval, or Renaissance authors who wrote in Latin—a bridge constructed of the same basic language, Latin.

VISUAL LEARNING

The Latin language and Roman culture have not only inspired writers throughout the ages and influenced modern life but have also left their legacy in the visual arts. Throughout the text, reproductions of paintings, drawings, sculptures, and other artworks demonstrate how Roman historical events and the tales of the gods and goddesses have inspired artists through the ages. *Latin for the New Millennium* presents an abundance of images of archaeological sites, buildings, objets d'art, and artifacts carefully chosen to represent the ethnic and geographic diversity that marked the Roman world. These full-color illustrations represent a visual panorama of the Roman world and support the written word in pictorial form, thus stimulating the imagination and memory for a more vibrant recollection of the text's content. Teachers are strongly encouraged to mine the illustrations as though a documentary of the Roman world and its later influence.

REVIEW COMPONENTS

After each set of three chapters there is a Review and supplementary readings.

REVIEW EXERCISES

The Review provides additional exercises to help the students give continued attention to the material in each unit. The review also includes a summary list of all the **Vocabulary to Learn** found in the chapters of each unit. This section features even more material to help the student understand Latin literature and its heritage today.

Preface • xi

CLASSICAL MYTHOLOGY

A passage on mythology, entitled **Considering the Classical Gods**, introduces the reader to stories about the Greek and Roman gods and heroes. A related passage in Latin about the gods reinforces the Latin lessons of the three chapters.

ASPECTS OF ROMAN LIFE

An English background essay, called **Connecting with the Ancient World**, discusses an important aspect of Roman daily life which connects to related material presented in the three chapters preceding the review.

EXPLORING ROMAN AND MODERN LIFE

Scholars from various universities throughout the United States graciously agreed to provide short essays that reflect upon the role that Latin and its culture play in our modern lives. The titles of these essays always start with the word **Exploring**.

MĪRĀBILE AUDĪTŪ

Each review ends with a section called *Mīrābile Audītū* that presents a series of Latin quotations, mottoes, phrases, or abbreviations currently used in English. The three supplementary essays and the *Mīrābile Audītū* section are designed to elicit classroom discussion about similarities and differences between the world of the Romans and America in the twenty-first century.

––––––––––––––––––

Milena Minkova wrote the Introduction; Chapters 1, 2, 3, 5, 7, 9, 13, 14, 17, 18, 20; Reviews 1, 3, 5, 6, and 7; the glossaries; and the appendices. Terence Tunberg wrote the Preface; Chapters 4, 6, 8, 10, 11, 12, 15, 16, 19, 21; and Reviews 2 and 4. Both authors have benefited, throughout the composition of the textbook, from continuous mutual advice and support.

M. M. and T. T.
2008

––––––––––––––––––

Join the *Latin for the New Millennium* Teachers' Lounge for access to electronic resources featuring a test bank, maps, worksheets, reading comprehension quizzes, and more. Go to the *LNM* web pages at www.bolchazy.com and find the Teachers' Lounge under "Support."

RESOURCE LIST

EDITORS' NOTE

We have attempted to assemble a comprehensive, representative resource list paying special attention to those topics or areas often less familiar. To that end, we provide an especially larger listing for the Late Empire, Early Christianity, and Middle Ages section. By no means is this resource list exhaustive. Teachers are encouraged to share titles they have found useful through the www.lnm.bolchazy.com website.

LATIN DICTIONARIES

Albert, S. *Imaginum vocabularium Latinum*. Saarbrücken: Societas Latina, 1998.

Egger, C. *Lexicon nominum locorum*. Rome: Libreria Editrice Vaticana, 1977.

———. *Lexicon nominum virorum et mulierum*. Rome: Studium, 1957.

———, ed. *Lexicon recentis Latinitatis*. 2 Vols. Rome: Libreria Editrice Vaticana, 1992–1997.

Lewis, Charlton T., and Charles Short. *A Latin Dictionary*. Rev. ed. New York: Oxford University Press, 1956.

New College Latin and English Dictionary, The. 3rd ed. Edited by John C. Traupman. New York: Bantam Books, 2007.

Oxford Latin Dictionary. 2nd ed. Edited by P. G. W. Glare et al. New York: Oxford University Press, 2012.

Smith, William, and Theophilus D. Hall. *Smith's English-Latin Dictionary*. Reprinted from the 1871 American Book Company edition, *A Copious and Critical English-Latin Dictionary*, with a new foreword by Dirk Sacré. Wauconda, IL: Bolchazy-Carducci Publishers, 2000.

LATIN GRAMMAR

Allen, J. H., and J. B. Greenough. *Allen and Greenough's New Latin Grammar*. Edited by Anne Mahoney. Newburyport, MA: Focus Publishing/R. Pullins, 2001.

Andresian, Anna. *Looking at Latin: A Grammar for Pre-College*. Wauconda, IL: Bolchazy-Carducci Publishers, 2006.

Bennett, Charles E. *New Latin Grammar*. 1908. Reprint, Wauconda, IL: Bolchazy-Carducci Publishers, 2006.

Gildersleeve, Basil L., and Gonzalez Lodge. *Gildersleeve's Latin Grammar*. 3rd ed. 1895. Reprint, Wauconda, IL: Bolchazy-Carducci Publishers, 2003.

Goldman, Norma, and Ladislas Szymanski. *English Grammar for Students of Latin*. 3rd ed. Ann Arbor, MI: Olivia and Hill Press, 2004.

Humphreys, James P. *Graphic Latin Grammar*. 1961. Reprint, Wauconda, IL: Bolchazy-Carducci Publishers, 2002.

Woodcock, E. C. *A New Latin Syntax*. 1957. Reprint, Wauconda, IL: Bolchazy-Carducci Publishers, 2005.

Young, Nicholas. *Instant Answers: A Quick Guide for Advanced Students*. Elmhurst, IL: L and L Enterprises, 2006.

LATIN COMPOSITION

Bennett, Charles E. *New Latin Composition*. 1912. Reprint, Wauconda, IL: Bolchazy-Carducci Publishers, 1996.

Minkova, Milena. *Introduction to Latin Prose Composition*. Wauconda, IL: Bolchazy-Carducci Publishers, 2007. First published 2001 by Wimbledon Publishing Co.

Minkova, Milena, and Terence Tunberg. *Readings and Exercises in Latin Prose Composition: From Antiquity to the Renaissance*. Newburyport, MA: Focus Publishing/R. Pullins, 2004.

———. *Answer Key to Readings and Exercises in Latin Prose Composition: From Antiquity to the Renaissance*. Newburyport, MA: Focus Publishing/R. Pullins, 2004.

Mountford, James F., ed. *Bradley's Arnold Latin Prose Composition*. Rev. ed. Wauconda, IL: Bolchazy-Carducci Publishers, 2006.

North, M. A., and A. E. Hillard. *Latin Prose Composition*. Reprint, Wauconda, IL: Bolchazy-Carducci Publishers, 1995.

———. *Key to Latin Prose Composition*. Reprint, Wauconda, IL: Bolchazy-Carducci Publishers, 1995.

LATIN LITERATURE

Albrecht, Michael von. *A History of Roman Literature: From Livius Andronicus to Boethius*. Leiden: Brill Academic Publishers, 1997.

Duff, J. Wight. *A Literary History of Rome*. 3rd ed. London: Ernest Benn, 1960.

Grant, Michael. *Greek and Latin Authors 800 B.C.–A.D. 1000*. New York: H. W. Wilson, 1980.

Howatson, C. M., and Ian Chilvers, eds. *The Oxford Companion to Classical Literature*. 3rd ed. Oxford: Oxford University Press, 2011.

IJsewijn, Jozef. *Companion to Neo-Latin Studies, Part I: History and Diffusion of Neo-Latin Literature*. Supplementa Humanistica Lovaniensia, 5. 2nd ed. Leuven: Leuven University Press, 1990.

IJsewijn, Jozef, and Dirk Sacré. *Companion to Neo-Latin Studies, Part II: Literary, Linguistic, Philological and Editorial Questions*. Supplementa Humanistica Lovaniensia, 14. 2nd ed. Leuven: Leuven University Press, 1998.

Rose, H. J. *A Handbook of Latin Literature*. 1954. Reprint, Wauconda, IL: Bolchazy-Carducci Publishers, 1996.

GENERAL LANGUAGE LEARNING AND METHODOLOGIES

Armstrong, Thomas. *Multiple Intelligences in the Classroom*. 3rd ed. Alexandria, VA: Association for Supervision and Curriculum Development, 2009.

Cook, Vivian. *Second Language Learning and Teaching*. 4th ed. London: Edward Arnold, 2008.

Gardner, Howard. *Intelligence Reframed: Multiple Intelligences for the 21st Century*. New York: Basic Books, 2000.

Kessler, Carolyn, ed. *Cooperative Language Learning: A Teacher's Resource Book*. Englewood Cliffs, NJ: Prentice Hall Regents, 1992.

Krashen, Stephen. *Principles and Practice in Second Language Acquisition*. New York: Pergamon Press, 1982.

Larsen-Freeman, Diane. *Techniques and Principles of Language Teaching*. 3rd ed. Oxford: Oxford University Press, 2011.

Oxford, Rebecca L. *Language Learning Strategies: What Every Teacher Should Know*. New York: Newbury House, 1990.

Pinker, S. *The Language Instinct*. New York: Harper Perennial, 1994.

Reid, Joy, ed. *Understanding Learning Styles in the Second Language Classroom*. Upper Saddle River, NJ: Prentice Hall, 1998.

Sparks, Richard L., Kay Fluharty, Leonore Ganschow, and Sherwin Little. "An Exploratory Study on the Effects of Latin on the Native Language Skills and Foreign Language Aptitude of Students with and without Learning Disabilities." *Classical Journal* 91 (1995): 165–184.

LATIN PEDAGOGY

Ancona, Ronnie, ed. *A Concise Guide to Teaching Latin Literature*. Norman, OK: University of Oklahoma Press, 2007.

Ball, Robert. *Reading Classical Latin: A Reasonable Approach*. 2nd ed. Lawrence, KS: Coronado Press, 1987.

Breindel, Ruth L. *De Discendi Natura: Learning Styles in the Teaching of Latin*. Oxford, OH: American Classical League TMRC, 2007.

Burns, Mary Ann T., and Joseph O'Connor. *The Classics in American Schools*. Atlanta, GA: Scholars Press, 1987.

Davis, Sally. *Latin in the American Schools*. Atlanta, GA: Scholars Press, 1991.

Distler, Paul. *Teach the Latin, I Pray You*. Wauconda, IL: Bolchazy-Carducci Publishers, 2001.

Gascoyne, Richard, et al. *Standards for Classical Language Learning*. Oxford, OH: American Classical League TMRC, 1997.

Gruber-Miller, John, ed. *When Dead Tongues Speak*. New York: Oxford University Press, 2006.

Hoyos, B. Dexter. *Latin: How to Read It Fluently: A Practical Manual*. Amherst, MA: Classical Association of New England, 1997.

LaFleur, Richard A. *Latin for the 21st Century: From Concept to Classroom*. Glenview, IL: Scott Foresman-Addison Wesley, 1998.

Salerno, Dorsey Price. *Latin in Motion*. Oxford, OH: American Classical League TMRC, 1985.

Standards for Classical Language Learning. Oxford, OH: American Classical League TMRC, 1997.

Strasheim, Lorraine A. *Total Physical Response*. Amherst, MA: Classical Association of New England, 1987.

Sweet, Waldo. *Latin: A Structural Approach*. Rev. ed. Ann Arbor, MI: University of Michigan Press, 1966.

CLASSROOOM AIDS

Amery, Heather. *First Thousand Words in Latin*. Edited by Mairi Mackinnon. London, UK: Usborne Books, 2008.

Couch, C. C., and Teddy Irwin. *Latin Verbs Rock!* Audio CD. Nashville, TN: Sound Inventions, 2006.

———. *Lyrical Latin: Learning Latin through Music.* Audio CD. Nashville, TN: Sound Inventions, 2004.

Curtis, William D. *Periculum Latinum: Latin Jeopardy.* Vol. 1. Oxford, OH: American Classical League TMRC, n.d.

———. *Periculum Latinum Secundum: Latin Jeopardy.* Vol. 2. Oxford, OH: American Classical League TMRC, n.d.

Demuth, Jocelyn. *Mendax: A Latin Card Game.* Wauconda, IL: Bolchazy-Carducci Publishers, 2003.

DuBose, Gaylan. *Farrago Latina.* With a list of resources by Judith Lynn Sebesta. Wauconda, IL: Bolchazy-Carducci Publishers, 1997.

Hanlin, Jayne, and Beverly Lichtenstein. *Learning Latin through Mythology.* Cambridge: Cambridge University Press, 1991.

Latin Tactic Grams. Atlanta, GA: World of Reading, n.d.

LUDI (at the Circus Maximus). Produced by Discere Ltd. Oxford, OH: American Classical League TMRC, 1989.

Mythites. Oxford, OH: American Classical League TMRC, 2003.

Osburn, LeaAnn. *A Latin Activity Book.* Elmhurst, IL: L and L Enterprises, 2000.

———. *Latin Crossword Puzzle Book.* Elmhurst, IL: L and L Enterprises, 1999.

———. *Latin Verbs Rock! Exercise Book.* Elmhurst, IL: L and L Enterprises, 2007.

———. *Lyrical Latin: A Teacher Resource Manual.* Elmhurst, IL: L and L Enterprises, 2004.

———. *22 Lively Latin Activities.* Elmhurst, IL: L and L Enterprises, 2005.

Sheikh-Miller, Jonathan. *Latin Words Sticker Book.* Tulsa, OK: EDC Publishing, 2006.

Wansbrough, M. B. *A Mundus Latinus Mystery.* 3 vols. Hamilton, Ontario: Tralco Educational Services, 2004.

ORAL LATIN

Abernathy, Faye, Jill Crooker, Margaret Curran, and David Perry. *The Development of Oral Skills in Latin with Visuals. A Supplementary Guide to the Syllabus, Latin for Communication.* Draft Copy. Albany: New York State Education Department, 1995.

Albert, S. *Cottidie Latine loquamur.* Saarbrücken: Societas Latina, 1987.

Allen, W. Sidney. *Vox Latina: A Guide to the Pronunciation of Classical Latin.* 2nd ed. New York: Cambridge University Press, 1989.

Capellanus, G. *Latin Can Be Fun.* Souvenir Press, 1997.

Daitz, Stephen G., ed. *The Living Voice of Latin.* Performed by Robert P. Sonkowsky. Madison, CT: Jeffrey Norton Publishing, 1984.

———. *The Pronunciation and Reading of Classical Latin: A Practical Guide.* DVD. Madison, CT: Jeffrey Norton Publishing, 1984.

Egger, C. *Latine discere iuvat.* Rome: Libreria Editrice Vaticana, 1982.

Latin Aloud: Audio AP Selections from Vergil, Catullus, Ovid, Cicero, and Horace. Performed by Robert P. Sonkowsky. CD-ROM. Wauconda, IL: Bolchazy-Carducci Publishers, 2007.

McCarthy, Thomas. *Nunc Loquamur: Guided Conversations for Latin.* 2nd ed. Newburyport, MA: Focus Publishing/R. Pullins, 2009.

Sweet, Waldo E. *Words of Wisdom from the Ancients: 1000 Latin Proverbs*. CD-ROM. Wauconda, IL: Bolchazy-Carducci Publishers, 2000.

Traupman, John. *Conversational Latin for Oral Proficiency*. 4th ed. *Audio Conversations*. Performed by Mark Robert Miner et al. Audio CDs. Wauconda, IL: Bolchazy-Carducci Publishers, 2006.

LATIN THROUGH MUSIC

Boynton, Sandra. *Grunt: Pigorian Chant*. Audio CD. New York: Workman Publishing, 1997.

Couch, C. C., and Teddy Irwin. *Carmina Popularia: Well-Known Songs in Latin*. Audio CD. Wauconda, IL: Bolchazy-Carducci Publishers, 2004.

———. *Latin Verbs Rock!* Audio CD. Nashville, TN: Sound Inventions, 2006.

———. *Lyrical Latin: Learning Latin through Music*. Audio CD. Nashville, TN: Sound Inventions, 2004.

———. *O Abies: Christmas Carols in Latin*. Audio CD. Wauconda, IL: Bolchazy-Carducci Publishers, 2003.

Kaldis, Cynthia. *Latin Music through the Ages*. 1991. Reprint. Text, Audio CD, and download. Wauconda, IL: Bolchazy-Carducci Publishers, 1999.

Meyer, Vernon L., trans. *Sing Along in Latin*. Oxford, OH: American Classical League TMRC, n.d.

Minkova, Milena, and Terence Tunberg. *Mater Anserina: Poems in Latin for Children*. Audio CD. Limited ed. Newburyport, MA: Focus Publishing/R. Pullins, 2006.

Orff, Carl. *Carmina Burana*. 1937. Enhanced reprint with critical text, introduction, and translation by Judith Lynn Sebesta. Wauconda, IL: Bolchazy-Carducci Publishers, 1996.

Osburn, LeaAnn. *Latin Verbs Rock! Exercise Book*. Elmhurst, IL: L and L Enterprises, 2006.

———. *Lyrical Latin: Learning Latin through Music: A Teacher Resource Guide*. Elmhurst, IL: L and L Enterprises, 2004.

Schlosser, Franz, trans. *Latine Cantemus*. Wauconda, IL: Bolchazy-Carducci Publishers, 1996.

Schola Cantans. Composed by Jan Novak, performed by *Voces Latinae*. Audio Cassette. Wauconda, IL: Bolchazy-Carducci Publishers, 1998.

YOUNG CHILDREN LATIN READERS

Bolchazy, Marie Carducci. "I Am Reading Latin" Series. Translated by Mardah B. C. Weinfield; narrated by James W. Chochola. Audio CD. Wauconda, IL: Bolchazy-Carducci Publishers, 2004.

———. *How Many Animals? Quot Animalia?* Translated by Mardah B. C. Weinfield. Wauconda, IL: Bolchazy-Carducci Publishers, 2002.

———. *What Color Is It? Quo Colore Est?* Translated by Mardah B. C. Weinfield. Wauconda, IL: Bolchazy-Carducci Publishers, 2002.

———. *What Will I Eat? Quid Edam?* Translated by Mardah B. C. Weinfield. Wauconda, IL: Bolchazy-Carducci Publishers, 2002.

———. *Who Loves Me? Quis Me Amat?* Translated by Mardah B. C. Weinfield. Wauconda, IL: Bolchazy-Carducci Publishers, 2002.

Williams, Rose. "I Am Reading Latin Stories" Series. Wauconda, IL: Bolchazy-Carducci Publishers, 2008.

———. *Octavus Octopus: Octavus the Octopus*. Wauconda, IL: Bolchazy-Carducci Publishers, 2008.

———. *Rena Rhinoceros: Rena the Rhinoceros*. Wauconda, IL: Bolchazy-Carducci Publishers, 2008.

———. *Taurus Rex: King Bull*. Wauconda, IL: Bolchazy-Carducci Publishers, 2008.

———. *Ursus et Porcus: The Bear and the Pig*. Wauconda, IL: Bolchazy-Carducci Publishers, 2008.

EASY READERS: BEGINNING LATIN

Barrett, Bonnie. *Nursery Rhymes*. Oxford, OH: American Classical League TMRC, n.d.

Chidley, Matt, and Brandon Morris. *Cinderella*. Oxford, OH: American Classical League TMRC, n.d.

Leaf, Munro. *Ferdinandus Taurus*. Translated by Elizabeth Hadas. Boston, MA: David R. Godine, Publisher, 2000.

Minkova, Milena, and Terence Tunberg. *Mater Anserina: Poems in Latin for Children*. Audio CD. Limited ed. Newburyport, MA: Focus Publishing/R. Pullins, 2006.

Noe, David C. *Tres Mures Caeci*. Purcellville, VA: Patrick Henry Press, 2005.

Tres Ursi. Adapted by Hanna Hutchinson, translated by LeaAnn Osburn. First edition in Latin. Cincinnati, OH: Another Language Press, 1995.

Williams, Rose. *Tres Porculi*. Elmhurst, IL: L and L Enterprises, 2006.

———. *The Young Romans*. Wauconda, IL: Bolchazy-Carducci Publishers, 2007. First published 2003 by Wimbledon Classics.

———. *The Young Romans: Teacher's Edition*. Wauconda, IL: Bolchazy-Carducci Publishers, 2007. First published 2003 by Wimbledon Classics.

———. *Vergil for Beginners*. Wauconda, IL: Bolchazy-Carducci Publishers, 2006.

GRADED READERS

Barocas, Victor. *Fairy Tales in Latin: Fabulae Mirabiles*. Edited by Susan Schearer. New York: Hippocrene Books, 2000.

Cobban, J. M., and R. Coleburn. *Civis Romanus*. 1967. Reprint, Wauconda, IL: Bolchazy-Carducci Publishers, 2003.

Dunlop, Philip. *Short Latin Stories*. Cambridge: Cambridge University Press, 1987.

Groton, Anne H., and James M. May. *Thirty-Eight Latin Stories: Designed to Accompany Wheelock's Latin*. 5th ed. Wauconda, IL: Bolchazy-Carducci Publishers, 1995.

Hillard, A. E., and C. G. Botting. *Latin Readings for Review*. With additions by Donald H. Hoffman. 1961. Reprint, Wauconda, IL: Bolchazy-Carducci Publishers, 2001.

Sweet, Waldo E. *Lectiones Primae*. 1966. Reprint, Wauconda, IL: Bolchazy-Carducci Publishers, 1996.

———. *Lectiones Secundae*. 1970. Reprint, Wauconda, IL: Bolchazy-Carducci Publishers, 1992.

Williams, Rose. *Lectiones de Historia Romana: A Roman History for Early Latin Study*. Wauconda, IL: Bolchazy-Carducci Publishers, 2001.

———. *Teacher's Notes for Lectiones de Historia Romana*. Wauconda, IL: Bolchazy-Carducci Publishers, 2001.

FAMILIAR CHILDREN'S BOOKS IN LATIN

Church, Francis Pharcellus. *"Yes, Virginia, There Is a Santa Claus" . . . in Latin: Vere Virginia, Sanctus Nicolaus est!* Translated by Walter Sauer and Hermann Wiegand. Wauconda, IL: Bolchazy-Carducci Publishers, 2001.

Milne, A. A. *Winnie the Pooh* [Winnie Ille Pu]. Rev. ed. Translated by Alexander Lenard. New York: Penguin, 1991.

Rowling, J. K. *Harry Potter and the Philosopher's Stone* [Harrius Potter et Philosophi Lapis]. Translated by Peter Needham. New York and London: Bloomsbury, 2003.

———. *Harry Potter and the Chamber of Secrets* [Harrius Potter et Camera Secretorum]. Translated by Peter Needham. Bloomsbury: New York and London, 2007.

Saint-Exupéry, Antoine de. *The Little Prince* [Regulus]. Translated by Augustus Haury. New York: Harcourt, 2001.

Seuss, Dr. *Cattus Petasatus: The Cat in the Hat in Latin*. Translated by Jennifer Morrish Tunberg and Terence O. Tunberg. Wauconda, IL: Bolchazy-Carducci Publishers, 2000.

———. *Green Eggs and Ham in Latin: Virent Ova! Viret Perna!!* Translated by Jennifer Morrish Tunberg and Terence O. Tunberg. Wauconda, IL: Bolchazy-Carducci Publishers, 2003.

———. *Quomodo invidiosulus nomine Grinchus christi natalem abrogaverit* [*How the Grinch Stole Christmas in Latin*]. Translated by Jennifer Morrish Tunberg with Terence O. Tunberg. Wauconda, IL: Bolchazy-Carducci Publishers, 1998.

Silverstein, Shel. *The Giving Tree in Latin: Arbor Alma*. Translated by Jennifer Morrish Tunberg and Terence O. Tunberg. Wauconda, IL: Bolchazy-Carducci Publishers, 2002.

White, E. B. *Tela Charlottae* [Charlotte's Web]. Translated by Bernice L. Fox. New ed. New York: Harper Collins, 1991.

ETYMOLOGY AND VOCABULARY

Adeleye, Gabriel G. *World Dictionary of Foreign Expressions*. With Kofi Acquah Dadzie. Edited by Thomas J. Sienkewicz and James McDonough. Wauconda, IL: Bolchazy-Carducci Publishers, 1999.

Ayres, Donald M. *English Words from Latin and Greek Elements*. 2nd ed. Tucson, AZ: University of Arizona Press, 2005.

Ayto, John. *Dictionary of Word Origins*. Reprint ed. New York: Arcade Publishing, 2011.

Beard, Henry. *X-Treme Latin: All the Latin You Need to Know for Survival in the 21st Century*. New York: Penguin Group, 2005.

Dictionary of Latin Words and Phrases. Edited by James Morwood. New York: Oxford University Press, 1998.

Dominik, William J., ed. *Words and Ideas*. Wauconda, IL: Bolchazy-Carducci Publishers, 2002.

———. *Words and Ideas: Answer Key*. Wauconda, IL: Bolchazy-Carducci Publishers, 2006.

Ehrlich, Eugene. *Amo, Amas, Amat and More*. New York: Harper and Row, 1987.

Heimbach, Elizabeth. *Latin Everywhere, Everyday: A Latin Phrase Workbook*. Wauconda, IL: Bolchazy-Carducci Publishers, 2004.

———. *Latin Everywhere, Everyday: A Latin Phrase Workbook: Teacher's Manual*. Performed by James Chochola. Compact disks. Wauconda, IL: Bolchazy-Carducci Publishers, 2005.

Janson, Tore. *The Natural History of Latin*. Translated by Merethe D. Sorensen and Nigel Vincent. Oxford and New York: Oxford University Press, 2007.

Krill, Richard. *Greek and Latin in English Today*. Book and two cassettes. 1990. Reprint, Wauconda, IL: Bolchazy-Carducci Publishers, 2003.

Masciantonio, Rudolph. *Build Your English Word Power with Latin Numbers*. Wauconda, IL: Bolchazy-Carducci Publishers, 1997.

———. *Build Your English Word Power with Latin Numbers: Teacher's Manual*. Wauconda, IL: Bolchazy-Carducci Publishers, 1997.

Morwood, James, and Mark Warman. *Our Greek and Latin Roots*. 2nd ed. Cambridge: Cambridge University Press, 2013.

O'Mara, Lesley, ed. *Which Way to the Vomitorium? Vernacular Latin for All Occasions*. Translated by Rose Williams. New York: Thomas Dunne Books, 1999.

Oxford Dictionary of English Etymology. Edited by C. T. Onions with G. W. S. Friedrichsen and R. W. Burchfield. New York: Oxford University Press, 1966.

Stone, Jon R. *Latin for the Illiterati*. 2nd ed. New York: Routledge, 2009.

MYTHOLOGY

Bierlein, J. F. *Parallel Myths*. New York: Ballantine Books, 1994.

Bolton, Lesley. *The Everything Classical Mythology Book*. 2nd ed. Peabody, MA: Adams Media Corporation, 2010.

Children's Books on Ancient Greek and Roman Mythology: An Annotated Bibliography. Compiled by Antoinette Brazouski and Mary J. Klatt. Westport, CT: Greenwood Press, 1994.

Chiron Dictionary of Greek and Roman Mythology, The. Translated by Elizabeth Burr. 1st English ed. New York: Continuum International Publishing Group, 1994.

Colakis, Marianthe, and Mary Joan Masello. *Classical Mythology and More: A Reader Workbook*. Wauconda, IL: Bolchazy-Carducci Publishers, 2007.

Couch, Malcolm. *Greek and Roman Mythology*. New York: Michael Friedman Publishing Group, 1998.

D'Aulaire, Ingri, and Edgar Parin D'Aulaire. *D'Aulaires' Book of Greek Myths*. New York: Doubleday, 1962.

Fleischman, Paul. *Dateline Troy*. Somerville, MA: Candlewick Press, 2006.

Gardner, Jane. *Roman Myths*. Austin: University of Texas Press, 1993.

Grant, Michael, and John Hazel. *Who's Who in Classical Mythology*. London: Routledge Press, 2002.

Grimal, Pierre. *The Dictionary of Classical Mythology*. Translated by A. R. Maxwell-Hyslop. 1996. Reprint, Malden, MA: Blackwell Publishing, 2001.

Harris, Stephen L., and Gloria Patzner. *Classical Mythology: Images and Insights*. 6th ed. Mountain View, CA: Mayfield Publishing Company, 2011.

Homeric Hymns. Translated by Diane Raynor. Updated edition. Berkeley and Los Angeles: University of California Press, 2014.

Kirkwood, G. M. *A Short Guide to Classical Mythology*. 1959. Reprint, Wauconda, IL: Bolchazy-Carducci Publishers, 2003.

Lowe, Cheryl, and Leigh Lowe. *D'Aulaires' Greek Myth Student Guide*. Louisville, KY: Memoria Press, 2006.

———. *D'Aulaires' Greek Myth Teacher Guide*. Louisville, KY: Memoria Press, 2006.

Mayerson, Philip. *Classical Mythology in Literature, Art, and Music*. Newburyport, MA: Focus Publishing/R. Pullins, 2001.

Morford, Mark P. O., and Robert J. Lenardon. *Classical Mythology*. 10th ed. New York: Oxford University Press, 2013.

Ovid. *Metamorphoses*. Translated by A. D. Melville. New York: Oxford University Press, 1998.

Russell, William F. *Classic Myths to Read Aloud*. New York: Crown Publications, 1989.

Vergil's Aeneid: Hero, War, Humanity. Translated by G. B. Cobbold. Wauconda, IL: Bolchazy-Carducci Publishers, 2005.

Williams, Rose. *Gods and Other Odd Creatures*. Austin, TX: CicadaSun Publishing, 2008.

———. *The Labors of Aeneas: What a Pain It Was to Found the Roman Race*. Wauconda, IL: Bolchazy-Carducci Publishers, 2003.

———. *The Original Dysfunctional Family: Basic Classical Mythology for the New Millennium*. Wauconda, IL: Bolchazy-Carducci Publishers, 2008.

ROMAN HISTORY

Bagnell, Nigel. *The Punic Wars*. New York: St. Martin's Press, 1990.

Beckett, Gilbert à. *The Comic History of Rome*. 1852. Reprint, Wauconda, IL: Bolchazy-Carducci Publishers, 1996.

Boardman, John, Jasper Griffin, and Oswyn Murray, eds. *Oxford History of the Roman World*. Oxford and New York: Oxford University Press, 1991.

Boatwright, Mary T., Daniel J. Gargola, and Richard J. A. Talbert. *A Brief History of the Romans*. 2nd ed. New York: Oxford University Press, 2013.

Connolly, Peter. *Greece and Rome at War*. London: Greenhill Books, 2006.

Constable, Nick. *Historical Atlas of Ancient Rome*. New York: Facts on File, 2003.

Cornell, Tim, and John Mathews. *Atlas of the Roman World*. New York: Facts on File, 1986.

Creighton, Mandell. *A Primer History of Rome*. 1855. Reprint, Wauconda, IL: Bolchazy-Carducci Publishers, 2001.

Goldsworthy, Adrian. *The Fall of Carthage: The Punic Wars 265–146 BC*. London: Cassell, 2000.

Haaren, John H., and A. B. Poland. *Famous Men of Rome*. Louisville, KY: Memoria Press, 2006.

Holland, Thomas. *Rubicon*. New York: Doubleday, 2003.

Jenkyns, Richard, ed. *The Legacy of Rome: A New Appraisal*. Oxford: Oxford University Press, 1992.

Kamm, Anthony. *Julius Caesar: A Life*. New York: Routledge, 2006.

Lowe, Cheryl, and Leigh Lowe. *Famous Men of Rome: Student Guide*. 2nd ed. Louisville, KY: Memoria Press, 2006.

Matyszak, Philip. *The Sons of Caesar: Imperial Rome's First Dynasty*. London: Thames and Hudson, 2006.

Mellor, Ronald, and Marni McGee. *The Ancient Roman World*. New York: Oxford University Press, 2004.

Oxford Classical Dictionary. 4th ed. Edited by Simon Hornblower and Anthony Spawforth. Oxford and New York: Oxford University Press, 2012.

Oxford Dictionary of the Classical World. Edited by John Roberts. New York: Oxford University Press, 2005.

Scarre, Chris. *Chronicle of the Roman Emperors*. 3rd ed. London: Thames and Hudson, 2007.

———. *The Penguin Historical Atlas of Ancient Rome*. New York: Penguin Putnam Inc., 1995.

Strauss, Barry. *The Death of Caesar*. New York: Simon and Schuster, 2015.

Ward-Perkins, Bryan. *The Fall of Rome*. Oxford and New York: Oxford University Press, 2005.

Williams, Rose. *Cicero the Patriot*. Wauconda, IL: Bolchazy-Carducci Publishers, 2004.

———. *Cicero the Patriot: Teacher's Manual.* Wauconda, IL: Bolchazy-Carducci Publishers, 2004.

———. *From Romulus to Romulus Augustulus: Roman History for the New Millennium.* Wauconda, IL: Bolchazy-Carducci Publishers, 2008.

———. *Once Upon the Tiber: An Offbeat History of Rome.* Wauconda, IL: Bolchazy-Carducci Publishers, 2007. First published 2002 by Wimbledon Classics.

Woolf, Greg, ed. *Cambridge Illustrated History of the Roman World.* Cambridge: Cambridge University Press, 2003.

ROMAN CULTURE AND DAILY LIFE

Adkins, Lesley, and Roy Adkins. *Dictionary of Roman Religion.* New York: Oxford University Press, 2000.

———. *Handbook to Life in Ancient Rome.* New York: Oxford University Press, 1994.

Allan, Tony. *Life, Myth, and Art in Ancient Rome.* Los Angeles: J. Paul Getty Trust Publications, 2005.

Apicius. *Cookery and Dining in Imperial Rome.* Edited by Joseph Dommers Vehling. New York: Dover, 1977.

Baker, Alan. *The Gladiator: The Secret History of Rome's Warrior Slaves.* New York: St. Martin's Press, 2006.

Baker, Charles, and Rosalie Baker. *The Classical Companion.* Peterborough, NH: Cobblestone Publishing, 1988.

Bonner, S. F. *Education in Ancient Rome from the Elder Cato to the Younger Pliny.* London: Methuen, 1977.

Bradley, Keith. *Slavery and Society at Rome.* Cambridge: Cambridge University Press, 1994.

Brucia, Margaret A., and Gregory Daugherty. *To Be a Roman: Topics in Roman Culture.* Wauconda, IL: Bolchazy-Carducci Publishers, 2007.

Buchanan, David. *Roman Sport and Entertainment.* London: Longman, 1976.

Carcopino, Jérôme. *Daily Life in Ancient Rome.* 2nd ed. New Haven and London: Yale University Press, 2003.

Casson, Lionel. *Travel in the Ancient World.* New ed. Baltimore: Johns Hopkins University Press, 1994.

———. *Libraries in the Ancient World.* New Haven, CT: Yale University Press, 2001.

Clackson, James, and Geoffrey Horrocks. *The Blackwell History of the Latin Language.* Cambridge: Blackwell Publishing, 2007.

Clarke, J. R. *Houses of Roman Italy 100 B.C.– A.D. 250.* Berkeley and Los Angeles: University of California Press, 1991.

Croom, A. T. *Roman Clothing and Fashion.* UK: Tempus Publishing, 2000.

D'Ambra, Eve. *Roman Art.* Cambridge and New York: Cambridge University Press, 1998.

———. *Roman Women.* Cambridge and New York: Cambridge University Press, 2007.

Goldsworthy, Adrian. *The Complete Roman Army.* London: Thames and Hudson, 2003.

Grant, Leigh. *Rome: A Fold-Out History of Ancient Civilization.* New York: Black Dog and Levanthal Publishers, 2005.

Grant, Mark. *Roman Cookery: Ancient Recipes for Modern Kitchens.* Rev. ed. London: Serif Publishers, 2008.

Hamey, L. A., and J. A. Hamey. *The Roman Engineers.* Cambridge: Cambridge University Press, 1981.

Harris, H. A. *Sport in Greece and Rome.* Ithaca, NY: Cornell University Press, 1972.

Herbert, Kevin. *Roman Imperial Coins*. Wauconda, IL: Bolchazy-Carducci Publishers, 1996.

Hodge, Peter. *The Roman Army*. White Plains, NY: Longman, 1984.

———. *Roman Family Life*. UK: Longman, 1984.

———. *The Roman House*. Rev. ed. White Plains, NY: Longman, 1976.

———. *Roman Towns*. Rev. ed. White Plains, NY: Longman, 1977.

———. *Roman Trade and Travel*. White Plains, NY: Longman, 1978.

Hopkins, Keith, and Mary Beard. *The Colosseum*. Cambridge, MA: Harvard University Press, 2005.

Humez, Alexander, and Nicholas Humez. *A, B, C Et Cetera: The Life & Times of the Roman Alphabet*. Boston, MA: David Gordon Publisher, 1985.

Hyland, Ann. *Equus: The Horse in the Roman World*. New Haven, CT: Yale University Press, 1990.

Jacobelli, Luciana. *Gladiators at Pompeii*. Los Angeles: J. Paul Getty Trust Publications, 2004.

James, Simon. *Ancient Rome*. Rev. ed. Eyewitness Books. New York: Alfred A. Knopf, 2004.

Jones, J. M. *A Dictionary of Ancient Coins*. London: Seaby, 1990.

Mannix, Daniel P. *The Way of the Gladiator*. New York: ibooks, 2001.

Massey, Michael. *Roman Religion*. White Plains, NY: Longman, 1984.

———. *Women in Ancient Greece and Rome*. New York: Cambridge University Press, 1986.

Olivová, V. *Sports and Games in the Ancient World*. London: Orbis Publishing, 1984.

Paoli, Ugo Enrico. *Rome: Its People, Life and Customs*. Translated by R. D. Macnaghten. New York: Longman, 1963.

Piggott, S. *The Druids*. Rev. ed. London: Thames and Hudson, 1985.

Sims, Lesley. *Roman Soldier's Handbook*. London: Usborne Books, 2006.

Solway, Andrew. *Rome: In Spectacular Cross-Section*. Oxford: Oxford University Press, 2004.

Stavely, E. S. *Greek and Roman Voting and Elections*. Ithaca, NY: Cornell University Press, 1972.

Treggiari, S. *Roman Marriage: Iusti Coniuges from the Time of Cicero to the Time of Ulpian*. Oxford: Clarendon Press, 1993.

Wallace, Rex E. *Introduction to Wall Inscriptions from Pompeii and Herculaneum*. Wauconda, IL: Bolchazy-Carducci Publishers, 2005.

Webster, G. *The Roman Imperial Armies of the First and Second Centuries A.D.* 3rd ed. London: A and C Black, 1998.

Westlake, Susan. *The Development of the Roman Alphabet*. Oxford, OH: American Classical League TMRC, 1992.

Yavetz, Z. *Slaves and Slavery in Ancient Rome*. New Brunswick, NJ: Transaction Books, 1988.

ROMAN ARCHAEOLOGY, ARCHITECTURE, AND ART

Aicher, Peter J. *Guide to the Aqueducts of Ancient Rome*. Wauconda, IL: Bolchazy-Carducci Publishers, 1995.

———. *Rome Alive: A Source Guide to the Ancient City*. 2 vols. Wauconda, IL: Bolchazy-Carducci Publishers, 2004.

Amery, Colin, and Brian Curran Jr. *The Lost World of Pompeii*. Los Angeles: J. Paul Getty Trust Publications, 2002.

Augenti, Andrea, ed. *Art and Archeology of Rome*. New York: Riverside Book Company, 2000.

Boardman, John. *Oxford History of Classical Art*. Oxford: Oxford University Press, 1997.

Campbell, Ann. *Roman Art and Architecture*. Rev. ed. Boulder, CO: Alarion Press, 1999.

Coarelli, Fillipo. *Rome and Environs: An Archeological Guide*. Translated by James J. Clauss and Daniel P. Harmon. Berkeley and Los Angeles: University of California Press, 2008.

Connolly, Peter. *Pompeii*. New York: Oxford University Press, 1990.

Corbishley, Mike. *Illustrated Encyclopedia of Ancient Rome*. Los Angeles: J. Paul Getty Trust Publications, 2004.

Davis, John T., and Deborah C. Wood. *Monumenta Romana Nostra*. Slide lectures, complete set. 1995. Revised, Wauconda, IL: Bolchazy-Carducci Publishers, 1997.

———. *Monumenta Romana Nostra: Roman Baths*. Slide lecture. 1995. Revised, Wauconda, IL: Bolchazy-Carducci Publishers, 1997.

———. *Monumenta Romana Nostra: The Forum in Rome and the Provinces*. Slide lecture. 1995. Revised, Wauconda, IL: Bolchazy-Carducci Publishers, 1997.

———. *Monumenta Romana Nostra: The Roman Basilica*. Slide lecture. 1995. Revised, Wauconda, IL: Bolchazy-Carducci Publishers, 1997.

———. *Monumenta Romana Nostra: The Roman Forum*. Slide lecture. 1995. Revised, Wauconda, IL: Bolchazy-Carducci Publishers, 1997.

———. *Monumenta Romana Nostra: The Roman Temple*. Slide lecture. 1995. Revised, Wauconda, IL: Bolchazy-Carducci Publishers, 1997.

Deiss, Joseph Jay. *Herculaneum: Italy's Buried Treasure*. 2nd ed., revised and updated. New York: Harper Collins, 1989.

de Franciscus, A. *Pompeii: Monuments Past and Present*. Los Angeles: J. Paul Getty Trust Publications, 2000.

D'Espouy, Hector, ed. *Greek and Roman Architecture in Classic Illustrations*. Mineola, NY: Dover Publications, 1999.

Dickison, Sheila K., and Judith P. Hallett, eds. *Rome and Her Monuments*. Wauconda, IL: Bolchazy-Carducci Publishers, 2000.

Heintze, Helga von. *Roman Art*. New York: Universe Books, 1971.

Lewis, Jon E., ed. *Mammoth Book of Eyewitness Ancient Rome*. New York: Carroll and Graf, 2003.

Ling, Roger. *Roman Painting*. Cambridge: Cambridge University Press, 1991.

Lovell, Isabel. *Stories in Stone from the Roman Forum*. Rockville, MD: Wildside Press, 2007.

Macaulay, David. *City: A Story of Roman Planning and Construction*. Boston, MA: Houghton Mifflin, 1974.

MacDonald, William L. *The Architecture of the Roman Empire: An Urban Appraisal*. New Haven, CT: Yale University Press, 1988.

MacKendrick, Paul. *The Mute Stones Speak: The Story of Archeology in Italy*. 2nd ed. New York: W. W. Norton, 1984.

Millard, Anne. *Welcome to Ancient Rome*. Edited by Jane Chisolm. London: Usborne Publishing, 1987.

Staccioli, R. A. *Ancient Rome: Monuments Past and Present*. Los Angeles: J. Paul Getty Trust Publications, 2000.

———. *The Roads of the Romans*. Los Angeles: J. Paul Getty Trust Publications, 2004.

Walker, Susan. *Roman Art*. Cambridge: Harvard University Press, 1991.

Wheeler, Mortimer. *Roman Art and Architecture*. 4th ed. New York: Praeger Publishers, 1969.

Winkes, Rolf. *Classical Collection: Roman Paintings and Mosaics*. Providence, RI: Museum of Art. Rhode Island School of Design, 1982.

LATE EMPIRE, EARLY CHRISTIANITY, AND MIDDLE AGES

Augustine. *Confessions*. Oxford World's Classics, translated by Henry Chadwick. Reprint, New York: Oxford University Press, 1998.

———. *Augustine: The City of God against the Pagans*. Translated by R. W. Dyson. Cambridge Texts in the History of Political Thought. Cambridge: Cambridge University Press, 1998.

———. *Augustine: Political Writings*. Translated by E. M. Atkins and Robert J. Dodaro. Cambridge Texts in the History of Political Thought. Cambridge: Cambridge University Press, 2001.

Barbero, Alessandro. *The Day of the Barbarians: The Battle That Led to the Fall of the Roman Empire*. Translated by John Cullen. New York: Walker and Company, 2007.

Barnes, Timothy D. *Athanasius and Constantius: Theology and Politics in the Constantian Empire*. Cambridge, MA: Harvard University Press, 1993.

Boethius. *The Consolation of Philosophy*. Translated by Victor Watts. Rev. ed. London: Penguin Books, 1999.

Boin, Douglas R. *Coming Out Christian in the Roman World: How the Followers of Jesus Made a Place in Caesar's Empire*. New York: Bloomsbury Press, 2015.

Bowersock, G. W., and Peter Brown. *Late Antiquity: A Guide to the Post Classical World*. Harvard University Press Reference Library. Cambridge, MA: Belknap Press, 1999.

Bowman, Alan, Averil Cameron, and Peter Garnsey, eds. *The Crisis of Empire, AD 193–337*. 2nd ed. Volume 12. *The Cambridge Ancient History*. Cambridge: Cambridge University Press, 2005.

Brown, Peter. *Augustine of Hippo: A Biography*. Rev. ed. Berkeley and Los Angeles: University of California Press, 2000.

———. *The World of Late Antiquity AD 150–750*. New York: W. W. Norton, 1989.

Cameron, Averil. *The Later Roman Empire. A.D. 284–430*. Cambridge, MA: Harvard University Press, 1993.

Cameron, Averil, Bryan Ward-Perkins, and Michael Whitby, eds. *Late Antiquity: Empire and Successors, A.D. 425–600*. Volume 14. The Cambridge Ancient History. Cambridge: Cambridge University Press, 2001.

Cameron, Averil, and Peter Garnsey, eds. *The Late Empire, A.D. 337–425*. Volume 13. The Cambridge Ancient History. Cambridge: Cambridge University Press, 1997.

Chadwick, Henry. *The Church in Ancient Society: From Galilee to Gregory the Great*. Oxford: Oxford University Press, 2001.

Corbishley, Mike. *The Middle Ages: Cultural Atlas for Young People*. 3rd ed. New York: Facts on File, 2007.

Doran, Robert. *Birth of a Worldview: Early Christianity in its Jewish and Pagan Context*. Lanham, MD: Rowman and Littlefield, 1999.

Edwards, Mark. *Constantine and Christendom: The Oration to the Saints. The Greek and Latin Accounts of the Discovery of the Cross. The Edict of Constantine to Pope Silvester*. Liverpool: Liverpool University Press, 2003.

Ferguson, Everett, ed. *Encyclopedia of Early Christianity*. 2nd ed. London: Garland Publishing, 1999.

Godfrey, A. W., ed. *Medieval Mosaic: A Book of Medieval Latin Readings*. Wauconda, IL: Bolchazy-Carducci Publishers, 2003.

Grant, Michael. *Constantine the Great: The Man and His Times*. New York: Charles Scribner's Sons, 1994.

———. *The Fall of the Roman Empire*. New York: Charles Scribner's Sons, 1997.

———. *The Collapse and Recovery of the Roman Empire*. London and New York: Routledge, 1999.

Harrison, F. E., ed. *Millennium: A Latin Reader A.D. 374–1374*. Reprint, Wauconda, IL: Bolchazy-Carducci Publishers, 2001.

Heather, Peter. *The Fall of the Roman Empire: A New History of Rome and the Barbarians*. New York: Oxford University Press, 2007.

Holmes, George. *The Oxford History of Medieval Europe*. Oxford: Oxford University Press, 2001.

Hopkins, Keith. *A World Full of Gods: Pagans, Jews and Christians in the Roman Empire*. London: Weidenfeld and Nicolson, 1999.

Howarth, Patrick. *Attila King of the Huns: Man and Myth*. New York: Barnes & Noble Books, 1995.

Jones, Terry. *Barbarians*. London: BBC Books, 2006.

Kulikowski, Michael. *Rome's Gothic Wars: From the Third Century to Alaric*. Cambridge: Cambridge University Press, 2007.

Lee, A. D., ed. *Pagans and Christians in Late Antiquity: A Sourcebook*. London: Routledge, 2000.

MacMullen, Ramsay, and Eugene N. Lane. *Paganism and Christianity, 100–425 C.E.: A Sourcebook*. Minneapolis: Fortress Press, 1992.

Mantello, Frank, and Arthur G. Rigg. *Medieval Latin: An Introduction and Bibliographical Guide*. Washington, DC: The Catholic University of America Press, 1996.

McEvedy, Colin. *The New Penguin Atlas of Medieval History*. Rev. ed. New York: Penguin Group, 1992.

Newman, Paul B. *Daily Life in the Middle Ages*. Jefferson, NC: McFarland and Company, 2001.

Smith, Jonathan Z. *Drudgery Divine: On the Comparison of Early Christianities and the Religions of Late Antiquity*. Chicago: University of Chicago Press, 1990.

Stambaugh, John E., and David Balch. *The New Testament in its Social Environment*. Philadelphia: Westminster Press, 1986.

Thompson, A. E. *The Huns*. Oxford: Blackwell Publishing, 1999.

Todd, Malcolm. *The Early Germans*. 2nd ed. Malden, MA: Blackwell, 2004.

Wells, Colin. *Sailing from Byzantium: How a Lost Empire Shaped the World*. New York: Bantam Dell, 2006.

Williams, Rose. *The Lighter Side of the Dark Ages*. London and New York: Anthem Press, 2006.

Wolfram, Herwig. *History of the Goths*. Translated by Thomas J. Dunlap. Berkeley and Los Angeles: University of California Press, 1988.

———. *The Roman Empire and Its Germanic Peoples*. Rev. ed. Translated by Thomas J. Dunlap. Berkeley and Los Angeles: University of California Press, 2005.

Young, Frances, Lewis Ayres, and Andrew Louth, eds. *The Cambridge History of Early Christian Literature*. Cambridge: Cambridge University Press, 2004.

CLASSICAL PERSPECTIVES

Highet, Gilbert. *The Classical Tradition*. New York: Oxford University Press, 1957.

Kopff, E. Christian. *The Devil Knows Latin: Why America Needs the Classical Tradition*. Wilmington, DE: ISI Books, 1999.

Maybury, Richard J. *Ancient Rome: How It Affects You Today.* 2nd ed. Placerville, CA: Bluestocking Press, 2004.

Murphy, Cullen. *Are We Rome?* New York: Houghton Mifflin, 2007.

Simmons, Tracy Lee. *Climbing Parnassus: A New Apologia for Greek and Latin.* 2nd ed. Wilmington, DE: ISI Books, 2007.

MAPS, POSTERS, AND CHARTS
Available from American Classical League TMRC. Hamilton, OH.

Map of Roman Empire; Map of Roman Italy; Rome, Central Archeological Area; Roma Archaica.

Circus Maximus, Colosseum; Constitution Preamble; Latin Abbreviations; Latin Phrases in Common Use; Legal Terms; Pantheon; Pompeii; Promotional Posters: Latin Is.

Derivative Tree Chart; Loan Word Chart; Romance Language Chart; Skeleton Chart.

Available from L and L Enterprises, Phoenix, AZ.

Ancient Civilization Wall Map (small and large size).

Using Latin Phrases; The Fabulous Five; Latin Promotional Mini-posters; Pater Noster; Pledge of Allegiance; Roman Scenes and Proverbs; Seven Hills of Rome; Remembering the Cases.

Available from Aims International Books, Cincinnati, OH.

Quo Modo Sentis Hodie Poster.

ADDITIONAL ITEMS
Available from Bolchazy-Carducci Publishers, Mundelein, IL.

Latin Buttons.

Toga Beats

Available from American Classical League TMRC. Hamilton, OH.

Latin-related CDs, DVDs, tapes, software; coins; greeting cards; games; accessories and jewelry; mimeographs; historical novels; Latin readers; and Junior Classical League items.

Available from L and L Enterprises, Phoenix, AZ.

Latin knowledge cards, British Museum book of postcards of Ancient Greece and of Rome.

Latin-related activity books; buttons; coloring books; key chain tags; note cards; origami projects; pencils; puzzle books; rulers; stampers; stickers; stuffed animals; tattoos; tote bags; and T-shirts.

MISCELLANEOUS
Available from American Classical League TMRC. Hamilton, OH.

2006 Updated Survey of Audio-Visual Materials and Textbooks in the Classics.
2007 Edition of ACL Software Directory for the Classics.

WEBSITES
For a regularly updated list of website resources, check www.lnm.bolchazy.com.

PROFESSIONAL ORGANIZATIONS

Most of these organizations offer a journal that teachers will find beneficial. Consult the organization's website to learn more.

American Classical League (ACL)

American Classical League: Teaching Materials and Resource Center (TMRC)

ACL Sponsored Activities:

   Junior Classical League

   National Committee for Latin and Greek

   National Greek Exam

   National Junior Classical League

   National Latin Exam

   National Senior Classical League

   National Mythology Exam

American Council on the Teaching of Foreign Languages (ACTFL)

Archaeological Institute of America (AIA)

Classical Association of Canada

Classical Association of New England (CANE)

Classical Association of the Atlantic States (CAAS)

Classical Association of the Middle West and South (CAMWS)

Classical Association of the Pacific Northwest (CAPN)

Classical Association of the Southwestern United States (CASUS)

Computer Assisted Language Instruction Consortium (CALICO)

Joint Association of Classical Teachers (JACT)

Society for Classical Studies (SCS)

Vergilian Society

In addition, many states and cities have classics-related organizations.

INTRODUCTION (PP. XXV–XXXVI)

PAGE XXV
Standard 4.1

EDITOR'S NOTE
The comprehension questions and answers as well as some of the **Teaching Tips** and **Teacher by the Way** notations in this teacher's manual were written by Elisa C. Denja, LeaAnn A. Osburn, Karen Lee Singh, and Donald E. Sprague, classics editors/educators at Bolchazy-Carducci Publishers.

HOW TO USE THIS BOOK
Please note that the correlations to the Standards for Classical Language Learning are printed just below page numbers from the student text. They correspond to the related activities or information presented on a given page or pages in the student text. For example, a set of standards is provided for the two pages devoted to the Latin reading with its background note, reading vocabulary list, and comprehension questions. The aural/oral activities that appear only in the teacher's manual are optional exercises that meet standard 1.2. As national standards are revised, see www.lnm.bolchazy.com for updated correlations.

Eisemann Communication assisted in preparing the correlations of *Latin for the New Millennium* with the national standards. For an overview of the standards themselves and the correlations, please consult www.bolchazy.com.

TEACHING TIP
The teacher may choose to use the picture of the Etruscan couple on this page and the brief mention of the Etruscan alphabet to open a discussion on what role the Etruscans played in early Roman times. Students may be directed to pp. xxxiv–xxxv (SE) to find Etruria on the map.

TEACHING TIP
The teacher may wish to discuss with the students the term "Romance languages." Many modern languages come from the language used by the ancient Romans: French, Italian, Portuguese, Spanish, Romanian, etc. Romansch (spoken by the descendants of the Raetians and one of the four official languages of Switzerland) is also derived from Latin.

TEACHER BY THE WAY
Based on archaeological evidence, it appears that Etruscan women were an important part of the social structure. Often the names of both mother and father were placed on funerary inscriptions. The freedom of women within society is likewise apparent on monuments where they can be seen reclining with their husbands on the same couch, attending games, and having a place of honor in the tomb itself. Notice the affectionate pose of the couple in the illustration on p. xxv (SE). Clearly married love was valued in Etruscan society and family life was important.

Tombs also provide evidence for the style of Etruscan homes. Some of these features were borrowed by the Romans, especially the central hall and three rooms at the back. This type of house was known at Pompeii as well as at Rome, according to Vitruvius, author of *Dē architectūrā*.

TEACHING TIP

The teacher may wish to have students read an English translation of Livy's traditional account of Tanaquil, wife of Tarquinius Priscus, the fifth king of Rome. The independence of Etruscan women is evident in this tale. Her behavior is the antithesis of the ideas of womanly decorum held by the Romans.

PAGE XXVI

TEACHING TIP

Students will enjoy singing the English "alphabet" song, replacing the English letter names with the Latin letter names. Students may be instructed to clap once where there is no Latin letter name (e.g., "J") equivalent to the English one.

TEACHING TIP

The teacher may choose to display any Latin words (a list is provided below for the teacher's convenience) and instruct the students to spell out the word using the Latin letter names. The students may become curious to know what the Latin words mean. Definitions are given below.

- *pars* – part
- *nox* – night
- *ruber* – red
- *ēgī* – I have done
- *familia* – family
- *carō* – flesh
- *dēcernō* – I decide
- *herba* – plant
- *Kalendae* – Kalends (first day of the month)
- *quoque* – also
- *timor* – fear
- *Pȳthia* – Pythia (name of Apollo's priestess)
- *iēcī* – I threw
- *fēlīx* – happy
- *ignis* – fire
- *mūtō* – I change

PAGE XXVII

Standards 1.2, 4.1

COMPREHENSION QUESTIONS AND ANSWERS FOR PAGES XXV–XXVII (SE)

Reproducible versions of the questions alone are available at **www.lnm.bolchazy.com**.

1. Trace the roots of the Latin alphabet from its beginnings forward.

   North-Semitic alphabet eleventh century BCE, Phoenician alphabet, Greek alphabet, Etruscan alphabet, Latin alphabet.

2. Which two letters in the English alphabet are not found in the Latin alphabet?

   W and J.

3. When does the letter J begin to appear in Latin?

   During the Middle Ages and the Renaissance.

4. Look at the Latin inscription on the sign from Pompeii (on the right of p. xxvii [SE]). Find at least three Latin words. List an English word you believe is based on the Latin word.

   duovir — virile, virility
   colonia — colonial, colony
   honoris — honor
   spectacula — spectacular, spectacle
   perpetvom — perpetual, perpetuity

PAGE XXVIII

TEACHING TIP
Students may want to know the English meanings of the Latin words in Exercises 1 and 2. The definitions are provided for the teacher's convenience.

▶ EXERCISE 1 ANSWERS

1. I nourish
2. student
3. frog
4. I scrape
5. I hold
6. I seek
7. smooth
8. seat
9. journey
10. I fear
11. I strive
12. wonderful
13. I approve
14. note
15. I put
16. gift
17. I howl
18. wolf
19. shoemaker
20. use
21. syllable
22. Pyrene (a name)

▶ EXERCISE 2 ANSWERS

1. summer
2. I make level
3. carriage
4. I praise
5. or
6. forecourt
7. or if
8. walls
9. and not
10. penalty
11. neither
12. Carthaginian
13. bronze
14. poem
15. ah
16. to this

Introduction • 3

PAGE XXIX

TEACHER BY THE WAY
Historical evidence can be cited for reading the first syllable of "*magnus*" as naturally long, but other evidence suggests it is naturally short. Thus in some grammar books, such as the one by Gildersleeve and Lodge, we find this syllable marked as long, but in other books as in *LNM* it is treated as short.

TEACHING TIP
The students may also wish to find out the meanings of the Latin words in Exercise 3. The definitions are provided for the teacher's convenience.

▶ EXERCISE 3 ANSWERS

1. food
2. I take
3. a heap
4. I grow
5. bud, jewel
6. a Gaul
7. glory
8. Zeus
9. library
10. philosophy
11. a girdle
12. theory
13. kidney bean
14. paper
15. I hide
16. old

PAGE XXX

TEACHING TIP
The teacher may wish to provide the students with some practice on syllables and stress accent. Here are some examples with the answers included for the teacher's convenience.

Underline the ultima in each word.

1. leg<u>ō</u>
2. rē<u>gis</u>
3. imperā<u>tor</u>

Underline the penult in each word.

1. <u>cau</u>sa
2. pū<u>nī</u>tum
3. ar<u>mā</u>tus

Underline the antepenult in each word.

1. <u>vul</u>nerō
2. <u>te</u>tigī
3. <u>sub</u>lātum

4 • Latin for the New Millennium: Teacher's Manual, Level 1

Underline the penult if it is long.
1. p<u>ō</u>nō
2. spē<u>lun</u>ca
3. pauperis

Underline the syllable that will receive the stress accent in each word.
1. ō<u>rā</u>culum
2. pe<u>tī</u>tum
3. cōn<u>stan</u>tia
4. ex<u>stīnc</u>tum
5. <u>vul</u>neris
6. <u>so</u>litus

PAGE XXXI
Standards 2.2, 3.1, 3.2, 4.1, 4.2

TEACHING TIP
Given the passage about the bathhouse on this page and the picture from Bath, England, the teacher may wish to open a discussion about baths during Roman times. The use of the *calidārium*, *frīgidārium*, *tepidārium*, and *sūdārium* may be explained by the teacher, and students may be encouraged to learn and/or pronounce these words.

TEACHER BY THE WAY
Baths were often constructed on locations having hot or mineral springs, such as Bath in England and Bāiae, a resort town on the Bay of Naples.

Modern Bath in Roman times was named after the Celtic goddess of healing, Sulis. In the first century, her shrine was taken over by the Romans and she was identified with the goddess Minerva. The site was then known as *Aquae Sulis Minerva*. In a temple relief she is represented with a Medusa-like head and a mustache!

The spa contained a great bath (73 ft. by 29 ft.) and three other swimming pools: the *calidārium* (hot bath), *tepidārium* (warm bath), and *frīgidārium* (cold bath). In the second century the spring was enclosed within a wooden barrel-vaulted building that housed these three pools. Hot air baths were fueled by coal fires. A constant flow of water was directed to the pools through lead pipes, which still function today.

Archaeological excavations have revealed many sacred votive offerings, curse tablets, and innumerable coins at the bottom of the springs. The curse tablets, written in Latin, heaped curses on anyone suspected of wrongdoing. The ancient tradition of throwing coins accompanied by a wish still prevails today in Rome at the Trevi Fountain where tourists/visitors do the same.

More information on bath complexes in Rome can be found on pp. 478–479 of this teacher's manual.

PAGE XXXII

Standards 2.1, 3.1, 3.2

TEACHING TIP
The teacher may wish to instruct the students to find the Tiber River, which is pictured here, on the map on pp. xxxiv–xxxv (SE).

COMPREHENSION QUESTIONS AND ANSWERS FOR PAGES XXXII–XXXIII (SE)

Reproducible versions of the questions alone are available at **www.lnm.bolchazy.com**.

1. Who were the legendary founders of Rome?
   Romulus and Remus.

2. According to legend, in what year was Rome founded?
   753 BCE.

3. Over the course of the monarchic period, how many kings ruled Rome?
   Seven.

4. What event occurred in 509 BCE?
   The beginning of the Roman Republic (with two consuls in charge).

5. What is the term associated with the two leaders of the Republic?
   Consul.

6. Which two leaders oversaw Rome's shift from a republic to a principate?
   Julius Caesar and Octavian/Augustus.

7. What major activity associated with empire-building took place during the principate?
   Territorial expansion.

8. Name two developments that characterized the late empire.
   Severe economic problems, internal political unrest, and/or frequent invasion by the Germanic tribes.

9. Describe Diocletian's response to the troubles of the empire.
   Diocletian divided the empire into two halves, the Eastern and Western empires, in order to make ruling the empire more manageable.

10. Explain the origin of the term "vandalism."
    The fifth-century invasion and pillaging of Rome by the tribe known as the Vandals, who occupied the Roman province of North Africa, led to the term "vandalism" meaning wanton destruction.

11. Describe Latin's role in the centuries after 476 CE.

    Latin flourished as the major literary language in the Western Roman Empire and was spread to non-Romanized places like Ireland, Scandinavia, and the New World.

TEACHING TIP
The teacher may ask the students to find the dates mentioned on this page in the timeline on pp. 405–408 (SE).

PAGE XXXIII
Standards 2.1, 3.1
RRA 1

TEACHING TIP
The teacher may instruct the students to locate Byzantium/Constantinople, discussed here in the second paragraph, on the map on pp. xxxiv–xxxv (SE).

TEACHING TIP
The teacher may ask the students to find the dates mentioned on this page in the timeline on pp. 405–408 (SE).

HOW TO USE THIS BOOK AND ITS ENRICHMENT TEXTS

Two enrichment texts are available for use with this book: *The Original Dysfunctional Family* (abbreviated ODF) and *From Romulus to Romulus Augustulus* (abbreviated RRA). RRA will be particularly useful in order to help students keep the time periods of the authors and of the events the authors wrote about straight in their minds. Chapter title pages will include, when appropriate, a notation on what chapter of RRA the teacher may wish to assign.

TEACHING TIP
The teacher may wish to assign Chapter 1 of the Roman history enrichment text *From Romulus to Romulus Augustulus* at this point.

COMPREHENSION QUESTIONS AND ANSWERS FOR PAGES XXXIII–XXXVI (SE)

Reproducible versions of the questions alone are available at **www.lnm.bolchazy.com**.

1. Whom did the Romans consider the father of Latin literature?
   Ennius.

2. What was Ennius's most famous work? Its subject matter?
   Annālēs was an epic poem about Rome's early history.

Introduction • 7

3. What famous Latin saying means "Carthage must be destroyed"?
   Carthāgō dēlenda est.

4. Who is the author of that saying?
   Cato the Elder/Cato the Censor.

5. When was Carthage said to have been destroyed?
   146 BCE, at the end of the Third Punic War.

PAGE XXXIV
Standard 3.1

TEACHING TIP
Ask students the English equivalent of countries such as *Britannia* and *Germānia* and the English equivalent of the cities *Neāpolis* and *Athēnae*.

TEACHING TIP
Additional reproducible worksheets, morphology charts, and their associated answer keys, related to this material, are available for download at www.lnm.bolchazy.com.

- **Map Work – Pages xxxiv–xxxv (SE)**
- **Maps and Geography – Pages xxxiv–xxxv (SE)**

PAGE XXXVI

TEACHING TIP
Students may be encouraged to find the city of Carthage, mentioned in the second paragraph, on the map on pp. xxxiv–xxxv (SE).

TEACHER BY THE WAY
Although the works of Ennius have been preserved only in fragments (about a thousand lines), he had a great influence on subsequent poets such as Vergil. Quotable quotes include:

- a test of friendship: *Amīcus certus in rē incertā cernitur* (A friend in need is a friend indeed);
- an application of wisdom to life: *Quī ipse sibi sapiēns prōdesse nequit nēquīquam sapit* (A man who himself is wise but unable to be useful to himself is wise for nothing);
- the famous description of Fabius Maximus: *Ūnus homō nōbīs cūnctandō restituit rem* (One man by delaying restored the state for us);
- and the line on Manius Curius: *Quem nēmō ferrō potuit superāre nec aurō* (Whom no one was able to defeat either by sword or by gold).

We also have preserved for us the example of excessive alliteration that has given rise to much laughter in Latin classrooms over the years: *Ō Tite tūte Tatī tibi tanta, tyranne, tulistī!* "O Titus Tatius you tyrant (all vocative), you brought to yourself such great (troubles)"—translated in context, which plays off the more literal ". . . you took/acquired for yourself such great things."

On the other hand, he composed his own epitaph, in which his high esteem among Romans proved to be prescient:

nēmō mē lacrumīs decōret neu funera flētū
faxit. Cūr? Volitō vivos per ōra virum.

(Let no one honor me with tears, or make a funeral pyre by weeping.
Why? I fly living through the mouths of men.)

TEACHER BY THE WAY

Plutarch's *Life of Cato* is a good source of snappy quotations attributed to this statesman, soldier, and author. For example, while discussing the power of women, he said: "All other men rule their wives; we rule all other men, and our wives rule us." Attempting to persuade the Roman people to forego a distribution of grain, he began his speech by saying, "It is a hard matter to argue with the belly, since it has no ears." And to a tribune who had been accused of using poison and was trying to pass a useless bill, he said, "I know not which is worse, to drink your mixtures or to enact your bills."

CHAPTER 1 (PP. 1–13)

GRAMMAR IN LANGUAGE FACTS

Parts of Speech; Nouns: Number, Gender, Case (Nominative and Accusative); First Declension Nouns

PAGE 1
Standards 1.1, 2.1
RRA 2 and 3

HOW TO USE THIS BOOK
The grammatical and syntactical topics that will be presented in each chapter of this book are listed at the top of the chapter title page.

HOW TO USE THIS BOOK
The illustration on each chapter's title page presents a visual introduction to the Latin reading passage that will follow. Teachers may choose to discuss the illustration in order to provide the context for the reading the students will encounter on the next page. As students' facility in Latin grows, this discussion could be conducted in Latin.

HOW TO USE THIS BOOK
On each chapter title page the phrase *Memorābile Dictū* ("A memorable thing to say") will be found. Below there will be a famous phrase, quotation, abbreviation, or motto in Latin that will connect these words to the topics in the chapter. These phrases often serve as springboards to discussion. As students' facility in Latin grows, this discussion could be conducted in Latin.

MEMORĀBILE DICTŪ VOCABULARY
populus, populī, *m.* – people

–que – and

senātus, senātūs, *m.* – Senate

TEACHER BY THE WAY
Rubens painted this picture of Romulus and Remus from 1615 to 1616 during what is called the Baroque period of art. The man approaching from the rear is Faustulus. The reclining figure is the god of the river Tiber. Ovid's *Metamorphōsēs* informed and inspired Rubens's mythological paintings.

HOW TO USE THIS BOOK AND ITS ENRICHMENT TEXTS

Two enrichment texts are available for use with this book: *The Original Dysfunctional Family* (abbreviated ODF) and *From Romulus to Romulus Augustulus* (abbreviated RRA). RRA will be particularly useful in order to help students keep the time periods of the authors and of the events the authors wrote about straight in their mind. Chapter title pages will include, when appropriate, a notation about what chapter of RRA the teacher may wish to assign.

PAGE 2
Standards 1.1, 2.2

TRANSLATION OF LATIN PASSAGE
Romulus and Remus

Mars is a god. Mars loves Rhea Silvia. And so Rhea Silvia has two sons: Romulus and Remus. Amulius locks up Rhea Silvia in chains. Amulius puts Romulus and Remus into the water. A she-wolf walks to the water. The she-wolf cares for (takes good care of) Romulus and Remus well and loves (them). Romulus and Remus grow up. Afterward (later) Romulus and Remus build Rome.

HOW TO USE THIS BOOK

Above each Latin reading passage, information is presented in English. This prereading provides background information about the author and establishes the context of the passage the students will read.

TEACHER BY THE WAY
The teacher may wish to introduce the class to the traditional abbreviations of AD (which stands for the Latin phrase *Annō Dominī*, "in the year of our Lord") and BC (which stands for the English phrase "Before Christ"). These older abbreviations continue to be used, but this book employs the abbreviations BCE (Before the Common Era) and CE (Common Era).

TEACHING TIP
Instruct the students to locate Alba Longa on the map on pp. xxxiv–xxxv (SE). When using the **Teaching Tips** for map work found throughout the text, teachers are encouraged to employ Latin: *Aperīte pāginam xxxiv! Spectāte chartam. Ubi est Alba Longa*, etc.?

TEACHER BY THE WAY
Though the twins were added to the sculpture in the Renaissance, the she-wolf has strong links with Etruscan mythology and shows characteristics of Etruscan sculpture.

TEACHING TIP
The teacher may wish to encourage the students to design an abbreviated family tree of Romulus and Remus.

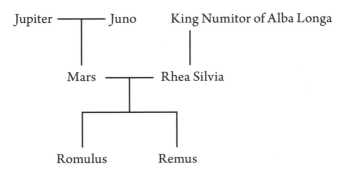

PAGE 3

HOW TO USE THIS BOOK
The English pronoun subject of a verb is not listed in the Reading Vocabulary if the pronoun is not needed in the translation.

HOW TO USE THIS BOOK
The students should **not** be expected to learn the words under the title **Reading Vocabulary**, whenever this title occurs in the book. Instead, instruct students to learn the vocabulary words listed under the title **Vocabulary to Learn** that will be found later in each chapter. In more advanced Latin texts, usually there are vocabulary and notes to help the students when reading a passage. This **Reading Vocabulary** will help prepare students for later, more advanced classes.

TEACHING TIP
Teachers may want to have students respond to the comprehension questions in Latin. This could begin with their citing the Latin that answers a given question and as their facility with Latin grows their answers need not be simple citation.

ANSWERS TO COMPREHENSION QUESTIONS
1. They are the sons of Mars and Rhea Silvia.
2. He locked up Rhea Silvia.
3. A she-wolf.
4. They built the city of Rome.

TEACHING TIP

While English derivatives from the asterisked words (i.e., the Vocabulary to Learn) are the topic of Exercise 2 later in this chapter, there are some interesting derivatives from the non-asterisked words and some of these show how words change through the years. The teacher may choose to discuss these derivatives with the students.

- *aedificant* (*aedificō*) – edify, edification, edifice

    This Latin word is built from two Latin words: *faciō* (to do, make) and *aedēs* (house, temple). The English derivatives retain this religious connection, for they mean "to build up the faith, morality; to instruct, especially morally." The word "edifice" is always used for an imposing structure, such as a "temple" or *aedēs*.

- *claudit* (*claudō*) – closet, conclusion, enclosure, sluice

    A "closet" is a small, shut-in space, and some people, if locked in one, suffer from "claustrophobia," a compound derivative, partly from Latin (to close, confine) and partly from the Greek (fear), hence "a fear of closed spaces."

    The word "sluice" does not look like a derivative of *claudō*, but it has undergone changes as it came into English via Middle English and Old French (*sclus*) from the Latin *exclūdō* which means "to shut out." A sluice has a gate at the top of the channel to <u>shut off</u> the flow of water as necessary.

- *crēscunt* (*crēscō*) – crescent, accrue, recruit, crew

    The word "crew" in middle English meant "reinforcement," so a body of soldiers <u>grew</u>. The word "recruit" has the same basic idea: Recruits increase the size of the army (from the Latin *recrēscō* meaning "to grow again").

- *deus* – deify, deity
- *duōs* – double, dozen, duet, duplicate

    The word "dozen" is a compound from the Latin word for "two" and the German word for "ten" (*zehn*).

- *pōnit* (*pōnō*) – depot, imposition, preposition

    A <u>depot</u> originally was a place where supplies were <u>put</u> for storage.

PAGE 4

Standards 1.1, 4.1

Workbook Exercise 1

HOW TO USE THIS BOOK

The Language Facts section of each chapter will contain both grammatical (morphological) and syntactical information, i.e., information about both the forms of the words and the structure of the sentence.

▶ EXERCISE 1 ANSWERS

1. noun
2. adverb
3. verb
4. preposition
5. verb
6. conjunction
7. noun
8. verb
9. noun
10. verb

TEACHING TIP

The teacher may wish to ask the students in Latin what part of speech a given word is. The teacher would say, "*Quae pars ōrātiōnis est?*" Student responses would be

- *nōmen substantīvum/substantīvum* – noun
- *prōnōmen* – pronoun
- *nōmen adiectīvum/adiectīvum* – adjective
- *verbum temporāle* – verb
- *adverbium* – adverb
- *praepositiō* – preposition
- *coniūnctiō* – conjunction
- *interiectiō* – interjection

PAGE 5

TEACHING TIP

Since this is the first set of Latin words that your students will be required to memorize, it is usually a good idea to suggest and discuss with them some different ways to memorize vocabulary. Some self-help options are listed below.

1. Look at the word in the book and say the word aloud.
2. Write down the word on a piece of paper along with its meaning and check to be sure there are no spelling errors. Color-coding the words by parts of speech is also helpful. Pronounce the word while writing it down and then repeat the word including the meaning and spelling.
3. Make handwritten flash cards with the Latin on one side and English on the other and be sure there are no spelling errors. Color-coding is a good strategy here also. Writing the word out helps some students cement the word in the brain. Bolchazy-Carducci Publishers has developed electronic vocabulary resources for those students for whom technological learning tools are an aid. See p. 117 for more information on electronic flash cards.
4. Use English derivatives to help remember meanings. But be careful since some derivatives may have meanings greatly changed from the original Latin word.
5. Find clip art pictures that illustrate the vocabulary words and use the pictures as a way to test yourself on the Latin words.
6. Students may also be directed to the digital vocabulary tools delineated on www.bolchazy.com.

TEACHER BY THE WAY

The teacher may wish to open a discussion about aqueducts and the water supply for ancient Romans while looking at the picture of the Pont du Gard on this page. For a history of aqueducts and their construction, Frontinus's book *Dē aquīs urbis Rōmae* is an excellent source. The book was written about 97 CE when he was Superintendent of Aqueducts. Other famous aqueducts include the following:

- The double high aqueduct in Segovia, Spain
- The *Aqua Appia* built in 312 BCE
- The *Aqua Trāiāna*
- The aqueduct built by Alexander Severus in 226 CE
- The *Aqua Claudia*
- The *Aqua Marcia*, which was probably named after Ancus Marcius, who was the first king of Rome by traditional accounts to build an aqueduct to bring water to Rome.

NB: The word "*Aqua*" when capitalized means "aqueduct."

Eleven aqueducts furnished 250,000 gallons of water to Rome every twenty-four hours.

PAGE 6
Standards 1.1, 3.1, 4.1
Workbook Exercise 2

HOW TO USE THIS BOOK
Ēn is a word that calls attention to something and means "Look at this!" The information given here draws attention to and further specifies different language facts.

HOW TO USE THIS BOOK
Study Tips give hints, rhymes, and mnemonics to help students learn grammar and vocabulary.

▶ EXERCISE 2 ANSWERS

1. filial   filia
2. agriculture   agricola
3. nautical   nauta
4. aquarium   aqua
5. terrain   terra
6. athletic   āthlēta
7. poetic   poēta

TEACHING TIP
Explain to the students that in English the words "a," "an," or "the" are usually placed before a noun and Latin does not have an equivalent for these words, known as articles.

Teachers may need to stress the absence of the article many times before students completely integrate this knowledge into their reading habits in Latin class.

TEACHING TIP

Latin, like many other languages, does not always observe biological gender. Often the gender of a Latin noun is determined by grammatical factors, such as the group to which a noun belongs.

TEACHING TIP

Although in Exercise 2 the students are directed to find only the derivatives based on the Vocabulary to Learn, they may be interested to learn that there are other derivatives in Exercise 2. The derivation of these words is provided for the teacher's convenience.

1. considerable – from *sīdus* (star) + *cum* (with, together) and from *cōnsīderō* (to examine, consider). respect – from *respectō* (to look back at, have regard for).
2. science – from *scientia* (knowledge) and *sciō* (to know). cultivating – from *colō* (to till, inhabit, worship).
3. necessary – from *necesse* (necessary). instruments – from *īnstruō* (to equip, build, provide) and from *īnstrumentum* (equipment, tool, etc.).
5. vehicle – from the Latin verb *vehō* (to carry).
6. competition – from *petō* (to seek, aim at, attack, etc.) + *cum* (with, together).
7. nature – from *nātūra* (nature).

PAGE 7

TEACHING TIP

Students may not know what the word "mnemonic" means; explain that a mnemonic device is something that helps a student to remember something. The teacher may also wish to use this opportunity to introduce Mnemosyne, the goddess of memory and the mother of the nine Muses.

Answers to "Find more examples of nominatives and their verbs from the reading passage at the beginning of the chapter."

Rhēa Silvia . . . habet

Amūlius . . . claudit

Amūlius . . . pōnit

Lupa . . . ambulat

Lupa . . . cūrat et amat

Rōmulus et Remus crēscunt

Rōmulus et Remus . . . aedificant

Answers to "Find more examples of accusatives and their verbs from the reading passage at the beginning of the chapter."

duōs fīliōs habet: Rōmulum et Remum

Rhēam Silviam . . . claudit

Rōmulum et Remum . . . pōnit

Rōmulum et Remum bene cūrat et amat

Rōmam aedificant

TEACHING TIP

Students may encounter difficulty when trying to translate Latin names used in cases other than the nominative. The teacher at some point will need to explain (and repeat whenever necessary) that when translating a Latin name the student should always use the nominative form of the word. On p. 7, students are asked to find examples of accusatives and their verbs in the reading passage. The answers listed above provide an opportunity to practice with this issue. Remind students to translate *duōs fīliōs habet: Rōmulum et Remum* as "he has two sons: Romulus and Remus." The other four answers may be used as practice with the students.

PAGE 8
Standards 1.1, 4.1
Workbook Exercise 3

TEACHER BY THE WAY

In conjunction with the picture and its caption, the teacher may wish to mention that the famililar acronym of SPQR is still in use and visible throughout modern Rome—on litter bins, sewer covers, etc.

▶ EXERCISE 3 ANSWERS

1. subject   vērum
2. direct objects falsum
3. direct object   falsum
4. subject   falsum
5. direct object   falsum
6. subject   vērum

TEACHING TIP

Additional reproducible worksheets, morphology charts, and their associated answer keys, related to this material, are available for download at www.lnm.bolchazy.com.

- **Noun Declensions**

PAGE 9
Standards 1.1, 3.1, 4.1
Oral Exercise 1; Workbook Exercise 4

TEACHING TIP
Ask the students what the Latin words selected from the reading and listed near the top of p. 9 mean.

TEACHING TIP
After the first declension has been presented to the students, encourage them, depending on their learning style, to say the declension aloud, to write down the words, or to invent a rap or a cheer. Alternatively, use Bolchazy-Carducci's *Toga Beats*.

TEACHER BY THE WAY
The pattern is called a declension because the other cases lean away (*dēclīnāre*) from the nominative, i.e., they do not follow the same form as the nominative.

ORAL EXERCISE 1
This exercise may be used after the first declension has been presented.

While looking at the declension of *lupa*, ask the students to decline *nauta*.

	Singular	**Plural**
Nominative	nauta	nautae
Genitive	nautae	nautārum
Dative	nautae	nautīs
Accusative	nautam	nautās
Ablative	nautā	nautīs

PAGE 10
Standards 1.1, 4.1

▶ EXERCISE 4 ANSWERS
1. genitive, dative   puellārum, puellīs
2. accusative   nautās
3. accusative   terrās
4. nominative   agricolae
5. genitive, dative   aquārum, aquīs
6. ablative   puellīs
7. ablative   āthlētīs

TEACHING TIP

As this is the second illustration of *SPQR* presented in this chapter, teachers are encouraged again to share the full phrase, S*enātus Populusque Rōmānus*, with their students. Place the full phrase on the board and have students give its meaning.

TEACHING TIP

Images of the she-wolf with the twins Romulus and Remus abound. As a classroom activity, divide students into groups to search for such images on the internet. The groups can be assigned images by medium (mosaic, fresco, statue, oil painting), by art historical period, or by location. The groups would then present their finds to the full class. When discussing location, students would point out the locations on the classroom map or on a projection of the map on pp. xxxiv–xxxv of their student text. For a homework activity, have students conduct an online search for a set number of examples and print out their favorite five or six images from that set. These should be small in size so that they could be pinned on the classroom map of the Roman world. As they pin them on the classroom map, students would explain why the image is a favorite.

PAGE 11

Standards 1.1, 4.1
Oral Exercise 2; Workbook Exercises 5, 6

TEACHING TIP

Students may wonder why the genitive singular without its ending must be used to find the base when the nominative singular without its ending works just as well. Explain that in other noun declensions the nominative will not always provide the same base or have the same spelling as the genitive.

▶ EXERCISE 5 ANSWERS

1. nominative   fīlia
2. dative, ablative   terrae, terrā
3. genitive   nautae
4. nominative   lupa
5. dative, ablative   aquae, aquā
6. genitive   poētae
7. nominative   agricola

HOW TO USE THIS BOOK

In this book the word "**base**" is used to refer to the noun without any ending. "**Stem**" is used for the part of the verb without any ending. "**Root**" is used for the Latin part of a derivative.

ORAL EXERCISE 2

This exercise may be used after Exercise 5.

Use one of the following classroom presentation options (hereafter referred to as CPO) (black/green/white/smart board, overhead or LCD projector, PowerPoint® presentation, etc.) to put this information on view.

quis?, "who?" (for the subject) and *quem?*, "whom?" (for the direct object).

Then ask the student to answer the following questions about the chapter reading either orally or in written form.

1. **Teacher:** Quis est Mārs? **Student:** Mārs est deus.
2. **Teacher:** Quem amat Mārs? **Student:** Rhēam Silviam Mārs amat.
3. **Teacher:** Quis amat Rhēam Silviam? **Student:** Mārs amat Rhēam Silviam.
4. **Teacher:** Quem habet Rhēa Silvia? **Student:** Rhēa Silvia duōs filiōs, Rōmulum et Remum, habet.
5. **Teacher:** Quis claudit Rhēam Silviam? **Student:** Amūlius claudit Rhēam Silviam.
6. **Teacher:** Quem claudit Amūlius? **Student:** Rhēam Silviam Amūlius claudit.
7. **Teacher:** Quis Rōmulum et Remum in aquam pōnit? **Student:** Amūlius Rōmulum et Remum in aquam pōnit.
8. **Teacher:** Quem Amūlius in aquam pōnit? **Student:** Amūlius Rōmulum et Remum in aquam pōnit.
9. **Teacher:** Quis ambulat ad aquam? **Student:** Lupa ambulat ad aquam.
10. **Teacher:** Quis Rōmulum et Remum bene cūrat? **Student:** Lupa Rōmulum et Remum bene cūrat.
11. **Teacher:** Quōs lupa bene cūrat? **Student:** Lupa Rōmulum et Remum bene cūrat.
12. **Teacher:** Quis Rōmulum et Remum amat? **Student:** Lupa Rōmulum et Remum amat.
13. **Teacher:** Quōs lupa amat? **Student:** Lupa Rōmulum et Remum amat.

PAGE 12
Standards 1.1, 1.2, 2.1, 4.1, 4.2
Oral Exercise 3; Workbook Exercise 7, Content Questions

TEACHER BY THE WAY
The teacher may mention that the most common word order (subject – direct object – verb) can often be changed. For example, if the verb is to be emphasized, it will take first position. If the subject or the direct object is to be emphasized, it will take the last position, which is the <u>most emphatic</u> one. In general, the more unusual the word's position is, the more emphasis is placed on this word.

▶ EXERCISE 6 ANSWERS

1. The farmer loves the land.
2. Āthlēta aquam amat.
3. The sailor loves (his) daughter.
4. Poēta Rōmam amat.
5. The farmer cares for (is taking care of) the land.
6. Lupa puellam cūrat.

TEACHING TIP
The teacher may start the class in Latin by saying *Salvēte, discipulī et discipulae!* and by teaching the students to say in return *Salvē, magister (magistra)!*

ORAL EXERCISE 3

This exercise may be used anytime after the students have learned the use of the accusative case or after Exercise 6.

Use one of the CPOs to put on display the forms *amō* and *cūrō*, and explain that they are in the first person singular, and how this differs from the third person singular learned in this chapter. Ask individual students to make sentences with them using the words they have learned.

Then tell the students that *nōn* means "not" and ask them to make similar sentences with *nōn amō* and *nōn cūrō*.

Examples:
(nōn) amō terram, fīliam, aquam, lupam, āthlētam
(nōn) cūrō terram, fīliam, puellam

PAGE 13
Standards 1.2, 4.1
Oral Exercises 4, 5, 6, and Dictation

TEACHING TIP
Have students read the dialogue aloud. This will help to build their pronunciation skills.

TRANSLATION OF THE LATIN CONVERSATION

Mary, Helen, and Christy are students.

Mary: Hello, Helen and Christy!
Christy: Hello, Mary!
Helen: Hello, Mary!
Mary: How are you, Helen? How are you, Christy?
Helen and Christy: Well. How are you doing, Mary?
Mary: Very badly.

Helen and Christy: Why?

Mary: I fear the Latin language.

Helen: I love the Latin language.

Christy: And I love the Latin language!

ORAL EXERCISE 4

This exercise may be used after the Latin dialogue has been presented.

Instruct the students to say "hello" in Latin to the student next to them. Divide the class into two parts. Tell one part to greet the other part using the plural greeting and vice versa. Do the same type of activity when saying "goodbye." You may wish to make greeting the class in Latin and saying "goodbye" in Latin a part of a daily routine.

Divide the students into pairs in which one person will ask how his/her partner is in Latin, and the other will answer.

ORAL EXERCISE 5

This exercise may be used after the Latin dialogue has been presented.

Tell the students that the particle *–ne* is added to the first syllable of a word that introduces a question. Then ask the following questions about the dialogue between Mary, Helen, and Christy. Individual students may answer orally, or the entire class may write the answers as the teacher asks them orally. The teacher should explain that the form *valēs* in the greeting *Quōmodo valēs?* is in the second person, which means "you." The third person form (referring to "her", "him," or "it") is *valet*. So the phrase "How is s/he doing" would be *Quōmodo valet?* The third person of *amō* is *amat*, and the third person of *timeō* is *timet*.

1. **Teacher:** Quōmodo Christīna valet?   **Student(s):** Christīna bene valet.
2. **Teacher:** Quōmodo Marīa valet?   **Student(s):** Marīa pessimē valet.
3. **Teacher:** Cūr (*why*) Marīa pessimē valet?   **Student(s):** Marīa timet linguam Latīnam.
4. **Teacher:** Amatne linguam Latīnam Helena?   **Student(s):** Helena linguam Latīnam amat.
5. **Teacher:** Linguamne Latīnam amat Christīna?   **Student(s):** Christīna linguam Latīnam amat.

ORAL EXERCISE 6 AND DICTATION

This combined exercise may be used to conclude the chapter or at any time after the students have learned the accusative case and chapter vocabulary.

Dictate the following sentences to the students. Then ask them to make the following changes either orally or in written form, at the discretion of the teacher.

1. **Teacher:** Agricola terram amat. (change the direct object into plural)
    Student: Agricola terrās amat.
2. **Teacher:** Lupa puellam cūrat. (change the direct object into plural)
    Student: Lupa puellās cūrat.
3. **Teacher:** Āthlēta puellās amat. (change the direct object into singular)
    Student: Āthlēta puellam amat.
4. **Teacher:** Fīlia terrās amat. (change the direct object into singular)
    Student: Fīlia terram amat.

Chapter 1 • 23

DERIVATIVES

agricola – A combination of *ager* (field) and *colō* (to till); hence a farmer is someone who "tills a field."

aqua – <u>Aqueous</u> rocks have been formed by matter deposited in or by water.

The word "ewer" (a pitcher with a wide spout) is derived from *aquārius* (of or for water; water carrier); through the Old French *eviere* (water pitcher). The astrological sign <u>Aquarius</u> is depicted as a bearded man pouring water out of a pitcher. The word "sewer" is derived through Anglo-French (*sewere*) and Old North French *sewiere* ("sluice from a pond") from a shortened form of *ex aquāriā* (out of something watery). The Middle French form was *esieveur*, referring to a drain for carrying water off.

āthlēta – This word is a transliteration from the Greek ἀθλήτης meaning "a prize fighter." It is based on the verb ἀθλέω (to contend in battle). The grammatical gender of "athlete" also mimics that of the Greek, e.g., a masculine noun in the first declension (consisting mostly of feminine nouns).

fīlia (feminine of *fīlius*) – The verb "filiate" is a legal term meaning "to determine judicially the paternity of a child."

The Spanish word *hidalgo* refers to a member of the lower nobility. The first syllable (*hi*) is derived from the Old Spanish *fijo, dalgo* from the Latin *dē* (from) and *aliquō* (something). The word meant literally, "a son with something, i.e., a person of property."

lupa – The word "lupus" is used of several diseases causing skin ulcerations, apparently because it "devours" the affected part (like a wolf).

The noun "lupine" is the name of a plant of the genus Lupinus. The reason for the association with "wolf" is unclear. It has been conjectured that the late fourteenth century considered these plants to be harmful to the soil. The adjective "lupine" means "savage, ravenous, predatory," traits considered characteristic of a wolf.

nauta – Like *āthlēta*, this word is a transliteration from the Greek (ναύτης, from ναῦς = ship).

poēta – This word is a transliteration of the Greek ποιητής. The Greek verb ποιέω (to do, to make) is the root of these words.

puella – No derivatives from the feminine, but *puer* gives us "puerile."

Puella is a diminutive form of *puer* (boy), perhaps a word coined to show affection for a young daughter (as other diminutives do, e.g., Catullus's *ocelle* for his beloved island Sirmio in Poem 31) in a society where sons were more important than daughters. Some families even named "extra" daughters with just numbers, e.g., *Secunda, Tertia*. Of course too many boys could also lead to this, e.g., *Quīntus, Sextus*!

Rōma – The adjective "Romance" was derived around 1300 through the Old French *romanz*, which meant "in the vernacular language," as opposed to Latin. It referred to a "story of a hero's adventures." A Romance language was one developed from Latin instead of Frankish. The connecting notion is that medieval vernacular tales were usually about chivalric adventure. By the 1660s the literary sense had been extended to "a love story." The idea of "adventure story" is first recorded in 1801; that of "love affair, idealistic quality" is from 1916.

The country "Romania" once constituted a large part of the Roman province of Dacia. Romanian is a Romance language.

The adjective "Romanesque" was coined in 1715 and originally meant "descended from Latin." By 1819 it was describing the architectural style in Europe from 800 to 1200 that had as its characteristics the arched barrel vault used extensively in Roman architecture.

terra – To "inter" a body means to bury it (in the ground = land).

The word "disinter" is the antonym of "inter." The synonym, "exhume," is also a Latin derivative (*ex* = out from; *humus* = ground, soil).

The word "subterranean" is composed of two Latin words – *sub* (under) and *terra*.

A "terrier" is so called because this breed of dog was used to start badgers from their burrows (from the Middle French *chien terrier* = dog of the earth).

amat (*amō*) – An "amateur" performs for the "love" of the sport or music.

An "amiable" person is agreeable, congenial. They were engaged in an amiable conversation.

The word "amicable" means "peaceable, marked by good will." They came to an amicable agreement on the point of contention.

The word "enemy" is derived from the Latin *inimīcus* (*in* is a negative here; not friendly) through the Middle English *enemi*.

The word "paramour," referring to an illicit lover, is derived from *amō* through the Middle English *par amour* (from the Old French) meaning "by love, passionately, with strong love or desire." Around 1300 it became a noun originally used as a term for Christ by women and for the Virgin Mary by men. By the mid-fourteenth century it came to mean "darling" or "sweetheart" and later in the century denoted a mistress, concubine, or clandestine lover.

ambulat (*ambulō*) – An "amble" is a slow walk. They ambled through the rose garden enjoying the beautiful flowers.

The word "ambulance" is derived through the French (hospital *ambul[ant]* = traveling hospital) from *ambulō*.

A "perambulator" is a baby carriage (often shortened to "pram") from the Latin *per* = through and *ambulō*.

The word "preamble" comes from the Latin *prae* = before and *ambulō* and means literally "walking before." It derives from the medieval Latin *preambulum*, a neuter adjective used as a noun meaning "preliminary" and came into English in the later fourteenth century through the Old French *preambule* (thirteenth century). Every American citizen should recognize the first words of the preamble to the Constitution, "We the People."

cūrat (*cūrō* = to care) – The word "accurate" is attested to in the 1610s and meant "done with care." The idea of doing something carefully led to that of being exact (1650s). The word "secure" means "free from care" (*sē* = without [on one's own] and *cūra*).

Johnny thought his job as vice president of the company would be a sinecure (*sine* = without and *cūra*) because his mother was the board chair.

The word "assure" dates from the late fourteenth century and was derived through the Old French *asseurer*, which was based on the Vulgar Latin *ad* (to, toward) and *sēcūrus* (free from care). It therefore means "to protect, calm, keep from care."

A "curate" is an assistant to a vicar or priest and helps "take care of" their parishioners.

A "curator" is one who "takes care of" the contents of a museum.

A "curio" is an article or object of art valued as a curiosity and is a shortened form of that word. The word "curious" dates to the mid-fourteenth century and meant "eager to know" (often in a bad sense). It was derived from the Latin *cūriōsus* (careful, diligent) through the Old French *curios* meaning "solicitous, anxious, inquisitive," but also "odd, strange," hence the varied nuances of the English word today.

He was <u>curious</u> to know the facts. The horse and buggy were a <u>curiosity</u> on the busy modern highway.

The word "procure" is based on two Latin words, *prō* (on behalf of) and *cūra*. It appears in English around 1300, derived through the Old French *procurer* (care for, acquire, provide). Its primary meaning today is "to obtain" (by the action of another) and has been used by the American military in that sense since 1949.

The word "proctor" is a contraction of *procurator* (c. 1300), which meant "manager of a household." In the late fourteenth century it referred to someone who spoke or acted for another, an advocate, and in the early fifteenth century to the financial administrator of a church or college. Today it is most often used to designate a supervisor of students during exams.

The word "proxy" is also a contraction of the related Latin *prōcūrātiō* (a caring for, management) and from the 1610s refers to a person who acts in place of another.

The word "scour" meaning "to clean or polish" is derived from the Latin *excūrāre* (*ex* = out and *cūra*) through the Old French *securer* and the Middle Dutch *scuren*. It may originally have been a technical term among Flemish workmen in England.

The word "sure" is derived from the Latin *sēcūrus* (without care) through the Old French *sur*, *seur* (safe) and entered the English language around 1300. It also means "yes" (from 1803), a usage based on the Middle English meaning "firmly established." Qualifiers were gradually added, resulting in such phrases as "sure enough" (1540s), "for sure" (1580s), and "to be sure" (1650s). "Surefooted" dates from the 1630s; "a sure thing" from 1836.

est – See *sum* in 1.1. (Note: References such as 1.1 refer to *LNM* Level 1, Chapter 1.)

bene – Most of the derivatives from *bene* are self-evident, but "benign" is not only pronounced differently but its spelling is more difficult. It is derived from the Latin *benignus* (*bene* = well, and *gignō* = to bear, beget); hence the spelling. It appears in English during the early fourteenth century and means "kind, merciful." Someone who was "wellborn" was expected to be kind and generous as well as honorable.

et, itaque – None

posteā (*post* = after, behind) – The word "posterity" refers to those born after the current generation. The judgment of current events will be left to posterity.

The "postern" gate was located "behind" the castle. It was a private entrance, apart from the main gate.

The word "posthumous" is erroneously associated with the Latin *humus* (ground), but in reality it comes from *postumus* = last, last born. It came into English during the mid-fifteenth century and meant "born after the death of the originator" (author or father) from the Late Latin spelling of the original Latin, which occurred because of the association with *humāre* (to bury) suggesting death. The one born after the father's death is obviously the last. The last novel of the author was published posthumously.

The adjective "preposterous" literally means "before behind" (from the Latin *praeposterus*) and describes something inverted, in reverse order; topsy-turvy, contrary to nature or reason. It came into English during the mid-sixteenth century.

The word "puny" is a variant spelling of "puisne," which derives from the Latin *post* and *nāscor* (to be born) through the Old French *puis* (after) from the Latin *posteā* (literally "after there") and Old French *ne* (to be born). It came into English during the sixteenth century and meant "inferior in rank." The sense of "small, weak, insignificant" is first recorded in the 1590s.

CHAPTER 2 (PP. 15–28)

GRAMMAR IN LANGUAGE FACTS

First and Second Conjugation Verbs; Principal Parts; Properties of Verbs: Number, Person, Tense, Stem; The Infinitive; Subject and Verb Agreement

PAGE 15
Standards 1.1, 2.1, 4.1, 4.2

RRA 4

TEACHER BY THE WAY
Plautus's comedy *Captives* is called *Captīvī* in Latin.

TEACHER BY THE WAY
In addition to Plautus's phrase "between the sacrificial animal and rock" and the more common English phrase "between a rock and a hard place," there is also the phrase "between Scylla and Charybdis," the narrow passage of water between the monster Scylla and the whirlpool Charybdis through which Odysseus had to navigate.

MEMORĀBILE DICTŪ VOCABULARY

inter + *accusative* – between

–que – and

sacer, sacra, sacrum – sacred; **sacrum** – a sacrificial animal

saxum, saxī, *n.* – rock

TEACHING TIP
The teacher may wish to explain that the reproduction of the wall painting on this page is a type of art called a fresco in which the colors are applied while the wall is still wet. Frescoes were a typical art form in ancient Rome.

First one to three coats of lime and sand were applied, then one to three coats of lime mixed with finely powdered marble were put on the wall. The colored pigments were mostly obtained from mineral, vegetable, and animal sources. One pigment came from the slimy secretion of the purple snail mixed with chalk, while the burning of pine wood chips or wine dregs produced black. Pliny the Elder's chapters on painting in his *Natural History* are a good source of this information.

TEACHING TIP
Chapter 4 of RRA may be assigned to be read in conjunction with Chapter 2 of this book but it also includes the historical events that accompany the literature of Chapter 3 of *Latin for the New Millennium*, Level 1.

PAGE 16
Standards 1.1, 2.1, 3.1, 3.2

TRANSLATION OF LATIN PASSAGE
About the Menaechmi

Messenio: By Jove! What do I see?
Menaechmus-Sosicles: What do you see?
Messenio: (*pointing at Menaechmus*) This (man) has your appearance.
Menaechmus-Sosicles: What story are you telling me?
Messenio: I am not telling stories. You ought to see.
Menaechmus-Sosicles: Wow! (*addressing Menaechmus*) How do they call you?
Menaechmus: They call me Menaechmus.
Menaechmus-Sosicles: You are telling stories! They call me Menaechmus also.
Messenio: They are like two drops of water!
Menaechmus-Sosicles: What fatherland do you have? ("Where are you from?")
Menaechmus: I am from Syracuse.
Menaechmus-Sosicles: I live there also. Therefore (and so) you are my brother. Hello, my brother! I am waiting for you for a long time.
Menaechmus: Hello, my brother! We ought to live with (our) father now.

TEACHER BY THE WAY
Chief among the Athenian writers after whom Plautus modeled his plays were Menander, Diphilus, and Philemon. This type of drama is known as "New Comedy" to distinguish it from the kinds of comedy that flourished in Athens a century earlier. Focused on common human experiences, such as the complications that arise in families over love, marriage, and conflicting values between parents and children, it shares many features with "situation comedy" today.

Over the course of the early second century BCE, the Romans conquered the Greek world, ultimately reducing Greece itself to a Roman province in 146 BCE. In the process, Roman society absorbed many Greek-speaking inhabitants, and both adopted and adapted many elements of Greek culture. The Roman comedies by Plautus and Terence, for example, are referred to as *fābulae palliātae*, "stories wearing Greek dress." Not only are they inspired by earlier Greek works, but they are also set in the Greek world. The *pallium* was a Greek cloak.

Evidence of Plautus's continuing popularity in the English-speaking world ever since the Renaissance includes William Shakespeare's adaptation of this work in *The Comedy of Errors*, and *The Boys from Syracuse,* a Broadway musical hit of 1938 based on Shakespeare's play.

TEACHING TIP
Instruct the students to locate the island of Sicily and the city of Syracuse on the map on pp. xxxiv–xxxv (SE) and to find Plautus and Terence on the timeline on pp. 405–408 (SE).

PAGE 17

ANSWERS TO COMPREHENSION QUESTIONS
1. They recognize each other.
2. Menaechmus-Sosicles's slave Messenio.
3. Both of them look absolutely alike and both are from Syracuse.
4. To live together with their father as a family.

TEACHER BY THE WAY
All social classes were represented in Plautus's audience. Admission was free. In the prologue to one of his plays (*Poenulus*), the ushers are asked not to walk in front of the spectators' faces, not to seat latecomers, and not to let slaves occupy seats intended for free men. Married women are to laugh where appropriate but watch silently and avoid chattering. Babies should be left at home. Special seats were reserved up front for dignitaries.

TEACHER BY THE WAY
In this Reading Vocabulary list, the Latin word *gutta* or "drop" occurs. This word is used in the famous proverb *gutta cavat lapidem nōn vī sed saepe cadendō* (a drop hollows a stone not by force, but by often falling), which is frequently shortened to *gutta cavat lapidem*. This Latin phrase can be found in Ovid's *Epistulae ex Pontō* 4.10.5.

PAGE 18
Standards 1.1, 1.2, 3.1, 4.1
Workbook Exercise 1

TEACHING TIP
The macron on the –*ē*– of the second conjugation infinitive should be memorized by students and its correct pronunciation should be stressed beginning with this chapter (as well as the macron on the –*ā*– of the first conjugation). When the third conjugation is presented later in this book, students will be able to distinguish between second and third conjugation infinitives more readily by both sight and sound.

TEACHER BY THE WAY
The word "conjugation" comes from the Latin verb *coniugāre* (join together) since it lists together person, number, tense, mood, and voice.

▶ **EXERCISE 1 ANSWERS**

1. second
2. first
3. first
4. second
5. first
6. first

TEACHING TIP

The teacher may choose to ask the students in Latin to what conjugation a given verb belongs. The teacher would say, "*Cūius coniugātiōnis est?*" Student responses would be

- *prīmae*
- *secundae*
- *tertiae*
- *quārtae*

PAGE 19

Standard 4.1

Workbook Exercise 2

HOW TO USE THIS BOOK

All the vocabulary entries will be given without abbreviations until the end of Level 1. In Level 2 and Level 3, the usual abbreviations will be used.

TEACHING TIP

The verbs from Vocabulary to Learn of Chapter 1 are repeated here in order to provide their principal parts.

Students need to memorize the first two principal parts of verbs, starting with this chapter. At this point in their Latin studies, whether or not students will also be required to memorize the third and fourth principal parts is a decision the teacher should make.

Remind the students that they learned *amat*, *ambulat*, and *cūrat* in Chapter 1.

▶ EXERCISE 2 ANSWERS

1. narrative — nārrō
2. habitat — habitō
3. expectations — exspectō
4. fabulous — fābula
5. video — videō
6. vocal — vocō
7. debit — dēbeō
8. patriotic — patria
9. preparations — parō
10. tentacles — teneō
11. ambulance — ambulō

TEACHING TIP

Although in Exercise 2 the students are directed to find only the derivatives based on the Vocabulary to Learn, they may be interested to learn that there are other derivatives in Exercise 2. The derivation of these words is provided for the teacher's convenience.

1. long – from *longus* (long).
2. humanity – from *hūmānitās* (humanity, human nature, kindness, courtesy, etc.).
3. results – from *resultō* (to rebound, spring back). exceeded – from *excēdō* (to go out, advance, overstep).
7. pay – from *pācō* (to subdue by force, pacify; later in medieval Latin – to satisfy or settle a debt; related to "peace"). credit – *crēdō* (to believe, trust).
9. festival – from *festīvus* (jolly, delightful). moving – from *moveō* (to move).
10. octopus – from *octo* (eight); and from Greek *pous, podos* (foot; related to *pēs* – foot in Latin). long – from *longus* (long)
11. siren – *Sīrēn* (a mythological figure)

PAGE 20
Standards 1.1, 1.2, 3.1, 4.1
Workbook Exercise 3

▶ EXERCISE 3 ANSWERS

1. second person singular
2. second person singular
3. third person singular
4. second person singular
5. second person singular
6. first person plural
7. third person plural
8. third person singular

Chapter 2 • 31

TEACHER BY THE WAY

If students notice that the stem vowel *–ā–* of the first conjugation is missing in the first person singular, explain that the original *–ā–* weakened (as in **nārrāō*) and only the *–ō* remains. In the second conjugation, however, the stem vowel *–ē–* does not weaken and does not disappear.

TEACHING TIP

Encourage the students to create a rap, cheer, or song to help them remember the personal endings. Alternatively, use Bolchazy-Carducci's *Toga Beats*.

TEACHING TIP

If the teacher wishes to ask a student in Latin what person a verb is, the question in Latin is "*Cūius est persōnae?*" Student responses would be

- *prīmae persōnae*
- *secundae persōnae*
- *tertiae persōnae*

If the teacher wants to ask what number the verb is, the question is "*Cūius est numerī?*" Student responses would be

- *numerī singulāris*
- *numerī plūrālis*

PAGE 21
Standards 1.1, 1.2, 4.1
Oral Exercise 1; Workbook Exercise 4

TEACHING TIP

The teacher may wish to explain briefly that each of the tenses has a set of endings peculiar to it.

TEACHING TIP

Emphasize to students that the subject pronoun (such as "she" or "it") of the Latin ending is expressed in English only when there is no noun subject (such as "the sailor" or "the soldier") present. Students may feel that it is necessary to repeat the pronoun subject when translating a sentence with a noun subject. The teacher can show why this is not needed.

TEACHER BY THE WAY

The first translation is the present simple tense that refers to a general action in the present. The second translation is emphatic in case the described action needs emphasizing. The third translation is the present progressive tense that is used for an action occurring at the moment of speaking.

▶ EXERCISE 4 ANSWERS

1. you call, do call, are calling
2. s/he sees, does see, is seeing
3. they wait for, do wait for, are waiting for
4. we take care, do take care, are taking care
5. you (plural) owe, do owe, are owing/you (plural) ought/you must/you should
6. I have, do have, am having

ORAL EXERCISE 1

This exercise may be used after the present tense of first and second conjugation verbs has been presented.
Ask the students to conjugate orally the verbs *amō* and *videō*.

> amō, amās, amat, amāmus, amātis, amant
>
> videō, vidēs, videt, vidēmus, vidētis, vident

PAGE 22

Standards 1.1, 1.2, 4.1
Oral Exercise 2; Workbook Exercise 5

▶ EXERCISE 5 ANSWERS

1. you see, do see, are seeing   vidētis
2. s/he/it owes/ought/must/should   dēbent
3. s/he/it walks, does walk, is walking   ambulant
4. I have, do have, am having   habēmus
5. you hold, do hold, are holding   tenētis
6. I love, do love, am loving   amāmus
7. s/he/it dwells, does dwell, is dwelling   habitant

ORAL EXERCISE 2

This exercise may be used after Exercise 6.
The teacher, holding a piece of chalk, says, "*Crētam teneō*," and asks a student "What am I doing? Answer in Latin!" The teacher may wish, after explaining its meaning, to substitute the phrase "*Respondē Latīnē*" for "Answer in Latin!"

The student should answer, "*Crētam tenēs.*"

The teacher then gives the piece of chalk to a student and asks another student: "What is William (or the appropriate name) doing? Answer in Latin!"

The student should answer, "*Crētam tenet.*"

Then the teacher takes a piece of chalk, gives pieces of chalk to several students, and asks a student from that group: "What are we doing? Answer in Latin!"

The student should answer, "*Crētam tenēmus.*"

Then the teacher asks the same question "What are we doing? Answer in Latin!" to a student who has no piece of chalk.

Chapter 2 • 33

The student should answer, "*Crētam tenētis.*"

Then the teacher puts away her/his piece of chalk and asks a student without a piece of chalk in his hand about the group that is holding pieces of chalk: "What are they doing? Answer in Latin."

The student should answer, "*Crētam tenent.*"

The same exercise can be done with a bottle of water held by the teacher/student(s) and the phrase *Aquam habeō*.

▶ EXERCISE 6 ANSWERS

1. we live/do live/are living   habitō
2. we love/do love/are loving   amō
3. they hold/do hold/are holding   tenet
4. they tell/do tell/are telling   nārrat
5. you (plural) have/do have/are having   habēs
6. we see/do see/are seeing   videō
7. you (plural) wait for/do wait for/are waiting for   exspectās

TEACHER BY THE WAY

Finite verbs have a specific personal ending attached to the stem. On the other hand, infinitives are infinite because the ending *–re* does not specify a person.

PAGE 23

Standards 1.1, 4.1
Oral Exercise 3

▶ EXERCISE 7 ANSWERS

1. to walk   first
2. to have   second
3. to tell   first
4. to wait for   first
5. to owe, ought   second
6. to see   second

ORAL EXERCISE 3

This exercise may be used after Exercise 7.

The teacher says "*Dēbeō exspectāre*" and then asks individual students: "What should you do (ought you to do)? Answer in Latin!"

Appropriate answers would be:

Dēbeō patriam amāre; puellam cūrāre; puellam vocāre; fābulam nārrāre; fōrmam cūrāre; poētam vidēre.

Then the teacher may wish to divide the class into groups, and the groups should devise an answer to the question "What should you do? Answer in Latin!"

The answer will start with *Dēbēmus . . .*

PAGE 24
Standards 1.1, 1.2, 4.1
Workbook Exercises 6, 7

▶ EXERCISE 8 ANSWERS
1. vident
2. nārrās
3. dēbēmus
4. dēbētis
5. habeō

TEACHING TIP
The teacher may choose to open a discussion on the differences between ancient Greek and Roman theatres. The Theatre of Ephesus, shown on this page, was built into a hillside in the Greek manner. Ask students to compare this theatre with the ones shown on p. 25 (SE) and p. 32 (SE), both of which were built as freestanding structures in the Roman style. The teacher may also wish to encourage students to locate Ephesus on a map. For a fuller discussion of theatres, see p. 70.

TEACHING TIP
Additional reproducible worksheets, morphology charts, and their associated answer keys, related to this material, are available for download at www.lnm.bolchazy.com.
- Verb Conjugations

PAGE 25
Standards 1.1, 1.2, 4.1
Workbook Content Questions

TEACHER BY THE WAY
The panel seen in the picture is called the *frons scenae*, "front of stage." Note that the center figure in the panel appears to be Mercury with the caduceus.

TEACHER BY THE WAY
Early plays were presented in the forum on a temporary wooden stage backed by a scene building, called both *scena* and *prōscaenium*, with three folding wooden doors behind which the actors could gather and dress. The doors represented entrances to houses located on an open street. Entrances on either side of the stage were used to signal an actor's offstage movements to the harbor or forum. Textual evidence suggests that a roof may have been positioned above at least one stage door. Wall paintings also provide evidence of staging props. Even after Pompey built the first permanent theatre (55 BCE), makeshift stages were used far into imperial times not only at Rome but also in towns.

▶ EXERCISE 9 ANSWERS

1. Dēbēmus exspectāre.
2. Dēbētis fābulam nārrāre.
3. Nunc patriam vident.
4. Fīliam cūrō.

▶ EXERCISE 10 ANSWERS

1. vērum
2. falsum
3. vērum
4. falsum

PAGE 26
Standards 1.2, 4.1, 4.2, 5.1

TEACHER BY THE WAY
The expression *Quid nōmen tibi est?* is used chiefly in Plautus, and even by him not consistently.

TEACHING TIP
This may be a good time to assign Latin names to students or to allow them to choose Latin names.

TEACHER BY THE WAY
More information on methods of naming in the Roman world is presented on pp. 106–107 (SE), including the fact that girls took the feminine form of their father's name. In order to prevent confusion, if there were several girls in one family, the girls might be called Prīma or Secuda or Tertia or Minor or Maior.

More choices for boys' names are provided for the teacher's convenience:

- D. = Decimus
- N. = Numerius
- S. or Sp. = Spurius
- Ti. = Tiberius

An adopted son took his adoptive father's name but his original name could be used as an adjectival cognomen. For example, Augustus's name was Gāius Iūlius Caesar Octāviānus (Octavian). The honorary title of Augustus decreed to Octavian by the Senate became the cognomen for all of his successors. The *tria nōmina* designation was a prerogative of Roman citizens.

TEACHING TIP
Encourage students to draw their own family tree or a fictional family tree, if this seems preferable, and to label each person in the real or fictional family with a Latin name.

PAGE 27
Standards 1.2, 4.1
Oral Exercises 4, 5, 6, and Dictation

TRANSLATION OF THE LATIN CONVERSATION
Mark is a new student.

Mary: Hello (everybody)! How are you?

Helen and Christy: We are well.

Mark: Hello (everybody)!

Mary: Hello! What is your name?

Mark: My name is Mark. What is your name?

Mary: My name is Mary. Where are you from?

Mark: I come from California. Where are you from?

Mary: I am American.

Mark: I also am American. But where do you come from?

Mary: I come from Washington, DC.

Helen: And I come from Washington, DC.

Christy: And I come from Washington, DC.

Mark: Certainly. Our school is in Washington, DC.

ORAL EXERCISE 4
This exercise may be used after the Latin dialogue has been presented.

Divide the students into pairs in which one will ask what his/her partner's name is in Latin, and the other will answer, and vice versa. Repeat the same with a question about each student's origin.

ORAL EXERCISE 5
This exercise may be used anytime after the students have learned the present tense or as a review exercise at the end of Chapter 2.

Ask the students to change the following forms into plural, if they are in singular, and into the singular, if they are in plural. When the teacher says the first form, the student should repeat it and then orally supply the changed form.

Teacher: parās	**Student:** parātis	**Teacher:** dēbēs	**Student:** dēbētis
Teacher: vocātis	**Student:** vocās	**Teacher:** habitant	**Student:** habitat
Teacher: vident	**Student:** videt	**Teacher:** ambulat	**Student:** ambulant
Teacher: vidēmus	**Student:** videō	**Teacher:** exspectātis	**Student:** exspectās
Teacher: amō	**Student:** amāmus	**Teacher:** tenēmus	**Student:** teneō

ORAL EXERCISE 6 AND DICTATION

This combined exercise may be used to conclude the chapter or at any time after the students have learned the present tense of the first and second conjugations.

Dictate the following sentences to the students. After they write down each sentence, ask a student to read the dictated Latin sentence and then to repeat it orally, changing the subject and the verb into the plural.

1. **Teacher:** Puella patriam amat.   **Student:** Puellae patriam amant.
2. **Teacher:** Nauta terram videt.   **Student:** Nautae terram vident.
3. **Teacher:** Agricola exspectāre dēbet.   **Student:** Agricolae exspectāre dēbent.
4. **Teacher:** Poēta fābulam nārrat.   **Student:** Poētae fābulam nārrant.

PAGE 28
Standard 4.1

DERIVATIVES

fābula – (*for* = to speak)

The word "fable" appeared in English around 1300, derived from the Latin through the Old French *fable* (story; fiction, falsehood). The sense of "animal story" came into English during the early fourteenth century, based on Aesop. In modern folklore the word refers to "a short, comic tale making a moral point about human nature, usually through animal characters behaving in human ways" (*Oxford Dictionary of English Folklore*, qtd. in OED). Most sources trace this type of story to Greece (cf. Aesop) or India.

The suffix "-ous" of "fabulous" means "full of" from the Latin *-ōsus* (cf. glorious, victorious, mischievous, etc.); hence the word describes something almost incredible, unusual, or superb. A <u>fabulous</u> dinner was served at the banquet.

fōrma – The Babylonians wrote in wedge-shaped letters called <u>cuneiform</u>.

The word "deformity" consists of the Latin preposition *dē* (down from) and *fōrma*; hence it describes something detracting from its normal shape. The soldier's <u>deformity</u> was caused by a bullet wound to his arm.

The word "formula" came into use by mathematicians in 1796, by chemists around 1846. It is a diminutive of *fōrma* (small form) and is derived directly from the Latin *formula*, spelling unchanged, which meant "form, draft, contract, rule, method."

A <u>platform</u> is a "flat form" and is derived through the Old French *plat* (cf. plateau) and the Latin *fōrma*. The French word *plat* itself is a derivative of the Greek πλατύς (level, flat). By the 1540s "platform" meant a plan of action, a scheme, a design. The literal sense of "level raised surface" dates to the 1550s. Its political sense is found first in 1803, probably from the physical platform on which the candidates stood to make their speeches.

The Latin verb *reformāre* (to form again, change) is the base for "reform, reformatory," and "reformation."

A <u>reformatory</u> is a penal institution designed to "change" young offenders back into useful citizens. The <u>Reformation</u>, begun in 1517 by Martin Luther, was a religious movement meant to "change" the perceived abuses in the Catholic Church.

Band members all look alike because they wear <u>uniforms</u> (*unus* = one, and *fōrma*).

Something <u>vermiform</u> in shape is long and slender, resembling a worm (*vermis* = worm, and *fōrma*).

38 • Latin for the New Millennium: Teacher's Manual, Level 1

An "informal" gathering is casual, one that does not require formal attire (*in* = not, and *fôrma*).

"To inform" means "to shape the mind," literally "into shape." The word "informer" originally (late fourteenth century) meant "instructor, teacher," but by 1500 it had combined with the Old French *enformeor* (one who gives information against another) and referred specifically to lawbreaking.

patria – (*pater* = father)

The land of one's birth is often called "the fatherland"; hence "patriot, patriotic," and "patriotism" refer to the loyalty one has to one's own country.

For *ambulō, amō,* and *cūrō,* see 1.1. The words are given there in the third person. (Note: References such as 1.1 refer to *LNM* Level 1, Chapter 1.)

dēbeō – A "debt" is something owed. A soldier does his duty because it is owed to his superior officer. A <u>debit</u> on Sarah's charge card indicated she owed $58.43.

The word "due" came into English in the fourteenth century meaning "customary" or "regular" and then "owing, payable" through the Old French *dei* (past participle of *devoir* from the Latin *dēbēre*).

The word "duly" is from "due" with the "-ly" suffix added (having the qualities of). The thieves were caught and <u>duly</u> punished (i.e., they received the punishment owed to them).

The word "endeavor" literally means "into duty" (*en* = in, into, and *dēbeō*) from the Old French phrase *mettre en deveir* (put in duty; make it one's duty). By the late fifteenth century it had acquired the meaning of "utmost effort."

exspectō – The meaning and spelling of the derivatives are clear. Do caution the students that the *s* has dropped in the English since it duplicates the sound of *x* and was therefore unnecessary.

habeō – One's <u>ability</u> depends on the talents and skills one has.

The word "inhibit" is derived directly from the Latin *inhibeō* (*in* = in, and *habeō*) and literally means "to hold in, keep back"; hence "to restrain, hinder." People often lower their inhibitions when they drink too much and act in ways they never would if they were sober.

The word "rehabilitate" consists of *re* = again and *hābilis* (manageable; *habeō* = to have, keep [in a certain condition, manage]). The guilty teenager was rehabilitated by doing community service.

habitō – (intensive or iterative form of *habeō* which indicates a forcible or repeated action) The word "habit" may refer to the garb often worn by a nun or to a customary practice or use, a behavior pattern.

An <u>inhabitant</u> is a permanent resident.

A <u>habitat</u> is a place that is natural for the life and growth of plant or animal, or human (as in Habitat for Humanity).

nārrō – The means and derivation of the English words are clear.

parō – The words "imperium, imperious, imperial" all derive from the Latin verb *imperō* (to command), which itself is a combination of *in* (into) and *parō*; hence "to arrange into" and then "to command."

The words "empire" and "emperor" come through the Old French *empire* (from the Latin *imperium*). The interchange of *e* and *i* can still be seen in such pairs as "enquire/inquire" and "insure/ensure."

Note the "-ous" ending of "imperious," meaning "full of."

The word "separate" literally means "to get ready apart" and appeared in English around 1600; the noun "separates," referring to clothing worn in various combinations, dates from 1945.

The word "sever" (appeared in English around 1300) derives from the same Latin verb (*sēparāre*) through the Vulgar Latin *sēperāre*, Old French *severer* and Anglo-French *severer*.

A "parapet" consists of the prefix "para" derived from *parō* and the Latin noun *pectus* (breast); hence it means a breast-high defensive wall. It also refers to a low protective wall often found on the edges of balconies and bridges. The word came into English in the 1580s directly from the Italian *parapetto* or the Middle French *parapet* (breastwork) in the 1600s.

The word "rampart" comes from the Latin *ante* (before) and *parō* (to prepare before) through the Middle French *remparer* (*re* = back again, and *emparer* = to take possession of, from the Old Provençal *amparar*). It refers to a mound of earth and stone raised as a fortification (prepared ahead of time).

The words "parachute" and "parasol" both exhibit the idea of "prepare against": "parachute" = to guard against a fall (from *cadō* through the Old French *cheoir* = to fall); "parasol" = to guard against the sun.

A "parade" is a show originally associated with the military that designated an assembly of troops for inspection, especially before battle; hence the idea of "prepared."

An apple can be prepared for eating by "paring" (cutting it into pieces and removing the skin).

sum – The <u>absent</u> student is away from school (*ab* = away from, and *sum* = be).

The word "essence" is formed from the infinitive *esse* and refers to that which is basic or "essential" as opposed to accidental or superficial.

The word "quintessence" (*quīntus* = five, and *esse*) refers to the "pure substance of which heavenly bodies are composed instead of the four elements: earth, air, water, fire that the ancients believed were the basic elements." The sense of "purest essence of a character or situation" is first recorded in the 1580s. This use of the "fifth" as the best is also reflected in <u>La Quinta</u> (The Fifth), the name of a motel reflecting the Spanish king's right to choose first fifth of all spoils (which of course would have been the best part).

The word "interest" is an exact transliteration of the Latin impersonal verb *interest* (literally = to be between [*inter* = between, among, and *sum*] but also came to mean "it is of importance, it makes a difference" [an extension from "be between"] and then "to intervene, take part in"). The Anglo-French (late fourteenth century) *interesse* meant "what one has a legal concern in," based on the medieval Latin noun use of *interresse* (from the Latin infinitive *interesse*) meaning "compensation for loss." The French noun *interest* (damage) influenced the meaning of the English form that is found in the mid-fifteenth century ("legal claim or right; concern; benefit or advantage"). The financial use of the word was distinguished from usury (forbidden by Church law) by referring to "compensation from a defaulting debtor." The idea of "curiosity" is first attested in 1771, interest rate by 1868.

The verb "present" is based on the Latin *praesentāre* (to place before, show, from the adjective *praesens* [*prae* = before, and *esse*]) and appeared in English around 1300. The adjective and noun meaning "at this point in time" (through the Old French *present* [evident, at hand]) are also derived from the Latin *praesens*, a word with multiple nuances such as in *rē praesentī* (on the spot, at the scene of the action).

teneō – The words "content, continent, contain," and "continual" all "hold something together" (*cum* = with, together).

The word "contentment" also literally means "to hold together" but with the added idea of "restrain" as in "hold yourself together, do not become agitated." Thus the Latin word *contentus* means "contained, satisfied" and results in the English adjective "content," which appeared around 1400; the verb in the early fifteenth century.

40 • Latin for the New Millennium: Teacher's Manual, Level 1

A person's "countenance" indicates a calm state of mind, a moderation (*continentia* from *contineō* = the way one holds himself). By the mid-fourteenth century its meaning had evolved from "appearance" to the "face" itself.

The word "entertain" (from *inter* = among, and *teneō* through the Old French *entretenir* = hold together, support) appeared in English during the late fifteenth century and meant "to keep (someone) in a certain frame of mind." The idea of "exercising hospitality" dates to the latter part of the fifteenth century, "to allow (something) for consideration" to the 1610s, "to amuse" to the 1620s.

The prefix of "impertinent" is negative; hence the word originally meant "not related to the point." The idea of "rudely bold" dates to the 1680s and arises from the earlier sense of "not appropriate to the situation."

A "lieutenant" literally "takes the place of another," i.e., he acts for a superior officer (from *locus* = place, and *teneō*). The spelling of *locus* was changed as it passed through Old French.

The word "maintain" is derived from the Latin *manus* "hand" and *teneō*. The word appears in the mid-thirteenth century meaning "to hold in hand; to practice habitually." From the mid-fourteenth century it came to mean "to carry on, keep up" and thus "to preserve, keep in good condition."

A "rein" is used to "hold back" a horse (*re* = back, and *teneō*). The spelling was affected by its passage through the Old French *re(s)ne* and the Middle English *rene*.

A "retinue" is a body of "retainers" (from *re* and *teneō*) who are attached (kept) in service to an important personage. The dental use of "retainer" dates to 1887, but its meaning as "a fee for services" is attested in the mid-fifteenth century.

"Tennis" was a favorite game of medieval knights, who used their palms instead of a racket. The server would call out *tenetz!* (hold, receive, take) to alert his opponent that the ball was coming. The use of the word for the modern game dates to 1874. A tennis court dating back to the Tudor period can still be seen at the manor in Falkland, Scotland.

The musical sense of "tenor" is attested in the late fourteenth century, the voice so called because it usually carried the sustained melody.

A "tenet" is an opinion, doctrine, or dogma that is held as true.

The word "tenure" refers to the holding of something, e.g., an office, faculty position, property, etc.

videō – The words "advice" and "advise" derive from the Latin *mihi est vīsum* (it seems to me) through the Old French *avis*, a shortened form of *ço m'est à vis*. The letter *d* is not historic, and seems to have been added to the English word during the fifteenth century, modeling it after Latin words beginning with *ad*. The *c* was substituted for *s* in the eighteenth century to distinguish the sounds in the noun (advice) and the verb (advise).

"Envy" and "envious" (note the "-ous" suffix) derive from the Latin *invidia* (literally, to look against; hence to hate, envy).

The word "evidence" derives from the Latin *ex* (out from) and *videō* and hence means "clear, obvious." From its appearance in the thirteenth century, it has meant "appearance from which inferences may be drawn." The Latin *ēvidentia* means "clearness, distinction," and thus "proof." The legal usage in English dates to the fifteenth century.

The prefix of "imprudent" means "not"; the Latin *prūdēns* is a contracted form of *prōvidēns* = to see before."

The word "jurisprudence" is derived from *iūris prūdentia* = a knowledge of the law.

Chapter 2 · 41

The word "purvey" comes into English during the late thirteenth century from the Old French *porveoir*, which itself is derived from *prōvideō* (to see on behalf of).

A "surveyor" is an overseer (*super* = over, and *videō*). In the mid-fifteenth century it referred to one who "examines the condition of." The idea of "measuring tracts of ground" dates to the 1540s.

The word "visit" is derived from the Latin *visitāre*, a frequentative of *vīsere* (to go to see) from the fourth principal part of *videō*.

The word "vista" came into English during the 1640s from the Italian *vista* (sight, view), a noun use of the feminine past participle of *vedere* (from the Latin *vidēre*).

The word "television" is derived from the fourth principal part of *videō* and the Greek adverb τῆλε meaning "far off, at a distance." What a viewer sees on television is "at a distance."

vocō – An "advocate" is a person who supports or pleads on another's behalf. It is derived from the Latin *advocō* (*ad* = to, toward, and *vocō*; hence, "call to [for the purpose of aiding]").

The word "avow" is also derived from *advocāre* through the Old French *avoer* meaning "to accept, recognize, especially as a protector," like an advocate.

The word "vouch" is derived from the Latin *vocitāre*, a frequentative of *vocāre* meaning "to summon insistently," and comes into English during the fourteenth century through the Old French *vocher* (to call, summon). The meaning "guarantee to be true or accurate" appeared in the 1590s.

When asked her opinion, Sue gave an <u>equivocal</u> (*aequus* = equal, and *vocō*) answer, favoring neither one side nor the other.

The <u>vocative</u> case in Latin is used for nouns of direct address.

Those people are fortunate who make successful careers out of their <u>vocations</u> (a "calling" to a particular activity).

diū – None

nōn – The derivatives listed are self-explanatory except for "umpire." This word appeared in English as noumper around 1400 from the Latin *nōn* and *par* (equal) through the Old French *nonper* meaning "odd number, not even." It referred to a third person who would act as arbitrator between two sides. The initial *n* was lost by the middle of the fifteenth century due to a faulty separation of "a noumper," heard as "an oumpere." The word assumed its sporting reference in 1714.

A "nonchalant" person is cool and calm (from *nōn* and *caleō* = to be warm) through the French *nonchaloir* (to be indifferent to). The word first appears in English in 1734.

nunc – None

42 • Latin for the New Millennium: Teacher's Manual, Level 1

CHAPTER 3 (PP. 29–42)

GRAMMAR IN LANGUAGE FACTS

Second Declension Masculine –*us*, –*er*, –*ir* Nouns; Genitive Case; Vocative Case; Prepositional Phrases

PAGE 29
Standards 1.1, 2.1, 4.1, 4.2
RRA 4

TEACHER BY THE WAY
Terence's comedy *The Self-Tormentor* is called *Heautontīmōroumenos* in Latin/Greek.

MEMORĀBILE DICTŪ VOCABULARY
ā mē – from me
aliēnus, aliēna, aliēnum – foreign
homō, hominis, *m*. – man
nihil hūmānī – nothing human
putō, putāre, putāvī, putātum – to think

TEACHER BY THE WAY
The teacher may wish to mention that both simple and detailed mosaics such as the one on this page were an exceedingly common form of art in ancient Rome. They became a method of decorating floors, walls, and sometimes ceilings.

Mosaics were composed of small pieces (*tessellae*) of colored glass, pebbles, marble, and other materials put in concrete. There were several techniques for making mosaics. *Opus sectile*, in which patterns were made of larger, specially cut pieces of tile or stone, was used for surfaces of walls and pavements. *Opus tesselātum*, a less expensive method, used small cubes of the same size. *Opus vermiculātum*, in which irregularly or wavy shaped *tessellae* were used, afforded the artist a wide range of colors.

Though continuing the Hellenistic Greek tradition, Roman mosaicists developed their own styles, especially the black and white geometric designs. The Romans in turn influenced the early Christian and Byzantine churches whose walls and ceilings were richly decorated with mosaics.

TEACHING TIP
The teacher may wish to assign Chapter 4 of RRA for reading or review. See p. 28.

PAGE 30
Standards 1.1, 2.1, 3.1, 3.2

TRANSLATION OF LATIN PASSAGE
About Two Brothers

Demea: (*knocking at the door*) Hey, my son!
Syrus and Ctesipho are inside the house.
Syrus: Who is calling? Who is this man?
Ctesipho: (My) father is calling me. I am very afraid.
Syrus: You ought not to (must not) fear. You have to (must, ought to) have good spirit.
Syrus answers the door.
Syrus: Who are you?
Demea: Hello, my good fellow! I am Demea, the father of Aeschinus and Ctesipho. I live in the countryside. I have to (must, ought to) see my son now.
Syrus: Do I have your son? Aeschinus is not at home.
Demea: Is Ctesipho at home?
Syrus: He is not. I do not have your sons.
Demea: Is my brother at home?
Syrus: He is not.
Demea: Where is Ctesipho?
Syrus: Ctesipho is with a friend.
Demea: Where does his friend live?
Syrus: First you walk on the road, then on the hill, then you see a stream. There is a gate and a cottage. Ctesipho is in the cottage with a friend.
Having sent Demea away on a "wild goose chase," Syrus returns inside to report his success to Ctesipho.

TEACHER BY THE WAY
Clever slaves such as Syrus, who both deceive and abet their masters, are stock figures in Greek and Roman comedy.

TEACHING TIP
The teacher may choose to introduce the topic of cultural diversity in ancient Rome after students have read that Terence came from North Africa.

TEACHING TIP
Instruct the students to find Terence on the timeline on pp. 405–408 (SE) and to locate Terence's homeland on the map on pp. xxxiv–xxxv (SE).

PAGE 31

TEACHING TIP
Instruct students to draw a picture and to label the following in their drawing:
- *domus Ctēsiphōnis*
- *domus Aeschinī*
- *casa amīcī*
- *via ad casam amīcī*
- *clīvus*
- *rīvus*

TEACHING TIP
While English derivatives from the asterisked words (i.e., the Vocabulary to Learn) are the topic of Exercise 2 later in this chapter, there are some interesting derivatives from the non-asterisked words. The teacher may choose to discuss these derivatives with the students.

- *bonus* – boon, bounty, bonbon, debonair

  The word "debonair" is derived from the French phrase *de bon aire*, which means "of good lineage." Wellborn people were expected to be courteous, gracious, and charming, to know how to behave properly, hence the modern meaning.
- *clīvus* – declivity
- *frāter* – fratricide, fraternity
- *pater* – patrilineal, patriarchal, patrician, patron
- *porta* – porch, portal, portico
- *prīmum* – primogeniture, prime, primeval, primitive
- *salvē* – salvation, salvage, safety

PAGE 32
Standards 1.1, 3.1, 4.1

ANSWERS TO COMPREHENSION QUESTIONS
1. To find his son Ctesipho.
2. No, he is afraid of his father and is hiding.
3. He is untruthful to him, and somewhat rude.
4. Syrus wants to help Ctesipho.
5. Syrus tells him that Ctesipho is visiting with a friend (which is untrue).

TEACHER BY THE WAY
The theatres built throughout the Roman world were meant to shed reflected glory on the emperor and patrons who provided funding and to impress the audience and visitors by their architectural magnificence and lavish productions. Bosra, conquered by Trajan in the second century CE, was once the capital of the Roman province of Arabia as well as the stopover site on the ancient trade route for pilgrims going to Mecca and Medina. When the Arabs conquered Bosra in the thirteenth century CE, they blocked all the doors and openings with thick walls and transformed the theatre into a citadel. A moat dug with a single bridge gave entry to the fortress. The sands of the desert covered the structure and the building inside for hundreds of years and thus preserved the theatre. The design is characteristic of permanent theatres: a freestanding structure on level ground with a large auditorium, a semicircular orchestral area, and a wide raised stage. The scenic facade (*scenae frons*) was embellished with painting and/or solid architectural decorations. The three doors are separated by the Corinthian capitals that line the stage facade. Excellent acoustics enabled the spectators to hear everything wherever they sat. Though there is no supporting evidence, it is said that during the performance a silk canopy sprayed with perfumed water refreshed the audience in the desert heat.

PAGE 33
Standards 1.1, 1.2
Oral Exercise 1

TEACHING TIP
The teacher may choose to call the students' attention to the word *filius* and its base, which results in the existence of a double set of the letter "i" in the genitive singular as well as in the nominative, dative, and ablative plural.

TEACHER BY THE WAY
There are some feminine nouns of the second declension (mainly names of trees, which are thought of as female beings, since they bear fruits) but only three neuter words: *pelagus* (sea), *vīrus* (venom), and *vulgus* (the public).

▶ EXERCISE 1 ANSWERS

1. accusative singular
2. accusative plural
3. dative singular or ablative singular
4. accusative plural
5. dative singular or ablative singular
6. genitive plural
7. genitive singular or nominative plural
8. dative plural or ablative plural

ORAL EXERCISE 1

*This exercise may be used after second declension **-us** nouns have been presented.*

While looking at the declension of *amīcus*, ask the students to decline *filius*:

	Singular	**Plural**
Nominative	fīlius	fīliī
Genitive	fīliī	fīliōrum
Dative	fīliō	fīliīs
Accusative	fīlium	fīliōs
Ablative	fīliō	fīliīs

PAGE 34
Standards 1.1, 1.2, 3.1, 4.1
Workbook Exercise 2

▶ EXERCISE 2 ANSWERS

1. egotism   ego
2. agrarian   ager
3. virility   vir
4. amicable   amīcus
5. timid   timeō
6. via   via
7. animated   animus
8. domestic   domī
9. puerile   puer

▶ EXERCISE 3 ANSWERS

1. rīvō   to/for the river
2. patriae   of the country
3. fīliī   the sons
4. animō   by/with the spirit
5. fōrmam   form, appearance
6. terrīs   by/with the lands

Chapter 3 • 47

TEACHING TIP

The teacher may wish to ask in Latin what case a noun is. The question is, "*Quō cāsū est?*" Student responses would be

- *nōminātīvō*
- *genitīvō*
- *datīvō*
- *accūsātīvō*
- *ablātīvō*

If the teacher wants to ask the number of a noun, the question is "*Cūius est numerī?*" Student responses would be

- *numerī singulāris*
- *numerī plūrālis*

TEACHING TIP

Although in Exercise 2 the students are directed to find only the derivatives based on the Vocabulary to Learn, they may be interested to learn that there are other derivatives in Exercise 2. The derivation of these words is provided for the teacher's convenience.

2. interested – from *interest* (from *intersum* [to be present]; it concerns, it is of importance).
3. violent – from *violēns* (raging, vehement). sign – *signum* (mark, sign, signal, etc.).
4. colleagues – from *legō* (to choose) + *cum* (together).
5. act – *agō* (to drive, do, discuss, live, spend, etc.). bravery – through ME and MF and It [*bravo*] and Vulgate Latin [*brabus*] from *barbarus* (foreign, savage).
6. Europe – *Eurōpa* (mythical princess of Tyre carried to Crete; name given to the continent).
7. joy – from *gaudium* (joy, delight). face – from *faciēs* (form, face).
8. meddle – from *misceō* (to mingle, blend, join, mix). affairs – from *faciō* (do, make, etc.).
9. adult – from *adolēscō* (to grow up, increase, burn).

PAGE 35
Workbook Exercise 1

TEACHING TIP

Emphasize to the students that the genitive should always be learned together with the nominative, no matter what declension is being studied.

TEACHING TIP

The teacher should stress how slight the differences between these subclasses of second declension nouns actually are. If the student knows the paradigm for *amīcus*, s/he essentially knows all of the types of masculine nouns in the second declension. The only additional necessity is that of knowing the nominative and the genitive forms for the subclasses. Stressing similarities and common elements will help students see how easy these forms are to learn.

TEACHING TIP
Additional reproducible worksheets, morphology charts, and their associated answer keys, related to this material, are available for download at www.lnm.bolchazy.com.
- **Noun Declensions**

PAGE 36
Standards 1.1, 1.2

▶ EXERCISE 4 ANSWERS
1. dative plural, ablative plural — agrō, agrō
2. genitive plural — lupae
3. dative singular, ablative singular — amīcīs, amīcīs
4. accusative plural — virum
5. nominative plural, genitive singular — rīvus, rīvōrum
6. genitive plural — animī

▶ EXERCISE 5 ANSWERS
1. agrīs — by/with the fields
2. puerō — to/for the boy
3. virīs — to/for the men
4. puellae — of the girl
5. filiōrum — of the sons
6. animum — the spirit

TEACHING TIP
The chart on second declension noun types on this page does not include the plural; teachers may wish to have students complete the chart by declining the plural of each of the nouns in the chart, either orally or in written form.

TEACHING TIP
Students are directed to identify the case and number of each noun in Exercise 4. Teachers may wish to conduct this exercise in Latin. The information on how to ask case and number in Latin and how the students should answer is on p. 48.

PAGE 37
Standards 1.1, 3.1, 4.1
Oral Exercise 2

TEACHER BY THE WAY
The name Ctēsiphō belongs to the third declension, which the students have not learned yet.

▶ EXERCISE 6 ANSWERS

1. agricolae — The daughter of the farmer/farmer's daughter loves an athlete.
2. poētae — The son of the poet/poet's son loves stories.
3. amīcōrum — We live in the cottage of friends/(our) friends' cottage.
4. lupae — The boys fear the appearance of the wolf/the wolf's appearance.
5. nautae — The mind of the sailor/sailor's mind expects the land.
6. poētārum — We tell the stories of poets/poets' stories.
7. patriae — You (pl.) love the fields of the fatherland/fatherland's fields.

ORAL EXERCISE 2

This exercise may be used anytime after the genitive case has been presented.

After explaining that these words are not yet to be memorized, use one of the CPOs to put the following nouns, and any others of the first and second declensions that seem appropriate, on view with their definitions.

Then ask the students to guess to whom the noun belongs by saying a phrase that consists of two nouns, one in the genitive. You may also draw things represented by the nouns in the Vocabulary to Learn of this chapter, such as *rīvus* and *casa*, and ask them to indicate the possessor in a similar way. If desired, you may draw an additional clue to help the student guess the possessor the teacher has in mind.

raeda, raedae, *f.* – car
anchora, anchorae, *f.* – anchor
liber, librī, *m.* – book
gladius, gladiī, *m.* – sword
tunica, tunicae, *f.* – coat
calamus, calamī, *m.* – pen

Possible answers may include:

Casa agricolae, amīcī, fīliae, fīliī, lupae, puellae, puerī, nautae, poētae, āthlētae, virī, Dēmeae, Aeschinī.

PAGE 38
Standards 1.1, 1.2
Oral Exercise 3

TEACHING TIP
The teacher may wish to take this opportunity to remind students that, although the nominative and vocative forms are frequently identical, the context, especially a conversation or dialogue, always tells the reader—or listener—which of the two cases is meant.

▶ EXERCISE 7 ANSWERS

1. amīce
2. agrīs
3. fīlium
4. amīcī
5. amīcō

ORAL EXERCISE 3

This exercise may be used anytime after the vocative case has been presented.

The teacher assigns the students different roles and names. Then the students greet each other with *Salvē, . . .* and a vocative.

Here are some of the possible roles and names in the nominative and the vocative.

fīlius	*fīlī*	*āthlēta*	*āthlēta*
fīlia	*fīlia*	*Aeschinus*	*Aeschine*
puer	*puer*	*Dēmea*	*Dēmea*
puella	*puella*	*Mārcus*	*Mārce*
agricola	*agricola*	*Marīa*	*Marīa*
nauta	*nauta*	*Christīna*	*Christīna*
poēta	*poēta*	*Helena*	*Helena*
vir	*vir*		

If the students want to have Latin names, this exercise may be done with the names they have chosen for themselves.

PAGE 39
Standards 1.1, 2.2, 4.1

TEACHING TIP

The teacher should stress that prepositions and prepositional phrases are a fundamental part of English, even though there are no case endings in English. Give a number of examples in English.

The teacher should also stress that the case that goes with a given preposition must be learned as a part of the Vocabulary to Learn.

TEACHING TIP

The teacher should choose whether to indicate briefly to students that *domī* is the locative case or wait until this form is learned. The irregular declension of *domus* and a brief explanation of the locative form *domī* is on p. 306 (SE).

Chapter 3 • 51

TEACHER BY THE WAY
More information on the construction of Roman roads is presented on pp. 275–277 (SE). The blocks of stone used to form the top layer of the *Via Sacra*, the Sacred Way, were made of volcanic stone, an abundance of which is found in Italy. Either here or later on, the teacher may consider introducing a discussion on travel during Roman times and the types of transportation that were available. (Some information on types of transportation is on p. 419 of this teacher's manual.)

TEACHER BY THE WAY
The Arch of Titus, seen in the background of the picture on this page, is one of several extant arches, a list of which can be found on p. 63. Notable, however, is how much the famous Arc de Triomphe in Paris recalls the Arch of Titus. Napoleon, who admired the Romans and had the title of "Consul," designed the Arc de Triomphe in 1806 to honor his army after the Austerlitz victory in 1805. The names of 128 battles with the name of the general of each are written on the walls under the vault. In 1920, the body of an unknown soldier was buried under the Arc, symbolizing the 1,500,000 French soldiers who died in World War I.

PAGE 40
Standards 1.1, 1.2
Oral Exercise 4; Workbook Exercises 3, 4, 5, 6, 7, Content Questions

▶ EXERCISE 8 ANSWERS
1. cum   The boy is waiting for the sailor with a girl.
2. in   In the story the she-wolf is taking care of the boys.
3. cum   We live with friends.
4. in   The man is on the road.
5. in   The she-wolf is in the field.

ORAL EXERCISE 4
This exercise may be used anytime after prepositional phrases have been presented.
The teacher says "*Ambulō cum puell . . .*" (saying the base of the noun without the ending) "I am walking with . . ." and asks the students to repeat the phrase, but also to fill in the right ending.

Possible exercise sentences would be: *Ambulō cum puellā/puellīs, cum puerō/puerīs, cum filiā/filiābus, cum filiō/filiīs, cum nautā/nautīs, cum agricolā/agricolīs, cum poētā/poētīs, cum virō/virīs, cum amīcō/amīcīs.*

TEACHING TIP
The teacher may choose to remind students that there is a special form *filiābus* for the daughters, which is used in order to avoid confusion with *filiīs*.

Then the teacher says *Sum in aqu . . .* "I am in . . ." and asks the students to repeat the phrase but also to supply the right ending. Possible answers would be:

Sum in aquā, in agrō/agrīs, in viā/viīs, in patriā, in rīvō, in terrā.

Remind the students simply to say *domī* to indicate that you are "at home."

An alternative exercise to what is above would be for the teacher to use gestures to get the student to say *Sum in aquā*. In this case the teacher might make arm movements such as are made during swimming to get the student to say *Sum in aquā*. Or a picture of water, a road, a field, etc., can be used to get the answer. This would become a type of little game if the teacher says first, "*Ubi sum?*" and then makes the gesture or holds up the picture before the student gives the answer.

▶ EXERCISE 9 ANSWERS

1. vērum
2. falsum
3. falsum
4. vērum

PAGE 41
Standards 1.2, 2.1, 4.1, 4.2
Oral Exercises 5, 6, 7, and Dictation

TRANSLATION OF THE LATIN CONVERSATION
Teacher: Hello, students!
Students: Hello, teacher!
Mark: Hey, Mary, Helen! Is the teacher good?
Teacher: Shh! Silence! We have a new student. What is your name?
Mark: My name is Mark.
Teacher: Get up and come to the board! Decline "filius" (son)!
Mark: (*to Mary*) I am afraid! (*to the teacher*) May I go to the bathroom?
Teacher: You may not. You have to write. Here is the chalk.

TEACHER BY THE WAY
The forms *surgās* and *veniās* in the dialogue are in the subjunctive used in a hortatory meaning, a milder form of a command.

TEACHING TIP
Teachers may choose to use some or all of these classroom expressions as part of daily classroom interaction.

Chapter 3 • 53

ORAL EXERCISE 5

This exercise may be used at the end of Chapter 3 as a review or anytime after the second declension and the vocative case have been presented.

Say a form in the singular and ask individual students to repeat the noun and then change it into plural.

Teacher: agrī	**Student:** agrōrum	**Teacher:** animus	**Student:** animī
Teacher: puer	**Student:** puerī	**Teacher:** fīlius	**Student:** fīliī
Teacher: amīcō	**Student:** amīcīs	**Teacher:** amīce	**Student:** amīcī
Teacher: lupa	**Student:** lupae	**Teacher:** puellā	**Student:** puellīs
Teacher: virum	**Student:** virōs	**Teacher:** aquae	**Student:** aquārum/aquīs

ORAL EXERCISE 6

This exercise may be used as a review exercise at the end of Chapter 3 or anytime after the vocative case has been presented.

The students may choose Latin names: Plautus, Mārcus, Aeschinus, Syrus, Marīa, Helena, Christīna, etc.

Instruct them to call each other: *Heus* ("hey, hi") *Plaute; Heus Mārce; Heus Aeschine; Heus Syre; Heus Marīa; Heus Helena; Heus Christīna*, etc.

Then divide the students into small groups and instruct them to draw the attention of the next group: *Heus Plaute et Helena; Heus Mārce et Christīna*, etc.

TEACHING TIP

If anybody chooses *Terentius* or another name ending in *-ius*, the teacher needs to remind the students that the vocative of such names ends in *-ī*: *Terentī*.

Tell the students that "teacher" in Latin is *magister, magistrī*, m., if a man, and *magistra, magistrae*, f., if a woman. The students may also use the vocatives of these words and get into the habit of greeting the teacher as well.

ORAL EXERCISE 7 AND DICTATION

This combined exercise may be used to conclude the chapter or at any time after the students have learned the second declension and prepositional phrases.

Dictate each sentence. Then ask individual students to read it and to change orally all singular forms into the plural.

1. **Teacher:** Vir fīlium vocat. **Student:** Virī fīliōs vocant.
2. **Teacher:** Fīlius virum nōn amat. **Student:** Fīliī virōs nōn amant.
3. **Teacher:** Vir in agrō habitat. **Student:** Virī in agrīs habitant.
4. **Teacher:** Fīlius in viā ambulat. **Student:** Fīliī in viīs ambulant.
5. **Teacher:** Fīlius amīcum exspectat. **Student:** Fīliī amīcōs exspectant.
6. **Teacher:** Fīlius fābulam nārrat. **Student:** Fīliī fābulās nārrant.

PAGE 42
Standard 4.1

DERIVATIVES

ager – An <u>agrarian</u> society depends primarily on farming.

The word "peregrination," which literally means "through a field," refers to travels, especially those on foot. The Latin participle *peregrinātus* meant "traveled abroad." A book containing the letters of Charles Stewart Hardinge, a nineteenth century British official in India, is titled *My Indian Peregrinations*.

The word "pilgrim" is derived through the Old French *pelerine, peregrine* (crusader, foreigner, stranger, pilgrim) from the Latin *peregrinus* (foreigner). The change of *r* to *l* is common in Romance languages by dissimilation (the speech sound becomes less like a neighboring sound or even disappears, e.g., we often say "gov-e-ner" for "governor"). The Italian *pellegrino* also demonstrates this change.

The word "acre" is derived from the Latin *ager* but goes back to a pre-Indo-European base as evidenced in the Proto-Germanic *akroy*, Old Norse *akr*, Middle Dutch *acker*, Gothic *akrs*, Greek αγρός, and Sanskrit *ajras* which all mean "tilled field" or "open land."

See also 1.1 (*agricola*) for other derivatives.

amīcus – See 1.1 (*amat*) for "amicable" and "inimical."

animus – The word "animadversion" literally means "turning the mind to." The idea of censure is in the Latin verb *animadvertō* (to pay attention to, notice, censure, punish). It was used as a euphemism for "to punish with death." Citizens have lately shown their <u>animadversion</u> against Congress.

The word "animosity" also exhibits this negative quality.

On the other hand, "magnanimity" and "magnanimous" (note the "-ous" suffix) are positive words literally meaning "great minded." The <u>magnanimous</u> man was generous in his forgiveness of the insult.

The word "pusillanimous," however, is again a negative, meaning "little courage" (from the Latin *pullus* = young animal; *pusillus* is a diminutive form = very little). Anna is very <u>pusillanimous</u> when it comes to decision-making.

The townspeople were of one mind on the need to build a new bridge and voted <u>unanimously</u> to raise taxes to pay for it.

casa – A <u>casino</u> is a place for gambling where people bet against the house.

domī – There is a movement in this country toward buying <u>domestic</u> goods and to avoid foreign products when possible.

It is now politically correct to call servants employed in a home <u>domestics</u> instead of "maids" or "hired help."

According to lawyers, a permanent legal residence is called a <u>domicile</u>.

Dogs were <u>domesticated</u> thousands of years before cats and horses. In fact, one source claims gray wolves, the ancestors of the dog, domesticated humans and not the other way around.

The word "domain" comes into English during the fifteenth century through the Middle French *domaine* (estate) and Old French *demaine* (lord's estate) from the Latin *dominium* (absolute ownership), which itself derives from *dominus* (master, owner of a house = *domus*). The Internet use of the word is attested by 1985.

Chapter 3 • 55

The word "dome" came into English during the 1650s through the Middle French *dome* and Italian *duomo* from the Latin *domus Deī* (the house of God) and therefore was a favorite roof formation for Christian churches. It is related to the Greek δῶμα which originally meant "chief room or hall" and in the plural "a whole house." The structural form itself dates to earlier times and can be seen in the igloos of Eskimos and the Pantheon of Rome. The use of domes in Islamic architecture has its roots in the Roman-Syria (Byzantine) style.

fīlius – See *fīlia*,1.1.

puer – See *puella*, 1.1.

rīvus – The words "derivation, derivative," and "derive" all literally mean "down from (*dē*) a stream." Thus the Latin *dērīvāre* means "to draw off" as in a diversion "from a stream." The Middle English *dirive(n)* meant "to flow, drain from a spring" (the origin of the water); hence a "derivative" "flows from" the word of origin.

A "rivulet" is a little stream. Note the diminutive suffix.

The word "rival" originally referred to one who used a stream in common with another farmer or herdsman (Latin *rīvālis*). The notion of competition seems to have been embedded in the word early and is commonly so used in classical Latin (cf. Catullus 57.9; Propertius 1.8.45; Ovid, *Amōrēs* 1.8.95).

Teachers are advised to warn students against false derivatives, i.e., the word "river" is not derived from *rīvus* (a common error) but from *rīpa* (bank of a stream).

via – A <u>devious</u> person departs "down from" the proper "way" and follows a circuitous or crooked path.

The word "impervious" (note the "-ous" suffix) is based on three Latin words: *in* (not), *per* (through), and *via*. Thus the word means "impenetrable," or "incapable of being affected." My mother remained <u>impervious</u> to any arguments for extending my nightly curfew.

The word "convey" consists of the Latin *cum* (together) and *via*; hence "to accompany on the way." By the late fourteenth century its meaning in English had expanded to "transport" from the Old French *convoier* (to escort). During the fifteenth to seventeenth centuries it was also used as a euphemism for "steal."

The word "convoy" appeared in the early sixteenth century meaning "the act of guiding or escorting for protection." It likewise was derived through the Old French *convoier*. It acquired its meaning of "a train of ships or wagons carrying munitions or wartime provisions under escort" around 1600.

An "envoy" today is a diplomatic agent but in the 1660s the word meant "messenger" and was derived through the twelfth century French *envoyé* (messenger) from the Late Latin *inviatus* (sent on the road [a journey]).

An "invoice" is a list of goods sent and was also derived through the French *envoyer* (to send). It appeared in English during the 1550s as a noun and as a verb during the 1690s.

The solution to the problem presented by the senators <u>obviated</u> the difficulties. The word consists of the preposition *ob* (in front of) and *via*; hence its meaning "to block."

On the other hand, something that stands "in front of" a person, "in the way of," is easily seen ("obvious").

The word "trivial" in Latin originally meant "where three roads meet" (*trēs* = three, and *via*).

56 • Latin for the New Millennium: Teacher's Manual, Level 1

The basic idea is "that which may be found anywhere." The Latin *trivium* meant "public street" as well as "crossroads." In medieval Latin the *trivium* consisted of the first three of the seven liberal arts (grammar, rhetoric, and dialectic, followed by music, arithmetic, geometry, and astronomy). The *trivium* was also part and parcel of a Roman boy's training, the subjects every educated Roman should know. The meaning "ordinary" is attested in English during the 1580s and "insignificant" during the 1590s.

The word "viaduct" is composed of *via* and *ductus* (leading). A viaduct is a bridge carrying (leading) a road over a valley or railroad tracks or another road.

In addition to "road, way, or street," *via* also means "journey." The related Latin noun *viāticum* meant "provisions for a journey." The Late Latin limited its meaning to "journey" and through this came the Old French *veiage* (travel, journey), which gave rise around 1300 to the English "voyage."

vir – The virility of the man was clearly seen in his masculine strength.

Virtue was considered the worth of a man, in his moral excellence, his goodness, and his righteousness. The phrase "by virtue of" appears in English during the early thirteenth century, preserving the Middle English sense of "efficacy" (from the Latin *efficiō* = to bring about). The Seven Cardinal (from the Latin *cardō* = hinge) Virtues were divided into the four natural (cf. Plato, *Protagoras* 330b, and Cicero, *Dē inventiōne* 2.53, the latter discussing them in many of his works)—wisdom, justice, courage, temperance—and the three theological—faith, hope, and charity.

The word "virtual" appears in English during the late fourteenth century meaning "influencing by physical virtues or capabilities" and derived from the Latin *virtūs* through the medieval Latin *virtuālis*. The meaning of "being something in essence though not in name" (e.g., virtual poverty) is first recorded in the 1650s. The computer use of "not physically existing but made to appear by software" dates to 1959.

In the 1610s a "virtuoso" was a scholar or connoisseur, the word derived through the Italian *virtuoso* (skilled, learned, of exceptional worth) from the Latin *virtūs* meaning "excellence, worth." The meaning of "a person with great skill," as in music, is first attested in 1743. Note the suffix "-oso" which means the same as "-ous" (full of). The word "virtuous" exhibits this suffix in English.

The teacher should warn the students about "lookalikes," i.e., such words as "virulence" (from *vīrus* = poison) and "viridian" (from *viridis* = green).

A "triumvirate" consists of three men ruling jointly as Caesar, Pompey, and Crassus did in 60 BCE. A triumvirate or troika of Stalin, Kamenov, and Zinouien was formed in 1923 against Trotsky.

ego – "Egoism" is the moral concept of self-interest as the substance of living as opposed to altruism which embodies a concern for the welfare of others. Ayn Rand based her novel *The Fountainhead* on the concept of egoism.

On the other hand, "egotism" is the practice of excessive and objectionable references to oneself based on overstated evaluations of one's mental prowess, looks, skills, etc. It is based on the misbelief that some of us are special and better than others.

tū – None

timeō – The word "intimidate" comes into English during the 1640s from the medieval Latin *intimidāre* (*in* = into and *timeō*; literally "into fear"). It is interesting to compare *intimidāre* to the classical Latin *intimidus* meaning "fearless." Here the prefix acts as a negative.

Note the "-ous" suffix of "timorous."

deinde – None

valdē – The word "valid" appears in English during the 1570s meaning "having force in law" and is derived from the Latin *validus* (strong). "Validate" (verb) and "validity" (noun) are likewise derived and have similar meanings.

cum – Compounds derived from *cum* will be dealt with under the main root, e.g., "compose" under *pōnō*; "comfort" under *fortis*; "concert" under *certo*; "concord" under *cor*, etc.

in – Compounds derived from *in* will be discussed under the main root, e.g., "incorporate" (*in* = into) under *corpus*; "invalid" (*in* = not) under *valeō*; "inflammable" (*in* = an intensive) under *flamma*.

REVIEW 1: CHAPTERS 1–3
(PP. 43–56)

PAGE 43

TEACHING TIP

One way to combine vocabulary review, student movement, and student ability to compose simple sentences in Latin is the following.

- Instruct the students to review individually the words on p. 43 (SE) for a short amount of time.
- Ask each student in the class to choose either a noun or a verb and to write the complete vocabulary entry of the chosen word in large letters on a piece of paper.
- Explain to the students that, at a given signal from the teacher, they will all need to stand up and hold their paper with the Latin word written on it in a way that is visible to other members of the class.
- After the students are standing, each student is to find another student whose word will combine logically with the student's own word. For example, the student holding *nārrō, nārrāre, nārrāvī, nārrātum* might pair up with the student whose word is *fābula, fābulae,* f.
- The two paired students then need to construct a sentence in Latin using their two words. Nouns may be used in different cases and verbs may be used in different persons. Encourage the students to make simple sentences since they are at the very beginning stage of learning Latin.
- After all the pairs of students have completed making their sentences, call on each pair in turn to say their sentence aloud to the rest of the class.
- The class, with the help of the teacher if necessary, will comment in an appropriate way on whether the sentence makes sense and whether it is correct grammatically.
- Some examples of pairs of words that have been turned into a Latin sentence include but are not limited to

Fābulam nārrāmus.	Agricolam vocō.
Aquam vident.	Lupam timēs.
Amīcōs cūrat.	Poēta est.
Domī habitātis.	Puerī ambulant.

After completing the activity, the teacher may wish to have the students exchange papers and do the activity again.

PAGE 44
Standards 1.1, 1.2

▶ EXERCISE 1 ANSWERS

Singular

Nominative	terra	rīvus	socer	liber
Genitive	terrae	rīvī	socerī	librī
Dative	terrae	rīvō	socerō	librō
Accusative	terram	rīvum	socerum	librum
Ablative	terrā	rīvō	socerō	librō
Vocative	terra	rīve	socer	liber

Plural

Nominative	terrae	rīvī	socerī	librī
Genitive	terrārum	rīvōrum	socerōrum	librōrum
Dative	terrīs	rīvīs	socerīs	librīs
Accusative	terrās	rīvōs	socerōs	librōs
Ablative	terrīs	rīvīs	socerīs	librīs
Vocative	terrae	rīvī	socerī	librī

▶ EXERCISE 2 ANSWERS

Infinitives: habēre – to have   exspectāre – to wait for   dēbēre – to owe, ought   cūrāre – to take care of

Singular

First person	habeō	exspectō	dēbeō	cūrō
Second person	habēs	exspectās	dēbēs	cūrās
Third person	habet	exspectat	dēbet	cūrat

Plural

First person	habēmus	exspectāmus	dēbēmus	cūrāmus
Second person	habētis	exspectātis	dēbētis	cūrātis
Third person	habent	exspectant	dēbent	cūrant

▶ EXERCISE 3 ANSWERS

1. fābulās   We tell stories.
2. vidēs   You see the friend.
3. poēta   I am not a poet.
4. cūrāre   We ought to take care of the son.
5. lupam   I do not fear the she-wolf.
6. nauta   The son is not a sailor.

PAGE 45
Standards 1.1, 1.2

▶ EXERCISE 4 ANSWERS

Dēmea <u>filium</u> vocat. Syrus Dēmeam convenit (*meets*) <u>et</u> dīcit (*says*): "Fīlius nōn est hīc (*here*)." Ctēsiphō autem (*however*) audit (*hears*) et Dēmeam <u>valdē</u> timet. Syrus dīcit: "Fīliōs tuōs (*your*) ego nōn teneō. Fīliōs tuōs ego nōn <u>habeō</u>." Dēmea rogat (*asks*): "Ubi (*where*) <u>est</u> Ctēsiphō? Ubi est <u>filius</u>?" Syrus dīcit: "Ctēsiphō est <u>in</u> casā <u>cum</u> amīcō." Itaque Dēmea ad (*to*) amīcum ambulāre <u>dēbet</u>.

Demea calls <his> <u>son</u>. Syrus meets Demea <u>and</u> says: "<Your> son is not here." Ctesipho however hears and fears Demea <u>greatly</u>. Syrus says: "I am not holding your sons. <u>I</u> do not <u>have</u> your sons." Demea asks: "Where <u>is</u> Ctesipho? Where is <my> <u>son</u>?" Syrus says: "Ctesipho is <u>in</u> the house <u>with</u> a friend." And so Demea <u>has</u> to walk to the friend.

TEACHING TIP
The teacher may wish to instruct the student to perform orally Exercise 4, after the answers have been given and corrected for accuracy. This will give the students more pronunciation practice and promote oral understanding of Latin.

▶ EXERCISE 5 ANSWERS

1. animī poētārum — the spirits of the poets
2. aqua āthlētae — the water of the athlete
3. terra filiārum — the land of the daughters
4. patria puerōrum — the fatherland of the boys
5. amīcus filiī — the son's friend
6. fōrma rīvōrum — the shape of the streams

TEACHING TIP
If the students need more practice like Exercise 5, here are some additional pairs of words. This may be done in oral or written format. The answers are provided for the teacher's convenience.

ager	agricola (singular)	ager agricolae	the field of the farmer or the farmer's field
animus	puella (singular)	animus puellae	the mind of the girl or the girl's mind
casa	amīcus (plural)	casa amīcōrum	the house of the friends or the friends' house
fābula	nauta (plural)	fābula nautārum	the story of the sailors or the sailors' story
filia	vir (singular)	filia virī	the daughter of the man or the man's daughter

Review 1: Chapters 1–3 • 61

PAGE 46
Standards 1.1, 2.1, 2.2, 3.1, 3.2, 4.2
Oral Exercise 1

TEACHER BY THE WAY
The actual books (membranes or papyrus rolls) on which Martial's poems were first written down have long since disappeared, as almost any text written in ancient times (except for the stone inscriptions and papyri, largely preserved in the sands of Egypt), and today we make judgments about nearly all the literary works of antiquity from the later manuscripts on which they were transcribed during the Middle Ages. More information about ancient books is given on p. 479.

TEACHING TIP
The caption on p. 46 (SE) does not give the Latin terms for the writing instruments. Have students do an internet search to find the Latin terms.

▶ EXERCISE 6 ANSWERS
I do not love you, Sabidius, and I cannot say why.
I can say only this: I do not love you.

TEACHER BY THE WAY
If the students notice that *amō* has a short *-o* here, the teacher may explain that it is for metrical reasons.

ORAL EXERCISE 1
This exercise may be used after Exercise 6.
The teacher may organize a game in which students supply other words/names in place of *Sabidī*.

TEACHING TIP
Instruct the students to find Martial on the timeline on pp. 405–408 (SE).

TEACHING TIP
Since Martial lived so much later than Plautus and Terence, the teacher may wish to have the students read the section about Martial in Chapter 6A of RRA.

CONSIDERING THE CLASSICAL GODS

PAGE 47
Standards 2.2, 3.1, 3.2
ODF 1, 2, 3.6

HOW TO USE THIS BOOK AND ITS ENRICHMENT TEXTS

The classical mythology enrichment text entitled *The Original Dysfunctional Family* and abbreviated ODF provides additional information about each of the deities discussed in this book. Notation will be found in the sections of this book entitled "Considering the Classical Gods" about what chapter in ODF coordinates with these sections.

TEACHING TIP
Instruct the students to find the Campus Martius and the Temple of Mars Ultor on the map on p. 233 (SE).

TEACHER BY THE WAY
Mars's priests, called Saliī, carried sacred shields called *ancīlia* around the city in his honor during the month of March. A depiction of the special animal sacrifice in his honor (*suovetaurīlia*) can be found both on the Āra Pācis, a monument dedicated to Augustus, and on Trajan's Column. His title "*Ultor*" means "Avenger."

TEACHING TIP
The teacher may wish to discuss with students the strict conditions required by the Senate for the celebratory procession of a victorious general (*triumphātor*) from the Campus Martius to the Temple of Jupiter Capitolinus. If this was not allowed, an *ovātiō* was often granted and the differences were notable.

TEACHER BY THE WAY
The general's *imperium* (right to command) was only valid in Rome for the day of the triumph. Until the Senate gave permission, the general and his army could not enter the city itself. Triumphal arches also commemorated such victories. Some famous triumphal arches are listed below:

- The triumphal arch in Orange, France, was built during the reign of Augustus to commemorate the town's beginning as a *colōnia* in 35 BCE.
- The arch of Trajan at Beneventum was built between 114 and 166 CE to honor Trajan.
- The arch of Titus was built and dedicated in 85 CE to commemorate Titus's capture of Jerusalem. The arch of Titus is located in the Roman Forum on the Via Sacra at its highest point.
- The arch of Septimius Severus, located in the Roman Forum, was dedicated in 203 CE to commemorate victories over Parthia.
- The arch of Constantine, located near the Colosseum, was built in 315 CE to honor the victory at the Milvian Bridge in 312 CE.

PAGE 48

Standards 2.1, 2.2, 3.1, 3.2
ODF 3.1, ODF 3.2

TEACHER BY THE WAY

Uranus is considered to be the personification of heaven.

TEACHER BY THE WAY

Myths about Jupiter's affairs with other goddesses and mortals include the stories of Europa, Io, Callisto, and Semele. Many of the women involved with Jupiter are now the names of the moons associated with the planet Jupiter.

TEACHING TIP

The teacher may wish to describe the roots of the word "pantheon" from the Greek "*pan*" meaning "all" and "*theon*" meaning "of the gods."

COMPREHENSION QUESTIONS AND ANSWERS FOR PAGES 47–49 (SE)

Reproducible versions of the questions alone are available at **www.lnm.bolchazy.com**.

1. In what ways did the Greeks and Romans differ in their consideration of Ares/Mars?

   While the Greeks depicted Ares unattractively, as unsuccessful in battle and engaging in embarrassing behavior, the Romans held him in higher esteem. They connected Mars to the origins of their city and made him the father of Romulus and Remus. The Campus Martius, the special sacrifice to Mars at census time, and the Temple of Mars Ultor attest to that esteem.

2. Explain what the census was about.

   Every five years, Rome conducted an official counting of its citizens.

3. What motivated Augustus to build the Temple of Mars Ultor?

   It honored Mars and commemorated Augustus's victory at the Battle of Philippi (42 BCE) in which he avenged the assassination of his adoptive father, Julius Caesar.

4. What characteristic in the fresco on p. 47 (SE) helps the viewer recognize Mars?

   The war helmet on the male figure to the left.

5. When would a Roman invoke the name of Jupiter?

   When swearing an oath calling upon Jupiter as a witness or in an exclamation.

6. How did Rhea outwit her husband?

   In order to outwit Cronus/Saturn, who had eaten all of his children, lest he suffer the same fate as his own father Uranus whom he had overthrown, Rhea substituted a stone for her last son Zeus, who subsequently rescued his siblings from Cronus's stomach.

7. What caused strife between Juno and her husband?

   Jupiter's many love affairs upset Juno, as did the offspring of those extramarital unions.

8. Explain the connection between the English word "money" and Juno.

   As a giver of advice, Juno was known as *Iūnō Monēta*. At the Temple of Juno Moneta in Rome, a mint produced coins. The Latin word *monēta* acquired the meaning "coined money" or "currency." Hence, English has the word "money."

PAGE 49
Standard 1.1

TEACHING TIP
The teacher may wish to instruct the students to locate the Temple of Juno Moneta, mentioned here, on the map on p. 233 (SE).

TEACHER BY THE WAY
Paestum, the Greek colony called Poseidonia and dedicated to the god Poseidon, features several examples of wonderfully preserved Greek temples like this one in the archaic style.

The numerous Greek cities in southern Italy were collectively referred to as *Magna Graecia*. Paestum became a Roman colony in 273 BCE and firmly resisted Hannibal in the Punic Wars. The temples located there present an impressive array of Doric architecture. These temples include an earlier sixth-century temple of Hera; a temple of Athena, known later as a temple of Ceres; a later temple dedicated to Hera (pictured). Most of the exterior parts of the pictured temple have survived, including the architraves, frieze, and pediments, in addition to the columns. The peristyle columns are made of local travertine, originally covered with stucco to resemble marble. Each column has twenty-four flutes. The metopes and pediments were lacking sculptural decorations so perhaps they were painted instead or even left undecorated. The division of the *cella* in three by internal columns suggests multiple dedications to Hera, Zeus, and an unknown third deity.

In the illustration on p. 49 (SE) a second Doric temple to Hera is visible on the side. Small terracotta figurines establish it as dedicated to the goddess. Both temples face east so the cult statue within the *cella* (sanctuary) will see the rising sun. The cult statue was probably made of wood since there are no traces of it on the floor where the statue should be. Worshippers performed rituals at an outside altar since only priests were allowed inside the sacred area. Paestum was famous for its flowers. Vergil mentions in the *Georgics* "the twice blooming roses of Paestum." Unfortunately the city had to be abandoned because malaria-infested swamps made it unhealthy.

READING PASSAGE TRANSLATION
Jupiter and Juno have a son. The son is Mars. Mars loves battles very much, and always prepares battles. Mars does not care for the life of men. And so the Greeks do not love him. In a certain battle men wound the god. The god runs away and the Greeks laugh.

PAGE 50

TEACHING TIP
Ask students to locate Mt. Olympus on the map on pp. xxxiv–xxxv (SE). Use this map to introduce the students to the various Latin words for places and to the geography of the ancient world.

TEACHER BY THE WAY
Mt. Olympus is the tallest mountain in Greece and is 2,919 meters or 9,600 feet high. Mt. Olympus is in the northern part of Greece while Olympia, site of a sanctuary sacred to Zeus where the Olympic Games were held, is on the Peloponnesus in southern Greece.

Mt. Olympus is situated in mainland Greece at 40°05′N, 22°21′E. Thessaloniki, the second largest city in Greece, is about 100 kilometers away from Mt. Olympus. The highest peak of Mt. Olympus is Mitikas at 2,919 meters tall and it is the highest peak in all of Greece. Trees and plant life, of which there are some 1,700 species, abound on this mountain.

Climbing Mt. Olympus is a favorite with both natives and tourists alike. Hikes to Mt. Olympus start at the town of Litochoro, which can be reached by bus from Athens and Thessaloniki. Christos Kakolos, Frederic Boissonas, and Daniel Baud-Bovy first reached the peak in 1913. It is a two-day climb to the top of Mt. Olympus, although experienced hikers have reached the top in one day, and there are hiking trails.

At the foot of Mt. Olympus is ancient Dion where there is an archaeological park and a museum. Alexander the Great made sacrifices to the gods here before leaving to conquer far-off places. In the restored ancient theatre located here, plays are performed during the August Olympus Festival. The ruins of a Temple of Isis are also located at Dion.

Mt. Olympus in Greece is not the only mountain with this name. There are also mountains of the same name in ancient Phrygia and in Cyprus as well as in Utah, Washington State, and San Francisco, California, all in the USA. There is also a Mt. Olympus on the planet Mars.

CONNECTING WITH THE ANCIENT WORLD

PAGE 51

Standards 2.1, 3.1, 3.2, 4.2

TEACHING TIP

The teacher may choose to introduce the various classes of Roman society (plebs, equites, patricians) in conjunction with the section on slavery. This may also lead to a discussion on patrons and clients. Additionally, given the ethnic diversity of the freed slaves (*lībertī*) who were added to the population, multiculturalism can again be considered.

COMPREHENSION QUESTIONS AND ANSWERS FOR PAGES 51–52 (SE)

Reproducible versions of the questions alone are available at **www.lnm.bolchazy.com**.

1. In what ways did slavery in ancient Rome differ from slavery in antebellum America?

    Roman slaves were not from a single race or culture but from all over the Roman world and its neighbors. As was customary in the ancient world, a victorious army would take captives who would become slaves. It seems that in the Roman world, a slave could liberate himself more readily than a slave in early America.

2. Identify the following terms related to Roman slavery: *mangōnēs, pecūlium, manūmissiō, FUG*.

    mangōnēs = slave dealers; *pecūlium* = a slave's accumulated savings; *manūmissiō* = liberation by one's master for good service; *FUG* = abbreviation for a runaway slave, a *fugitīvus*, who had been recovered. These letters would be branded on the recaptured slave's forehead.

3. What different roles did slaves perform in the Roman world?

    House slaves were often educated and served as teachers, tutors, or as literary and business assistants to their master. In addition to various household tasks, slaves also served in the fields and the mines.

4. How might a slave become a free man?

    He could purchase his freedom by means of his accumulated savings, *pecūlium*, or might be rewarded for good service with manumission (*manūmissiō*), freedom granted by his master. In addition, masters sometimes freed their slaves through their last will and testament.

5. Explain what took place during the Roman celebration of *Sāturnālia*.

    During *Sāturnālia*, the Roman holiday at the time of the winter solstice in December, social roles were reversed: slaves became masters, and masters became slaves. The normal rules of social conduct and class distinction were suspended and slaves even disrespected their masters.

PAGE 52

TEACHING TIP
Sāturnālia was one of many festivals (*fēriae*) celebrated in Rome. The teacher may wish to have students research some of the monthly public (celebrating a god) and private (celebrating a birthday) events. Ovid's *Fastī* provides information about the festivals of the first six months of the year. Only six of his twelve books were finished.

TEACHER BY THE WAY
With the advent of Christianity, some festivals were transformed into Christian celebrations. December 25th was the midwinter solstice at which time the god Sōl Invictus was honored. Christians choose to celebrate the birth of Christ instead. The medieval celebration called the Feast of Fools involved a similar reversal of roles as that which took place on the Sāturnālia. The role reversal for the slaves provided an outlet for pent-up resentment or ill feeling toward their masters or about their condition.

TEACHER BY THE WAY
The mosaic is housed at the Louvre. Teachers may wish to ask students how one would identify the overseer in the mosaic.

TEACHER BY THE WAY
Although Tiro had been freed in 53 BCE, nevertheless he accompanied Cicero to Cilicia during his term as governor there. Tiro was in poor health after that trip but he still outlived his former master and is believed to have collected and published Cicero's work. According to Aulus Gellius and Asconius, Tiro himself wrote several books on the Latin language and a biography of Cicero's life. He died at his estate near Puteoli in 4 BCE at the age of ninety-nine.

Tiro is credited with inventing a type of shorthand, although the renowned scholar and bishop St. Isidorus of Spain ascribes its invention to Ennius, who used 1,100 *notae*. Tiro's system, called the *notae Tīrōniānae*, is said to have included 4,000 *notae* and probably consisted of abbreviations for words. Tiro's system was the basis for later additions throughout the centuries. During the medieval period it was taught in monasteries and extended to about 13,000 signs. One of his *notae* (which looks very like our modern letter "z") is still used today for the sound "et" in *vidēlicet*, abbreviated *viz*.

EXPLORING ROMAN COMEDY

PAGE 53
Standards 2.2, 3.1, 3.2, 4.1, 4.2

 TEACHER BY THE WAY
During World War II, Hollywood movies similarly served as a distraction from the troubles and hardships of the war.

Plautus's use of colloquial Latin makes his plays a rich resource for scholars learning about everyday life and expressions in the early republican period of Rome.

COMPREHENSION QUESTIONS AND ANSWERS FOR PAGES 53–55 (SE)
Reproducible versions of the questions alone are available at **www.lnm.bolchazy.com**.

1. Why did ordinary Romans especially enjoy the festivals of *Megalensia* and *Lūdī Rōmānī*?
   Ordinary Romans enjoyed the free performances of Roman comedies, which offered a distraction from their troubles. During the Second Punic War and the setbacks caused by Hannibal's invasion, comedies provided Romans the opportunity to laugh away their cares and to identify with clever slaves who outwit their masters.

2. Describe the adaptations Plautus made to the Greek comedies.
   Plautus added song and dance, made fun of the Greek plots, only pretended to be mounting a Greek production, and he romanized and latinized non-Roman situations and half-Roman characters. (Romans especially enjoyed this last adaptation.)

3. Why did twins make for a rich comedic tradition?
   Twins can readily exchange identities and roles and trick others. When twins are separated and do not initially recognize each other, this can have great comedic effect.

4. In what ways are Terence's comedies different from those of Plautus?
   Terence did not try to make his plays funnier than those of the Greeks. He was especially interested in the human emotion felt by his characters. While Plautus used colloquial Latin, Terence's Latin was urbane.

5. Explain Terence's appeal as a "school author."
   The realistic characters and moral sentiments of Terence's plays along with their urbane Latin made his works ideal for reading in school both in antiquity and during the Renaissance.

6. The Renaissance saw a "rebirth," a heightened interest in the art and literature of Greece and Rome. Relate how that affected Terence's works.
   The Renaissance writer Petrarch admired Terence, which led him to write a biography of the Roman playwright and deposit an annotated manuscript of Terence's works in Florence. At the same city, for the first time since antiquity, a Terentian play was staged during the Renaissance. The Renaissance humanists used Terence as their model when writing their own comedies.

PAGE 54

TEACHER BY THE WAY

In conjuction with the photograph of the theatre on p. 54 (SE) or with other illustrations of theatres in the text, the teacher might wish to discuss what innovative structural design Roman architects added to Roman theatres, which at first followed the Greek design. Teachers might also choose to discuss ancient amphitheatres as a point of contrast and comparison with theatres.

With the advent of arches and concrete vaults in the first century BCE, the supporting hillside was no longer needed so the Roman theatre was built on its own foundation and enclosed on all sides. The auditorium (*cavea*) was semicircular and open at the top but covered with an awning (*vēlārium*). Vaults provided easy entrance to the rows of seats. The *prīma cavea* was reserved for the nobility and the *ultima cavea* was for the lower classes. A semicircular orchestra separated the seats from the stage and a raised platform (*prōscaenium*) in front of the stage separated it from the orchestra. Because the roofed stage was often three stories high, there was no view beyond the stage, which was typical of Greek theatres. In such a closed-in setting, the focus was on the play. Models of this architectural design are found in Sabratha, Libya; Orange, France; Aspendos, Turkey; and Taormina, Sicily.

The exterior of the Theatre of Marcellus in Rome became the paradigm for the architectural form of later theatres with its engaged columns in the Greek style with Doric at the base, Ionic on the second level, and perhaps Corinthian on the top level. The third story did not survive. The network of corridors, tunnels, arches, and ramps provided entrances to the inside of the theatre.

Amphitheatres shared many features of the theatres but were distinctly Roman in origin. Once again, Roman technology and the appearance of arches and concrete resulted in the monumental freestanding structures, such as the Colosseum, that became a familiar part of urban planning in the Roman Empire. The oval-shaped edifice was built in the round and spectacles took place in the oval arena. As in the circus, sand (*harēna*) covered the floor to soak up blood as well as to give the gladiators a firmer footing. Design and function went hand in hand. For spectators' protection iron bars were placed on the top of the arena walls when wild beast shows were part of the event. Here too an awning gave the audience some protection. The design allowed for underground chambers below the arena where props, men, and animals were kept. A hand-operated lift brought the animals up to the arena through trapdoors.

PAGE 55

TEACHER BY THE WAY

The word "Renaissance" is from the French word meaning "rebirth," which in turn is derived from the Latin *nāscor*, "I am born." Today's historians assert that the Italian Renaissance of the fifteenth century CE was not a total rebirth but a significant renewed emphasis on the classical world and its lessons.

TEACHING TIP
Point out to students that different authors and different genres appeal to later generations in different ways as was the case during the Renaissance.

TEACHER BY THE WAY
Publius Cornelius Scipio Africanus as a young man earned a reputation for his military deeds. He saved his father's life in battle and rallied the survivors at the disastrous battle of Cannae (216 BCE) in which Hannibal destroyed two consular armies. Scipio was technically disqualified from carrying on the war in Spain, as his father did, because he had not completed the steps of the *cursus honōrum* (a sequential order of political magistracies). Nonetheless, as a private citizen he was given proconsular powers by the people and successfully established Roman control in Spain by 206 BCE.

During his consulship, Scipio was determined to invade Africa, despite the Senate's opposition. He was momentarily victorious but then Carthage renewed the war in 202 BCE. Backed by a dedicated army with whom he had fought for ten years and by the cavalry of Massinissa, a Numidian king and ally, he defeated Hannibal at Zama that same year.

Most of Scipio's success was as a general rather than a statesman. Political antagonism and personal rivalries forced him later to withdraw into retirement as a private citizen. Scipio's daughter was Cornelia, mother of the Gracchi brothers known for their land reforms. Tradition says she esteemed her sons as her "jewels."

MĪRĀBILE AUDĪTŪ

PAGE 56
Standards 1.1, 3.1, 3.2, 4.1

PHRASES VOCABULARY

Drāmatis persōnae.
- **drāma, drāmatis,** *n.* – play
- **persōna, persōnae,** *f.* – mask (literally "where the sound comes through," per + sonus, "sound")

Exit. Exeunt.
- **exeō, exīre, exīvī, exitum** – to go out, to exit

Mīles glōriōsus.
- **glōriōsus, glōriōsa, glōriōsum** – boasting, bragging
- **mīles, mīlitis,** *m.* – soldier

Nōdum in scirpō quaeris.
- **nōdus, nōdī,** *m.* – knot
- **quaerō, quaerere, quaesīvī, quaesītum** – to seek
- **scirpus, scirpī,** *m.* – bulrush

Plaudite, ācta est fābula.
- **agō, agere, ēgī, āctum** – to do
- **plaudō, plaudere, plausī, plausum** – to applaud

TEACHING TIP

Find the script of a play that includes the phrases *drāmatis persōnae*, *exit*, and *exeunt*. Bring this into class and show it to the students in order to emphasize that these phrases truly are still in use today. Or ask the students to find a play with these words in Latin and to bring it to class.

TEACHING TIP

There will be many opportunities for students to act out dialogues or perform conversations orally during the course of using this book. Encourage the class, whenever a group of students has acted out a dialogue or performed a conversation orally, to say at the conclusion in unison, "*Plaudite, ācta est fābula.*"

CHAPTER 4 (PP. 57–68)

GRAMMAR IN LANGUAGE FACTS

Second Declension Neuter Nouns; Dative Case (Indirect Object); First and Second Declension –*us*, –*a*, –*um* Adjectives; Agreement of Nouns and Adjectives

PAGE 57

Standards 1.1, 2.1, 4.2
RRA 5

MEMORĀBILE DICTŪ VOCABULARY

aurum, aurī, *n*. – gold
famēs, famis, *f*. – hunger
sacer, sacra, sacrum – holy, accursed

TEACHING TIP
After the students have read the caption under the picture, ask them to locate Epirus on the map on pp. xxxiv–xxxv (SE).

TEACHER BY THE WAY
Pyrrhus was a second cousin of Alexander the Great and at one time (286 BCE) was the most powerful ruler in the European part of Alexander's empire.

TEACHING TIP
Instruct the students to find Pyrrhus's invasion of Italy on the timeline on pp. 405–408 (SE).

HOW TO USE THIS BOOK AND ITS ENRICHMENT TEXTS

Chapter 5 of RRA explains the historical events that occurred during the time that the literature in Chapters 4–9 of *Latin for the New Millennium*, Level 1 was being written. Teachers may wish to have students refer back to Chapter 5 of RRA as often as necessary.

PAGE 58

Standards 1.1, 2.1, 3.1, 3.2, 4.1

TRANSLATION OF LATIN PASSAGE
The Deserter Wants a Reward

Pyrrhus, the renowned king, is waging war with the Romans. He wants to have territory in Italy. A deserter secretly flees from the camp of Pyrrhus and walks into the camp of the Romans. The deserter is not afraid, but he wants to see Fabricius. Fabricius is the consul and general of the Romans. "You must give me a large reward," says the deserter; "if you give me a reward, I have in mind to enter secretly into the camp of Pyrrhus and to kill Pyrrhus by poison." Fabricius, however, does not want to have victory through treachery, but through open warfare. And so he summons armed men. He does not give a reward to the deserter, but chains. He orders the armed men to walk with the deserter to the camp of Pyrrhus and to give the deserter chained to Pyrrhus.

TEACHER BY THE WAY

During the subsequent centuries of the Roman Empire through the Middle Ages and especially in the Renaissance, Cicero's oratory set the standard for Latin eloquence. As long as Latin has survived as a literary language, his works have been viewed as a model of linguistic perfection.

A man of wide learning, Cicero popularized the idea of *hūmānitās*. This word signifies the mental cultivation worthy of a civic leader that can be derived from study of the subjects traditionally associated with the liberal arts—grammar, rhetoric, and dialectic—and it is the source of our word "humanities." Like many other contemporary Roman prose writers and poets, Cicero also strove to adapt Greek literary genres, verse meters, and modes of expression to the Latin language. In transforming Latin into a highly sophisticated literary language, these authors of the late first century BCE bequeathed to posterity Roman prose and poetic works, whose forms have earned the label "classical."

TEACHING TIP

Instruct the students to find Cicero on the timeline on pp. 405–408 (SE) and to locate the city of Tarentum on the map on pp. xxxiv–xxxv (SE).

TEACHING TIP

Since the story of Pyrrhus happened so much before Cicero's lifetime, the teacher may wish to instruct the students to review Chapter 3 of RRA.

PAGE 59

TEACHING TIP
The teacher may wish to point out to students the unusual short stem vowel in *dō, dăre*.

TEACHER BY THE WAY
Historical evidence can be cited for reading the first syllable of *"magnus"* as naturally long, but other evidence suggests it is naturally short. Thus in some grammar books, such as the one by Gildersleeve and Lodge, we find this syllable marked as long, but in other books it is treated as short.

TEACHING TIP
The teacher may wish to explain about the nature of Roman camps since the word *castra* is found in the Reading Vocabulary. Since military campaigns were usually long, there were both summer (*castra aestīva*) and winter camps (*castra hīberna*). Without exception, after every march soldiers were required to construct fortified camps, protected by a ditch, an earthen wall, and a palisade for which they carried the sticks themselves. It was Roman army policy never to spend the night in the open when in enemy territory. It took four to five hours to set up a camp. The commander's tent was in an open space near the middle. This compound gave the Romans protection against surprise attacks as well as refuge after a defeat.

TEACHER BY THE WAY
Fabricius, who was mentioned in the reading passage in this chapter, was famous for his incorruptibility and austerity, prized Roman virtues. In the underworld Anchises shows his son the spirit of Fabricius, "princely in poverty," waiting to be born.

ANSWERS TO COMPREHENSION QUESTIONS
1. With King Pyrrhus.
2. He wants land.
3. He needs to see Fabricius, the general.
4. He is prepared, for a reward, to enter Pyrrhus's camp secretly and kill the king with poison.
5. Fabricius wants victory in open warfare, not by treachery.

PAGE 60

Standards 3.1, 4.1

Oral Exercises 1, 2; Workbook Exercise 1

▶ EXERCISE 1 ANSWERS

1. dative or ablative plural
2. nominative singular
3. nominative or accusative plural
4. genitive plural
5. accusative singular
6. genitive singular or nominative plural
7. genitive singular

ORAL EXERCISE 1

This exercise may be used anytime after the declension of neuter nouns has been presented.

The teacher should carefully pronounce each of the following neuter nouns. If the noun is singular, students should respond orally with the corresponding plural form or with the singular form if the noun is plural. This exercise works best as a purely oral activity.

1. **Teacher:** venēnum   **Student:** venēna
2. **Teacher:** vinculīs   **Student:** vinculō
3. **Teacher:** bellī   **Student:** bellōrum
4. **Teacher:** praemiō   **Student:** praemiīs
5. **Teacher:** venēna   **Student:** venēnum
6. **Teacher:** bellōrum   **Student:** bellī
7. **Teacher:** praemiīs   **Student:** praemiō
8. **Teacher:** venēnō   **Student:** venēnīs

ORAL EXERCISE 2

This exercise may be used anytime after the declension of neuter nouns and castra, *a plural-only noun, has been presented.*

Ask a student to decline *castra*.

	Plural (only)
Nominative	castra
Genitive	castrōrum
Dative	castrīs
Accusative	castra
Ablative	castrīs

76 • Latin for the New Millennium: Teacher's Manual, Level 1

PAGE 61

TEACHING TIP
Instruct the students to look at the picture and read the caption and then turn to p. 397 (SE) to see Trajan's column in its entirety. Explain that Dacia is modern Romania and that Romanian is one of the Romance languages based on Latin.

TEACHING TIP
Additional reproducible worksheets, morphology charts, and their associated answer keys, related to this material, are available for download at www.lnm.bolchazy.com.
- **Noun Declensions**

PAGE 62
Standards 1.2, 3.1, 4.1
Workbook Exercise 2

▶ EXERCISE 2 ANSWERS
1. bellicose   bellum
2. jussive   iubeō
3. premium   praemium
4. venom   venēnum
5. bonus   bonus
6. army   armātus
7. entrance   intrō
8. malice   malus

TEACHING TIP
Although in Exercise 2 the students are directed to find only the derivatives based on the Vocabulary to Learn, they may be interested to learn that there are other derivatives in Exercise 2. The derivation of these words is provided for the teacher's convenience.

2. verb – from *verbum* (word). form – from *fōrma* (shape, appearance, etc.). convey – from *via* (way, road, street) + *cum* (with, together). order – from *ōrdō* (row, rank, regular arrangement).
3. product – from *prōdūcō* (to bring forward, bring out). quality – from *quālitās* (quality, nature).
4. fatal – from *fātālis* (fateful, destined, deadly).
5. receive – from *recipiō* (to take back, regain, rescue, etc.).
8. very – from *vērus* (true, real, actual). person – from *persōna* (mask, character, part, person, role). totally – from *tōtus* (whole, entire).

Chapter 4 • 77

TEACHING TIP

This is a mnemonic to help students remember the three major verbs that set up indirect objects: You **GIVE** the teacher a break when you present **SHOW** and **TELL**.

PAGE 63

Standards 1.1, 1.2, 2.1, 3.1, 3.2
Workbook Exercise 3

▶ EXERCISE 3 ANSWERS

1. profugae
2. Pyrrhō
3. profugae
4. armātīs virīs

▶ EXERCISE 4 ANSWERS

1. lupīs — We give poison to the she-wolves.
2. āthlētīs — You (plural) prepare water for the athletes.
3. nautīs — You (plural) owe rewards to the sailors.
4. agricolīs — They give land to the farmers.
5. puerō et puellae — We prepare a house for the boy and the girl.

TEACHING TIP

After the students have read the caption next to the picture on this page, the teacher may wish to introduce the topic of the various divisions within the Roman army (e.g., cohorts, centuries, legions). Clever students should be encouraged to investigate any discrepancies in the reenactors' garb. Some additional information about the Roman army is provided for the teacher's convenience.

The smallest unit of the Roman army was the *contubernium*, a group of eight men who shared a tent and eating utensils. These *contubernia* were grouped into centuries which, in spite of the name, historically numbered 60–80 men. Each century was commanded by a professional soldier called a centurion. Two centuries formed a maniple, which was under the centurion who commanded the century on the right in the line of battle. Three maniples constituted a cohort which, under Marius, replaced the maniple as the tactical unit of the legion. It was commanded by the centurion of the first century. The first cohort had only five centuries instead of six but also contained the clerks and specialists of the legion. It also had an extra centurion, called the *prīmipīlus*, who was the chief centurion of the legion. A legion consisted of ten cohorts.

PAGE 64
Standards 3.1, 4.1
Oral Exercise 3

 TEACHING TIP
Encourage students to see that the endings on first and second declension adjectives are the same endings used on first and second declension nouns.

ORAL EXERCISE 3

This exercise may be used after Exercise 6 or anytime after adjectives of the first and second declensions have been presented.

Use one of the CPOs to put the following adjectives on view, explaining that *parvus* is a new word.

iūstus, iūsta, iūstum – legitimate, open, just
magnus, magna, magnum – large, great
bonus, bona, bonum – good
malus, mala, malum – bad
parvus, parva, parvum – small

Also list the following interrogative phrases:

Quālis est . . . ? "Of what sort is . . . ?" (Of singular masculine and feminine things)

Quāle est . . . ? "Of what sort is . . . ?" (Of singular neuter things)

Quālēs sunt . . . ? "Of what sort are . . . ?" (Of plural masculine and feminine things)

Quālia sunt . . . ? "Of what sort are . . . ?" (Of plural neuter things)

The teacher should first explain that the answer to these questions is always an adjective. The students may now orally answer the following questions using one of the five adjectives provided (in most cases more than one of these adjectives can be appropriate). In their answers the students should repeat the *est* or *sunt* in the questions. The teacher may also explain—though this is not necessary at this point—that these answers involve the predicate use of the adjective, a concept to be explained in more detail later.

1. **Teacher:** Quālēs sunt amīcī?
   Student: Amīcī sunt iūstī/bonī/magnī/malī/parvī.

2. **Teacher:** Quāle est bellum?
   Student: Bellum est iūstum/magnum/bonum/malum/parvum.

3. **Teacher:** Quālia sunt castra?
   Student: Castra sunt magna/parva.

4. **Teacher:** Quālis est Fābricius?
   Student: Fābricius est iūstus/magnus/bonus/malus/parvus.

5. **Teacher:** Quāle est venēnum?
   Student: Venēnum est malum.

6. **Teacher:** Quālēs sunt agrī?
   Student: Agrī sunt bonī/magnī/malī/parvī.

7. **Teacher:** Quālēs sunt agricolae?
   Student: Agricolae sunt iūstī/bonī/magnī/malī/parvī.

Chapter 4 • 79

8. **Teacher:** Quālēs sunt poētae?
   Student: Poētae sunt iūstī/bonī/magnī/malī/parvī.

9. **Teacher:** Quālis est āthlēta?
   Student: Āthlēta est magnus/parvus/bonus/malus/iūstus.

10. **Teacher:** Quālis est casa?
    Student: Casa est magna/parva/bona/mala.

11. **Teacher:** Quālis est fābula?
    Student: Fābula est magna/parva/bona/mala.

12. **Teacher:** Quālēs sunt rīvī?
    Student: Rīvī sunt magnī/parvī.

TEACHER BY THE WAY
By the way, the word "quality" is based on the Latin word *quālis*.

PAGE 65
Standards 1.1, 1.2, 2.1, 3.1, 3.2
Workbook Exercises 4, 5, 7

TEACHING TIP
Instruct the students to repeat aloud the forms of *iūstus, iūsta, iūstum* after the teacher models the pronunciation of the words. Then encourage the students to create a rap, cheer, or song to help them remember the forms. Alternatively, use Bolchazy-Carducci's *Toga Beats*.

▶ EXERCISE 5 ANSWERS

1. In magnīs castrīs sum.   I am in the large camp.
2. Magnōs fīliōs habēmus.   We have great (important) sons.
3. Magnum bellum valdē timēmus.   We exceedingly fear a great war.
4. Magna praemia dēbēs.   You owe great rewards.
5. Magnam casam magnae poētae cūrāmus.   We take care of the large house of the great poet.
6. Magnus agricola ad magnum rīvum ambulat.   A great farmer walks to the large river.

▶ EXERCISE 6 ANSWERS

1. iūstīs praemiīs
2. agrō magnō
3. bellum malum
4. nauta armātus/nautārum armātōrum
5. poētīs praeclārīs
6. vinculum malum

80 • Latin for the New Millennium: Teacher's Manual, Level 1

▶ EXERCISE 7 ANSWERS

1. We should now expect the reward.
2. Fabricius does not esteem deception: he esteems legitimate victory.
3. We are not walking into the camp of the Romans.
4. We do not fear war, but poison.
5. You order <your> friend to give large rewards to the illustrious Romans.
6. You have good friends.

PAGE 66

Standards 1.1, 1.2, 2.1, 3.1, 3.2

Oral Exercises 4, 5; Workbook Exercise 6, Content Questions

▶ EXERCISE 8 ANSWERS

1. poētās   We call poets to <our> fatherland.
2. Agrōs magnōs   We are not giving large fields to the farmers.
3. Praemium iūstum I am preparing a just reward for the Romans.
4. victōriam iūstam Through war, not trickery we have legitimate victory.

▶ EXERCISE 9 ANSWERS

1. falsum
2. falsum
3. vērum
4. falsum
5. vērum
6. falsum
7. vērum

ORAL EXERCISE 4

This exercise may be used as a review exercise at the end of Chapter 4 or anytime after the dative case has been presented.

Use one of the CPOs to put on view the nouns *ager, aqua, lupa,* and *terra.* Also add the following unfamiliar nouns with English meanings.

raeda, raedae, *f.* – car   **liber, librī,** *m.* – book
gladius, gladiī, *m.* – sword   **pallium, palliī,** *n.* – coat
calamus, calamī, *m.* – pen   **pilleus, pilleī,** *m.* – cap
pōculum, pōculī, *n.* – cup   **marsūpium, marsūpiī,** *n.* – purse

The teacher should first explain to the students that *da mihi* means "give to me" and *dō tibi* means "I give to you," and that *mihi* and *tibi* in these phrases are indirect objects. Then point to each noun and say to a different student in turn *da mihi . . .* The student should reply *dō tibi* and add the indicated noun in the **accusative** case. The teacher can also use available objects that the student could actually give to the teacher for some or all of the nouns in the accusative case.

Chapter 4 • 81

ORAL EXERCISE 5

This exercise may be used as a review exercise at the end of Chapter 4 or anytime after adjectives of the first and second declensions have been presented.

The teacher should put the following **nominative** noun-adjective pairs on view, glossing new adjectives with English meanings. Then pointing to each pair **without** saying the words, the teacher will say to a different student in turn *vidēs* ("you see") . . . Each student should respond *videō* ("I see") and then say aloud the indicated adjective-noun pair, but in the **accusative case** as the object of *videō*.

lupa magna
fīlia praeclāra
dolī magnī
praemium praeclārum
aqua caerulea (blue)
casae parvae (small)

nauta iūstus
puellae lepidae (charming)
agricolae praeclārī
poēta doctus (learned)
puerī parvī (small)
rīvī magnī

amīcus iūstus
āthlētae magnī
fīlius bonus
patria cāra (dear)
via longa (long)

PAGE 67
Standards 1.2, 4.1, 4.2
Oral Exercise 6 and Dictation

TRANSLATION OF THE LATIN CONVERSATION

Mary: Do we have an assignment for tomorrow?

Helen: Yes indeed. We need to prepare a passage of Cicero.

Mary: Is the passage long?

Christy: It is not too long.

Mark: Who was Cicero?

Christy: Cicero was a philosopher.

Mary: Why do we need to read the words of philosophers? The philosophers do not tell about true life.

Helen: Cicero tells a true story about Fabricius. Fabricius does not want to have a victory with deception, but with a legitimate war.

Mark: This story is not true. Great men want to have victory even with deception.

Helen: However, Fabricius is not only great, but also just and distinguished. Just men ought not to have victory with deception.

Christy: And we ought to prepare the assignment.

TEACHING TIP
Some of the conversational Latin presented here may be used from now on in class when assigning homework. Students may also be encouraged to use *cūr, ita, ita vērō, minimē,* and *quis* when appropriate in the classroom.

ORAL EXERCISE 6 AND DICTATION

This combined exercise may be used to conclude the chapter.

First the teacher should use one of the CPOs to put on view the following interrogative words with their definitions:

quālis – of what sort?   **quid** – what?

quibuscum – with whom?   **quis** – who?

quōmodo – in what way?

Dictate the following sentences and then ask the students to answer the following questions orally, using the vocabulary in the sentences for their answers.

1. **Teacher:** Pyrrhus, vir praeclārus, terram in Italiā habēre vult.
   Teacher: Quālis est Pyrrhus? Quid in Italiā habēre vult?
   Student: Pyrrhus est vir praeclārus. Terram in Italiā habēre vult.

2. **Teacher:** Pyrrhus bellum cum Rōmānīs gerit.
   Teacher: Quibuscum Pyrrhus bellum gerit?
   Student: Cum Rōmānīs Pyrrhus bellum gerit.

3. **Teacher:** Profuga ē castrīs Pyrrhī ad Fābricium ambulat.
   Teacher: Quis ad Fābricium ambulat?
   Student: Profuga ad Fābricium ambulat.

4. **Teacher:** Profuga magnum praemium habēre vult.
   Teacher: Quid profuga habēre vult?
   Student: Habēre vult profuga magnum praemium.

5. **Teacher:** Profuga in animō habet Pyrrhum venēnō necāre.
   Teacher: Quid in animō habet profuga?
   Student: In animō habet Pyrrhum venēnō necāre.

6. **Teacher:** Fābricius autem victōriam bellō iūstō, non venēnō, habēre vult.
   Teacher: Quōmodo Fābricius victōriam habēre vult?
   Student: Victōriam bellō iūstō habēre vult Fābricius.

7. **Teacher:** Itaque Fābricius praemium nōn dat profugae, sed vincula.
   Teacher: Quid Fābricius dat profugae?
   Student: Fābricius vincula dat profugae.

PAGE 68
Standard 4.1

DERIVATIVES

bellum – A <u>belligerent</u> person is fond of waging war, whether it is against the rules of parents or of another country (*gerō* – to wage, carry on).

Mercenaries are <u>bellicose</u> because they earn a living by being eager to fight. Note the suffix which comes directly from the Latin, e.g., *glōriōsus*, *verbōsus*, etc., and has the same meaning as "-ous."

The word "duel" is derived from *duo* (two) and *bellum* through the medieval Latin *duellum*. It is a prearranged meeting between two combatants to settle a private quarrel with deadly weapons (sword, pistols).

The prefix of "rebel" means "against, again"; thus a "rebel" wages war against authority. Both the noun and the verb date back to the mid-fourteenth century, but the adjective appears earlier, around 1300.

Chapter 4 • 83

The noun "revel" appeared around 1300 meaning "riotous merry-making" through the Old French *reveler* (to be disorderly, raise a tumult, make merry) from the Latin *rebellō* (to revolt). The verb (to feast in a noisy manner) is first recorded during the early fourteenth century; the meaning "take great pleasure in" during 1754.

castra – The word "castle" is derived from the Latin *castellum* (a diminutive of *castra* meaning "fort, stronghold") through the Old French *castel* (attested in the twelfth century). A <u>castle</u> of a medieval city was its most strongly fortified part. It also was the residence of the ruling noble.

The word *castel* in Old English meant "village" from a biblical use of the word for the Greek κώμη (village). It later formed place names like Chester, Winchester, and Worcester.

The modern French word *chateâu* is derived from the same source as "castle."

A "chatelaine" is the wife of a castellan and mistress of a castle. The word also derives from the Latin *castellum* through the French *castel*.

The forward part of a ship was called the "forecastle" (pronounced "fo'c'sle" by sailors) and consisted of a short deck with railings raised like a castle to command an enemy's decks. The prefix meaning "before" is derived from the Middle English *fore*.

dolus – A <u>sedulous</u> person is diligent and careful. The word is derived from the Latin *sēdulus* (*se* = without, apart, and *dolus*) and appears in English during the 1530s. Note the "-ous" suffix. Do warn the students to be careful of "lookalikes," e.g., "indolent."

praemium – A <u>premium</u> is a reward that is given as an inducement to buy a certain product. The Latin *praemium* also means "profit derived from booty." It consists of *pre* (before) and *emere* (to buy, take). Insurance companies began using the word in the 1660s (something one buys before the need for services arises). Its meaning as "superior in quality" is first attested in 1925, originally in reference to butter.

venēnum – Note the "-ous" suffix on "venomous."

vinculum – None

armātus – The word "armature" refers to the protective gear (armor) worn by armed men (from the Latin verb *armō* = equip).

bonus – The word "debonair" is derived from the French phrase *de bon aire*, which means "of good lineage." Wellborn people were expected to be courteous, gracious, and charming, to know how to behave properly, hence the modern meaning.

The word "bounty" can refer to a generous gift or a reward.

The adjective "boon" as in "a boon companion" preserves the meaning of "good." The noun, which means "a petition," is derived from the Old Norse *bon* (petition, prayer).

iūstus – Although the word "adjust" originally derived from the Latin *adiungere* (to join) through the French *ajouter* (to join), it was influenced by folk etymology to come from *iūstus* (equitable, fair) and mean "to arrange something to conform with a standard, etc." This sense appears in the 1660s; the insurance sense dates to 1755; and the meaning "to get used to" appeared first in 1924.

"To justify" means literally "to do right" (*iūstus* and *facere* = to do, make). It refers to defending a claim in court and is derived through the Old French *justifier* (to submit to court proceedings), appearing in English around 1300. The idea of "to make exact" which appeared during the 1550s is now largely restricted to typesetting.

The prefix of "injustice" is a negative use of the preposition "in" (cf. note on *in* in 1.3).

84 • Latin for the New Millennium: Teacher's Manual, Level 1

magnus – The <u>magnanimous</u> donor gave generously (*magnus* and *animus*).

The <u>magnitude</u> of the problem was daunting (from the Latin *magnitūdō* = greatness, size, large amount).

A "magnate" is a person of great influence. Bill Gates is a <u>magnate</u> in the field of software development.

Be careful of "lookalikes," e.g., "magnolia," named after the French botanist Pierre Magnol, and "magnet" from the Latin *magnēs*.

malus – The word "malaria" literally means "bad air." The disease, now known to be caused by mosquitoes, was probably first named by the Italian physician Francisco Torti (1658–1741) because it was thought to be a result of bad air emanating from marshlands. The Pomptine Marshes were the reason wealthy Romans left the city during the summer. Numerous attempts to drain these marshes date back to 160 BCE, but success only came in the 1930s.

The word "dismal" appeared in English around 1400 through the Old French *dis mals* from the Latin *diēs malī* (*malus* = bad, evil, unlucky, and *diēs* = day). Up through the Middle Ages two days of each month were considered unlucky, supposedly based on the calculations of Egyptian astrologers. Its meaning as "gloomy or dreary" is first recorded during the 1590s.

A "malediction" is a curse (as opposed to a benediction which is a blessing).

"Maleficent" was the name of the bad fairy, a "bad doer," in the Disney movie *Sleeping Beauty*.

Abraham Lincoln used the word "malice" in his second inaugural address. "With <u>malice</u> toward none, with charity for all . . ." It is derived from the Latin *malitia* (badness, illwill, spite) through the Old French *malice* (spite, wickedness).

The word "malady" is derived through the Old French *maladie* (sickness, disease) from the Latin *male habitus* (literally, "holding badly"; hence "doing poorly, feeling sick").

Cinderella's stepmother was certainly <u>malevolent</u> (*malus* and *volō* = to wish; hence "to wish ill") toward her.

A <u>malignant</u> tumor is cancerous (from the Latin *malignus* [*malus* and *gignō* = to cause, produce] = unkind, stingy, unfruitful). Students should be cautioned about the spelling and pronunciation of "malign." Latin helps here, of course.

praeclārus – Derivatives will be presented in 2.2 with *clārus*.

Rōmānus – See 1.1 under *Rōma*.

dō – The <u>data</u> on the project were compiled into a final report (*dātum* = that which has been given). Students should be cautioned that <u>data</u> is a plural form (Latin neuter plural). A single statistic would be termed a *datum* (fourth principal part of *dō*).

The "dative" case indicates to or for whom something is given.

The word "addition" appears in English during the late fourteenth century and is derived from the Latin *addere* (to join to; *ad* = to, and *–dere*, the combinative form of *dāre*). The idea of "to do sums" also dates from that period.

Benedict Arnold <u>betrayed</u> his country (from the Latin *trādere* [*trāns* = across, over, and *dare*] = to give over). The *be-* prefix has a wide range of meanings (thoroughly, make, cause, at, on, for, etc.) and probably derives from, or at least a cognate of, the Latin *ambi* (about).

The noun "die" (plural "dice") derives from the French *de* (die, dice), which is of uncertain origin but may come from *datum* (fourth principal part of *dō*) which may refer to "what is given by Fortune." The common form in Romance languages (Spanish, Portuguese, and Italian = *dado*, Provençal = *dat*, Catalan = *dau*) strengthens this possibility.

Chapter 4 • 85

A "dowry" is given by a woman's family as a gift to the man she marries. It is derived from the Latin *dōs, dōtis* (gift) which itself comes from *dō, dare*, through the Anglo-French *dowaire* and Old French *doaire*. The burden on the bridal family of this custom, found throughout the world even today, has been mitigated to a large extent by the presentation of gifts from relatives and friends. However, it was one of the reasons male offspring were so long preferred over girls.

The words "edit, editor, and edition" all derive from the Latin *ēdō* which literally means "to give out" (*ex* = out from, and *dō, dare*).

Voltaire apparently coined the word *extradition* from the Latin *ex* (out from) and *traditiō* (giving over, handing over) which came into English in 1833 to signify the delivering up of criminals who had fled to other countries to the government of their own.

The word "render" appeared in English during the early fourteenth century and is derived through the Old French *render* (to give back, present, yield) from the Latin *reddere* (to give back, return, restore). The nurse <u>rendered</u> valuable assistance to the wounded soldiers. The word today can also mean to convey the meaning as of a play or a work of art. The critic <u>rendered</u> the play unfit for youngsters.

The word "rendezvous" is a French word from *rendez-vous* (to present yourselves), which refers to an agreement to meet at a certain time and place.

The word "rent" is derived from the Old French *rente* (from *rendere* and the Latin *reddere*) and meant "payment for use of property" (a giving back for something).

The word "sacerdotal" is an adjective meaning "of priests, priestly" and is derived from the Latin word for priest (*sacerdos*, which literally meant "giver of holy things"). The new priest rapidly became acquainted with his <u>sacerdotal</u> duties in his assigned parish.

The prefix of "surrender" is from the Latin *supra* (over); hence the word means "to give over, give up."

The word "traitor" is derived from the Latin *trāditor* (betrayer, literally, one who delivers) from *trādō* (to deliver, give over).

The word "treason" is likewise derived from *trādō* through the Middle Engloish *tre(i)so(u)n* and Old French *traison*. It is a doublet of "tradition."

The word "vendor" appeared in English during the late fourteenth century and is a contraction of the Latin *venum* (for sale) and *dō, dare*. The term "vending machine" dates to 1889.

intrō – None. Related words are derived from *inter* and *intrā* (from which *intrō* itself is derived).

iubeō – A <u>jussive</u> subjunctive is the form used to give polite commands, e.g., Let's do it.

ad – Compounds derived from *ad* (to, toward, near) will be considered under the main root, e.g, "adhere" under *haereō*; "admit" under *mittō*; "admonition" under *moneō*; "adjacent" under *iaceō*, etc.

ex – Compounds derived from *ex* (out, out from) will be considered under the main root, e.g., "exit" under *eō*; "emit" under *mittō*; "evident" under *videō*; "evict" under *vincō*, etc.

in – See 1.3 under *in*.

autem, sed – None

CHAPTER 5 (PP. 69–81)

GRAMMAR IN LANGUAGE FACTS

First and Second Conjugation Verbs: Present Tense Passive, Present Passive Infinitive; Ablative of Agent; First and Second Declension –*er* Adjectives

PAGE 69

Standards 1.1, 2.1
RRA 5

MEMORĀBILE DICTŪ VOCABULARY
sī – if
valeō, valēre, valuī, —— – to be well

TEACHER BY THE WAY
The wall painting shown on this page is another example of a fresco. Many of the extant examples of this art form were found in Herculaneum and Pompeii.

TEACHING TIP
Teachers may wish to point out that the modern equivalent of STVBEEV is "If you're okay, I'm okay."

Teachers may have students compare this image with that on p. 46 (SE).

TEACHER BY THE WAY
The teacher may wish to begin discussing Pompeii and Herculaneum since many of the illustrations in the textbook are from these two cities. Pompeii experienced many influences: Oscan, Etruscan, Greek, Samnite, and finally Roman. Sulla colonized it with veterans in 80 BCE. The town covered about 163 acres of which 103 have been excavated. There were seven gates; an eighth one was closed off in ancient times. It was laid out along two east-west (*decumānī*) and three north-south (*cardinēs*) streets. Commerce brought prosperity. Products in demand were perfume, cloth, and fish sauce (*garum*). Recent studies suggest that the restorations in progress in 79 CE were to repair damages caused by earthquakes more recent than the one in 62 CE. Excavations reveal how different Herculaneum was from Pompeii. The town was small with about 4,000–5,000 people and covered 26 acres. Fishing was the main industry. The upper class took residency here and the homes suggest wealth and taste. Pedestrian stepping stones and painted notices on walls are absent. Public buildings were richly designed.

TEACHING TIP
Teachers may wish to assign Chapter 5 of RRA for reading or review. See p. 73.

PAGE 70
Standards 1.1, 2.1, 3.1, 3.2

TRANSLATION OF LATIN PASSAGE
Cicero Says a Very Great Greeting to Terentia

I am holding now your letter, my Terentia. Nevertheless, I am reading your letter not only with joy, but also with tears. For I am wretched far from (my) fatherland, far from (my) family. I always think of you, of (our) daughter, and of (our) son. My heart (soul) hurts. Bad plans are being devised against me by bad men, and help ought to be given to me by good men (i.e., good men ought to help me). I love you very much, my Terentia, and I am awaiting long letters from you. If I read your letters, I see you in my mind. You should take good care of yourself, of (our) son, of (our) beautiful daughter. Goodbye!

TEACHING TIP
Now is an appropriate time to introduce students to the Latin words for other members of a family after completing this reading. *Avus, avia, avunculus, amita, mātertera,* and *cōnsōbrīnus* are examples of family member words that belong to declensions that the students already know. Other words (*soror, pater, frāter, māter*) may also be introduced if the students are expected to use only the nominative singular forms. Students may be encouraged to create their own or fictional family trees in Latin.

TEACHER BY THE WAY
Some immediate members of Cicero's family are:

- Quintus Tullius Cicero, his younger brother, quick tempered and easily offended. A good soldier and administrator but a poor politician. His marriage to Atticus's sister Pompōnia was trying. To assist Cicero in his bid for the consulship, he probably authored *Commentāriolum Petītiōnis*, a pamphlet on electioneering advice. He died in the proscriptions of 43 BCE along with Cicero.

- Titus Pomponius Atticus, wealthy childhood friend of Cicero, both a confidant and supporter who always tried to protect Cicero's interests. He chose to live in Athens to avoid Roman politics, hence his cognomen.

- Marcus Tullius Cicero junior, who was educated under his father's tutelage but who lacked the intellectual capacity and drive of his father. He was mildly successful in the military. After the defeat of Antony, he was co-consul with Octavian; both men participated in his father's murder in 43 BCE.

- Tullia, beloved daughter, married three times but separated from her third husband Dolabella whom Cicero disliked. When her father returned from his year of exile in Thessaloniki, Greece (58 BCE), she met him at Brundisium, to his great joy. Her death in childbirth (45 BCE) devastated him. Cicero considered building a temple to his Tulliola.

- Publilia, Cicero's ward whom he married after divorcing Terentia in 46 BCE. When Tullia died, he divorced her as well. Terentia is discussed below in the Teacher by the Way.

PAGE 71

ANSWERS TO COMPREHENSION QUESTIONS
1. Away from his fatherland.
2. Three: his wife Terentia, his son, his daughter.
3. Cicero is afraid that bad men are designing bad plots against him.
4. He sees Terentia in his mind.
5. To write long letters to him.

TEACHING TIP
After reading Cicero's letter to Terentia, students can be assigned to write a letter in Latin to one of their family members. This can be an in-class assignment that students then share aloud or a homework activity that the teacher will grade as an assessment.

TEACHER BY THE WAY
Terentia came from a wealthy family. Her half sister, a Vestal, was suspected of having an affair with Catiline. Little wonder that she encouraged Cicero to prosecute him! Cicero's letters mention her bravery and strength while he was in exile and how much she advocated on his behalf during that difficult year (58 BCE). Nonetheless, when he returned, their marriage deteriorated because he considered her dishonest in managing financial matters and insensitive in family affairs. He often complained that she gave him and Tullia too little money. During Cicero's absence in Cilicia as proconsul (51 BCE), the headstrong Terentia arranged the marriage of then divorced Tullia to Dolabella, much to Cicero's chagrin. The young man was a supporter of Caesar and had a reputation for debt and dissipation. In 46 BCE Cicero divorced Terentia after thirty years of marriage. She remarried twice and died at the age of 103.

TEACHING TIP
The teacher may wish to review how to say the parts of speech in Latin in conjunction with this Reading Vocabulary. This information was presented on p. 15 of this teacher's manual.

PAGE 72

Standards 1.1, 3.1, 4.1
Oral Exercise 1

TEACHING TIP
If the students notice that the stem vowel *–ā–* of the first conjugation is missing in the first person singular of the passive voice, explain that the original *–ā–* weakened in **paraōr* and only the *–or* remains. In the second conjugation, however, the stem vowel *–ē–* does not weaken and does not disappear. The same condition exists in the first person singular of the active voice.

Chapter 5 • 89

ORAL EXERCISE 1

This exercise may be used anytime after the present passive of the first and second conjugations has been presented.
Ask the students to conjugate in the present passive *vocō* and *videō*.

vocor, vocāris, vocātur, vocāmur, vocāminī, vocantur

videor, vidēris, vidētur, vidēmur, vidēminī, videntur

TEACHING TIP
Additional reproducible worksheets, morphology charts, and their associated answer keys, related to this material, are available for download at www.lnm.bolchazy.com.
- **Verb Conjugations**

PAGE 73
Standards 1.1, 1.2

▶ EXERCISE 1 ANSWERS
1. third person plural — videntur
2. third person singular — vocātur
3. first person plural — iubēmur
4. second person plural — cūrāminī
5. first person singular — amor
6. third person plural — dēbentur
7. second person singular — daris
8. third person singular — exspectātur

TEACHING TIP
Since the verb *dō* is used in Exercise 1, if necessary, remind the students that this verb, as an exception, has a short vowel *-a* in its stem.

TEACHING TIP
As noted on p. 32, if the teacher wishes to conduct Exercise 1 in Latin, the questions for the teacher to pose are "*Cūius est persōnae?*" and "*Cūius est numerī?*" The answers to Exercise 1 in Latin are printed for the teacher's convenience.

1. *tertiae persōnae, numerī plūrālis*
2. *tertiae persōnae, numerī singulāris*
3. *prīmae persōnae, numerī plūrālis*
4. *secundae persōnae, numerī plūrālis*
5. *prīmae persōnae, numerī singulāris*
6. *tertiae persōnae, numerī plūrālis*
7. *secundae persōnae, numerī singulāris*
8. *tertiae persōnae, numerī singulāris*

This may be the appropriate point at which to introduce the class to the question *"Cūius generis est?"* or the later Latin *"Cūius vōcis est?"* both of which mean "What voice is it?"

Note that the earlier term has a disadvantage: *genus* also means "grammatical gender." Appropriate student responses to this question are (*generis*) *āctīvī* or *passīvī* or (*vōcis*) *āctīvae* or *passīvae*. *"Cūius temporis est?"* means "What tense is it?" An appropriate response at this point in the student's knowledge of Latin is *"praesentis."*

PAGE 74
Standards 1.1, 1.2, 4.1
Workbook Exercise 2

▶ EXERCISE 2 ANSWERS

misery	miser
malicious	malus
malignant	malus
auxiliary	auxilium
counsel	cōnsilium
pulchritude	pulcher
longitude	longus

TEACHING TIP
Although in Exercise 2 the students are directed to find only the derivatives based on the Vocabulary to Learn, they may be interested to learn that there are other derivatives in Exercise 2. The derivation of these words is provided for the teacher's convenience.

- mini-series – from *minimus* (least, smallest) and *seriēs* (row, sequence, succession).
- auction – from *augeō* (to increase).
- malicious – from *malus* (bad) and *malitiōsus* (wicked, crafty).
- counsel – from *cōnsilium* (deliberation, consultation; deliberating body).
- constitution – from *cōnstitūtiō* (state, condition, regulation) and *cōnstituō* (to establish, build, create, organize, determine, etc.).
- mall – (short from pall-mall), from *malleus* (mallet).

TEACHER BY THE WAY
The portraiture that flourished in the time of the Roman Republic is distinctive for its realism. The bust of Cicero shows his age with the furrows in his forehead, his receding hairline, and the crow's feet around his eyes. During the Augustan and imperial periods, portraiture tended to be idealized.

▶ EXERCISE 3 ANSWERS

1. tenētur — Terentia's letter is being held by Cicero.
2. miser; misera — Cicero is wretched and Terentia is wretched.
3. parantur — Good plans are being designed by good men.
4. exspectantur — Long letters are being expected by Cicero.
5. vidētur — Terentia is being seen in Cicero's mind.

PAGE 75

Standards 1.1, 1.2, 3.1, 3.2, 4.1
Oral Exercise 2; Workbook Exercise 1

▶ EXERCISE 4 ANSWERS

1. cōgitārī — to be thought
2. vocārī — to be called
3. habērī — to be had
4. amārī — to be loved
5. dēbērī — to be owed
6. vidērī — to be seen
7. exspectārī — to be expected
8. nārrārī — to be told

ORAL EXERCISE 2

This exercise may be used anytime after the present passive infinitives of the first and second conjugations have been presented.

Ask the students to say the active and the passive infinitives of the following verbs and to translate both forms.

1. **Teacher:** habeō   **Student:** habēre (to have)   habērī (to be had)
2. **Teacher:** amō   **Student:** amāre (to love)   amārī (to be loved)
3. **Teacher:** dēbeō   **Student:** dēbēre (to owe)   dēbērī (to be owed)
4. **Teacher:** cūrō   **Student:** cūrāre (to care)   cūrārī (to be cared)
5. **Teacher:** iubeō   **Student:** iubēre (to order)   iubērī (to be ordered)
6. **Teacher:** nārrō   **Student:** nārrāre (to tell)   nārrārī (to be told)

PAGE 76

Standards 1.1, 1.2, 3.1, 4.1
Oral Exercise 3; Workbook Exercise 5

 TEACHING TIP

Draw the students' attention to the fact that the passive voice is much less regularly used in contemporary English, but that it is widely used in Latin. English writing tends to avoid the passive voice.

▶ EXERCISE 5 ANSWERS

1. Epistula ā virō tenētur. — The letter is held by the man.
2. Puella ā virō amātur. — The girl is loved by the man.
3. Āthlēta ā puerō nōn vidētur. — The athlete is not seen by the boy.
4. Fīlius et fīlia ā Terentiā cūrantur. — The son and the daughter are cared for by Terentia.
5. Auxilium agricolae miserō ā virō datur. — Aid is given to the wretched farmer by the man.
6. Fīlius ā nautā cūrātur. — The son is cared for by the sailor.
7. Cōnsilia bona ā virō parantur. — Good plans are being prepared by the man.
8. Cōnsilia mala ā fēminā timentur. — Bad plans are feared by the woman.
9. Praemia praeclāra ab āthlētā exspectantur. — Distinguished rewards are expected by the athlete.
10. Fābulae longae ā poētīs nārrantur. — Long stories are being told by the poets.
11. Puella ā puerō vocātur. — The girl is being called by the boy.
12. Epistula ā puellā habētur. — The letter is had by the girl.

ORAL EXERCISE 3

This exercise may be used anytime after the ablative of agent has been presented.

Use one of the CPOs to put these two questions on view: *Quid faciō?* "What am I doing?" and *Quid fit?* "What is happening?". Explain that the first one would require an answer in the active and the second one in the passive voice. Explain to the students that "by you" is *ā tē*. Then the teacher may draw pictures, or imitate several actions, and ask the students about them. If the students have trouble guessing the initial statement, s/he can help them with it.

Teacher: Fābulam nārrō. Quid faciō?   **Student:** Fābulam nārrās.
Teacher: Quid fit?   **Student:** Fābula nārrātur.

Teacher: Fīlium teneō. Quid faciō?   **Student:** Fīlium tenēs.
Teacher: Quid fit?   **Student:** Fīlius ā tē tenētur.

Teacher: Fīliam cūrō. Quid faciō?   **Student:** Fīliam cūrās.
Teacher: Quid fit?   **Student:** Fīlia ā tē cūrātur.

Teacher: Nautam exspectō. Quid faciō?   **Student:** Nautam exspectās.
Teacher: Quid fit?   **Student:** Nauta ā tē exspectātur.

Teacher: Praemium dō. Quid faciō?   **Student:** Praemium dās.
Teacher: Quid fit?   **Student:** Praemium datur.

Teacher: Epistulam parō. Quid faciō?   **Student:** Epistulam parās.
Teacher: Quid fit?   **Student:** Epistula ā tē parātur.

PAGE 77
Standards 1.1, 3.1, 4.1

TEACHING TIP

Some students may not be familiar with the phrase "adjectives agree with nouns" but may know instead "adjectives modify nouns" or "adjectives refer to nouns."

TEACHING TIP

The teacher may wish to point out that the reason for learning all genders of the nominative singular of an adjective is comparable to the reason why students must learn not just the nominative singular of a noun, but also its genitive singular.

In dictionary entries for adjectives such as *iūstus*, in which there is no change in the base, often the masculine form is followed just by the endings for the feminine and the neuter. In the case of *pulcher*, *miser*, and similar words, the three forms should always be written in full in order to avoid errors and to make clear how the base of the word is joined to the endings throughout all the cases.

TEACHING TIP

Instruct the students to repeat aloud the forms of *pulcher* after the teacher models the pronunciation of the words. Then encourage the students to create a rap, cheer, or song to help them remember the forms. Alternatively, use Bolchazy-Carducci's *Toga Beats*.

TEACHING TIP

The teacher may wish to have the students compare the chart that includes the forms of *pulcher* on this page with the chart that shows the forms of *iūstus* on p. 64 (SE). Encourage students to see how little difference there is between the two.

PAGE 78

Oral Exercise 4; Workbook Exercise 3

ORAL EXERCISE 4

This exercise may be used as a review exercise at the end of Chapter 5 or anytime after -er adjectives have been presented.

Use one of the CPOs to put on view "*Quālis est . . . ?*" explaining that the phrase means "What kind of . . . is s/he/it?" and that it requires an answer with an adjective and the verb *est* ("is"). The teacher may want to use only masculine and feminine forms, in order to avoid the neuter *Quāle est . . . ?* Then put on view the following adjectives that have been learned recently. *Parvus*, used in Chapter 4, may again be added.

armātus, armāta, armātum – armed
bonus, bona, bonum – good
longus, longa, longum – long
magnus, magna, magnum – big
malus, mala, malum – bad
praeclārus, praeclāra, praeclārum – famous, distinguished
pulcher, pulchra, pulchrum – beautiful, nice
miser, misera, miserum – wretched

Afterward, the teacher may ask the students questions containing the phrase *Quālis est . . . ?* The students should be encouraged to ask the teacher to repeat the question any number of times, if they do not understand the sentence immediately or recall all of its words. Repetition is beneficial. In fact, the teacher can teach them to ask in Latin for the question to be repeated. They can say such phrases as *Repete, sīs*, "Please, repeat!" or *Nōn intellegō*, "I don't understand."

The following are samples for such questions and answers:

1. **Teacher:** Quālis est ager? **Student:** Ager est magnus/parvus.
2. **Teacher:** Quālis est fābula? **Student:** Fābula est longa/parva/bona/pulchra.
3. **Teacher:** Quālis est epistula? **Student:** Epistula est longa/parva/bona.
4. **Teacher:** Quālis est puella? **Student:** Puella est bona/mala/misera/magna/parva.
5. **Teacher:** Quālis est puer? **Student:** Puer est magnus/parvus/bonus/malus/miser.
6. **Teacher:** Quālis est vir? **Student:** Vir est bonus/malus/pulcher/praeclārus/miser.
7. **Teacher:** Quālis est fēmina? **Student:** Fēmina est bona/mala/pulchra/praeclāra/misera.

If the teacher considers it appropriate, s/he can ask questions about the students.

Example
Teacher: Quālis est Mārcus? **Student:** Mārcus est magnus.
Teacher: Quālis est Marīa? **Student:** Marīa est magna.

This exercise will include only the masculine and feminine singular in order to avoid the introduction of the forms *Quāle est?* for neuter singular, *Quālēs sunt?* for masculine and feminine plural, and *Quālia sunt?* for neuter plural.

PAGE 79
Standards 1.1, 1.2
Workbook Exercises 4, 6, 7, Content Questions

TEACHING TIP
In the caption to the picture, the word "Cicero" is misspelled. Explain to students that the Latin word *sīc*, "thus," is used in this type of context to indicate that the error comes from the source and not from the author of the statement. This annotation is often seen in letters to the editor in newspapers.

▶ EXERCISE 6 ANSWERS
1. lacrimīs miserīs — to/for, by/with wretched tears
2. viam longam — a long road
3. āthlētārum pulchrōrum — of beautiful athletes
4. virō iūstō — to/for, by/with a just man
5. poētā armātō — by/with the armed poet
6. patriā pulchrā — by/with the beautiful fatherland
7. vinculōrum miserōrum — of wretched chains
8. puerī miserī — wretched boys, of the wretched boy
9. familiīs bonīs — to/for, by/with good families
10. animus magnus — a great mind (spirit)

Chapter 5 • 95

TEACHER BY THE WAY
In Exercise 6, #5 brings to mind Horace, who describes his military career as lamentable in *Epistulae* 2.2.46–49.

▶ EXERCISE 7 ANSWERS
1. falsum
2. falsum
3. vērum
4. falsum
5. vērum
6. falsum
7. falsum
8. vērum

PAGE 80
Standards 1.2, 4.1, 4.2
Oral Exercise 5 and Dictation

TRANSLATION OF THE LATIN CONVERSATION
Mary: I want to become a lawyer. For my father is a lawyer. Lawyers have a lot of money.

Christy: I want to become a doctor. Not only lawyers, but also doctors have a lot of money. However, doctors always help men and women, boys and girls. I want to take care of boys and girls.

Helen: I do not think about money. I am an artist and I think about art. What job do you want to have, Mark?

Mark: I am an athlete. My father, however, is an astronaut. In California he flew in the sky. Now in Washington, DC, he has a job in the government.

Girls: Wow!

TEACHING TIP
The teacher may use this opportunity to open a discussion on the occupations typical of ordinary and wealthy Romans.

ORAL EXERCISE 5 AND DICTATION
This combined exercise may be used to conclude the chapter or anytime after the passive voice has been presented. Dictate the following sentences. After each sentence, the teacher will ask an individual student to read it, and then to change it orally into passive voice.

1. **Teacher:** Nauta longās epistulās exspectat. **Student:** Longae epistulae ā nautā exspectantur.
2. **Teacher:** Āthlēta pulchram puellam amat. **Student:** Pulchra puella ab āthlētā amātur.
3. **Teacher:** Virī vincula misera timent. **Student:** Vincula misera ā virīs timentur.
4. **Teacher:** Poēta praeclārus fābulam nārrat. **Student:** Fābula ā poētā praeclārō nārrātur.

PAGE 81
Standard 4.1

DERIVATIVES

auxilium – (from *augeō* = to increase)

An <u>auxiliary</u> verb, like "has," "does," and "am" in verb phrases, is called a "helping" verb by elementary teachers instructing their young charges in grammar.

<u>Auxiliary</u> forces come to the aid of front line troops if they meet overwhelming odds.

Note: A knowledge of Latin helps the spelling of "auxiliary," for the English pronunciation hides the second *i*.

cōnsilium – The verb "counsel" enters into English in the late thirteenth century from the Old French *conseiller* "to advise," from Latin *cōnsiliārī* based on *cōnsilium*. Counseling meaning "giving professional advice on social or psychological problems" dates from 1940 (OED).

The noun derivative "counsel" meaning "advice" comes into English at the same time from the Old French *counseil*, which meant "advice, counsel; deliberation, thought." As a synonym for "lawyer" it is first attested in the late fourteenth century. Today, that meaning is usually expressed as "counselor at law."

Note the "-or" agent or doer ending on "counselor." From the early thirteenth century, "counselor" came from the Old French *conseillier* from the Latin *consilātor*. The specialized meaning "one who gives professional legal advice" dates from the 1530s while marriage counselor and related psychological senses is from 1940.

A tendency to confuse "council" in form and meaning with "counsel" has been consistent since the sixteenth century (OED). "Council" and related words derive from the Latin *cōncilium*, "a meeting, a gathering of people."

epistula – A formal or didactic letter is often called an <u>epistle</u>.

The letters of the apostles (e.g., Paul to the Romans) are called <u>epistles</u>.

An <u>epistolary</u> novel is written in the form of letters, e.g., Saul Bellow's *Herzog*, Bel Kaufman's *Up the Down Staircase*, Anne Bronte's *The Tenant of Wildfell Hall*, or Stephen King's *Carrie*.

familia – The word "family" came into English around 1400 meaning "servants of a household" from the Latin *familia*, which meant "family servants" (from the Latin *famulus* meaning "servant"). The extension of the meaning to "all those connected by blood" did not occur until the 1660s.

From the Latin adjective *familiāris* was derived the English word "familiar," which, like the Latin, meant "intimate, friendly, on a family footing." The noun form meaning "demon, evil spirit that answers one's call" dates to the 1580s.

gaudium – The word "gaudy" now means "excessively showy, without taste," but it is derived from *gaudium*. The pejorative connotation probably comes from the Anglo-French *gaudir*, which meant "to be merry," but also "to scoff" through the Middle English "gaud" (deception, trick).

The word "joy" appeared in English early, around 1200, meaning "a feeling of pleasure or delight." The idea of "a source of pleasure or happiness" is found around 1300. It derives from *gaudium* through the Old French *joie* (eleventh century).

Note the "-ous" suffix on "joyous."

The prefix "re-" in "rejoice" is an intensive. The word appears in English around 1300 and is derived from the Latin through the Old French *rejoissant*, the present participle of *rejoir*.

Chapter 5 • 97

The prefix of "enjoy" is a word-forming element derived from the Latin *in* (in, into). For instance, it is used to make verbs out of nouns and adjectives, e.g., "encircle" (to put in or on), "endear" (to cause or make). Hence, "enjoy" means "to make glad, take delight in, give joy." The verb appears in English during the late fourteenth century. The modern use of "enjoy" tends to lose its connection with pleasure, e.g., "to enjoy bad health" is a common phrase in northern and western England. A picture of a girl may be labeled "Susie is <u>enjoying</u> an ice cream cone" when all she is doing is eating it.

lacrima – The <u>lachrymal</u> glands, which are located one above each eye, secrete tear film.

<u>Lachrymal</u> ducts carry the tears to and from the eye.

The <u>lachrymose</u> woman was obviously still in deep mourning over the death of her husband.

A good white Italian wine is named <u>*Lacrima*</u> *Christi* (the Tears of Christ).

longus – A rubber band can be easily <u>elongated</u> so that it can stretch over a package (from the Latin *ex* = out from, and *longus*; in Late Latin there appears a verb *elongāre* = remove to a distance from *e*, and *longāre* = to lengthen out). The verb appears in English during the 1530s; the noun "elongation" during the late fourteenth century.

The word "longevity" is derived from *longus* and *vīta* (life). The word appeared in English during the 1610s: Increased <u>longevity</u> in America is putting a strain on the Social Security system.

The word "longitude" is derived directly from the Latin *longitūdō* (length) and appears in English during the late fourteenth century. <u>Longitudinal</u> measurements of the globe begin at the Prime Meridian in Greenwich, English.

The word "lunge" appears in English in 1735 and was originally a fencing term (to thrust with a sword). It was a shortened form of the French *allonger* (to extend, thrust) from the Old French *alongier* (to lengthen, make long; derived from the Latin *longus*). The meaning "to make a sudden forward rush" dates from 1821.

The Latin word *oblongus* means "somewhat long" or "more long than broad" with *ob* (to, toward) becoming more like an intensive than a directional.

The prefix of "prolong" is derived from the Latin *prō* (in front of) which gives the sense of forward movement; hence "extend." To <u>prolong</u> life means to "extend" it (make it longer).

The word "purloin," which now means "to steal," originally meant "remove" in Anglo-French, from the Old French *purloigner* (to put off, delay, be far away; cf. the Latin *prō* and *longus*). The word appeared in English during the mid-fourteenth century, but its meaning "to steal" is a development in English which occurred during the 1540s.

See also the non-asterisked word list in 1.2.

miser – The word "commiserate" is derived from the Latin *cum* (together) and *miser*: The mourners at the funeral <u>commiserated</u> with Javier over the death of his father ("felt sorrow together").

The word "miser" appeared in English during the 1540s and meant "unhappy person, a wretch." The modern meaning of "money hoarder" dates back to the 1560s, acquired on the presumption that such people are unhappy.

pulcher – A song "There's Nothin' Like a Dame" in the musical *South Pacific* extols the <u>pulchritude</u> of women.

Selection to fill vacancies on the Cowboy Cheerleading Squad depends largely on the <u>pulchritudinous</u> attributes of the applicants.

Both derivatives come from the Latin *pulchritūdō*.

cōgitō – This Latin word is a combination of *cum* (together) and *agō* (to drive, do, discuss). It literally means "to drive together, put in constant motion," as a thinker does when turning over ideas in his mind. The coach <u>cogitated</u> over ways to improve his team's chances to win the game.

doleō – Many <u>condolences</u> were given to the team which lost the championship game ("con" = *cum*; hence "grieving together").

The name "Delores" is derived from the Latin through the Spanish "Maria de los Dolores" (Mary of the Sorrows).

The prefix of "indolent" is negative. An "indolent" person is "without pain, lazy, or disinterested." The sense of "living easily" dates to 1710.

Note the "-ous" suffix of "dolorous."

The route Jesus took to Calvary while carrying his cross is called the *Via <u>Dolorōsa</u>* (the Road of Pain).

parō – See 1.2.

longē – See *longus*, 1.5.

semper – *Semper parātus* (always prepared) is the motto of both the Boy Scouts and the Coast Guard. *Semper fidēlis* is the motto of the Marine Corps, often shortened to *Semper Fi*.

A diamond is <u>sempiternal</u> because it lasts forever.

ab – Compounds from *a, ab* will be discussed under the main root, e.g., "abduct" under *dūcō*, "abdicate" under *dīcō*, and "abridge" under *brevis*. Students should be warned to be careful about words beginning with *a* as they come from several different sources such as "ascent" from *ad*, and not always from Latin, e.g., "abacus," "acorn," and "alcove."

dē – Compounds derived from *dē* (down from, about concerning) will be discussed under the main root, e.g., "deduct" under *dūcō*, "depress" under *premō*, "depend" under *pendeō*, "depict" under *pingō*, etc.

nam – None

tamen – None

Chapter 5 • 99

CHAPTER 6 (PP. 83–94)

GRAMMAR IN LANGUAGE FACTS

Present Tense and Present Infinitive of *Sum* and *Possum*; Complementary Infinitive; Transitive and Intransitive Verbs

PAGE 83

Standards 1.1, 3.1, 3.2, 4.1

RRA 5

MEMORĀBILE DICTŪ VOCABULARY

ālea, āleae, *f.* – a die, game of dice, risk (in general)

iacta . . . est – is cast (literally, "has been cast")

TEACHING TIP

Instruct the students to locate the Rubicon River on the map on pp. xxxiv–xxxv (SE) and to find Caesar in the timeline on pp. 405–408 (SE).

TEACHER BY THE WAY

In Florence in 1597, Jacopo Peri produced a new entertainment, *Dafne*, in which singers and dancers enacted an entire drama telling of Daphne fleeing from the god Apollo. This and the similar works that followed it, as they incorporated virtually all the performing arts—singing, dancing, instrumental music, and acting, plus elaborate costuming and settings—were called "operas" from the Latin word *opera* or perhaps from the plural of "*opus, operis.*" Both Latin words mean "work."

The opera *Norma*, with musical score by Vincenzo Bellini and libretto or text by Felice Romani, was a high point of the *bel canto* or "beautiful singing" style. It was based on Alexandre Soumet's play about a Druid priestess, daughter of the Archdruid, who has secretly married Pollione, a Roman proconsul commanding the forces occupying Gaul around 50 BCE. Although they have two children, Pollione decides to reject Norma and flee with a young temple virgin, Adalgisa. When the girl confesses to Norma, the priestess decides to kill her children, but instead denounces her husband to the Druids and then dies on the funeral pyre with him. The opera's popularity springs not only from its beauty but from the wide range of human experiences it encompasses: loyalty in public and private life, love, motherhood, friendship, desperation, and resignation.

TEACHING TIP
The teacher may wish to assign Chapter 5 of RRA for reading or review. See p. 73.

PAGE 84
Standards 1.1, 2.1, 3.1, 3.2

TRANSLATION OF LATIN PASSAGE
About the Druids

Among the Gauls are great (i.e., of high standing) men who are called Druids. The sacred rites of the Gauls are handled by the Druids. The Druids are exceedingly feared by the Gauls: for they have great authority, and are accustomed to make judgment about good and bad men. Rewards and punishments are given by the Druids. The life (i.e., the lives) of the Gauls is managed by the Druids. Because of the great knowledge of the Druids, many boys stay with the Druids for a long period. The boys learn from the Druids: the Druids teach the boys. The Druids have great knowledge about sacred rites, but they do not like books and literature. For sacred rites seem to the Gauls to be great, if they lie (hidden) in shadows. So the sacred rites of the Gauls are not preserved by writings, but by memory. The Druids are able to preserve a large body of knowledge by means of memory. So while the Druids teach examples and tell stories, the boys strengthen their memory (i.e., memories).

TEACHER BY THE WAY
Cicero's style is noteworthy for its complex structures. Caesar, however, writes in a straightforward, unadorned, and precise manner. He is one of the few classical Roman authors born in the city of Rome itself; his family, in fact, claimed direct descent from Iulus, son of Aeneas, the mythical ancestor of Rome, the son of Venus, and one of Rome's early kings

TEACHER BY THE WAY
The chapter reading passage has been adapted from *Dē bellō Gallicō*, 6.13–14.

TEACHING TIP
The teacher may wish to instruct the students to find *Gallia* (Gaul) on the map on pp. xxxiv–xxxv (SE).

PAGE 85

ANSWERS TO COMPREHENSION QUESTIONS
1. Because of their great authority, both civil and religious.
2. They want to learn from the Druids, who have much knowledge.
3. Sacred rites seem more impressive to them if they are hidden from most people and not accessible in writings.
4. The sacred rites of the Gauls are preserved by memory—specifically the memory of the Druids.
5. The students of the Druids must especially develop their memory skills/ability to memorize.

TEACHER BY THE WAY
The Celts were an ethnic group of many clans and subgroups with no central organization. Their laws and beliefs were transmitted orally rather than being written down. Thus we know relatively little about the Druids. Caesar says Gaul has two powerful social groups, knights or military leaders and Druids. The Druids, who neither went to war nor paid taxes, controlled religion, education, and law both criminal and civil. Their judgments in all these areas were final, and anyone not obeying them was prohibited from attending the sacred sacrifices. The sacrifice of criminals was believed to propitiate the gods and provide safety against disease and danger; thus people who were not allowed to attend were shunned by everyone.

The Druids, when not judging law cases or conducting religious rites, taught the young about astronomy, geography, nature, and religion. They were ruled by an Archdruid, whose power over them was absolute. There is no certain information about whether or not there were Druid priestesses. Their regular meetings were held in groves of oak trees, one of which was in the land of the Canutes (near Chartres) because this was the center of Gaul. (*Dē bellō Gallicō*, 6.13–16)

TEACHING TIP
Teachers may wish to point out to students that not all verbs have four principal parts—e.g., *iaceō* and *soleō* in the Reading Vocabulary and Vocabulary to Learn of this chapter.

PAGE 86
Standards 1.1, 1.2, 3.1, 3.2, 4.1
Oral Exercise 1

▶ EXERCISE 1 ANSWERS
1. The Druids are great men.
2. You are Druids: you teach good examples and you tell stories.
3. We are not Druids.
4. I am a just man.
5. I, on the other hand (however), am a great athlete.
6. You are not an athlete; you are a poet.
7. The book is good.

ORAL EXERCISE 1

This exercise may be used anytime after the present tense of sum *has been presented.*

Use one of the CPOs to put the following interrogative words on view with their meanings. Also add the adjectives that have been in the Vocabulary to Learn:

quālis – what sort – (masculine/feminine nominative singular)
quālēs – what sort – (masculine/feminine nominative plural)
quāle – what sort – (neuter singular nominative)
quālia – what sort – (neuter plural nominative)

bonus, iūstus, longus, magnus, miser, malus, praeclārus, pulcher.

Then the teacher may ask different students in turn the following questions. Each question involves a form of *sum*: in the answers the students must supply the correct form of *sum*, along with an adjective in the correct number and gender.

1. **Teacher:** Quālis es? **Student:** Sum bonus/a, iūstus/a, etc.
2. **Teacher:** Quālis est vīta? **Student:** Vīta est longa, pulchra, bona, etc.
3. **Teacher:** Quāle est auxilium? **Student:** Auxilium est bonum, iūstum, etc.
4. **Teacher:** Quālia sunt gaudia? **Student:** Gaudia sunt bona, praeclāra, etc.
5. **Teacher:** Quālēs sunt lacrimae? **Student:** Lacrimae sunt miserae, malae, etc.
6. **Teacher:** Quālēs estis? **Student:** Sumus pulchrī, bonī, etc.
7. **Teacher:** Quālis est lupa? **Student:** Lupa est pulchra, bona, mala, etc.
8. **Teacher:** Quāle est venēnum? **Student:** Venēnum est malum, etc.
9. **Teacher:** Quālēs sunt amīcī? **Student:** Amīcī sunt bonī, praeclārī, etc.
10. **Teacher:** Quālēs sunt āthlētae? **Student:** Āthlētae sunt magnī, praeclārī, etc.
11. **Teacher:** Quālis est Rōma? **Student:** Rōma est magna, praeclāra, pulchra, etc.

PAGE 87

TEACHER BY THE WAY

The discovery of Pompeii has allowed the modern world to see into the lives of not only the upper class with its villas and treasures but also those of the innkeepers, the merchants, and the lower classes. However, it is the graffiti (not just the inscriptions on stone)—ranging from political electioneering, advertisements for rental property, and comments on sporting figures to messages by and about friends, lovers, and prostitutes—which make the Romans of the first century very real people to us.

Paul MacKendrick in *The Mute Stones Speak* (Second Edition) gives lively and detailed accounts of election posters (p. 249)—"Vote for X: he won't squander public funds"—and everyday life (pp. 264–266). Graffiti keep accounts of daily purchases, wine prices, rewards for stolen goods, apartments for rent, erotic art, messages ("I am yours—for two *assēs*"), and even literary quotations (including the first line of the *Aeneid* written in a childish scrawl). In fact, there were so many graffiti everywhere that some Pompeiian wag wrote a couplet, which has been translated (p. 166):

I wonder, wall, that you do not go smash,

Who have to bear the weight of all this trash. (*Corpus Inscrīptiōnum Latīnārum* 4.1904)

Other examples from the *Corpus Inscrīptiōnum Latīnārum*, Volume 4 include:

- The finances officer of the emperor Nero says this food is poison (8075)
- Palmyra, the thirst-quencher (8475)
- I made bread (8792)
- What a lot of tricks you use to deceive, innkeeper. You sell water but drink unmixed wine (3498)
- Ampliātus Pedānia is a thief (4993)
- Romula hung out here with Staphylus (2060)
- If anyone does not believe in Venus, s/he should gaze at my girlfriend (6842)
- May Love burn in some lonely mountains whoever wants to rape my girlfriend (1645)

And then there are those that are like the scribblings on the stall doors of modern public restrooms:

- Crescēns is sweet and charming (4783)
- Phileros is a eunuch (1826)
- Serena hates Isidorus (10231)
- Virgula to her friend Titus: You are disgusting (1881)
- Auge loves Allotenus (1808)

People haven't changed much in 2,000 years!

PAGE 88
Standards 1.1, 1.2, 3.1, 4.1
Workbook Exercise 2

▶ EXERCISE 2 ANSWERS

1.	letter	littera		confirmation	firmō
2.	conservation	servō			
3.	essence	sum, esse			
4.	adjacent	iaceō			
5.	library	liber			
6.	illiterate	litterae		remain	maneō
7.	memorandum	memoria			
8.	multivitamin	multus, vīta			
9.	permanent	maneō			
10.	potent	possum			
11.	vital	vīta			

Chapter 6 • 105

TEACHING TIP
Although in Exercise 2 the students are directed to find only the derivatives based on the Vocabulary to Learn, they may be interested to learn that there are other derivatives in Exercise 2. The derivation of these words is provided for the teacher's convenience.

1. please – through ME and MF from *placeō* (to please, satisfy). delivery – from *līberō* (to set free).
2. museum – from Greek *mouseion* and *Mūsa* (Muse in Latin).
5. largest – from *largus* (copious, ample, liberal, bountiful). country – from *contrā* (against) = "that which is opposite, hence landscape."
6. past – from *passus* (step). people – from *populus* (people, nation, large crowds, populace). school – from *schola* (school), which is from the Greek *scholē* (meaning leisure since only the wealthy had the time for education).
8. recommended – from *commendō* (to entrust, commit, recommend).
9. license – from *licet* (it is permitted, it is allowed).
10. very – from *vērus* (true, real, actual). agent – from *agō* (to drive, do, discuss, live, spend, etc.). prescription – from *prae* (before) + *scrībō* (to write).
11. signs – from *signum* (sign, standard, signal). hospital – from *hospes* (guest, host) and *hospitium* (friendship, lodging) and *hospitālis* (hospitable).

PAGE 89
Standards 1.1, 1.2, 3.1, 3.2
Workbook Exercise 1

▶ EXERCISE 3 ANSWERS
1. Puerōs docēre possumus. We can/are able to teach the boys.
2. Scientiam magnam habēre potes. You can have great knowledge.
3. Memoriam firmāre possum. I am able to strengthen (my) memory.
4. Sacra Gallōrum cūrāre nōn possunt. They are unable to administer the sacred rites of the Gauls.
5. Druidēs amāre nōn potest. He cannot esteem the Druids.
6. Druidēs timēre potes. You can fear the Druids.

TEACHING TIP
When explaining to students how easy the forms of *possum* in the present tense are to learn if one can see the form of *sum* inside the form of *possum*, the teacher may choose to use this saying to help students remember this: Prefix "pos" when the form of *sum* begins with an "s" and "pot" when it begins with an "e."

106 • Latin for the New Millennium: Teacher's Manual, Level 1

PAGE 90

▶ EXERCISE 4 ANSWERS

1. You ought not to fear the darkness.
2. We can strengthen and preserve <our> memory.
3. We are accustomed to preserve literature in books.
4. Good men can give good examples.
5. You (pl.) ought to think always.
6. Armed men ought to take care of the fatherland.
7. I am accustomed to tell long stories.
8. Life is accustomed to give not only tears, but also joys.
9. You ought to see Rome.

TEACHING TIP
Additional reproducible worksheets, morphology charts, and their associated answer keys, related to this material, are available for download at www.lnm.bolchazy.com.

- **Verb Conjugations**

PAGE 91

Standards 1.1, 1.2, 3.1, 3.2, 4.1
Oral Exercise 2; Workbook Exercises 3, 4

▶ EXERCISE 5 ANSWERS

1. Librōs servāre solēmus.
2. Druidēs timēre nōn dēbētis.
3. Memoria firmārī potest.
4. Fābulae ā Druidibus nārrārī solent.
5. Praemia habēre possumus: praemia ā Druidibus darī possunt.
6. Puerī docērī dēbent.

Chapter 6 • 107

ORAL EXERCISE 2

This exercise may be used anytime after the complimentary infinitive with possum, dēbeō, *and* soleō *has been presented.*

The teacher should recite orally each of the following verb forms. Then the student should respond orally with the corresponding plural form if the verb is singular or vice versa.

1. **Teacher:** possum   **Student:** possumus
2. **Teacher:** sumus   **Student:** sum
3. **Teacher:** potestis   **Student:** potes
4. **Teacher:** dēbēmus   **Student:** dēbeō
5. **Teacher:** solent   **Student:** solet
6. **Teacher:** dēbet   **Student:** dēbent
7. **Teacher:** es   **Student:** estis
8. **Teacher:** sunt   **Student:** est
9. **Teacher:** possunt   **Student:** potest
10. **Teacher:** soleō   **Student:** solēmus
11. **Teacher:** dēbēs   **Student:** dēbētis
12. **Teacher:** estis   **Student:** es

TEACHING TIP
Ask the students to look at Caesar's crown in the picture and explain that the laurel wreath represented victory. Then explain that the modern expression "Rest on one's laurels" means to live off previously earned praises.

TEACHING TIP
The following list of transitive and intransitive verbs is from the Vocabulary to Learn, Chapters 1–6. Teachers might ask the students to recall from memory verbs learned thus far that are transitive or intransitive. Alternately, teachers might read the verbs from this list and ask the students whether they are transitive or intransitive.

Transitive

- *amō, amāre*
- *dēbeō, dēbēre*
- *dō, dare*
- *doceō, docēre*
- *exspectō, exspectāre*
- *firmō, firmāre*
- *habeō, habēre*
- *intrō, intrāre*
- *iubeō, iubēre*
- *nārrō, nārrāre*
- *parō, parāre*
- *servō, servāre*
- *teneō, tenēre*
- *timeō, timēre*
- *videō, vidēre*
- *vocō, vocāre*

Intransitive

- *ambulō, ambulāre*
- *habitō, habitāre*
- *iaceō, iacēre*
- *maneō, manēre*
- *possum, posse*
- *sum, esse*

PAGE 92

Standards 1.1, 1.2, 3.1, 3.2
Workbook Exercises 5, 6, 7, Content Questions

▶ EXERCISE 6 ANSWERS

1. transitive   I hold the girl's letter.
2. intransitive   In the family there are beautiful memories.
3. intransitive   Great men often lie in chains.
4. transitive   Help is given by good men.
5. transitive   I love (my) son and daughter exceedingly/very much.
6. intransitive   A friend always remains in the memory.

▶ EXERCISE 7 ANSWERS

1. Amīcī bonī auxilium dant.   Good friends give help.
2. Fābula ā puellā nārrātur.   The story is told by a girl.
3. Puerī familiam amant.   The boys love the family.
4. Litterae ā poētīs iūdicantur.   The letters are judged by the poets.
5. Rōmānī mala cōnsilia nōn parant.   The Romans do not prepare evil plans.

▶ EXERCISE 8 ANSWERS

1. vērum
2. vērum
3. falsum
4. falsum
5. vērum
6. vērum

Chapter 6 • 109

PAGE 93

Standards 1.2, 4.1, 4.2

TEACHING TIP

Many of these conversational phrases and sentences may be used by teachers and students during classtime.

PAGE 94

Standards 1.2, 4.1
Oral Exercise and Dictation 3, Oral Exercise 4

TRANSLATION OF THE LATIN CONVERSATION

Teacher: Today you all will take a quiz.
Christy: Why do we need to take a quiz today?
Teacher: Because you all need to keep knowledge in <your> memory. Don't you love Latin literature?
Christy: I love Latin literature.
Teacher: Therefore you need to learn the passage of Caesar.
Christy: In that passage of Caesar there are many new words. We are not Druids. We are not Gauls. We are not accustomed to retain a large <amount of> knowledge and many words by memory.
Teacher: You already retain by memory the passage of Caesar. You are a good student! Are you now ready, students?
Students: We are ready.
Teacher: Take up your pens. Write on empty pieces of paper. Write your names on the back of the paper.

ORAL EXERCISE AND DICTATION 3

This combined exercise may be used to conclude the chapter.

After putting these two words on view, the teacher should read the following passage slowly and clearly so the students can write it with understanding.

inimīcus, inimīcī, *m.* – the opposite of *amīcus*
necō, necāre, necāvī, necātum – to murder

Caesar et Cicero sunt magnī virī. Caesar tamen et Cicero nōn sunt amīcī. Nam Caesar dē bellīs cōgitāre solet. Cicero autem patriam semper cūrat. Et Caesar et Cicero litterās amant. Et Cicero et Caesar ab inimīcīs necantur.

Next the teacher should use one of the CPOs to put these words with explanations on view. Then ask the students the following questions about the passage just dictated. The students should answer using as far as possible the actual words in the dictated text.

–ne (asking a general question)   **quid** – what?
quālēs – of what sort or character   **ā quibus** – by whom?
dē quibus rēbus – about what?

110 • Latin for the New Millennium: Teacher's Manual, Level 1

Teacher: Quālēs sunt Cicero et Caesar?
Student: Cicero et Caesar sunt magnī virī.

Teacher: Suntne Cicero et Caesar amīcī?
Student: Cicero et Caesar nōn sunt amīcī.

Teacher: Dē quibus rēbus cōgitāre solet Caesar?
Student: Caesar dē bellīs cōgitāre solet.

Teacher: Quid Cicero semper cūrat?
Student: Cicero patriam semper cūrat.

Teacher: Quid amant Caesar et Cicero?
Student: Caesar et Cicero litterās amant.

Teacher: Ā quibus Caesar et Cicero necantur?
Student: Caesar et Cicero ab inimīcīs necantur.

ORAL EXERCISE 4

This exercise may be used after the Latin dialogue has been presented.

The teacher may ask the following questions about the dialogue, which the students will have read and studied with the help of the teacher. In their answers, the students should use, as far as possible, the words in the dialogue, changing the endings only where appropriate for a correct answer. The teacher should use one of the CPOs to put the following interrogative words/phrases with meanings on view:

quid – what?

quem – whom/what?

ubi – where?

–ne (an interrogative particle added to the end of the first word of a question, used to indicate the sentence is a question)

1. **Teacher:** Cūr probātiunculam hodiē subīre dēbent discipulī?
   Student: Quia scientiam memoriā servāre dēbent.

2. **Teacher:** Litterāsne Latīnās amat Christīna?
   Student: Christīna litterās Latīnās amat.

3. **Teacher:** Quem locum discere dēbet Christīna?
   Student: Christīna locum Caesaris discere dēbet.

4. **Teacher:** Suntne in locō Caesaris multa verba?
   Student: In locō Caesaris sunt multa verba.

5. **Teacher:** Solentne multa verba memoriā servāre Christīna et amīcī?
   Student: Christīna et amīcī nōn solent multa verba memoriā servāre.

6. **Teacher:** Quid iam memoriā tenet Christīna?
   Student: Locum Caesaris iam memoriā tenet Christīna.

7. **Teacher:** Suntne discipulī parātī?
   Student: Discipulī sunt parātī.

8. **Teacher:** Ubi scrībere dēbent discipulī?
   Student: In chartīs vacuīs scrībere dēbent discipulī.

Chapter 6 • 111

DERIVATIVES

exemplum – (from *ex* = out from, and *emō* = to buy, procure, win over; *eximō* = to take out, remove, release, banish)

The vendor took out a sample of cloth from the showcase to show as an <u>example</u> to his customer. The word appears in English during the late fourteenth century.

The word "sample" appeared in English around 1300 meaning "something which confirms a proposition or statement" from the Latin *exemplum* (meaning "sample, example, precedent"). The meaning of "a small part of a larger item" dates to the early fifteenth century; the sense of "a scientific specimen" to 1878.

The word "exemplary" can refer to something negative, as in "exemplary punishment," or to something postitive, as in "exemplary behavior," and dates back to the 1580s.

liber – The word "libel" is derived from the Latin diminutive *libellus* (little book) which in Middle English also referred to a formal document, especially the statement of a plaintiff, as did Pliny in his letter to Trajan about the Christians (10.96). It appeared in English through the Old French *libelle* (small book, legal charge) during the mid-fifteenth century.

A "library" is a place for books. The word dates from the late fourteenth century. In Latin a *librārium* was "a chest for books."

A "libretto" is the text of an opera or similar musical composition. It is derived from *liber* through the Italian diminutive of *liber*, hence the retention of the short *i*. (Other derivatives from *liber* have a long *i* like "libel" and "library.") The reverse is true of derivatives from *liber* (free). Those derivatives have a short *i*, e.g., "liberal, liberty, deliver," and "livery."

littera – The prefix "ob" of "obliterate" means "against"; hence the word literally means "against a letter, document, something learned from a book." "To wipe out of mind, to forget"; "to erase, cancel" are the meanings of the Latin *oblitterō*: The hard rain <u>obliterated</u> the tracks of the animal.

The word "alliteration" consists of *ad* (to, toward, near) and *littera* and literally means "to the letter." It appears in English during the 1650s meaning "beginning with the same letter." We call that process assimilation (the *ad* changes to "as" as it changes to "al" in "alliteration."

The prefix "il" of "illiterate" and "illiteracy" also demonstrates this type of spelling change ("in" becomes "il"). It is a negative here. "Alliteration" can be seen in such lines as "Peter Piper picked a peck of pickled peppers" in which the initial letter of the words is the same.

The word "literature" is derived from the Latin *literatūra* ("something written with letters" and then "entire bodies of writing" or "having permanent worth through excellence"). Its meaning in English as a "literary production or work" is first attested in 1779 (cf. Ben Johnson's "Lives of the English Poets"; that of "body of writings from a period or people," e.g., classical literature, dates to 1812.

The word "letter" is derived from *littera* through the Old French *letre* (tenth century) and appeared in English early (around 1200). The use of the word to designate a sports award (as in "She earned a [school] letter in softball") is attested by 1908. The expression "to the letter," meaning "precisely," is from the 1520s; "letter-perfect" dates to 1845 and may have its origin in the theatre, referring to an actor who knew his lines perfectly.

memoria – A "memoir" is a record of facts or events as known to the writer. The word appeared in English during the early fifteenth century derived from the Latin *memoria* (from *memor* = mindful) through the Anglo-French *memoire*.

tenebrae – The <u>tenebrific</u> (from *tenebrae* and *faciō* = to make) eclipse brought darkness on the face of the earth.

The kingdom of Hades had a <u>tenebrous</u> atmosphere. Note the "-ous" suffix of "tenebrous."

vīta – "Vital" statistics concern human life as recorded in deaths, births, and marriages.

<u>Vitamins</u> are essential to human health.

The word "victuals" appeared around 1300 in English but was spelled *vitaylle* (through the Old French *vitaille*). The spelling was altered during the early sixteenth century to conform with the Latin *victuālis* from the fourth principal part (*victus*) of *vīvō* (to live), but the pronunciation remains "vittles." More related derivatives will be found later under *vīvō* in 1.19.

multus – The word "multiply" is derived from *multus* and *plicō* (to fold); hence the literal meaning is "many folds." If one sheet of paper is folded once, it becomes two; if folded again, it becomes four; another fold yields eight, etc. The Latin verb *multiplicō* means "to enlarge" from which the Old French *multiplier* (to increase, flourish, extend, enrich) is derived. The English form appears early, in the mid-twelfth century.

The word "multitude," like latitude and longitude, is derived directly from the Latin *multitūdō* = crowd). The suffix ("-tude") forms abstract nouns from adjectives and participles and is derived through the French *-ude* from the Latin *-ūdō* (genitive *-ūdinis*).

Note the "-ous" suffix of "multitudinous."

doceō – A <u>docile</u> child is more easily taught.

A "doctor" was originally a teacher (Latin *doctor* = teacher, instructor, from *doceō* = to show, teach). The word came into English around 1300 directly from the medieval Latin *doctor*. A holder of the highest university degree acquired the title of "doctor" during the late fourteenth century. It came to refer to a medical professional about the same time but was not common until the late sixteenth century. It replaced the term "leech."

A TV "documentary" is an instructional film.

The word "document" derives from the Latin *documentum* (lesson, example, proof) and appears as a noun in English during the early fifteenth century, as a verb during the 1640s when it meant "to teach." The meaning "to support by documentary evidence" dates to 1711.

The word "doctrine" refers to a particular position or policy advocated (i.e., taught) by a religion or government.

firmō – The witness <u>confirmed</u> the details of the accident (*con* = *cum* and *firmō*).

The immigrant <u>affirmed</u> his loyalty to his new country (*ad* = to, toward, and *firmō* = to strengthen, establish). Note the assimilation in the English derivative, which is not done in the Latin *adfirmō*).

The prefix of "infirm" is negative.

The word "firmament" appeared in English during the mid-thirteenth century directly from the Latin (*firmāmentum*) and meaning the same thing (a support or strengthening). It was used in the Vulgate to translate the Greek στερρέωμα which in turn translated the Hebrew *raqia* (a word used both for the vault of the sky and for the floor of the earth in the Old Testament).

The noun "farm" appeared in English around 1300 meaning "fixed payment" (taxes or rent) derived from the Old French *ferme* (rent, lease) from the medieval Latin *firma* (fixed payment) and the Latin *firmō* (to fix, settle, confirm). It first referred to a tract of leased land in the early fourteenth century, then to cultivated land in the 1520s. The verb usage (to rent land) appeared during the mid-fifteenth century; the agricultural sense dates to 1719. The phrase "to buy the farm," meaning "to die," dates from World War II if not earlier and perhaps cynically referred to a soldier's dream of getting out of the war and going home, in many cases during that period when farms were prolific throughout the country, to a peaceful farmstead.

iaceō – The house <u>adjacent</u> to mine became an eyesore (*ad* = to, toward, near, and *iaceō* = to lie, be situated).

The word "gist" appeared in English in 1711 and referred to "the real point" of an argument or law case. It was derived through the Anglo-French legal phrase *c'est action gist* (this action lies = is sustainable by law) and the Old French *gésir* (to lie) from the Latin *iaceō*. The medieval practice of writing a classical Latin consonantal *i* as a *j* led to the *g* in French.

From the same French verb came the noun *giste* meaning "a beam supporting a bridge." This gave rise to the sense of boards "lying down" on the beam. *Giste* appeared in English during the early fourteenth century as "joist."

iūdicō – Note again how the consonantal *i* changes to a *j* in judge, judicial, etc. The verb "to judge" appears in English around 1300 and the noun during the mid-fourteenth century through the Old French *jugier* from *iūdicō*.

Note the "-ous" suffix of "judicious."

The word "prejudice" consists of the prefix "pre" (Latin *prae* = before) and *iūdicō*. The Latin word *praeiūdicium*, meaning "example, prejudgment," underwent some minor spelling changes as it passed through the medieval Latin *preiūdicium* and the Old French *prejudice* (injustice). Around 1300 the English derivative meant "contempt." The meaning "preconveived opinion," which dates to the late fourteenth century, is not necessarily unfavorable. The critic was <u>prejudiced</u> in our favor.

maneō – A <u>mansion</u> is literally "a place to stay" (from the Latin noun *mansiō*). The idea of a large and stately house, its image today, dates to the 1510s. During the mid-fourteenth century it referred to the chief residence of a lord which probably led to the modern meaning. Originally it referred to any house or abode as in thirteenth-century Old French and "a place to stay" as in John 14:2: "In my father's house are many mansions. . . ."

The word "manor" is first attested in a July 1859 article in *The Times* about the Emperor of France's visit to Austria. "Before Solferino, Austria was only an intruder in Italy; now she is as one 'to the manor born'" (one accustomed by birth to a high position). It may have been a misspelling or a wordplay on Shakespeare's "to the manner born" (*Hamlet* 1.4.15). However, the Elizabethan playwright was referring to a general custom, not a "person accustomed by birth to a high position." The latter meaning (and the word "manor") may have been popularized by the very successful British sitcom "To the Manor Born" (1979), and it is now the accepted one. It is interesting to note that the confusion between the two words has continued, for the "manor" meaning is found in the *Random House Collegiate Dictionary* under "manner" and not "manor." The word "manner" is derived from *manus*, not *maneō*.

A <u>manse</u> is the home of a minister (the place where he stays).

114 • Latin for the New Millennium: Teacher's Manual, Level 1

The word "menagerie" appears in English in 1712 meaning "a collection of wild animals kept in captivity" from the French *menagerie* (housing for domestic animals), which itself is derived from the Old French *manage*. That in turn comes from the Latin *mansiō* (a place to stay, from *maneō*).

In the later fourteenth century the word "menial" referred to a household servant (through the Anglo-French *meignial* and the Old French *mesnie* from the Latin *mansiō*). Its broader meaning, "lowly, humble, suited to a servant," dates to the 1670s: No job should be considered too <u>menial</u> to derive pleasure in the work well done.

The prefix of "permanent" means "through, throughout." The former prisoner was granted a <u>permanent</u> annuity to last through his life as recompense for false imprisonment.

The word "remain" is derived from the Latin *remaneō* (*re* = back, behind, and *maneō*).

A <u>remnant</u> sale is a good place to find smaller pieces of material or carpet which remain after the larger ones have been bought to cover floors and make drapes.

possum – (from *potis* = having the power, able to, and *sum*)

The structure of this word explains the presence of *t* in the paradigm; assimilation explains the interchange of *s* and *t* in the present tense.

The prefix of "impossible" is a negative.

The spelling of "puissant" was affected by its passage from the Latin *possum* through the Old French *poeir* (to be able) and Middle French *puissant* (strong, mighty, powerful) of the twelfth century. It appears in English during the mid-fifteenth century: The <u>puissant</u> governor gathered all the reins of governance into his hands.

servō – The owner of the restaurant held back the <u>reserved</u> wines for himself (from *re* = back, and *servō* = to preserve, save).

The word "preservation" consists of the prefix "pre" (from the Latin *prae* = before) and *servō*, hence the word basically means "to save ahead of time." The black rhino <u>preservation</u> saved the animals from being hunted to extinction before their numbers dwindled irreparably.

<u>Preserves</u> are made during the summer from fresh fruit and saved for the winter months.

The <u>conservation</u> of our natural resources should be championed by everyone.

The word "reservoir" is first attested in English during the 1680s and meant "a place where something tends to collect" (from the Old French *reserver* = to reserve, through the French *reservoir* = storehouse). Its specific reference to an artificial basin for storing a large body of water dates to 1705.

The word "observe" came into English during the late fourteenth century meaning "to hold to a manner of life or course of conduct" from the Latin *observō* (*ob* = over, and *servō*; hence to watch over, look to, guard, comply with). Its meaning of "watch, perceive, notice" dates to the 1560s; that of "to say by way of remark" to around 1600.

soleō – The prefix of "obsolescent" here means "against" or "away from." Thus an item that is termed "obsolescent" is one that people no longer use.

The meaning of "unusual" gradually became "excessive," then "overbearing, haughty." When the word came into English during the late fourteenth century, it meant "immoderate, arrogant, contemptuous." The meaning "contemptuous of rightful authority" dates to the 1670s.

sum – The word "present" as a noun meaning "a gift" entered English early, around 1200. This usage was derived from the Old French in such phrases as *en present* ("[to offer] in the presence of") or *mettre en present* (to place before, give).

The word "entity" is said to derive from the Late Latin *entitās*, itself based on the nonexistent present participle of *sum*. It came into English during the 1590s meaning "a thing" and was originally an abstract noun; its concrete sense dates to the 1620s. A "nonentity," therefore, is something which does not exist. The meaning of "a person or thing of no importance" is attested from 1710.

In a "presentation," something is offered before a group of people, e.g., a theatre performance or a business report.

The prefix "re" in "represent" is intensive. The word came into English during the late fourteenth century and meant "to bring to mind by description," i.e., to make something seem present, at hand, real. The Latin root (*repraesentō*) also exhibits the intensive "re" and meant "to exhibit, reproduce."

saepe – None

propter – None

dum – None

REVIEW 2: CHAPTERS 4–6
(PP. 95–111)

PAGE 95

TEACHING TIP

Digital flash cards are an engaging way for students to learn Latin vocabulary. Based on the time-proven technique of paper flash cards, electronic flash cards provide students with a way to use technology while mastering the words of Latin.

Flash cards have been used as a strategy for learning and reviewing vocabulary for a very long time. Often homemade, these cards contained the vocabulary on one side, and the definition on the reverse, at times supplemented by cognates, case or declension, gender, and more. While solid in content, these flash cards suffered from three flaws: (1) the cards were not very portable; they were bulky and often boxed or held together with an elastic band; (2) individual cards could get lost and, as a result, students who had studied the flash cards diligently in preparation for a test or quiz would find (*horribile dictū!*) that a word had not been learned because it had slipped from the deck; (3) students would often copy the word or definition inaccurately and thus, unless checked by the teacher (an exceedingly time-consuming task), the students would learn the errors they had created.

Digital flash cards are prized for their mobility. To learn about the latest electronic vocabulary learning aids available for *Latin for the New Millennium*, check the website www.lnm.bolchazy.com for the latest offerings.

NB: Remind students when using flash cards to concentrate effort on the words that pose problems for them.

PAGE 96
Standards 1.1, 1.2

▶ EXERCISE 1 ANSWERS

Singular

Nominative	exemplum	gaudium
Genitive	exemplī	gaudiī
Dative	exemplō	gaudiō
Accusative	exemplum	gaudium
Ablative	exemplō	gaudiō
Vocative	exemplum	gaudium

Plural

Nominative	exempla	gaudia
Genitive	exemplōrum	gaudiōrum
Dative	exemplīs	gaudiīs
Accusative	exempla	gaudia
Ablative	exemplīs	gaudiīs
Vocative	exempla	gaudia

▶ EXERCISE 2 ANSWERS

Infinitive

servārī – to be preserved   firmārī – to be strengthened   docērī – to be taught   habērī – to be had

Singular

First person	servor	firmor	doceor	habeor
Second person	servāris	firmāris	docēris	habēris
Third person	servātur	firmātur	docētur	habētur

Plural

First person	servāmur	firmāmur	docēmur	habēmur
Second person	servāminī	firmāminī	docēminī	habēminī
Third person	servantur	firmantur	docentur	habentur

▶ EXERCISE 3 ANSWERS

1.	magnō	We are able to think about a great reward.
2.	miserae	We are giving aid to the miserable family.
3.	bonīs	The reward is being given to the good men.
4.	pulchrā	I always think about (my) beautiful daughter.
5.	iūstī	The memory of the just man is preserved by books.
6.	praeclārōrum	The life (lives) of distinguished Romans can be preserved by literature.

PAGE 97
Standards 1.1, 1.2

▶ EXERCISE 4 ANSWERS

1. Epistula Terentiae ā virō Rōmānō nunc tenētur.
   Terentia's letter is now being held by the Roman man.
2. Virī armātī ā Fābriciō vocantur.
   Armed men are being called by Fabricius.
3. Mala cōnsilia ā virīs malīs parantur.
   Bad plans are being prepared by bad men.
4. Memoria ā puerīs firmātur.
   The memory is being strengthened by the boys.
5. Auxilium patriae ā virīs praeclārīs datur.
   Help is being given to the homeland by the distinguished men.
6. Patria ā virīs iūstīs cūrātur.
   The homeland is being cared for by the just men.

TEACHER BY THE WAY

The picture on p. 97 of the student text contains a *gladius* and its scabbard. This offensive weapon carried by soldiers was about two feet long and two-edged. The common soldier wore his sword on his right side suspended by a shoulder band; officers wore theirs on the left side attached to a belt around the waist. The two-edged sharp-pointed dagger in the picture was called a *pūgiō* and was worn by officers in the army and persons of high rank to indicate their power over life and death.

The chief offensive weapon during the monarchy and early Republic was the *hasta*, a long thrusting spear with a point at each end. This was replaced by the *pīlum* or javelin, a throwing spear about six feet long, able to penetrate both shield and armor when well thrown. Marius had it so constructed that, if the point stuck in the shield of an enemy, the iron was bent by the weight of the wooden shaft, thus rendering the weapon useless and, because it was difficult to draw out, making the shield unmanageable.

One weapon that was not used by the military was the *sīca*, or dagger, which had a sharp point and a curved blade. It was particularly useful for stabbing or ripping up and was used by gladiators. Among the Romans it was considered the weapon of ruffians and assassins.

PAGE 98
Standards 1.1, 2.1

▶ EXERCISE 5 ANSWERS

1. Propter memoriam multa exempla servārī possunt.
   Because of memory many examples can be preserved.
2. Exempla animum firmāre solent.
   Examples are accustomed to strengthen the spirit.
3. Praemium virō nōn dare dēbētis.
   You ought not to give the reward to the man.
4. Epistulās Terentiae exspectāre soleō.
   I am accustomed to await Terentia's letters.
5. Poētae praeclārī esse possumus.
   We can be outstanding poets.
6. Puerōs docēre solent.
   They are accustomed to teach the boys.

Review 2: Chapters 4–6 • 119

▶ EXERCISE 6 ANSWERS

In books there are many and good examples (for us). Because of literature the good examples do not lie in darkness. Examples are provided by just men, whose life (i.e., lives) is preserved in books. While I take care of (my) country, I see the excellent men, whose memory is kept (held) in literature. Because of literature, just and good and distinguished men remain in life and they call on me. Help and advice are supplied by literature. The spirit is always strengthened by literature. Literature is at home with us, it is with us in the fields, it stays with us on the road . . .

Transitive verbs	**Intransitive verbs**
dantur	*sunt*
servātur	*iacent*
cūrō	*manent*
videō	
tenētur	
vocant	
firmātur	

PAGE 99

TEACHER BY THE WAY

The basilica served as a prominent civic building in Roman cities. It was a large, usually rectangular, hall divided into central and side aisles by a series of columns. In his treatise, *Dē architectūrā*, Vitruvius, the Roman architect and city planner from Augustus's time, stated that the basilica should be located alongside the forum in its warmest location so that businessmen could meet there without being inconvenienced by bad weather. He also set forth guidelines for a pleasing symmetry of the basilica's elements. As the Romans built cities or renovated cities, a basilica following Vitruvius's guidelines was often erected.

The central meeting area of the Roman Forum was flanked by the second century CE Basilica Aemilia and the larger Basilica Julia, which replaced an older basilica. Julius Caesar planned the latter in his renovations of the Forum and efforts to bring greater symmetry to an area that had evolved organically. Trajan's Forum included the Basilica Ulpia.

The early Christians adapted the basilica form to become the predominant building type for their churches because the basilica did not represent an explicit Roman religious connotation and from the outside was a fairly inconspicuous building. While the Roman basilica was entered from the long side, one entered the Christian basilica from the short side and one's eyes were immediately drawn down the center aisle to the altar, the focal point of the Christian liturgy. The basilica of St. John Lateran in Rome built by Constantine follows this pattern as did the original St. Peter's, which was also built by Constantine. Today, a Roman Catholic church may be granted the designation "basilica" because of its preeminence as a site of worship whether it is in the traditional architectural form of a basilica or not.

TEACHING TIP

Instruct the students to locate the Roman Forum on the map on p. 233 (SE).

CONSIDERING THE CLASSICAL GODS

PAGE 100
Standards 2.1, 2.2, 3.1, 3.2
ODF 3.3

TEACHER BY THE WAY
In the picture note the horses, which Neptune created and which are associated with his sea chariot.

TEACHER BY THE WAY
Neptune was a water deity more than a sea god since the early Romans did not take to the seas. He was a rain-giver and related to the growth of vegetation. His festival was celebrated in July when the summer heat was intense. Participants built huts of branches for protection against the sun. But soon enough he shared the attributes of Poseidon. Since he was also worshipped as patron of horses and horsemen, there was a temple to him in the Circus Flaminius.

Plato writes about the legendary lost island of Atlantis in two of his dialogues. The story starts in the *Timaeus* and resumes in the fragments of the *Critias*. No mention is made of this fabled place in Greek mythology but it has fascinated people ever since.

Solon, an Athenian lawgiver (*fl.* 594 BCE), while traveling in Egypt was told by one of the priests about an ancient tradition that related to a war fought in the far past by Athens against the people of Atlantis. Atlas, the oldest of Poseidon's five sets of twin boys, was given supreme authority and he divided the island into ten districts. The descendants of the ten sons of Poseidon ruled the ten districts, and the descendant of Atlas ruled them all. Atlantis was highly civilized, wealthy, and rich in both minerals and vegetation. Gold, copper, iron, and other metals were in abundance. But once mortal blood mixed with divine blood, the benevolent kings became tyrannical and tried to conquer the remaining nations. Under the leadership of Athens they were subsequently defeated after a long war. Destroyed by an earthquake, the island disappeared into the sea and the accompanying floodwaters killed both the Atlantians and Athenians. All this occurred 9,000 years before the time of Plato.

The belief in such a place still exists. On the Greek island of Thera (Santorini) work is being done on ruins of an ancient city that lies beneath a thick volcanic covering. Some have hopes that this is the lost island. Currently research is being done on the island of Cyprus by Robert Sarmast, who has discovered evidence of a sunken land mass that may be the prehistoric Atlantis. It was the first time fifty physical matches were made that coincide with Plato's description. A second expedition took place in 2006.

TEACHING TIP
Any student who wants to learn more about this project should read Robert Sarmast's book *Discovery of Atlantis: The Startling Case for the Island of Cyprus*, Origin Press, 2003.

PAGE 101

Standards 2.1, 2.2, 3.1, 3.2
ODF 3.4

TEACHER BY THE WAY

This description represents the Homeric Greek picture of the underworld. Teachers may take this opportunity to introduce students to some of the geography and residents of the mythical underworld. In addition to the rivers Styx and Acheron, which are mentioned on this page, the rivers Phlegethon and Lethe are also said to be located in the underworld. The three-headed dog Cerberus likewise inhabits this realm. Both Tartarus, where famous sinners such as the Danaids, Sisyphus, Tantalus, and Ixion are punished, and the Elysian Fields, the home of the blessed, are also part of the kingdom of the dead as depicted by Vergil, if not in earlier sources.

TEACHING TIP

Encourage students to research the crimes that the Danaids, Sisyphus, Tantalus, and Ixion committed or explain the following:

- Danaids: commanded by their father to kill their fifty bridegrooms; forty-nine complied, one (Hypermnestra) did not. They ceaselessly refill leaky jars.
- Sisyphus: chained Thanatos (Death), who had come to claim him. He eternally pushes a rock uphill only to have it fall down again. (Odysseus saw Sisyphus toiling away when he visited the underworld.)
- Tantalus: tried to trick the gods by giving them human flesh, by revealing divine secrets, and by giving ambrosia and nectar to undeserving mortals. Tormented by an insatiable hunger and thirst, whenever he tries to pluck fruit from a branch, it goes out of reach. Whenever he bends to drink, the pool of water recedes. (Odysseus also saw Tantalus.)
- Ixion: murdered a kinsman and was unable to be purified by god or man. Nevertheless, Zeus purified him and invited him to dinner. The reprobate tried to seduce Hera. He is bound to a fiery wheel that revolves eternally in Tartarus.

There are other accounts of the crimes committed by some of the above individuals. The teacher might suggest that students research the alternate versions.

TEACHING TIP

The description of Charon and his skiff on this page may also be used to open a discussion of burial customs that the Romans followed. Ask students to compare and contrast the two depictions of Neptune.

PAGE 102

Standards 2.1, 2.2, 3.1, 3.2
ODF 3.5, ODF 4.1

TEACHER BY THE WAY
The Vestal Virgins were maintained at public expense. The high respect in which the Vestal Virgins were held is exemplified by the fact that Augustus entrusted his will, the document outlining the disposition of his army, the account of his expenses on behalf of the Roman Republic, and the *Rēs Gestae Dīvī Augustī* (his autobiography) to the Vestal Virgins.

TEACHING TIP
Some students may not understand what the word "hearth" means. Explain that it is a brick, stone, or concrete area in front of a fireplace; the floor of a fireplace; the focal point of the home, which has evolved to mean a vital or creative center.

The teacher may also wish to discuss the derivation of the word "pontifex" from *pōns, pontis + faciō* = bridge maker. The priest acts as a bridge between the people and the gods. The Roman Catholic Pope of Rome is also known as the Pontiff, a word derived from the same Latin word.

COMPREHENSION QUESTIONS AND ANSWERS FOR PAGES 100–103 (SE)

Reproducible versions of the questions alone are available at **www.lnm.bolchazy.com**.

1. Name Rhea and Cronus's three sons. Over which part of the universe did each preside?

    Jupiter: heaven; Neptune: the ocean; Pluto: the underworld.

2. What symbol distinguishes Neptune?

    His trident, a three-pronged, fork-like instrument with which he ruled the waves.

3. Describe the Greek concept of the world with its three divisions.

    The plane of the earth is surrounded by the river of the ocean; the vault of heaven, which included cloudy Mt. Olympus; and the underworld. (Beneath the underworld lay Tartarus, a gloomy black pit reserved as a prison for the enemies of the gods.)

4. Explain the mythological origins of the English words "tantalize" and "Sisyphean."

    Tantalus's eternal punishment was to stand in a pool of water with luscious fruits hanging just above his head. As he reached to drink, the water would recede and as he reached for the fruit, the branches similarly receded from his grasp. Thus, the water and drink so close to his reach perpetually teased or "tantalized" him as he sought to slake his thirst and sate his hunger. Sisyphus was doomed to roll a boulder up a mountain and then watch it roll back to the bottom from which he must again push it toward the mountaintop. A difficult and seemingly endless task is called Sisyphean.

5. Explain why Vesta and her temple would be so important to ancient people.

   Vesta protected the hearth, the very heart of the home—the source of heat and food. Her temple contained a sacred flame, which was carefully guarded so that Rome would symbolically never suffer the loss of fire.

6. What Roman institution and practice emphasizes the importance of Vesta and her temple?

   Rome established a special group of priestesses, the Vestal Virgins, who followed a strict regimen and met high standards, to watch over the temple and its flame. Should the flame go out, the person guarding it was beaten.

7. Discuss how the story of Proserpina's abduction explains a natural phenomenon.

   Having been abducted by Pluto, god of the underworld, Proserpina ate some seeds of the pomegranate, a symbol of sexual knowledge, which bound her to Pluto. Because she had so eaten, she was expected to spend part of the year in the underworld with Pluto and the other part with her mother. Thus, when Proserpina is in the underworld it is autumn and winter. Her return to the upper world and her mother signals spring and summer.

PAGE 103
Standards 1.1, 2.1

LATIN PASSAGE TRANSLATION
Ceres walks on earth. Ceres cannot see her daughter Proserpina and she looks for Proserpina. Proserpina, however, is being held by Pluto in the darkness. The spirit of the goddess is grieving exceedingly/very much. The goddess cannot take care of the earth and the earth is wretched.

Then Jupiter orders: "Proserpina needs to stay for six months on the earth and for six months in the darkness."

Ceres takes care of the earth for six months and the earth is beautiful. While, however, (her) daughter is with Pluto, the earth is not being taken care of by the goddess.

TEACHING TIP
Since the Latin phrase *per sex mēnsēs* occurs in this reading passage, the teacher may wish to take this opportunity to introduce students to the accusative of duration of time, which is used without a preposition. The preposition *per* is only employed to emphasize the notion "throughout."

TEACHER BY THE WAY
The child Triptolemus pictured as an adult in the postage stamp is part of the story behind the Eleusinian Mysteries. The teacher may choose whether to introduce this religious concept to the students. The myth of Proserpina is considered aetiological in nature since it explains the existence of the seasons.

While Ceres was mourning the kidnapping of her daughter Proserpina, she was treated hospitably by Celeus and Metaneira and taken as a nurse for their son Demophon. Out of gratitude for the warm reception, she wanted to make Demophon immortal but when Metaneira saw her putting Demophon in the fireplace in order to burn away his mortality, she was terrified. As a result, Ceres bestowed gifts on their other son, Triptolemus. In another version, Triptolemus was given seed wheat, instructions on how to use a plow, and a chariot drawn by winged dragons with which he journeyed throughout the world teaching the arts of agriculture to mankind. The goddess also taught him her sacred rites and mysteries, which offered initiates some hope of life after death.

TEACHING TIP
The teacher might suggest to students that they look up Johnny Appleseed and compare his activities to those of Triptolemus.

TEACHER BY THE WAY
Proserpina's Greek name was Persephone or Kore, the latter meaning "the Maiden."

CONNECTING WITH THE ANCIENT WORLD

PAGE 104

Standards 2.1, 2.2, 3.1, 3.2

TEACHING TIP
The teacher may wish to have students compare ancient and modern wedding preparations and traditions.

COMPREHENSION QUESTIONS AND ANSWERS FOR PAGES 104–105 (SE)

Reproducible versions of the questions alone are available at **www.lnm.bolchazy.com**.

1. Explain the term *paterfamiliās*.

   The Roman *paterfamiliās*, father of the household, ruled over both his family and over the slaves that they owned. As *paterfamiliās*, especially in privileged households, he arranged his daughter's marriage.

2. Discussing at least six customs, compare and contrast Roman marriage with American marriage. [This question can serve as a class discussion item to be asked after the students have read the essay and made some notes in their notebooks. Others might present the question prior to reading the essay.]

Similarities:
   a. Marriage betrothals are signified by the man giving his fiancée an engagement ring.
   b. The engagement ring is worn on the finger next to the little finger on the left hand.
   c. The modern prenuptial agreement lends a financial aspect to marriage; the Roman ritual called *coēmptiō* involved the financial arrangements for funding a marriage.
   d. The most traditional form of Roman marriage took place in the presence of a priest, the Pontifex Maximus, and before ten witnesses. Similarly, American weddings often take place with a priest or religious leader officiating and two individuals serving as witnesses.
   e. Both Roman and American brides wear white gowns.
   f. The Roman bridal torch is echoed in the candles at American wedding services.
   g. The groom carries the bride over the threshold.
   h. Both the Roman and the American wedding involve much celebration. Roman and American married women are called matrons. In America, when the bride's principal wedding attendant is a married woman, she is called the matron of honor while an unmarried woman in the same role is called the maid of honor.

Differences:
   a. While Americans consider May a desirable time for marriage, the Romans thought May brought bad luck.
   b. In Roman marriage, the wife came under the legal control of her husband, while in America the husband and wife have, for the most part, evolved as coequals in marriage.

126 • Latin for the New Millennium: Teacher's Manual, Level 1

c. Bachelor and bachelorette parties in America sometimes become bawdy and raucous while the wedding reception is tamer. The Roman custom of shouting obscene verses would not be appropriate at an American wedding.
d. Carrying the bride across the threshold signifies the bride leaving her father's home but no longer connotes the transfer of power or control from father to husband as it did in ancient Rome.

PAGE 105

TEACHING TIP
Ask students to explain the case of "*Talassiō*." It is dative, "for Talassius."

TEACHER BY THE WAY
When Romulus had obtained sole power after the death of his brother, he fortified the Palatine, instituted laws for his people, and increased the population by providing a place of asylum for fugitives, such as slaves and criminals, from nearby states. He also attended to social organization by creating a hundred senators whose descendants were called patricians.

However, great as Rome was becoming, the city seemed likely to last only a generation because it did not have enough women, and intermarriage with the upstart community had been forbidden by its neighbors, which rejected its overtures. Therefore, Romulus hid his resentment and planned to solve this problem by inviting all the people of the surrounding countryside to help celebrate the *Consuālia*, a festival in honor of Neptune. Curious to see the new town, the crowds came. Then the show began, and all the able-bodied Romans raced through the multitude seizing the young women. The rest of the visitors managed to escape. Reassured by the words of Romulus, who promised them civic and property rights as well as free choice, and treated well by their new husbands, the women in time lost their resentment. Although there were raids and skirmishes with the other communities involved, the struggle with the Sabines was the most serious. However, the women themselves intervened during a battle and appealed to their husbands on one side and to their fathers and brothers on the other. Peace was made, and the two states were united under one government. (Livy 1.7–13)

EXPLORING ROMAN FAMILIES

PAGE 106
Standards 2.1, 2.2, 3.1, 3.2, 4.2

TEACHING TIP
The teacher may wish to have students look at the funerary busts on this page and then think about what symbols might represent a couple in modern times. Wax masks/portraits (*imāginēs*) of distinguished ancestors were kept in the cupboards of the *ālae* (alcoves) of Roman houses. These masks were also used in the funeral procession.

TEACHING TIP
Instruct the students to locate Syria on the map on pp. xxxiv–xxxv (SE).

TEACHER BY THE WAY
Funerary representations of the dead were carved on tombs and urns by the Greeks and by the Etruscans. These often depicted scenes from the everyday life of the deceased, like the Greek Hegeso choosing a necklace from a jewelry box or the Etruscan figure reclining on the lid of a crematory urn holding a wine cup. The Roman funerary monuments often continued this tradition. For example, the one depicted on p. 104 of the student text shows a woman holding a distaff and spindle, items she used throughout her life to spin the thread she would then weave into the cloth needed to make clothes for her family.

The distaff, called a *colus*, was made out of a cane stick about a yard in length and was held in the left hand or under the left arm. Carded wool was wrapped around it from which the woman drew out the fibers with her right hand and attached them to the spindle (*fūsus*), a stick about a foot long, which she then set to spinning with her fingers. The rotation of the spindle as it hung suspended twisted these fibers into a thread (*fīlum*), which was constantly fed from above by drawing out more fibers from the distaff. When the thread was long enough for the spindle to reach the ground, the thread was wound around it, and the process was repeated until the spindle was full. The thread was then broken from the distaff and rolled up into a ball ready for use. (See Catullus 64.312–318, where this process is described.)

PAGE 107

TEACHER BY THE WAY
Statuettes and reliefs from sarcophagi give evidence of what was popular with Roman children. Pets included:

- dogs (*canēs*), then as now, were a favorite
- doves (*columbae*)
- ducks (*anatēs*)
- geese (*anserēs*)
- goats (*caprī*)
- lambs (*agnī*)

Children's toys included:
- balls stuffed with feathers, hair, or air
- hobbyhorses
- hoops
- rag dolls (*pūpae*) and dolls of wood, wax, or bone, some with moveable limbs
- small terracotta toys such as a fan, a dog, and a horseman

Ancient representations in museums show children playing with animal chariots and go-carts, and boys walking on stilts and playing ball games. On vases there are scenes of hoops driven with sticks, swings, and seesaws. Sarcophagi panels show a child playing with a scooter and a group of children playing with nuts (*nucēs*) and pebbles (*calculī*), much like our own game of marbles.

Baby rattles (*crepundia*) were in the form of a charm necklace to entertain the infant with its jingling. A flower, a sword, a tool, and a half moon for luck might be hung on the necklace. The *crepundia* also served as an identification if the child was lost or kidnapped.

The famous teacher Quintilian talks about ivory letters, which are probably akin to our alphabet blocks. Horace mentions hitching mice to carts and riding on hobbyhorses. Ovid gives directions for a game played with nuts, and girls are pictured playing knucklebones (*tālī*), a game like jacks perhaps. Cicero refers to a game of *pār impār* in which one's partner has to guess whether the number in one's hand is odd or even. Ball games were also common. Balls of different sizes were used. In some private homes and public baths there is said to have been a handball court.

PAGE 108

TEACHER BY THE WAY
A well-to-do Roman served as *patrōnus* "patron" for those *clientēs* "clients" who sought his assistance or whose well-being was dependent on the patron's generosity. The teacher may use this opportunity to open a discussion on the difference between what the word "client" means today and what it meant in Roman times.

COMPREHENSION QUESTIONS AND ANSWERS FOR PAGES 106–109 (SE)

Reproducible versions of the questions alone are available at **www.lnm.bolchazy.com**.

1. Explain how the funerary bust on p. 106 illustrates gender roles in ancient Rome.

    The husband is depicted holding a scroll while the wife is holding a spindle and distaff, which are tools employed in cloth making.

2. Discuss the role of the state in protecting children in today's world and in the Roman world.

    While the Roman state played no role in protecting children who were totally subject to the control of their fathers, modern states like the United States have enacted laws that protect a child and require parents to care properly for their children.

3. Explain to what extent the Roman father's control of his child was absolute.

    A Roman father could choose to accept the child or to reject it and to commit the child to infanticide. A Roman citizen father's acceptance was necessary for a child to be considered a Roman citizen. Should the child of a Roman citizen father survive rejection and abandonment, s/he would not be entitled to Roman citizenship.

4. What took place on the *diēs lūstricus*? What is its modern equivalent?

    On this day, the Romans named the child and the baby was given *crepundia*, trinkets worn on a necklace. Children were also given a *bulla*, an amulet that protected the child against evil spirits. The Christian tradition of a christening and the Jewish rite of bris for male babies are similar to this Roman tradition.

5. Who did the Romans believe protected a young boy? A young girl?

    A *genius* and *Iūnō* respectively.

6. Using the specific Latin terms, explain the naming customs of the Romans.

    The firstborn son of an upper-class family received the same three names as his father—a *praenōmen*, the clan name or *nōmen*, and a *cōgnōmen*. A girl's name was the feminine form of her clan name—Julia, Claudia, etc. For example, Cicero named his son Marcus Tullius Cicero and his daughter Tullia. Additional daughters would be distinguished by the addition of *maior* and *minor* for two girls and *prīma*, *secunda*, *tertia*, etc., for more than two.

7. To what extent did a Roman child engage in activities similar to those of a modern child?

    Roman children learned to read and write at home and many modern children learn the basics of reading prior to formal schooling. Both Roman and modern children play with toys, balls, dolls, hoops, dice, gaming boards, and pets.

8. What two aspects of Roman education indicate that education was for the most part limited to the well-to-do?

    Schools were private and fee based. Young boys were accompanied by a *paedagōgus*, a slave who took his charges to and from school and oversaw their studies. Though slaves, these individuals could punish the pupil for failing to pay attention.

130 • Latin for the New Millennium: Teacher's Manual, Level 1

9. In what ways was Roman education geared toward public life?

   After mastering skills in reading, writing, and arithmetic, a young Roman boy undertook the study of history, philosophy, literature, and rhetoric. These subjects would serve him well in a political career. Mathematics and science were not school subjects, as they were used by contractors and not necessary for public life.

10. What signified a Roman boy's coming of age?

    At age fourteen or more likely sixteen, a Roman boy placed his *toga praetexta* along with his *bulla* on the altar of the household gods, the *Larēs*. He then put on the *toga virīlis*, the white toga of a Roman citizen.

11. What signified a Roman girl's coming of age?

    Just as the Roman boy left his *bulla* at the altar of the household gods, the *Larēs*, so too did the young Roman girl on the day of her wedding. She also dedicated her toys, the symbol of her childhood. Then she left her parent's home to enter her husband's household.

MĪRĀBILE AUDĪTŪ

PAGE 110
Standards 1.1, 4.1

PHRASES AND ABBREVIATIONS VOCABULARY

Annuit coeptīs.

annuō, annuere, annuī, —— – to nod upon in consent

coepta, coeptōrum, *n. pl.* – undertakings

Caveat ēmptor.

caveat – a third person sg. present active subjunctive of **caveō, cavēre, cāvī, cautum** – to beware

ēmptor, ēmptōris, *m.* – buyer

Dē factō.

factum, factī, *n.* – a done thing

In vitrō.

vitrum, vitrī, *n.* – glass

Quid prō quō?

quid – what

prō + *ablative* – for, on behalf of

quō – which

Sine quā nōn.

condiciō, condiciōnis, *f.* – condition

quā – which

sine + *ablative* – without

Status quō.

quō – which

status, statūs, *m.* – status

Tempus fugit.

tempus, temporis, *n.* – time

fugiō, fugere, fūgī, —— – to flee, run away

Urbī et Orbī.

orbis, orbis, *m.* – world

urbs, urbis, *f.* – city (of Rome)

Vice versā.

versus, versa, versum – converted

vice – ablative of a word lacking nominative and meaning "turn"

132 • Latin for the New Millennium: Teacher's Manual, Level 1

Semper parātus.

> **semper** (*adv.*) – always
>
> **parō, parāre, parāvī, parātum** – to prepare

@

> **apud** + *accusative* – at, at the home of

etc.

> **cēterus, cētera, cēterum** – other, the rest

P.S.

> **postscrībō, postscrībere, postscrīpsī, postscrīptum** – to write after

TEACHER BY THE WAY
Dē factō, "in practice," is often mentioned in contrast to *dē iūre*, "by law." For instance, a precedent can be established in English Common Law based on a practice done over a period of time even though it did not follow a specific law.

TEACHING TIP
As a regular assignment or for extra credit, students can be on the lookout for everyday written evidence of these phrases as employed in the newspaper or other printed media. (A secondary benefit of such an assignment is encouraging students to look at printed media.)

In class discussion when first introducing these phrases, ask students how these phrases make sense to them or how they would use them in a sentence. While *in vitrō* and *Urbī et Orbī* are more readily understood, the other phrases may require some explication and discussion.

The following is suggested as a "quick quiz" for the day following the introduction of these phrases.

1. Which of the phrases might be taught in a consumer economics class?   *Caveat ēmptor*
2. Which abbreviation is often found at the end of a list of items?   *etc.*
3. Which phrase means an absolute necessity?   *sine quā nōn*
4. Which phrase might be cited when establishing precedent?   *dē factō*
5. People who oppose or fear change, want to preserve what instead?   the *status quō*
6. Which phrase is related to retaliation?   *quid prō quō*
7. In discussing opposites, one might employ which phrase?   *vice versā*

Extra Credit/Bonus Question

What other familiar Latin phrase includes a form of *caveat*?   *Cavē canem*, "beware of the dog."

CHAPTER 7 (PP. 113–124)

GRAMMAR IN LANGUAGE FACTS

Third Declension Masculine and Feminine Nouns; Indirect Statement: Accusative and Infinitive

PAGE 113

Standards 1.1, 2.1

RRA 5

MEMORĀBILE DICTŪ VOCABULARY

ōdī – I hate

TEACHING TIP

The chapter image of Catullus and Lesbia can be used as a prereading activity. Ask students what the painting seems to tell us about the relationship between the poet standing on the left and Lesbia lying on the couch. After having read the chapter reading, students can again examine the depiction of Catullus and Lesbia and relate it to the Latin reading. Teachers are encouraged to have students conduct these discussions in Latin. Alternatively, students could write their responses in Latin and then share them with the class.

TEACHER BY THE WAY

The name of Lesbia, the lover of Catullus, is usually considered a pseudonym for Clodia, who was the second of three daughters born to Appius Claudius Pulcher. He served as consul in 79 BCE and won some victories in Macedonia while governor there. She thus belonged to the distinguished family of the Claudii in spite of her name, which she changed to the "popular" form as her brother did when he was adopted into a plebeian *gēns* in 59 BCE. Her mother was the daughter of another patrician, Metellus Baliaricus, and the ties between the two families were continued when Clodia married her cousin, Metellus Celer, the grandson of Baliaricus.

Metellus was a brother-in-law of Pompey, whose policies he supported in concert with his brother, Metellus Nepos. He held the praetorship in 63 BCE and, in collusion with Caesar, terminated the sham trial of Rabirius. He was given the governorship of Cisalpine Gaul in 62 and was offered a special command against Catiline by Cicero. He supported his brother against the consul when Nepos and Caesar attempted to acquire a special command for Pompey against Catiline. While Nepos continued to support Pompey, Metellus, who had served as consul in 60 BCE, turned against him because the general divorced Mucia, the sister of Celer and Nepos, on the grounds of her licentious behavior while he had been campaigning against Mithridates. Nevertheless, Nepos himself remained a Pompeian although he did oppose the Senate for a while and protected Clodius, a strong Caesarian and his former brother-in-law, when Cicero returned from exile in 57. Like the on-again, off-again relationship of Pompey and Caesar, the Metelli of this period certainly demonstrate how family alliances affected politics and how fluid these political alliances could be.

Metellus died in 59 before he could go to his province, Gallia Transalpina; some say he was poisoned by his wife Clodia, although that may be hard to believe in the face of the continuing support of her family by her erstwhile brother-in-law. Nonetheless, she lived a very profligate life. Her affair with Catullus began before the death of her husband, and even the poet attests to her inconstancy. Cicero hated her for her "moral decadence" (even though she is said to have once offered marriage to him!) but also because of his enmity for her brother Clodius. In 56 BCE, Cicero pulled out all the stops in his defense of Caelius, who had been Clodia's lover and was now accused of attempting to poison her. He called her "the Medusa of the Palatine" and even accused her of incest with her brother. Clodia was so humiliated by the speech that she retired from the political and social scene, although there is evidence she was still alive in 45 BCE.

TEACHING TIP
The teacher may wish to assign Chapter 5 of RRA for reading or review. See p. 73.

PAGE 114
Standards 1.1, 2.1, 3.1, 3.2

TRANSLATION OF LATIN PASSAGE
About Love

My girl has a sparrow. Oh, sparrow, a pet of my girl! My girl plays with the sparrow, holds the sparrow, gives (her) finger to the sparrow, the finger is bitten by the sparrow. The girl says she loves the sparrow. The girl loves the sparrow more than (her) eyes. For the sparrow is sweet as honey. Catullus sees that sparrow is always on the girl's lap. The sparrow always chirps to (his) mistress. Catullus, however, wants to be with the girl and to be loved by the girl. And so Catullus envies the sparrow. You, girl, need to love Catullus, not the sparrow. However, severe old men think that the girl ought not to love Catullus. Girl, we cannot care a bit about the words of the old men. For life is not long.

TEACHER BY THE WAY
The Greek Hellenistic writers were devoted to writing small poems that abounded in learned, often obscure allusions.

TEACHER BY THE WAY
One hundred sixteen poems written by Catullus survive.

TEACHING TIP

Instruct the students to find Catullus, Tibullus, Propertius, and Ovid on the timeline on pp. 405–408 (SE).

PAGE 115

ANSWERS TO COMPREHENSION QUESTIONS

1. The poet feels envy. In fact, the girl displays too much affection for the sparrow.
2. The grumpy old men.
3. Life is short.

TEACHING TIP

Ask the students to determine which nouns in the Reading Vocabulary do not follow the format of the first and second declension nouns that they have already learned.

TEACHER BY THE WAY

In addition to the sparrow, doves and pigeons appear in statues as children's pets. Romans loved their gardens so the realistic depiction of various bird species in their frescoes is not surprising. Birds also figured prominently in Roman religion and myth. Augurs observed the flights of birds to determine whether a proposed action was auspicious or not. Romulus and Remus based their respective claims to kingship on the number of birds each one saw. Remus, stationed on the Aventine Hill, saw the first sign, a flight of six vultures (*vulturēs*). Romulus, on the Palatine Hill, saw twelve vultures. A fight ensued in which Remus was killed and Romulus became the eponymous (name-giving) founder of Rome. The vulture and woodpecker (*pīcus*) were sacred to Mars, the twins' father.

The eagle (*aquila*) was a prominent symbol on the Roman legionary standard. To lose it to the enemy was disgraceful and sometimes resulted in the disbandment of the legion. Varus in 9 CE lost three legions to the Germans, which prompted him to commit suicide.

TEACHING TIP

Remind students that the aviary is the location for the birds (*avēs*) at the zoo.

Birds may have been a delightful and decorative element in everyday life, but beekeeping was big business. Civil laws even made provisions for this occupation. Bees in hives were a beekeeper's property and to steal them was theft and punishable. Pliny the Elder and Columella, a Spaniard interested in reviving Roman agriculture, discuss in depth how to build and maintain hives, how to harvest honeycomb, and how to alleviate a bee's stress. Romans were obviously very involved in the care of their bees. Vergil glorifies this interest in the *Georgics* (Book 4) in his story of Aristaeus, whose bees were destroyed. It was considered a sign of good hospitality to offer guests fresh honey. Soldiers carried honey in their packs to treat burns and wounds. Physicians recommended honey for those having problems sleeping. It was used to make *mulsum* (honey wine), for food preparation, and for wax. Romans learned many tricks of the trade from Greece, Spain, and Carthage.

Chapter 7 • 137

TEACHING TIP
The term "apiary," a place where bees are kept for their honey, derives from the Latin word for bee, *apis*.

PAGE 116
Standards 1.1, 1.2, 3.1, 4.1
Oral Exercise 1

▶ EXERCISE 1 ANSWERS

amōre	ablative singular
passerem	accusative singular
passer	vocative singular; nominative singular
passere	ablative singular
passerī	dative singular
senēs	nominative plural
senum	genitive plural
assis	genitive singular

ORAL EXERCISE 1
This exercise may be done anytime after the third declension has been presented.

While looking at the declension of *passer*, ask the students to decline *amor*.

amor, amōris, amōrī, amōrem, amōre, amor

amōrēs, amōrum, amōribus, amōrēs, amōribus, amōrēs

TEACHING TIP
Additional reproducible worksheets, morphology charts, and their associated answer keys, related to this material, are available for download at www.lnm.bolchazy.com.
- **Noun Declensions**

PAGE 117
Standard 4.1
Workbook Exercise 2

▶ EXERCISE 2 ANSWERS

1. delicious   dēliciae
2. sorority   soror
3. senior   senex
4. amorous   amor
5. digital   digitus
6. estimate   aestimō
7. dominion   domina
8. verbal   verbum
9. severe   sevērus
10. computer   putō

TEACHING TIP
Although in Exercise 2 the students are directed to find only the derivatives based on the Vocabulary to Learn, they may be interested to learn that there are other derivatives in Exercise 2. The derivation of these words is provided for the teacher's convenience.

2. college – from *collēgium* (college, guild, association in office). member – from *membrum* (limb, member, part, division).
3. purchase – from *prō* (for); the root is not Latin. discount – from *computō* (to reckon, number) + *dis* (apart, away). price – from *pretium* (price, value, worth).
4. story – from *historia* (history, inquiry, story). relationship – from *relātiō* (retorting [in law], magistrate's report [pl.], repetition).
6. repair – from *parō* (to prepare, get ready); *reparō* (to retrieve, recover, restore, repair).
7. power – from *possum* (to be able).
9. me – from *ego* (I, me [*mē*, acc.]).
10. computer – from *putō* (to think); *computō* (to reckon, number); *cum* (with, together).

PAGE 118

Standards 1.1, 1.2, 3.1, 4.1
Workbook Exercises 1, 3

▶ EXERCISE 3 ANSWERS

	Singular	Plural
Nominative	soror	sorōrēs
Genitive	sorōris	sorōrum
Dative	sorōrī	sorōribus
Accusative	sorōrem	sorōrēs
Ablative	sorōre	sorōribus
Vocative	soror	sorōrēs

▶ EXERCISE 4 ANSWERS

1. Sorōrēs pulchrās habeō.
2. Multae sunt lacrimae amōris.
3. Pācem nōn timēmus.
4. Puella ā sorōre cūrātur.
5. Poēta passerī invidet.
6. Senēs poētae invident.
7. Poēta fābulam senibus nārrat.

▶ EXERCISE 5 ANSWERS

1. praemium magnum — great reward
2. sorōribus pulchrīs — to/for, by/with beautiful sisters
3. amōrī miserō — to/for wretched love
4. senis armātī — of the armed old man
5. lacrimās multās — many tears
6. senum sevērōrum — of the strict old men
7. passerēs miserī, passerēs miserōs — wretched sparrows
8. senex iūstus — a just old man

TEACHER BY THE WAY

Senis armātī (#4 in Exercise 5) recalls King Priam of Troy as an armed old man with a "powerless sword" (*Aeneid* 2.509–510).

PAGE 119

TEACHER BY THE WAY
This construction is called by various names including "accusative and infinitive," "indirect statement," "indirect discourse," and "*ōrātiō oblīqua*."

TEACHER BY THE WAY
Venus was a very ancient Italian goddess who presided over the fertility of gardens and their lovely appearance. Wall paintings give an idea of how very fond of gardens the Romans were. Flower, vegetable, and herb gardens were common. It was only much later that Venus was identified with Aphrodite.

Several temples in her honor commemorate her various aspects. When war was about to erupt over the rape of the Sabine women, the men were held back from fighting by the women themselves. Myrtle branches (sacred to Venus) were used to purify the opposing armies. On the spot where they reconciled, a temple was erected to the goddess as Venus the Purifier. Pompey was widely criticized for building such a lavish stone theatre; so he built a small temple to Venus within the confines. When it was ready for consecration, the opportunity presented itself to put on plays and games. Julius Caesar constructed a temple to the goddess as Venus Genetrix (mother) in 46 BCE. The Julian *gēns* claimed descent from Aeneas's son Iulus (Ascanius), grandson of Venus herself. Roman matrons worshipped Venus Verticordia, who turned women's hearts to chastity. The largest and most spectacular temple in Rome was the Temple of Venus and Rome designed by the emperor Hadrian in 121 CE. It was the only example of a structure having ten columns across its principal facade. The two main chambers housed the cult statues, one of Venus, the goddess of love, and the other of Roma, the ancestress of Rome. Roma faced west and viewed the Roman Forum while Venus looked over the Colosseum facing east. Hadrian deliberately placed the statues back to back to create symmetry, which was extended with the choice of names because AMOR is ROMA spelled backward.

Once assimilated to Aphrodite, symbols of the goddess became pronounced in her myths. She was awarded the golden apple by Paris. Hippomenes/Milanion was given three golden apples by Aphrodite to help him win the foot race against Atalanta. Doves led Aeneas to the golden bough. Swans bore her chariot. Today the rose still symbolizes love. Aphrodite's companions were Eros and the three Graces. The *Grātiae* were *Āglāia* (Radiance), *Euphrosyne* (Joy), and *Thalīa* (Festivity).

PAGE 120
Standards 1.1, 1.2
Oral Exercise 2

Answer to "Find one more indirect statement in the Latin reading passage."

Senēs autem sevērī putant puellam Catullum amāre nōn dēbēre.

"However, severe old men think that the girl ought not to love Catullus."

▶ EXERCISE 6 ANSWERS

1. Catullus sees that the sparrow is being loved by the girl.
2. The poet tells that the sparrow bites the finger of the girl.
3. Catullus tells that he envies the sparrow.
4. The girl thinks that she loves the sparrow more than Catullus.
5. Catullus thinks that he loves the girl more than his eyes.
6. Catullus thinks that life is not long.

ORAL EXERCISE 2

This exercise may be used anytime after Exercise 6.

Use one of the CPOs to put on view this series of sentences.

Sum āthlēta.	*Poēta sum.*
Praeclārī sunt āthlētae.	*Propter amōrem doleō.*
Amor est semper bonus.	*Domī saepe maneō.*
In agrīs saepe ambulō.	

Then the teacher asks individual students to read them. After each sentence is recited, the teacher asks another student: *Quid nārrat* (the name of the person who just read the sentence, e.g., *Mārcus*)? or *Quid putat* (the name of the person who just read the sentence, e.g., *Mārcus*)? The student in question answers *Mārcus nārrat . . .* or *Mārcus putat . . .* , followed by the indirect statement.

Student 1: Sum āthlēta.　　　　　　　　　**Teacher:** Quid nārrat Mārcus?
Student 2: Mārcus nārrat sē esse āthlētam.

Student 1: Poēta sum.　　　　　　　　　　**Teacher:** Quid nārrat Mārcus?
Student 2: Mārcus nārrat sē esse poētam.

Student 1: Praeclārī sunt āthlētae.　　　　　**Teacher:** Quid nārrat Mārcus?
Student 2: Mārcus nārrat āthlētās esse praeclārōs.

Student 1: Propter amōrem doleō.　　　　　**Teacher:** Quid nārrat Mārcus?
Student 2: Mārcus nārrat sē propter amōrem dolēre.

Student 1: Amor est semper bonus.　　　　　**Teacher:** Quid putat Mārcus?
Student 2: Mārcus putat amōrem esse semper bonum.

Student 1: Domī saepe maneō.　　　　　　　**Teacher:** Quid nārrat Mārcus?
Student 2: Mārcus nārrat sē saepe domī manēre.

142 • Latin for the New Millennium: Teacher's Manual, Level 1

Student 1: In agrīs saepe ambulō.
Student 2: Mārcus nārrat sē saepe in agrīs ambulāre.

Teacher: Quid nārrat Mārcus?

Student 1: Senēs malam vītam habent.
Student 2: Mārcus putat senēs malam vītam habēre.

Teacher: Quid putat Mārcus?

Student 1: Vīta senum nōn est semper misera.
Student 2: Mārcus putat vītam senum nōn esse semper miseram.

Teacher: Quid putat Mārcus?

PAGE 121
Standards 1.1, 1.2
Oral Exercise 3; Workbook Exercises 4, 5, 6, 7, Content Questions

ORAL EXERCISE 3

This exercise may be used anytime after Exercise 6.

The teacher should mimic different actions and ask individual students the question *"Quid vidēs?"* To this question the student should answer either *"Videō tē . . ."* or *"Videō magistrum/magistram."* Therefore, the students need to know that as subject of the indirect statement *tē* is accusative singular of "you," *magistrum* accusative singular of "male teacher," and *magistram* accusative singular of "female teacher."

Teacher: (*Mimicking pain.*) Quid vidēs?
Student: Videō tē dolēre.

Teacher: (*Mimicking deep thought.*) Quid vidēs?
Student: Videō tē cōgitāre.

Teacher: (*Holding a book.*) Quid vidēs?
Student: Videō tē librum habēre.

Teacher: (*Lying down, being inert.*) Quid vidēs?
Student: Videō tē iacēre.

▶ EXERCISE 7 ANSWERS
1. Vir cōgitat oculōs puellae esse pulchrōs.
2. Poēta nārrat puellam ā familiā amārī.
3. Catullus videt puellam dēliciās amāre.
4. Puella putat passerem esse pulchrum.
5. Poēta cōgitat sē dolēre.
6. Senēs nārrant vītam nōn semper esse pulchram.
7. Poēta et puella putant malās fābulās ā senibus nārrārī.

▶ EXERCISE 8 ANSWERS
1. The boy thinks that the girl is serious.
2. Puella putat amōrem esse gaudium.
3. The old man tells that life is wretched.
4. Poēta nārrat bellum esse longum.
5. The mistress sees that the poet is waiting.
6. Agricola videt lupam puerōs cūrāre.
7. The athlete thinks that he loves rewards.
8. Nauta cōgitat patriam vocāre.

Chapter 7 • 143

PAGE 122
Standards 2.1, 4.1

TEACHING TIP
Pictures of the foods listed on these pages or children's plastic play foods may be used as visual reinforcement for the Latin words for foods. The teacher may also teach the Latin words for other foods not listed here. This would also be an opportunity for the teacher to open a discussion on how Roman meals differ from our own and which are healthier.

TEACHING TIP
The picture of the *thermopōlium* presents an opportunity for the teacher to discuss how fast-food counters in ancient times are different from modern fast-food restaurants. The word means "a hot-drink shop."

TEACHING TIP
Teachers may wish to have students create a new conversation, modeled on the one on p. 123 (SE) but substituting different names of foods for the ones used in the original dialogue. Or, students may simply become curious to know the names of more food items in Latin. More food names are provided here for the teacher's convenience:

- **būbula <carō>, būbulae,** *f.* – beef
- **cereālia, cereālium,** *n. pl.* – cereal
- **cuppēdiae, cuppēdiārum,** *f. pl.* – candy
- **embamma (embammatis,** *n.*) **ex lycopersicīs factum** – ketchup
- **gallīnācea <carō>, gallīnāceae,** *f.* – chicken
- **hilla calēns, hillae calentis,** *f.* – hot dog
- **laganum, laganī,** *n.* – pancake
- **laganum ex ōvīs, laganī ex ōvīs,** *n.* – omelet
- **līmonāta, līmonātae,** *f.*/**sūcus (sūcī,** *m.*) **ex citrīs expressus** – lemonade
- **pāniculus, pāniculī,** *m.* – roll
- **perna, pernae,** *f.* – ham
- **piper, piperis,** *n.* – pepper
- **pretiola, pretiolae,** *f.* – pretzel
- **saccharum, sacchari,** *n.* – sugar
- **sāl, sālis,** *n.* – salt
- **salgama, salgamōrum,** *n. pl.* – pickle
- **sāvillum, sāvillī,** *n.* – cheese cake
- **scriblīta, scriblītae,** *f.* – muffin
- **sināpi, sināpis,** *n.* – mustard
- **socolāta, socolātae,** *f.*/**theobrōma, theobrōmatis,** *n.* (meaning "food of the gods") – chocolate
- **squilla, squillae,** *f.* – shrimp

PAGE 123

Standard 1.2
Oral Exercises 4, 5, Dictation

TRANSLATION OF THE LATIN CONVERSATION

Mark: Hello, Mary!

Mary: Hello, Mark!

Mark: What will you eat? Do you want a banana?

Mary: I want to eat not only a banana, but also a hamburger. For I am very hungry. What will you eat?

Mark: I want to eat a sandwich.

Christy and Helen: Hello, Mark and Mary!

Christy (*to the waiter*)**:** Give me pizza, please. Thank you.

Mark: How does the pizza taste?

Christy: Good. How does the sandwich taste?

Mark: Excellent. The food is very delicious. I ate well.

Helen: You say, Mark, that the food is very delicious. But I want to eat Mexican food. I do not care a bit for pizza and hamburger.

Mary: There is no Mexican food here.

Helen: Then I want to eat only cookies. For I love cookies a lot.

Mark (*to himself*)**:** I love you, Helen. I want you to be my girl . . .

TEACHING TIP
This dialogue lends itself well to being acted out by four students for the rest of the class.

ORAL EXERCISE 4

This exercise may be used after the Latin dialogue has been presented.

When the students have read the dialogue, ask them the following questions (they may answer while looking at the text).

TEACHING TIP
Remind the students that *quis* means "who," *vult* "want," and that *–ne* asks a question.

Teacher: Quis est in thermopōliō?   **Student:** Mārcus, Marīa, Christīna, Helena.

Teacher: Quid Mārcus comedere vult?   **Student:** Mārcus pānem īnfersum comedere vult.

Teacher: Quōmodo pānis īnfersus sapit?   **Student:** Pānis īnfersus bene sapit.

Teacher: Quid Marīa comedere vult?   **Student:** Marīa banānam et īsicium Hamburgēnse comedere vult.

Teacher: Quid Christīna comedere vult?   **Student:** Christīna placentam Neāpolitānam comedere vult.

Teacher: Quid Helena comedere vult?   **Student:** Helena cibum Mexicānum comedere vult.

Teacher: Estne in thermopōliō cibus Mexicānus?   **Student:** In thermopōliō nōn est cibus Mexicānus.

Teacher: Amatne Helena crūstula?   **Student:** Helena crūstula amat.

Teacher: Quid Mārcus nārrat sē amāre?   **Student:** Mārcus nārrat sē Helenam amāre.

DICTATION AND ORAL EXERCISE 5
This combined exercise may be used to conclude the chapter.

Puellam amō

Puellam valdē amō. Dē puellā semper cōgitō. Amor animum tenet. Ambulāre nōn possum. Oculī tenebrās vident. Verba nōn manent. Cōnsilia habēre nōn possum.

The teacher should ask individual students to read one sentence at a time and then ask a question that would require an answer in an indirect statement.

TEACHING TIP
Remind the students that *quid* means "what."

Student 1: Puellam amō.
Student 2: Poēta nārrat sē puellam amāre.   **Teacher:** Quid nārrat poēta?

Student 1: Puellam valdē amō.
Student 2: Poēta nārrat sē puellam valdē amāre.   **Teacher:** Quid nārrat poēta?

Student 1: Dē puellā semper cōgitō.
Student 2: Poēta nārrat sē dē puellā semper cōgitāre.   **Teacher:** Quid nārrat poēta?

Student 1: Amor animum tenet.
Student 2: Poēta putat amōrem animum tenēre.   **Teacher:** Quid putat poēta?

Student 1: Ambulāre nōn possum.
Student 2: Poēta putat sē ambulāre nōn posse.   **Teacher:** Quid putat poēta?

Student 1: Oculī tenebrās vident.
Student 2: Poēta putat oculōs tenebrās vidēre.   **Teacher:** Quid putat poēta?

Student 1: Verba nōn manent.
Student 2: Poēta putat verba nōn manēre.   **Teacher:** Quid putat poēta?

Student 1: Cōnsilia habēre nōn possum.
Student 2: Poēta nārrat sē cōnsilia habēre nōn posse.   **Teacher:** Quid nārrat poēta?

PAGE 124
Standard 4.1

DERIVATIVES

amor – See *amat* 1.1.

dēliciae – Note the "-ous" suffix of "delicious."

The word "delight" appeared in English around 1200 but was spelled *delit* (through the Old French *delitier* from the Latin *dēlectāre*) until the sixteenth century when it changed to its modern form under the influence of "flight, light, bright," etc.

The word "dilettante" came into English in 1733, borrowed from the Italian *dilettante* (a lover of music or painting), which itself was derived from the Latin *dēlectāre*. Originally there was no negative connotation; it meant "devoted amateur." The pejorative sense emerged by the later eighteenth century in contrast to "professional."

digitus – Toes and fingers are called <u>digits</u>. The noun "digit" appeared in English during the late fourteenth century meaning "a number below 10" because those numerals were counted on fingers. The sense of "finger or toe" arose by the 1640s.

The adjective "digital" appeared during the 1650s pertaining to fingers. The meaning "using numerical digits" dates to 1938, especially referring to computers after 1945. It also was used in reference to recording or broadcasting from 1960.

The Digital Age is the period characterized by a shift from traditional industry to an economy based on information computerization, which created a knowledge-based society beginning with the advent of the computer in the 1970s.

domina – The word "dame" entered English during the early thirteenth century through the Old French *dame* from the Late Latin *domna* (Latin *domina*). It was the title of a knight's wife. The slang sense of "woman" is first attested in 1902 in American English.

A "damsel" is a young woman, originally one of noble birth. The word is derived through the Old French *dameisele* from a diminutive of *domina*.

The name "Donna" is derived through the Italian *donna* meaning "lady."

The name "Madonna" also is derived through the Old Italian *ma donna* (modern Italian = *mia donna*) meaning "my lady." The association of the name with the Virgin Mary dates to the 1640s.

The word "madam," from the same source, appears in English around 1300; the form "madame" in the 1590s. It was originally a title of respect for a woman of rank but is now given to any married woman. The *Oxford English Dictionary* recommends "madam" as an English title, "madame" in reference to foreign women.

The word "mademoiselle" is a French diminutive originally meaning "my noble young lady" but now is a general title of respect for a girl or unmarried woman.

According to the *Oxford English Dictionary*, the word "granny" appeared during the 1660s and was most likely a diminutive and contraction of "grannam," itself a shortened form of *granddame* rather than from "grandmother."

gremium – None

oculus – The "antler" of a stag is located "before the eyes" (*ante* = before, and *oculus*). The word came into English during the late fourteenth century through the Anglo-French *auntiler*.

Chapter 7 • 147

A pair of <u>binoculars</u> is used by both eyes (*bi* = twice, from *bis*).

The Latin word *oculus* also means "bud" as well as "eye"; therefore the word "inoculate," which appeared in English during the mid-fifteenth century, meant "to implant a bud into a plant" (i.e., to graft). The medical use meaning "to plant a germ to produce immunity" is first recorded in 1714, originally in reference to smallpox.

An "eyelet" is a small, finished hole in fabric through which a small cord or metal ring is drawn. The word came into English during the late fourteenth century through the Middle French *oeillet*, a diminutive of *oeil* (eye) from the Latin *oculus*.

The word "inveigle" came into English during the late fifteenth century meaning "to blind (someone's) judgment" (through the Middle French *aveugler* [to delude, make blind] from the Latin *ab* [away from] and *oculus* [away from sight, blind]). The meaning "to win over by deceit" dates to the 1530s.

A "monocle" is a glass piece for one (Greek μόνος) eye. The word appeared in English in 1886, derived through the French adjective *monocle* (one-eyed) from the Latin *monoculus* (one-eyed).

passer – None

senex – The French words *messieurs*, *monsieur*, and *seigneur* derive through the Old French *monseigneur* from the Latin *meus* (my) and *senior* (comparative of *senex*) and were titles of honor meaning "my lord." Note the similarity to, and between, the Spanish *señor*, *señora* (fem.), *señorita* (girl or unmarried woman) and the Italian *signor*, *signora*, *signorina*.

The Latin *senātus*, literally "a council of elders," was the legal and administrative body of ancient Rome. By the late fourteenth century, it referred to governing bodies of free states in Europe and to national governing bodies by the 1550s. The upper house of Congress was so called in 1775.

"Senility" refers to the decrease of mental faculties and is a characteristic of old age, although certainly not all elders suffer from it to such an extent that they become infirm.

The word "sir" is a variant of "sire" which is derived from *senior* through the medieval Latin *seior* (hypothetical). It was a respectful term of address indicating a person of high rank, e.g., a knight. Using the term "sire" by itself meaning "Your Majesty" is attested in the early thirteenth century. The word "sir" was generalized as a respectful form of address by the mid-fourteenth century and was used as a salutation in letters by the early fifteenth century.

soror – The word "cousin" came into English during the mid-twelfth century through the Old French *cosin* from the Latin *consōbrīnus* (*cum* = together, and *sōbrīnus* from *soror*). A *consōbrīnus* (or *consōbrīna*) was a boy (or girl) born on the mother's side, originally "a mother's sister's son (or daughter)." Unlike modern English, Latin carefully delineated family relationships.

verbum – The word "adverb" literally means "that which is added to (*ad* = to, toward) a verb."

The suffix "-ose" of "verbose" means the same as "-ous" and comes directly from the Latin, e.g., *glōriōsus*, *bellicōsus*, *verbōsus*, etc.

The word "verbiage" appears in English from the French *verbiage* in 1721. Its meaning, "wordiness," comes from the Middle French *verbier* (to chatter).

"Proverb" is derived from the Latin *prōverbium*, meaning "saying, old adage, maxim," literally "words put forward." In Latin the prefix *prō-* gives a sense of prominence, of priority in time, as well as forward movement.

sē – None

148 • Latin for the New Millennium: Teacher's Manual, Level 1

meus – The word "me" is more accurately the accusative form of the related pronoun *ego* "I" but is found with varied spellings throughout Indo-European languages, e.g., Greek, Old Irish, Old English, Old Saxon, Old High German, etc.

sevērus – In the Latin *perseverō* the prefix has an intensive force, hence the verb means "to persist, endure" (literally, "to be very strict, earnest"). The word "persevere" appeared in English during the mid-fourteenth century.

The word "asseveration" comes directly from the Latin *adseverō* (*ad* = to, toward, and *sevērus*) meaning "to assert strongly" (with assimilation). It came into English during the 1550s; the verb "asseverate" is first found in 1791. The president made a solemn <u>asseveration</u> that he would work on the issue relentlessly.

aestimō – The word "aim" came into English during the early fourteenth century meaning "to estimate, calculate" through the Old French *aesmer* (to value, rate, estimate) from *aestimō*. From "to calculate with a view toward an action" (c. 1400) came the meaning "to direct a blow, a missile, etc." (1570s).

The verb "esteem" was derived through the Middle French *estime(r)* from the Latin *aestimō* and came into English during the mid-fifteenth century; the noun a century earlier. The idea of "high regard" dates to the 1610s.

The prefix of "inestimable" is negative.

invideō – The Latin prefix is a negative, hence the verb means "to look at in a negative way (with ill will)." The English adaptation appeared around 1600. Note the "-ous" suffix of "invidious" (the equivalent of the Latin *invīdiōsus*).

The noun "envy" came into English during the late thirteenth century through the Old French *envie* from the Latin noun *invīdia*; the verb appeared in the late fourteenth century.

Note the "-ous" ending of "envious."

putō – The prefix "com" of "compute" intensifies the action of *putō*, e.g., Matt was thinking hard as he <u>computed</u> the answer to the difficult math problem. The word came into English during the 1630s.

The noun "computer" appeared in English during the 1640s and originally meant "one who calculates." The meaning of "a calculating machine" dates to 1897, of "a programmable digital electronic computer" to 1945.

The verb "count" appeared in English during the mid-fourteenth century through the Old French *conter* (to add up, to tell a story) from *computāre*.

The prefix of "account" comes from the Latin *ad* by assimilation and here is emphatic, meaning "with regard to." It arrived in English earlier (c. 1300) than the verb "count" through the Old French *aconter* (to count, render account).

Although most English derivatives from *putō* reflect its meaning "to think, ponder, assess," the first one of the nine given in the *Oxford Latin Dictionary* is "to make clean, prune or cut back, scour, purify or refine." It is on this meaning that the word "amputate" is derived (from *amputō* = to cut off; *am* = *ambi* [round, about]; hence, the English meaning "to cut all around," i.e., "to cut off completely").

The Latin *dēputō* means, first, "to cut off (*dē* = down from) completely"; then, "to consider as, to allot, to assign away." Thus the word "deputy," which came into English around 1400, refers to one who has been assigned by a superior with full powers to a duty but without holding the office. A sheriff gave his <u>deputy</u> the job of bringing in the fugitive. The related noun "deputation" and verb "depute" came into English a little earlier, during the late fourteenth century, both derived from the same source.

Chapter 7 • 149

The prefix "dis-" of "discount," "disputable," and "disreputable" has a negative connotation from its meaning "apart" (from *dē* = down from). A <u>disputable</u> point needs to be examined, weighed, and discussed (see *putō*).

The word "reputation" is derived from the Latin *reputō* and reflects the meaning of the Latin verb (*re* = back, again, and *putō*; hence, "to think back, think over, consider"). Nelson Mandela's <u>reputation</u> rests on the high international estimation of his work in combatting apartheid.

The prefix "in-" of "indisputable" is a negative.

On the other hand, the same prefix on the verb "impute" means "into." Literally the Latin word *imputō* means "to think into," and thus "to ascribe, charge" as in "ascribing a debt to" or "laying a charge on": Be careful not to <u>impute</u> unsubstantiated motives to the woman's comments.

CHAPTER 8 (PP. 125–137)

GRAMMAR IN LANGUAGE FACTS

Third Conjugation Verbs: Present Tense Active and Passive, Present Active and Passive Infinitive; Ablatives of Manner, Instrument, Separation, Place from Which, Place Where; Accusative of Place to Which

PAGE 125

Standards 1.1, 3.1, 3.2
RRA 5

MEMORĀBILE DICTŪ VOCABULARY

melius (*adv.*) – better

pugnābimus – we will fight (future tense)

umbra, umbrae, *f.* – shade

TEACHER BY THE WAY

The story of Leonidas and his 300 is also recounted in the Greek historian Herodotus's *Histories*. Students may know the story from the 2006 movie *300* or from Frank Miller's graphic novel, *300*, on which the movie is based.

TEACHER BY THE WAY

The wars with Persia actually began in 499 BCE when the Ionian Greeks, living on the western coast of Asia Minor under the rule of Persia, rose up in revolt. Athens responded to their pleas for help, and its soldiers reached and burned Sardis, the headquarters of the Persian governor. The Persians in turn crushed the Greek fleet at Lade in 494 BCE, but Darius, who had succeeded to the throne in 521, never forgave the interference of the mainland Greeks and in 490 sailed to Marathon. The Athenians won that encounter, and Darius died before he could try again. However, he passed on the humiliation to his son Xerxes, who became king in 485. The new king planned carefully for three years and won over several Greek states as well as the Delphic Oracle through diplomacy. By a bridge of boats Xerxes's army crossed the Hellespont and marched upon northern Greece through Thrace.

In the meantime, Themistocles, who had come to power in Athens, convinced the city to use the output from the silver mines at Laurium to build a fleet and persuaded the Greeks to unify. Sparta took command of the land forces under Leonidas and the naval forces under Eurybiades. Leonidas held the Persians for two days at Thermopylae while the fleet challenged Xerxes at Artemisium. After both these positions were lost, the Greeks retreated to

• 151 •

Salamis, where Themistocles and Eurybiades forced a naval battle in the Straits there before the very eyes of Xerxes, who had been so confident of victory that he set up a golden throne on the promontory to watch the battle. Needless to say, he promptly retreated to Asia but left an army under Mardonius. Under the Spartan commander Pausanias, the allied forces defeated the Persians in 479 BCE at Plataea, while the Greek fleet destroyed that of the Persians at Mycale.

It is interesting to note the subsequent careers of the main leaders. Xerxes retired home, built extensively at Persepolis, and was murdered during a court intrigue; Themistocles lost influence to more conservative leaders, was ostracized in 471 BCE, and eventually became a Persian governor under Artaxerxes I; and Pausanias, after a somewhat checkered career, was accused of fomenting a helot revolt. He took sanctuary in a temple in Sparta where he was left to starve.

TEACHER BY THE WAY
Herodotus tells us that Pheidippides had run from Athens to Sparta and back seeking the Spartans' aid against the Persians. Tradition tell us that he then marched with the Athenians in full armor to Marathon and following the battle ran to Athens to announce the Athenian victory. After reporting "Rejoice! We conquer!" Pheidippides dropped dead.

Today's marathon is named for and based roughly on the distance (26 miles, 385 yards/ 42.195 km) from Marathon to Athens.

PAGE 126
Standards 1.1, 2.1, 3.1, 3.2

TEACHING TIP
The teacher may wish to assign Chapter 5 of RRA for reading or review. See p. 73.

TRANSLATION OF LATIN PASSAGE
Themistocles Saves the Greeks

Themistocles is the general of the Athenians and <is> a very clever person. Xerxes, king of the Persians, is said to prepare war against the Greeks with great care. Xerxes has many soldiers and many ships and he is sailing toward Greece with many armed men. The Athenians fear war and decide to seek the oracles of the Pythian priestess. The Pythian priestess lives at Delphi, and she gives the counsels of Apollo to people. The Pythian priestess says these words to the Athenians in the Delphic temple: "The Athenians can be saved by means of wooden walls." Only Themistocles thinks he understands the advice of Apollo. He says that the wooden walls are ships. The Athenians think the words of Themistocles are good. They flee from their land, but they build many ships. Then, with great courage, they attack the ships of the Persians and they defeat the Persians. The Athenians are freed from fear.

TEACHER BY THE WAY
Nepos, for example, notes that the Romans of his day considered it shameful for a nobleman to perform on stage, behavior the Greeks found totally acceptable.

TEACHER BY THE WAY
Inasmuch as Greek city-states were constantly at odds with one another, this collaborative undertaking by a large and diverse group of Greek communities was highly unusual.

TEACHING TIP
Instruct the students to locate Persia, Athens, Delphi, and Thermopylae on the map on pp. xxxiv–xxxv (SE) and to find Nepos on the timeline on pp. 405–408 (SE).

PAGE 127

ANSWERS TO COMPREHENSION QUESTIONS
1. Xerxes's intentions are to conquer Greece.
2. The Athenians consult Pythia, a priestess who predicts the future.
3. Pythia advises the Athenians to be protected by wooden walls, by which she means ships.
4. Yes, the Athenians built a fleet, and won.

TEACHER BY THE WAY
Although a full Athenian citizen of the Lycomid clan, Themistocles seems to have had a non-Greek mother, hence the hostility shown to him by the noble class. He was an ambitious politician (eponymous archon in 493 BCE, general of his tribe in 490) and, in spite of repeated attempts to ostracize him (no less than 542 of the 1,500 known *ostraka* bear his name), managed to exile his opponents instead (Hipparchus, Megacles, Xanthippus, and Aristides).

However, Themistocles was able to subordinate this ambition to the good of the state as can be seen when he freely relinquished the naval command to the Spartan Eurybiades for the battle at Artemisium in 480 BCE. When the Greeks were unwilling to place their faith in another sea battle against an enemy that was plundering their cities and destroying their lands, Themistocles forced their hand by secretly sending word to Xerxes of their intentions. The Persian king responded by bottling up the Greek fleet in the bay of Salamis. This gave the advantage to the Greeks because their smaller, swifter ships outmaneuvered the larger, slower Persian vessels and won a decisive battle. Themistocles was the hero of the hour.

Nevertheless, his political enemies took the chief Athenian commands in the following year and recalled their leaders from exile. Themistocles did remain important for a time, using diplomatic delaying tactics at Sparta while Athens rebuilt its walls, an act Sparta opposed, and also Piraeus was fortified on his motion. However, his influence continued to wane, and in 471 he himself was ostracized. He lived for a while in several Peloponnesian cities that were leaning toward democracy. This disturbed the Spartans, who accused him of conspiring with Persia. He was condemned by the Athenians *in absentiā* but escaped to Persia where the son of Xerxes, King Artaxerxes I, who had formerly put a price on his head, made him one of his favorites and appointed him governor of three cities. According to Thucydides, Themistocles died in Magnesia of sickness, although some say he committed suicide. His bones were carried to Attica where the Athenians demonstrated their belated gratitude by honoring him with a magnificent tomb.

PAGE 128

Standards 3.1, 4.1
Workbook Exercises 1, 3

TEACHING TIP
Unlike other third conjugation verbs, *dīcō* and *dūcō* do not have a final *-e* in the singular imperative. Some teachers will feel comfortable using the rhyme that follows to teach this, although third *-iō* verbs and the irregular verb *ferō* have not yet been learned. Others may choose to delay using this rhyme until Chapter 10 where third *-iō* verbs appear or until Level 2 where irregular verbs are presented.

> Dīc, dūc, fac, and fer
> Don't look for the *-e*
> 'cause it isn't there.

TEACHING TIP
Additional reproducible worksheets, morphology charts, and their associated answer keys, related to this material, are available for download at www.lnm.bolchazy.com.
- **Verb Conjugations**

PAGE 129

Standards 1.1, 1.2
Oral Exercise 1

▶ EXERCISE 1 ANSWERS
1. putātur
2. parāmur
3. iubēminī
4. solēre
5. iūdicās
6. docēmus
7. intellegunt
8. petuntur
9. vincitis
10. aestimārī

ORAL EXERCISE 1

This exercise may be used anytime after Exercise 1.

Use one of the CPOs to put the following passive sentences on view with an additional nominative singular or plural noun. The teacher should call on students individually to repeat each sentence orally, but include the singular or plural noun in the sentence and change it to an ablative of agent with *ā/ab*.

1. Cōnsilium datur. (rēx)   Cōnsilium **ā rēge** datur.
2. Persae vincuntur. (rēgēs)   Persae **ā rēgibus** vincuntur.
3. Ōrāculum dīcitur. (homō)   Ōrāculum **ab homine** dīcitur.
4. Ōrācula nōn intelleguntur. (hominēs)   Ōrācula **ab hominibus** nōn intelleguntur.
5. Bona verba dīcuntur. (dux)   Bona verba **ā duce** dīcuntur.
6. Multī virī armātī vincuntur. (mīlitēs)   Multī virī armātī **ā mīlitibus** vincuntur.
7. Verba Pȳthiae nōn intelleguntur. (mīles)   Verba Pȳthiae **ā mīlite** nōn intelleguntur.
8. Delphī petuntur. (ducēs)   Delphī **ā ducibus** petuntur.
   Delphī, Delphōrum, *m. pl.* – Delphi
9. Cōnsilium ducis intellegitur. (Graecī)   Cōnsilium ducis **ā Graecīs** intellegitur.

PAGE 130

Standards 1.1, 1.2, 3.1, 4.1
Workbook Exercise 2

▶ EXERCISE 2 ANSWERS

duchy	dux
fortitude	fortitūdō
human	homō
decree	dēcernō
dictum	dīcō
intelligent	intellegō
liberated	līberō
navigation	nāvigō
petition	petō
contrary	contrā
military	mīles
oracular	ōrāculum
regal	rēx
timorous	timor

Chapter 8 • 155

▶ EXERCISE 3 ANSWERS

Present active
intellegō
intellegis
intellegit
intellegimus
intellegitis
intellegunt

Present passive
intellegor
intellegeris
intellegitur
intellegimur
intellegiminī
intelleguntur

Present active infinitive
intellegere

Present passive infinitive
intellegī

PAGE 131

TEACHING TIP
The teacher may wish to remind the students about the use of the ablative of agent.

Athēniēnsēs ā duce servantur.

The Athenians are being saved by the general.

TEACHING TIP
Additional reproducible worksheets, morphology charts, and their associated answer keys, related to this material, are available for download at www.lnm.bolchazy.com.

- Case Uses

PAGE 132

Standards 1.1, 1.2

Workbook Exercises 4, 5

TEACHER BY THE WAY
The eighteenth century CE, called the Age of Enlightenment or the Age of Reason, was accompanied by the artistic style called neoclassicism, which sought inspiration in the stories and figures of classical Greece and Rome. Jacques-Louis David, an avid supporter of the French Revolution and republicanism and subsequently of Napoleon, painted many classical scenes.

▶ EXERCISE 4 ANSWERS

1. Praemium meum cum gaudiō exspectō.   ablative of manner
   I await my reward with joy.
2. Multōs miserōs senēs oculīs meīs vidēre possum.   ablative of means
   I can see many wretched old men with my eyes.
3. Nautae fābulam lacrimīs multīs nārrant.   ablative of manner
   The sailors tell the story with many tears.
4. Persās cum fortitūdine exspectāre possumus.   ablative of manner
   We can wait for the Persians with courage.
5. Animus magnus tenebrīs nōn vincitur.   ablative of means
   A great mind is not conquered by shadows.
6. Iūstī hominēs vinculīs līberārī dēbent.   ablative of separation
   Just men ought to be freed from chains.
7. Ad castra ā casā ambulāmus.   ablative of place from which
   We walk to the camp from the house.

PAGE 133
Standards 1.1, 1.2, 3.1, 4.1

▶ EXERCISE 5 ANSWERS

1. Ōrācula cum gaudiō petimus.
2. Bellō nōn līberāminī/līberāris.
3. Puerōs et puellās praemiīs docēmus.
4. Miserī hominēs vinculīs tenentur.
5. Mīlitēs Persārum (cum) magnō timōre/magnō cum timōre exspectās/exspectātis.

TEACHER BY THE WAY

The early Christians like St. Augustine found themselves attracted to the philosophy of Plotinus and others who promoted Neoplatonic thought. They found that platonic notions of the ideal melded quite well with Christian thought. When Aristotle was rediscovered by Christian Europe through the writings of the Muslim scholar Averroës (Ibn Rushd 1126–1198) and the inter-religious discussions fostered by the Muslim court at Cordoba in Spain, Neoplatonism fell out of favor. St. Thomas Aquinas (1225–1274) synthesized Aristotelian and Christian thought in his *magnum opus*, the *Summa Theologica*. This Thomist philosophy continues as the foundation for official Roman Catholic teaching. However, with the Italian Renaissance's heightened interest in the texts and writings of the ancient Greeks and Romans, Plato was rediscovered. Cosimo de Medici commissioned the translation of Plato into Latin. This spurred the development of a new group of Neoplatonic scholars and writers.

This renewed Renaissance interest in Neoplatonism influenced both the literature and the art of the Renaissance. The human form in all its beauty became a metaphor for the soul's desire for God. Thus, for example, the naked Venus in Botticelli's famous *The Birth of Venus* is an image used allegorically to represent divine love and beauty. Michelangelo's Sistine Chapel ceiling demonstrates a synthesis of biblical narrative, Christian theology, Neoplatonist philosophy, and classical allusions, all of which serve to demonstrate the beauty and truth of divine, i.e., Christian, revelation. The Delphic Sybil illustrated on p. 133 (SE) joins the "pagan" Cumaean, Libyan, Erythreaean, and Persian sibyls in a series of panels on either side of the ceiling's center, with their scenes from the Bible, which alternate with the Hebrew prophets: Isaiah, Daniel, Joel, Ezekiel, and Jeremiah. Together these figures herald the coming of Christ. According to the Neoplatonists, God's word was revealed in the prophecies of pre-Christian seers.

PAGE 134
Standards 1.1, 1.2

▶ EXERCISE 6 ANSWERS

1. ad patriam
   The sailors sail toward the fatherland.

2. In pulchrā casā
   We live in a beautiful little house.

3. In casam/ad casam
   We come into the little house/toward the little house.

4. in castrīs
   The soldiers remain in the camp.

5. in agrīs/in agrōs
   The farmer is walking in the fields/into the fields.

6. in castra Rōmānōrum
   Armed men enter by means of a trick into the camp of the Romans.

7. in templō, ex templō, ad castra/in castra
   The commander remains in the temple; then he comes out of the temple and walks to the camp/into the camp.

PAGE 135

Standards 1.1, 2.1, 4.1

Oral Exercise 2 and Dictation; Workbook Exercises 6, 7, Content Questions

▶ EXERCISE 7 ANSWERS

1. To what place are the Athenians walking?
   Ad templum Delphicum ambulant Athēniēnsēs.
   The Athenians are walking to the Delphic temple.

2. To what place is the king of the Persians sailing?
   Ad Graeciam rēx Persārum nāvigat.
   The king of the Persians is sailing to Greece.

3. From where is the king of the Persians sailing?
   Ex Āsiā rēx Persārum nāvigat.
   The king of the Persians is sailing from Asia.

4. Where are the Athenians awaiting war?
   In castrīs bellum exspectant Athēniēnsēs.
   The Athenians are awaiting war in the camp.

5. Where can the Athenians not remain?
   In terrā manēre nōn possunt Athēniēnsēs.
   The Athenians cannot remain on land.

6. To what place are the Athenians sailing?
   Ad nāvēs Persārum Athēniēnsēs nāvigant.
   The Athenians are sailing toward the ships of the Persians.

TEACHER BY THE WAY

The ancient Greeks considered Delphi a very special place for its beautiful natural setting nestled on the side of Mt. Parnassus (a modern-day ski resort is located on the mountain) and for its mythological associations. The Greeks believed Delphi was the center of the world and erected a statue of a belly button or *omphalos* to symbolize this belief. According to tradition, when Zeus set two eagles to fly in opposite directions in search of the earth's center, they met at Delphi. As the sanctuary, sacred to Apollo, evolved, it included a series of small buildings or treasuries that held the votive offerings of a given city-state, the sibyl's seat, the temple to Apollo, a theatre, a stadium, and a circus which collectively celebrated the religious, intellectual, and physical aspects of human endeavor. Every four years, Delphi hosted the Pythian Games, which were similar to the more familiar Olympic Games. Like Olympia, Delphi was a religious sanctuary and not a settlement.

ORAL EXERCISE 2 AND DICTATION

This combined exercise may be used to conclude the chapter.

The teacher should dictate the following passage slowly and clearly. The students should be allowed to ask the teacher to repeat words, phrases, and sentences as often as needed. When the dictation is finished, the teacher may ask the following questions about the passage the students have written down: the teacher should remind the students they can and should use the words they have actually written in their answers, changing only what is needed to produce a correct answer. The teacher should use one of the CPOs to put the following interrogative words on view.

cūius – whose?   **quid?** – what?

quis? – who?   **quī?** – who (plural)?

quō? – to what place . . . ?   **quōmodo?** – in what way?

The Reading Vocabulary may be consulted.

Xerxēs rēx Persārum cum multīs virīs armātīs ad Graeciam nāvigat. Athēniēnsēs bellum magnō timōre exspectant. Sed Themistoclēs cōnsilium Apollinis in templō Delphicō petit. Pȳthia verba Apollinis dīcit: "Athēniēnsēs mūrōs ligneōs parāre dēbent." Verba Apollinis ā Themistocle intelleguntur. Themistoclēs dīcit: "Multae nāvēs ab Athēniēnsibus parārī dēbent. Nāvibus servārī possunt Athēniēnsēs."

1. **Teacher:** Quis cum multīs virīs armātīs nāvigat?
    Student: Xerxēs rēx Persārum cum multīs virīs armātīs nāvigat.

2. **Teacher:** Quō Xerxēs cum multīs armātīs nāvigat?
    Student: Xerxēs cum multīs armātīs ad Graeciam nāvigat.

3. **Teacher:** Quōmodo Athēniēnsēs bellum exspectant?
    Student: Athēniēnsēs bellum magnō (cum) timōre exspectant.

4. **Teacher:** Quid Themistoclēs in templō Delphicō petit?
    Student: Themistoclēs cōnsilium Apollinis in templō Delphicō petit.

5. **Teacher:** Cūius verba Pȳthia dīcit?
    Student: Pȳthia verba Apollinis dīcit.

6. **Teacher:** Quī mūrōs ligneōs parāre dēbent?
    Student: Athēniēnsēs mūrōs ligneōs parāre dēbent.

7. **Teacher:** Cūius verba ā Themistocle intelleguntur?
    Student: Verba Apollinis ā Themistocle intelleguntur.

8. **Teacher:** Quid Themistoclēs dīcit?
    Student: Themistoclēs dīcit: "Multae nāvēs ab Athēniēnsibus parārī dēbent. Nāvibus servārī possunt Athēniēnsēs."

160 • Latin for the New Millennium: Teacher's Manual, Level 1

PAGE 136
Standard 1.2

TRANSLATION OF THE LATIN CONVERSATION
Mary: Hello, Mark! What are you going to do in the afternoon?

Mark: I want to ride a skateboard. What are you going to do?

Mary: I have to do homework.

Christy approaches.

Mark: Hello, Christy! What are you going to do in the afternoon?

Christy: I want to watch television.

Mark: Do you want to ride a skateboard with me? You will be able to turn on the television afterward.

Christy: Yes indeed! I want to ride a skateboard with you.

Helen approaches.

Mark: Hello, Helen! What are you going to do in the afternoon?

Helen: I want to play ball, then to have a snack.

Mark: Do you want to ride a skateboard with me and Christy? You will be able to play ball and have a snack afterward.

Helen: Yes indeed. I want to ride a skateboard with you. And you, Mary, what are you going to do?

Mary: I have to do homework.

Helen: Oh! Oh! You should ride a skateboard with us. You will be able to do homework afterward.

Mary: Yes indeed. You are right (you say well). I will be able to do homework afterward. Where are the skateboards?

PAGE 137
Standards 1.2, 4.1
Oral Exercise 3

ORAL EXERCISE 3
This exercise may be used after the Latin dialogue has been presented.

Ask the following questions about the dialogue, which the students will have read and studied with the help of the teacher. Before beginning the exercise, the teacher should use one of the CPOs to put on view all the following Latin phrases with the English equivalents.

. . . an . . . ? *(in a question)*	. . . or . . .
. . . ne . . . ? *(added to the first word)*	. . . asks a question
Nōlō . . . *(usually with infinitive)*	I don't want . . .
Quid facere vult . . . ?	What does ____ want to do?
Quid faciet . . . ?	What will ____ do?
Vīsne . . . ?	Do you want . . . ?
Volō . . . *(usually with infinitive)*	I want . . .

Chapter 8 • 161

A. The students should use in their answers, as far as possible, the words in the dialogue, changing the endings only where appropriate for a correct answer.

1. **Teacher:** Quid post scholās facere vult Mārcus?
   Student: Mārcus vult post scholās tabulā subrotātā vehī.

2. **Teacher:** Quid post scholās facere dēbet Marīa?
   Student: Marīa post scholās pēnsum domesticum perficere dēbet.

3. **Teacher:** Quid post scholās facere dēcernit Christīna, tēlevīsiōnem spectāre an tabulā subrotātā vehī cum Mārcō?
   Student: Christīna dēcernit post scholās tabulā subrotātā vehī cum Mārcō.

4. **Teacher:** Quid post scholās facere dēcernit Helena, pilā lūdere et merendāre an cum Mārcō et cum Christīnā tabulā subrotātā vehī?
   Student: Helena dēcernit post scholās tabulā subrotātā vehī cum Mārcō et cum Christīnā.

5. **Teacher:** Dēcernitne Marīa pēnsum domesticum perficere an cum amīcīs tabulā subrotātā vehī?
   Student: Dēcernit Marīa cum amīcīs tabulā subrotātā vehī.

B. Now the teacher should ask individual students the following questions.

1. **Teacher:** Vīsne tēlevīsōrium accendere? **Student:** Volō/Nōlō tēlevīsōrium accendere.

2. **Teacher:** Vīsne tēlevīsōrium exstinguere? **Student:** Volō/Nōlō tēlevīsōrium exstinguere.

3. **Teacher:** Vīsne tēlevīsiōnem spectāre? **Student:** Volō/Nōlō tēlevīsiōnem spectāre.

4. **Teacher:** Vīsne pilā lūdere? **Student:** Volō/Nōlō pilā lūdere.

5. **Teacher:** Vīsne tabulā subrotātā vehī? **Student:** Volō/Nōlō tabulā subrotātā vehī.

6. **Teacher:** Vīsne pēnsum domesticum perficere? **Student:** Volō/Nōlō pēnsum domesticum perficere.

DERIVATIVES

dux – (from *ducō* = to lead; related derivatives will be listed and discussed there)

The Latin verb *condūcō* gives English such words as "conduct" (noun and verb), "conductor," "conducive," "conduit," and the Italian *condottiere* (originally "leader" of a private band of mercenaries and later a mercenary soldier of fortune himself; the Vatican's Swiss Guards are the modern remnants of such a mercenary army). The various meanings of *condūcō* (to bring together, hire, rent, undertake, be of use, profit) are seen in "conductor," which appared in the 1520s and meant "a leader or guide." The idea of "orchestra leader" dates to 1784; "one who guides passengers and collects fares on a train" to 1832.

The atmosphere in the classroom was <u>conducive</u> to learning ("be of use").

The teacher is a <u>conduit</u> of learning through whom knowledge flows to her students ("bring together").

A "duke" was originally a sovereign prince and later the highest rank below prince among the English aristocracy. His wife is called a "duchess."

A "ducat" coin was named after the Duke of Apulia (Roger II of Sicily) who first minted them around 1140. Over the years it was a popular currency in Holland, Russia, Sweden, Venice, etc., but of varying value.

162 • Latin for the New Millennium: Teacher's Manual, Level 1

The "doge" was the chief magistrate of Venice or Genoa.

All of these derivatives reflect the meaning of the Latin *dux* ("leader").

fortitūdō – The form and meaning of the English word "fortitude" reflect its origins in *fortitūdō*, which itself is based on the Latin *fortis*. Related derivatives will be listed and discussed there.

homō – The word "homage" appeared in English during the late thirteenth century through the Old French *homage* meaning "allegiance or respect to one's feudal lord" from the Latin *homō*. The figurative sense of "reverence, honor shown" dates to the late fourteenth century.

The word "human" derives from the Latin adjective related to *homō* (*hūmānus*) meaning "of man."

The words "humanity, humanist," and "humanism" all derive from the related noun *hūmānitās* which meant "mankind, human nature," but also "kindness, courtesy," and "culture."

The word "humanist" came into English during the 1580s and meant "a student of classical humanities." The philosophical sense dates to 1903, referring to one who "strives to understand human problems by the resources of the human mind."

The prefix of "inhuman" is negative.

A "superhuman" effort goes over and above (*super* = over, above, beyond) ordinary human power, as the achievements of Herakles and Superman demonstrate.

mīles – The word *mīles* is the root of the Latin *mīlitia* (military service, the army), which came into English unchanged in form or meaning. The idea of "a citizen army" as opposed to professional soldiers arose during the 1690s. In 1777 the word in American English came to refer to "the whole body of men declared amenable to military service."

A "militant" is an aggressive, combative person who advocates warfare.

ōrāculum – (from *ōrō* = to speak, plead, beg, pray)

The <u>oracular</u> shrine of Apollo at Delphi was consulted by Croesus. The word came into English during the 1670s.

The word "oracle," derived directly from the Latin, is attested in the late fourteenth century.

rēx – (from *regō* = to rule)

The word "realm" came into English during the late thirteenth century meaning "kingdom" through the Old French *reaume* and *roiaume* from the Latin *rēx* (note the French *roi* for "king" in *roiaume*).

Note the spelling of "regal" and "regicide" (to kill a king) and "reign," which reflects the root verb *regō* and the base of *rēx* (gen. *rēgis*).

Students should be cautioned about the usage of "reign." It has been confused with "reins" even in quality newspapers, e.g, "He held the reigns of government tightly." (The correct word here is "reins" as in the "reins of a horse.") "He reigns over all he surveys" illustrates the correct usage.

The spelling of "royal," which is derived from *rēx*, is affected by its passage through the Old French *roial* from the Latin *rēgālis*.

A "viceroy" is a representative of a sovereign (from the Latin ablative *vice* = in place of) through the French *roi* (king).

templum – A *templum* was "a place for taking auguries." The verb *contemplor* meant "to observe" as in taking auguries. Hence, "to contemplate" means "to regard, study, observe thoughtfully." The Latin prefix *con* in *contemplor* expresses joint action or partnership, as occurs when gods commune with the priests through auguries.

Chapter 8 • 163

timor – See *timeō*, 1.3

Note the "-ous" suffix of "timorous."

dēcernō – (from *cernō* = to discern, understand, decide, determine)

The word "decree" appears in English during the fourteenth century and is derived from the fourth principal part of *dēcernō* (*dēcrētum*) through the Old French *decret* (twelfth century). A "decree" is issued when a decision has been made.

Related derivatives will be listed and discussed under *cernō*.

dīcō – A "benediction" is something "said well," a blessing; a "malediction" is something "said badly," a curse.

A "prediction" (*pre* = before) is something "said before" it actually happens, a forecast; a "contradiction" is something "said against" (*contrā* = against), a contrary opinion or denial.

The word "verdict" is derived from the Latin *vērum dictum* (a true word, saying, command). It came into English during the 1530s through the Anglo-French *verdit* and Old French *voirdit* and referred to "a jury's decision in a case." Juries are supposed to decide the truth of the matter being disputed.

The word "ditty" appeared in English around 1300 and meant "a short song." It was derived through the Old French *ditie* (a composition, poem) from the Latin *dictāre* (to dictate, compose), a frequentative (showing repeated action) of *dīcō*.

An "indictment" is a "saying" or "charge against (*in* = against) someone." The word appeared in English around 1300 as "endytement" from the Anglo-French *enditement*. The Latin spelling was restored during the seventeenth century, but the pronunciation stayed the same.

The Latin *addīcō* (*ad* = to, toward) literally meant "to declare for, speak favorable of," then, "to award, yield, devote to." An "addiction" is a habit of awarding oneself. The modern connection to drugs was first attested in 1906 in reference to opium although one instance occurs in 1779 in reference to tobacco.

The word "addict" appeared in 1909 in reference to morphine.

The word "condition" derives from the Latin *condīcō* (agreement, situation; from *condīcō* = to speak with, talk together). It appeared in English during the early fourteenth century.

intellegō – (from *legere* = to choose, gather, read, etc.)

The English derivatives come directly from *intellegō* (the g and c spelling changes reflect those in the principal parts).

līberō – The philanthropist was known for his <u>liberality</u>.

A <u>libertine</u> acts with such freedom both morally and sexually that he is more commonly known as a rake or profligate.

The word "livery" originally meant "household allowance of any kind to servants." It is derived through the Old French *livreé* (allowance, ration, pay) and *librer* (to deliver, hand over, dispense) from the Latin *līberō* which, in addition to "to free (a slave, state, etc.)" can also mean "to discharge, fulfill (an obligation, debt), pay for, cover (an expense)." By the mid-fifteenth century the English sense was reduced to "servants' rations" and "provision for horses." The former led to "distinctive clothing given to servants"; the latter is now obsolete except in the term "livery stable" (1705).

The word "delivery" is derived from the Latin *dēlīberō* (*dē* = from; to consider, consult, etc.). It came into English around 1200 meaning "to save, rescue, liberate." A "delivery" involves the action of handing over to another, a release of an item: The pitcher's <u>delivery</u> of his fast ball was famous. (This usage dates back to 1702.)

See also Teaching Tip 1.6.

164 • Latin for the New Millennium: Teacher's Manual, Level 1

nāvigō – This verb consists of *nāvis* (ship) and *agō* (to drive); hence "to drive a ship" means "to sail."

Words like "navigator," which end in "-tor" or "-or" (inventor, professor, doctor, pastor), indicate the person doing the action. An inventor "finds" something new; a professor "claims to be an expert in some field and is a teacher of the highest rank"; a doctor teaches; a pastor leads his flock, etc. A "navigator" directs the course of a ship.

petō – The word "compete" appears in English during the 1610s and is derived from *cum* (= together) and *petō* (to strive, seek, attack). Hence, athletes enter "competitions" striving with each other as they seek to win the event.

The word "competence" entered English during the 1590s meaning "rivalry," but it soon came to mean "adequate supply" and by the 1630s referred to "a sufficiency of means for living at ease." It derives from the Latin *competō* meaning "to agree, coincide, be capable or fitting."

The Latin word *impetus* (*in* = against, and *petō* = aim for, rush at) means "attack." It came into English unchanged and refers to a "forward movement, a rushing forward."

An "impetuous" person rushes into things, often without giving the situation due thought. Note the "-ous" suffix.

The Latin *appetō* (*ap* = *ad* by assimilation) means "to attack, grasp, desire." The derivatives came into English around 1300 limited to "a craving for food." Other desires were added during the late fourteenth century. His appetite for war was well documented.

An "appetizer" is the first course of a dinner designed to whet the desire to eat.

"Impetigo," derived directly from the Latin *impetigō*, refers to a contagious "attack" on the skin marked by pustular eruptions.

The word "perpetual" consists of the Latin *per* (thoroughly, through to the end) and *petō*; hence "to be sought forever." Perpetual motion never ends.

George Washington will be honored by Americans in perpetuity.

Asking repeatedly with no response can certainly lead to irritability or peevishness (="petulance" from the Latin word *petulantia* meaning "boisterous aggressiveness, impudence, effrontery"). The word appeared in English around 1600 and meant "insolence." The meaning of "peevishness" is first recorded in 1784.

The word "repeat" is derived through the Middle French *repeter* from the Latin *repetere* (*re* = again, back). The spelling was affected by the Great Vowel Shift, a major change in the pronunciation of English between 1350 and 1700. The long diphthong *ea* is also seen in "beak, peace, leader," etc. However, that same diphthong could also remain short (depending on the subsequent consonant) as in "dead, head," and "wealth." Modern English is indeed a complicated language and difficult to learn!

vincō – The prefix of "invincible" is negative.

Note the "-ous" suffix of "victorious.

The prefix of "conviction" is intensive. His strong convictions regarding justice for the unfortunate guided the actions of his life.

The Latin root for "convict" (verb and noun) and "convince," as well as "conviction," is *convincō* (to overcome, refute, prove wrong).

The word "vanquish" came into English during the early fourteenth century through the Old French *venquis* (past tense of *veintre*) from the Latin *vincō*. Note the vowel changes which occurred during its passage to English.

Chapter 8 · 165

tunc – None

contrā – The Latin meaning carries over into such derivatives as "contrary, contrast, contradict," etc.

The verb "counter," meaning "to go against," appeared in English during the late fourteenth century through the Old French *countre* (facing opposite) from the Latin *contrā*. The spokesman for the assembled crowd <u>countered</u> each of the commissioner's proposals with one of their own.

The prefix of "encounter" comes from the Latin *in* through the French *en-*. A Late Latin form *incontrā* (= in front of, against) is attested. An "encounter" then is a meeting of adversaries. The weakened sense of "casually meet" is first recorded in English during the early sixteenth century.

The word "country" appears in English during the mid-thirteenth century meaning "district, native land," and was derived through the Old French *contree* from the Latin *contrā*. The medieval Latin *contrātā* referred to "that which is opposite," hence "landscape." The sense narrowed during the 1520s to rural areas, as opposed to cities.

See also Teaching Tips 1.6 and 1.7.

166 • Latin for the New Millennium: Teacher's Manual, Level 1

CHAPTER 9 (PP. 139–151)

GRAMMAR IN LANGUAGE FACTS

Fourth Conjugation Verbs: Present Tense Active and Passive, Present Active and Passive Infinitive; Third Declension Neuter Nouns; Third Declension *I*–Stem Nouns

PAGE 139

Standards 1.1, 2.1
RRA 5

MEMORĀBILE DICTŪ VOCABULARY

mōs, mōris, *m.* – custom, *pl.* morals
tempus, temporis, *n.* – time

TEACHER BY THE WAY

Cicero's four famous orations, Against Catiline 1–4, are titled *In Catilīnam 1–4*. Catiline was defeated by Cicero for the consulship of 63 BCE. Since he was twice rejected for that office, in desperation he conspired to overthrow the government.

Cicero's focus in his speeches against Catiline was on the immediate threat to the state. His interest was purely on the politics of the moment, and, if he did malign Catiline's character, especially in the first two orations, it was to enhance his viewpoint that Catiline was a dangerous man. The charge that he murdered his wife and son to make way for a new bride was part of a common type of invective, and no law of libel prevented Cicero from giving full rein to it. That Cicero was successful in alienating the Senate from Catiline is clear from the picture on p. 139 (SE) of the text, which is based on the description in Chapter 7 of the First Catilinarian. The second speech, delivered on the following day, continued in this vein with a list of the types of men who had joined Catiline, from landowners deeply in debt, to bankrupt but ambitious politicians, and criminals of every class, to effeminate and dissolute youths *proprium Catilīnae* (*Cat.* 2.10.18). In a superb paragraph (*Cat.* 2.11) he uses parallel structure and antithesis to highlight the moral differences between the revolutionaries and "the Senate and the people of Rome": *aequitās, temperantia, fortitūdō,* and *prūdentia* on the one side, and *inīquitās, luxuria, ignāvia,* and *temeritās* on the other.

Sallust, however, set Catiline in a larger frame and saw these negative characteristics as indicative of an entire society in decay. According to the historian, Catiline was born of a noble family and possessed great intellectual and physical strength but used his talents to satisfy his greed for power. Cicero also admitted his good qualities, e.g., his ability to endure hunger and cold (*Cat.* 1.10), but promptly accused him of using such skills in nefarious ways to further his argument that Catiline was plotting to overthrow the state. Sallust, however, depicted

Catiline as an example of *virtūs* corrupted, the product of a society weakened by a love of luxury and money (*Dē coniūrātiōne Catilīnae* 20). He also cautioned his readers about the rumors regarding the young men who gravitated to the revolutionary camp, saying that they probably stemmed from the general lifestyle of that generation rather than from actual knowledge.

Nevertheless, if Sallust's description of Catiline seems a bit more evenhanded than that of Cicero, it must be remembered that the historian nursed a biased attitude toward the *nōbilēs* and supported Caesar during the Civil War who, like Catiline, championed the cause of the *populārēs*. This time, however, the revolt was successful.

TEACHING TIP
As a prereading activity employing the chapter page image, teachers may ask the students to examine the painting. *Spectāte pictūram! Quis est Cicero? Quis est Catilīna? Quōmodo scis?*

TEACHING TIP
The teacher may wish to assign Chapter 5 of RRA for reading or review. See p. 73.

PAGE 140
Standards 1.1, 2.1, 3.1, 3.2

TRANSLATION OF LATIN PASSAGE
About the Conspiracy of Catiline

The city (of Rome) is perturbed. In the place of peace and joy come fear and sadness. People walk <being> miserable, believe nobody, fear greatly. Women's cries are heard in the city.

Catiline's mind is devising bad plans. Catiline, however, comes into the Senate, seeks a seat, behaves like a good man. Then the consul Marcus Tullius Cicero delivers a long and splendid speech in the Senate. With great courage Cicero tells that Catiline is a bad man, and that he is preparing death for Roman citizens. Cicero says that he can save the Romans with weapons and remove Catiline from the city of Rome. Catiline is listening and looking at the floor (earth). At last Catiline says that the senators should not listen to Cicero's words. The senators, however, do listen to Cicero's words and decide to save the city.

TEACHER BY THE WAY
Sallust writes tersely, concisely, and somewhat obscurely, with many archaic touches; his style was imitated and evidently admired by the late first century CE Roman historian Tacitus.

TEACHING TIP
Instruct the students to locate Numidia on the map on pp. xxxiv–xxxv (SE) and to find Sallust on the timeline on pp. 405–408 (SE).

TEACHER BY THE WAY
Lucius Sergius Catilina (108–62 BCE) was a member of one of the oldest patrician families in Rome. Vergil connects the family to Sergestus, a companion of Aeneas. The last Sergius to be consul had held office in 380 BCE. One of Catiline's ambitions was to restore the political heritage and financial power of his family, which had not been prominent for several generations. It is possible he was married to Gratidia, a sister of Marcus Marius Gratidianus, but changing allegiances severed that Marian connection when Catiline killed his brother-in-law at the request of Catulus.

PAGE 141

ANSWERS TO COMPREHENSION QUESTIONS
1. The city was perturbed and the people were worried and full of mistrust.
2. Catiline intended to make a revolution in Rome.
3. Cicero discredited Catiline in his speeches.
4. Catiline pretended to be a good citizen and came to the Senate.

TEACHING TIP
While English derivatives from the asterisked words (i.e., the Vocabulary to Learn) are the topic of Exercise 2 later in this chapter, there are some interesting derivatives from the non-asterisked words. The teacher may choose to discuss these derivatives with the students.

- *clāmor* – clamorous, clamor
- *locus* – local, locality, locomotive, lieutenant, lieu

    Both "lieu" (in place of) and "lieutenant" (place-holding) are derived from the Latin *locus* through the OF, *liu*, hence the spelling change.

- *spectō* – spectacles, spectator, spectacular

TEACHER BY THE WAY
The word *sella* that is in this Reading Vocabulary list, when combined with the word *curūlis*, denotes a special object. The *sella curūlis* was a stool with bent legs, which could be folded shut for easy transportation and was especially useful on military campaigns. Whereas today canvas or leather is attached to the legs and remains a part of such a camp stool, the Romans had a separate wooden bench, which would be fitted into notches in the top of each leg when the chair was opened. Such seats were introduced from Etruria and originally were used in Rome exclusively by the kings. Subsequently, this privilege was granted to consuls, praetors, and curule aediles. In early times they were enriched with ivory, but later decorations consisted of gold ornaments.

PAGE 142
Standards 3.1, 4.1
Oral Exercise 1; Workbook Exercise 1

ORAL EXERCISE 1
This exercise may be used anytime after the present active and passive of the fourth conjugation have been presented.
While looking at the conjugation of *audiō*, ask the students to conjugate *sentiō* in the present active and passive, including the active and passive infinitives.

    sentiō, sentīs, sentit, sentīmus, sentītis, sentiunt

    sentior, sentīris, sentītur, sentīmur, sentīminī, sentiuntur

    sentīre, sentīrī

TEACHING TIP
Additional reproducible worksheets, morphology charts, and their associated answer keys, related to this material, are available for download at www.lnm.bolchazy.com.
- **Verb Conjugations**

PAGE 143
Standards 1.1, 1.2

▶ EXERCISE 1 ANSWERS
veniunt – third person plural active

TEACHING TIP
At this juncture, the teacher may wish to review with students how to say in Latin to what conjugation a verb belongs. The information on how to say this in Latin was presented on p. 30 of this teacher's manual. For the teacher's convenience a combined list of new verbs presented on this page and other verbs previously learned in this book is given. The teacher may choose to say these verbs orally, ask in Latin to what conjugation the verb belongs, and call on a student to answer in Latin.

- **sciō, scīre, scīvī, scītum** – know (*quārtae*)
- **parō, parāre, parāvī, parātum** – prepare (*prīmae*)
- **dīcō, dīcere, dīxī, dictum** – say (*tertiae*)
- **teneō, tenēre, tenuī, tentum** – hold (*secundae*)
- **maneō, manēre, mansī, mansum** – remain (*secundae*)
- **dō, dare, dedī, datum** – give (*prīmae*)
- **petō, petere, petīvī, petītum** – seek (*tertiae*)
- **sentiō, sentīre, sēnsī, sēnsum** – feel (*quārtae*)
- **vincō, vincere, vīcī, victum** – conquer (*tertiae*)
- **veniō, venīre, vēnī, ventum** – come (*quārtae*)
- **crēdō, crēdere, crēdidī, crēditum** – believe (*tertiae*)
- **invideō, invidēre, invīdī, invīsum** – envy (*secundae*)

TEACHER BY THE WAY

The consul was the supreme military and civil magistrate during the Republic. Two consuls of equal authority were elected annually by the *Comitia Centuriāta* on October 24th and took office on January 1st (after 154 BCE). The duality of the office was probably in answer to the threat of a return to monarchical rule. The consuls alternated supreme authority monthly, with the presiding consul always preceded in public by twelve lictors carrying the *fascēs*, the symbol of the power "to command and coerce." The other consul would be accompanied by a crier, with his lictors (minus the *fascēs*) walking behind. This may have been done to assuage the fear of the populace upon seeing two men of equal rank perhaps facing off against one another. Thus the "equal authority" was tempered by the custom of alternating months and by the Valerian Law, which stated that the elder consul was *prior*.

The consuls presided over the Senate and were the supreme military leaders until the empire became too large, when it became customary to appoint ex-consuls to the provinces. The consuls also gave their names to the year, e.g., *C. Caesare et M. Bibulō cōnsulibus* = 59 BCE. However, in this instance, Caesar so dominated the political scene that a wag dubbed the year "in the consulship of Julius and Caesar!"

During the Empire, the consulship became a mere title beginning with Augustus, who separated the power of the office from the magistracy itself and shortened the term, thus ensuring the election or appointment of several more consuls each year. This allowed him to honor more nobles (and to keep them in check), who seemed satisfied to hold only the trappings of power and the prestige of the office. The consulship deteriorated to such an extent that under the emperor Commodus there were 25 consuls in one year.

PAGE 144

Standards 1.1, 1.2, 4.1
Workbook Exercise 2

▶ EXERCISE 2 ANSWERS

1. capital — caput
2. civil — cīvis
3. gesture — gerō
4. audience — audiō
5. credit — crēdō
6. temporary — tempus
7. corporal — corpus
8. exemplary — exemplar
9. mortality — mors
10. urban — urbs
11. armed — arma
12. consulate — cōnsul
13. animals — animal
14. science — sciō
15. marina — mare
16. oratory — ōrātiō
17. sentimental — sentiō

▶ EXERCISE 3 ANSWERS

1. s/he/it is known
2. to come
3. they know
4. they are known
5. we come
6. you (plural) are known
7. s/he knows
8. to be known

TEACHING TIP

Although in Exercise 2 the students are directed to find only the derivatives based on the Vocabulary to Learn, they may be interested to learn that there are other derivatives in Exercise 2. The derivation of these words is provided for the teacher's convenience.

1. punishment – from *pūniō* (to punish, avenge).
2. insist – from *īnsistō* (to stand on, stand firm, etc.).
4. received – from *recipiō* (to take back, get back, receive).
6. position – from *pōnō* (to put, place, set, etc.).
7. punishment – from *pūniō* (to punish, avenge). schools – from *schola* (school) from the Greek *scholē* meaning leisure since only the wealthy had the time for education.
8. courage – from *cor* (heart).
9. rate – from *prō ratā parte* (according to a fixed part; proportionally): *reor* (to think, suppose). significantly – from *significātiō* (indication, signal, sign of approval).
10. poverty – from *paupertās* (moderate means, poverty). area – from *ārea* (vacant site, open space, playground). country – from *contrā* (against, opposite); that which is opposite, hence landscape.
11. adversaries – from *adversārius* (opponent); *adversus* (opposite, in front, hostile).
12. apply – from *applicō* (to attach, place close to); *plicō* (fold) + *ad* (to). visa – from *vīsō* ([freq. of *videō*] – to see); short for *carta vīsa* (the document has been examined).
13. agency – from *agō* (to drive, do, discuss, live, spend, etc.). protection – from *prōtegō* (to cover over, shield, protect).
14. vast – from *vastus* (empty, desolate, enormous). improvements – [back formation from] *prōsum, prōdesse* (to be useful, to benefit). in – from *in* (in, on, at).
15. let – from *lassus* (tired, exhausted).
16. famous – from *fāmōsus* (celebrated; infamous, scandalous); *fāma* (humor, fame, reputation).
17. letter – from *littera* (letter of the alphabet [sing.], letter, letters [pl.]). received – from *recipiō* (to take back, get back, receive). very – from *vērus* (true); *vērāx* (truthful).

PAGE 145
Standards 1.1, 1.2

▶ EXERCISE 4 ANSWERS
1. audītur — Cicero is heard by Catiline.
2. sentītur — Fear is felt by the women.
3. venīre — The senators are accustomed to come to the Senate.
4. audīrī — The words of Cicero ought to be heard by the senators.
5. sciunt — The senators know that Catiline is a bad man.

TEACHER BY THE WAY
The Roman Senate House, pictured on this page, as well as the one that preceded it was called the *Cūria* by the Romans. The term "Curia" lives on in Vatican City, where the Pope's chief advisors and their assistants are called the Curia.

The original structure, called the *Cūria Hostīlia*, was thought to have been built by Tullus Hostilius, the third king of Rome. The Diocletian-era Senate House served as a church for centuries and was deconsecrated as a church and then restored during Mussolini's rule. Benito Mussolini (1883–1945), fascist dictator of Italy from 1922 to 1943, enthusiastically connected his rule with that of the imperial Romans. He staged triumphal processions, financed the excavations of Rome's harbor city, Ostia, and restored many Roman monuments.

TEACHING TIP
Instruct the students to find Julius Caesar, Augustus, and Diocletian on the timeline on pp. 405–408 (SE).

PAGE 146
Standards 1.1, 1.2, 3.1, 4.1
Oral Exercise 2

▶ EXERCISE 5 ANSWERS
1. timōrēs (malus) — timōrēs malī, timōrēs malōs — bad fears
2. ducī (sevērus) — ducī sevērō — to/for the serious leader
3. corporis (pulcher) — corporis pulchrī — of the beautiful body
4. tempus (longus) — tempus longum — a long time
5. corporibus (multus) — corporibus multīs — to/for, by/with many bodies
6. in ōrātiōne (meus) — in ōrātiōne meā — in my speech

Chapter 9 • 173

ORAL EXERCISE 2

This exercise may be used anytime after third declension neuter nouns have been presented.

Ask the students to decline *caput* and *corpus*.

	Singular	**Plural**
Nominative	caput	capita
Genitive	capitis	capitum
Dative	capitī	capitibus
Accusative	caput	capita
Ablative	capite	capitibus
Vocative	caput	capita

	Singular	**Plural**
Nominative	corpus	corpora
Genitive	corporis	corporum
Dative	corporī	corporibus
Accusative	corpus	corpora
Ablative	corpore	corporibus
Vocative	corpus	corpora

PAGE 147
Standards 3.1, 4.1

TEACHING TIP
If the students think the word *pater, patris*, m., "father" should be an *i*–stem, the teacher may explain that it declines like *passer*, although it has the same number of syllables in the nominative and genitive. Together with *māter, mātris*, f., "mother," and *frāter, frātris*, m., "brother," it is an exception to the rule.

TEACHER BY THE WAY
The word *os, ossis*, n., "bone," like masculine and feminine nouns that have a one-syllable nominative singular and a genitive singular base ending in two consonants, has an *i*–stem genitive plural ending (i.e., *–ium*). Since *os* is neuter, however, its accusative singular is *os* and its nominative and accusative plural show the third declension *–a* ending, not the *i*–stem ending *–ia*.

TEACHING TIP
Additional reproducible worksheets, morphology charts, and their associated answer keys, related to this material, are available for download at www.lnm.bolchazy.com.
- **Noun Declensions**

PAGE 148
Oral Exercise 3; Workbook Exercises 3, 4

ORAL EXERCISE 3
This exercise may be used anytime after masculine, feminine, and neuter i–stem nouns have been presented.

While looking at the declension of *urbs*, ask the students to decline *mors*.

	Singular	**Plural**
Nominative	mors	mortēs
Genitive	mortis	mortium
Dative	mortī	mortibus
Accusative	mortem	mortēs
Ablative	morte	mortibus
Vocative	mors	mortēs

While looking at the declension of *mare*, ask the students to decline *animal*.

	Singular	**Plural**
Nominative	animal	animālia
Genitive	animālis	animālium
Dative	animālī	animālibus
Accusative	animal	animālia
Ablative	animālī	animālibus
Vocative	animal	animālia

TEACHER BY THE WAY
The term "Mediterranean" derives from the Latin word *mediterrāneus* meaning "middle of the Earth." To the ancient Romans, the Mediterranean was the center of the Earth known to them. It was more commonly called *Mare Nostrum* "Our Sea" by both the Greeks and Romans because its waters washed both coasts. The term *Mare Internum* characterizes its position as a landlocked body of water that is enclosed by Europe on the north, by Africa on the south, and on the east by Asia. Its connection to the Atlantic, the Strait of Gibraltar, is only nine miles wide. With Rome's far-flung empire, the Mediterranean allowed merchants and travelers the opportunity for trade and cultural exchange between countries. Sailing in the Mediterranean meant that people had to rely on personal experience, familiar landmarks, and local winds and currents. Unfortunately, the pirates were more adept at navigating than the Romans. In the first century BCE, Pompey was commissioned to clear the sea of pirates, which he did in a short period of three months.

TEACHING TIP
The teacher may wish to have students read about Julius Caesar's encounter with pirates, available in the *Cīvis Rōmānus* text listed in the Resource Guide.

Chapter 9 • 175

PAGE 149

Standards 1.1, 1.2

Workbook Exercises 5, 6, 7, Content Questions

▶ EXERCISE 6 ANSWERS

1. marī — to/for the sea; by/with the sea
2. animālium — of the animals
3. urbī — to/for the city
   urbe — by/with the city
4. exemplāribus — to/for the examples; by/with the examples
5. cīvis — the citizen
   cīvem — the citizen
6. mortis — of death

▶ EXERCISE 7 ANSWERS

1. Hominēs timōrem intellegunt.   Men understand fear.
2. Catilīna in cūriam ambulat.   Catiline walks into the Senate.
3. Cicero scit Catilīnam arma parāre.   Cicero knows that Catiline is preparing weapons.
4. Cicero dīcit Catilīnam contrā cōnsulem Rōmānum sentīre.   Cicero says that Catiline has feelings against the Roman consul.
5. Verba Cicerōnis ā patribus exspectantur.   The words of Cicero are expected by the senators.
6. Catilīna est exemplar malī hominis.   Catiline is an example of an evil man.
7. Patrēs nārrant Cicerōnem bene dīcere.   The senators say that Cicero speaks well.

TEACHING TIP

The teacher may wish to ascertain whether the students can determine which nouns are *i*–stems and which are not. It is not necessary for the student to have learned the word to make this determination. The following list of nouns, which the teacher can ask the students to identify as an *i*–stem or not, contain some nouns that have already been seen in this book and some that have not. Answers are provided for the teacher's convenience.

1. **ōrātiō, ōrātiōnis,** *f.* – oration, speech — not an *i*–stem
2. **mōns, montis,** *m.* – mountain — an *i*–stem
3. **caput, capitis,** *n.* – head — not an *i*–stem
4. **cōnsul, cōnsulis,** *m.* – consul — not an *i*–stem
5. **nūbēs, nūbis,** *f.* – cloud — an *i*–stem
6. **lēx, lēgis,** *f.* – law — not an *i*–stem
7. **nox, noctis,** *f.* – night — an *i*–stem
8. **mīles, mīlitis,** *m.* – soldier — not an *i*–stem

PAGE 151
Standards 1.1, 1.2, 2.1, 4.1
Oral Exercises 4, 5, and Dictation

TRANSLATION OF THE LATIN CONVERSATION

Mary: What are you going to wear today, Christy?

Christy: I will wear a skirt and a nice blouse. What are you going to wear, Mary?

Mary: I would like to wear jeans.

Helen: Jeans are not very nice.

Mary: What are you going to wear, Helen?

Helen: I would like to wear a dress.

Mary: Is Mark coming to the party?

Christy: Yes.

Mary: Now I understand . . . I think that Mark loves Helen and is loved by Helen. Put on your dress, Helen, and you, Christy, put on the skirt and the nice blouse. I, however, would like to wear jeans and sneakers.

Helen: Fine. We ought to get ready now. Are you coming?

ORAL EXERCISE 4

This exercise may be used after the Latin dialogue has been presented.

The teacher should give commands to the students that they must carry out. Then have individual students exchange commands so all are involved.

> Indue tunicam. Sūme pilleum. Sūme amictōrium. Sūme digitābula. Sūme perspicillum fuscātum. Sūme umbellam.

> Exue tunicam. Pōne pilleum. Pōne amictōrium. Pōne digitābula. Pōne perspicillum fuscātum. Pōne umbellam.

The teacher may also ask individual students the following question *Quid gestās?*, to which the students may answer:

> Brācās, brācās Genāvēnsēs, castulam, camīsiam, stolam, subūculam, calceāmenta, tībiālia, umbellam, perspicillum, perspicillum fuscātum, pilleum, tunicam.

Chapter 9 • 177

TEACHING TIP

Teachers may wish to have students create a new conversation, modeled on the one on p. 151 (SE) but substituting different names of articles of clothing for the ones used in the original dialogue. Or, students may simply become curious to know the names of more articles of clothing in Latin. More clothing vocabulary is provided here for the teacher's convenience:

- **breviōrēs brācae, breviōrum brācārum,** *f. pl.* – shorts
- **cingulum, cingulī,** *n.* – belt
- **digitālia, digitālium,** *n. pl.* – gloves
- **fōcāle, fōcālis,** *n.* – tie (necktie)
- **pērula, pērulae,** *f.* – purse
- **sandalium, sandaliī,** *n.* – sandal
- **soccī, soccōrum,** *n. pl.* – slippers
- **subligar natātōrium, subligāris natātōriī,** *n.* – swim trunks
- **thōrax lāneus, thōrācis lāneī,** *m.* – sweater
- **tunica, tunicae,** *f.* – jacket
- **vestis natātōria, vestis natātōriae,** *f.* – swimsuit

DICTATION AND ORAL EXERCISE 5

This combined exercise may be used to conclude the chapter.

The teacher should dictate the following text representing Cicero's famous speech against Catiline.

Ō tempora, ō mōrēs! Scīmus Catilīnam cīvibus Rōmānīs mortem parāre. Magnum timōrem sentīmus. Et virī et mulierēs Catilīnam ducem hominum malōrum timent. Nam Catilīna cīvium Rōmānōrum corpora vinculīs dare potest. Ego tamen cōnsul armīs urbem servāre dēbeō.

Use one of the CPOs to put on view the following words:

quis? – Who?
quid? – What?
cūr? – Why?

Ask the students the following questions.

Teacher: Quis mortem cīvibus Rōmānīs parat?   **Student:** Catilīna mortem cīvibus Rōmānīs parat.

Teacher: Quid Catilīna cīvibus Rōmānīs parat?   **Student:** Catilīna mortem cīvibus Rōmānīs parat.

Teacher: Quid sentīmus?   **Student:** Magnum timōrem sentīmus.

Teacher: Quis Catilīnam timet?   **Student:** Virī et mulierēs Catilīnam timent.

Teacher: Cūr virī et mulierēs Catilīnam timent?   **Student:** Catilīna cīvium Rōmānōrum corpora vinculīs dare potest.

Teacher: Quis urbem servāre dēbet?   **Student:** Cicero cōnsul urbem servāre dēbet.

DERIVATIVES

animal – (from *anima* = breath, life, soul, spirit; related derivatives will be discussed there)

arma – The word "alarm" is derived from the Latin *arma* through the Old French *alarme* and Italian *all'arme* (literally, "to arms"). It came to be used as a warning. The weakened sense of "apprehension" dates to 1833. "Alarm clock" is attested from the 1690s.

An "armada" is a fleet of warships. The word is derived from *arma* through the Spanish *armada* (an armed force) and refers especially to the fleet sent against England by Philip II of Spain in 1588 and which was defeated largely by the efforts of Sir Francis Drake and Elizabeth's other "sea dogs" (e.g., John Hawkins, Martin Frobisher, Sir Walter Raleigh).

An "armadillo" is armed with protective covering of bony plates. The suffix is a diminutive.

An "armistice" is a temporary suspension of armed conflict (from *arma* and *stō* = to stand, stop).

caput – The word "achieve" is derived from the Old French *achever* meaning "to finish, accomplish," which itself comes from the phrase *à chef* (*venir*), meaning "come to a head = at the end," and the Late Latin *ad caput* (*venīre*). The Latin *caput* toward the end of the Empire took on the sense of "end." The *ie* spelling indicates the pronunciation of a long *e* as in "chief"; without the *i*, the derivative has a short *e* as in "chef."

The word "biceps" is singular despite the final *s* and refers to a muscle on the front of the arm, so called because of its structure. It is derived directly from the Latin *biceps* meaning "two-headed."

The word "cabbage" came into English during the mid-fifteenth century through the Middle French *caboche* (head and Old French *caboche* [head]), a diminutive from *caput*. It was introduced to Canada in 1541 by Jacques Cartier but does not appear in American written record until the 1660s.

The word "cadet" is attested in English around 1610 from *capitulum* (diminutive of *caput* = small head) through the Gascon *capdet* (chief, youth of a noble family) and the French *cadet* (military student officer). In Late Latin the diminutive (*capitellum*) came to indicate "inferior head of a family." Since the eldest son was regarded as the first head of the family, the second son became the *cadet* (little head). Younger sons of Gascon families were sent to the French court to serve as officers, which gave the word its military meaning.

"Cad" is a shortened form of "cadet," found in 1730 referring to servants; in 1831 it was used to designate town boys by British university students. From 1838 it came to mean "a person who lacked finer feelings."

The word "capitulate" appeared in English during the 1570s meaning "to draw up in chapters (i.e., under 'heads'), arrange conditions." By the 1680s it meant "to yield on stipulated terms."

A "capital" letter was so called because it was located at the head of a sentence or word (late fourteenth century).

The term "capital" indicates the city where the government of a state or nation is located. It also refers to the type of letter found at the beginning of a sentence.

The "Capitol" is the building housing the legislative branches of government itself.

The word "capital," meaning "principal," dates to the early fifteenth century. The financial use appeared during the 1620s referring to trading heads of cattle.

The word "cattle" originally meant "property" (mid-thirteenth century) from the Latin *caput* through the Old French *chattel* and Anglo-French *catel*. It originally referred to moveable property but gradually came to be limited to cows and bulls (late sixteenth century).

Chapter 9 • 179

"Chattel," like "cattle," meant "property or goods" in the late thirteenth century (from the Old French *chattel*). The application of the word to slaves (1640s) by the abolitionists is a rhetorical figure.

A "kerchief" is a piece of cloth that covers the head and ties under the chin. A "handkerchief" is a one-word contradiction in terms, for it also is a small piece of cloth (like a kerchief) but is carried in the hand (or pocket) and used to wipe moisture from the face or hands. King Richard II of England is widely believed to have invented the handkerchief. Written sources attest to his using square pieces of cloth to wipe his nose.

The prefix "mis" of "mischief" comes through the Old French *mes-* (bad, wrong) from the Latin *minus* (less), which was not used as a prefix. It is the opposite of "achieve" (see above); its root also derives from *caput* through the Old French *chever* (to happen, come to a head). When the word appeared in English around 1300, it meant "evil condition, misfortune, need, want." The meaning "harm or evil done by some agent" dates to the later fifteenth century; the sense of "playful malice" to 1784.

Note the "-ous" suffix of "mischievous."

The word "precipice" is derived from the Latin *praeceps* (steep, headlong, head first) which consists of *prae* (before) and *caput*.

The verb "precipitate" is also derived from *praeceps* through *praecipitō* (to throw down, rush headlong, fall).

To "recapitulate" means "to go back (re-) to the beginning" (the head).

cīvis – The word "city" appeared in English during the early thirteenth century through the Old French *cite* (tenth century) from an earlier *citet* which derived from *citatem*, a Late Latin shortened form of *cīvitātem*. Remember that the Latin word for "city" was *urbs*, but a resident was a *cīvis*. *Cīvitās* seems to have replaced *urbs* as Rome lost its prestige. The sense of *cīvitās* thus transferred from inhabitant to place.

A "citadel" is a fortress commanding a city. The word came into English during the 1580s through the Middle French *citadelle* from the Italian *cittadella*, a diminutive of the Old Italian *cittade* (from the Latin *cīvitātem*).

To "civilize" (around 1600) meant "to bring out of barbarism," i.e., to make someone fit to be a citizen.

cōnsul – The "consulate" (late fourteenth century) referred to the government of Rome by consuls. It also denoted the government of France 1799–1804.

corpus – "Corporal" punishment refers to a punishment of the body as opposed to a fine or exile (1580s).

A "corporal" is the lowest noncommissioned officer (1570s), so called either from *corpus* because he was in charge of a "body" of troops or from *caput* because he was the "head" of those troops. The OED suggests that *corpus* was the source and *caput* the influence.

A Latin diminutive of *corpus* (*corpusculum* = little or puny body) is the source for the English "corpuscle" which, in the 1650s, referred to any small particle but was later applied to blood cells (1845).

A "corporation" consists of persons united (from *cum* = together, with) in a body for some purpose (mid-fifteenth century).

The prefix of "incorporate" means "into."

The antonym of "corporeal" is "spiritual."

180 • Latin for the New Millennium: Teacher's Manual, Level 1

The Latin *corpulantus*, meaning "fat, fleshy," is the source for "corpulent."

The English word "corps" was derived from *corpus* through the French *cors* and meant simply "body" (late thirteenth century). It then evolved to mean a "body of citizens" (fifteenth century) and then a "body of knights" (mid-fifteenth century). The modern military sense dates to 1704 based on the French *corps d'armee*. The letter *p* was restored in French (fourteenth century) and then in English (fifteenth century), but the letter remained silent. The singular and plural are spelled the same, but the singular is pronounced "cor" and the plural "cors."

The word "corpse" is a variant spelling of "corps" (1540s) in which the *p* is now sounded and which refers specifically to a dead body.

The word "corsage" appears in English during the later fifteenth century meaning "size of the body," from the Old French *cors*. The meaning "body of a woman's dress, bodice," dates to 1818. The sense of "a bouquet worn on the bodice" appears in 1911, apparently an American adaptation of the French *bouquet de corsage* (bouquet of the bodice).

The thirteenth-century French word *corset*, meaning "bodice, tunic," is a diminutive of *cors*. In 1300 it meant "a kind of laced bodice"; the meaning "stiff supporting and constricting undergarment" appears in 1795.

exemplar – See *exemplum* in 1.6.

mare – "Marinated" meat has been soaked for hours in a seasoned mixture of vinegar and oil. The word appeared in the 1640s through the French *mariner* (to pickle in brine [seawater]) from the Latin adjective *marīnus* (of the sea).

The "rosemary" plant is an evergreen used as a seasoning as well as in perfumery and medicine. It is also a symbol of remembrance. The word derives from the Latin *ros* (dew, water) and *mare* and was probably so called because it grew near the Mediterranean coasts. It came into English during the mid-fifteenth century from the earlier form *rosmarine* (around 1300), its spelling having been altered by the influence of "rose" and "Mary."

A "submarine" travels under (*sub* = under) water.

mors – The prefix of "immortal" is the negative "in"; its spelling is due to assimilation.

The word "mortification" is derived from *mors* and *faciō* (literally, "to make dead"). It has been practiced through the centuries by those attempting to rid their bodies of sin and to strengthen their will (e.g., by fasting, self-flagellation, etc.).

The word "mortgage" came into English during the late fourteenth century meaning "to convey property as security for a loan or agreement" through the Old French *mortgage* (*mort gage*, literally, "dead pledge"). It was so called because the deal died when the loan was repaid or when payment failed. The root of "-gage" lies in the Old French *guage* (pledge).

mulier – Some women lack <u>muliebrity</u>, i.e., femininity.

ōrātiō – (from *ōrō* = to speak, pray, beg)

The word "oratory" can refer to formal public speaking, or to a small chapel which is a place for prayer. The Oratory of St. Philip Neri in Rome was noted for its musical services. By 1727 the word "oratorio" appeared meaning "a long musical composition usually with a text based on Scripture."

The "peroration" is the concluding part of a speech (*per* = through to the end).

Chapter 9 • 181

pāx – After crossing the Isthmus of Panama, Balboa came upon the ocean he named the <u>Pacific</u> because it looked so calm and peaceful.

The word "peace" came into English druing the mid-twelfth century through the Anglo-French *pes* and the Old French *pais* (eleventh century) from *pāx*. The modern spelling came into being during the sixteenth century, reflecting the vowel shift.

A "pacifist" opposes war and violence and prefers to "make peace" (*faciō* = to do, make, and *pāx*) with an enemy. The word first appears in English in 1903.

The word "appease" came into English around 1300 meaning "to reconcile." It is derived from the Latin *ad* (to, toward) and *pāx* through the Old French phrase *a paisier* (bring to peace).

When the verb "pay" came into English around 1200, it meant "to satisfy, appease." This meaning died out by 1500, but the word remained a reflection of the Old French *paier* (to pay up) which acquired its financial meaning from the Medieval Latin *pacāre* (to satisfy a creditor).

The word "taxpayer" is based on two Latin roots: *taxāre* (to evaluate, estimate) and *pacāre* (to satisfy).

tempus – "Contemporaries" live at the same time ("con-" from *cum* = together, with).

An "extemporaneous" speaker talks on the spur of the moment (*ex* = out of and *tempus*) without taking time to prepare. Nowadays the word often means "without notes or teleprompter."

The word "tempest" appears in English during the mid-thirteenth century meaning "a violent storm" and is derived from the Latin *tempestās* (storm, weather, season). The meaning evolved from "period of time" to "period of weather" to "bad weather" to "storm." It is interesting to note that words for "weather" were originally words for "time" in languages from Brittany to Russia.

Note the suffix "-ous" of "tempestuous."

The "tense" of a verb refers to the time of the action it is describing (present, future, etc.)

urbs – "Interurban" buses run between cities (*inter* = between, among, and *urbs*).

City dwellers moved to the "suburbs" to get away from urban problems but still remained close enough (*sub* = close to, up to) in order to enjoy the city's amenities.

An "urbane" person possesses the polish regarded as characteristic of sophisticated social life in major cities.

audiō – An "audience" listens.

The sound of church bells was "audible" all over the city.

The prefix of "inaudible" is negative.

The word "audit" came into English during the fifteenth century meaning "a hearing, an official examination of accounts," so called because the procedure was oral.

After listening to instructions, the children "obeyed" them. The word comes from the Latin *oboediō* (*ob* = for the sake of, on account of, for, and *audiō*) and literally means "to listen to."

The noun "obeisance" appeared in English during the late fourteenth century derived from the same source through the Old French present participle (*obeisant*) from the verb *obeir*.

The prefix of "disobedient" also is derived from Latin (*dis* = separate, apart, reversal). It has a negative sense.

crēdō – Note the "-ous" suffix of "credulous." Be sure to distinguish between "credulous," which describes people "so full of belief that they are naïve," and "credible" meaning "believable."

182 • Latin for the New Millennium: Teacher's Manual, Level 1

The word "credit" appeared in English during the 1520s through the Middle French *credit* meaning "belief or trust" from the Latin participle of *crēdō*, used as a noun, meaning "loan." The original sense was commercial; the idea of honor dates to 1600, the academic sense to 1904, the movie/broadcasting sense to 1914. The term "credit rating" surfaced in 1958.

The invention of the telephone is <u>accredited</u> to Alexander Graham Bell (*ad* = to). The French *acréditer* (to credit someone with a sum) is the source for the English word (1610s).

"Credentials" are the *bona fidēs* given as evidence of trust, authority, and rights to privileges.

"Creed" is a spelling version of the Old English *creda*, referring to a statement of Christian belief. Its meaning broadened during the seventeenth century to mean "any statement of belief." The diphthong appeared during the Great Vowel Shift to reflect the long sound.

The prefix of "incredible" is negative as in the Latin *incrēdibilis* (not believable). It describes something so extraordinary as to seem unbelievable.

The noun "grant" came into English around 1200, meaning "consent, permission" through the Old French *granter*, a variant of *creanter* from the present participle of *crēdō*. The verb appeared a century later meaning "to allow, permit" and shortly thereafter "to admit, acknowledge."

During the fourteenth century "miscreant" meant "unbeliever" ("mis" from *minus* = less), derived from the Old French *mescreant*. The sense of "villain" was first recorded in 1590 when it was used by Spenser in *The Faerie Queene* 5.2.6.8.

gerō – A <u>belligerent</u> person likes to wage war.

One of the meanings of *gerō* is "to bring." The prefix of "congestion" is derived from *cum* (with, together); hence the word means "a gathering together." The medical sense dates to the 1630s; the meaning "a crowding together" appears in 1883.

The word "digest" appeared during the late fourteenth century meaning "a collection of writings" from the Latin *digerō* (*dis* = apart, and *gerō* = to carry) which meant "to divide, distribute, arrange." The medical meaning "to assimilate food in bowels" is attested during the late fourteenth century, also.

A "gerund" is a verbal noun and indicates something that is to be carried on, e.g., Eating is necessary for life.

The word "gesture" came into English during the early fifteenth century meaning "a way of carrying the body." The restricted sense of "a movement by a part of the body" dates to the 1550s; the figurative sense of "action undertaken in good will to express feeling" to 1916.

A "jest" in the early thirteenth century meant "a narrative of exploits" through the Old French *geste* (action, exploits) from the Latin participle *gesta* (deeds) of *gerō* (to carry, behave, act). The sense of "jest" descended through "idle tale" (fifteenth century) to "mocking speech" (1540s) to "joke" (1550s).

The Latin *regerō* (literally, "to carry back, to record") is the root of "register" which appeared in English during the late fourteenth century through the Old French *registre* (thirteenth century) and the medieval Latin *registrum* (list, matters, recorded). The musical sense dates to 1811 in reference to "the range of a voice or instrument." A "cash register" (1875) automatically records currency transactions.

The word "suggest" appears in English during the 1520s, derived from the Latin *suggerō* (to supply, bring up; *sub* = up to, and *gerō*). The sense evolved from the Latin "to heap up, build" to "bring forward an idea." The related noun "suggestion" appeared earlier (during the mid-fourteenth century) and meant "a prompting to evil." This original notion is preserved in "suggestive" (1630s); the indecent aspect appeared in 1888. Its use in hypnotism began in 1887.

Chapter 9 • 183

sciō – The Latin *conscientia* (*cum* = with, together) means "joint knowledge, knowledge within oneself, moral sense"; hence "conscience" refers to one's innermost thoughts, feelings, or intentions.

Note the "-ous" suffix of "conscientious."

On the other hand, the word "conscious" is derived from the Latin *conscius* (knowing, aware, sharing knowledge). It came into English around 1600.

The prefix of "subconscious" means "under, below"; hence "not wholly conscious." The word appears in English in 1823. Its psychological sense is attested in 1886.

A <u>prescient</u> person knows of events before they happen (*pre* = before, in front of).

An <u>omniscient</u> person knows everything (*omnis* = all, every).

The word "plebiscite" came into English in 1860 derived from the Latin *plebs* (the people) and *scitum*, the past participle of *sciscō* (to approve, decree, appoint), the inchoative form of *sciō*.

The word "nice," which came into English during the late thirteenth century meaning "foolish, stupid, senseless" is derived from the Latin *nescius* (*nē* = not) meaning "ignorant, unaware." The sense developed from "timid" (pre-thirteenth century); to "fussy, fastidious" (late fourteenth century); to "dainty, delicate" (around 1400); to "precise, careful" (1500s) which is preserved in the phrase "nice distinction"; to "agreeable, delightful" (1769); to "kind, thoughtful" (1830). In *Northanger Abbey* Jane Austen wrote:

> Catherine: ". . . it is a <u>nice</u> book . . ."
>
> Henry: ". . . and this is a very <u>nice</u> day, and we are taking a very <u>nice</u> walk; and you are two very <u>nice</u> ladies. Oh. It is a very <u>nice</u> word indeed! It does for everything."

See what happens when a word is used to describe anything and everything—it is the bane of an English teacher's existence!

sentiō – The prefix of "consent" means "with, together" (*cum*); hence the word means "agreement in sentiment."

The prefix of "assent" (from *ad* by assimilation) means "toward, with regard to, etc." The word derives from the Latin *adsentor* (to agree with).

The prefix of "dissent" is negative as is that of "insensible."

The word "nonsense" means "no sense" (*nōn* = not); hence, "foolish, of little or no use." It came into English during the 1610s.

The prefix of "resent" means "again" and is also an intensive here. The word is derived from the Latin through the Old French *resentir* (to feel again) and appeared in English around 1600 meaning "to be angry or provoked at."

The Latin verb *sentiō* means "to perceive by any one of the five senses"; hence something "perceived by the nose" is a "scent."

The word "sensuous" was coined by Milton (1640s) to recover the original meaning of "sensual," which had acquired a lascivious connotation, but by 1870 "sensuous" had started down the same path.

The word "sentence" appeared in English during the late thirteenth century meaning "doctrine." By 1300 it meant "punishment imposed by a court." The idea of a "grammatically complete thought" is attested during the mid-fifteenth century from the Latin *sententia* (opinion, judgment), itself derived from the present participle of *sentiō*.

A person who is "sententious" is full of self-righteousness and engages in excessive moralizing. The word is definitely pejorative.

184 • Latin for the New Millennium: Teacher's Manual, Level 1

Humans are "sentient" beings because they have the power of perception, of feeling.

A "sentiment" can be a feeling, emotion, or opinion.

veniō – "Advent" (*ad* – to, toward, and *veniō*) is the period leading up to Christmas. It celebrates the impending arrival (*adveniō*) of the Christ Child.

The Latin *adventīcius* means "foreign, extraneous, unearned." Meeting an old friend on the street of New York was <u>adventitious</u>, but it led to a delightful lunch and lots of chatter.

The word "adventure" appeared in English around 1200 meaning "chance, fortune, wonder, miracle." By 1300 it had acquired the nuance of risk or danger through the idea of "a trial of one's chances." The meaning of "perilous undertaking" was added in the late fourteenth century, and by the 1560s it also meant "a novel or exciting incident."

An "avenue" is a "way of approach." The word appeared in English around 1600 and was military in origin. The meaning shifted to "a broad tree-lined roadway" in the 1650s, then to "a wide main street" in 1846, especially in the United States.

The word "convent" came into English around 1200 through the Anglo-French *covent* from the Latin *conventus* (*cum* = together, and *veniō*; an assembly). In Medieval Latin it referred to a "religious house," but such houses were not exclusively feminine until the eighteenth century. The Middle English spelling remains in London's "Covent Garden."

The Latin *conveniō*, which can also mean "to agree, be suitable" as well as "to meet, assemble," is the source for the meaning of "covenant."

The prefix of "inconvenient" is negative.

The Latin *ēveniō* (*ex* = out, and *veniō*; come out, result, happen) is the source for "event."

The words "invent" and "inventive," which did not appear in English until the early fifteenth century, are derived from the Latin *inveniō* (*in* = in, into, and *veniō*) meaning "to come upon, find, discover." The meanings "to make up, to think up, produce by original thought" date to the 1530s.

A "parvenue" is an upstart. The word is first seen in English in 1802 through the French *parvenu*, referring to an obscure person who "has made his fortune, come up in the world," from the Latin *praeveniō* (*prae* = before and *veniō*).

The Latin *reveniō* (to come back) is the source for the Old French *revenue* (a return) and the English "revenue," which meant "a return on property or possessions," i.e., income (early fifteenth century). The meaning of "public income" appeared in the 1680s.

The Latin *subveniō* (*sub* = up to, and *veniō*) means "to come to the support of, provide help" and then (of ideas) "to come to the mind." Therefore, a "souvenir" helps call to mind a particular occasion, event, or person. Years after she became famous, the pianist found a program of her first concert which she had kept as a <u>souvenir</u>. The word is first attested in 1775, coming through the French *souvenir* (to remember) from the Latin.

The word "venture" is a shortened form of "adventure" (see above).

tandem – None

REVIEW 3: CHAPTERS 7–9
(PP. 153–166)

PAGE 153

TEACHING TIP

One way to conduct a fun vocabulary review is to play principal part baseball with verbs, a game that can easily be converted to accommodate nouns also.

- Instruct the students to review individually the words on p. 153 (SE) for a short amount of time; meanwhile the teacher should use one of the CPOs to put on display a drawing of a baseball diamond with each of the four bases labeled.
- Divide the class into two teams and instruct each team to line up in the batting order their team chooses to use. The teacher is always the pitcher.
- Toss a coin to see which team is at bat first.
- The teacher pitches a verb, either in English or the first principal part of the verb in Latin, whichever way the teacher prefers.
- The person at bat, if the verb is pitched in English, replies with as many principal parts of the pitched verb as possible and gains one base for each part correctly given. If the verb is pitched in Latin, the person at bat replies with the remaining three principal parts and the verb's meaning in English.
- If the person at bat cannot give the first principal part, if the verb is pitched in English, or the second principal part, if the verb is pitched in Latin, he is out.
- Normal baseball rules apply. Three outs and the next team is up. There are no strikes, bunts, or fouls.
- If the person at bat makes a one, two, or three base hit, the number of correct answers the next person up gives will determine how many bases the person will advance or if he will be driven home by that next player.

To play baseball with nouns, if the teacher pitches the noun in English, the four parts of the answer are the nominative singular, genitive singular, gender, and derivative. If the nominative singular of the noun is pitched in Latin, the four parts of the answer are the genitive singular, gender, meaning, and derivative.

PAGE 154

Standards 1.1, 1.2

▶ EXERCISE 1 ANSWERS

	Active	Passive	Active	Passive	Active
Singular					
First person	gerō	geror	crēdō	crēdor	veniō
Second person	geris	gereris	crēdis	crēderis	venīs
Third person	gerit	geritur	crēdit	crēditur	venit
Plural					
First person	gerimus	gerimur	crēdimus	crēdimur	venīmus
Second person	geritis	geriminī	crēditis	crēdiminī	venītis
Third person	gerunt	geruntur	crēdunt	crēduntur	veniunt
Infinitive	gerere	gerī	crēdere	crēdī	venīre

▶ EXERCISE 2 ANSWERS

Singular					
Nominative	cōnsul	caput	fortitūdō	nox	rēte
Genitive	cōnsulis	capitis	fortitūdinis	noctis	rētis
Dative	cōnsulī	capitī	fortitūdinī	noctī	rētī
Accusative	cōnsulem	caput	fortitūdinem	noctem	rēte
Ablative	cōnsule	capite	fortitūdine	nocte	rētī
Vocative	cōnsul	caput	fortitūdō	nox	rēte

Plural					
Nominative	cōnsulēs	capita	fortitūdines	noctēs	rētia
Genitive	cōnsulum	capitum	fortitūdinum	noctium	rētium
Dative	cōnsulibus	capitibus	fortitūdinibus	noctibus	rētibus
Accusative	cōnsulēs	capita	fortitūdinēs	noctēs	rētia
Ablative	cōnsulibus	capitibus	fortitūdinibus	noctibus	rētibus
Vocative	cōnsulēs	capita	fortitūdinēs	noctēs	rētia

▶ EXERCISE 3 ANSWERS

1. Poēta dīcit passerem esse dēliciās mulieris.
   The poet says that the sparrow is the pet of the woman.
2. Catullus sentit sē verba senum sevērōrum unīus assis aestimāre.
   Catullus feels that he does not care a bit for the words of the severe old men.
3. Catullus scit amōrem semper vincere.
   Catullus knows that love always wins.

PAGE 155

Standards 1.1, 1.2

▶ EXERCISE 3 ANSWERS, CONTINUED

4. Pȳthia scit nāvēs Graecōs servāre posse.

 Pythia knows that the ships can save the Greeks.

5. Themistoclēs sentit sē verba Pȳthiae intellegere.

 Themistocles feels that he understands the words of Pythia.

6. Themistoclēs scit Graecōs nāvigāre dēbēre.

 Themistocles knows that the Greeks ought to sail.

7. Cicero intellegit Catilīnam mortem cīvium petere.

 Cicero understands that Catiline seeks the death of the citizens.

8. Cicero scit Rōmam ā Catilīnā līberārī dēbēre.

 Cicero knows that Rome ought to be freed from Catiline.

9. Hominēs audiunt cōnsulem pācem servāre posse.

 People hear that the consul can save the peace.

▶ EXERCISE 4 ANSWERS

1. cum timōre   We think about Catiline with fear.
2. armīs   Catiline can be conquered with weapons.
3. ad mare   Men and women ought to go to the sea and sail.
4. Ab urbe   They come from the city to the fields.
5. in gremiō   The sparrow remains on the lap of the girl.

PAGE 156

Standards 1.1, 1.2, 2.1

▶ EXERCISE 5 ANSWERS

1. Oculīs meīs videō.
2. Timōre līberārī dēbēmus.
3. Ad urbem venīre dēbēs.
4. In urbe manēre dēcernitis.
5. Cum amōre verba audiō.
6. Exemplar ā rēge et ā ducibus darī dēbet.

▶ EXERCISE 6 ANSWERS

Catullus feels that he is miserable. For the girl does not want to save <their> love. Catullus ought to understand that love cannot be preserved. Love does not remain in the spirit (heart) of the girl. The girl does not seek Catullus. The girl does not want to hear the words of Catullus. The girl does not want to give Catullus kisses. And so Catullus must strengthen his spirit and walk away from the girl.

Review 3: Chapters 7–9 • 189

TEACHING TIP

The Latin paragraph in Exercise 6 is based upon Catullus 8, which is provided here for the teacher's convenience. The teacher may wish to share this poem with the students and point out some of the phrases that illustrate grammar points that the students have already learned such as the vocative "*miser Catulle*" in line 1, the present tense "*vidēs*" in line two, and the third declension noun "*sōlēs*" in lines 3 and 8, etc.

Catullus 8

1   Miser Catulle, dēsinās ineptīre,
    et quod vidēs perisse perditum dūcās.
    fulsēre quondam candidī tibi sōlēs,
    cum ventitābās quō puella dūcēbat
5   amāta nōbīs quantum amābitur nūlla.
    ibi illa multa cum iocōsa fīēbant,
    quae tū volēbās nec puella nōlēbat,
    fulsēre vērē candidī tibi sōlēs.
    nunc iam illa nōn vult; tū quoque inpotē<ns nōlī>,
10 nec quae fugit sectāre, nec miser vīve,
    sed obstinātā mente perfer, obdūrā.
    valē, puella, iam Catullus obdūrat,
    nec tē requīret nec rogābit invītam.
    at tū dolēbis, cum rogāberis nūlla.
15 scelesta, vae tē! quae tibi manet vīta?
    quis nunc tē adībit? cui vidēberis bella?
    quem nunc amābis? cuius esse dīcēris?
    quem basiābis? cui labella mordēbis?
    at tū, Catulle, destinātus obdūrā.

CONSIDERING THE CLASSICAL GODS

PAGE 157

Standards 2.1, 2.2, 3.1, 3.2
ODF 3.7

TEACHER BY THE WAY

Other myths that include Apollo and which may be mentioned in conjunction with this reading about him are the myths of Marsyas, Pan, Typhaon, Tityus, Daphne, Niobe, Sibyl, and Aesculapius.

The emperor Augustus was especially devoted to Apollo and named his legion, which probably served with him at Actium (31 BCE), *Apollināris* after the god. Augustus built a temple to Apollo on the Palatine Hill in gratitude for his victory at Actium.

In the beginning Delphi was sacred to Mother Earth and was guarded by the terrible serpent Python, who was later killed by Apollo. Thus, the Olympian deities supercede the earlier, chthonic, earth-connected deities. Recent collaboration between archaeologists and geologists leads them to believe that the priestess's trance may also have been stimulated by the gases emitted from the area.

COMPREHENSION QUESTIONS AND ANSWERS FOR PAGES 157–158 (SE)

Reproducible versions of the questions alone are available at **www.lnm.bolchazy.com**.

1. What Greek ideal does Apollo represent?

   Apollo represents the Greek ideal of physical beauty and emotional tranquility: possessing both perfectly proportioned body and rational intellect.

2. With what realm of human endeavor is Apollo identified and with whom does he share this interest?

   Apollo, as god of reason and intellect, is associated with the arts. He is the leader of the nine Muses who each preside over a specific art.

3. How did Juno's jealousy about Leto reveal itself?

   Juno attempted to prolong Leto's birth pangs and did so for nine days, at which point Leto delivered her twins Artemis and Apollo on the island of Delos.

4. Where would one travel to visit the site most special and sacred to Apollo? What makes that site so special?

   One would travel to Delphi, Greece, to the sanctuary of Apollo, where the Pythian priestess presided over the oracle and provided cryptic responses to inquiries.

5. What was the Delphic Oracle's response to the Athenians' inquiry about the war with Xerxes and the Persians? How is the response characteristically difficult to interpret?

    The oracle prophesied, *"Athēniēnsēs mūrīs ligneīs servārī possunt."* This response was obscure and the Athenians did not initially realize that *"mūrīs ligneīs"* referred to their ships with which they defeated the Persians at the famous Battle of Salamis.

6. Why do you suppose that NASA named its space expeditions to the moon after Apollo?

    Apollo was chosen because he represented rational intellect (and was god of the sun).

PAGE 158

TEACHER BY THE WAY
Some of the youths with whom Apollo was in love died and were turned into flowers and plants, for example Hyacinthus (whose name was given to the flower hyacinth), or Cyparissus (whose name was given to the cypress tree).

Apollo became enamored of the beautiful Hyacinthus. During a discus-throwing game, a gust of wind or perhaps an accident caused the discus to hit and kill Hyacinthus. Several versions of the story claim that Zephyrus (the west wind) was a jealous rival for the boy's attention. From his blood came the hyacinth (not our version of the flower) whose petals are marked with the syllables of lament *"ai, ai."*

Another beautiful young man loved by Apollo was Cyparissus. He was so attached to a pet stag that when it was accidentally killed by his throw of the javelin, he was inconsolable. Yearning for death, he shed so many tears that his body was drying up. Apollo took pity on him and turned him into a cypress tree, a common symbol of mourning.

Both of these tales are examples of aetiological myths that explain the origin of a flower and tree respectively and are likewise examples of etymological myths that explain the origin of the name of something.

TEACHING TIP
Instruct the students to locate Delos on the map on pp. xxxiv–xxxv (SE).

PAGE 159
Standards 1.1, 2.1

TEACHER BY THE WAY
The Temple of Apollo built in the archaic Doric style dates from the sixth century BCE and replaced an earlier temple on the same site. Note that the columns are monolithic, carved from a single piece of stone. The Greeks also made columns built from a set of pieces called drums.

Tradition states that Corinth was perhaps founded by Sisyphus. When Poseidon and Helius vied for control of the city, the sea god was awarded the isthmus. His temple is there and the Isthmian games are celebrated in his honor.

In ancient times ships were sometimes placed on rollers and dragged across the isthmus to avoid the lengthy route around the Peloponnesus. Corinth became a very wealthy and powerful city because of its commercial importance. It was destroyed by Rome in 146 BCE. The temple in the illustration on p. 159 (SE) was the only structure to survive the sack of the city. Julius Caesar did much restoration work in 46 BCE.

PASSAGE TRANSLATION
Cassandra is the daughter of the Trojan king. Apollo loves Cassandra, but is not loved by Cassandra. Apollo gives Cassandra a gift, if Cassandra wants to love Apollo. The gift is this: Cassandra can know the future. Cassandra has the gift, but at last she decides not to love Apollo. Then Apollo gives Cassandra another gift. The other gift is this: people do not believe Cassandra.

The Greeks prepare a wooden horse and give it to the Trojans. Then Cassandra says that the Greeks design death for the Trojans. The Trojans, however, do not listen to Cassandra. The horse enters the city of the Trojans, and with the horse, death comes to the Trojans.

TEACHER BY THE WAY
Cassandra was one of the twelve daughters of Priam. There are two versions regarding how she became a prophetess. As a child she was sleeping in Apollo's temple while her parents were attending his festival. Two sacred snakes licked her ears and she acquired the gift of prophecy. In another more familiar version, Apollo promised her the ability to foretell the future if she returned his love. She agreed to the bargain, but then rejected him. The god could not withdraw his gift but cursed her by making her an unheeded predictor of impending doom. She warned Priam that there were armed men inside the wooden horse and tried to burn it. When she became the captive of Agamemnon, she foretold his death and hers. She also predicted the wanderings of Odysseus. Cassandra did not speak again until she reached Argos. Then in a frenzied speech she alluded to the the bloody feasts, past and present, and the coming of Agamemnon's avenger (Orestes). She prayed to the gods for a swift death and entered the palace where Clytemnestra killed her.

CONNECTING WITH THE ANCIENT WORLD

PAGE 160
Standards 2.1, 2.2, 3.1, 3.2

TEACHING TIP
The teacher may instruct students to research what was worn by other classes of society and what other items were symbolic of rank. Examples include red shoes for senators and the ring for equites.

TEACHER BY THE WAY
Two other special kinds of togas were the *toga picta*, which was crimson with gold embroidery and worn in triumphal processions by victorious generals. The *toga pulla* was a dark gray color and worn by men in mourning. This tradition continues even today since black is often worn as a sign of mourning.

TEACHER BY THE WAY
The spinning and weaving of woolen material to make togas was done at home. However, the finishing process was usually given to a professional. A semicircular cut was made about five yards long and four yards wide. Part of this was pressed into long narrow folds by a fuller (*fullō*) which were then gathered together over the left shoulder.

When a toga needed to be cleaned and whitened, it was again sent to the fuller, who washed it by treading on it in a large vat of water mixed with an alkaline detergent, usually urine collected from vessels placed in corners of the streets for this purpose. It was then beaten with wooden sticks or mallets to close up the texture, then washed and dried again to clean and shrink it. After being dried on a semicircular frame, the toga was placed over a pot of sulphur for bleaching. It was then hung up, brushed to raise the nap, and put in a press to smooth and condense it.

Cleaning was a necessary expense because the togas, which were white and heavy, had to look fresh and be draped properly. This required professional handling and could not be done at home.

PAGE 161

COMPREHENSION QUESTIONS AND ANSWERS FOR PAGES 160–161 (SE)

Reproducible versions of the questions alone are available at **www.lnm.bolchazy.com**.

1. Explain how tombstones reveal important information about the ancient Romans.

   Tombstone inscriptions provide all kinds of information that helps us learn about the Romans. For instance, the inscription *Domum servāvit, lānam fēcit* documents the significance of the woman's role as a maker of wool.

2. What would a Roman's clothing tell you about the person's status?

   Roman male citizens could be identified by their *toga virīlis*, while those holding high political office wore a *toga praetexta*, with its purple border. Triumphant military leaders wore gold-embroidered garments called *togae pictae*. It was more difficult to distinguish a woman's status—one would have to judge based on the quality of the *stola* she wore.

3. Explain the history of the English word "candidate."

   Romans running for political office wore a snow-white toga called a *toga candida*. *Candidātus* in Latin means "dressed in a *toga candida*." The English word "candidate" is thus derived from the Latin *candidātus*, a word closely connected to *candida*.

 TEACHER BY THE WAY

Gold necklaces (*monīlia*) and bracelets (*armillae*) in the form of snakes, pendants of a single pearl (*ūniōnēs*), and brooches (*fībulae*) of bronze, silver, or gold studded with jewels were all part of Roman women's adornments. Rings, worn by both men and women, could be set with gems. A brooch (*fībula*) was used to fasten cloaks. Most prized gems were opals, emeralds, and pearls. Engagement rings were often made of iron. The wealthy had lighter rings for summer and heavier ones for winter. Cameos of semiprecious stones were especially popular. Suetonius mentions the single pearl Caesar gave to Servilia, the mother of Brutus. Its cost was exorbitant.

EXPLORING ROMAN GOVERNMENT

PAGE 162
Standards 2.1, 3.1, 3.2, 4.2

COMPREHENSION QUESTIONS AND ANSWERS FOR PAGES 162–164 (SE)

Reproducible versions of the questions alone are available at **www.lnm.bolchazy.com**.

1. In what ways were Athenian democracy and Roman republicanism similar?

    Both systems were developed in response to all political power being in the hands of an individual—the tyrant in Athens and the king in Rome. The collective will of the citizens, not the individual will of an autocrat, decided public policy. Both Athens and Rome encouraged political debate and discussion of the issues. Both systems excluded women from the political process and neither system enfranchised all the males.

2. How did the Roman education system prepare young men to participate in the political process?

    Since public speaking played an important role in public life and the political process, young Roman men learned history, philosophy, literature, and rhetoric, as these subjects would prepare them for engaging in public debate.

3. Why did Cicero entitle his speeches against Mark Antony the "Philippics"?

    Cicero entitled his admonitions against Mark Antony's political ambitions to rule Rome the "Philippics" consciously alluding to Demosthenes's speeches that warned the Greeks about Philip II of Macedon's plan to conquer the Greek city-states.

4. What does the use of "Philippics" connote today?

    "Philippics" connotes very bitter opposition speeches.

5. To what was a Roman referring when he cited *mōs maiōrum*?

    In citing *mōs maiōrum*, a Roman was calling on the tradition of his ancestors, of the traditional lawgivers and the traditional political practices of the revered past.

6. How did Greece and Rome differ with respect to citizen naturalization and how did that difference affect the size or scale of their respective citizen communities?

    The Athenians jealously guarded citizenship and seldom naturalized those who had not been born to Athenian parents. Rome, on the other hand, granted citizenship to Roman allies and conquered peoples, and even to former slaves. Thus Rome enlarged its citizenship with a population of citizens in the millions by the first century BCE while the Athenian citizenry numbered only in the tens of thousands.

7. Explain how the Athenian policy of limited citizenship led to Athens's downfall.

    Despite the advice of politicians who sought to enlarge the citizen body in the face of the Macedonian threat, Athenians persisted in maintaining the status quo with respect to citizenship. Subsequently, when trying to stop the Macedonians as they invaded Greece, Athens could not staff an army of sufficient size to withstand the invaders.

196 • Latin for the New Millennium: Teacher's Manual, Level 1

8. How did the difference in scale between Athens and Rome affect the experience of popular politics?

Athenian citizens, irrespective of socioeconomic or education status, voted directly on legislation in the assembly, *ekklêsia*, while Romans voted as members of very large voting blocks, the "centuries," *Comitia Centuriāta*, or tribes, *Comitia Tribūta*. A large percentage of Athenian citizens themselves served as a juror, board member, or participant in the Council of 500, *boulê*. In Rome, however, important public offices were monopolized by a small elite group of wealthy and well-connected families, and the Senate, which handled most of the real work of government, was highly hierarchical.

9. Discuss the two crucial mistakes made by the Athenians in the course of their democracy.

Prone to overambitious projects and snap judgments, the Athenians launched imperialistic wars like the disastrous Sicilian expedition during the Peloponnesian Wars and executed the famous philosopher Socrates.

10. The final paragraph in Professor Ober's essay presents a series of historical cause and effect developments and events. In bullet or outline form, present this series.

  • Ambitions of powerful individuals (Marius, Sulla, Caesar, et alii) led them to retain command of their armies and convert citizens to obedient clients

  • Rome's wars of expansion created a large class of impoverished citizens and the army was the best way to improve their lot

  • Legionary soldiers owe allegiance more to their leaders than to the state and this allegiance led citizen-soldiers to fight their fellow citizens

  • A series of civil wars led to the collapse of the Republic and the creation of the Roman imperial principate

11. What did the collapse of the Roman Republic portend for future centuries?

The collapse of the Roman Republic brought to an end a long history of popular government in antiquity. Not until the Italian Renaissance would the forms of republic and democracy reappear.

Review 3: Chapters 7–9 • 197

PAGE 164

TEACHER BY THE WAY

Marius and Sulla are often portrayed as opposites—the equestrian versus the patrician, the *populāris* versus the optimate. However, as was usual in Rome, such political and social categorizations are far too simplistic.

Marius gained distinction while fighting under Scipio Aemilianus in Spain and, with the help of the Metelli, became a tribune in 119 BCE. However, he opposed Metellus Delmaticus on election procedures and was later prosecuted (unsuccessfully) for bribery. He became praetor in 115, served as governor of Spain where he impressed his peers, and married into the aristocratic Julian family, thereby becoming the uncle of the yet unborn Julius Caesar. In 109 the brother of Dalmaticus was elected consul, forgave the promising Marius for past differences, and took him as his senior legate to fight Jugurtha. This alliance, however, did not last long as Marius intrigued against his commander in the consular elections and was successful in 107 BCE.

Marius took over the war against Jugurtha and, with the help of his quaestor Sulla, captured the Numidian leader. Sulla continued to serve under Marius during the wars against the Germans, but, chafing underneath because Marius claimed all the credit for winning the Jugurthine War, he brought the feud to a head in 91 by supporting the *optimātēs* who disapproved of Marius's actions concerning the exile of Metellus Numidicus. This alliance was strengthened by marriage ties when Sulla wed the daughter of Metellus Delmaticus.

After gaining the consulship in 88 BCE, Sulla was given the command against Mithridates. However, the tribune Sulpicius Rufus had it transferred to Marius. In response, Sulla marched on Rome with his army and took it by force. Sulpicius was killed while Marius and his supporters with difficulty escaped the bloodshed. Sulla then left for the East and by 86 had driven Mithridates from Greece (taking the time to sack Athens during his pursuit). The two negotiated mutually advantageous terms of peace, and Sulla, who had been relieved of his command by the *populārēs* in control at Rome, invaded Italy. Marius had died in 86 BCE during his seventh consulship, but a vicious civil war ensued with his adherents, which ended with the Battle of the Colline Gate in 82.

Appointing himself dictator, Sulla set out to overhaul the government. His many constitutional reforms were designed to put the *optimātēs* firmly in control of the state, but these were largely rescinded by 70 BCE. He himself abdicated his position, became consul in 80, retired in 79 BCE, and died the following year.

Marius is most famous for holding seven consulships and, more importantly, for reforming the army by discarding the property qualification for enlistment. He thus relieved Rome of its overpopulation of landless citizens and fashioned a fighting force loyal only to its commander. Ironically, it was this new military organization that allowed Sulla to march successfully on Rome. He was the first general to do so but not the last, for the age of "nabobs on horseback" had begun.

MĪRĀBILE AUDĪTŪ

PAGE 165
Standards 1.1, 4.1

PHRASES AND MOTTOES VOCABULARY

Ē plūribus ūnum.
    plūribus – more, an increasing number of
    ūnum – one

Ex officiō.
    officium, officiī, *n.* – office

PAGE 166

Audēmus iūra nostra dēfendere.
    audeō, audēre, ausus sum – to dare
    dēfendō, dēfendere, dēfendī, dēfēnsum – to defend
    iūs, iūris, *n.* – right
    noster, nostra, nostrum – our

Ense petit placidam sub lībertāte quiētem.
    ensis, ensis, *m.* – sword
    lībertās, lībertātis, *f.* – freedom
    plācidus, plācida, plācidum – quiet
    quiēs, quiētis, *f.* – rest
    sub + *ablative* – under

Iūstitia omnibus.
    iūstitia, iūstitiae, *f.* – justice
    omnis, omne – every, all

Montānī semper līberī.
    montānus, montānī, *m.* – mountaineer

Salūs populī suprēma lēx estō!
    estō (*future imperative*) – let it be
    populus, populī, *m.* – people
    salūs, salūtis, *f.* – salvation
    suprēmus, suprēma, suprēmum – supreme

Sīc semper tyrannīs.
    sīc (*adv.*) – thus
    tyrannus, tyrannī, *m.* – tyrant

TEACHER BY THE WAY
Assassin John Wilkes Booth, after shooting President Abraham Lincoln, while crossing the stage of the Ford Theater, shouted "*Sīc semper tyrannīs*" to the audience.

TEACHING TIP
The teacher may wish to run a competition in which students can design the best seal with the best motto for the Latin class. Students need not be good at drawing to do this. Any picture a student would like to use on the class seal can be found on the internet.

TEACHING TIP
A matching exercise may be used to assess how well the students have mastered the mottoes on this page. The answers are provided for the teacher's convenience.

Matching: Choose the correct answer from both column A and column B

1. *Salūs populī suprēma lēx estō!*
2. *Ense petit placidam sub lībertāte quiētem.*
3. *Sīc semper tyrannīs.*
4. *Audēmus iūra nostra dēfendere.*
5. *Iūstitia omnibus.*
6. *Montānī semper līberī.*

Column A
A. He seeks with a sword quiet rest under freedom.
B. The people of the mountains are always free.
C. Let the salvation of the people be a supreme law.
D. Justice to all people.
E. Thus always <it happens> to tyrants.
F. We dare to defend our rights.

Column B
G. motto of West Virginia
H. motto of Virginia
I. motto of Alabama
J. motto of the District of Columbia
K. motto of Massachusetts
L. motto of Missouri

Answers:
1. C – L
2. A – K
3. E – H
4. F – I
5. D – J
6. B – G

CHAPTER 10 (PP. 167–182)

GRAMMAR IN LANGUAGE FACTS

Third Conjugation –*iō* Verbs: Present Tense Active and Passive, Present Active and Passive Infinitive; Third Declension Adjectives; Substantive Adjectives

PAGE 167

Standards 1.1, 2.1

RRA 6A

MEMORĀBILE DICTŪ VOCABULARY

Danaī, Danaōrum, *m. pl.* – the Greeks

et – even (sometimes *et* has this meaning rather than "and")

ferentēs (accusative plural) – bearing

id – it

quidquid – whatever

TEACHER BY THE WAY

The discovery of Troy near Hissarlik in modern Turkey is testament to the power of story. For it was childhood tales of the Trojan War that inspired Heinrich Schliemann to make finding the historical Troy his life's passion. His dream led him to conduct excavations beginning in 1870. While the stratum that he considered Homeric Troy was misidentified and the authenticity of the finds he called "Priam's Treasure" remains debated, Schliemann did find an ancient site, quite probably Troy. Subsequent excavations and studies have found evidence of inhabitation since 3000 BCE and some nine distinct strata, with level VI contemporaneous with what is believed to have been the time of the Trojan War. Excavations at this important site that is dominated by a large wooden horse continue.

TEACHING TIP

Many students will recognize the Trojan horse as the subject of the chapter page image. Teachers might ask students *Quid est?* To help students with the vocabulary needed to answer the question, direct them: *Spectāte titulum in pāginā.* The teacher may point to the story title while giving the command.

TEACHING TIP

Chapter 6A of RRA explains the events that happened during the time the literature of Chapters 10–18 of *Latin for the New Millennium* was being written. Teachers may wish to have students consult Chapter 6A of RRA as often as necessary during these chapters.

PAGE 168

Standards 1.1, 2.1, 3.1, 3.2

TRANSLATION OF LATIN PASSAGE
About the Trojan Horse

The Greeks listen to the words of Ulysses and make plans. A great wooden horse is built by the Greeks. Brave soldiers are hidden in the horse. Bad things and things deadly for the Trojans are prepared by the Greek soldiers hidden in the horse. Then the horse is moved to the gate of the city. The Trojans see the horse and say that they do not now fear war: the horse is a gift; the Greeks are giving the horse to the gods. But the Trojans are not fortunate. For they believe that the Greeks are absent, nor do they wish to know about the danger. Now the horse is in the city. The Greeks hidden in the horse wait for night and shadows/darkness. Night comes. The armed Greeks go out from the horse into the city. The unprepared Trojans must fight against prepared and fierce enemies. The city of the Trojans cannot be saved. Troy is destroyed by the weapons of the Greeks and flames. Few are able to flee.

TEACHER BY THE WAY
Vergil had come to Augustus's attention through his literary patron, Augustus's close friend Gaius Maecenas, as well as through his earlier works. The *Eclogues* or *Bucolics*, a collection of short poems, were about the lives of mythical shepherds who reflect on nature, love, and poetry itself, and the *Georgics*, a didactic poem in four books, was about farming. Like the *Aeneid*, both were modeled on earlier works of Greek poetry.

TEACHER BY THE WAY
In the course of his forty-five-year reign, Augustus's achievements were many. He laid the foundation for the Roman Empire. After nearly a century of civil strife, Rome enjoyed domestic peace and stability. Having solidified Rome's conquests in both the West and the East, Augustus wisely planted his retired soldiers in these territories where he built cities complete with the amenities Rome offered—fora, basilicae, baths, temples, theatres, aqueducts, and amphitheatres. A system of roads policed by the army and a navy to protect sea routes ensured good communication and trade. Augustus was especially pleased with his work restoring Rome, which had fallen victim to deferred maintenance. His civic improvements included restoring some eighty plus temples, finishing the Basilica Julia, the Forum of Julius Caesar and the Theatre of Marcellus, and building some dozen temples including that of Mars Ultor in his forum. Suetonius tells us that Augustus boasted that he transformed Rome from a city of brick to one of marble.

PAGE 169

ANSWERS TO COMPREHENSION QUESTIONS
1. Odysseus's plan was to build a big wooden horse and fill it with Greek warriors, who would emerge from the horse at night in the city of Troy and begin the destruction of the city.
2. The Trojans thought that the horse was a gift from the gods.
3. The Greeks came out of the horse and captured Troy.

TEACHER BY THE WAY
There is a non-Homeric tradition that Anticleia was seduced by Sisyphus before she married Laertes, Odysseus's father. If so, Odysseus inherited his genes for deviousness and cleverness honestly. Additionally his maternal grandfather was a rogue and a thief. The nurse Eurycleia asked Autolycus to choose a name for his grandchild. He decided on Odysseus, whose Greek root signifies "to be angry at," since he had experienced so much animosity from so many people. It was while visiting his grandfather that he received the famous boar scar that his nurse recognized when he returned home.

Like most royal sons, Odysseus was one of Helen's many suitors, but he preferred to pursue her cousin Penelope. Odysseus shrewdly advised King Tyndareus, who feared violence once Helen made her choice, to command all the suitors to take a vow to defend and protect Helen if necessary. In gratitude, Tyndareus spoke on his behalf to Penelope's father Icarius and Penelope became Odysseus's wife.

Another dilemma soon presented itself. Odysseus heard that the time had come to make good the vow since Helen had been abducted. His strategy was to fake insanity when the ambassadors arrived. They found him plowing a field with a horse and an ox and sowing salt in the ground. Suspecting trickery, Palamedes grabbed Odysseus's baby son Telemachus and put him in front of the plow. Odysseus, not wanting to go to war but unwilling to plow over his son, accepted the inevitable and went to war.

PAGE 170
Standards 1.1, 1.2, 3.1, 4.1
Oral Exercise 1; Workbook Exercise 1

▶ EXERCISE 1 ANSWERS
1. we are desired
2. they desire
3. you flee
4. to desire
5. we flee
6. I am desired
7. you (plural) are desired
8. you (plural) are fleeing

ORAL EXERCISE 1

This exercise may be used anytime after the present tense of third –iō verbs has been presented.

While looking at the conjugation of *capiō*, ask the students to conjugate *cupiō* in the present active and passive, including the active and passive infinitives.

cupiō, cupis, cupit, cupimus, cupitis, cupiunt

cupior, cuperis, cupitur, cupimur, cupiminī, cupiuntur

cupere, cupī

TEACHING TIP

Additional reproducible worksheets, morphology charts, and their associated answer keys, related to this material, are available for download at www.lnm.bolchazy.com.

- **Verb Conjugations**

PAGE 171

Standards 1.2, 4.1
Workbook Exercise 2

▶ EXERCISE 2 ANSWERS

1.	nocturnal	nox	7.	deleted	dēleō	13.	fugitives	fugiō
2.	celebrities	celeber	8.	captured	capiō	14.	hostile	hostis
3.	paucity	paucī	9.	donation	dōnum	15.	motion	moveō
4.	perilous	perīculum	10.	fortitude	fortis	16.	felicitous	fēlīx
5.	flammable	flamma	11.	pugnacious	pugnō	17.	edifice	aedificō
6.	equine	equus	12.	cupidity	cupiō			

TEACHING TIP

Although in Exercise 2 the students are directed to find only the derivatives based on the Vocabulary to Learn, they may be interested to learn that there are other derivatives in Exercise 2. The derivation of these words is provided for the teacher's convenience.

1. creatures – from *creō* (to create, beget, produce).
2. votes – from *vōtum* (vow, prayer, wish, longing). in – from *in* (in, on, at). political – from *politicus* (political) but the root is really the Greek word πόλις, *polis* for "city."
3. despite – from *dēspiciō* (to look down on). defenders – from *dēfendō* (to repel, defend, protect). fort – from *fortis* (strong, sturdy, brave). relief – from *relevō* (to lift up, lighten, comfort, ease).
4. dense – from *dēnsus* (thick, dense). very – from *vērus* (true, real, actual); *vērāx* (truthful).
5. extremely – from *extrēmus* (outermost, last, utmost, etc.).

6. in – from *in* (in, on, at). parts – from *pars* (part, share, fraction). country – from *contrā* (against, opposite); that which is opposite, hence landscape. sports – from *portō* (to carry) through "disport." popular – from *populāris* (popular, democratic); from *populus* (the people).

7. second – from *secundus* (following, next). chapter – from *caput* (head, top, extremity). line – from *līneus* (flaxen, linen) [used as a guiding rule, rope, etc.]. author – from *augeō* (to increase, enrich); *auctor* (from the fourth principal part = one who increases, enriches).

8. in – from *in* (in, on, at).

9. accession – from *accessiō* (coming, visiting, attack; from *accēdō* – to attack, come, approach). emperor – from *imperātor* (general, commander-in-chief). Roman – from *Rōmānus* (Roman). soldiers – from *solidus* (solid, firm, dense, whole, complete). used – from *ūtor* (to use, possess, enjoy, experience). donation – from *dōnō* (to give, present). loyal – from *lēx* (law, rule, principle, contract).

10. simple – from *simplex* (single, simple, natural). remedy – from *remedium* (cure, remedy, medicine). adversity – from *adversitās* from *adversus* (opposite, in front, hostile).

11. personality – from *persōna* (character, part, person, mask) [*per* = through; *sonō* = sound: sound through a mask].

12. politicians – from *politicus* (political); from the Greek word πόλις, *polis* for "city." simply – from *simplex* (single, simple, natural).

13. in – from *in* (in, on, at). forest – from *forīs* (outside).

14. governor – from *gubernātor* (pilot). encountered – from *in* (in, on, at) + *contrā* (against). very – from *vērus* (true, real, actual); *vērāx* (truthful). reception – from *recipiō* (to take back, get back, etc.). in – from *in* (in, on, at). city – from *cīvitās* (community, state, city, citizenship).

15. picture – from *pictūra* (picture); *pingō* (to paint, decorate). industry – *industria* (diligence).

17. post office – from *pōnō* (to put, place, etc.) + *officium* (service, duty). imposing – from *impōnō* (to inflict, assign, impose, put in, lay on, etc.).

PAGE 172
Standards 1.1, 1.2

▶ EXERCISE 3 ANSWERS
1. cupimus   The Greeks say: "We desire to construct a large wooden horse."
2. capere   The Trojans must make plans against fierce enemies.
3. capiuntur Plans against the Greeks are made by me.
4. fugere   I say that few Trojans are fleeing.
5. fugiō   I flee from the city of the Trojans.

TEACHER BY THE WAY
Odysseus encounters more challenges that test his spirit and cunning upon returning to Ithaca. The Phaeacians transport him home and leave him asleep on the shore. He awakens, worried that he has been tricked, until Athena in disguise welcomes him home. She warns him about the suitors, disguises him as a beggar, and puts her plan in motion. Odysseus and his son Telemachus reunite at the hut of the swineherd Eumaeus and plan the destruction of the suitors. The disguised Odysseus goes to the palace and the first of several recognition scenes takes place. His dog sees him, wags his tail, and dies. At the palace he witnesses for himself the abuse of hospitality, the insolence of the suitors, and the predicament of his family. He is in turn mocked, insulted, and attacked by his "guests." Penelope comes to greet the stranger and orders Eurycleia, his old nurse, to wash his feet. She recognizes the boar scar but is urged to hold her tongue. Then suddenly his wife decides to hold a contest. Whoever is able to string Odysseus's bow and shoot an arrow through twelve axheads will claim her as a wife. Odysseus asks if he can participate but his request is rudely rejected by the suitors. Penelope, however, gives him permission, and Telemachus sends her to her room and puts himself in charge of the bow and the contest. Odysseus in disguise completes the task. With the help of Athena, the swineherd, and the goatherd, the bloodbath begins. The suitors and the disloyal servants are killed, but the herald and bard are spared. Odysseus does not gloat over his victory, but cautions the overjoyed Eurycleia that it was impious to gloat over slain men. When Penelope hears the news that her husband has returned and killed the suitors, she is not convinced. As a test she orders the marriage bed to be moved so he can sleep there. Odysseus protests and reveals the secret of the marriage bed that cannot be moved. It was made from the trunk of an olive tree and the whole house was built around it. Penelope is assured that he is indeed Odysseus; they are reunited and talk far into the night about all his travels. The next day he lets his father Laertes know he is alive. Meanwhile the fathers of the suitors want revenge and are ready for war. Athena stops them, and Zeus seconds the motion with a thunderbolt. Peace is restored.

PAGE 173
Standards 3.1, 4.1

TEACHING TIP
After students see the example of three, two, and one termination adjectives on p. 173 (SE), it is sometimes helpful to present them with a list of other third declension adjectives. Students may then be asked to indicate how many terminations each adjective has. While this is a simple matter for three termination adjectives, it is not always as easy for students to differentiate between two and one termination adjectives. After the students have seen the paradigms for third declension adjectives on pp. 174–175 (SE), this list of adjectives may be used again for additional declension practice. Although these adjectives will not be presented until later in this book, it is helpful to have more words to work with and the exposure to future vocabulary is good for the student.

- *celer, celeris, celere* – swift
- *crūdēlis, crūdēle* – cruel
- *difficilis, difficile* – difficult
- *dīves, dīvitis* – rich
- *dulcis, dulce* – sweet
- *facilis, facile* – easy
- *ferōx, ferōcis* – fierce, ferocious
- *omnis, omne* – every, all
- *pauper, pauperis* – poor
- *similis, simile* – like, similar
- *terribilis, terribile* – terrifying

Other third declension adjectives that are not found in this book but which may be used for the purposes described above follow.

- *dissimilis, dissimile* – unlike, dissimilar
- *gracilis, gracile* – slender, thin
- *humilis, humile* – humble
- *lēnis, lēne* – smooth, soft
- *memor, memoris* – mindful
- *reclīnis, reclīne* – leaning backward
- *sōlāris, sōlāre* – solar
- *tenuis, tenue* – thin, fine
- *vetus, veteris* – old

PAGE 174

TEACHING TIP

Instruct the students to repeat aloud the forms of *ācer*, then of *fortis*, and then of *fēlīx* after the teacher models the pronunciation of the words. Then encourage the students to create a rap, cheer, or song to help them remember the forms. Alternatively, use Bolchazy-Carducci's *Toga Beats*. The teacher may also wish to have the students compare the charts of the third declension adjectives on pp. 174–175 (SE) with the charts of the first and second declension adjectives on pp. 64 (SE) and 77 (SE).

A fun activity that includes movement and that will reinforce the differences between third declension adjectives of one, two, and three terminations follows.

- Divide the students into three teams that are as equal in number as possible.
- One group will be the masculine group, another the feminine group, and a third the neuter group.
- Move the tables and chairs in the classroom to the sides of the room.
- Instruct each group of students to line up at the back of the classroom.
- First announce a three termination adjective in Latin such as *celeber, celebris, celebre*.
- On a given signal, each group will advance one step forward and, in order, the first person of each group will say aloud in Latin the nominative singular masculine, then the feminine nominative singular, and finally the neuter form.
- On the next signal, each group moves one more step forward and, in order, the second person in each group will give the genitive singular masculine, then feminine, and finally the neuter form in Latin. The activity proceeds this way through all the singular and plural forms of *celeber*. It may be necessary, depending on the size of the classroom, to instruct the students to start taking steps backward at some point.
- This activity becomes even more fun when a two termination adjective is announced. When a word such as *fortis, forte* is given by the teacher, the masculine and feminine groups need to move close to one another while the neuter group remains separated from them. On the given signal, the groups now only two in number, one double group and one single group, advance one step forward and the first person of both the masculine and the feminine group say in unison the nominative singular of the adjective in the masculine/feminine form and the one first person in the neuter group says his form. The activity continues in this way.
- When a one termination adjective such as *fēlīx, fēlīcis* is announced, all three groups merge together into three lines close to one another. On the given signal, all three groups now standing close to one together but still in three lines, step forward and say in unison the nominative singular of the adjective in Latin. Play proceeds until the accusative neuter singular when the neuter group must move apart from the masculine and feminine groups. The merged masculine and feminine groups will say the accusative singular of the masculine/feminine gender in unison but the neuter group will say its accusative form alone. After the accusative singular, the neuter group must merge back with the masculine and feminine groups until it is time to separate from them again when the neuter has a form different from the masculine/feminine one.

208 • Latin for the New Millennium: Teacher's Manual, Level 1

PAGE 175
Oral Exercise 2; Workbook Exercise 3

ORAL EXERCISE 2

This exercise may be used anytime after third declension adjectives have been presented.

The teacher should ask three students to use one of the CPOs to put on view (from memory) the declension of three previously learned nouns: *cōnsul*, m.; *via*, f.; and *templum*, n. Then the teacher should ask individual students to supply orally the correct forms of the third declension adjective *celeber, celebris, celebre* (renowned), to agree with each of the nouns. As the student supplies the form, the teacher should put the adjective next to the appropriate form of the noun.

Singular

Nom.	cōnsul celeber	via celebris	templum celebre
Gen.	cōnsulis celebris	viae celebris	templī celebris
Dat.	cōnsulī celebrī	viae celebrī	templō celebrī
Acc.	cōnsulem celebrem	viam celebrem	templum celebre
Abl.	cōnsule celebrī	viā celebrī	templō celebrī
Voc.	cōnsul celeber	via celebris	templum celebre

Plural

Nom.	cōnsulēs celebrēs	viae celebrēs	templa celebria
Gen.	cōnsulum celebrium	viārum celebrium	templōrum celebrium
Dat.	cōnsulibus celebribus	viīs celebribus	templīs celebribus
Acc.	cōnsulēs celebrēs	viās celebrēs	templa celebria
Abl.	cōnsulibus celebribus	viīs celebribus	templīs celebribus
Voc.	cōnsulēs celebrēs	viae celebrēs	templa celebria

PAGE 176
Standards 1.1, 1.2

▶ EXERCISE 4 ANSWERS

1.	verba celebria	frequent words
2.	dominārum fēlīcium	of the happy mistresses
3.	duce miserō	by/with the wretched leader
4.	cīvis fortis	brave citizen, of the brave citizen
5.	verba ācria	fierce/harsh words
6.	hostī fēlīcī	to/for the fortunate enemy
7.	mīlitum fortium	of the brave soldiers

Chapter 10 • 209

TEACHING TIP

After the students have completed Exercise 4 and the correct answers have been given, the teacher may wish to return to the beginning of Exercise 4 and ask in Latin what case(s) and number each phrase in the student edition is. The Latin way to ask for case and number was given on p. 48 of this teacher's manual. The answers are provided for the teacher's convenience.

- 1. *nōminātīvō aut accūsātīvō <cāsū>, numerī plūrālis*
- 2. *genitīvō, numerī plūrālis*
- 3. *ablātīvō, numerī singulāris*
- 4. *genitīvō, numerī singulāris*
- 5. *nōminātīvō aut accūsātīvō, numerī plūrālis*
- 6. *datīvō aut ablātīvō, numerī singulāris*
- 7. *genitīvō, numerī plūrālis*

▶ EXERCISE 5 ANSWERS

1. The enemies are destroying the well-known city.
2. We fear the strong enemies.
3. A happy man loves a happy woman.
4. The king is captivated by fierce love.
5. People feel that death is fierce.
6. Dangers are not feared by the brave soldiers.
7. A strong camp is being built.
8. Many listen to the well-known poet.

▶ EXERCISE 6 ANSWERS

1. Hostēs ācrēs in equō nōn audīmus.
2. Trōiānōs esse fēlīcēs nōn putās.
3. Graecī urbem Trōiānōrum capiunt.
4. Dē mīlitibus ācribus nōn cōgitant.
5. Urbem cīvium fēlīcium vidēmus.
6. Dōnum Graecōrum nōn cupiō.
7. Ab hostibus Trōiānōrum fortium capior.

PAGE 177

Standards 1.1, 1.2, 3.1, 4.1
Workbook Exercises 4, 5, 6

▶ EXERCISE 7 ANSWERS

1. We do not always save beautiful things.
2. The brave do not always win.
3. The fortunate are freed from fear.
4. Many men seek justice.
5. The good feel joy, the bad <feel> fear.
6. We seek fortunate and beautiful things, we fear bad ones.

PAGE 178

Standards 1.1, 1.2
Workbook Exercise 7, Content Questions

▶ EXERCISE 8 ANSWERS

1. Ulixis cōnsiliō equus ligneus aedificātur.
   The wooden horse is being built with the advice of Ulysses.
2. Trōiānī equum esse dōnum crēdunt.
   The Trojans believe the horse is a gift.
3. Trōiānī Graecōs abesse crēdunt, sed Graecī nōn absunt.
   The Trojans believe that the Greeks are away, but the Greeks are not away.
4. Mīlitēs ācrēs in equō occultantur.
   Fierce soldiers are hidden in the horse.
5. Graecī armātī ex equō in urbem exeunt.
   The armed Greeks go out from the horse into the city.

TEACHING TIP
Here is a quick activity to reinforce the translation of substantive adjectives. This may be done in oral or written format. Instruct the students after hearing the adjective said or after reading the adjective to translate it into English including the word "man," "woman," or "thing" depending on the gender of the adjective. In some cases there may be more than one answer.

- ācrēs   paucae   sevērō
- miserā   iūstōrum   pulchram
- celebre   praeclārī   fortia
- fēlīcī   armātōs   meīs

Chapter 10 • 211

PAGE 179

 TEACHER BY THE WAY

Vergil intended to spend three years in Greece and Asia adding finishing touches to his epic. There are more than fifty unfinished verses. Augustus, whom he met in Athens, persuaded him to return to Rome, but Vergil died en route. His executors had been ordered to burn the *Aeneid* if anything happened to him. Augustus intervened and published the unfinished poem just as Vergil had left it.

In addition to the two Muses mentioned in the illustration on p. 179 (SE), there are seven more. The nine Muses are the daughters of Zeus and Mnemosyne, the goddess of memory. The meaning of the Greek name, the generally accepted function, and the symbol of each are listed for the teacher's convenience.

- Calliope, "fair voice" (epic poetry), stylus and tablets
- Clio, "renown" (history), heroic trumpet and scrolls
- Erato, "lovely" (lyric and love poetry), lyre
- Euterpe, "gladness" (flutes), double flute
- Melpomene, "singing" (tragedy), tragic mask and ivy wreath
- Polyhymnia, "many songs" (mime and heroic hymns), thoughtful, with a finger on her mouth
- Terpsichore, "joy in dance" (lyric poetry/dance), cithara/lyre
- Thalia, "abundance, good cheer" (comedy), comic mask, shepherd's staff
- Urania, "heavenly" (astronomy), celestial globe and compass

The Muses were in the company of Apollo, the god of music and prophecy, who was their leader. With him they entertained the gods at festivals on Mt. Olympus. The Muses also attended Achilles's funeral.

PAGE 180

Standards 1.2, 2.1, 4.1, 4.2
Oral Exercise 3

ORAL EXERCISE 3

This exercise may be used anytime after the present passive voice has been presented or as a review of the same topic at the end of this chapter.

The teacher should ask individual students to repeat each sentence orally (some students may need to hear the sentence more than once before they can do this). Then the students must change each sentence into the passive.

1. **Teacher:** Graecī verba audiunt. **Student:** Verba ā Graecīs audiuntur.
2. **Teacher:** Graecī cōnsilia capiunt. **Student:** Cōnsilia ā Graecīs capiuntur.
3. **Teacher:** Graecī magnum equum aedificant. **Student:** Magnus equus ā Graecīs aedificātur.
4. **Teacher:** Graecī in equō mala parant. **Student:** Mala ā Graecīs in equō parantur.

5. **Teacher:** Graecī equum ad urbem movent.   **Student:** Equus ad urbem ā Graecīs movētur.
6. **Teacher:** Graecī in equō noctem exspectant.   **Student:** Nox ā Graecīs in equō exspectātur.
7. **Teacher:** Trōiānī perīculum nōn vident.   **Student:** Perīculum ā Trōiānīs nōn vidētur.
8. **Teacher:** Trōiānī urbem servāre nōn possunt.   **Student:** Urbs ā Trōiānīs servārī nōn potest.

PAGE 181
Standard 1.2
Oral Exercise 4

TRANSLATION OF THE LATIN CONVERSATION
Christy: When are you used to getting up, Mark?

Mark: If I have to attend classes, I get up early in the morning. Then I am woken up by the alarm clock. However, I always desire to sleep late and for a long time. On the weekend, I can sleep longer.

Christy: When are you accustomed to getting up, Mary?

Mary: I always get up early in the morning.

Christy: I also desire to get up early in the morning. Then I can prepare a good breakfast. I love breakfast.

Helen: I also love breakfast. What sort of breakfast do you prepare? What do you eat?

Christy: I eat fruits and eggs and toast with butter. What time is it now?

Mark: It is eight o'clock now.

Christy: I want to prepare a good breakfast now. We can have breakfast before the Latin class. Do you want to have breakfast with me?

Mark, Helen: Yes indeed!

Mary: I want to have breakfast with you, but I ought to study. Therefore I ought to have breakfast quickly and easily. In Latin class tomorrow there will be an exam. So I concentrate on studies not only in the evening, but also in the morning. I ought to be prepared.

Christy: We ought to be prepared, but not prepared too much.

Mary: I cannot be prepared too much.

Christy: But the teacher is fair. The exam will not be difficult. The teacher says so.

Mark: If we all pass the exam, ten extra points will be given to us all. The extra points are gifts!

Mary: I think about the words of the poet Vergil. In the *Aeneid* a Trojan says: "Whatever it is, I fear the Greeks even carrying gifts."

Christy: You should not fear. The teacher is a friend, not an enemy.

TEACHING TIP
See also Latin Conversation, Chapter 6.

ORAL EXERCISE 4

This exercise may be used after the Latin dialogue has been presented.

After the students have carefully read and understood the dialogue, the teacher should ask individual students the following questions. In preparation for the exercise, the teacher should use one of the CPOs to put on view the following words, which are also useful for questions and answers. The students should try to answer while looking at the dialogue, and should be told they can frame their answers using the actual words in the text—with the appropriate adjustments of endings and person.

-ne added to the first word of a sentence asks a question
cūr? – why?
quia – because
quōmodo – how, in what way?

1. **Teacher:** Quandō Mārcus surgere solet, sī scholās adīre dēbet?
   Student: Sī Mārcus scholās adīre dēbet, bene māne surgit.

2. **Teacher:** Cupitne Mārcus semper bene māne surgere?
   Student: Mārcus nōn cupit semper bene māne surgere.

3. **Teacher:** Quandō Mārcus diūtius dormīre potest?
   Student: Mārcus exeunte hebdomade diūtius dormīre potest.

4. **Teacher:** Soletne Marīa semper bene māne surgere?
   Student: Marīa semper bene māne surgere solet.

5. **Teacher:** Cūr Christīna bene māne surgere cupit?
   Student: Christīna bene māne surgere cupit, quia ientāculum amat, et tunc ientāculum bonum parāre potest.

6. **Teacher:** Quāle ientāculum parat Christīna?
   Student: Christīna pōma et ōva et pānem tostum cum būtȳrō parat.

7. **Teacher:** Cupiuntne Mārcus et Helena ientāre ante scholam Latīnam cum Christīnā?
   Student: Mārcus et Helena ientāre ante scholam Latīnam cum Christīnā cupiunt.

8. **Teacher:** Putatne Marīa quoque sē dēbēre ientāre ante scholam Latīnam cum Christīnā?
   Student: Marīa sē nōn dēbēre ientāre ante scholam Latīnam cum Christīnā putat.

9. **Teacher:** Cūr Marīa sē nōn dēbēre ientāre ante scholam Latīnam cum Christīnā putat?
   Student: Marīa sē in studia incumbere tunc dēbēre putat.

10. **Teacher:** Itaque quōmodo Marīa sē dēbēre ientāre putat?
    Student: Marīa sē dēbēre expedītē ientāre putat.

11. **Teacher:** Cūr Marīa sē expedītē ientāre et in studia incumbere dēbēre putat?
    Student: Marīa sē expedītē ientāre et in studia incumbere dēbēre putat, quia in scholā Latīnā crās erit probātiō, et Marīa parārī cupit.

12. **Teacher:** Putatne Christīna Mārīam parārī dēbēre?
    Student: Christīna putat Mārīam parārī dēbēre, sed nōn nimium parārī.

13. **Teacher:** Quālem esse magistram putat Christīna?
    Student: Christīna magistram esse iūstam putat.

14. **Teacher:** Quālia dōna ā magistrā dantur?
    Student: Pūncta superaddita ā magistrā dantur.

15. **Teacher:** Cūr Marīa timēre nōn dēbet?
    Student: Marīa timēre nōn dēbet, quia magistra est amīca.

214 • Latin for the New Millennium: Teacher's Manual, Level 1

PAGE 182
Standard 4.1

DERIVATIVES

deus – The word "adieu" is French from the phrase *adieu (vous) commant* (I commend you to God). It derives from the Latin *ad* (to) and *deus*. It was originally said by those departing to those left behind; "farewell" was said to those setting forth.

The word "deify" is a compound of *deus* and *faciō* (to make); hence the word means "make (someone) a god."

A <u>deist</u> believes in a supreme god but denies revelation.

For related derivatives, see *dīvīnus* 1.20.

dōnum – (from the verb *dōnō*; its meaning is limited to "to present, bestow" whereas its root *dō* has other shades of meaning, e.g., permit, grant, cause, devote, etc.). The derivation from *dōnum* of "donation" and "donate" is clear, but "dower" is derived from a related verb, *dōtō*, which means "to endow" as in "dowry" (the Latin *dōs*). A "dowry" (money, land, jewelry, etc.) was presented to a bride on her wedding by her family. It was intended to support the woman in widowhood (hence "dowager") and eventually to support her sons and daughters. However, this did not always occur as in many instances the husband used the dowry for his own benefit unless legally prevented by strictures on his rights to that dowry. Disputes could, and often did, result in domestic violence, and dowry deaths occurred when husbands and in-laws murdered, tortured, or drove to suicide a young wife in order to gain control of the dowry.

For related derivatives, see *dō* 1.4.

equus – The word "equestrienne" refers to a female rider (it is a pseudo-French feminine dating to 1848). The word "equestrian" entered English during the 1650s derived from the Latin *equester* (horseman).

The word "equine" appeared in English in 1765. It is better to describe people with long faces as "equine" in appearance than "horsefaced"!

flamma – The words "flammable" and "inflammable" are synonyms. A common misconception makes the "in" prefix negative; it is an intensive. The word is derived from the Latin *inflammō* (to set on fire; literally, into flame). The Latin *flammō* also means "to set on fire" but can also be used intransitively, i.e., "to burn, blaze."

An "inflammation" is a swollen, reddened area of the body, so called because of its color.

The crowd was roused to fury by the speaker's <u>inflammatory</u> remarks.

hostis – There are two possible sources for the root of "hostage": one is the Latin *hostis*, which can mean "stranger, foreigner" as well as "enemy" (strangers could be friends or foes); or two, the Latin *hospes* (guest, host, visitor, stranger). A third, less likely, possibility is the Latin word for "hostage" (*obses*, from *ob* = in front of, and *sedeō* = to sit; therefore, "to sit in front of" as prisoners would before their captors).

The word "host" from *hostis* refers to a multitude of people. It should not be confused with the "host" from *hospes*.

nox – The autumnal <u>equinox</u> and the vernal <u>equinox</u> are the two days of the year when the time of the night is equal (*aequus*) to that of the day.

The owl is a <u>nocturnal</u> bird, hunting by night and sleeping by day.

Chapter 10 · 215

A "nocturne" is a musical composition having a dreamy character appropriate to the evening or night. The word was coined in 1814 by John Field, who wrote many of them in a style mastered by Chopin.

"Nocturn" is the term for a division of the office of matins (early thirteenth century) derived through the Old French *nocturne* (evening service, curfew) and the medieval Latin *nocturna* (a group of Psalms used in the "nocturns," from the classical Latin *nocturnus* [adjectival form of *nox*]).

perīculum – The <u>Perils of Pauline</u> was a Saturday matinee serial popular in 1914 and again during the 1930s. There were also four full-length features made with that title, the last in 1967.

Edmund Hilary was the first to make the <u>perilous</u> climb up Mt. Everest in 1953.

Note the "-ous" suffix of "perilous."

The prefix of "imperil" means "into"; hence the literal translation is "into danger." The incompetent commander made decisions which <u>imperiled</u> his whole army.

ācer – There was an <u>acrimonious</u> exchange today between the two leaders of the Senate ("full of sharp words"; note the "-ous" suffix).

The <u>acrid</u> smoke made my eyes tear.

The word "eager" came into English during the late thirteenth century meaning "strenuous, ardent, fierce, angry," through the Old French *aigre* (sour, acid, harsh, rough, greedy, active, lively) from the Latin *ācer*.

The word "vinegar" appeared in English around 1300 through the Old French *vinaigre* (*vin* = wine, and *aigre* = sour) from the Latin which called the same produce *vīnum acētum* (wine turned sour).

celeber – This adjective, meaning "crowded, honored, famous," is the basis for "celebrity" (an honored or famous person) and "celebration," which honors a day, event, or person and usually includes well-attended festivities. The verb "to celebrate" appeared in English during the mid-fifteenth century, the noun "celebration" during the 1520s, the adjective "celebrated" in the 1660s, the noun "celebrant" in 1731, and the adjective "celebratory" in 1855.

fēlīx – The word "felicity," meaning "happiness," came into English during the late fourteenth century. It has also been a proper noun, used as a girl's name.

Note the "-ous" suffix of "felicitous." The bride and groom received many <u>felicitations</u>, wishes for happiness, at their wedding reception.

fortis – The prefix of "comfort" ("com" = *cum*) is intensive. The word came into English during the late thirteenth century derived through the Old French *conforter*, which meant "to strengthen, help, solace."

The "dis" prefix of "discomfort" is negative.

An "effort" is made "out of strength." The word appeared in English during the late fifteenth century through the Old French *esforcier* (to force out, exert oneself) from the Latin *ex* (out from) and *fortis*.

The verb "enforce" came into English during the early fourteenth century through the Old French *enforcier* (to make, put in, make an effort, compel).

A "fort" is a stronghold.

The word "forte" (pronounced "fort" when referring to a person's strong point) had an *e* added to it in the eighteenth century in imitation of the Italian *forte*. It is also pronounced in the Italian way when it is used as a term in music.

216 • Latin for the New Millennium: Teacher's Manual, Level 1

The word "fortification" is derived from *fortis* and *faciō* (to make); hence it refers to a place "made strong" for protection.

A "fortress" is also a "strong place" with the fairly uncommon English suffix "-ess" (cf. largess, duress) which was derived from the Latin suffix "-itia" (quality or condition).

The word "pianoforte" was coined in 1767 by the inventor Cristofori as a name for the piano because it could vary tones (soft and loud), unlike the harpsichord.

The "re" of "reinforce" means "again"; thus the word means "to strengthen again." It referred to an augmentation as in military reinforcements during the 1650s.

See also *fortitūdō* in 1.8; "fort" in Teaching Tip 1.10.

paucī – The paucity of the grain supply caused great hardship, especially among the poor.

aedificō – (from *aedes* = temple; plural, house, and *faciō* = to make; hence "to build")

Today the word "edifice" is used for a large or imposing building.

To "edify" meant literally "to build or construct" (mid-fourteenth century), but it was also used figuratively, meaning "to build up morally, instruct, or teach."

The principal's remarks on drug use were very edifying to the students attending the school assembly.

capiō – The verb "accept" comes from the fourth principal part of the Latin *accipiō* (to take, receive, etc.); the noun "concept" from that of *concipiō* (to take in and hold, understand, commit); "precept" from that of *praecipiō* (*prae* becomes "pre"; to anticipate, teach, admonish, take beforehand). The nouns "reception," "inception," "deception," etc., are also derived in like fashion, e.g., "reception" from *recipiō* (to take back, recover, occupy), "deception" from *decipiō* (to deceive, ensnare; the prefix is pejorative), "inception" from *incipiō* (to begin, to undertake, literally, to take into). The corresponding verbs ("to conceive, deceive, receive") all show the lengthening of the root vowel by making it a diphthong.

Eggs are incipient life.

The word "reception" entered English during the late fourteenth century and was used in astrology to mean "the effect of two planets on each other." The sense of "act of receiving" dates to the late fifteenth century; that of a "ceremonial gathering" to 1882.

The noun "receipt" appeared in English during the late fourteenth century at first meaning "act of receiving." The manager was in receipt of the delivery. Around 1600 the word came to mean "a written acknowledgment of goods or money received."

The word "recipe" is the Latin imperative *recipe* (take!) of *recipiō*, written by physicians at the head of prescriptions, and appeared during the 1580s in English meaning "medical prescription." This sense only survives today in the abbreviation Rx. The meaning "direction for preparing food" was first recorded in 1743.

The word "cable" is first found in English around 1200 and was derived through the medieval Latin *capulum* (rope, halter) from *capiō*. Its nautical meaning referred to rope more than 10 inches in circumference; non-nautical usage referred to "rope made of wire." The term "telegraphic cable" dates to 1883, "cable car" to 1879, "cable television" to 1963.

The word "capable" derives through the Latin *capābilis* used by theologians meaning "able to grasp or hold" from the Latin *capax* (adjectival form of *capiō*) meaning "able to hold much."

Note the "-ous" suffix of "capacious."

Chapter 10 • 217

The noun "caption" appeared in English during the late fourteenth century and meant "taking, seizure" (from the fourth principal part of *capiō*). From the seventeenth century it was used in law at the head of a legal document involving seizure (Certificate of Caption). The meaning was extended to refer to the head of any document like a chapter (1789) and "a description or title below an illustration" (1919). Note that "caption" does not derive from *caput* as the word "chapter" does.

The word "catch" is derived from the Latin *captō*, the frequentative form of *capiō*. The word "chase" also derives from *captō* through the Old French *chacier* (to hunt, pursue, try to seize).

The word "conceit" originally meant "something formed (taken) in the mind" (late fourteenth century). By the 1510s it had evolved to mean "witty notion," by 1600 to "vanity." The prefix is intensive.

The word "emancipation" consists of the Latin *ex* (out of), *manus* (hand), and *capiō*; hence the literal meaning "to take out from (under) the hand of." In Roman law it meant "freeing from the authority of the pater familias." It was adopted by the cause of religious toleration during the seventeenth century and then by the antislavery movement in 1776.

The prefix of "incapable" is negative, that of "inception" and "incipient" is not.

The word "municipal" appeared in English during the 1540s and is derived from the Latin *municipium* (*munus* = duty, gift, and *capiō*). It meant "a free town, one whose citizens have Roman privileges but are governed by their own laws." It now refers to the local government of a town or city.

A "participant" takes part in an event (from *pars* = part, and *capiō*).

A "participle" is so called because it "takes part of" (shares) the nature of a verb and an adjective (called "a verbal adjective").

The word "prince" is derived from the Latin *princeps* (*prīmus* = first, and *capiō*) meaning "first, chief," etc.

A principal is the leader of a school. The word may also mean "most important," hence "the four principal parts of a Latin verb."

The noun "principle," however, is derived from the related *principium*, which means "beginning or origin" from the "take first" of *princeps*. Thus a "principle" is an axiom, a "first rule," the basics of a philosophy or discipline. The English *l* was probably inserted analogous to "participle," "manciple," etc.

The prefix of "purchase" is the Anglo-English equivalent of the Latin *prō* (before, in place of, on behalf of, in exchange for); hence, the literal meaning "to take in exchange for," i.e., "to buy with money, to acquire" (around 1300). The meaning "to hold for applying power" dates to 1711: His special boots gave him enough purchase to scale the rock.

The word "recover" entered English around 1300, derived from the medieval Latin *recuperāre* (to take back). The OLD cites the preferred spelling in classical Latin as *recipere* (*re* = back, and *capiō*). It meant "to regain consciousness" from the Old French "get again, procure, regain health."

The word "recuperate," derived from the same root as "recover," appeared in English during the 1540s and meant "to revive, convalesce." The meaning "to recover from sickness or loss" dates to 1864.

The word "susceptible" is derived from the fourth principal part of *suscipiō* (to undertake, support, catch from below, take into one's mind; *sub* = under, up to, and *capiō*) and came into English around 1600. Today it means "accessible to treatment, capable of being affected." See also "capable" above.

cupiō – Note that "recuperate" and "recover" do not derive from *cupiō*. The spelling may lead to false derivation.

The prefix of "concupiscence" is intensive. The word is derived from *concupiscō* (to long for, be very desirous of). Unlike "concupiscence," which limits desire to "lust," "cupidity," which entered English during the mid-fifteenth century through the Anglo-French *cupidite* from the Latin *cupiditās* and originally meant "passionate desire, ambition," gradually came to mean especially "desire for wealth, greed, avarice."

The word "covet" came into English during the mid-thirteenth century through the Old French *conveitier* (to lust after) and, like "cupidity," reflected at first the erotic sense of the Latin *cupiō* but today refers primarily to a "wrongful or excessive desire to another's property." However, the Latin verb and its related nouns, adjectives, and verbs are all used pejoratively and retain that erotic nuance.

Note the "-ous" suffix of "covetous."

dēleō – Indelible ink cannot be removed. The prefix is negative.

Taking drugs socially can be very deleterious to one's health (*dēleō* = to blot out, destroy). Note the "-ous" suffix.

Aaron hit one wrong key, and the computer deleted his entire term paper.

fugiō – The Latin word from which we derive "centrifugal" (literally, "to flee the center") was coined by Sir Isaac Newton in his *Principia* (written in Latin, 1687).

The word "refuge" was derived from the Latin *refugium* (a place to flee back to) and appeared in English during the late fourteenth century.

The noun "subterfuge" derives from the Latin *subterfugiō* ("to escape by stealth, evade," from *subter* = beneath and *fugiō*). Politicians seeking to evade the consequences of immoral or illegal acts often resort to subterfuge.

A "fugue" is a musical composition based upon a theme that then "flees" to other parts or voices in turn.

moveō – All the derivatives listed that contain a "mot" root are derived from the fourth principal part of *moveō*. The prefixes limit the meaning, e.g., "remote" (*re* = back; to move back, withdraw; hence, "be distant" as in "remote control"); "locomotive" (*locō* = ablative of place from which; therefore, "to move from a place"); "commotion" (from *cum* = together, thoroughly; hence, "to move together, disturb, shake, agitate"); "promote" (to move forward).

The word "motif" entered English in 1848 through the Old French *motif* (dominant idea, theme = that which moves someone). The *f* of "motif" and *v* of "motive" are allophones (from the Greek = another sound).

The "-or" suffix of "motor" indicates someone or something which does the action, e.g., an actor acts, an inventor invents, a doctor teaches, a motor moves (something) or has moving parts.

The letter *b* in early texts before 800 represented *v*. This has been retained in "mobile," "automobile" (a self-mover; from the Greek αὐτός = "self").

The word "mob" is a slang shortening of "mobile." The Latin phrase *mōbile vulgus* (fickle common people) was used around 1600 in English. The word is used in Australia and New Zealand to refer to a crowd but not pejoratively. The word is not a synonym for the Mafia but refers to a group organized to produce and supply liquor during Prohibition in America.

The word "moment" derives from the Latin *momentum* (contraction of *movimentum*) meaning "movement" but also "a short space of time (*momentum temporis*)" or "importance" (*momentum vertere* = to turn the scale).

Note the "-ous" suffix of "momentous."

The *o* to *u* spelling change of the root seen in "mutiny" (from the fourth principal part of *moveō*) is also seen elsewhere, as in the spelling of "mommy" (American) and "mummy" (British).

A "mutiny" is a revolt reflecting the stronger nuances of *moveō* (change, dislodge, expel).

Note the "-ous" suffix of "mutinous."

pugnō – The word "repugnant," meaning "contrary, contradictory," appeared in English during the late fourteenth century from the Latin *repugnō* (to oppose, literally, "to fight back"). The meaning "distasteful, objectionable" dates to 1777.

Note the "-ous" suffix of "pugnacious," a word used to describe someone "full of fight," like a bully.

In the pronunciation of the verb "impugn," the *g* sound has been lost (as in "resign, malign, sign," etc.); however, it reappears in related words, e.g., "malignant, resignation, signal," etc. The word is derived from *impugnō* (*in* = to, against, and *pugnō*; hence, to fight against, to attack): The politician retorted to an aggressive question from the audience, "Are you <u>impugning</u> my motives?"

nec – None

220 • Latin for the New Millennium: Teacher's Manual, Level 1

CHAPTER 11 (PP. 183–196)

GRAMMAR IN LANGUAGE FACTS

Imperfect Tense Active and Passive of All Conjugations; Imperfect Tense of *Sum* and *Possum*; Enclitics –*que* and –*ne*

PAGE 183

Standards 1.1, 2.1, 3.1, 3.2

RRA 6A

MEMORĀBILE DICTŪ VOCABULARY

condō, condere, condidī, conditum – to found

erat (*third person singular*) – was

gēns, gentis, *f.* – race, nation

mōlēs, mōlis, *f.* – weight, mass, trouble, effort; *tantae mōlis* is a genitive of quality

tantus, tanta, tantum – so much, so great

TEACHING TIP
Since the love story of Aeneas and Dido is so far removed from Vergil's lifetime, the teacher may wish to instruct the students to review Chapter 2 of RRA.

TEACHING TIP
As a prereading activity employing the chapter page image, teachers may ask the students to examine the painting. *Spectāte pictūram! Quid vidētis? Quid faciunt?*

TEACHER BY THE WAY
Aeneas's toils and sufferings began even before he set out on his divine mission to found the new Troy, the future Rome. He witnessed the deaths of King Priam and his son Polites as the Greeks captured the citadel at Troy; he had to convince his reluctant father to accompany him on his journey; and he lost his wife Creusa in the chaos of departing the city. In the course of his journey and after his arrival in Italy, his trials and travails include:

- his father Anchises misinterpreting the omens, which resulted in a false start in Crete
- an encounter with the Harpies and the perils of Scylla and Charybdis
- the death of his father
- a horrible storm that blows his fleet off course
- the temptation of Dido

- the ongoing interference of the resentful Juno
- his ships set aflame at Sicily
- his descent to the underworld
- war with the Latins
- the death of Pallas, who had been entrusted to Aeneas's care
- the battle with Turnus

TEACHING TIP
Chapter 6A of RRA contains information on Vergil. The teacher may wish to assign this chapter for reading or review. See. p. 201.

PAGE 184
Standards 1.1, 2.1, 3.1, 3.2

TRANSLATION OF LATIN PASSAGE
About Queen Dido

Dido the queen was burning with love. For she deeply loved Aeneas. Aeneas and Dido walk in the forest. A great storm comes. While it thunders and rains, Aeneas and Dido remain in a cave. Aeneas realizes (understands) that he is loved by Dido, and he says that he also loves Dido. Afterward in Carthage Aeneas and Dido were often seen together. Then because of <their> love Aeneas and Dido were happy. But Jupiter, the king of the gods, sends Mercury to Aeneas. Mercury orders Aeneas to leave Dido and to seek a new land. Aeneas says to Dido that he cannot stay. Dido thinks Aeneas is behaving wrongly. Aeneas seems to Dido to be cruel. But Aeneas leaves Dido and heads for Italy. Dido was a brave woman, but she was not able to conquer <her> grief. Life seemed to Dido to be bad, and she wished to seek death.

TEACHER BY THE WAY
Book 4 of Vergil's *Aeneid* recounts Aeneas's time in Carthage where he is received graciously by Queen Dido, whose hospitality and other attentions he enjoyed until Mercury arrived reminding him of his mission to found a new Troy. Driven by duty (so he claimed), Aeneas departed, rejecting Dido's pleas to stay. Considering herself betrayed by Aeneas with whom she had fallen deeply in love and whose relationship she had considered a marriage, Dido sought to end her life. She enlisted the aid of her unwitting sister Anna, who had previously encouraged Dido to yield to her attraction to Aeneas and had served as go-between trying to persuade Aeneas to postpone his departure until the wintry seas had settled. Dido pretends that she needs to perform a special ritual that will rid her of her misery and memories of Aeneas. Anna dutifully readies an altar and fire to consume the effigy of Aeneas. Only later, after leaving Dido alone to perform her ritualistic purging, does Anna realize that Dido has tricked her into setting up her funeral pyre. Sick with grief, Anna asked her dying sister Dido why she had deceived and abandoned her.

PAGE 185

ANSWERS TO COMPREHENSION QUESTIONS
1. Aeneas and Dido found refuge in the same cave and confessed their love for each other.
2. Not too long, until Jupiter sent Mercury to remind Aeneas of his duty.
3. Aeneas had to find a new land.
4. Dido could not overcome her grief and did not remain in life.

TEACHING TIP
In **Considering the Classical Gods**, after Chapters 3, 6, and 9, the students have already read in English about Mars, Jupiter, Juno, Neptune, Pluto, Vesta, Ceres, and Apollo. In this chapter the students read about Mercury. Teachers may wish to take the time at this juncture to introduce the students to the gods' names in Latin. They are listed here for the teacher's convenience in the order in which they are encountered in this book.

- **Iuppiter, Iovis,** *m.* – Jupiter/Zeus
- **Iūnō, Iūnōnis,** *f.* – Juno/Hera
- **Mārs, Mārtis,** *m.* – Mars/Ares
- **Neptūnus, Neptūnī,** *m.* – Neptune/Poseidon
- **Vesta, Vestae,** *f.* – Vesta/Hestia
- **Cerēs, Cereris,** *f.* – Ceres/Demeter
- **Apollō, Apollinis,** *m.* – Apollo
- **Mercurius, Mercuriī,** *m.* – Mercury/Hermes
- **Minerva, Minervae,** *f.* – Minerva/Athena
- **Diāna, Diānae,** *f.* – Diana/Artemis
- **Venus, Veneris,** *f.* – Venus/Aphrodite
- **Bacchus, Bacchī,** *m.* – Bacchus/Dionysus
- **Volcānus/Vulcānus, Volcānī/Vulcānī,** *m.* – Vulcan/Hephaestus

PAGE 186
Standards 3.1, 4.1

TEACHER BY THE WAY
Note that the stem of fourth conjugation verbs ends in a long vowel. But the *–i–* is short before endings

- of the imperfect
- of the future
- of the first person singular present active
- of the third person singular present active

- of the third person plural present active
- of the first person singular present passive
- of the third person plural present passive

As a result, the stem of *audī-ēba-m* is marked long here on p. 186 but on p. 188 where *audiō* is conjugated in the imperfect tense (*audiēbam*) the stem vowel is short.

TEACHER BY THE WAY

On p. 91 of this teacher's manual the question "*Cūius temporis est?*" was introduced. At that juncture there was only one correct answer "*praesentis.*" With the introduction of the imperfect tense in this chapter, one more answer will be added. That answer is "*imperfectī.*"

PAGE 187

TEACHING TIP

Additional reproducible worksheets, morphology charts, and their associated answer keys, related to this material, are available for download at www.lnm.bolchazy.com.

- **Verb Conjugations**

PAGE 188

Standards 1.1, 1.2

Oral Exercise 1; Workbook Exercises 1, 3, 4

▶ EXERCISE 1 ANSWERS

1. you (plural) were seeking
2. you (plural) were being driven
3. I was left behind
4. we were thinking
5. s/he was saving
6. you were understanding
7. they were grieving
8. they were regarded
9. we were freed
10. I was coming

ORAL EXERCISE 1

This exercise may be used after the imperfect tense has been presented.

The teacher should recite slowly and clearly each of the following verbs in the imperfect tense. After saying each verb the teacher should call on individual students to repeat the verb first, then change it into the corresponding plural form if it is singular and into the singular if it is plural.

Teacher: aedificābāmus	**Student:** aedificābam
Teacher: dabantur	**Student:** dabātur
Teacher: docēbāminī	**Student:** docēbāris
Teacher: sentiēbās	**Student:** sentiēbātis
Teacher: fugiēbātis	**Student:** fugiēbās
Teacher: movēbāris	**Student:** movēbāminī
Teacher: agēbantur	**Student:** agēbātur
Teacher: dēlēbātis	**Student:** dēlēbās
Teacher: vincēbāmur	**Student:** vincēbar
Teacher: capiēbātis	**Student:** capiēbās
Teacher: erāmus	**Student:** eram
Teacher: dolēbat	**Student:** dolēbant

PAGE 189

Standards 1.2, 4.1
Workbook Exercise 2

▶ EXERCISE 2 ANSWERS

1. active   agō
2. regicide   rēgīna, rēx
3. ardent   ārdeō
4. conspicuous   cōnspiciō
5. tempestuous   tempestās
6. agent   agō
7. relinquish   relinquō
8. novelty   novus
9. unanimous   ūnā
10. missive, mission   mittō
11. dolorous   dolor
12. arson   ārdeō, ārdēre, ārsī
13. sylvan/silvan   silva

Chapter 11 • 225

TEACHING TIP

Although in Exercise 2 the students are directed to find only the derivatives based on the Vocabulary to Learn, they may be interested to learn that there are other derivatives in Exercise 2. The derivation of these words is provided for the teacher's convenience.

1. longer – from *longus* (long).
2. republic – from *rēs pūblica* (thing, matter; public). established – from *stabiliō* (to make stable, establish).
3. confession – from *confessiō* (acknowledgment, confession); *confiteor* (to confess, acknowledge, reveal).
5. affair – from *adficiō* (to affect, endow, afflict with); from *faciō* (to do make). quieter – from *quiētus* (at rest, peaceful, calm, etc.).
6. foreign – from *forās* (outside). state – from *status* (position, situation, form of government, condition).
7. advise – from *ad* (to, toward) + *vīsō* (to look at, survey, see to). plans – from *plānus* (level, flat, plain, clear). completely – from *compleō* (to fill up, fulfill, finish). move – from *moveō* (to move).
8. exciting – from *excitō* (to rouse, wake up, summon, raise).
9. decision – from *decīdō* (to settle, put an end to, cut off).
11. perpetually – from *perpetuus* (continuous, entire, universal). expression – from *exprimō* (to squeeze out, force out, press up).
12. accused – from *accūsō* (to reproach, prosecute, accuse); from *ad causam* ([call] to account).
13. mysterious – *mystērium* (secret religion, mystery, secret) from the Greek *mystērium* (*myō* – to shut out, close). deities – from *deus* (god).

PAGE 190

Standards 1.1, 1.2, 3.1, 3.2, 4.1

▶ EXERCISE 3 ANSWERS

1. capiēbar — I was captured
2. līberābāmur — we were freed
3. audiēbāminī — you (plural) were heard
4. timēbantur — they were being feared
5. aestimābātur — s/he was regarded
6. firmābāmur — we were strengthened
7. crēdēbāris — you were believed

▶ EXERCISE 4 ANSWERS

Aenēās et Dīdō in silvā ambulābant. Aenēās sē ā Dīdōne amārī et sē quoque Dīdōnem amāre intellegēbat. Sed tempestās ab Aeneā et Dīdōne timēbātur. In spēluncā manēbant. In spēluncā autem nōn timōrem sed gaudium sentiēbant. Nam dē amōre cōgitābant. Posteā saepe ūnā esse solēbant.

Aeneas and Dido were walking in the forest. Aeneas realized that he was loved by Dido and that he also loved Dido. But a storm was feared by Aeneas and Dido. They were waiting in a cave. In the cave, however, they were not feeling fear, but joy. For they were thinking about love. Afterward they were accustomed to be together often.

TEACHING TIP

If students need more practice changing verbs from the imperfect active to passive or the reverse, here is a suggestion. After the students have changed the imperfect active verbs into the imperfect passive according to the directions in Exercise 3 and after the answers have been checked for accuracy, instruct the students to close their books. Ask the students, while looking only at the imperfect passive answers on their paper, to turn those answers back into the imperfect active. This may be done in an oral or written format.

PAGE 191

Standards 1.1, 1.2, 3.1, 3.2, 4.1
Oral Exercise 2; Workbook Exercise 5

▶ EXERCISE 5 ANSWERS

1. poterāmus
2. erat
3. poteram
4. erant
5. erātis
6. poterās
7. poterat
8. erāmus

ORAL EXERCISE 2

This exercise may be used after the imperfect of sum *and* possum *has been presented.*

The teacher should recite the following imperfect forms of *sum* or *possum*. The students will orally convert each form of *sum* into the equivalent form of *possum*, and vice versa.

Teacher: eram	**Student:** poteram
Teacher: poterāmus	**Student:** erāmus
Teacher: erant	**Student:** poterant
Teacher: erās	**Student:** poterās
Teacher: poterat	**Student:** erat
Teacher: erātis	**Student:** poterātis

Teacher: erāmus   **Student:** poterāmus
Teacher: poteram   **Student:** eram
Teacher: poterātis   **Student:** erātis
Teacher: poterant   **Student:** erant

PAGE 192

TEACHER BY THE WAY

Some information about the later Punic Wars against Carthage is included here for the teacher's convenience. There is also a good description of this era in the enrichment text *From Romulus to Romulus Augustulus*.

First Punic War (264–241 BCE)

As Rome gradually extended her territory outward, she readily came in conflict with the Carthaginians who had intervened in 264 BCE in a dispute between the Greek cities of Syracuse and Messina on the island of Sicily. Recognizing Sicily as a critical location for Mediterranean trade and an area at that time especially rich in wheat fields, the Romans attacked Messina and forced the Carthaginians to withdraw. A subsequent foray failed to gain Sicily for Rome but resulted in forcing the Carthaginians from the island of Corsica. In 256 BCE, Rome gained a foothold in Africa. The Carthaginians found Rome's terms for surrender too harsh and drove the enemy off the following year. The war continued until 241 when the Romans defeated the Carthaginian navy. Having captured a Carthaginian warship, the Romans had copied it and adapted it to accommodate their skill in hand-to-hand combat. The Romans would ram an enemy ship, board it, and dispatch its occupants. The terms of the peace treaty forced Carthage to cede both Sicily and the Lipari islands to Rome.

Second Punic War (218–201 BCE)

In the years following the First Punic War, Rome seized both Corsica and Sardinia from Carthage and exacted a greater indemnity payment. The Council of the Hundred, an oligarchy of select families that ruled Carthage, chose to maintain the status quo, pay the indemnity, and avoid conflict with Rome. Hamilcar Barca led his family and a group of like-minded Carthaginians to Spain where they established a base from which they planned to attack Rome. Tradition holds that Hamilcar, a veteran of the First Punic War, made his son Hannibal as a young boy dedicate his life to avenging Carthage's humiliation at the hands of the Romans.

In 219 BCE, Hannibal captured Saguntum, which lay south of the Ebro River, Rome's area of interest. When Carthage did not recall him, the Romans considered the seizure an act of aggression and declared war. Recognizing Rome's control of the sea, Hannibal chose to march to Italy. Gifted with a shrewd appreciation of psychology, Hannibal knew the Romans would not be expecting a land-based attack and that he could cultivate his men's sense of superiority with their conquest of the Alps. In the battles at the River Trebia and Lake Trasimene, Hannibal used the topography to his advantage and deftly ensnared the Romans in dual slaughters. Fabius was called to serve as dictator and he waged a guerrilla war of attrition, hoping to demoralize the Carthaginians by denying a battle and depriving them of supplies. The Romans were not happy with this tactic and called him *Cunctātor*, "Delayer." However, when the consuls who succeeded him suffered a devastating loss at the

Battle of Cannae in 216 BCE, Fabius was vindicated and elected consul. Scholars debate why Hannibal did not directly attack Rome. In 211, Rome won Capua back and by 203, Hannibal was summoned back to Carthage. Meanwhile, in Spain, Publius Scipio with a victory at Ilipa in 206 had driven the Carthaginians off the peninsula. Scipio took the war to Africa and, in the Battle of Zama, Hannibal was defeated by his own tactics. Scipio earned the honorific title *Africānus* and Carthage relinquished Spain and the Mediterranean islands, paid a heavy indemnity, and surrendered its navy.

Third Punic War (149–146 BCE)

The Romans did not appreciate Carthage's continued prosperity as a commercial power. When they violated the peace treaty, Scipio Aemilianus, following in his adoptive grandfather's footsteps, blockaded Carthage and eventually destroyed the city and enslaved those Carthaginians remaining after the slaughter.

PAGE 193
Standard 2.1

TEACHING TIP
The teacher may choose to take this opportunity to compare and contrast the journey that Aeneas took to Italy from Troy with the route that Odysseus followed from Troy to Ithaca. Ask students to locate Ithaca on the map on pp. xxxiv–xxxv (SE).

TEACHER BY THE WAY
Geographers and scholars, both ancient and modern, base their conjectures about where Odysseus (Ulysses) might have stopped on his way home to Ithaca on their interpretation of the Homeric text. Troy, Ithaca, and perhaps Scheria (Corfu) are actual sites as are the Aegean, Ionian, Tyrrhenian, and Adriatic Seas. The area around and beyond Sicily was not well known to Homer. Many of the adventures take place there. The stops, in chronological order, and their *possible* locations are listed for the teacher's convenience.

- Troy — Troy
- Cicones — Ismaros, southwest coast of Thrace
- Lotus Eaters — island of Djerba, off Tunisia
- Cylopes — western edge of Sicily
- Aeolus — Ustica, off northern coast of Sicily
- Laestrygonians — southern Corsica
- Circe — Aeaea/Mt. Circeo on west coast of Italy
- Underworld — near the Bay of Naples
- Sirens — off the southwest coast of Italy in Tyrrhenian Sea
- Thrinacia — south of Sicily
- Scylla & Charybdis — narrowest point in Straits of Messina
- Calypso — Ogygia, in Maltese Islands
- Scheria — Corcyra/Corfu, within 80 miles of Ithaca
- Ithaca — perhaps the modern island of Ithaca, perhaps not

Chapter 11 • 229

TEACHING TIP
The teacher might wish to compare the journey of Odysseus to that of Aeneas provided on the map on p. 193 (SE). A map of Odysseus's journey can be found in *Classical Mythology and More* from Bolchazy-Carducci Publishers. The teacher may also ask the students to research whether Ithaca/Ithaki is the true island home of Odysseus. The internet provides plenty of information on this topic.

PAGE 194
Standards 1.1, 1.2, 2.1
Workbook Exercises 6, 7, Content Questions

▶ EXERCISE 6 ANSWERS
Mercurius: Hello! Are you Aeneas?

Aenēās: Aenēās sum. Valdē magnus esse vidēris! Esne deus?

Mercurius: I am a god! I am Mercury. What are you preparing now?

Aenēās: Ego Dīdōque esse Carthāgine rēx rēgīnaque cupimus. Casam aedificō. Casane pulchra vidētur?

Mercurius: Yes indeed! But you cannot stay with Dido and live in Carthage.

Aenēās: Crēdisne amōrem esse malum? Intellegisne Aenēam Dīdōnemque ūnā manēre dēbēre?

Mercurius: The gods are not accustomed to think about the love of humans. I do not care a bit for the love of Aeneas and Dido. Aeneas must hear the words of Jupiter and not stay with Dido!

Aenēās: Dēbeōne Dīdōnem relinquere et ad Italiam nāvigāre?

Mercurius: Jupiter orders you to leave Dido and seek Italy.

Aenēās: Iuppiter est crūdēlis! (Tū) es crūdēlis! Deī sunt crūdēlēs!

Mercurius: Not the gods, but the Fates are cruel. The Fates say Aeneas must seek Italy.

Aenēās: Dēbentne hominēs esse miserī?

Mercurius: Yes indeed. However, afterward Aeneas will be renowned and a poet shall say: "Of so much trouble it was to found the Roman race!"

TEACHER BY THE WAY
While English prefers "Dido and I," Latin prefers *"ego Dīdōque."* In the same line *Carthāgine* has a locative sense.

TEACHING TIP
After the students have completed Exercise 6 and the teacher has checked to make sure the translations are correct, ask pairs of students to perform this dialogue orally in Latin.

PAGE 195
Standards 1.2, 2.1, 3.1, 3.2, 4.1
Oral Exercise 3, Dictation and Oral Exercise 4

TRANSLATION OF THE LATIN CONVERSATION

Mark: For a long time I was saving money. For I wanted to have a car. And so I bought a car.

Christy: Are you accustomed to come to school in (by means of) your car, Mark?

Mark: Yes, indeed. And Helen is accustomed to come with me in my car. How are you, Christy, accustomed to come to school?

Christy: I am accustomed to come to school in (by means of) a bus or in (by means of) the subway train. For I do not have a car and we live far from school. Every day I have to make a long trip.

Mark: How are you, Mary, accustomed to come to school?

Mary: I am accustomed to come to school on a bicycle or on foot. For we live close to school. Therefore sometimes I can walk to school. Why, Mark, does Helen always come to school with you?

Mark: Helen and I always desire to make the trip to school together. First I make a trip to Helen's house. Helen is waiting. I pick Helen up. Then we make (the) trip to school together.

ORAL EXERCISE 3

This exercise may be used after the Latin dialogue has been presented.

After the students have carefully read and understood the dialogue, the teacher should ask individual students the following questions. In preparation for the exercise, the teacher should use one of the CPOs to put on view the following words that are also useful for questions and answers. The students should try to answer while looking at the dialogue, and should be told they can frame their answers using the actual words in the text—with the appropriate adjustments of endings and person.

quid? – what?   **quōmodo** – how, in what way?
cūr? – why?   **quandō** – when?
quia – because   **quis** – who?

1. **Teacher:** Quid Mārcus diū servābat?
    Student: Mārcus pecūniam diū servābat.
2. **Teacher:** Cūr Mārcus pecūniam diū servābat?
    Student: Quia raedam habēre cupiēbat.
3. **Teacher:** Habetne Mārcus raedam?
    Student: Mārcus raedam habet.
4. **Teacher:** Quōmodo Mārcus ad scholam venīre solet?
    Student: Mārcus raedā ad scholam venīre solet.
5. **Teacher:** Quis cum Mārcō ad scholam venīre solet?
    Student: Helena cum Mārcō ad scholam venīre solet.
6. **Teacher:** Habetne raedam Christīna?
    Student: Christīna raedam nōn habet.
7. **Teacher:** Quōmodo Christīna iter ad scholam facit?
    Student: Christīna raedā longā aut trāmine subterrāneō iter ad scholam facit.

Chapter 11 • 231

8. **Teacher:** Habitatne prope scholam Christīna?
   Student: Christīna longē ā scholā habitat.

9. **Teacher:** Habitatne longē ā scholā Marīa?
   Student: Marīa prope scholam habitat.

10. **Teacher:** Quōmodo Marīa iter ad scholam facit?
    Student: Marīa iter ad scholam birotā aut pedibus facit.

11. **Teacher:** Cūr Helena ad scholam cum Mārcō venīre solet?
    Student: Quia Mārcus et Helena iter ad scholam semper ūnā facere cupiunt.

DICTATION AND ORAL EXERCISE 4

This exercise may be used to conclude the chapter.

The teacher should dictate the following passage to the students, and then ask individual students the questions written below. To answer the questions, the students should make use of the words in the passage that they have just written—with the appropriate adjustments of endings and person. Before asking the questions, the teacher should put on view the vocabulary below the passage.

Trōiānī iter longum Carthāginem faciunt. Nāvibus Carthāginem veniunt. Dīdō rēgīna Carthāgine habitat. Aenēās Dīdōque iter pedibus in silvam ūnā facere cupiunt. Diū ambulant. In spēluncam veniunt. Aenēās dīcit sē Dīdōnem amāre. Aenēās novum iter facere nōn cupit, sed cupit ūnā cum Dīdōne manēre et longē ab Italiā habitāre. Deī autem iubent Aenēam novum iter facere. Itaque Aenēās Dīdōnem relinquere et nāvibus Italiam petere dēbet.

Carthāgine – Carthage
Carthāginem – to Carthage
cūr? – why?
Italia, Italiae, *f.* – Italy
iter faciō (**facere, fēcī, factum**) – I make a journey, travel
nāvis, nāvis, *f.* – ship
pēs, pedis, *m.* – foot

quandō – when?
quia – because
quid – what?
quis – who?
quō – to what place?
quōmodo – how, in what way?
Trōiānus, Trōiānī, *m.* – Trojan
ubi – where?

1. **Teacher:** Quō Trōiānī iter longum faciunt?
   Student: Trōiānī iter longum Carthāginem faciunt.

2. **Teacher:** Quōmodo Trōiānī Carthāginem veniunt?
   Student: Trōiānī nāvibus Carthāginem veniunt.

3. **Teacher:** Ubi Dīdō rēgīna habitat?
   Student: Dīdō rēgīna Carthāgine habitat.

4. **Teacher:** Quōmodo Aenēās Dīdōque iter in silvam ūnā facere cupiunt?
   Student: Aenēās Dīdōque iter pedibus in silvam ūnā facere cupiunt.

5. **Teacher:** Quō pedibus Aenēās Dīdōque veniunt?
   Student: Aenēās Dīdōque in spēluncam pedibus veniunt.

6. **Teacher:** Quid Aenēās dīcit?
   Student: Aenēās dīcit sē Dīdōnem amāre.

7. **Teacher:** Cupitne Aenēās novum iter facere?
   Student: Nōn cupit Aenēās novum iter facere.

232 • Latin for the New Millennium: Teacher's Manual, Level 1

8. **Teacher:** Quid cupit Aenēās?
    Student: Aenēās cupit ūnā cum Dīdōne manēre et longē ab Italiā habitāre.
9. **Teacher:** Quid Deī iubent?
    Student: Deī iubent Aenēam novum iter facere.
10. **Teacher:** Quō novum iter facere dēbet Aenēās?
    Student: Aenēās novum iter ad Italiam facere dēbet.

PAGE 196
Standard 4.1

DERIVATIVES

dolor – The names "Delores" and "Dolores" are derived from the Latin *dolor* through the Spanish proper name, *Maria de los Dolores* (Mary of the Sorrows).

Note the "-ous" suffix of "dolorous." The *Via Dolorōsa* is the road Jesus walked carrying his cross. Note how the *-ōsa* suffix of the Latin becomes the "-ous" in English.

See the verb *doleō* 1.5 for related derivatives.

rēgīna – For related derivatives, see *rēx*.

silva – The Roman *Silvanus* was the god of the forests.

"Silviculture" is a concern of the US Forest Service (from *silva* and *colō* = to cultivate).

The <u>sylvan</u> was surrounded by trees.

The state <u>Pennsylvania</u> is equivalently "Penn's woods."

The word "savage" came into English around 1300 meaning "wild, undomesticated, untamed" from the Latin *silva* through the Old French *sauvage* (wild, untamed). The meaning expanded to include "reckless, ungovernable" (around 1400) and "implications of human ferocity" (1570s).

spēlunca – Amelia and her husband often go <u>spelunking</u>, as they love to investigate caves.

tempestās – See *tempus* 1.9.

crūdēlis – The words "cruel" and "cruelty" appeared in English during the early thirteenth century through the twelfth century Old French *cruel* (earlier form *crudel*) from the Latin *crūdēlis*.

novus – The word "novel" as an adjective meaning "new, strange, unusual" appeared in English during the early fifteenth century, derived from the Latin diminutive of *novus* (*novellus*). The noun, referring to a "fictitious narrative," came into English during the 1560s. This type of literature first appeared among the Romans who called such writings *novella* (new things), e.g., Apuleius's *The Golden Ass*. Boccaccio's *Decameron*, (literal meaning = ten days), a collection of short loosely connected stories set in the year of the Black Death (1348), is the first example of a "novel" in more modern literature.

The word "novice," meaning "a probationer in a religious order," entered English during the mid-fourteenth century. This period of a religious novice's life is called a "novitiate." The meaning of "an inexperienced person" is attested from the early fifteenth century.

The verb "innovate," meaning "introduce as new," appeared in English during the 1540s, derived from the fourth principal part of the Latin *innovō* (to change into something new, alter).

A skilled restorer can <u>renovate</u> an old painting to make it look like new again.

Chapter 11 • 233

The word "novelty" came into English during the late fourteenth century meaning "a new manner or fashion, something new or unusual." The sense of "a useless but amusing object" is attested from 1901.

agō – These words are just a representative sample of the derivatives based on *agō*.

The "act" base of "act, action, and actual" derives from the fourth principal part of *agō*.

The prefix of "inaction" is negative.

Note the "-tor" suffix of "agitator" (a person who "drives" others to action).

An "ambiguity" can lead to several possible meanings (*ambi* – Latin prefix meaning "round, about" and *agō*).

The verb "coagulate" appeared in English during the early fifteenth century, its form and meaning derived from the Latin *cogō* (*cum* = together, and *agō*; hence, "to drive together, collect, compel, thicken, etc.): Blood <u>coagulates</u>; to <u>curdle</u> milk means to thicken it.

A "cogent" argument is a compelling one.

To "cogitate" means "to think, ponder" from the Latin *cogitō* (to think; *cum* and *agitō*, a frequentative form of *agō*; literally, "to put into motion together").

The noun "essay" appeared in English during the 1590s and was first attested in the writings of Francis Bacon. It was derived through the Middle French *essai* (trial, attempt) from the Latin *exigō* (*ex* = out from, and *agō*; hence, "to drive out, demand [payment], dispose of, test, consider"). It was thus used as the term for a "short, nonfiction literary composition" with the suggestion of unpolished writing.

The word "exact" is also from *exigō* (the fourth principal part), deriving from the meaning "to demand, require, measure," for the verb (mid-fifteenth century) and leading to the adjective meaning "precise, accurate" about a century later (1530s).

From the same Latin verb come "exigency" (1580s) meaning "urgency" and "exigent" (1660s), also meaning "urgent, requiring immediate action" (*exigō* = demand, require, drive out).

A "navigator" drives (steers) a ship (*nāvis* = ship).

The word "prodigal" came into English during the mid-fifteenth century, derived through the Middle French *prodigal* from the Latin *prōdigus* (wasteful, lavish; from *prōdigō* = to squander, from *prō* = forth, and *agō* = drive, spend, etc.). The first reference to a "prodigal son" is found in Luke 15:11–32 (*filius prōdigus*). A "prodigal person" dates to the 1590s.

The verb "squat," meaning "to crouch on the heels," appeared in English during the early fifteenth century, derived through the Old French *esquatir* (to press down, crush) from the Latin *ex* = out, and *coactus* (drive together, force). The adjective sense of "short, thick" dates to the 1620s.

The word "squatter" (settler occupying land without legal title) appears in 1788, and is used to designate "paupers or homeless people inhabiting (sitting in) empty buildings" from 1880.

See also Teaching Tips 1.6, 1.9.

ārdeō – The word "ardent" in the early fourteenth century referred to alcohol like brandy (ardent spirits) but was also used figuratively to describe passions.

The noun "arson," derived from the fourth principal part of *ārdeō*, appeared in English during the 1670s; "arsonist" in 1864.

cōnspiciō – (from *speciō* = to see, consider)

234 • Latin for the New Millennium: Teacher's Manual, Level 1

The prefix of "conspicuous" is intensive. Note the "-ous" suffix. The word came into English during the 1540s (from the Latin *conspicuus*) meaning "visible, striking." Today it refers to someone or something attracting special attention, often with a pejorative nuance. Social and economic prejudice is still very <u>conspicuous</u> in America. However, it can be a positive description. The soldier's <u>conspicuous</u> bravery earned him the Congressional Medal of Honor.

mittō – Most of the derivatives listed are easily understood, their meanings altered by prefixes, e.g., "admit" (to send to, let go into), "remission" (a sending back), "emit" (to send out), "dismiss" (to send away).

The word "mission," meaning "a sending abroad" (1590s), originally referred to the Jesuits sent to foreign countries during the "Age of Exploration" to convert inhabitants to Christianity. The diplomatic sense dates to the 1620s. Military usage dates to 1929, that of space exploration to 1962.

The word "committee" derives from the Latin *committō* (to send together, join, undertake). It originally referred to a person to whom something is assigned (late fifteenth century). From the seventeenth century it has referred to a group of such people.

The word "promise" is derived from the Latin noun *prōmissum* (*prō* = before, and *mittō*; hence *prōmittō* = to send forth, foretell, assure beforehand).

A "compromise" is a "promise together, a joint promise" to abide by an arbiter's decision (early fifteenth century). The modern sense of "coming to terms" dates to the latter part of that century.

The word "demise" is derived through the Middle French *démettre* from the Latin *dis* (away) and *mittō* (to let go). In the mid-fifteenth century it referred to "a transfer of estate by will." The meaning was extend to "death" in 1754 because that was the occasion for such a transfer.

The word "manumission," meaning "freedom," came into English around 1400, derived from the Latin *manūmissiō* which referred to the freeing of a slave (*manū* = from the hand, i.e., from the power of a master, and *mittō*).

The verb *mittō* can also mean "to thrust, put," hence the Late Latin meaning "to put, place." The noun *missus* thus meant "a placing on the table, a course at dinner." This gave rise to the Old French *mes* (a course at dinner, a portion of food) and thus to the English "mess" (around 1300). The idea of a "common eating place," especially a military one, is found in the 1530s. In 1738 the word is found to mean "mixed food, especially for animals," which led to the contemptuous use for "jumble, mixed mass" (1828). The figurative use of the word meaning "confusion" dates to 1834 and the "condition of untidiness" to 1851. Using the verb "mess" to mean "make a mess" dates to 1853. The meaning "to interfere" is attested in 1903; "to make a mistake, get into trouble" in 1933.

Like "mess," the word "message" derives from the fourth principal part of *mittō* (to send) through the Old French *message* (news, tidings, embassy). It appeared in English around 1300 meaning "communication transmitted by a messenger."

The spelling of the word "messenger" is interesting. This noun appeared in English early, around 1200, derived from the Latin *missus* through the Old French *messagier* (from the eleventh century *message*). The letter *n* seems to have been inserted for no other reason than that people liked to say it that way (cf. passenger, scavenger, Dillinger).

"Omit" comes directly from the Latin *omittō* (to let go, disregard, overlook); "permit" from *permittō* (to let go, let pass, allow); "premise" from *praemittō* (to send in advance); "submit" from *summittō* (*sub* = up to, and *mittō*; hence, to send up, dispatch; note the assimilation); "surmise" from *super* (upon) and *mittō*.

Chapter 11 • 235

"Surmise" appeared in English as a verb around 1400 meaning "to charge, allege" (send upon) through the French *surmettre* (to accuse). The meaning "to infer" dates to 1700. The noun "surmise" is found in English as a legal term a little bit later (early fifteenth century) meaning "a charge" and evolved to mean "guess, inference" by the 1580s.

relinquō – The spelling of "relic" reflects that of the fourth principal part of *relinquō* (*relictus*).

A <u>derelict</u> building has been abandoned (*derelinquō*; the prefix *de* = entirely). The fourth principal part *derelictus* was used in Latin as an adjective meaning "abandoned, deserted." The English derivative dates to the 1640s.

A related Latin verb, *delinquō*, meaning "to fail, do wrong," is the source for "delinquent," which appeared during the late fifteenth century.

ita – None

minimē – This is the adverbial form of the superlative of *parvus* (small), hence the derivatives "minimal, minimum, and minimize." The Latin adverbial form was used by the Romans as a strong negative response: "By no means, no way."

quoque – None

ūnā – See *ūnus* 2.7.

CHAPTER 12 (PP. 197–209)

GRAMMAR IN LANGUAGE FACTS

First, Second, and Third Person Personal Pronouns; First and Second Person Possessive Adjectives; Declension of *Vīs*

PAGE 197
Standards 1.1, 1.2
RRA 6A

MEMORĀBILE DICTŪ VOCABULARY
adiuvō, adiuvāre, adiūvī, adiūtum – to help
fortūna, fortūnae, *f.* – fortune, fate

TEACHER BY THE WAY
Like Jacques-Louis David (cf. p. 132 [SE]), Pecheux paints in the neoclassical style.

TEACHING TIP
The story of Mucius Scaevola occurred in a much earlier time than when its author Livy was writing. Hence the teacher may wish to instruct the students to review Chapter 3 of RRA.

TEACHER BY THE WAY
There were several groups of very powerful cities in Etruria, the region of Italy lying between Florence and Rome. Twelve cities were united into a league only for celebrating religious festivals. The most famous were Tarquinii, Caere, Veii, Vetulonia (the oldest settlement), and Clusium. The last mentioned was the stronghold of Lars Porsenna. Because of their rivalry with each other, the Etruscans were not united by a firm alliance and this affected their struggles with those who would try to prevent their encroachment beyond Etruria. Toward the end of the seventh century BCE, the Etruscans crossed the Tiber and occupied Latium. Then they soon advanced south into Campania and also established colonies from Milan to Bologna. By the fifth century BCE their expansion, domination, and civilization reached its height. They struggled with the Greeks at Cumae on land and sea and lost. Next the Romans expelled the last Etruscan king in 509 BCE. Tradition claims that Tarquinius Superbus asked

Lars Porsenna for help and Rome was besieged, but the outcome is unclear. Porsenna retired and did not involve himself any further with the deposed Etruscan king. Hieron of Syracuse in 474 BCE saved Cumae by sending a fleet and putting an end to Etruscan sea power. An Etruscan helmet that commemorates this victory was found at Olympia in 1817. With the capture of Veii in 396 BCE and the Gallic invasion in 390 BCE, their power declined and in the next two hundred years all the great Etruscan cities were subdued by Rome.

TEACHING TIP
Chapter 6A of RRA contains information on Livy. The teacher may wish to assign this chapter for reading or review. See p. 201.

PAGE 198
Standards 1.1, 2.1, 3.1, 3.2

TRANSLATION OF LATIN PASSAGE
About Mucius Scaevola

"I am a Roman citizen," said Mucius. "People call me Mucius. I sought to kill you, an enemy. I was not afraid of your soldiers. Now I am not afraid of death. The Romans do not fear the force of enemies. There are many Romans like me and prepared to do what I was not able to do. Therefore you must always fear our citizens. You wage war against us not only in camp (i.e., in the field), but also at home, where there are hidden enemies seeking you." The king is stirred by anger. He orders the Etruscan soldiers to place fires near Mucius. Then the king said: "Do you say that there is danger for me from hidden enemies? I say there is now danger for you from the fires! You must now fear the fires, unless you tell me immediately the names of the hidden enemies!" Mucius, however, suddenly places his right hand in the fire. There he stayed, nor did he show pain. The astounded king sees the right hand of Mucius consumed by flames. Then the king decides to free Mucius; for he understands that he (Mucius) is extremely brave and he judges that such great bravery cannot be conquered!

TEACHER BY THE WAY
There are summaries of the missing books, called *Periochae*. Livy worked on this history of Rome for forty years.

TEACHING TIP
Instruct the students to locate Padua and Etruria on the map on pp. xxxiv–xxxv (SE) and to find Livy, Mucius Scaevola, and Lars Porsenna on the timeline on pp. 405–408 (SE).

TEACHER BY THE WAY

Books 1–5 of Livy's *Ab Urbe Conditā* cover the years from the earliest legends through the early Republic to the destruction of Rome by the Gauls in 390 (387) BCE. Books 6–10 describe the internal politics (389–366 BCE), the Samnite Wars, and the settlement of Latium. Books 21–30 cover the Second Punic War. Books 31–45 describe the Second and Third Macedonian Wars, the arraignment of Scipio Africanus, and the Bacchanalia in Rome and Italy.

PAGE 199

ANSWERS TO COMPREHENSION QUESTIONS

1. Mucius tells Porsenna that many more Romans are ready to do what he has just tried to accomplish.
2. Mucius thrusts his right hand into the fire.
3. Porsenna frees him in admiration of his courage.

TEACHING TIP

Students may be interested in learning about the word *occīdō* that is based on the verb *caedō*, which means in general "to strike, beat, punch, slap, beat, flog, scourge" but also "to kill, slay, murder, defeat." *Occīdō* seems to be even more intense and lethal: "to kill, slaughter," then "to involve in disaster or failure, bring about the ruin of," and finally, "to cut up, crush to pieces."

From this root comes a series of English words derived from "-cide" meaning "the killing of."

- fratricide   a brother
- genocide   a race
- homicide   a man, a person
- infanticide   an infant
- matricide   a mother
- parricide   any close relative; a "kin-killer"
- patricide   a father
- pesticide   an insect
- regicide   a king
- sororicide   a sister
- suicide   one's self
- uxoricide   a wife

Chapter 12 • 239

PAGE 200
Standards 3.1, 3.2, 4.1

TEACHING TIP
Instruct the students to repeat aloud the forms of the personal pronouns of the first and second person after the teacher models the pronunciation of the words. Then encourage the students to create a rap, cheer, or song to help them remember the forms. Alternatively, use Bolchazy-Carducci's *Toga Beats*.

TEACHING TIP
Remind students that the nominative singular of the first and second person pronouns are usually only needed in a Latin sentence for emphasis, since the verb endings also indicate the person of the verb. On the other hand, when the other cases of the personal pronouns are needed in a sentence, they cannot be omitted.

TEACHING TIP
The teacher may wish to use the oral Latin grammar terms already presented in this teacher's manual on p. 32 and p. 48 to ask students about the personal pronouns (*prōnōmen persōnāle*) in the paradigm on p. 200 (SE). The teacher may ask these questions with the students looking at the paradigm in the student edition or with the book closed. Some questions are listed for the teacher's convenience.

- *Ego – quō est cāsū?* Answer: *nōminātīvō <cāsū>*
- *Meī – cūius est numerī?* Answer: *<numerī> singulāris*
- *Mihi – cūius est persōnae?* Answer: *prīmae <persōnae>*
- *Mē – quae pars ōrātiōnis est?* Answer: *prōnōmen persōnāle*

The same types of questions may be asked about the forms of the second person singular personal pronoun and the first and second person plural personal pronouns.

PAGE 201
Standards 1.1, 1.2

▶ EXERCISE 1 ANSWERS

1. nōbīs
   You (plural) give gifts to us. Therefore we ought to give gifts to you (plural).
2. Vōs
   We love you very much. Therefore you also ought to love us.
3. Tē
   I really love you. Therefore you also ought to love me.
4. nōbīs
   You are always thinking about us. Therefore we must always think about you.

5. mē
   You (plural) are always thinking about me.
   Therefore I must think about you (plural) always.
6. Nōs
   We are happy.
   vōs
   Are you happy?
7. Ego
   I am happy.
   tū
   Are you happy?

TEACHING TIP

After the students have completed Exercise 1 and the correct answers have been given, some oral practice can be done using the words in bold in Exercise 1. For each of the bold words, the teacher may ask individual students the following questions:

- *Cūius temporis est?*   Answer: *praesentis*
- *Cūius persōnae est?*   Answers: *prīmae, secundae, tertiae*
- *Cūius generis/vōcis est?*   Answer: *āctīvī/āctīvae*
- *Cūius est numerī?*   Answers: *singulāris, plūrālis*
- *Quae pars ōrātiōnis est?*   Correct Answer: *verbum temporāle*
- *Estne verbum inaequāle (irregular)?*   Correct Answers: *ita, minimē*

PAGE 202

Standards 1.1, 1.2, 4.1
Workbook Exercise 2

▶ EXERCISE 2 ANSWERS

1. facts — faciō
2. ostentatious — ostendō
3. position — pōnō, positum
4. consumers — cōnsūmō
5. simile — similis
6. dexterity — dextra
7. ignition — ignis

TEACHING TIP

Although in Exercise 2 the students are directed to find only the derivatives based on the Vocabulary to Learn, they may be interested to learn that there are other derivatives in Exercise 2. The derivation of these words is provided for the teacher's convenience.

1. please – from *placeō* (to please, satisfy). state – from *status* (posture, attitude, position) from *statuō* (to set up, decide, decree, propose, etc.).
2. simple – from *simplex* (single, simple, natural, straightforward).

Chapter 12 • 241

3. proud – from *prōsum, prōdesse* (to be useful to). social – from *socius* (friend, companion, partner, ally) from *sociō* (to unite, associate, share).
4. various – from *varius* (diverse, changeable, various).
5. figure – from *figūra* (shape, form) from *fingō* (to form, shape, make, etc.). comparison – from *comparō* (to match, pair with).
6. gladiator – from *gladius* (sword).

▶ EXERCISE 3 ANSWERS

1. Mē esse hostem crēdit. — S/he believes that I am an enemy.
2. Vōs tempestātem cōnspicere cupiēbāmus. — We wanted you to look at the storm.
3. Senēs nōbīs similēs nōn sunt. — The old men are not like us.
4. Dē mē mulier nōn cōgitat. — The woman does not think about me.
5. Dīcimus vōbīs ē flammīs esse perīcula. — We say that there are dangers to you from the flames./We say to you that there are dangers from the flames.
6. Prope nōs pōnuntur ignēs. — The fires are placed near us.

PAGE 203

Standards 3.1, 4.1
Oral Exercise 1; Workbook Exercises 3, 5

ORAL EXERCISE 1

This exercise may be used anytime after is, ea, id *has been presented.*

The teacher should pronounce the forms of *is, ea, id* in either singular or plural, and then ask individual students to change the forms that are singular into plural and vice versa. For some, more than one answer is possible.

Teacher: eī	**Student:** is; eīs
Teacher: ea	**Student:** eae; id
Teacher: eā	**Student:** eīs
Teacher: eōrum	**Student:** eius
Teacher: eīs	**Student:** eī; eā; eō
Teacher: eae	**Student:** ea
Teacher: id	**Student:** ea
Teacher: eārum	**Student:** eius
Teacher: eum	**Student:** eōs
Teacher: eās	**Student:** eam
Teacher: eō	**Student:** eīs

TEACHING TIP

Instruct the students to say the declension of *is, ea, id* aloud after the teacher models the pronunciation of these words. Then encourage the students to create a rap, cheer, or song to help them remember the forms. Alternatively, use Bolchazy-Carducci's *Toga Beats*.

PAGE 204
Standards 1.1, 1.2

TEACHER BY THE WAY
The cross at the top of the Temple of Antoninus and Faustina in the picture on this page shows how the conversion of this Roman temple into a Christian church preserved this building. Perhaps the best example of this, however, is the Roman Pantheon (see pp. 392–393 [SE] for pictures of this edifice), which continues to function as a Catholic church, Santa Maria della Rotunda. Although the Pantheon has lost some of its decorative elements and the sculptures from its pediment, its fundamental structure with its magnificent dome and *oculus* stands as a testament to Roman architectural and engineering achievement. Some of the temple's bronze accoutrements were melted and incorporated into the baldachino in St. Peter's Basilica. While Roman structures often served as quarries for later generations, the conversion of a Roman building to a different use preserved it quite well.

▶ EXERCISE 4 ANSWERS

1. Dolōrem eārum vidēmus.   We see their grief.
2. Magna praemia eīs dantur.   Great rewards are given to them.
3. Mūcius ex eius castrīs nōn fugit. Mucius does not flee from his camp.
4. Mūcius eam ē rēge nōn petēbat. Mucius did not seek it from the king.
5. Mīles id nōn timēbat.   The soldier was not afraid of it.
6. Lacrimīs eārum movēbāmur.   We were moved by their tears.
7. Rēx eī nōn crēdit.   The king does not believe him.
8. Dē eā saepe cōgitāmus.   We think about it often.
9. Templum ab eō aedificātur.   The temple is built by him.

TEACHER BY THE WAY
Ab is used most frequently and always before words beginning with vowels and the letter *h*. *Ex* is used more frequently than *ē* and, similarly, always before vowels and *h*.

TEACHING TIP
Instruct the students to find Antoninus Pius on the timeline on pp. 405–408 (SE).

Chapter 12 • 243

PAGE 205

Standards 1.1, 1.2, 3.1, 4.1

Oral Exercise 2; Workbook Exercise 1

▶ EXERCISE 5 ANSWERS

1. fīlius meus
2. fīliōrum meōrum
3. fīliae nostrae
4. fīliās nostrās
5. verbō tuō
6. verba tua
7. equō vestrō
8. equīs vestrīs

ORAL EXERCISE 2

This exercise may be used after the personal pronouns and possessive adjectives of the first and second persons have been presented.

The following oral exercise is designed to help students internalize their understanding of the first and second person pronouns and the first and second person possessive adjectives. In preparation for the exercise, the teacher should use one of the CPOs to put on view the following interrogative words with the English translation. Then the teacher makes a statement assumed to be true for the purpose of the activity. Next the teacher should ask a student about the statement just made. When answering, the student can (and should) use all the words in the statement, but will have to change the personal pronouns and possessive adjectives to fit the point of view of the person who answers. For a quicker understanding of the questions, the teacher should point to the interrogative word on view that is used in each question. Both the statement and the question should be repeated as many times as needed.

cūius? – whose (genitive singular)?

quōrum? – whose (genitive plural)?

cui? – to whom (dative singular)?

quem? – whom (accusative singular)?

Statement: Nōmen meum nōn scīs.
Teacher: Cūius nōmen nōn scīs?
Student: Nōmen tuum nōn sciō.

Statement: Dextrās vestrās nōn ostenditis. (The teacher should indicate by gesturing that s/he is referring to the whole class and the student should respond accordingly.)
Teacher: Quōrum dextrās nōn ostenditis?
Student: Dextrās nostrās nōn ostendimus.

Statement: Amīcum tuum doceō.
Teacher: Cūius amīcum doceō?
Student: Amīcum meum docēs.

Statement: Dē verbīs meīs nōn cōgitās.
Teacher: Cūius dē verbīs nōn cōgitās?
Student: Dē verbīs tuīs nōn cōgitō.

Statement: Librum tuum vidēre cupiō.
Teacher: Cūius librum vidēre cupiō?
Student: Librum meum vidēre cupis.

244 • Latin for the New Millennium: Teacher's Manual, Level 1

Statement: Librōs vestrōs nōn videō. (The teacher should indicate by gesturing that s/he is referring to the whole class and the student should respond accordingly.)
Teacher: Quōrum librōs nōn videō?
Student: Librōs nostrōs nōn vidēs.

Statement: Librum meum tibi dare cupiō.
Teacher: Cui librum meum dare cupiō?
Student: Librum tuum mihi dare cupis.

Statement: Fābulam tuam mihi nārrāre cupis.
Teacher: Cui fābulam tuam nārrāre cupis?
Student: Fābulam meam tibi nārrāre cupiō.

Statement: Casam meam tibi ostendere cupiō.
Teacher: Cui casam meam ostendere cupiō?
Student: Casam tuam mihi ostendere cupis.

Statement: Tē librum novum habēre sciō.
Teacher: Quem librum novum habēre sciō?
Student: Mē librum novum habēre scīs.

PAGE 206

Standards 1.1, 1.2, 3.1, 4.1
Workbook Exercise 4

▶ EXERCISE 6 ANSWERS

1. vestrōrum — of your names
2. nostrō — The horse was being led by our son.
3. tuum — You are taking your reward.
4. meās — The king loved my daughters.
5. nostram — The men were observing our land.
6. tuam — You must not leave your right hand in the fire.

TEACHING TIP

Some students may experience difficulty distinguishing between the forms of *vīs* and *vir*. The irregular noun *vīs* is declined on p. 206 of the student text. The teacher may wish to instruct the students to look back at p. 35 (SE) where the declension of *vir* will be found. Using these two pages as a reference, the students may be asked to identify the case, number, and meaning (force [singular] vs. strength [plural] vs. man) of the following words. This exercise may be done orally or in written format. The answers are provided for the teacher's convenience.

- *Vīrēs* — nominative or accusative plural – strength
- *Virīs* — dative or ablative plural – men
- *Vim* — accusative singular – force
- *Virōs* — accusative plural – men
- *Virī* — nominative plural or genitive singular – men/man

- *Vī*   ablative singular – force
- *Vīrium* genitive plural – strength
- *Virum*   accusative singular – man
- *Vīribus* dative or ablative plural – strength

PAGE 207
Standards 1.1, 1.2
Workbook Exercises 6, 7, Content Questions

TEACHER BY THE WAY
The teacher may wish to point out that in the picture of the Roman soldiers on this page, two of them are carrying standards *(signa mīlitāria)* which identified the legion. A legion could be dissolved if the standard was lost in battle. Julius Caesar's favorite was LEGIŌ X.

▶ EXERCISE 7 ANSWERS
1. Nunc intellegō, Mūcī, fortitūdinem tuam flammīs vincī nōn posse.
2. Dē morte meā cōgitāre cupis, sed fortitūdinem meam vidēs.
3. Ea tibi, rēx, videntur esse perīcula, sed nōn mīlitibus nostrīs Rōmānīs.
4. "Dēbēs mihi," inquit rēx, "nōmina hostium meōrum statim dīcere."
5. "In urbe meā," inquit Mūcius, "sunt mihi similēs multī."
6. "Fortitūdinem mīlitum nostrōrum," inquit Mūcius, "intellegere nōn potes."

TEACHING TIP
Instruct the students to find Marcus Aurelius on the timeline on pp. 405–408 (SE).

TEACHER BY THE WAY
The Latin terms for the clothing and accoutrements seen in the relief are printed for your convenience.

- breastplate – *lōrīca*
- cloak fastened in front with a brooch – *sagum*
- greaves – *ocreae*
- helmet – *galea*
- javelin – *pīlum*
- leather tunic (worn under the *lōrīca* to protect the thighs and shoulders) – *tunica*
- sandals (heavy and hobnailed) – *caligae*
- shield – *scūtum*

The two soldiers wearing *saga* are each carrying a *signum*, the standard of a century. These soldiers were called *signiferī*.

PAGE 208
Standards 1.2, 4.1

TEACHING TIP
Divide the class into four groups and assign one season to each group. The groups should draw a picture that represents the season assigned to them. Then they should label in Latin objects in their picture.

Examples:
arbor
caelum
folium
fulgur
gemma
nix
nubēs
tonitruum

Then instruct the students to write short Latin sentences that describe their picture.

Examples:
Folia sunt rubra.
Fulgur in caelō est.
Nix in foliīs est.

Students may wish to consult the dialogue on the next page for ways of describing their picture in Latin. Finally, each group may show its picture and orally describe it in Latin to the rest of the class.

PAGE 209
Standards 1.2, 4.1
Oral Exercise 3, Dictation and Oral Exercise 4

TRANSLATION OF THE LATIN CONVERSATION
Helen: It is snowing today. I do not like snow. If it snows, I want to remain at home.
Mary: I like snow. It is good to play in the snow. What sort of weather do you like?
Helen: I like clear and bright weather/sky. I like summer. I like heat. I like the sea. In fact, during the summer I can play near the sea. Do you like the summer, Mark?
Mark: I like the summer. I like all the seasons. What season do you like, Christy?
Christy: I like the spring. Then the sky is bright, but cloudy. The clouds seem beautiful to me. Also during the spring there are buds on the trees.
Mary: I like spring too. But I love the fall very much. Then the leaves are beautiful: red and yellow. During the fall there are also storms. I am happy if I hear thunder and see lightning.

ORAL EXERCISE 3

This exercise may be used after the Latin dialogue has been presented.

After the students have carefully read and understood the dialogue, the teacher should ask individual students the following questions.

TEACHING TIP
Instruct the students to look at the dialogue while answering.

quid? – what?

quae rēs? – what things?

Teacher: Amatne nivēs Helena?
Student: Helena nivēs nōn amat.

Teacher: Sī ningit, quid facere cupit Helena?
Student: Sī ningit, Helena domī manēre cupit.

Teacher: Quid in nivibus facere cupit Marīa?
Student: Marīa cupit in nivibus lūdere.

Teacher: Quāle caelum Helenae placet?
Student: Caelum sūdum et serēnum Helenae placet.

Teacher: Quod annī tempus Helenae placet?
Student: Placet Helenae aestās.

Teacher: Quid dē calōribus sentit Helena?
Student: Placent Helenae calōrēs.

Teacher: Quod annī tempus Mārcō placet?
Student: Omnia annī tempora Mārcō placent.

Teacher: Quid dē vēre sentit Christīna?
Student: Vēr Christīnae placet.

Teacher: Quid dē nūbibus putat Christīna?
Student: Christīna putat nūbēs esse pulchrās.

Teacher: Quod annī tempus valdē amat Marīa?
Student: Marīa autumnum valdē amat.

Teacher: Quae rēs Marīae autumnō placent?
Student: Folia rubra et flāva. Tonitrua et fulgura Marīae autumnō placent.

DICTATION AND ORAL EXERCISE 4

This exercise may be used to conclude the chapter.

The teacher should dictate the following passage to the students, and then ask individual students the questions written below. Before asking the questions, the teacher should use one of the CPOs to put on view the words below the passage. To answer the questions, the students should make use of the words in the passage that they have just written—with the appropriate adjustments of endings and person.

Rōmānī Mūcium esse mīlitem fortem crēdēbant. Rōmānī mittunt eum ad rēgem Etrūscōrum. Mūcius autem rēgem Etrūscōrum occīdere nōn potest, sed ab Etrūscīs capitur. Rēx Mūciī amīcōs valdē timet. Sed Mūcius nōmina amīcōrum eī nōn dīcit. Mūcius sē nōn timēre ostendit. Rēx Mūciī fortitūdinem vincere nōn potest.

quid? – what?

quis? – who?

quō? – to what place?

Teacher: Quid dē Mūciō crēdēbant Rōmānī?
Student: Rōmānī Mūcium esse mīlitem fortem crēdēbant.

Teacher: Quō Mūcium mittunt Rōmānī?
Student: Rōmānī mittunt Mūcium ad rēgem Etrūscōrum.

Teacher: Quid rēgī Etrūscōrum facere cupit Mūcius?
Student: Mūcius rēgem Etrūscōrum occīdere cupit.

Teacher: Potestne Mūcius rēgem Etrūscōrum occīdere?
Student: Mūcius rēgem Etrūscōrum occīdere nōn potest.

Teacher: Quī Mūcium capiunt?
Student: Etrūscī Mūcium capiunt.

Teacher: Quid ē Mūciō audīre cupit Etrūscōrum rēx?
Student: Etrūscōrum rēx ē Mūciō nōmina eius amīcōrum audīre cupit.

Teacher: Dīcitne eī Mūcius nōmina amīcōrum?
Student: Mūcius nōmina amīcōrum eī nōn dīcit.

Teacher: Quid rēgī ostendit Mūcius?
Student: Mūcius rēgī sē nōn timēre ostendit.

Teacher: Quid ā rēge vincī nōn potest?
Student: Mūciī fortitūdō ā rēge vincī nōn potest.

DERIVATIVES

dextra – (from the adjective *dexter*)

An "ambidextrous" person can use both hands equally (*ambo* = two, both, and *dexter*; literally "two right hands"). Globally only about 12% of men and 10% of women are left-handed; therefore, the right hand is usually the dominant one and is thus the reference for skill. This obviously held true among the Romans as well. A fascinating article in *Scientific American* (April 2012) discusses the proportion of left-handers and their talents.

Manual <u>dexterity</u> is needed for occupations requiring skillful hands.

ignis – Turning on the <u>ignition</u> of a car fires the spark plugs to <u>ignite</u> the fuel in the cylinder.

<u>Igneous</u> rocks come from a volcano where they are formed under intense heat.

<u>Ignescent</u> stones emit sparks when struck with steel. The suffix has an inchoative force from the Latin *-scō* as in *crēscō, nōscō,* and *irāscor.*

īra – The <u>irascible</u> old woman was filled with <u>ire</u> at the noisy children playing across the street.

Chapter 12 • 249

nōmen – The word "renown" entered English around 1300, derived through the Old French *renon* (fame, reputation) and *renomer* (*re* = again, repeatedly, and *nomer* = to name) from the Latin *nōmen*.

"Ignominious" (note the "-ous" suffix) is derived directly from the Latin *ignominiōsus* (disgraceful, shameful). The prefix is an assimilated form of *in*, here a negative; hence the word literally means "not a (good) name" or "loss of a good name."

The prefix of "denomination" is intensive and means "completely." The noun came into English during the late fourteenth century meaning "act of giving a name to." The monetary sense dates to the 1650s; that of "religious sect" to 1716.

A "noun" is the name of a person, place, thing, or idea.

A "pronoun" is a word standing in place of (*prō* = instead of) a noun.

The prefix of "misnomer" is derived through the Old French *mes* (badly, wrongly) from the Latin *minus* (less). The word refers to a misapplied designation or error in naming a person or thing.

vīs – The word "violation" comes directly from the verb *violō* (to treat without respect, pollute, defile), which apparently is related to *vīs* although the "formation has not been satisfactorily explained" (OLD). It appeared in English during the early fifteenth century.

The prefix of "inviolate" is negative; the word describes someone or something intact or unhurt.

is, ea, id – The neuter form *id* has been in use since 1924 to denote the unconscious instinct in Freud's psychoanalytical theory.

Id combined in Latin with the suffix *–em* to form *idem* (the same). The *d* was retained in other forms of the paradigm by misdivision, i.e., *i-dem* instead of *id-em* (OLD). The final *m* changes to an *n* in its combinative form; hence "identity." The Latin phrase *idem et idem* (the same and the same) was abbreviated to *identidem* (over and over, repeatedly). This is the source for the English derivatives which appeared during the seventeenth century. A person's <u>identity</u> stays the same under varying aspects or conditions.

nōs – None

vōs – None

noster – The word "nostrum" began referring to "quack medicine" around 1600, derived from the Latin *nostrum remedium* meaning "our remedy" (one presumably prepared by the person offering it).

similis – Related to *similis* (like) are *simulitūdō* (likeness, imitation), *simulō* (to imitate, impersonate, pretend, counterfeit). From these roots are derived English words whose meanings vary with the prefixes.

An "assembly" consists of a group of people coming together for a common (similar, like) purpose. The prefix is an "assimilation" of *ad* (to) in which the letter *d* is made "like" the following consonant.

"To dissemble" means "to disguise or conceal," derived from "dis" (from the Latin *dis* = away, apart from) and *simulō*. The same prefix is seen in "dissimilar."

The word "simulation" should be very familiar since it always appears on the bottom of the TV screen when space explorations being shown are imitations because no real photographs are available.

"Simultaneous" events occur at the same (similar) time. Note the "-ous" suffix.

The word "ensemble" appeared in English during the mid-fifteenth century as an adverb (together, at the same time) from the Latin *in*, the intensive prefix, and *similis* through the Middle French *ensemblée* (all parts considered together). The noun usage dates to 1703; the musical sense to 1844.

250 • Latin for the New Millennium: Teacher's Manual, Level 1

The prefix of the word "resemblance" is intensive: The brothers bore a remarkable <u>resemblance</u> to their father.

tantus – The verbal phrase "tant amount" appeared in English during the 1620s meaning "be equivalent" (amount to as much) and was made one word during the 1640s: Some new Latin students consider their class <u>tantamount</u> to torture, but most change their minds over time.

tuus – None

vester – None

cōnsūmō – The verb "consume" came into English during the late fourteenth century, the noun "consumer" a little later. The prefix *"con-"* (from *cum*) is an intensive; hence the Latin *cōnsūmō* means "use up, waste, squander," from *sūmō* = take, use, spend). When the word "consumption" came into English, it meant "wasting of the body by disease." The meaning "using up of material" was in vogue by the 1530s. Tuberculosis, known as "consumption" for centuries, could not begin to be controlled until the discovery of streptomycin in the early 1940s.

faciō – The verb "affect" is derived from the frequentative form of *afficiō* (*adfectō*; *ad* = to, and *faciō* = to do; hence, to aim at, try to win over, make a pretense of) and came into English during the early fifteenth century meaning "to aim at, desire, aspire." During the seventeenth century it came to mean "to act upon" and "to make a pretense of."

"Defect" derives from *dēficiō* (to fail, desert, cease; *dē* = down from, and *faciō*, to make; hence "to make less") as does "deficit," which is the third person singular of *dēficiō* and came into English in 1782 meaning "a wanting, a lack."

A "benefactor" "does well" in his actions and helps others. Note the suffix "-or" indicating agent.

A "certificate" makes certain that requirements have been met or authorization given.

Something "artificial" is made by the skill of man (*ars* = craft, skill, and *faciō*) as opposed to "natural" (made by nature).

The verb "chafe" appeared in English during the early fourteenth century derived from a combination of the Latin *caleō* (to be warm) and *faciō* through the Old French *chaufer* (to heat).

The word "chauffeur" appeared in English in 1896 originally meaning a "motorist." It was derived from the French *chauffeur* meaning "a stoker, an operator of a steam engine" which then became a nickname for early motorists whose early cars were steam-driven. The sense of professional or paid driver dates to 1902.

The prefix of "confection" means "with"; hence the word meant "to do with (something)" and referred to pharmaceutical mixtures. The idea of "making with ingredients" was extended to candy or light pastry during the sixteenth century and has remained the predominant meaning today.

"Confetti" originally referred to sweets thrown during carnivals in Italy, a custom adapted for weddings and such in England by the symbolic tossing of paper (1815).

The word "face" and its cognates, e.g., deface, efface, etc., come more directly from *faciēs* (face, appearance, form, shape) which is formed from *faciō* like *speciēs* from *speciō*.

A "facade" is the front (appearance, shape) of a building.

The word "defeat" appeared in English during the late fourteenth century derived from the Latin *dis-* (not) and *faciō* through the Old French *desfaire* (to undo; hence to destroy) and originally meant "to bring to ruin." The military sense of "to conquer" dates to around 1600. The *ea* spelling ensures the long vowel pronunciation as opposed to "defect, confection, affect," etc.

Chapter 12 • 251

<u>Factitious</u> enthusiasm is forced or contrived. Note the "-ous" suffix.

The word *factiō* in Latin means, literally, a "making" or "doing," hence a group "doing," like a political party, is called a "faction."

The noun "affair" is derived through the Old French *afaire* (from the infinitive phrase *à faire* = to do) from the Latin *ad* (to) and *faciō*. Thus the word meant (around 1300) "what one has to do." The general sense of "vague proceedings" in war or romance dates to 1702.

The verb "counterfeit" appeared in English during the late thirteenth century meaning "to imitate" from the Latin *contrā* (opposite, contrary, in violation of) and *faciō*.

The adjective "difficult" is derived directly from the Latin *difficilis* (*dis* = not, away from, and *facilis* = well-suited, ready, prosperous, easy, from *faciō*).

The spelling of "fashion" comes from the Old French *façon* (a thing done, design, beauty, etc.), which was derived from *faciō* through *factiō*.

The word "fetish" was derived, like "factitious," from the Latin *facticius* (manufactured, artificial) but came into English as *fatisso* (1610s) through the Portuguese *feitiço* (charm, sorcery). This word was replaced by the French *fétiche* about 1760.

The prefix of "forfeit" is derived from the Latin *forīs* (outside, beyond). The word came into English around 1300 meaning "misdeed" (from *forīs factum* = something done outside [the law]). The sense shifted from the crime to the penalty during the mid-fifteenth century.

The "perfect" tense indicates completed action (*per* = throughout to the end); the "imperfect" shows incomplete action (*in* = not). The "pluperfect" tense indicates action more (*plus*) in the past.

"Maleficent" is the name of the mean fairy who does bad things in Walt Disney's *Sleeping Beauty*.

The term "matter-of-fact" appeared during the 1570s as a translation of the Latin *rēs factī* (that portion of an inquiry concerned with the truth or falsehood of the alleged facts).

The Latin word *officium* was derived from *ops* (power, ability) and *faciō*; hence the "power to do one's duty, to give aid or service." From this come such derivatives as "office" meaning a "post, an employment" (mid-thirteenth century) which later referred to "a place for conducting business" (1560s); "official," "officer," and "officious." Note the "-ous" suffix, which today emphasizes the bad sense of "too zealous, meddlesome," instead of the original "full of duty, service, courtesy." The Latin *officiōsus* could also have that pejorative sense.

Someone who is "proficient" makes progress (*prō* = forward, and *faciō* = *prōficiō*) in accomplishing a designated task.

The word "profit" likewise is derived from *prōficiō* and means "to advance, success, increase." It appeared in English during the mid-thirteenth century meaning "income, benefit, advantage."

The word "ratification" derives from the Latin *ratus* (fixed, settled, valid) and *faciō*.

The Latin *reficiō*, meaning "to remake, restore," is the source for the English "refectory" through the medieval Latin *refectōrium*, a room where monks "restored themselves," i.e., a dining hall.

The word "suffice" is derived from the Latin *sufficiō* (to supply, be adequate). The *sub-* prefix indicates a reduced intensity in the verb (one does what is necessary but just enough).

The word "surface" is derived from the French *sur-* (from the Latin *super* = above) and *faciēs* (from *faciō* = *superficiēs*) and thus means "above the face" (i.e., the surface).

"Superficial" is another derivative from the same source. As is the word "surfeit" meaning "overdone" (an excess amount). The guests were <u>surfeited</u> by the seven-course meal.

The English derivatives ending in "-fy" (from *faciō*) are so numerous they can form the basis of games in the classroom. Here are some examples of such learning activities:

(1) The students are given a couple of minutes to make individual lists of words ending in "-fy." Then a check is made to see who has the most words.

(2) The students are organized into a "spelldown" format in which each person has to come up with a word not used before (the teacher must keep a list) or is out of the game.

(3) Groups can work competitively in an allotted time to make lists.

(4) The next step for the students would be to see who can come up with the most basic definitions correctly, e.g., "mortify" = to make dead; "deify" = to make a god. This makes them look up the words they cannot explain.

This list contains a goodly number of such words but is not exhaustive: amplify, beautify, clarify, classify, deify, dignify, disqualify, diversify, edify, electrify, exemplify, falsify, fortify, glorify, gratify, horrify, identify, indemnify, intensify, justify, liquefy, magnify, modify, mollify, mortify, mystify, notify, nullify, ossify, pacify, personify, petrify, purify, putrefy, qualify, rectify, sanctify, satisfy, simplify, solidify, specify, stratify, stupefy, testify, typify, unify, verify, vilify, vivify.

inquit – None

occīdō – "Occidental" means "west" for that is where the sets from *occidēns*.

ostendō – An "<u>ostensible</u> reason, one that can easily be seen (right in front)" is not always the real reason behind an action.

The words "ostentation" and "ostentatious" are pejorative (too much showing off).

pōnō – The word "compost" literally means "put together" and appeared in English during the late fourteenth century derived through the Old French *composte* (a mixture of leaves, etc., for fertilizing land) from the Latin *compōnō*.

The word "compound" as a verb and adjective came into English during the late fourteenth century as "compounen" derived through the Old French *compondre* or *componre* from the Latin *compōnō*. The *d* was added to the English word during the 1500s.

The word "depot" meaning "warehouse" came into English in 1795 through the French *dépôt* (a place of deposit; a deposit or pledge) from the Latin *dēpōnō* meaning "to lay aside" (literally, "to put down").

The Latin prefix *dis-* indicates a scattering, a dispersal; therefore, *dispōnō* means "to place here and there" but also "to scatter at definite intervals." From this we arrive at "disposition," meaning "a placing of the troops, an arrangement, or state of mind."

The adjective "exponential" (Latin *expōnō* = to put forth) came into English during the 1580s; the noun "exponent" in 1706 at first as a mathematical term. The sense of "one who puts forth" (explains, advocates, etc.) dates to 1812.

An "imposter" puts on the identity or character of someone else in order to deceive or cheat.

An "outpost" is a military position detached from the main body. The word was used first by George Washington in 1759. The mercantile sense of "trading settlement" dates to 1802. The adverb "out" is not a Latin derivative but has a common Indo-European origin with *ūsque* (all the way to).

The words "post" and "postage" came into English early in the sixteenth century from the Latin *pōnō* through the Middle French *poste* (a place where one is stationed). Riders and horses were "posted" (stationed) along the route to speed the mail by relays. This idea dates back to ancient Persia (Herodotus, *The Histories* 8.98) and was used by the Pony Express in America.

"Postilion" riders were mounted on the left side of a pair of horses drawing a carriage. They were hired, along with the coach, at a post house from a postmaster situated at set intervals along the road.

The adjective "positive" came into English during the early fourteenth century as a legal term meaning "formally laid down" from the Latin *positīvus* (arbitrarily imposed). The sense of "confident in opinion" dates to the 1660s; its mathematical use to 1704.

One's "posture" is determined by the position of the body (the meaning around 1600) or by an artificial state of mind (1877).

The word "provost" is derived from the Latin *prōpōnō* (to put ahead = in charge of). The spelling change of *p* to *v* is due to the Old French *provost*, related to the Old English *profost* and the Old High German *probost*.

A "supposition" was a term in logic, which appeared in English during the early fifteenth century meaning "assumption" (to assume as the basis of argument) from the Latin *suppōnō* (to put under, add on, apply, substitute).

See also Teaching Tips 1.1, 1.9, and 1.10.

ibi – None

statim – The abbreviation of this word "stat" is used in hospitals today whenever doctors and nurses are called to an emergency.

subitō – None

prope – The word "approach" is based on the Latin *ad* and the comparative of *prope* (*propior*) literally meaning "nearer to." The addition of *a* keeps the *o* long, as in "boat, coat, soak," etc.

The word "approximate" is based on the Latin *ad* and the superlative of *prope* (*proximus*). Thus the word means "next to." The verb form originally meant "to bring or put close" (early fifteenth century). The meaning "to come close to" dates to 1789.

The Latin *propinquus* derives from *prope* and is the root of "propinquity," which entered English during the late fourteenth century meaning "nearness in relationship." The sense of "physical nearness" dates to the early fifteenth century.

The derivation of "reproach" is in dispute. Some French etymologists claim the Old French *reprochier* comes from the Latin *re* (opposite of, back) and *prope*, with suggestions of "to get near to" as in "to get in someone's face." This interpretation may also have been colored by the similar form of "reproach" to "approach." However, this may be a false comparison, as others argue "reproach" is derived from *re* (opposite of) and *probus* (excellent in quality). The latter explanation seems more probable given the meaning of "reproach" (rebuke, blame, censure).

The word "rapprochement," which entered English in 1809, refers to "a reunion, a reconciliation" (*re* = again, and *prope*).

254 • Latin for the New Millennium: Teacher's Manual, Level 1

REVIEW 4: CHAPTERS 10–12
(PP. 211–223)

PAGE 211

TEACHING TIP
Another way to conduct a fun vocabulary review is to play vocabulary Jeopardy.

- Instruct the students to review individually the words on p. 211 (SE) for a short amount of time; meanwhile the teacher should use one of the CPOs to put on display as many categories as the teacher wishes (four or five usually work well) and to label the categories nouns, adjectives, verbs, adverbs, etc. Other parts of speech may be added as a category if there are at least five words in that category to be learned in the vocabulary review. Underneath each category there should be five boxes, each labeled with an increasing number of points. Points may be labeled in English or Latin or Roman numerals and may be from 1 to 5, 10 to 50, or 100 to 500.
- Divide the students into three teams with as equal an amount of players as possible. It will work more easily if the three teams sit or stand in rows.
- The teacher plays the role of Alex Trebek on the television show.
- For the first question, the teacher chooses a category and an amount. For example, the teacher might say, "Nouns for 100." Then the teacher gives either the nominative singular of the noun in Latin or the English meaning of the noun. Only the first person in each row/team may raise his/her hand if s/he knows the answer. The first person with his/her hand up is called upon by the teacher and, if the correct answer is given, 100 (or 1 or 10) points are awarded to the team of the winning student. The second question in the game is only for students who are in the second place on each team. The category and amount is chosen by the team that won the preceding answer. Play continues in this way until all the number amounts have been used. A correct answer gains the labeled amount of points for the whole team while an incorrect one causes the points to be subtracted from the team's current total.

If there is sufficient time, a second complete round, called "Double Jeopardy," may be played. Different words should be used during the second round. Points continue to accumulate for each team. "Final Jeopardy" should consist of one very difficult question. Each team decides how many of their points they wish to bet on whether they will get the "Final Jeopardy" question correct. Each team should be instructed to write down their bet on a piece of paper and not show the bet to the other teams. After the "Final Jeopardy" question is announced, the whole team may work to together to write their answer on the same paper on which they wrote their bet. The teacher then checks the paper of each team. If the answer is correct, the team receives the amount of points they bet. If the answer is incorrect, the amount bet is subtracted from the team score. This game is usually a favorite with students.

PAGE 212

Standards 1.1, 1.2

▶ EXERCISE 1 ANSWERS

	Singular	Plural	Singular	Plural
Nominative	dōnum tuum	dōna tua	rēgīna crūdēlis	rēgīnae crūdēlēs
Genitive	dōnī tuī	dōnōrum tuōrum	rēgīnae crūdēlis	rēgīnārum crūdēlium
Dative	dōnō tuō	dōnīs tuīs	rēgīnae crūdēlī	rēgīnīs crūdēlibus
Accusative	dōnum tuum	dōna tua	rēgīnam crūdēlem	rēgīnās crūdēlēs
Ablative	dōnō tuō	dōnīs tuīs	rēgīnā crūdēlī	rēgīnīs crūdēlibus
Vocative	dōnum tuum	dōna tua	rēgīna crūdēlis	rēgīnae crūdēlēs

	Singular	Plural	Singular	Plural
Nominative	hostis noster	hostēs nostrī	equus celeber	equī celebrēs
Genitive	hostis nostrī	hostium nostrōrum	equī celebris	equōrum celebrium
Dative	hostī nostrō	hostibus nostrīs	equō celebrī	equīs celebribus
Accusative	hostem nostrum	hostēs nostrōs	equum celebrem	equōs celebrēs
Ablative	hoste nostrō	hostibus nostrīs	equō celebrī	equīs celebribus
Vocative	hostis noster	hostēs nostrī	eque celeber	equī celebrēs

▶ EXERCISE 2 ANSWERS

Present Active

	Singular	Plural
First person	cōnspiciō	cōnspicimus
Second person	cōnspicis	cōnspicitis
Third person	cōnspicit	cōnspiciunt

Present active infinitive cōnspicere

Present Passive

	Singular	Plural
First person	cōnspicior	cōnspicimur
Second person	cōnspiceris	cōnspiciminī
Third person	cōnspicitur	cōnspiciuntur

Present passive infinitive cōnspicī

▶ EXERCISE 3 ANSWERS

Imperfect Active

	Singular	Plural
First person	pugnābam	pugnābāmus
Second person	pugnābās	pugnābātis
Third person	pugnābat	pugnābant
First person	fugiēbam	fugiēbāmus
Second person	fugiēbās	fugiēbātis
Third person	fugiēbat	fugiēbant
First person	veniēbam	veniēbāmus
Second person	veniēbās	veniēbātis
Third person	veniēbat	veniēbant

Imperfect Passive

	Singular	Plural
First person	movēbar	movēbāmur
Second person	movēbāris	movēbāminī
Third person	movēbātur	movēbantur
First person	ostendēbar	ostendēbāmur
Second person	ostendēbāris	ostendēbāminī
Third person	ostendēbātur	ostendēbantur

PAGE 213
Standards 1.1, 1.2

▶ EXERCISE 4 ANSWERS

1. poētā celebrī
2. puellārum fortium
3. lupae fortis/lupae fortī/lupae fortēs
4. praemia celebria
5. cōnsulēs ācrēs
6. rēgum fēlīcium
7. viā fēlīcī

▶ EXERCISE 5 ANSWERS

1. mē — You say I am severe. But I believe that you do not understand my mind.
2. vōs — We can see you (plural). But we are not observed by you (plural).
3. mē — You are deeply loved by me. But you do not seem to love me very much.
4. tē — You seem to me to have many friends. Therefore I think you are fortunate.
5. mē mē — The girl is loved by me, but she does not care a bit for me. So I grieve and am miserable.
6. tē — I realize, Mucius, that your bravery cannot be overcome. So I am deciding to free you.

Review 4: Chapters 10–12 • 257

TEACHING TIP

If students need more practice on noun-adjective agreement using third declension adjectives, here are phrases to use. Follow the same directions as the ones for Exercise 3. This may be done in oral or written format. Answers are provided for the teacher's convenience.

- rēgīnae nostrae (crūdēlis)   rēgīnae crūdēlis/rēgīnae crūdēlī/rēgīnae crūdēlēs
- dōna nova (similis)   dōna similia
- equōrum paucōrum (ācer)   equōrum ācrium
- deum tantum (celeber)   deum celebrem
- dolōre novō (crūdēlis)   dolōre crūdēlī

PAGE 214
Standards 1.1, 1.2. 2.1

▶ EXERCISE 6 ANSWERS

1. Dēbentne hominēs deōs timēre?
2. Dīcisne eōs virōs esse fēlīcēs?
3. Bona praeclāraque semper amāre dēbēmus.
4. Hostēs crūdēlēs occīdēbantur.
5. Eōs castra vestra relinquere nōn vidēmus.
6. Graecīne dōna nōbīs dant? Nōn crēdō ea esse bona.
7. Mala nōn semper ā nōbīs cōnspiciuntur.
8. Prō vīribus pugnābāmus.
9. Eamne relinquēbās?

▶ EXERCISE 7 PASSAGE TRANSLATION

Cloelia and some women flee from the camp of the Etruscans and head for Rome. Then Porsenna is seized by great anger and sends ambassadors to the Romans: "None of you ought to neglect (not care a bit for) our treaty. And so Cloelia ought to return to the camp of the Etruscans. If Cloelia returns to our camp, I will free her." Cloelia does this and the king of the Etruscans frees her. He understands that not only Roman men, but also the Roman women are very courageous.

TEACHING TIP

The teacher may wish to contrast this legend with that of Tarpeia. While the story of Cloelia celebrates the noble courage of Roman womanhood, the story of Tarpeia presents a different female response in the face of conflict. After the Romans had made off with the Sabine women and made them their wives, the Sabine parents protested to their king Titus Tatius demanding that he redress this violation. So, the Sabines made war against the Romans.

In the course of their attack, Titus Tatius approached a young woman named Tarpeia, the daughter of the commander of the Capitolium at the time, and tried to enlist her aid.

As the story goes, her eyes immediately caught sight of the beautiful gold bracelets the Sabine soldiers wore on their left arms. She agreed to assist the Sabines in exchange for "what they wore on their left arms." So, Tarpeia led the enemy troops into the city, thus betraying her country, and then asked for her reward. In response, the soldiers immediately crushed the girl to death with their shields, which they also wore on their left arms. Ruthlessly, the soldiers tossed the dead girl's body over a cliff on the side of the Capitoline Hill.

This story is a perfect example of both an aetiological and an etymological legend. It explains how the Tarpeian Rock or cliff received its name and its special use. The Romans hurled murderers and traitors over the Tarpeian Rock.

The ancient Greeks and Romans used myths and legends to present morals. The story of Tarpeia brings to mind the modern notion "Be careful, you just might get what you ask for." Tarpeia's greed led her both to betray her father and the Romans and to bring about her own death.

The stories of noble Cloelia and greedy Tarpeia stand as counterpoints ripe for comparison and discussion.

CONSIDERING THE CLASSICAL GODS

PAGE 215

Standards 2.1, 3.1, 3.2

ODF 3.11

TEACHER BY THE WAY

Hermes is often pictured holding the winged herald's staff (*cādūceus*) with two intertwined snakes. It is said that the god came upon the two snakes fighting and used his staff to make peace between them. Then they curled themselves around his staff and became symbolic of peace and prosperity. In modern times the caduceus is used not only as an emblem of commerce but also by physicians. The serpents represent wisdom, the rod power, the wings diligence and activity.

COMPREHENSION QUESTIONS AND ANSWERS FOR PAGES 215–216 (SE)

Reproducible versions of the questions only are available at **www.lnm.bolchazy.com**.

1. Many myths are stories about the origin of a name, a custom, an object. Recount the tale about the creation of the lyre.

   Having stolen the cattle of his brother, Apollo, Mercury later reconciled with him by presenting Apollo with the gift of the newly invented lyre, which Mercury had made by carving the shell of a tortoise and stretching strings over it.

2. If you were looking at a statue of Mercury, how would you recognize him? Why is he dressed as he is?

   As the official herald of the gods and the patron of travelers, Mercury is recognized by his travel attire—a traveler's hat (*petasus*), winged shoes, and the caduceus, which could serve as a walking stick.

TEACHING TIP

Encourage students to look closely at the gods pictured in the clouds in Albani's painting and to identify the names of the deities. This activity may be done in English or in Latin.

TEACHER BY THE WAY

Mercury's invention of the lyre is considered an aetiological myth since it explains how the lyre came into being.

PAGE 216
Standards 1.1, 2.1

PASSAGE TRANSLATION
Mercury was the messenger of the gods. He was often sent to men. Jupiter sends Mercury to Aeneas: for Jupiter does not want Aeneas to stay with Dido. So Aeneas is ordered by him to set out for Italy, and he hears his commands from Mercury. Mercury not only reported the commands of the gods to men, but he also led the ghosts of the dead to the underworld. Therefore men did not always love Mercury: they often feared him!

TEACHING TIP
The teacher may wish to take the opportunity to mention other occasions when Hermes acted as Zeus' messenger. In the *Iliad* he accompanied Priam to Achilles's tent to recover his son Hector's body, and in the *Odyssey* he helped Odysseus end his stays with Circe and Calypso. It was also Hermes who negotiated with Hades the terms of Persephone's release.

TEACHER BY THE WAY
The teacher may direct these questions about the photograph to the students. In addition to the caduceus, what else identifies this figure as Mercury? Why do you think Mercury came to be associated with the railroad? As an extra credit assignment, ask students to research the grand railroad terminals like Grand Central and to what Roman public building type(s) the train stations might be compared.

CONNECTING WITH THE ANCIENT WORLD

PAGE 217

Standards 2.1, 2.2, 3.1, 3.2, 4.2

TEACHING TIP
Ask students to think about the etymology of *trīclīnium*.

tres, tria + *clīnō* = "three + bend, turn"

COMPREHENSION QUESTIONS AND ANSWERS FOR PAGES 217–218 (SE)
Reproducible versions of the questions alone are available at www.lnm.bolchazy.com.

1. What are the Latin terms and English equivalent for the three main Roman meals? What did Romans customarily eat at each meal?

    ientāculum, breakfast: water, bread with cheese

    prandium, lunch: bread, cold meat, fruit, vegetables, wine

    cēna, dinner: three to seven courses consisting of meat, fowl, fish, vegetables, fruits, sweets

2. The main meal, Roman dinner, consisted of three courses. Provide the Latin and English meaning for each course and the Roman equivalent of "from soup to nuts."

    gustātiō, the appetizer or hors d'oeuvres course

    prīma mēnsa, the main course

    mēnsa secunda, "second table," and the dessert course

    ab ōvō ūsque ad māla, "from eggs to apples," the equivalent of "from soup to nuts"

3. If one were to characterize a dinner party as worthy of Trimalchio, what would that reference suggest?

    An event marked by questionable taste and both culinary and behavioral excess.

TEACHER BY THE WAY
Since the Romans ate with their fingers, sauces like the famous *garum* fish sauce could make for a messy meal. So, dinner napkins were an absolute necessity. While hosts sometimes provided napkins, guests were expected to bring their own napkins, *mappae*. In addition, a slave boy would provide water for pouring over one's hands for cleansing. Guests were also known to bring leftovers from the meal back to their own home in their napkin. In poem 13, Catullus chastises Marrucinus for stealing another guest's napkin.

262 • Latin for the New Millennium: Teacher's Manual, Level 1

PAGE 218

TEACHER BY THE WAY

Wines were usually classified by color (black, red, white, yellow) or by taste (dry, harsh, light, sweet). The different varieties usually were based on locality. For example, Praeneste, Velitrae, and Formiae were known for their Alban wine. The Caecuban wine, which Augustus favored, was made a little further south, near Terracina, and the Falernian, perhaps even more famous, was produced in Campania. Horace mentions both the Caecuban (*Odes* 2.14.25) and the Falernian (*Odes* 3.1.43) wines in his poems. Pliny the Elder in his huge work entitled *Historia Nātūrālis* (Book 14) claims that over eighty choice wines were available to the Romans during his time, two-thirds of which were produced in Italy.

Family dinners were usually spent in conversation, or a trained slave might read aloud. At "men-only" dinners, entertainment might include music, professional jugglers, and "ladies of the night."

TEACHING TIP

The teacher may wish to instruct students either to prepare as authentic a Roman meal as possible or simply to write a menu in Latin for a fictional meal. The *vādemēcum* for students who wish to prepare authentic Roman food is *The Classical Cookbook* by Andrew Dalby and Sally Grainger (British Museum Press, 2000). It uses the information found in several sources such as Apicius, Cato the Elder, Archestratus, and Athenaeus but recreates the recipes for the modern kitchen and even suggests where less well-known ingredients may be found. The book also contains a wealth of historical information on dining, drinking, and festivity in the classical world. Not to be missed is the wonderful section on *garum* and how to recreate a modern equivalent without the malodorous smell of its preparation offending the entire neighborhood (pp. 19–21)!

Students should follow the basic pattern in designing a menu for a Roman meal: the *gustus* or *gustātiō* during which uncooked vegetables and shellfish were served; eggs were almost invariably on the menu. The antipasti served at an Italian dinner is the modern equivalent. The main part of the meal (*cēna* or *prīma mēnsa*) may have been served in several courses and would have consisted of meat, fish, fowl, and vegetables. The *mēnsa secunda* of pastry, sweets, nuts, and fruit (often apples) would have closed the meal. The names of some food items are on p. 180 of the student text in Latin.

EXPLORING THE MYTH OF THE TROJAN HORSE

PAGE 219
Standards 2.1, 2.2, 3.1, 3.2

 TEACHER BY THE WAY
The bust of Homer reflects the tradition that he was a blind bard. Hence, note the manner in which the eyes are depicted.

COMPREHENSION QUESTIONS AND ANSWERS FOR PAGES 219–222 (SE)
Reproducible versions of the questions alone are available at **www.lnm.bolchazy.com**.

1. What are the two main literary sources for the story of the Trojan horse? How do the two versions differ?

   Homer's *Odyssey* and Vergil's *Aeneid* are the main literary sources for this story.

   Homer's account does not mention the Greek agent Sinon, who in the Vergilian version convinces the Trojans that the horse is a gift to the gods, a symbolic offering to replace the stolen Palladium. In addition, the story of Laocoön, the priest of Apollo who advises against bringing the horse into the city and is subsequently killed by two serpents from the sea, is mentioned in Vergil but not in Homer.

2. The original accounts of the Trojan War and the Trojan horse were handed down by word of mouth. Citing elements in Professor Catto's essay, show evidence for an oral tradition with multiple variations.

   The epic poems of Homer and Vergil include different aspects of the Trojan horse story. Sophocles makes mention of Laocoön in a fragment of one of his plays. Quintus Smyrnaeus's version includes additional Greek warriors hidden in the horse and the Trojan priestess Cassandra's warnings about the horse.

3. How might the Trojan horse story serve as a mythological explanation for a natural phenomenon?

   Neptune, the god who created horses and to whom horses were sacrificed, was never paid for helping build the walls of Troy. Thus he sided with the Greeks in the Trojan War. As earthshaker, Neptune is associated with earthquakes. Perhaps the Trojan horse refers symbolically to the enmity of Neptune. This hostility was the cause of an earthquake that destroyed Troy.

4. For what purpose might a political cartoonist employ the image of the Trojan horse?

   By using the image of the Trojan horse, the political cartoonist might suggest that a particular political policy, plan, or decision will have disastrous results rather than the good consequences the plan's proponents would suggest.

5. Why is it fitting that a computer virus be called a Trojan horse?

   Like the Trojan horse which held disaster in its belly in the form of the Greek warriors, a computer virus causes significant damage to one's computer and its programs.

PAGE 220

TEACHER BY THE WAY

Timeō Danaōs et dōna ferentēs. "I fear the Greeks even when they bear gifts." (Vergil *Aeneid* 2.49) Laocoön's passionate warning to his fellow Greeks underscores his mistrust of the Greeks in general and of the wooden horse. Perhaps his advice would have prevailed but for the appearance and ploy of the sneaky Greek Sinon. Of course, Sinon's success is sealed when, just after his persuasive yet deceitful appeal to the Trojans, twin snakes arrive from the sea and devour Laocoön and two sons.

While Sinon appears in Quintus Smyrnaeus's *The Fall of Troy*, this account is based on Vergil's *Aeneid* 2. Vergil's depiction of Sinon demonstrates an insightful psychological portrayal of the spy and his audience. While the Trojans debate the purpose of the horse, Sinon contrives an encounter with Trojan shepherds who bring him before the assembled crowd. Vergil notes that Sinon is prepared to meet his death or to weave his lies. Young Trojans taunt the Greek who plays to their prejudice proclaiming that he is a man without a country driven from the Greeks and assailed by the Trojans. When asked his identity, Sinon readily admits that he is Greek, thereby immediately establishing credibility with the all-too-unsuspecting Trojans. Ironically, he avers that his desperate position would not make him a liar. Identifying himself as a comrade of Palamedes who had opposed the war and was convicted of treason due to trumped charges instigated by Ulysses, Sinon casts himself as a pariah among the Greeks, persecuted by Ulysses with whose forked tongue he suggests the Trojans are familiar.

At this point, believing he has gained the Trojans' interest in the tale of his plight, he breaks from his narrative, brilliantly playing to the Trojans' prejudice by accusing them of considering all Greeks in the same light and at the same time insinuating (note allusion to Sinon's name) that harming him would play into the hands of Ulysses and the Greeks themselves. Confident that he has the Trojans ensnared with curiosity, Sinon continues his tale, explaining that the Greeks were prepared to return home but needed a favorable wind to do so. Calchas, the ready seer, claimed that just as their departure required a human sacrifice, so now the Greeks' return requires a like sacrifice. Sinon states that all eyes fell upon him but he broke his shackles and escaped. As he ends his masterful speech, Sinon begs his rapt listeners for pity. Priam readily offers him safety and asks the purpose of the horse. Sinon, again citing Calchas and his interpretation of the gods' wishes, explains that the horse is an expiatory votive, whereupon the snakes arrive and kill Laocoön and the Trojans break down the walls and bring the horse into the city. While the Trojans are dead asleep from their wine and revelry, Sinon signals the Greek fleet to return and lets his comrades out of the horse.

PAGE 221

TEACHER BY THE WAY

In Book 2 of the *Aeneid*, Aeneas describes in graphic detail the death of King Priam and his son Polites at the hands of the young warrior son of Achilles, Neoptolemus (his name can be construed as meaning "new war"). Having ignored Hector's advice that he leave Troy at once, Aeneas had reentered the war and assisted in the defense of the royal palace. The Trojans, however, could not withstand the onslaught of the Greeks and chief among them, Pyrrhus (the other name for Neoptolemus). Likened to a snake who has fed on poisonous grasses and exults in his new skin, Pyrrhus rages through Priam's palace.

In fright Hecuba and her daughters and daughters-in-law have taken refuge alongside the altar in the palace's inner courtyard. She begs her aged husband Priam to join her but he, driven by the warrior ethic, dons his armor ready to meet his death. Suddenly, their son Polites racing through the halls with Pyrrhus on his heels arrives only to be brutally slaughtered before his parents' eyes. Outraged, Priam verbally accosts Pyrrhus stating that he could not be the son of Achilles who had shown pity toward Priam when he asked for his son Hector's body back. At the same time, Priam hurls his spear, which lamely bounces off the young warrior's armor. To Priam's charge, Pyrrhus sarcastically tells him to go tell that to his father Achilles as he drags the old man slipping in the blood of his son Polites to the altar, where he kills him with a steady plunge of the sword to its very hilt.

The sight of Priam's death knocks Aeneas to his senses as he thinks of his own father and his wife and realizes his Trojan comrades have been killed or in desperation taken their own lives. So, he leaves the palace to find his family.

PAGE 222

TEACHER BY THE WAY

One of the first to hide in the Trojan horse, according to some accounts, was Neoptolemus, son of Achilles, who proved himself a good fighter in the war. Like his father, a prophecy declared that his presence was needed at Troy for victory. So Odysseus was selected to retrieve him from Scyros where he was then living because Thetis had hidden his father on that island, disguised as a girl, knowing Achilles would die at Troy. Odysseus also was responsible for unmasking Achilles by showing him weapons among various trinkets, which he immediately chose, and this sealed his fate. While there, Achilles mated with Deidameia, daughter of the king of Scyros, and they had a son Neoptolemus. In the *Aeneid* (Book 2), the death of the aged Priam is retold to Dido. Neoptolemus, also known as Pyrrhus, kills King Priam. Neoptolemus does pay for this sacrilege according to Pindar the poet. Apollo, angered that the young Greek warrior had desecrated the altar by a killing, swore he would never reach home. Supposedly he is killed in a dispute with the servants of the shrine at Delphi when he goes there. In the *Odyssey* (Book 4) Menelaus and Helen are celebrating the wedding of their daughter Hermione whom they are sending to Neoptolemus as a bride. In post-Homeric versions, he goes to Delphi to inquire about his wife's infertility and is killed by Orestes, son of Agamemnon, to whom she had been betrothed. In other accounts Andromache, Hector's wife, becomes his concubine, her son Astyanax is thrown off the cliff by Neoptolemus, and Neoptolemus also sacrifices Polyxena, the youngest daughter of Priam and Hecuba, to the spirit of his father. Many writers have added to the story of his life after Troy.

MĪRĀBILE AUDĪTŪ

PAGE 223
Standards 1.1, 2.1, 3.1, 3.2, 4.2

PHRASES AND QUOTATIONS VOCABULARY

Arma cēdant togae.

cēdō, cēdere, cessī, cessum – to go, yield

cēdant – should yield, a present jussive imperative

toga, togae, *f.* – toga, a Roman garment worn in time of peace

Cāsus bellī.

cāsus, cāsūs, *m.* – accident, occasion

Dīvide et imperā!

dīvidō, dīvidere, dīvīsī, dīvīsum – to divide

imperō, imperāre, imperāvī, imperātum – to rule

Dulce et decōrum est prō patriā morī!

decōrus, decōra, decōrum – decorous, proper

dulcis, dulce – sweet

morior, morī, mortuus sum – to die

prō + *ablative* – for

Sī vīs pācēm, parā bellum!

sī (*conj.*) – if

vīs (*2nd person singular*) – want

Ubi sōlitūdinem faciunt, pācem appellant.

appellō, appellāre, appellāvī, appellātum – to call

sōlitūdō, sōlitūdinis, *f.* – desert, wilderness

ubi – where

Vae victīs!

vae + *dative* – woe to . . . !

victus, victa, victum – conquered

Review 4: Chapters 10–12 • 267

CHAPTER 13 (PP. 225–238)

GRAMMAR IN LANGUAGE FACTS

Present Tense Positive and Negative Imperatives; First and Second Person Personal Pronouns, Genitive Case; Third Person Possessive Pronoun and Adjective

PAGE 225

Standards 1.1, 2.1

RRA 6A

MEMORĀBILE DICTŪ VOCABULARY

carpō, carpere, carpsī, carptum – to pluck

diem (*accusative singular*) – day

TEACHER BY THE WAY

The Roman Forum, also called the Forum Romanum, was the political and religious center of Rome. In its present state as shown on the picture on this page, one can see the remains of the following buildings, many of which date from the imperial period since the emperors were regularly renovating this important public space.

Basilicas

- Basilica Aemilia
- Basilica Julia
- Basilica of Maxentius, also called the Basilica Nova or the Basilica of Constantine

Temples and Religious Buildings

- Fountain of Juturna
- *Lapis Niger*
- *Porticus Deōrum Cōnsentium*
- *Sacellum* of *Venus Cloācīna*
- Temple of Antoninus and Faustina
- Temple of Castor and Pollux, the Dioscuri
- Temple of Concordia
- "Temple of *Dīvus Rōmulus*" (Some scholars think this might actually be the headquarters of the *praefectus urbis*.)

- Temple of Saturn
- Temple of the Deified Julius Caesar
- Temple of the Deified Vespasian
- Temple of Vesta and House of the Vestal Virgins
- Temple of Venus and Rome

Arches
- Arch of Augustus
- Arch of Septimius Severus
- Arch of Titus

Other Buildings
- *Cūria*
- *Rēgia*
- *Rostrum*

In addition, the central open square of the Forum contains the remains of commemorative columns including one for Phocas, a seventh century CE Eastern or Byzantine Roman emperor.

PAGE 226
Standards 1.1, 2.1, 3.1, 3.2

TEACHING TIP
Chapter 6A of RRA contains information on Horace and Maecenas. The teacher may wish to assign this chapter for reading or review. See p. 201.

TRANSLATION OF LATIN PASSAGE
About a Boorish Man

I was walking on the Sacred Way and thinking about my trifles. A man known to me only by name runs to me. He seizes my arm and says: "What are you doing, dear fellow?" "I am fine (<I am doing> well)," I say, "and I desire all the things which you desire (i.e., I wish you all the best)." Then I withdraw. However, he walks with me. I ask him: "What can I do for you?" "Do not run," says the boor, "but remain with me!" "I cannot (it is not allowed to me)," I answer, "for I have to visit a friend on the other side of Tiber. Goodbye!" "Hear me!" says the boor, "I do not have to do anything else and I am not lazy. I do not want to leave you. I can come with you." I walked, a miserable man; for I desired him to withdraw from me. The boor, however, asked about Maecenas and his friends. "Each one of us," I answered, "has his place at the house of Maecenas: not only the rich and learned men." We were already close to the temple of Vesta. I desired very much to be left by the boor, but he was not leaving me. Then a man suddenly comes to us and calls the boor: "To what place are you walking? You should come with me to the judge." Then he leads the boor to the judge and saves me.

TEACHER BY THE WAY
Because of Maecenas's generosity to several different writers of this era, his name has become a proverbial designation for a wealthy patron of the arts.

TEACHING TIP
Instruct the students to find Vergil, Horace, Maecenas, and the battle at Actium in the timeline on pp. 405–408 (SE).

TEACHER BY THE WAY
The Battle of Actium took place on September 2nd, 31 BCE, off the western coast of Greece. Octavian had trapped Antony's forces camped at Actium. At Cleopatra's suggestion, Antony commenced a naval engagement. Octavian's "right-hand man" Agrippa commanded the Roman ships in a fiercely contested battle. When Cleopatra fled with her ships to Egypt, Antony followed. Shortly thereafter, his fleet surrendered and later his land forces did as well. This decisive victory not only cemented Octavian's power but marked the end of the Ptolemaic Dynasty, which had ruled Egypt since the death of Alexander the Great.

PAGE 227

ANSWERS TO COMPREHENSION QUESTIONS
1. Horace was walking on the Sacred Street in the Roman Forum.
2. A boorish man accosted Horace and walked with him.
3. Everybody has his own place in Maecenas's circle, not only rich and learned people.
4. The boorish man who was annoying Horace was led away by someone to court.

TEACHING TIP
While English derivatives from the asterisked words (i.e., the Vocabulary to Learn) are the topic of Exercise 2 later in this chapter, there are a few interesting derivatives from the non-asterisked words. The teacher may choose to discuss these derivatives with the students.

- *bracchium* – bracelet, brace, brachial
- *importūnus* – importune, importunous
- *nōtus* – notable, notorious
    Notice that the derivatives can have a positive or negative connotation.
- *sacer* – sacred, consecrate, desecrate, sacrilege

Chapter 13 • 271

TEACHER BY THE WAY
In *Odes* 1.1.1, Horace attests to the royal antecedents of Maecenas (*atavīs ēdite rēgibus*) who claimed descent from Etruscan kings. Although he never held public office, Maecenas remained an important adviser to Augustus up to the last years of his life when a rift may have occurred over his wife Terentia. Nevertheless, when he died, Maecenas left all his extensive property to the emperor.

During the civil wars, Maecenas accompanied Octavian to Philippi and was an active negotiator in the diplomacy that resulted in the pacts of Brundisium (40 BCE) and Tarentum (37 BCE). He also arranged Octavian's marriage to Scribonia, the mother of his only offspring Julia, to conciliate Sextus Pompeius. However, it was as a patron of letters that Maecenas is remembered. The circle that formed about him included Vergil, Horace, and Propertius, all of whom he brought to the attention of Augustus. Thus art and politics were well coordinated by the patronage of Maecenas, a combination that became a cornerstone of the Golden Age of literature.

PAGE 228
Standards 3.1, 3.2, 4.1
Oral Exercises 1, 2; Workbook Exercises 1, 3

TEACHER BY THE WAY
A **mood** shows whether the action expressed by the verb is represented as really happening, or as desired to happen.

ORAL EXERCISE 1
This exercise may be used after the present active imperative has been presented.

While looking at the chart of imperative forms, the students should say the present active imperatives, singular and plural, of the following verbs.

TEACHING TIP
Remind the students that the *–i* in third conjugation *–ite* is short but long in the fourth conjugation *–īte*.

Teacher: agō	**Student:** age	agite
Teacher: ambulō	**Student:** ambulā	ambulāte
Teacher: cōgitō	**Student:** cōgitā	cōgitāte
Teacher: cōnsūmō	**Student:** cōnsūme	cōnsūmite
Teacher: cupiō	**Student:** cupe	cupite
Teacher: crēdō	**Student:** crēde	crēdite
Teacher: doceō	**Student:** docē	docēte
Teacher: doleō	**Student:** dolē	dolēte

Teacher: iaceō	**Student:** iacē	iacēte
Teacher: līberō	**Student:** līberā	līberāte
Teacher: maneō	**Student:** manē	manēte
Teacher: moveō	**Student:** movē	movēte
Teacher: petō	**Student:** pete	petite
Teacher: relinquō	**Student:** relinque	relinquite
Teacher: vincō	**Student:** vince	vincite
Teacher: veniō	**Student:** venī	venīte

ORAL EXERCISE 2

This exercise may be used after the present positive and negative commands have been presented.

Use one of the CPOs to put on view the following infinitives. Ask individual students to form either a singular or a plural imperative of each verb, and to address it either to another individual student or to a group of students. Then the individual student or the group of students should perform/mimic the commanded action. The student should use a negative command to stop a student/group of students from performing the indicated action.

aedificāre – aedificā, aedificāte, nōlī aedificāre, nōlīte aedificāre

audīre – audī, audīte, nōlī audīre, nōlīte audīre

capiō – cape, capite, nōlī capere, nōlīte capere

cōgitāre – cōgitā, cōgitāte, nōlī cōgitāre, nōlīte cōgitāre

cōnspicere – cōnspice, cōnspicite, nōlī cōnspicere, nōlīte cōnspicere

dēlēre – dēlē, dēlēte, nōlī dēlēre, nōlīte dēlēre

discēdere – discēde, discēdite, nōlī discēdere, nōlīte discēdere

dare – da, date, nōlī dare, nōlīte dare

dolēre – dolē, dolēte, nōlī dolēre, nōlīte dolēre

Additional verbs for oral practice:

fugiō – fuge, fugite, nōlī fugere, nōlīte fugere

iaceō – iacē, iacēte, nōlī iacēre, nōlīte iacēre

moveō – movē, movēte, nōlī movēre, nōlīte movēre

ostendere – ostende, ostendite, nōlī ostendere, nōlīte ostendere

pōnere – pōne, pōnite, nōlī pōnere, nōlīte pōnere

pugnāre – pugnā, pugnāte, nōlī pugnāre, nōlīte pugnāre

relinquere – relinque, relinquite, nōlī relinquere, nōlīte relinquere

tenēre – tenē, tenēte, nōlī tenēre, nōlīte tenēre

venīre – venī, venīte, nōlī venīre, nōlīte venīre

vocāre – vocā, vocāte, nōlī vocāre, nōlīte vocāre

PAGE 229

Standards 1.1, 2.1

▶ EXERCISE 1 ANSWERS

1. Pugnāte!   Fight! (plural)
2. Ostende!   Show! (singular)
3. Mittite!   Send! (plural)
4. Sentī!   Feel! (singular)
5. Invidē!   Envy! (singular)
6. Timē!   Fear! (singular)
7. Aestimā!   Regard! (singular)
8. Fuge!   Flee! (singular)

TEACHING TIP

A total physical response activity is perfect to use when practicing imperatives. Teachers may wish to play the children's game called "Simon Says" with commands. The teacher will say the following commands and direct each to a student, using his/her name. If Simon has said this and the student performs the action correctly, the student stays in the game. If Simon has not said the command or the student does not perform the command correctly, the student is out of the game. Some examples follow for the teacher's convenience.

- Simon dīcit, "Discēde!" Simon dīcit, "Discēdite!"
- "Respondē 'minimē!'" "Respondēte 'minimē!'"
- Simon dīcit, "Movē caput!" Simon dīcit, "Movēte capita!"
- "Ambulā!" "Ambulāte!"
- "Fuge!" "Fugite!"
- Simon dīcit, "Venī ad mē!" Simon dīcit, "Venīte ad mē!"
- "Da magistrō (magistrae) crētam!" "Date magistrō (magistrae) crētam!"
- Simon dīcit, "Iacē!" Simon dīcit, "Iacēte!"
- "Manē!" "Manēte!"
- "Intrā!" "Intrāte!"
- Simon dīcit, "Tenē librum!" Simon dīcit, "Tenēte librōs!"
- Simon dīcit, "Pōne in mēnsā librum!" Simon dīcit, "Pōnite in mēnsā librōs!"

To practice with plural imperative forms, divide the students into several small groups of two to four people. Let each group choose a Latin name for their group. Then use the sentences above using the plural imperatives in the second column. The teacher may wish to give the plural commands above in a different order than was used the first time.

PAGE 230

Standards 1.2, 4.1
Workbook Exercise 2

TEACHER BY THE WAY

The constantly burning fire in the temple of Vesta represented the goddess, who was not portrayed by statues. Mussolini (cf. p. 173) restored the Temple of Vesta to its present form as seen in the illustration. A relief sculpture in the Uffizi Gallery in Florence shows what the temple looked liked in ancient times.

▶ EXERCISE 2 ANSWERS

1. judicial — iūdex
2. nihilism — nihil
3. alienation — alius
4. doctorate — doctus
5. response — respondeō
6. valedictory — valē
7. license — licet
8. interrogation — rogō
9. omnipotent, omniscient — omnis
10. aqueduct — dūcō

TEACHING TIP

Although in Exercise 2 the students are directed to find only the derivatives based on the Vocabulary to Learn, they may be interested to learn that there are other derivatives in Exercise 2. The derivation of these words is provided for the teacher's convenience.

1. power – from *possum* (to be able). separate – from *sēparō* (to part, divide, distinguish). executive – from *exsequor* (to follow, pursue, accomplish).
2. frequently – from *frequēns* (crowded, numerous). encounter – from *in* (in, on, at) + *contrā* (opposite, against). attitude – [*aptitūdō*] from *aptō* (to adapt, prepare, equip, fit). people – from *populus* (people, nation, populace).
3. cities – from *cīvitās* (state, community, city, citizenship).
5. accusation – from *accūsō* (to prosecute, reproach, accuse).
6. in – from *in* (in, on, at). school – from *schola* (school, sect, followers) from the Greek word *scholē* for leisure since only the wealthy had the time for education.
8. provide – from *prōvideō* (to take care, see ahead, make provision).
9. omnipotent – [from *omnis* in the vocabulary] + from *potēns* (powerful, strong, capable). omniscient – [from *omnis* in the vocabulary] + from *sciō* (to know).
10. aqueduct – [from *dūcō* in the vocabulary] + *aqua* (water). structure – from *struō* (to pile up, build, erect). transported – from *trāns* (across) + *portō* (to carry).

Chapter 13 • 275

PAGE 231

Standards 1.1, 2.1, 3.1, 3.2, 4.1

▶ EXERCISE 3 ANSWERS

1. Nōlīte pugnāre!   Don't fight! (plural)
2. Nōlī discēdere!   Don't leave!
3. Nōlīte dolēre!   Don't grieve! (plural)
4. Nōlīte mittere!   Don't send! (plural)
5. Nōlī vincere!   Don't conquer!
6. Nōlīte putāre!   Don't think! (plural)
7. Nōlī petere!   Don't rush to!
8. Nōlī capere!   Don't take!
9. Nōlīte venīre!   Don't come! (plural)

▶ EXERCISE 4 ANSWERS

Horace:

1. Līberā mē!
2. Discēde!
3. Fuge!
4. Nōlī nārrāre!
5. Relinque mē!

Boor:

1. Audī!
2. Crēde mihi!
3. Exspectā!
4. Manē!
5. Respondē!

276 • Latin for the New Millennium: Teacher's Manual, Level 1

PAGE 232
Standards 1.1, 1.2

▶ EXERCISE 5 ANSWERS
1. Few of us desire to hear words of a boorish man.
   nostrum – partitive genitive
   hominis importūnī – modifying genitive
2. All of you seem to flee from annoying people.
   vestrum – partitive genitive
3. The boor was not seized by fear of me, but walked with me.
   meī – objective genitive
4. Give me help, because of your love for me!
   meī – objective genitive

TEACHER BY THE WAY
The teacher may wish to remind the students that the verb *dō* has a short stem and is therefore an exception.

TEACHING TIP
The partitive genitive is sometimes called a genitive of the whole.

PAGE 233
Standard 2.1

TEACHING TIP
Remind the students that Rome was built on seven hills. Not all of the hills are placed on the map. The teacher may wish to tell students where the additional hills are located. This mnemonic will help students learn the names of the hills.

Please	**P**alatine
Consume	**C**apitoline
All	**A**ventine
Exquisite	**E**squiline
Cookies	**C**aelian
Very	**V**iminal
Quickly	**Q**uirinal

Chapter 13 • 277

TEACHER BY THE WAY
Two other hills, the *Jāniculum* and *Vāticānus*, were located on the right bank of the Tiber River.

TEACHING TIP
Additional reproducible worksheets, morphology charts, and their associated answer keys, related to this material, are available for download at www.lnm.bolchazy.com.
- **The City of Rome in Ancient Times**

Teachers may wish to use the more detailed plan of the Roman Forum found in the materials for Level 3 in the *LNM* Teachers' Lounge.

PAGE 234
Standards 1.1, 1.2, 3.1, 3.2, 4.1
Oral Exercise 3

▶ EXERCISE 6 ANSWERS
1. The rich farmers take care of their land.
2. All love their life.
3. The leader is seized by anger. The soldiers fear his anger.
4. The king is being consumed with anger. And so he fears his own anger.
5. The city is on fire. Flee (pl.) its flames!
6. The citizens ought to protect their own houses from the flames.
7. The friend is giving a horse. Take his horse!
8. You (all) see our friends. You (all) desire to know their names.

ORAL EXERCISE 3
This exercise may be used after the possessive pronoun and adjective for the third person have been presented.
Use one of the CPOs to put on view a list of expressions that indicate what objects different students possess.

liber Mārcī – the book of Mark
calamus (calamī, *m.***) Mariae** – the pen of Mary
sacculus (sacculī, *m.***) Helenae** – the bag of Helen
liber Mārcī et Helenae – the book of Marcus and Helen

The teacher should first put on view the word *cūius?*, "whose?" and then give the book to Mark to hold, and ask another student:

Cūius librum tenet Mārcus?

The answer is supposed to be: *Mārcus librum suum tenet.*

Then the teacher gives the book to Helen and asks:

Cūius librum tenet Helena? Please, answer twice: once with the name of the possessor, and once with a demonstrative pronoun instead.

The answer is supposed to be: *Helena librum Mārcī tenet. Helena eius librum tenet.*

And in a smiliar way with the other expressions:

Cūius calamum tenet Marīa? Marīa calamum suum tenet.

Cūius calamum tenet Mārcus? Mārcus calamum Marīae tenet. Mārcus calamum eius tenet.

Cūius sacculum tenet Helena? Helena sacculum suum tenet.

Cūius sacculum tenet Mārcus? Mārcus sacculum Helenae tenet. Mārcus eius sacculum tenet.

Cūius librum tenent Mārcus et Helena? Mārcus et Helena librum suum tenent.

Cūius librum tenet Marīa? Marīa librum Mārcī et Helenae tenet. Marīa librum eōrum tenet.

PAGE 235
Standards 1.1, 1.2
Workbook Exercises 4, 5, 6, 7, Content Questions

▶ EXERCISE 7 ANSWERS

1. eius   I fear the judge and I wait for his words.
2. suā   Rome is the fatherland of the soldiers. The soldiers fight for their fatherland.
3. eōrum   We want to hear the words of the poets. For we love their words.
4. suō   The girl loves the sparrow and holds the sparrow on her lap.

▶ EXERCISE 8 ANSWERS

1. Venī mēcum!
2. Dēbeōne tēcum venīre?
3. Venīte mēcum!
4. Dēbēmusne tēcum venīre?
5. Nōlī discēdere!
6. Nōlīte discēdere!
7. Nōlīte nōs ad iūdicem dūcere!
8. Āthlēta corpus suum cūrābat.
9. Vir importūnus rogābat et poēta nihil respondēbat. Poēta eius verba nōn audiēbat.
10. Omnēs nostrum vōs rogābāmus. Omnēs vestrum respondēre dēbēbātis.
11. Poēta importūnō dīcēbat: "Relinque mē propter amōrem meī."

Chapter 13 • 279

TEACHING TIP
After the students have completed Exercise 8 and the correct answers have been given, the teacher may give the students some additional practice by instructing them to find all the imperatives in Exercise 8 and to change positive imperatives to the negative and negative imperatives to the positive, keeping the same number as the original imperative. The answers to this additional practice are listed here for the teacher's convenience.

1. Nōlī venīre mēcum!
3. Nōlīte venīre mēcum!
5. Discēde!
6. Discēdite!
7. Dūcite!
11. Nōlī relinquere!

PAGE 236
Standards 1.2, 4.1

TEACHING TIP
The teacher may choose to use this opportunity to indicate that cardinal numerals from *quattuor* to *decem* are indeclinable.

TEACHING TIP
Obtain a large clock with moveable hands. Move the hands of the clock around into a different position and ask a student "*Quota hōra est?*" Instruct the student to answer in Latin. Ask several students the same question, each time with the clock hands in different positions.

TEACHING TIP
Prepare several easy addition and subtraction problems written in Roman numerals. Instruct the students to answer with a Latin cardinal number. This may be done in written or oral format.

PAGE 237
Standards 1.2, 2.1, 4.2
Dictation

TEACHING TIP
In this dialogue, *schola* is used to mean "school" in some places, and "class" in other places. The teacher may wish to remind students of the two meanings of this word.

280 • Latin for the New Millennium: Teacher's Manual, Level 1

TRANSLATION OF THE LATIN CONVERSATION

Helen: Hurry, Mark! We are late.

Mark: Should we hurry?

Helen: Yes, we ought to hurry.

Mark: What time is it?

Helen: It is 8:15.

Mark: Then we do not need to hurry. For school starts at 8:30.

Helen: However, we should enter school at 8:15. For we ought to prepare (our) books.

Mark: I, however, wait for one o'clock.

Helen: Why?

Mark: Classes end at one o'clock.

Helen: Don't think now about the end of classes, but come with me!

TEACHING TIP

The teacher may use this information on numbers and telling time to open a discussion on how the Romans calculated a date by using these three special days: Kalends, Nones, and Ides.

DICTATION

This exercise may be used to conclude the chapter.

The teacher should dictate sentences containing a subject, a verb, and a direct object, which the students have to transform, either orally or in a writing, into a phrase containing: (1) a noun (for the verb); (2) a possessive adjective (for the subject); (3) an objective genitive (for the direct object).

Example:

Teacher: ego tē amō   **Student:** meus amor tuī

Teacher: tū mē amās   **Student:** tuus amor meī
Teacher: nōs tē amāmus   **Student:** noster amor tuī
Teacher: tū nōs amās   **Student:** tuus amor nostrī
Teacher: vōs mē amātis   **Student:** vester amor meī
Teacher: ego vōs amō   **Student:** meus amor vestrī
Teacher: vōs nōs amātis   **Student:** vester amor nostrī
Teacher: nōs vōs amāmus   **Student:** noster amor vestrī

TEACHING TIP

If you would like to give your students some practice with times and dates, some exercises (with answers) are provided for your convenience.

Time: The teacher may read these sentences aloud and allow the students some time to work on converting the Roman time to English time.

1. Banquets beginning before <u>the ninth hour</u> were called *tempestīva convīvia*.
   Answer: 3 P.M.

2. Caesar aroused his soldiers <u>during the third watch</u> to prepare for battle.
   Answer: between 12 midnight and 3 A.M.

3. Lucius told his friend to meet him in the Forum at the <u>second hour</u>.
   Answer: 8 A.M.

4. *Prandium* was usually served at the <u>fifth hour</u>.
   Answer: 11 A.M.

5. What was the hour before sunset called?
   Answer: *hōra duodecima*; 6 P.M.

6. Complete the couplet: The English hour you may fix,
   If to the Latin you add _____.
   Answer: 6

7. Because each Roman hour was 1/12 of the time between sunrise and sunset, the length of the hour varied from season to season. When were the hours of night equal to the hours of day?
   Answer: During the vernal equinox and the autumnal equinox (March 20th and September 22nd)

Dates:

Originally the Romans only had four months in their calendar—March to June—since it was an agricultural society, and the growing season was the most important. Six more months were added but only given numerical names (*Quintīlis–December* = July–December). As town life became more important, King Numa added the two months of January and February. The year still began on March 1st.

Each month had three set dates: The Kalends, which fell on the 1st of each month, the Nones on the 5th or 7th, and the Ides on the 13th or 15th. An old poem helps students remember the system:

In March, July, October, May,
The Ides fall on the 15th day,
The Nones the 7th; and all besides
Are two days less for Nones and Ides.

There are two other points to remember about changing Roman dates into modern equivalents. First, the Romans practiced inclusive dating, which means they counted both ends. For example, we would say that Sunday is the second day after Friday; the Romans called it the third day. Secondly, the Romans counted backward from one of the three set dates. Here is an example:

a(nte) d(iem) III Nōn. Iān. (on the third day before the Nones of January) = January 3rd because the Nones falls on the 5th in January and you count both ends.

The teacher may use one of the CPOs to put these dates on display to give students practice on this.

1. a.d. VIII Kal. Iān.   Answer: December 25th
2. a.d. III Īd. Iūl.   Answer: July 13th
3. a.d. V Nōn. Oct.   Answer: October 3rd
4. prīdiē Īd. Māi.   Answer: May 14th
5. a.d. XII Kal. Nov.   Answer: October 21st
6. a.d. IV Nōn. Feb.   Answer: February 2nd

TEACHER BY THE WAY

Our calendar today begins on January 1st because in 154 BCE the Romans voted to move back the beginning of their calendar year to that date. Because the empire was growing so large, the day on which the new consuls took their oath of office was advanced so that the ex-consuls could get out to their provinces in time for the start of the campaign season. This travel often took a few months, and if the new generals left in March, military activities would already have been well under way by May or June. Finally, Julius Caesar in 46 BCE reformed the calendar, which was too short for the solar year, and Pope Gregory XIII revised it again to the one we have today. Some of the Orthodox Christian churches still follow the Julian calendar for their holy days.

PAGE 238
Standard 4.1

DERIVATIVES

iūdex – Note that the prefix "in-" of "injudicious" is negative. Note also the "-ous" suffix.

The prefix of "misjudge" is also negative. It comes from the Old English *mis-* meaning "bad or wrong," and is related to the Old French *mes-*, which has the same meaning but is derived from the Latin *minus*.

See also *iūdicō* 1.6.

nihil – The spelling of "annihilate" is easy for Latin students who can see *nihil* in it. The prefix "an-" comes from *ad* by assimilation; hence the literal meaning "to nothing."

quid – The original classical meaning of *quid* survived in "quiddity" (the real essence or nature of a thing) during the late fourteenth century when the word appeared in English. By the 1530s it meant "a trifling nicety in argument, a quibble," a sense that developed from scholastic disputes over the nature of things.

Chapter 13 • 283

The word "quid" per se still exists in British slang for "one pound sterling" (from 1680s), perhaps derived from the phrase *quid prō quō* or directly from the Latin *quid* meaning "what, something, anything." It is a parallel to the French *quibus*, a slang term for "money, cash," said to be short for *quibus fiunt omnia*.

The word "quibble" came into English during the 1610s meaning "a pun, a play on words," derived perhaps from an overuse of *quibus* in legal jargon (see "quiddity" above). By the 1650s it meant "equivocation, evasion of the point."

The word "quip" is perhaps derived from *quippe* which was formed from *quid* and the suffix *–pe* (OLD) and meant "of course, indeed" (used sarcastically). Both the noun and verb forms appeared in English during the sixteenth century.

alius – The derivatives listed come more directly from the Latin adjective *aliēnus*, which was formed from *alius* and the *-ēnus* suffix. This clarifies the spelling of the English words which appeared during the mid-fourteenth century.

"Inalienable" dates to the 1640s. The prefix is negative.

The verb "alienate" is derived from the fourth principal part of *aliēnō* (to estrange, transfer property by sale) and came into English during the 1540s.

dīves – None

doctus – For derivatives, see *doceō* in 1.6.

omnis – The earliest appearance of the "omni-" words occurred during the early fourteenth century (omnipotent). "Omnipotence" came into English during the mid-fifteenth century, "omnipresent" and "omniscient" in 1600, and "omnivorous" during the 1650s. The noun "omnivore" did not appear until 1890.

suus – See the pronoun *suī* for related derivatives.

discēdō – None

dūcō – The English words derived from the fourth principal part of *dūcō* are numerous. The meaning is changed by the prefixes, e.g., "abduct" = to lead away, "deduct" = to lead down (to take away), "induction" = to lead into, etc.

The Latin *aquae ductus* (a leading or drawing of water) gave rise to "aqueduct" (mid-sixteenth century).

The purpose of a "viaduct" (early nineteenth century) is to carry (lead, guide) a road over a chasm, river, train tracks, or another road.

The word "conduit" came into English around 1300, derived through the Old French *conduit* meaning "escort, protection, pipe, channel" from the Latin *conductus* (a leading, a pipe). It is a doublet of "conduct" but differentiated in meaning during the fifteenth century.

The verb "conduct" dates to the early fifteenth century, also derived from *conductus* (to lead or bring together). The sense of "manage, direct" dates to the 1630s, that of "behave in a certain way" to 1710. The noun appears during the mid-fifteenth century meaning "guide." The sense of "behavior" is first recorded during the 1670s.

A "redoubt" is a small, enclosed military place for *retreat* (*re* = back, and *dūcō*). The word appeared in English, spelled "redout," around 1600. The *b* was added by the influence of derivatives from *dubitō*, e.g., "redoubtable."

The prefix of the Latin word *sēdūcō* meant "apart, away," hence the verb meaning of "to lead away, lead astray." This gave rise to the English verb in the 1520s meaning "to persuade someone to desert his allegiance or service." The sexual sense, which now prevails, dates to the 1550s, although the noun "seduction," which originally referred to actions or beliefs, did not acquire that sense until 1769.

The verb "subdue" (late fourteenth century), meaning "to conquer," was derived from the Latin *subdūcō* (literally, to withdraw from underneath, remove, steal) through the Old French *soudire* (to deceive, seduce). The sense seems to have been taken in Anglo-French from the Latin *subdō* (put under, make subordinate).

See *dux* in 1.8 for related derivatives.

licet – The word "license," meaning "to give permission to do something," came into English during the mid-fourteenth century. The sense of "excessive liberty and disregard of propriety" dates to the mid-fifteenth century.

Note the "-ous" suffix of "licentious." The word is always pejorative.

The prefix of "illicit" is derived from *in* by assimilation and is a negative.

The word "leisure," meaning "the time or opportunity to do something," appeared in English during the early fourteenth century derived from the Latin *licet* through the Old French *leisir* (be permitted). The *u* appeared during the sixteenth century, probably influenced by such words as "pleasure."

See also Teaching Tip 1.6.

nōlō – None (from *nōn volō*; for related derivatives, see *volō, velle*.)

respondeō – The prefix of "irresponsible" is derived from *in* by assimilation and is a negative.

rogō – The word "abrogate" is derived directly from the Latin *abrogō* (*ab* = away, and *rogō* = to ask, propose, move; hence "to request [a law] away" = to repeal, annul) and came into English during the 1520s.

The word "derogatory" also comes directly from the Latin. *Dērogō* means "to take away, diminish, detract from" (*dē* = away, and *rogō*; hence, "to propose away" = to repeal, amend). Many words which were once in common use, like "Jap," "Bohunk," or "Dago," are now rightfully considered <u>derogatory</u>.

A "surrogate" is a substitute. The word is derived from the Latin *subrogō* (to propose in place of).

The word "prerogative" came into English during the late fourteenth century meaning "a special right granted to someone." It is derived from the Latin *praerogatīva* (the tribe or century with the first vote, literally "asked before").

The word "interrogation" is derived from the Latin *interrogō* (to ask among = to seek information from others).

The word "arrogance" is derived from the Latin *adrogō* (*ad* = to, toward, and *rogō*; hence, "to ask for oneself") and the noun *adrogantia* (insolence, presumption). Note the assimilation.

valē – (from *valeō* = to be strong, be well).

The prefix of "convalescent" is intensive (= "completely"); the base is inchoative.

Note the "-ous" suffix of "valorous."

In chemistry the word "valence" refers to the combining power of atoms.

The word "avail" is a combination of the Latin *ad* and *valeō*: The courage of the military patrol was to no <u>avail</u> in the face of overwhelming odds.

In the end, the stronger team <u>prevailed</u> (from *praevaleō* = to have great power; *prae* = pre).

Chapter 13 • 285

Students should be cautioned about the prefix "in-." In the word "invalid" it is a negative, but in "invaluable" it has intensive force.

The "value" of something is what it is worth (*valeō* = to be strong, have power, be effective, be worth).

tantum – See *tantus* 1.12.

tum – None

apud – None

prō – The word "pro" by itself stands for "for, on behalf of" as opposed to "contra" (against): The committee discussed the <u>pros</u> and cons of the issue.

The list of derivatives, which is not exhaustive by any means, gives examples of various meanings of *prō*, e.g., "provide, protect" = on behalf of; "prologue" = before; "proponent" = for; "procrastinate, proceed, progress" = in front, forward; "pronoun" = in place of. Although almost countless words in English begin with "pro," not all such words are derived directly from the Latin preposition. They might derive from *prope* (propinquity) or *prōles* (proletariat) or *probus* (proof), etc. See the main root for the meanings of these "pro" derivatives.

See also Teaching Tip 1.7.

atque – None

enim – None

286 • Latin for the New Millennium: Teacher's Manual, Level 1

CHAPTER 14 (PP. 239–251)

GRAMMAR IN LANGUAGE FACTS

First and Second Conjugation Verbs: Future Tense Active and Passive; Future Tense of *Sum* and *Possum*; Relative Pronouns; Relative Clauses

PAGE 239
Standards 1.1, 2.1
RRA 6A

TEACHER BY THE WAY
Lucas Cranach is a German artist who wore many hats in his profession. He is named after his place of birth in southern Germany, Kronach. He was an etcher and woodcut designer, portrait painter, engraver of copper plates, and painter of erotic nudes for a large clientele of private collectors. A close friend of Martin Luther, he was committed to the Protestant Reformation, but this did not prevent him from working for many Catholic clients. His portraits of Luther are among the finest as are the woodcuts illustrating the first German translation of the New Testament, done in 1522. It is thought that he may have been the inventor of the full-length independent portrait. He also had several business interests that included apothecary, printing, and a bookshop. In Wittenberg the sale of medicine was exclusively his, as was the patent for publishing bibles. Martin Luther even used his presses. Religious art, especially the pictorial representation of sin and grace, was a preference, but Cranach also painted mythological scenes. Notice in the illustration on p. 239 the detailed landscape, the German costumes on the Babylonian lovers, and the decorative quality of the picture, all characteristic of his paintings of this type.

TEACHER BY THE WAY
Pyramus and Thisbe became a favorite theme in both art and literature. An old French poem in 1170 and another Anglo-Norman poem in the twelfth or thirteenth century retold the lovers' story. Giovanni Boccaccio (1313–1375) mentions the two in *The Decameron* in which a desperate housewife carries on a romance with her neighbor and communicates with him through a crack in the wall. Geoffrey Chaucer was among the first to tell the story in English in a poem entitled *The Legend of Good Women*. In the Prologue Cupid is angry because Chaucer wrote about so many women who betrayed men, so as a penance he must focus on good women. Of course, his variations on the original make the poem more comic than tragic, especially in his phrasing "blood flows like broken plumbing." Shakespeare includes it in *A Midsummer Night's Dream* as a play within a play, but here too as "tragical mirth." The story is poorly performed by

a band of lower-class laborers in honor of the newlyweds Theseus and Hippolyta. Louisa May Alcott, author of *Little Women*, retells the story in a children's version entitled *A Hole in the Wall*. Even the Beatles took a turn with this tale. In 1964 they did a performance for British TV. Paul played the part of Pyramus, John was Thisbe, and Ringo the lion.

TEACHING TIP

Chapter 6A of RRA contains information on Ovid. The teacher may wish to assign this chapter for reading or for review. See p. 201.

PAGE 240
Standards 1.1, 2.1, 3.1, 3.2

TRANSLATION OF LATIN PASSAGE
About Pyramus and Thisbe

Pyramus lived near Thisbe. He loved her and was beloved by her. However, because of the hatred which was between their parents, Pyramus and Thisbe could not be together. They often said words to the wall which was dividing them: "O bad wall, you are always dividing lovers!" But they also asked the wall: "Is it permitted, O good wall, to send words through you?"

Pyramus and Thisbe finally decide to meet secretly. "Tonight I will see you in the fields near the tree in which there are white berries," says Pyramus. Thisbe comes first and waits. Suddenly a lioness approaches Thisbe. The lioness has blood in her mouth. For the lioness was eating an animal. Thisbe is afraid and runs into a cave, but the veil of the girl falls on the ground. The lioness touches the veil with her mouth and the blood remains on the veil.

Pyramus comes and sees the veil, on which blood is observed. Thisbe does not now seem to be alive. Pyramus grieves deeply and kills himself with a sword. In the meantime, Thisbe walks out of the cave and sees that Pyramus is lying dead on the ground. Thisbe takes the sword from Pyramus's chest and kills herself as well. The blood of Pyramus and Thisbe flows into the earth. The berries of the tree will soon be red.

TEACHING TIP

The teacher may wish to have the students locate Pontus, the country where Ovid lived in exile, on the map, pp. xxxiv–xxxv (SE), and find Ovid on the timeline on pp. 405–408 (SE).

TEACHER BY THE WAY

A myth like that of Pyramus and Thisbe, which explains something such as the red color of the mulberry tree, is called aetiological.

PAGE 241

ANSWERS TO COMPREHENSION QUESTIONS

1. They were in love, but were not allowed to love each other because of their parents' hatred.
2. They decided to meet secretly.
3. Pyramus saw Thisbe's veil stained with blood. In fact, Thisbe had hidden herself from a lioness, but had lost her veil while fleeing. It was then stained by the mouth of the lioness who had just devoured an animal.
4. Coming out of her hiding place, she saw Pyramus's dead body and killed herself using Pyramus's sword.

TEACHING TIP

As a postreading activity, teachers may have students return to the chapter page image and explain in Latin what it depicts and how it connects to the chapter reading.

TEACHER BY THE WAY

While some Latin words for different animals, like *leaena* in this Reading Vocabulary, are different in the masculine and feminine genders, others are exactly alike in both genders, and still others differ between the two genders only by declension/gender ending.

- *ariēs*, m.; *ovis*, f.   ram, sheep
- *asinus, asina*   donkey
- *cervus, cerva*   stag, doe
- *equus, equa*   stallion, mare
- *gallus, gallīna*   cock, hen
- *lacertus, lacerta*   lizard
- *leō*, m.; *leaena*, f.   lion, lioness
- *lupus, lupa*   wolf
- *mūlus, mūla*   mule
- *taurus*, m.; *vacca*, f.   bull, cow
- *ursus, ursa*   bear

- *bōs*, m./f.   ox, cow
- *canis*, m./f.   dog
- *lynx*, m./f.   lynx
- *sūs*, m./f.   pig

- *būfō*, m.   toad
- *elephāns* (or *elephantus*), m.   elephant
- *mūs*, m.   mouse
- *sciūrus*, m.   squirrel
- *tigris*, f. (usually) or m.   tiger

Chapter 14 • 289

- *fēlēs*, f.   cat
- *mūstēla*, f.   weasel
- *panthēra*, f.   panther
- *rāna*, f.   frog
- *vulpēs*, f.   fox

The Romans celebrated a festival called the *suovetaurīlia* because at it they sacrificed a pig (*su-*), a sheep (*-ove-*), and a bull (*-taur-*).

PAGE 242

Standards 3.1, 4.1
Oral Exercise 1; Workbook Exercise 1

TEACHING TIP
The teacher may choose to tell students that another correct translation for the first person singular and plural is "shall." "I shall ...," "we shall ..."

TEACHING TIP
The teacher may wish to point out to students that the future indicative endings of the first and second conjugation verbs are the same as the present tense endings of the third conjugation verbs:

parāb**ō**, parāb**is**, parāb**it**, parāb**imus**, parāb**itis**, parāb**unt**

pet**ō**, pet**is**, pet**it**, pet**imus**, pet**itis**, pet**unt**

tenēb**or**, tenēb**eris**, tenēb**itur**, tenēb**imur**, tenēb**iminī**, tenēb**untur**

pet**or**, pet**eris**, pet**itur**, pet**imur**, pet**iminī**, pet**untur**.

ORAL EXERCISE 1

This exercise may be used after the future tense of first and second conjugation verbs has been presented.

While looking at the future of *parō* and *teneō*, ask the students to conjugate the verbs *aestimō* and *doceō* in the future active and passive.

aestimābō, aestimābis, aestimābit, aestimābimus, aestimābitis, aestimābunt

aestimābor, aestimāberis, aestimābitur, aestimābimur, aestimābiminī, aestimābuntur

docēbō, docēbis, docēbit, docēbimus, docēbitis, docēbunt

docēbor, docēberis, docēbitur, docēbimur, docēbiminī, docēbuntur

TEACHER BY THE WAY

With the introduction to the future tense on this page, the answers to *"Cūius temporis est?"* expand to

- *temporis praesentis*
- *temporis imperfectī*
- *temporis futūrī*

PAGE 243

Standards 1.1, 1.2
Oral Exercise 2

TEACHER BY THE WAY

Another expression for "please" is *sīs* (*sī vīs*).

▶ EXERCISE 1 ANSWERS

1. iūdicābō — I will/shall judge
2. aedificābunt — they will build
3. docēbis — you will teach
4. dolēbimus — we will/shall grieve
5. servābit — s/he will save
6. iubēbitis — you (plural) will order
7. parābunt — they will prepare
8. iacēbō — I will/shall lie
9. solēbitis — you (plural) will be accustomed
10. pugnābit — s/he will fight

ORAL EXERCISE 2

This exercise may be used after the future tense of first and second conjugation verbs has been presented.

The teacher should put on view these three words: *herī*, "yesterday," *hodiē*, "today," *crās*, "tomorrow," as well as three questions: *Quid hodiē facis?* "What are you doing today?," *Quid herī faciēbās?* "What were you doing yesterday?," *Quid crās faciēs?* "What will you be doing tomorrow?"

The teacher should also list some verbs from which the students can choose when answering the questions:

ambulō, cōgitō, doleō, exspectō, iaceō, domī maneō, fābulās nārrō, pugnō, timeō.

Then the teacher should ask different students any of the three questions above, and the students should answer, choosing a verb from the list, and putting it in the appropriate form.

Chapter 14 • 291

Teacher: Quid hodiē facis? Student: Hodiē ambulō, cōgitō, doleō, exspectō, iaceō, domī maneō, fābulās nārrō, pugnō, timeō.

Teacher: Quid herī faciēbās? Student: Herī ambulābam, cōgitābam, dolēbam, exspectābam, iacēbam, domī manēbam, fābulās nārrābam, pugnābam, timēbam.

Teacher: Quid crās faciēs? Student: Hodiē ambulābō, cōgitābō, dolēbō, exspectābō, iacēbō, domī manēbō, fābulās nārrābō, pugnābō, timēbō.

PAGE 244
Standards 1.2, 4.1
Oral Exercise 3; Workbook Exercise 2

▶ EXERCISE 2 ANSWERS

1. expectorant — pectus
2. parental — parēns
3. tact — tangō
4. fluent — fluō
5. separation — sēparō
6. convention — conveniō
7. sanguine — sanguis
8. album — albus
9. rubric — ruber
10. oral — ōs
11. gladiators — gladius
12. odious — odium
13. prime — prīmus
14. arboretum — arbor
15. cadence — cadō

TEACHING TIP
Although in Exercise 2 the students are directed to find only the derivatives based on the Vocabulary to Learn, they may be interested to learn that there are other derivatives in Exercise 2. The derivation of these words is provided for the teacher's convenience.

2. attentive – from *attendō* (to direct the attention, attend to, notice).
3. please – from *placeō* (to please, satisfy). approach – from *ad* (to, toward) + *propior* (nearer). delicate – from *dēlicātus* (delightful, tender, soft).
4. in – from *in* (in, on, at).
5. in – from *in* (in, on, at). country – from *contrā* (opposite, against); that which is opposite, hence landscape. state – from *status* (attitude, position, standing, situation, state, condition).
6. representatives – from *praesentō* (to exhibit, present).
7. difficulties – from *difficultās* (distress, hardship, difficulty).
8. please – from *placeō* (to please, satisfy). pictures – from *pictūra* (painting, picture) from *pingō* (to paint, decorate).
9. issue – from *exeō* (to go out, march out, issue forth, leave). property – from *proprius* (one's own, personal).
10. class – from *classis* (a political class, army, fleet). prepare – from *prae* (before) + *parō* (to get ready, prepare). presentations – from *praesentō* (to exhibit, present).

11. arena – from (h)arēna (sand, desert, seashore).

13. elected – from ēligō (to pick, pluck out, choose). minister – from minister (attendant, servant, helper, agent) from minor (less).

14. in – from in (in, on, at).

15. lovely – from libet [lubet] (it pleases). in – from in (in, on, at). voice – from vōx (voice, sound, cry, call).

ORAL EXERCISE 3

This exercise may be used after the Vocabulary to Learn has been presented.

The students have learned the words *albus*, "white," and *ruber*, "red." Put on view other words denoting color as well as the word *rem* (accusative singular of *rēs*, f. "thing"), and explain what it means. Then the teacher should tell the students to perform the commands listed below.

niger, nigra, nigrum – black   **flāvus, flāva, flāvum** – yellow
viridis, viride – green   **spādīx, spādīcis** – brown
caeruleus, caerulea, caeruleum – blue

Teacher: Tange rem albam, rubram, nigram, viridem, caeruleam, flāvam, spādīcem!

Teacher: Da mihi rem albam, rubram, nigram, viridem, caeruleam, flāvam, spādīcem!

Teacher: Ostende nōbīs rem albam, rubram, nigram, viridem, caeruleam, flāvam, spādīcem!

Teacher: Pōne prope amīcum rem albam, rubram, nigram, viridem, caeruleam, flāvam, spādīcem!

PAGE 245

Standards 1.1, 1.2, 3.1, 4.1
Workbook Exercises 4, 5

▶ EXERCISE 3 ANSWERS

1. you responded/used to respond/were responding   respondēbis   you will respond
2. s/he is being set free   līberābitur   s/he will be set free
3. you are being separated   sēparāberis   you will be separated
4. s/he sails   nāvigābit   s/he will sail
5. we thought/used to think/were thinking   cōgitābimus   we will think
6. I destroy   dēlēbō   I will/shall destroy
7. you (plural) owed/used to owe/were owing   dēbēbitis   you (plural) will owe
8. they taught/used to teach/were teaching   docēbunt   they will teach
9. you (plural) are strengthened   firmābiminī   you (plural) will be strengthened
10. we are envied   invidēbimur   we will/shall be envied
11. they were being judged/used to be judged   iūdicābuntur   they will be judged
12. I am moved   movēbor   I will/shall be moved

Chapter 14 • 293

▶ EXERCISE 4 ANSWERS

Puer puellam amābit. Puer ā puellā amābitur. Puer et puella ad arborem in agrīs ambulāre dēbēbunt. Puella ibi exspectābit et leaenam vidēbit. Puella cum leaenā nōn pugnābit, sed timēbit et in spēluncā manēbit. Tum puer ad arborem ambulābit. Puella apud arborem nōn vidēbitur. Puer rogābit: "Ubi eris, amīca?" Puer et puella in morte nōn sēparābuntur. Semper poteritis vōs amāre, puer et puella!

The boy will love a girl. The boy will be loved by the girl. The boy and the girl will have to walk in the fields to a tree. The girl will wait there and will see a lioness. The girl will not fight with the lioness, but will fear and will remain in a cave. Then the boy will walk to the tree. The girl will not be seen at the tree. The boy will ask: "Where will you be, friend?" The boy and the girl will not be separated in death. You will be able to love yourselves (each other) always, boy and girl!

TEACHING TIP

After the students have completed Exercises 3 and 4, the teacher may wish to ask individual members of class in Latin about the verbs in the exercise. Some questions include:

- *Cūius temporis est?*   Answers: *praesentis, imperfectī, futūrī*
- *Cūius persōnae est?*   Answers: *prīmae, secundae, tertiae*
- *Cūius generis/vōcis est?*   Answers: *āctīvī/āctīvae, passīvī/passīvae*
- *Cūius est numerī?*   Answers: *singulāris, plūrālis*

TEACHING TIP

The teacher may wish to have the students look back in their texts at the paradigms of *sum* and *possum* in the present and imperfect tenses on p. 86, p. 89, and p. 191 in order to review those forms before proceeding to introduce the future tense of these two verbs.

PAGE 246
Standards 1.1, 1.2

▶ EXERCISE 5 ANSWERS

1. poteritis   you (plural) were able/could   you (plural) will be able
2. erunt   they were   they will be
3. poterit   s/he/it can/is able   s/he/it will be able
4. erimus   we are   we will/shall be
5. poterunt   they can/are able   they will be able
6. eris   you were   you will be
7. eritis   you (plural) were   you (plural) will be
8. poterit   s/he/it was able/could   s/he/it will be able
9. poterō   I was able/could   I will/shall be able
10. erit   s/he/it was   s/he/it will

PAGE 247
Standards 1.1, 1.2, 3.1, 4.1

▶ EXERCISE 6 ANSWERS
1. Possum fābulam audīre. Poteram fābulam audīre. Poterō fābulam audīre.
2. Pȳramus nōn est fēlīx. (Is) nōn erat fēlīx. (Is) nōn erit fēlīx.
3. Tū, Pȳrame, nōn es fēlīx. Tū, Pȳrame, nōn erās fēlīx. Tū, Pȳrame, nōn eris fēlīx.
4. Possuntne (eī) convenīre? (Eī) nōn poterant convenīre. (Eī) poterunt convenīre.
5. Vōs, Pȳrame et Thisbē, nōn potestis ūnā esse. Vōs, Pȳrame et Thisbē, poterātis ūnā esse, sed nōn poteritis ūnā esse.
6. Poterāmus dē amōre nārrāre, possumus et poterimus.

TEACHING TIP

In order to provide more practice with the forms of *sum* and *possum*, after the students have completed Exercise 6 and the correct answers have been given, instruct the students to change the verbs in each sentence in Exercise 6 in the following way.

1. Change each part of this sentence to the second person singular.
2. Change Pyramus to Pyramus and Thisbe and make all other required changes.
3. Change Pyramus to Pyramus and Thisbe and make all other required changes.
4. Change each part of this sentence to the third person singular.
5. Change each part of this sentence to the third person plural and make all other required changes.
6. Change each part of this sentence to the first person singular.

PAGE 248
Standards 3.1, 4.1
Oral Exercise 4; Workbook Exercise 3

TEACHING TIP

Although the genitive singular of the relative pronoun does not resemble the genitive singular of any noun declension, *cūius* does resemble *eius*, the genitive singular of *is, ea, id*, and it also resembles *huius* and *illīus*, the genitive singular forms of two demonstrative pronouns and adjectives that the students will learn later in this book.

TEACHING TIP

Instruct the students to repeat the forms of the relative pronoun after the teacher models their pronunciation.

Chapter 14 • 295

ORAL EXERCISE 4

This exercise may be used after the relative pronoun has been presented.

The teacher should say a form of the relative pronoun either in the singular or in the plural, and the student will change it into singular, if it is plural, or into the plural, if it is singular. For some, more than one answer is possible.

Teacher: quibus	**Student:** cui, quō, quā
Teacher: cūius	**Student:** quōrum, quārum
Teacher: quī	**Student:** quī
Teacher: quae	**Student:** quod, quae
Teacher: quōs	**Student:** quem
Teacher: quam	**Student:** quās
Teacher: quō	**Student:** quibus
Teacher: quod	**Student:** quae
Teacher: quā	**Student:** quibus

PAGE 249

Standards 1.1, 1.2

Workbook Exercises 6, 7, Content Questions

▶ EXERCISE 7 ANSWERS

Propter odium tamen, quod erat inter eōrum parentēs, Pȳramus et Thisbē ūnā esse nōn poterant.

"However, because of the hatred which was between their parents, Pyramus and Thisbe could not be together."

Quod is neuter singular, because it refers to the word *odium*; it is nominative, because it is the subject of *erat*.

Parietī, quī eōs sēparābat, verba saepe dīcēbant.

"They often said words to the wall which was dividing them."

Quī is masculine singular because it refers to *parietī*; it is nominative, because it is the subject of *sēparābat*.

Pȳramus venit et videt vēlāmen, in quō sanguis cōnspicitur.

"Pyramus comes and sees the veil, on which blood is observed."

Quō is neuter singular because it refers to *vēlāmen*; it is ablative because of the preposition *in*.

▶ EXERCISE 8 ANSWERS

1. Parentēs, quōs rogō dē multīs, multa sciunt.
2. You will fight with soldiers who will not have fear in their hearts (chests).
3. Cīvēs quibus gladiī dantur sunt fortēs.
4. The poet from whose mouth we are now hearing words is renowned.
5. Passer petit digitum dominae quae eum tenet.
6. Animal quod ea timet discēdit.
7. Tears were flowing from the eyes of the person to whom the story was being told.
8. Odium quod est in animō tuō habēre nōn dēbēs.
9. The girl about whose life he was grieving was alive.

296 • Latin for the New Millennium: Teacher's Manual, Level 1

PAGE 250

Standard 1.2

Oral Exercises 5, 6, Dictation

TRANSLATION OF THE LATIN CONVERSATION

Helen: Mark, were you able to do your homework yesterday?

Mark: I was not able. For I had to do many other things.

Helen: Were you surfing in the internet?

Mark: Aaa . . .

Mary (*enters*): Hello, Mark and Helen! Mark, yesterday you were sending me nice instant messages.

Helen: Instant messages?!

Mary: Mark and I were surfing in the internet for a long time yesterday, and we were having an internet chat. Today we will surf again. Won't we, Mark?

Helen: So, Mark, you were unable to prepare your homework because of the messages you were sending to Mary. (*leaves*) Goodbye!

Mark: Stay, Helen! Don't get angry at me! Today I will not surf in the internet. I will prepare my homework. We also will be able to walk together. Are we going to walk together today?

Helen: We shall see . . . I will call you.

ORAL EXERCISE 5

This exercise may be used after the Latin dialogue has been presented.

The teacher should ask students questions related to the dialogue. The students may look at the dialogue while responding. The teacher should use one of the CPOs to put on view the words *cūr?* "why?" and *gaudeō, gaudēre,* "to rejoice/be glad."

Teacher: Poteratne Mārcus pēnsum suum herī facere?
Student: Mārcus pēnsum suum herī facere nōn poterat.

Teacher: Cūr Mārcus pēnsum suum herī facere nōn poterat?
Student: Herī Mārcus diū in interrētī nāvigābat et ad Marīam nūntiōs subitāneōs mittēbat.

Teacher: Gaudetne Helena dē nūntiīs subitāneīs quōs Mārcus ad Marīam mittēbat?
Student: Helena nōn gaudet dē nūntiīs subitāneīs quōs Mārcus ad Marīam mittēbat.

Teacher: Quid Helena tunc facit?
Student: Helena discēdit.

Teacher: Quid Mārcus tunc dīcit?
Student: Mārcus dīcit: "Manē, Helena! Nōlī mihi īrāscī!"

Teacher: Nāvigābitne Mārcus hodiē quoque in interrētī?
Student: Hodiē Mārcus in interrētī nōn nāvigābit.

Teacher: Ambulābitne Mārcus cum Helenā?
Student: Mārcus cum Helenā ambulāre cupit.

Teacher: Ambulābitne Helena cum Mārcō?
Student: Helena dīcit: "Vidēbimus."

Chapter 14 • 297

DICTATION AND ORAL EXERCISE 6

This exercise may be used to conclude the chapter.

Dictate the following pairs of sentences. Then ask the students to transform them (orally or in a written form) into one sentence using a relative pronoun. Demonstrate by putting an example on view.

Example:

Teacher: Multī sunt et eī veniunt.   **Student:** Multī sunt quī veniunt.

Teacher: Videō puellam et eam amō.   **Student:** Videō puellam quam amō.

Teacher: Parābam epistulās et eās mittēbam.   **Student:** Parābam epistulās quās mittēbam.

Teacher: Nārrō fābulās et eīs movēminī.   **Student:** Nārrō fābulās quibus movēminī.

Teacher: Videō hominēs et eōrum nōmina dīcō.   **Student:** Videō hominēs quōrum nōmina dīcō.

Teacher: Vocābō puellam et eī fābulam nārrābō.   **Student:** Vocābō puellam cui fābulam nārrābō.

Teacher: Amāmus amīcōs et eīs dōna damus.   **Student:** Amāmus amīcōs quibus dōna damus.

PAGE 251

Standard 4.1

DERIVATIVES

arbor – Squirrels are <u>arboreal</u> animals, for they live in trees.

gladius – A <u>gladiator</u> uses a sword. Note the "-tor" suffix indicating "one who uses," etc.

A <u>gladiolus</u> (also <u>gladiola</u>) plant has sword-shaped, i.e., <u>gladiate</u>, leaves.

See also Teaching Tip 1.2.

odium – Note the "-ous" suffix on "odious."

The verb "annoy" appeared in English during the late fourteenth century from the Latin *esse in odiō* (literally, "to be in hatred," therefore, "hateful to me") through the Late Latin *inodiāre* and the Old French *anuier* (*enoiier*). It meant "to weary, vex, anger; be troublesome to."

The word "noisome" also is derived from the Latin through the French *anoier*, appearing in English during the late fourteenth century and meaning "harmful, noxious." The meaning "bad-smelling" was first recorded in the 1570s, as in "odorous." However, the Random House dictionary defines "odoriferous" as "bringing (especially) a fragrant smell."

"Ennui" came into English as a French word during the 1660s, derived from the Old French *ennui* (annoyance) which itself was formed from *invier*. The word was fully naturalized by 1758, but the pronunciation has remained French since there is no English analogy. The French meaning of *ennui* (displeasure) carried over into the English definition, "a displeasure resulting in boredom; weariness; satiation."

ōs – Note the difference between *ōs* (mouth) and *os* (bone).

The word *ōrificium* in Latin meant "an opening" (literally, "mouth-making") and is the root of "orifice," which came into English during the early fifteenth century and refers to a mouth-like opening.

The Latin word *ostium* is related to *ōs* and meant "a door or entrance." An *ostiārius* was a doorkeeper. The word "usher," which entered English in the late fourteenth century, is derived from that Latin through the Old French *ussier* and meant "a servant in charge of doors who admits people into a hall or chamber." The verb dates to the 1590s; the feminine form ("usherette") to 1925.

298 • Latin for the New Millennium: Teacher's Manual, Level 1

parēns – (from *pariō* = to give birth to)

A "repertoire" is a stock of plays, songs, etc., which a performer or company is ready to perform. The word consists of the intensive prefix "re" and the Latin verb *pariō* (to produce, bring forth). The word came into English from the French in 1847.

"Repertory" is based on the same roots but came into English earlier (1550s) meaning "a list, a catalogue." Its reference to a list of performances is dated to 1845.

pectus – <u>Pectoral</u> muscles are located in the chest area. The slang shortening "pec" dates to 1966.

The word "parapet" is derived from two Latin words: *para* from *parāre* (to get ready, to ward off for protection or defense) and *pectus* (through the Italian *petto* from *pectus* and meaning "breast"). It came into English during the 1580s. The soldiers built a <u>parapet</u> behind which they could shoot at the oncoming enemy. The word can also refer to the wall around the balcony of a house.

The word "expectorate" was first used as a euphemism for "spit" in 1827. The word came into English around 1600 meaning "to clear out the chest or lungs" (*ex* = out, and *pectus*).

sanguis – The derivatives are a bit tricky because they do not seem to mean the same thing. A <u>sanguinary</u> battle is a bloody one, but a <u>sanguine</u> person is "cheerful, hopeful, confident." This meaning was first attested around 1500 because these qualities were considered representative of an "excess of blood" (one of the four humors). Thus, a <u>sanguine</u> complexion is ruddy in color and denotes good health.

"Consanguinity" (from *cum* = together, and *sanguis*) indicates a close relationship by blood. Brothers are <u>consanguineous</u>.

quī, quae, quod – None, but see the related *quid* in 1.13.

albus – "Albumen" is the white part of an egg. The word came into English during the 1590s.

People with a deficiency in pigmentation are called "albinos." They have pale, milky skin, light hair, and pink eyes. The word was first used by the Portuguese in 1777 of dark-skinned Africans whose skin had splotches of white.

The word "auburn" appeared in English during the early fifteenth century through the Old French *auburn* and the medieval Latin *alburnus* meaning "off-white, whitish" from the Latin *albus*. In English it meant "yellowish-white" but shifted during the sixteenth century to "reddish-brown" influenced by the Middle English *brun*.

The verb "daub" appeared in English during the late fourteenth century, but "Dauber" as a surname is recorded from the mid-thirteenth century. It is derived through the Old French *dauber* (to whitewash, plaster) perhaps from the Latin *dealbāre* (*dē* = thoroughly, and *albus*) meaning "to whiten, whitewash." The painting sense dates to the 1620s.

prīmus – Longfellow's poem "Evangeline," written in dactylic hexameters (which is a great way to introduce Vergil students to the meter), begins "This is the forest <u>primeval</u>." The word is formed from the Latin *prīmus* and *aevum* (age).

The word "primogeniture" refers to the right of succession of the firstborn.

A young student enters the <u>primary</u> grades first.

The word "primate" first referred to a high bishop (around 1200). Later (1876) it came to denote members of the biological order that includes monkeys and humans, so called from supposedly being the highest (the first in rank) order of mammals.

The "primrose" flower is so called (from the Latin *prīma rosa*) because it blooms early in the spring.

The word "prince" (around 1200) is derived from the Latin *princeps*, which is composed of *prīmus* and *capere* (to take first place). "Princess" is the feminine form of "prince" based on the Italian *principessa* and the Old French *princesse*.

The word "principal" can be both a noun and an adjective, and is derived from the Latin *principālis* (original, first in importance).

On the other hand, the word "principle" can be used only as a noun. It derived from the Latin *principium* (beginning, origin, first part). It appeared in English during the late fourteenth century meaning "origin, axiom." The letter *l* in English was added apparently by analogy of "participle," etc.

See also Teaching Tip 1.3 for *prīmum*.

ruber – The word "rubric" came into English around 1300 meaning "directions in religious services" because they were often written in red ink. It is derived from the Latin *rubrīca* meaning "red ocher," a substance that was especially used as a pigment. Students and teachers know well the use of <u>rubrics</u> with respect to assignments and grading.

cadō – The word "accident" is derived from the Latin *accidō* meaning "to fall on, happen (usually misfortune)." Note the assimilation of *ad* and the common change of *a* to *i* from *cadō* and *accidō* (as in *faciō* to *afficiō*, etc.).

"Cadence," meaning "a flow in rhythm," came into English during the late fourteenth century derived through the Old Italian *cadenza* (conclusion of a movement in music; literally, a falling) from *cadō*.

The adjective "casual" appeared in English during the late fourteenth century meaning "subject to or produced by chance." Describing a person as someone not to be depended on dates to 1883, as in a "casual" acquaintance. The meaning "showing a lack of interest" is first attested in 1916; a reference to informal clothes began in 1939. The noun "casualty" appeared during the early fifteenth century meaning "chance, accident." The military reference to losses in numbers from a troop is from the late fifteenth century; to individuals lost or killed in battle dates to 1844. Both words derive from the Latin noun *cāsus* (derived from the fourth principal part of *cadō*).

The noun "chance" came into English around 1300 meaning "an occurrence, a happening" (more often bad than good) through the Old French *cheance* from a Vulgar Latin term used in dice derived from the Latin participle *cadentia*. The verb "chance" is found in English during the late fourteenth century meaning "to happen." The idea of risk is not in evidence until 1859 whereas that idea is associated with the noun earlier, e.g., the mathematical and odds-making sense which dates to 1778.

The verb "cheat" came into English during the mid-fifteenth century, a shortening of the French *escheat* meaning a revision of property to the state when an owner dies without heirs (literally, "that which falls to one" from the Latin *ex* = out, and *cadō*). The royal officers evidently had a low reputation, for the meaning of the word evolved from "confiscate" (mid-fifteenth century) to "deprive unfairly" (1580s). The noun appeared earlier (late fourteenth century) meaning simply "forfeited property," but it, too, evolved into "a deceptive act" (1640s) and "a swindler" (1660s).

The word "chute" came into American English in 1725 meaning "a fall of water." It was derived from the French *chute* (from the Old French *cheoite*, participle of *cheoir* which came from the Latin *cadō*). The meaning of "tube, inclined trough" dates to 1804; that of "a narrow passage for cattle" to 1881. It is also used as a shortened form for "parachute," a word coined in 1784 by Blanchard, the year in which its first use was attempted. The "para" comes from the Latin *parō* (to get ready, prepare) and *cadō* (to fall); hence, "a guard against falling."

"Deciduous" trees lose their leaves every year in the fall (*dē* = down, and *cadō*).

"Decay" and "decadence" also derive from the *dē* and *cadō* combination. The noun "decay" appeared in English during the mid-fifteenth century referring to deterioration or decline in value. The verb came into English a little later (late fifteenth century) meaning "to decrease." The idea of "decompose" dates to the 1570s. The noun "decadence" appeared during the 1540s, the adjective "decadent" in 1837.

The word "coincide," which appeared in 1715, is a composite of the Latin *cum* (together), *in* (into), and *cadō* (to fall), hence "to fall into (upon) together."

The noun "incident" derives from the Latin *incīdō* (to fall upon, meet, occur, happen). In the early fifteenth century it simply meant an occurrence casually connected to something else. Its reference to "an event that might trigger a crisis or cause unrest" dates to 1913.

The word "occident" derives from the Latin *occīdō* (from *ob* by assimilation, and *cadō*), meaning "to fall, set, die, perish," and refers to the West (where the sun sets; Latin *sōlis occāsus*). It is the antonym for "orient" which refers to the East (where the sun rises; Latin *orior* = to rise).

The words "occasion" and "occasional" derive from the Latin *occāsiō* (from the fourth principal part of *occīdō*) meaning "opportunity, convenient time."

Students who know their Latin will readily spell words like "occasion" correctly.

comedō – (from *cum* = thoroughly, and *edō* = to eat; hence "to eat up, consume")

The word "comestible" is first found in English in 1837 meaning "article of food." In modern times it is also used as an adjective to describe something that is edible.

Note that the noun "comedo" is a medical name for blackheads, secretions that look like the worms that devour the body to which the word originally referred.

conveniō – See *veniō* 1.9.

fluō – What city is located near the <u>confluence</u> of the Ohio and the Mississippi Rivers? (Cairo, Illinois)

The word "affluence" is derived from the Latin *affluō* (*ad* by assimilation) meaning "to flow toward"; hence "to abound in." The sense of wealth dates to around 1600.

The <u>effluent</u> Mississippi River flows out into the Gulf of Mexico.

The <u>fluctuating</u> current flowed back and forth.

The noun "flux" appeared in English during the late fourteenth century meaning "an excessive flow" (of blood or excrement). It was an early term for dysentery.

Although the word "flume" (late twelfth century) referred in general to running water like a stream, in the United States today it usually denotes artificial streams channeled for some industrial purpose.

The word "influence" derives from the Latin *influō* (to flow into). The reference to an exercise of personal power by humans dates to the mid-fifteenth century. The phrase "under the influence" (drunk) is first found in 1866.

The spelling of this word was changed to "influenza" when it came to refer to an illness in 1743 from the Italian *influenza*, which originally meant "a visitation of the stars" (reflecting the astrological meaning of "influence" [late fourteenth century]).

The <u>mellifluous</u> sounds of the string quartet flowed sweetly through my memory (*mel, mellis* = honey). Note the "-ous" suffix.

The word "superfluous" consists of the Latin *super* (over, above) and *fluō*. The literal meaning of "overflowing" easily evolved to "unnecessary" (early fifteenth century). Note the "-ous" suffix and stress the correct pronunciation of the word, with the accent on the antepenult.

Chapter 14 • 301

sēparō – (from *sē* = apart, aside, and *parō* = prepare, make ready)

The word "sever" comes from *sēparō* through the Old French *sevrer* (to separate).

The adjective "several" came into English during the early fifteenth century meaning "existing apart" but by 1500 it meant "various, diverse, different" and by the 1530s was being used to indicate "more than one."

tangō – Derivatives with the "tang" base derive from *tangō* (tangible, tangent, etc.); those with "tact" come from the fourth principal part *tāctus* (intact, contact); those with "ting" follow the usual *a* to *i* shift when a prefix is added (contingent). "Contiguous" and "contagious" lose the *n* as *tangō* does in the third and fourth principal parts.

A "contagious" person should not come into close contact with others (Latin *contāgiō* = contact, infection, contamination).

Forty-eight of the fifty states of America are <u>contiguous</u>.

The related Latin verb *contāminō* (to defile, spoil; from the pre-Indo-European root tag meaning "to touch" and which also serves as the base of *tangō*) is the source for the English "contaminate."

An "integer" is an untouched or whole number.

To "integrate" means "to make something whole" (Latin *integrō* = to renew, replenish, repair). The prefix of "disintegrate" means "do the opposite of" as it does in "distaste."

The word "taste" entered English during the late thirteenth century meaning "to touch, handle" and derived through the Old French *taste* (from *tangō*), which earlier meant "to feel or touch" and then "to taste, explore by touching." (The tongue touches the food to explore its taste or flavor.) The sense of aesthetic judgment dates to the 1670s.

The adjective "entire" (late fourteenth century) is derived through the Old French *entire* (whole, intact) from the Latin *integer*.

The word "attain" is derived from the Latin *attingō* (*ad* = toward, and *tangō*) through the Old French *ataindre* (to touch, reach toward, arrive at). The Latin has a wide range of meanings, e.g., to attack, strike, arrive at, undertake, etc., but all relate to the idea of "touch."

iam – None

mox – None

per – This is a commonly used prefix in English. For meanings of such words, e.g., permeate, permanent, permission, percolate, etc., see the Latin root verb.

CHAPTER 15 (PP. 253–266)

GRAMMAR IN LANGUAGE FACTS

Third and Fourth Conjugation Verbs: Future Tense Active and Passive; Interrogative Pronouns and Adjectives

PAGE 253

Standards 1.1, 2.1, 3.1, 3.2
RRA 6A

MEMORĀBILE DICTŪ VOCABULARY

fātum, fātī, *n.* – destiny

nōlēns, nōlentis – unwilling

trahō, trahere, trāxī, trāctum – to drag

volēns, volentis – willing

TEACHER BY THE WAY
Cleanthes wrote during the third century BCE and Seneca's *Moral Letters* are named *Epistulae Mōrālēs* in Latin.

TEACHER BY THE WAY
Giordano was an influential Italian artist of the late Baroque period known for his speed of execution and huge output. A painter primarily of mythological and religious subjects, he was noted for his use of lively and showy color. Influenced by such decorative painters as Veronese, he is considered to be a forerunner of Tiepolo and other great eighteenth-century painters.

TEACHER BY THE WAY
Seneca was commanded to commit suicide in 65 CE because he was implicated in the Pisonian conspiracy by Antonius Natalis, one of its chief organizers. According to Tacitus, Natalis may have done this to win the favor of Nero, "who hated Seneca" (*quī īnfēnsus Senecae omnīs ad eum opprimendum artēs conquīrēbat, Annālēs* 15.56). The death of Seneca was "a special joy to the emperor" (*caedēs Annaeī Senecae, laetissima principī, Annālēs* 15.60). Whether or not Seneca was actually involved is unclear, but Nero had often been the recipient of his free speech (*Annālēs* 14.52; 15.61) and in his rage took the opportunity to order his suicide. The death of

Seneca is described by Tacitus in excruciating but sympathetic detail (15.62–64): "Because of his age and frugal diet, the blood flowed too slowly from the arteries he had severed in his arms, so he also cut those in his legs. Still living and in pain, he asked for hemlock, but that was also unsuccessful. Finally, he was taken to a heated bath where he suffocated from the steam."

TEACHING TIP

Chapter 6A of RRA contains information on Seneca and Nero and provides a chart of the Julio-Claudian emperors. The teacher may wish to assign this chapter for reading or review. See p. 201.

PAGE 254
Standards 1.1, 2.1, 3.1, 3.2

TRANSLATION OF LATIN PASSAGE
Seneca Meets His Old Age

Seneca wishes (says) good health to Lucilius.

I see indications of my old age everywhere. A rural country house belongs to me (there is for me a rural country house). I come to my country house and the steward tells me that he must repair many things in the country house. He says that he does everything, that he neglects nothing, but the country house is old. But I had built the country house! What will be <in store> for me? Will my body collapse, just like the stones of my country house?

"You," I said, "are neglecting the trees: they don't have leaves. Do you give water to the trees?"

"I always took care of the trees," he said, "and will take care of them, and they will never be neglected by me. But they are old."

I shall tell you something, Lucilius, which you will perhaps not believe is true: I planted the trees!

Then I look at the door. There stands an old man, who is staring at me.

"Who is the old man?" I said. "Why is he staring at me?"

"Don't you recognize me?" said the old man. "I am Felicio, with whom you used to play as a boy. I was once your little friend."

It is difficult for me to recognize my friend! For the old man who stands in front of me, who has no teeth, does not seem like the little boy with whom I used to play!

My country house seemed to say to me: "Look! <Here is> your old age!" Old age will come to all of us even <when we are> unprepared. So we ought to expect it. We ought to be prepared.

TEACHER BY THE WAY

Seneca's distinctive style of expression is noteworthy for its short, epigrammatic sentences. His thoughts are briefly worded; they express a paradox, contrast, or surprising observation. They are often easily quotable as mottoes or proverbs.

304 • Latin for the New Millennium: Teacher's Manual, Level 1

TEACHING TIP

Instruct the students to locate Corsica on the map on pp. xxxiv–xxxv (SE) and to locate Claudius and Nero on the timeline on pp. 405–408 (SE).

PAGE 255

TEACHER BY THE WAY

In addition to the *Epistulae Mōrālēs*, Seneca also wrote the following:

- *Apocolocyntōsis* – a satire on the death of the emperor Claudius
- *Dē beneficiīs* – on the nature of and problems connected with gratitude and ingratitude including examples of heroic self-sacrifice
- *Dē clementiā* – praise of Nero's early years
- *Dialogī* – ten ethical treatises
- *Nātūrālēs quaestiōnēs* – an examination of nature to find in it a foundation for Stoic ethics
- Nine tragedies including *Herculēs Furēns, Mēdēa, Trōadēs, Phaedra, Agamemnōn, Oedipūs, Hercules Oetaeus, Phoenissae,* and *Thyestēs*

There are also three epigrams collected in the *Anthologia Latīna* that contain some references to his own life and family.

TEACHING TIP

Since the word *iānua* is listed in the Reading Vocabulary on this page, the students might be interested in the following.

The word *iānua*, which refers to the outer door of the house, is connected to the word *iānus*, which properly means a gate. These were often freestanding and used for ceremonial purposes. For instance, an army setting out for war would formally march through a *iānus*, and a closing of the gates on the temple of Janus signified Rome was at peace.

The god Janus was originally the *nūmen* of these gates, and therefore it was easy to associate him with the door of a house, which was used for entrance to a dwelling as a gate was for a city. Thus he became the god of beginnings. Because of this connection to going in and coming out, Janus came to be depicted in art with two faces, one facing forward, the other backward.

It was the Etruscans who probably introduced their calendar into Rome, and *Iānuārius* was no doubt meant to mark the beginning of the year since Janus had become a very important god and was always the first one invoked in a list of gods during prayer. However, this reform was stopped when the Etruscans were expelled, and March continued to be the first month of the Roman year until 154 BCE when January finally became the first month as it is today.

PAGE 256
Standards 1.1, 3.1, 4.1

ANSWERS TO COMPREHENSION QUESTIONS
1. Everything was very old.
2. Seneca's childhood friend. He had grown old.
3. Old age comes even if we do not think about it.

TEACHING TIP
After the students have studied the paradigms on p. 257 (SE), the teacher may wish to ask three questions in Latin about each of these verbs that the students have already learned in this book. Answers are provided for the teacher's convenience. This exercise may be done in oral or written format.

Cūius coniugātiōnis est? – What conjugation is it?
Cūius temporis est? – What tense is it?
Cūius generis/vōcis est? – What voice is it?

1. cadēs — Answer: *tertiae, futūrī, āctīvī/āctīvae*
2. comedit — Answer: *tertiae, praesentis, āctīvī/āctīvae*
3. sēparāminī — Answer: *prīmae, praesentis, passīvī/passīvae*
4. tenēberis — Answer: *secundae, futūrī, passīvī/passīvae*
5. neglegentur — Answer: *tertiae, futūrī, passīvī/passīvae*
6. tanguntur — Answer: *tertiae, praesentis, passīvī/passīvae*
7. rogābit — Answer: *prīmae, futūrī, āctīvī/āctīvae*
8. dūcēmur — Answer: *tertiae, futūrī, passīvī/passīvae*
9. agam — Answer: *tertiae, futūrī, āctīvī/āctīvae*
10. aedificātur — Answer: *prīmae, praesentis, passīvī/passīvae*
11. pugnant — Answer: *prīmae, praesentis, āctīvī/āctīvae*
12. cōnsūment — Answer: *tertiae, futūrī, āctīvī/āctīvae*

PAGE 257
Oral Exercise 1; Workbook Exercise 1

ORAL EXERCISE 1

This exercise may be used after the future tense of the third and fourth conjugations has been presented.

The teacher should say a present tense form and ask the students to change it into the corresponding future tense.

Teacher: agō	**Student:** agam
Teacher: dēcernitur	**Student:** dēcernētur
Teacher: neglegis	**Student:** neglegēs
Teacher: audītur	**Student:** audiētur
Teacher: cōnspiciuntur	**Student:** cōnspicientur
Teacher: fugimus	**Student:** fugiēmus
Teacher: intellegimur	**Student:** intellegēmur
Teacher: mittiminī	**Student:** mittēminī
Teacher: sentiunt	**Student:** sentient
Teacher: dīceris	**Student:** dīcēris
Teacher: stās	**Student:** stābis

PAGE 258
Standards 1.1, 1.2
Workbook Exercise 4

▶ EXERCISE 1 ANSWERS

1. s/he is sent — mittētur — s/he will be sent
2. they know — scient — they will know
3. we were eating/used to eat — comedēmus — we will/shall eat
4. you (plural) were being led/used to be led — dūcēminī — you (plural) will be led
5. you (plural) abandon — relinquētis — you (plural) will abandon
6. I was shown/used to be shown — ostendar — I will/shall be shown
7. we were being killed — occīdēmur — we will/shall be killed
8. s/he was doing — faciet — s/he will do

TEACHING TIP
Additional reproducible worksheets, morphology charts, and their associated answer keys, related to this material, are available for download at www.lnm.bolchazy.com.
- **Verb Conjugations**

Chapter 15 • 307

PAGE 259

Standards 1.1, 1.2, 3.1, 4.1
Workbook Exercise 2

▶ EXERCISE 2 ANSWERS

1. difficulty — difficilis
2. neglect — neglegō
3. AM (ante merīdiem) — ante
4. rustic — rūsticus
5. senile — senectūs
6. static — stō
7. verified — vērus
8. argumentation — argūmentum
9. ubiquitous — ubīque
10. village — vīlla

TEACHING TIP

Although in Exercise 2 the students are directed to find only the derivatives based on the Vocabulary to Learn, they may be interested to learn that there are other derivatives in Exercise 2. The derivation of these words is provided for the teacher's convenience.

1. source – from *surgō* (to rise, spring up).
3. usually – from *ūsus* (experience, custom, familiarity, usage).
4. unrefined – from *fīnis* (border, end, summit, aim, purpose). recipe – from *recipiō* (to take back, regain, accept, undertake).
5. debility – from *dēbilitās* (weakness, infirmity). age – from *aevum* (age, lifetime, eternity).
6. moves – from *moveō* (to move).
7. documents – from *doceō* (to teach, inform).
8. internally – from *internus* (internal, civil). coherent – from *cum* (with, together) + *haereō* (to cling, stick, stay close). valid – from *validus* (strong, powerful, healthy, effective).
9. advertisements – from *advertō* (to turn, direct toward, call attention to).
10. in – from *in* (in, on, at).

PAGE 260

TEACHING TIP

Instruct the students to repeat the forms of the interrogative pronoun aloud after the teacher models their pronunciation.

308 • Latin for the New Millennium: Teacher's Manual, Level 1

TEACHING TIP

Encourage the students to create a rap, cheer, or song for both the interrogative pronoun and the interrogative adjective that are on pp. 260–261 (SE). Alternatively, use Bolchazy-Carducci's *Toga Beats*.

TEACHING TIP

A quick oral exercise that can be used to practice comprehension of the various cases of the interrogative pronoun follows.

Instruct the students that, after they are asked a question in Latin, they may reply with one of these words only but in whatever case is needed. The words for the replies are *puer, puella, discipulus, discipula, magister, magistra.*

The teacher should move around the room asking students in a random order any one of the following questions. The teacher should carry any available book with him/her to use as a prop with these questions. The answers are provided for the teacher's convenience.

- *Quis es?*   Answers: (*Sum*) *puer, puella, discipulus, discipula*
- *Quis sum?*   Answers: (*Es*) *magister, magistra*
- *Cūius liber est?*   Answers: (*Est liber*) *magistrī, magistrae*
- Hand the book to another student and then ask, "*Cui librum dō?*"   Answers: (*Dās librum*) *puerō, puellae, discipulō, discipulae*
- *Quem vidēs?*   Answers: (*Videō*) *puerum, puellam, discipulum, discipulam, magistrum, magistram*
- Point to the book and then say, "*Quid vidēs?*"   Answer: (*Videō*) *librum*
- Tell the student to stand next to you and say, "*Quōcum stās?*"   Answers: (*Stō*) *cum magistrō, magistrā*

PAGE 261
Oral Exercise 2

TEACHER BY THE WAY

A shrine to the household gods (*Larēs*) was located in a corner of the atrium. They were honored on the Kalends, Nones, and Ides of each month. The images of the *Penātēs* (pantry gods) were also located in the atrium. Since both were guardians of the household, a part of the meal was set aside and thrown into the hearth fires for them.

TEACHING TIP

Instruct the students to say the forms of the interrogative adjective aloud in Latin. The students have already learned how to pronounce those forms that are the same as those of the relative pronoun.

Chapter 15 • 309

ORAL EXERCISE 2

This exercise may be used after the interrogative pronoun and adjective have been presented.

The teacher should use one of the CPOs to put on view the following sentences and then ask individual students to change each sentence so that the underlined nouns or adjectives are replaced by the correct form of the interrogative pronoun or adjective. All other words in each sentence will remain the same. In making these changes, of course, the students will change the sentences from statements into questions. The students should make the changes entirely orally. The students may refer to the charts in case they have not yet thoroughly learned the forms.

Example: (statement) <u>Seneca</u> nōn timet. (question) <u>Quis</u> nōn timet?

1. Senātōrēs <u>Rōmānī</u> in urbe habitābant.   <u>Quī</u> senātōrēs in urbe habitābant?
2. Vīllae ā <u>senātōribus</u> habēbantur.   Ā <u>quibus</u> vīllae habēbantur?
3. Praemia <u>senātōribus</u> dantur.   <u>Quibus</u> praemia dantur?
4. Exempla <u>nova</u> ā senātōribus dabuntur.   <u>Quae</u> exempla ā senātōribus dabuntur?
5. <u>Perīcula</u> in urbe timēbantur.   <u>Quae</u> in urbe timēbantur?
6. <u>Senātōrum</u> vīllae erant magnae.   <u>Quōrum</u> vīllae erant magnae?
7. Senātōrēs terram <u>rūsticam</u> amābant.   <u>Quam</u> terram senātōrēs amābant?
8. <u>Saxum</u> in viā ā Senecā cōnspicitur.   <u>Quid</u> in viā ā Senecā cōnspicitur?
9. Agrī ab <u>agricolā</u> cūrantur.   Ā <u>quō</u> agrī cūrantur?
10. Vīlla <u>Senecae</u> est vetusta.   <u>Cūius</u> vīlla est vetusta?

TEACHER BY THE WAY

It was common practice for wealthy Romans to own several homes—a city home in Rome, a country house often attached to a farm in the hills outside of Rome, and a home on the sea on the Bay of Naples. Roman owners of these maritime villas vied with one another in terms of size, scale, and luxurious decoration. Vesuvius's eruption provides a glimpse into this lavish lifestyle via the excavated villas at Boscoreale and Stabiae, the Villa of the Papyri at Herculaneum, and the magnificent villa at Oplontis. Just outside Pompeii lie two "suburban" villas—the Villa of Diomedes and the Villa of the Mysteries. Magnificent frescoes were the key decorative element of these villas.

The Villa of the Mysteries, consisting of some sixty rooms, commands an excellent view of the sea. The villa was built and rebuilt over the course of three centuries. At the time of the eruption, the owners had not yet finished renovations.

A 15' x 21' room in what are probably the private apartments of the villa boasts a group of paintings whose subject matter gave the villa its name. The two panels depicted in the illustration on p. 261 (SE) are part of this series of frescoes that shows the rich color called Pompeian red, a hue derived from the local soil. The panels of the dressed woman on the left and the bare-chested male dancer on the right are the tamer pictures in this series that illustrates Dionysus and what is probably a depiction of the mystery rites of initiation into his cult. Other panels include Silenus, satyrs, cupids, and several scenes including women. Because the Dionysiac rituals were mysteries, references and allusions along with these paintings provide only a shadowy understanding of what actually took place.

PAGE 262

Standards 1.1, 1.2, 2.1
Workbook Exercises 3, 5

▶ EXERCISE 3 ANSWERS

1. Cūius vīlla est vetusta?
2. Quōrum vīllae sunt vetustae?
3. Quae vīlla est vetusta?
4. Quae vīllae sunt vetustae?
5. Quem cōnspicit senex?
6. Quōs amīcōs cōnspicit senex?
7. Quī senex mē cōnspicit?
8. Cui agricolae agrum dabis?
9. Quibus agricolīs agrōs dabis?
10. Quī agricolae agrōs mihi dabunt?
11. Quōcum ad vīllam ambulābis?
12. Quibuscum in vīllā manēbis?

▶ EXERCISE 4 ANSWERS

1. To whom does the steward say that he must repair many things in the villa?
   Senecae vīlicus dīcit sē dēbēre multa in vīllā reparāre.
   The steward says to Seneca that that he must repair many things in the villa.

2. What does the steward say that he neglects?
   Vīlicus dīcit sē nihil neglegere.
   The steward says that he neglects nothing.

3. What does Seneca think about himself?
   Seneca cōgitat sē esse vetustum sīcut vīllam.
   Seneca thinks he is old just like <his> vīlla.

4. What leaves are in the trees?
   Arborēs nōn habent folia.
   The trees do not have leaves.

5. By whom were the trees always cared for and shall not ever be neglected?
   Vīlicus arborēs semper cūrābat nec eās negleget.
   The steward always cared for the trees and will not neglect them.

6. Which trees are said to be old?
   Arborēs Senecae dīcuntur esse vetustae.
   Seneca's trees are said to be old.

Chapter 15 • 311

7. Whom does the old man, who stands in the door, observe?
   Senecam cōnspicit senex, quī in iānuā stat.
   The old man, who stands in the door, observes Seneca.

8. To which people will old age come?
   Ad omnēs hominēs veniet senectūs.
   Old age will come to all people.

PAGE 263
Workbook Exercises 6, 7

TEACHING TIP
The topic of ancient villas is encountered in this chapter and a diagram of a *domus* is included on this page. Here one might compare and contrast the layout of an ancient *vīlla*, *domus*, and *īnsula*. The teacher may wish to discuss the use of the rooms labeled on this diagram. An *exedra*, for example, was a sitting room. The teacher may also want to include the names of other rooms and areas (e.g., *compluvium, cubiculum, culīna, impluvium, taberna, trīclīnium*) not shown on this diagram. Another diagram of a *domus* is on p. 306 (SE).

TEACHING TIP
Additional reproducible worksheets, morphology charts, and their associated answer keys, related to this material, are available for download at www.lnm.bolchazy.com.

- **The Roman House**

PAGE 264
Standards 1.1, 1.2
Workbook Exercise 8, Content Questions

▶ EXERCISE 5 ANSWERS
Fēlīciō: Quis nunc ad vīllam venit? Quem cōnspiciō?
Seneca: I am Seneca. The villa is mine.
Fēlīciō: Quid dīcis? Seneca esse nōn potes!
Seneca: I cannot be Seneca? I AM Seneca!
Fēlīciō: Seneca mihi esse nōn vidēris: vidēris mihi esse senex!
Seneca: I am an old man—and Seneca.
Fēlīciō: Quem hominem mē esse putās?
Seneca: I think you are an old man who does not have teeth.
Fēlīciō: Quī puer tēcum puerō lūdere solēbat?
Seneca: Fēlīciō, <my> little friend, used to play with me as a boy.
Fēlīciō: Quis tibi esse videor? Eram Fēlīciō. Sum Fēlīciō. Erō Fēlīciō.
Seneca: You are Fēlīciō! I am happy! It was difficult for me, Fēlīciō, to recognize you. For you too, just as Seneca, are an old man. But at last I see my friend!

312 • Latin for the New Millennium: Teacher's Manual, Level 1

PAGE 265

Standards 1.2, 4.1
Oral Exercise 3, 4, Dictation

TRANSLATION OF THE LATIN CONVERSATION

Mary: Tomorrow I will go to the country together with (my) parents.

Helen: Do you love the countryside?

Mary: I love the countryside very much. (My) parents also love it. If we have leisure, we go to the countryside.

Mark: What are you going to do in the country, Mary?

Mary: The fields are beautiful, the trees are beautiful. My parents and I will look for trails in the woods. It pleases my parents to walk there.

Christy: Does it please you to take a walk in the woods, Mary?

Mary: Yes indeed. But (my) parents do not remain in the woods for a long time. After a few hours they get tired and want to go to the country house. They are older.

Christy: What do you do then? Do you go with them to the country house?

Mary: Sometimes. But sometimes I go to the fields and woods alone. There I ride a bicycle for a long time. Sometimes I have with me a backpack and a foldable tent. Then I do not go to the country house, but sleep in the open.

TEACHING TIP

The teacher may choose to tell students that *rūrī*, like *domī*, which has been seen before in this book, is in the locative case.

ORAL EXERCISE 3

This exercise may be used after the Latin dialogue has been presented.

After the students have carefully read and understood the dialogue, the teacher should ask individual students the following questions. (NB: the students may look at the dialogue while they answer.)

Teacher: Quibuscum rūs petet Marīa?
Student: Marīa cum parentibus rūs petet.

Teacher: Amatne terram rūsticam Marīa?
Student: Marīa terram rūsticam amat.

Teacher: Quid faciunt Marīa et parentēs, sī ōtium habent?
Student: Sī ōtium habent, terram rūsticam petunt.

Teacher: Quid rūrī faciunt Marīa et parentēs?
Student: Marīa et parentēs in silvīs sēmitās petunt et ibi deambulāre solent.

Teacher: Parentēsne Marīae diū in silvīs manent?
Student: Parentēs Marīae nōn diū in silvīs manent.

Teacher: Quid Marīa sōla in agrīs et silvīs facere solet?
Student: Marīa sōla in agrīs et silvīs diū birotā vehitur. Interdum manticam dorsuālem et tentōrium plicātile habet. Tunc vīllam nōn petit, sed sub dīvō dormit.

DICTATION AND ORAL EXERCISE 4

This exercise may be used to conclude the chapter.

In preparation for the exercise, the teacher should put on view the vocabulary below the passage. Then the teacher should dictate the following passage to the students and ask individual students the questions listed below. To answer the questions, the students should make use of the words in the passage that they have just written—with the appropriate adjustments of endings and person. The students should also refer to the Reading Vocabulary, where needed.

Ubīque argūmenta senectūtis ā Senecā cōnspiciuntur. Venit ad vīllam, quam ante multōs annōs aedificāverat. Ibi saxa ē mūrīs ceciderant. In arboribus nōn erant folia. Vīlla, arborēs, saxa erant vetusta, sīcut Seneca ipse. Tunc Seneca senem videt, quī prope vīllam stat. Seneca puer ante multōs annōs fuerat amīcus virī, sed eum nunc cōgnōscere nōn potest. Itaque dē senectūte cōgitāre dēbet Seneca, quae ad omnēs hominēs venit.

aedificāverat – he had built (pluperfect tense)
annus, annī, *m.* – year
ceciderant – had fallen (pluperfect tense)
fuerat – had been (pluperfect tense)

ipse – himself (nominative singular agreeing with *Seneca*)
mūrus, mūrī, *m.* – wall

Teacher: Ā quō argūmenta senectūtis cōnspiciuntur?
Student: Argūmenta senectūtis ā Senecā cōnspiciuntur.

Teacher: Quis ad vīllam venit?
Student: Seneca ad vīllam venit.

Teacher: Quid ante multōs annōs aedificāverat Seneca?
Student: Seneca vīllam ante multōs annōs aedificāverat.

Teacher: Cūius in arboribus nōn erant folia?
Student: In arboribus Senecae nōn erant folia.

Teacher: Quem videt Seneca?
Student: Seneca senem videt.

Teacher: Prope quid stat senex?
Student: Senex prope vīllam stat.

Teacher: Quis ante multōs annōs fuerat amīcus senis, quī prope vīllam stat?
Student: Seneca puer ante multōs annōs fuerat amīcus senis, quī prope vīllam stat.

Teacher: Quem nunc cōgnōscere nōn potest Seneca?
Student: Senem nunc cōgnōscere nōn potest Seneca.

Teacher: Quis dē senectūte cōgitāre dēbet?
Student: Seneca dē senectūte cōgitāre dēbet.

Teacher: Quid ad omnēs hominēs venit?
Student: Senectūs ad omnēs hominēs venit.

314 • Latin for the New Millennium: Teacher's Manual, Level 1

PAGE 266
Standard 4.1

DERIVATIVES

argūmentum – (from *arguō* = to prove, make known, accuse, blame, denounce)

    An <u>argumentative</u> person always wants to prove that his point is the correct one.

saxum – A <u>saxifrage</u> grows wild in rock clefts and, in spite of its puny size, is well-named (rock-breaker).

    <u>Saxatile</u> plants live and grow on or among rocks.

senectūs – See *senex* in 1.7.

vīlla – The word "village" came into English during the late fourteenth century, denoting a place "larger than a hamlet but smaller than a town." Around the <u>villas</u> of wealthy Romans grew up small collections of houses and other buildings for the people who served or worked on the country estate, hence the name.

    Originally (around 1300) the word "villain" meant a "base or lowborn rustic." This gradually evolved to mean "boor, clown, knave," and finally, "scoundrel." Today the word is used only in the pejorative sense.

    Note the "-ous" suffix on "villainous."

    The word "villein" (early fourteenth century) is a variant spelling of "villain," but its meaning is limited to a feudal class of half-free peasants.

quis, quid – See *quid* in 1.13.

difficilis – See *faciō* in 1.12 and Teaching Tips 1.11 and 1.14.

parvus – The word "paraffin" is derived through the German *Paraffin*, coined by the chemist von Reichenbach (1788–1869) who first obtained the substance from wood tar. The word is derived from *parvus* (small) and *adfīnis* (neighboring, associated with) because "paraffin" is not closely related chemically to other substances.

quī, quae, quod – None

rūsticus – (from *rūs, rūris* = country)

    The adjective "rustic" came into English during the mid-fifteenth century meaning, like its root, "country-like, simple, rough, coarse." The noun "rusticity" appeared in English during the 1530s meaning "country life." "Rustication" appeared during the 1620s and meant "to reside in the country." The old lord preferred <u>rustication</u> to urban life.

vērus – The word "verdict" derives from the Latin *vērum dictum* (true word) and appeared in English during the 1530s meaning "a jury's decision" (a jury is impaneled to decide the truth of a dispute).

    The name "Verity" was popular among the Puritans and, although quite rare today, it can be found in the Harry Potter series and the Poldark novels.

    The word "verisimilitude" (*vērus* = true, and *similis* = like) can mean "the probability of truth" or "having merely the appearance of truth." It can therefore be a positive or negative word.

    To "verify" a statement means "to make sure it is the truth" (*vērus*, and *faciō* = to make).

Chapter 15 • 315

The word "very" appeared in English during the mid-thirteenth century spelled *verray* and meaning "real, genuine." It was derived from *vērus* through the Old French *verai*. Its meaning, "greatly, extremely," was first used during the mid-fifteenth century. As an adjective it can also mean "precise, particular." That is the <u>very</u> book I was reading just last night.

The verb "aver" (late fourteenth century) is derived from the Latin *ad* (to) and *vērus* through the Old French *averer* (to prove to be true). Today it has the sense of "stating positively, affirming with confidence."

See also Teaching Tips 1.6 and 1.10.

vetustus – None

inquam – None

neglegō – (from *nec* = not, and *legō* = to choose, gather, read, etc.)

The word "negligee" came into English in 1756 meaning "a loose gown worn by women" from the Latin verb *neglegō* (to not heed, disregard, make light of), so called in comparison to the elaborate costumes worn by women of that period (OED). The modern sense of a "semitransparent flimsy dressing gown" appeared in 1930. The word was also used by the American funeral industry during the mid-twentieth century for "the shroud of a corpse."

Other derivatives listed also come directly from *neglegō*, e.g., the verb "neglect" (1520s) and the noun "neglect" (1580s), the adjective "neglectful" (1640s), the noun "negligence" (mid-fourteenth century) through the Latin *neglegentia* (carelessness, neglect), and negligible (1819).

stō – The long list of derivatives given for this Latin verb is representative, not exhaustive. After two general observations about them, a more detailed examination will be made of words with interesting derivations, meanings, or spellings.

The derivatives with "stat" as their base come from the fourth principal part, e.g., statue, estate, interstate, station. Those based on "sta" come from the second principal part, e.g., obstacle, distance, stay, substantial, circumstance, constable, constant.

From the related Latin verb *sistō* come the "sti" derivatives, e.g., constitution, destination, destitute, solstice, etc.

The summer and winter <u>solstices</u> occur when the sun seems to "stand still" before beginning its journey across the sky in the opposite direction.

The word "exist" (from the Latin *exstō* = to stand out, be visible) came into English around 1600. The OED notes: "The late appearance of the word is remarkable."

The adjective "extant" appeared in English during the 1540s meaning "to stand out above a surface," but shortly thereafter (1560) it also meant "in existence." Only twenty of the plays of Plautus are <u>extant</u>.

Note the difference in meaning created by one vowel between "stationary" (standing still) and "stationery" (from "stationer," a dealer who sells books and papers in a shop that stands in a permanent location as opposed to peddlers and vendors). Both words derive from the Latin *statiō* (standing still, post, station) through the medieval Latin *stationārius* (stationary seller = one who remains in one place).

The word "substantial" (literally "stand under or be present," hence "having reality, material") is derived directly from the Latin *substantia* meaning "wealth, means."

The word "destination," from the Latin *dē* (completely) and *stāre*, came into English during the 1590s meaning "act of appointing" (Latin *dēstinātiō* = resolution, appointment). The modern sense of "place where one is destined to go" dates to 1787.

316 • Latin for the New Millennium: Teacher's Manual, Level 1

The Latin *dēstituō* (to forsake, set apart; from the causative of *stare* and *dē* = away) is the source for "destitute," which entered English during the late fourteenth century.

"Distance" originally (late thirteenth century) meant "quarrel, discord" from the Latin *distantia* (standing apart, separate).

Note that the "in" prefix may be negative as in "inconsistent," or mean "in, into, or upon" as in "institute" (from *instituō* = to establish) or "instant" (standing near, present, urgent from *instō*).

The word "state" has several related meanings. The verb (1590s) means "to put in a position, place on the record" from the Latin *status* (manner of standing, position, condition). The noun (early thirteenth century) can refer to "the circumstances of a person or thing," but during the 1530s it also came to mean the political organization of a country, a sense that grew out of the meaning "condition of a country."

The Latin *stabulum* (a standing place) is the source for the word "stable" which is a place for cows and horses. From the related Latin *stabilis* (firm, steadfast, literally, "able to stand") comes the adjective.

The word "stage" is derived through the Old French *estage* (a floor of a building) from the Latin *statum* (a place for standing). Its meaning "a platform for the presentation of a play" dates to the late fourteenth century.

The word "obstetrics" (from the Latin *obstetrix* = midwife) literally means "the one standing opposite the woman giving birth."

The word "cost" is derived from the Latin *constō* (literally, "to stand with" but with a wide range of figurative meanings including "cost"). For example, if an auctioneer says, "The current bid stands at [or with] $1,000," he means "the current cost of the item."

The word "rest" meaning "the remainder" is derived from the Latin *restō* (to stand back, be left). The word "rest" meaning "sleep" is not Latin in origin but is derived from the Old English *reste* (sleep).

The adjective "restive" came into English during the early fifteenth century through the Middle French *restif* (brought to a standstill) from the Latin *restō*. The idea of "unmanageable" (1680s) evolved via the notion of a horse refusing to go forward.

The word "prostitute" comes from the Latin *prostituō* meaning "to put up for sale" (literally, "to stand before; hence, to expose publicly"). The notion of "sex for hire" is not inherent in the etymology, which rather suggests "exposed to lust," or sex "indiscriminately offered."

The noun "statistics" came into English in 1770 meaning "the science with data about the condition of a state or community."

The word "stanza," derived through the Italian *stanza*, originally meant "a stopping place" and was applied (1580s) to a group of rhymed verse lines because of the stop at the end of it.

The word "arrest" appeared in English during the fourteenth century meaning "to cause to stop" through the Old French *arester* from the Latin *ad* (to) and *restō* (to stop, remain behind). The figurative sense of "to catch the attention of" dates to 1814: The attention of the audience was <u>arrested</u> by the strange aroma wafting through the room.

The word "stature" can refer to "height" as it did originally (around 1300) derived from the Latin *statūra*, e.g., He failed to make the football team because of his diminutive <u>stature</u>; or it can be used figuratively (from 1834), e.g., She became a scientist of world <u>stature</u>.

Note the "-ous" suffix of "superstitious," which mirrors the *-ōsus* suffix of the Latin *superstitiōsus*. The word literally means "standing over or above" and originally had a religious connotation ("state of religious exaltation" and then "excessive fear of the gods"). The sense of "unreasonable notion" dates to 1794.

See also Teaching Tips 1.11, 1.12, and 1.14 under *status*.

cūr – None

etiam – None

fortasse – None, but see *fortūna* for related derivatives.

sīcut – None

ubīque – Note the "-ous" suffix of "ubiquitous." The word is a late arrival in English (1837). "Omnipresent" is a synonym.

umquam – None

ante – The word "antediluvian" means "before the flood" (Noah's) and was coined during the 1640s by the English physician Sir Thomas Browne. Today it can also refer to anything antiquated or primitive, e.g., antediluvian ideas.

The Latin phrases *ante merīdiem* (before noon) and *post merīdiem* (after noon) give us the abbreviations AM and PM.

The prefix of such words as "antebellum," "antecedent," or "antepenult" means "before," but not all words beginning with "ante" are derived from that Latin preposition, e.g., antelope or antenna.

The word "antler" is derived from *ante* and *oculus* (eye) and means, literally, "before the eyes," referring to the placing of the branched horns of deer.

The word "anterior" (1610s) is the Latin comparative of *ante* and refers to something situated in front or before. Its antonym is "posterior."

The words "antique" (1530s) and "antiquity" (late fourteenth century) come from the Latin *antīquus* and *antīquitās*, respectively.

The word "antic(s)" came into English in the 1520s through the Italian *antico*, which originally referred to "the strange and fantastic representations in ancient murals unearthed around Rome," hence "a grotesque or comical gesture." The extension to "any bizarre behavior" was the sense of the word when it first appeared in English.

The word "advance" came into English during the mid-thirteenth century spelled *avauncen* and derived through the Old French *avancier* (to move forward) from the Latin *abante* (from before). The *d* was inserted during the sixteenth century on the mistaken notion that the initial *a* was from the Latin *ad*.

Note the "-ous" suffix of "advantageous."

"Advantage" came into English during the early fourteenth century meaning, literally, "position of being before, ahead of another" from the Late Latin *abante* through the Old French *avantage*. The meaning "a favoring circumstance" dates to the late fifteenth century; the sense of a tennis score to the 1640s (first recorded in John Milton).

The word "vantage" has the same derivation as "advantage." The phrase "vantage point" dates to 1865 although a similar idea is attested in the 1610s (vantage ground).

The word "vanguard" (mid-fifteenth century) was derived through the Middle French *avant-garde* from the Latin *ante*. It means "the front part of an army." The word was shortened to "van" around 1600.

Care should be taken with words beginning with "anti." For example, "anticipate" is based on "ante," but "antiphony" is derived from the Greek "anti" (against).

ecce – None

REVIEW 5: CHAPTERS 13–15
(PP. 267–280)

PAGE 267

TEACHING TIP

Another way to conduct a fun vocabulary review is to play family feud vocabulary.

- Instruct the students to review individually the words on pp. 267–268 (SE) for a short amount of time.
- Divide the class into two families (teams) and instruct each family to line up in the order in which they will give the answers. It is often best to move the tables and chairs to the side of the room to make room for two long groups of students to face one another.
- Each family should choose a Roman family name for itself (e.g., the Claudii, the Metelli, the Cicerones, the Scipiones, the Julii, etc.).
- Toss a coin to see which family goes first.
- Ask one of the questions about pp. 267–268 (SE) listed below for the teacher's convenience. The family that won the toss goes first. The first person in line in the family that is playing gives an answer in Latin to the question posed by the teacher. The second person gives another, different answer to the same question. The family gets one point for each correct answer to the question. Whenever a member of a family gives an incorrect answer, that is one strike. At three strikes the family is out and the opposing family only needs one more correct but different answer to the same question to steal the points away from the previous family. If the first family to play gets all the answers correct, they retain the points, and the teacher poses another question to the other family. Play continues in this fashion.
- Possible questions (the answers for each are on pp. 267–268 [SE]).
  1. Name seven third declension nouns in Latin and what they mean.
  2. Name four second declension nouns in Latin and what they mean.
  3. Name five pronouns in Latin and what they mean.
  4. Name nine first and second declension adjectives in Latin and what they mean.
  5. Name three third declension adjectives in Latin and what they mean.
  6. Name seven third conjugation verbs in Latin and what they mean.
  7. Name one irregular verb, one fourth conjugation verb, and one verb that only introduces direct speech, each in Latin and what they mean.
  8. Name ten adverbs in Latin and what they mean.
  9. Name four prepositions with the case that follows and what each means.
  10. Name two conjunctions and one interjection.

PAGE 268

Standards 1.1, 1.2

▶ EXERCISE 1 ANSWERS

Future Active

	Singular	**Plural**
First person	respondēbō	respondēbimus
Second person	respondēbis	respondēbitis
Third person	respondēbit	respondēbunt
First person	cadam	cadēmus
Second person	cadēs	cadētis
Third person	cadet	cadent
First person	conveniam	conveniēmus
Second person	conveniēs	conveniētis
Third person	conveniet	convenient

Future Passive

	Singular	**Plural**
First person	rogābor	rogābimur
Second person	rogāberis	rogābiminī
Third person	rogābitur	rogābuntur
First person	cōnspiciar	cōnspiciēmur
Second person	cōnspiciēris	cōnspiciēminī
Third person	cōnspiciētur	cōnspicientur

▶ EXERCISE 2 ANSWERS

1.	comede	comedite	nōlī comedere	nōlīte comedere
2.	discēde	discēdite	nōlī discēdere	nōlīte discēdere
3.	convenī	convenīte	nōlī convenīre	nōlīte convenīre
4.	neglege	neglegite	nōlī neglegere	nōlīte neglegere
5.	respondē	respondēte	nōlī respondēre	nōlīte respondēre
6.	rogā	rogāte	nōlī rogāre	nōlīte rogāre
7.	sēparā	sēparāte	nōlī sēparāre	nōlīte sēparāre
8.	tange	tangite	nōlī tangere	nōlīte tangere
9.	fuge	fugite	nōlī fugere	nōlīte fugere

PAGE 269
Standards 1.1, 1.2

▶ EXERCISE 3 ANSWERS
1. quam — Near which tree will I see you?
2. quam — The old age, which many fear, is not always bad.
3. quī — Answer to the man who is asking you!
4. quā — The rural country house, in which I did not live for a long time, seemed to me old.
5. Quibus — With what arguments will you show that old age is good?

▶ EXERCISE 4 ANSWERS
1. sua — People often like their (own) words, but do not like the words of the others.
2. suum — The boy and the girl desired to save their love, but because of the hatred of the parents <it> was difficult to do this.
3. eius — The boy thought that the girl did not live any more and was grieving about her death.
4. suam — All people fear their old age.
5. eōrum — The learned people and their words teach many things about old age.

TEACHER BY THE WAY
Seneca calls his home a *vīlla rūstica* (country farmhouse), but whether it was a modest place or something more stately is not alluded to in the reading. The needs and taste of the owner determined the size and location of the country estate. The simple *vīlla rūstica* consisted of a courtyard with a main house surrounded by barns and work areas. Seneca talks with his *vīlicus*, which suggests he is an urban, absentee owner. On large estates, which depended on profits from successful farming, there were a variety of establishments. Vitruvius, the practical architect, advises that the press and storage rooms for wine should face north and those for making olive oil should face south. In addition, there were stables, granaries, woodsheds, and accommodations for slaves. The overseer lived near the gate to keep his eye on things. Pliny the Younger complains about how much time he spends on accounts and the affairs of his tenants. Horace had his beloved Sabine farm, and Cicero had other farms in addition to the one at Tusculum. Whether they were for profit or pleasure determined the structure. A *vīlla urbāna* was also a rural retreat for wealthy Romans. This establishment was more like a Roman *domus* but much more extensive and luxurious. Some villas included baths, libraries, orchards, game preserves, fishponds, and other amenities for outdoor pleasures and relaxation. The proximity to the city and the beauty of the surroundings influenced the owner's choice of locations. The *vīlla maritima* was another such pleasure palace. Baiae, a resort town at the north end of the Bay of Naples, boasted of imposing villas built by Caligula, Nero, and others.

PAGE 270
Standards 1.1, 1.2

TEACHER BY THE WAY

Augustus's breastplate, also called a cuirass, celebrates the return of the standard that had been lost by Crassus at the Battle of Carrhae against the Parthians in 53 BCE. In his autobiography, *Rēs Gestae Dīvī Augustī*, Augustus notes this achievement of regaining the triple standards lost to the Parthians. In the center on the right, the Parthian king surrenders a Roman standard that has an eagle on its top and is decorated with garlands and disks. The Roman receiving the standard may be Romulus with the she-wolf or perhaps Tiberius, who was commander of the Roman expedition in 20 BCE. The figures to the right and left represent conquered Roman provinces. The breastplate's shoulder straps are sphinxes, which were part of Augustus's seal. The upper register of the cuirass includes representations of Sky (Uranus) whose outstretched hands open the canopy of the heavens, Apollo driving the chariot of the Sun on the left, and on the right, Aurora, the Dawn, holding her urn. Above Aurora is Luna, the moon, holding a torch. The bottom register depicts a reclining Mother Earth (Gaea) holding a cornucopia. On her left Apollo rides a griffin and on the right Diana rides a stag.

Some consider Augustus's youthful appearance a deliberate echo of Alexander the Great. Augustus is depicted as *imperātor*, the commander of the army, dressed in military clothing. The raised hand with pointing finger outstretched is a symbolic gesture used when addressing the troops. In his left hand, Augustus holds the consular baton.

The images on this breastplate reflect the new imperial vision of peace that is supported by divine providence, a theme reiterated in the literature, art, and coins of the Augustan age.

▶ EXERCISE 5 ANSWERS

1. tuī   Objective genitive.
   I will always remain with you because of love for you.
2. meī   Objective genitive.
   The enemies observe my sword and because of fear of me stand and do not move.
3. vestrī   Objective genitive.
   You are cruel soldiers. Fear of you moves (i.e., "affects") us.
4. nostrum   Partitive genitive.
   We do not fear difficult things. In fact, many of us seek difficult things.
5. nostrī   Objective genitive.
   It is permitted to many men to come to our country house, but <they> do not come because of hatred for us.

PAGE 271
Standards 1.1, 1.2, 3.1, 3.2

▶ EXERCISE 6 ANSWERS
"Now I will teach you your fate (NB: in Latin this is plural). You will sail for a long time, you will fight for a long time, and finally you will arrive home. For you will found a new city. The name of the city will be Rome. The Romans will spare subjected people and will conquer the proud people. Finally an emperor will give peace to all people," says Anchises.

"What emperor will give peace, Father?" asks Aeneas.

"Peace will be given to all people by Emperor Augustus, whose name will be heard everywhere," answers Anchises.

TEACHING TIP
Since the story of Aeneas happened so long before the time when it was written, the teacher may wish to instruct the students to review Chapter 2 of RRA.

TEACHER BY THE WAY
The interrelationship of myth and history is at the heart of Aeneas's visit to the underworld to see his father. Aeneas hears the tormented screams of the sinners, familiar from Greek mythology but with some variations. Finally, upon seeing his father in the Elysian Fields he makes a futile attempt to embrace him. A discussion of reincarnation segues into a parade of people, yet unborn, namely his son, grandson, and their descendants, as well as Romulus, the legendary founder of Rome, and Augustus, the second founder of Rome, who will bring the golden age to Italy. Next come the early kings of Rome and Brutus, who ended the monarchy and established the Republic. Pompey and Caesar wear armor because they will bring about civil wars. In another group are the men who won victories in war, namely Fabricius, Fabius, and the Scipios. Young Marcellus, whom Augustus adopted as his successor, appears last. All Rome mourned his untimely death. Aeneas's hardships are not yet over. War with the Latins awaits him. Nonetheless, Anchises's revelation of Rome's future greatness has strengthened Aeneas's resolve to fulfill his destiny and see to his task of sparing the humble and bringing down the proud—*parcere subiectīs et dēbellāre superbōs* (Aeneid 6.853).

CONSIDERING THE CLASSICAL GODS

PAGE 272

Standards 2.1, 2.2, 3.1, 3.2

ODF 3.10

COMPREHENSION QUESTIONS AND ANSWERS FOR PAGES 272–274 (SE)

Reproducible versions of the questions alone are available at **www.lnm.bolchazy.com**.

1. Describe the unusual circumstances of Minerva's birth.

    Fearing that the offspring of Metis might overthrow him, Jupiter swallowed the pregnant Metis and delivered the baby Minerva from his own head. When she emerged, Minerva was helmeted and fully armored.

2. How did Minerva become the patron of Athens?

    When Neptune challenged Minerva's position as patron of Athens, the Athenians decided to choose their divine patron by a democratic election. To gain popular support, Neptune offered a spring of salt water and Minerva offered an olive tree. The olive tree won the Athenian vote and to this day maintains a significant presence in the Mediterranean world.

3. Diana is associated with self-contradictory elements. Cite at least two of them.

    Diana is mistress of animals but also a hunter.

    Though a virgin, she also protects childbirth.

    While she possesses youthful beauty and charm, she is characterized as having a cold heart.

4. Mortals learned not to challenge the gods. Summarize a story in which a mortal is punished for "pushing the envelope" with Diana.

    Because the hunter Actaeon dared to look upon her bathing, Diana turned him into a stag and set his own hunting dogs upon him who devoured him.

    OR

    When Niobe bragged that her children were greater than those of Leto, Diana and Apollo, taking offense at this insult to their mother, cruelly slaughtered Niobe's fourteen children. Overwhelmed by grief, Niobe was turned into a stone.

5. Citing evidence from the statue of Diana on p. 273 (SE), explain how one would recognize this statue as being Diana.

    The woman is youthful, she has a quiver over the right shoulder, she is wearing a skirt unlike other goddesses who wear a full-length garment, and a hunting dog stands beside her.

324 • Latin for the New Millennium: Teacher's Manual, Level 1

PAGE 273

Standards 2.1, 2.2, 3.1, 3.2
ODF 3.8, ODF 3.9

TEACHER BY THE WAY

There are two versions of the story about Venus's birth. One of them simply states that she is daughter of Jupiter and the goddess Dione. The other story tells of an earlier time. Uranus (the sky) was one of the primordial deities. His wife was Gaea (the earth). Uranus repeatedly embraced his wife, impregnating her again and again. His son Cronus (whose Latin name is Saturn), acting on his mother's advice, ambushed his father and severed his genitals, which fell into the sea. From the blood that dripped into the sea foam emerged the lovely goddess Venus (actually the Greek name Aphrodite means "coming from the sea foam").

TEACHER BY THE WAY

Zeus decided it was time to give Aphrodite a taste of her own medicine. Too many times she had wielded her power causing many divinities, including Zeus himself, to fall in love with mortals. The handsome Anchises, a descendant of Dardanus and Ilus, founders of the Trojan race, was his choice. While Anchises was tending his flocks on Mt. Ida, Aphrodite came to him disguised as the daughter of a king, claiming she had been kidnapped by Hermes. With this bit of trickery, his fate was sealed. She even proposed marriage, and though suspicious, Anchises succumbed and happily lay with her. When Aphrodite revealed her true identity, Anchises was terrified, realizing he would be punished. The goddess reassured him and promised a son (Aeneas) who would be like a god. Nymphs would raise him until his fifth year. However, she begged Anchises not to reveal the name of the child's mother. But Anchises got drunk at a feast and did just that. Retribution followed. Zeus struck him with a thunderbolt, which made him lame. Aeneas does carry his aged father out of Troy on his shoulders in keeping with the finale of this myth.

Aphrodite was also worshipped as a goddess of the heavens (Urania) and the winds. Thus many of her temples were on elevated sites such as the one at Eryx in Sicily. Aeneas built a shrine to Idalian Venus there as well and left those who were tired of traveling with King Acestes.

TEACHING TIP

The teacher may wish to consult the "Homeric Hymn to Aphrodite" for a detailed account of this myth.

PAGE 274

Standards 1.1, 2.1

TEACHER BY THE WAY
In the *Odyssey*, after the dinner at which Odysseus dines with the Phaeacians, the bard Demodocus tells this tale of Mars and Venus ensnared by Vulcan.

TEACHING TIP
The teacher may wish to mention "arachnophobia," the excessive fear of spiders, in connection with the story of Arachne and Minerva.

PASSAGE TRANSLATION

Arachne was able to weave very well. She thought that she could defeat Minerva. Arachne was saying: "Minerva is a goddess, but I will fight with her and defeat her. Her art is not very great." Minerva heard the words of Arachne and was moved by great anger. "Now you will be turned into a spider," says Minerva. "You will always weave, but you will not be able to say words." Because of the anger of the goddess the poor Arachne will now have the body of a spider.

PASSAGE TRANSLATION

Venus was burning with love for Adonis. For Adonis was very handsome. Mars was moved by hatred. "Who is Adonis?" says Mars. "A human being who is loved by a goddess." Mars sends a boar to Adonis, who kills him. Blood flows from the chest of Adonis. Venus sees the blood and calls Adonis: "Do not be separated from me! For I am held by love for you." Adonis, however, does not seem to live any more. Then Venus changes Adonis into a red flower.

TEACHER BY THE WAY
This is another example of an aetiological myth. According to the poet Bion, from each tear that Venus shed, a red rose came forth; from each drop of Adonis's blood, a red anemone appeared.

CONNECTING WITH THE ANCIENT WORLD

PAGE 275

Standards 2.1, 2.2, 3.1, 3.2

COMPREHENSION QUESTIONS AND ANSWERS FOR PAGES 275–277 (SE)

Reproducible versions of the questions alone are available at **www.lnm.bolchazy.com**.

1. In what significant way did the city of Rome differ from the new cities Rome built throughout the empire?

    Because Rome evolved in an organic and haphazard way, except for the imperial *fora*, the city was a maze of winding streets and alleys. When they built new cities, the Romans used a grid pattern with streets running perpendicular to one another.

2. Name at least five public buildings that graced a Roman city.

    Public baths, public latrines, council building, *basilicae*, libraries, marketplaces.

3. Explain the civic tradition which led wealthy aristocrats to underwrite the costs of erecting public monuments or adorning public buildings.

    Classical Greece developed a civic tradition that obligated those with considerable financial means to accept responsibility for directing some of their wealth to improving the public fabric of the city-state.

4. For what reasons did Rome maintain an extensive system of well-paved roads?

    The road system was critical to the movement of troops and military supplies and facilitated trade and travel throughout the empire.

5. Identify the key components of a Roman road.

    fossae, trenches dug to the bedrock

    pavīmentum, a foundation of lime mortar or sand, formed a level base; a second layer consisted of concrete with stones, gravel, or sand and lime poured in layers

    summum dorsum, the top surface consisted of six-inch or thicker polygonal blocks of stone

6. What do you suppose was the function of a *mīliārium*?

    The *mīliārium*, a milestone, was placed alongside a Roman road to provide the traveler with information about the distance to the next town and how many miles they had traveled along the road.

PAGE 276

TEACHER BY THE WAY

Vitruvius's text *Dē architectūrā* provides many insights into Roman architecture, engineering, and city planning. Vitruvius intended his book to serve as a manual to be used as the Romans built and Romanized cities throughout the empire. The urban amenities that Rome provided helped gain the favor of the local populace.

TEACHING TIP
The time during which Appius Claudius lived and the Appian Way was built may be reviewed in Chapter 3 of RRA.

TEACHER BY THE WAY
The earliest circus at Rome was the Circus Maximus, constructed during the monarchy and rebuilt by Julius Caesar. Chariot races (*lūdī circēnsēs*) were held in this open-air stadium that held about 200,000 spectators. The U-shaped course (*harēna/arēna*) had a low barrier (*spīna*) marked at each end by turning posts (*mētae*). At the open end of the U were the starting gates for twelve teams of horses who competed four, six, or more at a time. The four-horsed chariots (*quadrīgae*) had to complete seven laps, about five miles. Toward each end of the *spīna* were movable eggs and dolphins that measured the laps. The *spīna* was decorated with sculptures, obelisks, and fountains. The emperor or official started the race by dropping a white cloth (*mappa*) as a signal.

Chariot racing was a lucrative business for both victorious charioteers (*aurīgae*) and the owners of the company (*factiōnēs*) for whom they rode. Huge sums of money were spent on horses, importing them from Greece and Spain. The training stables were also grandiose. Inscriptions sometimes give the names of all the horses. Before the race, a list with the names of horses and drivers was posted for those wanting to place bets. Competition was so fierce that sometimes the rival company would drug the horse. Bribery was an inducement for a driver to switch companies. The pay was extravagant since there was a bidding war for the best charioteers. Each company had its own colors. At first there were only the "Reds" (*russātī*) and "Whites" (*albātī*), but then the Greens (*prasinī*) and "Blues" (*venetī*) were added. It is said that one charioteer drove for twenty-four years and won 1,462 victories. Skillful driving was necessary but ramming and "fouling" were permitted. The driver's tunic was the color of his company and was laced around his body with leather thongs. The reins were also tied together around his body so that if he was thrown from the chariot, a knife in his belt allowed him to extricate himself from the tangle of reins and not be crushed under the horse. Rich gifts and a bag of gold were awarded to the winner. Even though the drivers were freedmen or slaves, they became like pop stars and everyone, highbrow or low, courted them.

For more information on chariot racing, see p. 355 of this teacher's manual.

PAGE 277

 TEACHER BY THE WAY

Some of the many roads that the Romans built are as follows:

- Via Aemilia: this road extended from Rome to Placentia for a distance of 162 English miles. It was built by Marcus Aemilius Lepidus and later extended 45 more miles to Mediolanum (Milan) and, as the reading notes, was paved by Augustus.
- Via Aurēlia: this road was constructed ca. 241 BCE from Rome along the coast of Etruria to Pisa. In 109 BCE it was extended 45 more miles to Mediolanum.
- Via Egnātia: begun in 130 BCE by the proconsul Gāius Egnātius, it stretched from Dyrrachium to Thessalonica and then to Byzantium, a distance of 696 English miles.
- Via Flāminia: this road was the older route from Rome to Ariminum and was 193 English miles in length. The newer route was 222 miles. It was built by Gāius Flāminius during his censorship in 220 BCE.
- Via Latīna: this road was built at least twenty years prior to the construction of the Via Appia and it stretched from Rome to Capua.

EXPLORING ROMAN LAW

PAGE 278
Standards 2.1, 3.1, 3.2, 4.2

TEACHER BY THE WAY
lēx tāliōnis = law of retribution. An "eye for an eye" was a judicial concept held by the Mesopotamians and the Hebrews.

COMPREHENSION QUESTIONS AND ANSWERS FOR PAGES 278–279 (SE)
Reproducible versions of the questions alone are available at **www.lnm.bolchazy.com**.

1. Professor Keenan's essay exemplifies the role Roman literature plays in helping reconstruct aspects of the Roman world and daily life. Explain how.

   Horace's *Satire* 1.9 and its narrative about Horace and his encounter with the Boor include technical language associated with the elements of a Roman civil lawsuit.

2. Discuss the Twelve Tables.

   The Twelve Tables, dating from 451 to 450 BCE, were a set of bronze tablets inscribed with the codification of Roman law. The tablets themselves were probably destroyed during the Gallic invasion of the 390s BCE. Because later Roman authors make reference to the laws on the tablets, scholars have been able to compile a representative set of the laws that are distinctively local, agrarian, and archaic in nature.

3. Why is the state of Louisiana's code of law different from that practiced in the rest of the United States?

   Because Louisiana was once French territory, the state follows a civil code based on the Napoleonic Civil Code of 1804, which, in turn, is based on the Roman emperor Justinian's great codification of Roman law in the sixth century CE. The rest of the United States follows laws rooted in the English Common Law tradition.

4. In the American legal system, a plaintiff can use the power of the subpoena to compel witnesses to appear in court. How was the Roman practice different?

   The plaintiff himself, if necessary, seized the defendant by force (*per manum*) but required a competent witness to make this legal. This practice is illustrated in Horace's satire.

5. What are two major differences between lawyers in Rome and in America?

   In the United States, lawyers attend law school and pass the state bar examination in order to practice law, whereas in Rome lawyers and judges were not necessarily trained specifically for such a profession. In addition, American lawyers, unless doing *prō bonō* work, charge for their legal services, while the Romans provided legal services from a sense of social obligation or friendship.

PAGE 279

TEACHER BY THE WAY

The Roman privileged class, the patricians, and the common folk, the plebeians, seeing the need to codify the practices and customs in place, appointed a commission of ten men, the Decemviri, ca. 455 BCE to construct a binding code of law. The Decemviri drew up ten tablets of laws but some, especially the plebeians, found them inadequate. A second commission appointed in 450 BCE wrote up an additional two tablets. The Twelve Tables cover a variety of agrarian, property, and social concerns and there are many interesting bits of information in the full text, which the teacher may consult if s/he wishes. A condensed version of what is included in the Twelve Tables follows for the teacher's convenience.

- Table 1 – A person summoned by a magistrate must go. A compromise made by the disputing parties should be announced. With no compromise, each should state his case before noon in the *comitium*. If either party does not appear, the judgment goes to the one present.
- Table 2 – A witness who does not appear may be summoned every third day by loud calls outside his house.
- Table 3 – A debtor has thirty days to pay what is owed. After that the creditor may bring the debtor before a magistrate.
- Table 4 – A deformed child may be killed. A man's will is binding. The power over an insane person without a guardian belongs to the members of his family. A child born ten or more months after his father's death is not entitled to an inheritance from him.
- Table 5 – A female should continue to have a guardian even after she has reached legal age.
- Table 6 – A legal transfer of property of one person to another by a bond is binding. Legal possession of movable things requires one year's possession. A woman who does not wish to become the legal possession of her husband should be absent three successive nights each year.
- Table 7 – If a road is not paved, a man may drive his team where he wants. If a tree on a neighbor's farm becomes bent and leans over your farm, you can remove the tree legally. You may pick up fruit falling on your land from your neighbor's tree.
- Table 8 – If one has hurt another person's limb, he should compromise with that person or pay a freedman 300 coins or a slave 150 coins. It is permitted to kill a person committing theft at night. An arsonist may be put to death. A person who has given false witness shall be hurled from the Tarpeian Rock.
- Table 9 – Capital punishment is the penalty for a judge who takes a bribe and a person committing treason.
- Table 10 – Corpses may not be burned or buried inside the city and women may not tear their faces because of a funeral.
- Table 11 – There should be no marriage between plebeians and patricians.
- Table 12 – If a slave steals or harms property with his owner's knowledge, the action for the damages are in the slave's name.

TEACHING TIP

Students are often intrigued by such codes as Rome's Twelve Tables. A comparison of the Hebrews' Ten Commandments, Rome's Twelve Tables, the Bill of Rights of the United States of America, and the Code of Hammurabi makes for a rich class discussion. The teacher may encourage students to do the following:

- Compare/contrast analyses of the codes mentioned above.
- Find examples of *lēx tāliōnis*, the principle of retaliation or "an eye for an eye."
- Discuss how ancient laws have modern-day counterparts.
- Discuss why they consider some ancient laws "archaic."
- Identify the law's concern as social, proprietary, agrarian, etc.
- Discuss the value which the law protects.

MĪRĀBILE AUDĪTŪ

PAGE 280
Standards 1.1, 3.1, 4.1

PHRASES AND QUOTATIONS VOCABULARY
Alibi.
   alibi (*adv.*) – elsewhere

Cui prōdest?
   prōsum, prōfuī, prōdesse, —— + *dative* – to benefit

Dē iūre.
   iūs, iūris, *n.* – law

Flagrante dēlictō.
   dēlictum, dēlictī, *n.* – crime
   flagrō, flagrāre, flagrāvī, —— – to blaze

Sub poenā.
   poena, poenae, *f.* – penalty, punishment
   sub + *ablative* – under

TEACHING TIP
For extra credit or otherwise, the teacher may wish to ask students to make a note of whenever they hear a Latin legal phrase uttered on one of the many law shows on TV and to bring this information into class.

In order to ascertain the student's mastery of the phrases on p. 280 (SE), the teacher may wish to ask the following questions in class. The answers are provided for the teacher's convenience.

1. What phrase indicates that a lawyer has done legal work without expecting a fee? *prō bonō*
2. If a defendant in a court case can prove that he did not commit the crime, he is said to have what? An *alibi*.
3. When a person receives a legal notice to appear in court, what has he received? A *sub poenā*.
4. What phrase is referenced when a person is kept in jail illegally? *habeās corpus*
5. When something has been done legally, it is said to have been done how? *dē iūre*
6. What phrase could be used to describe a thief's action when a police officer actually sees him stealing an object that does not belong to him? *flagrante dēlictō*
7. A judge who wants to know who had a motive for committing a crime might say what Latin phrase? *Cui prōdest?*

Review 5: Chapters 13–15 • 333

CHAPTER 16 (PP. 281–295)

GRAMMAR IN LANGUAGE FACTS

Perfect Tense Verbs; Perfect Stem, Perfect Tense Active of All Conjugations; Perfect Tense of *Sum* and *Possum*; Dative of Possession

PAGE 281

Standards 1.1, 1.2

RRA 6A

MEMORĀBILE DICTŪ VOCABULARY

sī – if

caelum, caelī, *n.* – sky, heaven, weather

ruat (*subjunctive mood*) – should/would fall

ruō, ruere, ruī, —— – to fall with violence, to plunge headlong

Terence's comedy *The Self-Tormentor* is called *Heautontimoroumenos* in Latin/Greek.

TEACHER BY THE WAY

Jean Baptiste François Genillon was a painter from the Vernet school and his subjects included shipwrecks, seaports, combats at sea, and eruptions near a body of water, such as the illustration on this page.

TEACHER BY THE WAY

The eruption of Mt. Vesuvius, depicted in the illustration on this page, covered not only the towns of Pompeii and Herculaneum but also Stabiae and Oplontis. Although less familiar, both towns have villas and luxury items as impressive and beautiful as those of Pompeii. Stabiae was famous for its thermal mineral waters, and with its advantageous position overlooking the Bay of Naples, it was prime real estate for wealthy Romans. The layout did not follow the usual grid pattern of most Roman towns but accommodated the needs of a spa center. Pliny the Elder died there en route to help his friend. The floating pumice forced him to sail toward Stabiae rather than Pompeii. Though the town was spared the lava flow, it was still buried in the heavy ash flow.

Excavations started in the mid-eighteenth century CE and then resumed in 1949. Several villas have been partially excavated thus far. The remains attest to the wealth and taste of the Roman elite who went there in the first centuries BCE and CE for both business and pleasure. There are miles of luxurious villas. One such example is the Villa of San Marco, so called because of its proximity to a chapel dedicated to St. Mark. It was originally built during the

Augustan age and expanded during the Claudian age. This summer residence consists of extensive gardens, colonnaded walks, a reflecting pool in the atrium, a private bath complex decorated with cupids, remains of a stairway in travertine marble, and a triclinium with a view of the bay. Adjacent to the peristyle is a *nymphaeum* (a shrine connected with water). Another site, the Villa Arianna, is still partly buried. The triclinium decorated with a fresco of Theseus abandoning Ariadne is the source of its name. This seaside resort has servant quarters, baths, a summer triclinium, and a *palaestra* that dates from the Flavian era. The floors are done with black and white mosaic. A tunnel ran from an entrance under the living quarters to the seashore. In what are perhaps the rooms belonging to the women of the house, the famous frescoes of Flora gathering flowers with her basket, Medea gripping a sword, Diana with a bow and arrow, and Leda cradling a swan were found. The blue, red, and green of the frescoes were well preserved by the ash covering.

Of the two villas excavated in Oplontis, only the Villa of Poppaea, the wife of Nero, can be visited. An inscription labels it as hers and says that she had been murdered by the emperor eleven years before. When the eruption occurred, the place was stripped of furniture and undergoing restoration. Part of the back of the villa has a number of reception and service rooms that overlook a rectangular pool and extended gardens. Excavations reveal a triclinium with a view of the bay, a colonnaded courtyard, a private bath complex, and frescoes that show architectural perspective with their columns, doors, etc. A second villa housed many amphorae, tools, jewels, and coins.

PAGE 282
Standards 1.1, 2.1, 3.1, 3.2

TEACHING TIP

Chapter 6A of RRA contains information on Pliny the Elder and Pliny the Younger. The teacher may wish to assign this chapter for reading or review. See p. 201.

TRANSLATION OF LATIN PASSAGE
About the Eruption of Mt. Vesuvius

My uncle was the commander of the fleet at Misenum. On the day, in which the beginning of such a large disaster took place, <my> uncle was lying outside and studying books. My mother suddenly pointed out to him a new and unusual cloud, which appeared to be in the sky near Mt. Vesuvius. The cloud had a shape similar to the shape that we often see in trees. For the top of the cloud was being separated into many parts—just as into branches. <My> uncle, a man <who was> extremely interested in nature, wanted to understand the cause of the cloud. So he ordered ships to be prepared: for he wished to sail to the coast which is next to Mt. Vesuvius. Then a sailor gave a letter to <my> uncle. Said the sailor: "A woman who lives near Mt. Vesuvius has sent the letter to you." <My> uncle read the letter and at once understood that there was a large conflagration in Mt. Vesuvius: that the woman feared the danger and wanted to escape by means of ships. My uncle had a brave spirit (literally: "for/to my uncle there was a brave spirit"). Therefore he made a new plan. He decided to sail to the people who were living near Mt. Vesuvius and to free them from the great danger. For stones and hot ashes were falling upon them from the sky. So he sailed to that region, but he never came back. For there deadly smoke and ashes overwhelmed him with many others.

TEACHING TIP
Instruct the students to locate Bithynia, Mt. Vesuvius, Pompeii, and Stabiae on the map on pp. xxxiv–xxxv (SE) and to find Pliny the Younger, Pliny the Elder, and the eruption of Mt. Vesuvius on the timeline pp. 405–408 (SE).

PAGE 283

ANSWERS TO COMPREHENSION QUESTIONS
1. A cloud in the shape of a tree appeared near Vesuvius.
2. Pliny's uncle decided to investigate the strange phenomenon.
3. Pliny received a letter from an inhabitant near Vesuvius asking for help.
4. Pliny's uncle decided to help people who were suffering from the eruption of Vesuvius, but died himself.

TEACHING TIP
As a postreading activity, teachers may have students return to the chapter page image and explain in Latin what it depicts. This activity encourages students to employ the new vocabulary of the chapter.

TEACHER BY THE WAY
A fascinating account of the days leading up to and including the day of destruction is Robert Harris's well-researched book *Pompeii*.

TEACHING TIP
The teacher may wish to instruct the students to draw their own picture of the eruption of Mt. Vesuvius and to label in Latin on their picture the following:
- *caelum*
- *cinis calidus*
- *classis*
- *fūmus*
- *incendium fūnestum*
- *lītus*
- *nāvis*
- *nūbēs*
- *summus mōns*
- *Vesuvius*

PAGE 284

Standards 1.1, 1.2, 2.1, 3.1, 4.1

▶ EXERCISE 1 ANSWERS

cupīvit	s/he it wanted, desired
dēcrēvit	s/he decided
intellēxit	s/he understood
iussit	s/he ordered
mīsit	s/he sent
nāvigāvit	s/he sailed
ostendit	s/he pointed out
oppressērunt	they overwhelmed
revēnit	s/he/it returned

 TEACHER BY THE WAY

If the students need some additional practice on distinguishing between the use of the imperfect and perfect tenses, some sample sentences are listed for the teacher's convenience.

1. I kept seeing the smoke. — I saw the smoke.
2. The ship was sailing to the shore. — The ship sailed to the shore.
3. Mother habitually observed the sky. — Mother finally observed the sky.
4. The judge usually prepared an argument. — The judge did not prepare an argument.
5. We felt ill while traveling. — We felt ill yesterday.
6. The rocks kept falling from the mountain. — The rocks fell from the mountain.
7. Who was building a country house? — Who has built a country house?
8. Was the advice good? — Was the advice good then?
9. The parents were asking for help. — The parents have asked for help.
10. My uncle was able to save his friends. — At last my uncle was able to save his friends.
11. The citizen kept leaving the city. — The citizen left the city.
12. The queen sensed danger. — The queen finally sensed danger.
13. Dangers usually frightened people. — The dangers frightened the people.
14. Were you giving a reason? — Did you give a reason?
15. The enemy was entering the camp. — The enemy has entered the camp.

PAGE 285

Standards 1.2, 4.1
Workbook Exercise 2

▶ EXERCISE 2 ANSWERS

1. celestial — caelum
2. cinerary — cinis
3. causality — causa
4. incendiary — incendium
5. naval — nāvis
6. class — classis
7. avuncular — avunculus
8. littoral — lītus
9. maternity — māter
10. oppressed — opprimō
11. feminine — fēmina
12. fumigated — fūmus
13. lecture — legō
14. partially — pars
15. student — studeō

TEACHING TIP

Although in Exercise 2 the students are directed to find only the derivatives based on the Vocabulary to Learn, they may be interested to learn that there are other derivatives in Exercise 2. The derivation of these words is provided for the teacher's convenience.

1. interest – from *interest* (it is of importance, it concerns). me – *mē* (accusative singular of *egō*, I). Note, however, that the Latin impersonal verb *interest* is NOT the simple equivalent in meaning to the modern English expression "it interests me."
2. several – from *sēparō* (to part, divide, distinguish). urns – from *ūrna* (water jar, voting urn, cinerary urn, money jar). site – from *situs* (situated, lying, founded).
3. people – from *populus* (people, nation, populace). introducting – from *intrōdūcō* (to bring in, institute). totally – from *tōtus* (entire, whole, all). subjective – from *subiectus* (exposed, subject) from *subiciō* (to put under, bring under, submit, etc.). mode – from *modus* (measure, size, way, method).
4. terrible – from *terribilis* (terrifying, dreadful). destruction – from *dēstruō* (to demolish, destroy). city – from *cīvitās* (citizenship, community, state).
5. very – from *vērus* (true, real, actual); *vērāx* (truthful). exacting – from *exigō* (to drive out, enforce, demand, claim). science – *scientia* (knowledge) from *sciō* (to know).
6. advocated – from *advocō* (to summon, call in the assistance of); *advocātus* (supporter in a lawsuit, counsel). entire – from *integer* (whole, complete). history – from *historia* (history, inquiry, story). based – from *basis* (pedestal, base). conflict – from *cōnflīgō* (to pierce, shoot) + *cum* (together, with).
7. very – from *vērus* (true, real, actual); *vērāx* (truthful).
8. region – from *regiō* (direction, quarter, region, district). sustains – from *sustineō* (to hold up, support, control, maintain). variety – from *varietās* (difference, diversity). plant – from *planta* (shoot, slip). animal – from *animal* (animal, living creature).
9. hospital – from *hospitālis* (host's, guest's, hospitable); from *hospes* (host, guest, stranger, friend).

Chapter 16 • 339

10. underprivileged – from *prīvus* (single, own, private) + *lēx* (law). people – from *populus* (people, nation, populace). in – from *in* (in, on, at). Roman – from *Rōmānus* (Roman). cruelly – from *crūdēlis* (hard-hearted, cruel).
11. gender – from *generō* (to breed, procreate). noun – from *nōmen* (name).
12. carpet – from *carpō* (to pluck, tear off, gather). in – from *in* (in, on, at). apartment – from *ad* (to, toward) + *pars* (part, share, fraction).
13. present – from *praesum* (to be at the head of, take the lead, protect).
15. lifelong – from *longus* (long).

PAGE 286
Standards 1.1, 1.2, 2.1, 3.1, 4.1

▶ EXERCISE 3 ANSWERS

1. The sailors were remaining near the shore. They were always observing the sky. Then they formed a plan. They decided to prepare the ship.
2. We sent a letter immediately to the people who were waiting on the road, and we ordered them to come to us.
3. We were waiting for the sailors. Now we can see their ships. "The sailors have come," said my friend.

TEACHER BY THE WAY

Volcanologists now use the term "plinian" to describe the kind of eruption that Pliny the Younger witnessed (Chapter 16 reading). During the day ash and pumice carried by the wind rained down on Pompeii and Stabiae. It is estimated that the eruption column was twenty miles tall. Within four to five hours roofs had collapsed from the weight. Anyone trying to escape by sea was endangered because of the weight of the pumice. By nighttime around ten feet of pumice had fallen, and fiery clouds of poisonous gas and fine ash fell like an avalanche. Those who did not escape died of suffocation or were buried by the fallout. The volcanic matter gradually cooled and hardened. Because the wind direction was southeast, Herculaneum was slower to feel the impact. Since at first about two inches of ash had fallen at Herculaneum, the people were not seriously worried. When the column later collapsed, a cascade of lava and boiling mud filled the town and harbor. It probably took about five minutes to asphyxiate, burn, or bury the victims under the debris. The four blocks that were excavated were empty of people. However, most of the skeletons found were huddled together under seaside stone terraces or on the beach. The shoreline, which once came right up to the city, was pushed far back into the bay. It is easier to dig through soft pumice and ash at Pompeii than to excavate Herculaneum where the solidified mud-lava is hard as concrete.

PAGE 287
Workbook Exercise 1

TEACHING TIP
Encourage the students to create a rap, cheer, or song that will help them remember the perfect tense active endings. Alternatively, use Bolchazy-Carducci's *Toga Beats*.

TEACHER BY THE WAY
With the introduction of the perfect tense, there is another correct answer to "*Cūius temporis est?*" This is "*temporis praeteritī perfectī*" or more simply "*temporis perfectī.*"

TEACHING TIP
Additional reproducible worksheets, morphology charts, and their associated answer keys, related to this material, are available for download at www.lnm.bolchazy.com.
- **Verb Conjugations**

PAGE 288
Standards 1.1, 1.2
Oral Exercise 1

▶ EXERCISE 4 ANSWERS
1. sēparāvērunt — they separated/did separate/have separated
2. lēgimus — we read/did read/have read
3. discessit — he departed/did depart/ has departed
4. tetigistī — you touched/did touch/have touched
5. ārsērunt — they burned/did burn/have burned
6. respondistis — you (plural) answered/did answer/have answered
7. cecidistī — you fell/did fall/have fallen
8. dēlēvērunt — they destroyed/did destroy/have destroyed
9. oppressit — s/he overwhelmed/did overwhelm/has overwhelmed
10. neglēximus — we neglected/did neglect/have neglected
11. stetērunt — they stood/have stood/did stand

ORAL EXERCISE 1

This exercise may be used after the perfect active indicative tense has been presented.

The teacher should read each sentence slowly and clearly and then ask individual students to repeat each sentence changing the present tense verbs to the corresponding perfect tense. The teacher should be ready to repeat any sentence as often as necessary so the student answering can reproduce it only by listening.

Teacher: Classis Rōmānōrum ad lītus venit.   **Student:** Classis Rōmānōrum ad lītus vēnit.
Teacher: Nūbem novam vidēmus.   **Student:** Nūbem novam vīdimus.
Teacher: Fēminae epistulās nostrās tenent.   **Student:** Fēminae epistulās nostrās tenuērunt.
Teacher: Nāvēs igitur parās.   **Student:** Nāvēs igitur parāvistī.
Teacher: Ad urbem nāvigāre cupimus.   **Student:** Ad urbem nāvigāre cupīvimus.
Teacher: Multa saxa ē caelō cadunt.   **Student:** Multa saxa ē caelō cecidērunt.
Teacher: Epistulam ad tē mittō.   **Student:** Epistulam ad tē mīsī.
Teacher: Multōs librōs legere dēcernis.   **Student:** Multōs librōs legere dēcrēvistī.
Teacher: Flammae sunt magnae.   **Student:** Flammae fuērunt magnae.
Teacher: Montem vidēre potestis.   **Student:** Montem vidēre potuistis.

PAGE 289

Standards 1.1, 1.2, 2.1, 3.1, 4.1
Workbook Exercises 3, 4

▶ EXERCISE 5 ANSWERS

1.	lēgimus	<My> uncle and I read books.
2.	cōnspeximus	We observed a new cloud in the sky.
3.	intellēxērunt	People interested in nature understood the cause of the new cloud.
4.	Dīxit, iussistī	The sailor said: "You ordered me to prepare the ships at once."
5.	timuistis, dēbuistis	You (plural) were very afraid of the danger. Therefore you (plural) ought to have formed a new plan.
6.	cecidērunt	Stones and hot ashes suddenly fell from the sky.
7.	lēgī	I have just now read their letter.

TEACHING TIP

You may wish to point out to students that *legimus* in sentence 1 in Exercise 5 has a short *e* in the present and a long *ē* in the perfect. This is also true of *venimus* with a long *ē* and *fugimus* with a long *ū* in the perfect tense but with a short *e* and *u* respectively in the present tense.

TEACHING TIP

The teacher may choose to ask the students to change the present tense verbs in Exercise 5 (#1, 2, 6, and 7 only) to the imperfect tense after they have completed Exercise 5 according to its directions. Then ask the students how using the imperfect tense in sentences 1, 2, 6, and 7 changes the meaning of the sentence.

PAGE 290

TEACHING TIP
Review the present, imperfect, and future tenses of *sum*, either before presenting the perfect tense forms or afterward.

TEACHER BY THE WAY
The House of the Faun is thus named because of the presence of the bronze "faun" in the house's atrium. If excavators at Pompeii found no documentation of a home's owner, they named houses based on the subject matter of a fresco or a statue. The faun is a mythological creature with the body of a man and various attributes of a goat—horns, ears, hands, and sometimes legs as well. The faun is similar to the Greek satyr, which is part man and part goat. Both figures are connected to Bacchus/Dionysus and his wine-induced revelry. The faun might be descended from an Italic woodland deity or spirit. However, scholars have come to believe that the statue depicts a satyr rather than a faun.

The original bronze statue is housed at the Museo Nazionale in Naples. The copy shown in the photograph on this page is faithful to the original except for the modesty panel covering the original's genitalia. The photograph's frontal view hides the figure's telltale tail at his rear. The satyr's stance is as fully suggestive of movement as a stationary object allows—a twisted figure playing on the s-curve refined in classical Greek sculpture with arms thrust into space and his legs just touching the base. The dancing satyr speaks of Bacchic revelry or orgiastic ritual. A marble statue from Pompeii also at the Museo Nazionale presents a definitive faun, complete with a goat's ears and lower torso but with human genitals, depicted seducing the young Pan with his syrinx.

The "faun" is one of a number of artistic elements in the home that speak to the owners' cosmopolitan taste. The second century home with some nine thousand square feet makes it the largest home in Pompeii. Its rich decoration befits its size. Mosaics include an erotic encounter between a satyr and a nymph; a Nilotic river scene with crocodile, fowl, doves, and hippopotamus; food arrangements; and Dionysus riding the tiger symbolizing his conquest of India. The most important mosaic is the famous scene of Alexander meeting Darius in the Battle of Issus, which decorated the floor of the house's exedra (a room used for conversation and formed by an open or columned recess often semicircular in shape and furnished with seats). This exedra looks out to the larger peristyle, a space larger than some of the public spaces in Pompeii.

PAGE 291

Standards 1.1, 1.2, 2.1, 3.1, 4.1

Oral Exercise 2; Workbook Exercise 5

▶ EXERCISE 6 ANSWERS

1. Saxane et cinerēs calidōs in caelō vidēre potuistis?/Potuistisne saxa et cinerēs calidōs in caelō vidēre?

2. Eō tempore hominem/virum ad eōs mittere potuistī quī prope montem Vesuvium habitābant.

3. Verba fēminae legere nōn potuimus.

4. Tunc incendium in monte subitō fuit.

5. Fēminae epistulam iam legere potuī. Nunc nāvēs parō.

6. Hominēs magnō perīculō līberāre potuistī.

ORAL EXERCISE 2

This exercise may be used after the perfect tense and dative of possession have been presented.

In preparation for the exercise, the teacher should use one of the CPOs to put on view the following words.

postquam – after

quālem (*accusative singular*)? – what sort of?

quālis (*nominative singular*)? – what sort of?

ubi? – where?

The teacher should ask the students to return to the Latin reading passage and then ask individual students the following questions. (NB: the students should be looking at the passage while responding.) The students use the actual words in the passage, changing endings and forms only where needed to fit the answer.

Teacher: Ubi erat Plīniī avunculus classis praefectus?

Student: Plīniī avunculus Mīsēnī erat classis praefectus.

Teacher: Quid faciēbat avunculus eō diē, quō tantae clādis initium fuit?

Student: Eō diē, quō tantae clādis initium fuit, avunculus forīs iacēbat librīsque studēbat.

Teacher: Quid avunculō māter Plīniī ostendit?

Student: Māter Plīniī nūbem novam et inūsitātam avunculō ostendit, quae in caelō prope montem Vesuvium vidēbātur esse.

Teacher: Quālem fōrmam habuit nūbēs?

Student: Nūbēs fōrmam habuit similem fōrmae, quam in arboribus hominēs saepe vident.

Teacher: Quālis erat Plīniī avunculus?

Student: Plīniī avunculus homō rērum nātūrae valdē studiōsus erat.

Teacher: Postquam māter Plīniī nūbem novam avunculō ostendit, quid facere cupīvit avunculus?

Student: Postquam māter Plīniī nūbem novam avunculō ostendit, avunculus causam nūbis intellegere cupīvit, et ad lītus nāvigāre, quod est prope montem Vesuvium.

Teacher: Quid deinde nauta avunculō dedit?

Student: Deinde nauta epistulam avunculō dedit.

Teacher: Quis epistulam ad avunculum mīsit?

Student: Fēmina, quae prope montem Vesuvium habitābat, epistulam ad avunculum mīsit.

344 • Latin for the New Millennium: Teacher's Manual, Level 1

Teacher: Postquam avunculus epistulam lēgit, quid facere dēcrēvit?
Student: Postquam avunculus epistulam lēgit, ad hominēs nāvigāre dēcrēvit, quī prope montem Vesuvium habitābant, et eōs perīculō magnō līberāre.

Teacher: Quid tunc fēcit avunculus?
Student: Avunculus illūc nāvigāvit, sed numquam revēnit.

Teacher: Quālis animus avunculō erat?
Student: Animus fortis avunculō erat.

PAGE 292
Standards 1.1, 1.2
Workbook Exercise 6

▶ EXERCISE 7 ANSWERS
1. The uncle had many books, which he studied throughout his life.
2. The boy heard the words of the (his) uncle/(his) the uncle's words and read many books.
3. The uncle heard about the disaster and made decisions. For he had to give help to others.
4. Fire, smoke, ash overwhelmed the mountain and the shore. The uncle, however, always had a strong spirit.
5. The uncle told the sailors: "You (plural) have prepared a ship. Now prepare the fleet!" The sailors heard the words of the uncle.
6. "Do not fear!" the uncle said to everybody. But the fear held many people.

▶ EXERCISE 8 ANSWERS
1. Habēsne avunculum?   Estne tibi avunculus?
2. Ōs parvum habet.   Eī est ōs parvum.
3. Hostēs crūdēlēs habēmus.   Nōbīs sunt hostēs crūdēlēs.
4. Quae nōmina habētis?   Quae nōmina vōbīs sunt?
5. Vīllās rūsticās habent.   Eīs vīllae rūsticae sunt.

TEACHER BY THE WAY
The discovery of Pompeii was preceded by that of Herculaneum. The King of Naples began the excavations in Herculaneum in 1738 and at Pompeii in 1748 but tunneling through tufa, hard volcanic stone, was very slow. Convicts were used for the project. However, even though the buildings collapsed at Herculaneum more than at Pompeii, furnishings were better preserved because they were encased in mud kept wet by water from the nearby river. Then, at the end of the sixteenth century an architect doing some reclamation work stumbled upon a number of inscriptions. He had no clue the whole city of Pompeii was buried there. Later, in 1748, a farmer noticed a piece of land that had caved in and discovered the remains of a painting and marble statues. This prompted digging by military engineers who realized that the Herculaneum technique would not work because the softer pumice and ash covering, though less than twenty feet thick, might trigger a tunnel collapse. When Fiorelli took over in 1860, the excavations became more systematic, more intense, and definitely more scientific. Unfortunately, the remains in plaster casts cannot be studied. When in 1980 workers discovered a new batch of

skeletons near the beach in Herculaneum, Dr. Sarah Bisel, a physical anthropologist, began her work of preserving the bones. Of the eighty skeletons found, thirty-six have been taken out. She washes, dries, and dips the bones in a solution to harden them. Examining the bone structure has yielded information about the occupations, lifestyles, and ailments of the victims.

Findings from Dr. Bisel's study of twenty-six adults have thus far determined that the average man was about 5' 7" and the average woman about 5' 1½" tall. Teeth are in good condition perhaps because sugar was not part of the diet. Minor arthritis seems to be common, but nothing more serious.

PAGE 293
Standards 1.1, 1.2
Workbook Exercise 7, Content Questions

▶ EXERCISE 9 ANSWERS

Pliny: Mother has already observed the large cloud, which is in the sky near Mt. Vesuvius. Can you see the cloud, Uncle?

Uncle: I can see the cloud. I am an old man, but I have good and healthy eyes.

Pliny: What is this cloud? Its shape seems to me to be unusual. Trees usually have such a shape, not clouds.

Uncle: As soon as your mother showed me the cloud, I realized it was not usual. So I wanted to sail to the mountain and investigate the cause of the cloud. But I changed <my> plan.

Pliny: Why did you change <your> plan?

Uncle: A woman, whose country house is not far from Mt. Vesuvius, sent me a letter, in which she said flames were coming from the mountain: stones and hot ashes were falling on people: there was great danger in that place.

Pliny: You therefore thought about the people who live there?

Uncle: Yes indeed.

Pliny: What will you do?

Uncle: I will sail there and free the people from great danger.

Pliny: You have a brave spirit!

TEACHER BY THE WAY
Pliny the Elder was born to an equestrian family that afforded him a good education and sparked an intellectual curiosity that he pursued up to his death. Pliny served in the military and under the emperor Vespasian undertook several postings as procurator responsible for the emperor's personal finances and possessions as well as for the administration of justice. While serving as prefect of the Roman fleet stationed at Misenum on the Bay of Naples, Pliny, the author of an encyclopedic natural history, sought both to investigate the cloud formed by the eruption of Mt. Vesuvius and to bring aid to those in need. His nephew Pliny the Younger describes his uncle's death by asphyxiation en route in a letter to the Roman historian Tacitus.

PAGE 294

Standard 1.2

Oral Exercise 3

TRANSLATION OF THE LATIN CONVERSATION

Helen: When did you return from the beach to the city, Christy?

Christy: Both I and my parents returned yesterday. We had good holidays. For we love the beach a lot.

Mary: You do not seem to me suntanned. Surely you and (your) parents are accustomed to sunbathe?

Christy: We never lay down outside unless smeared with sunscreen. The doctors say that people should not remain for a long time in the sun unless smeared with sunscreen(s).

Helen: What else did you do on the beach with your parents?

Christy: We built sandcastles. We played volleyball. In the evening, we were always used to barbecue food in the open.

Mark: All this you did on land. Did you fear water? Weren't you in the habit of swimming?

Christy: In the morning, I used to swim in the swimming pool. However, in the afternoon hours, I was often lying on the seashore under an umbrella and I was studying books.

Mark: Even on the beach, even on vacation you were paying attention to books! Which person was ever so diligent as you?

Christy: Before the vacation in the Latin class we read about the eruption (fire) of Mt. Vesuvius. At the time when there was eruption (fire) in the mountain, Pliny and his uncle were lying down outside and were studying books!

ORAL EXERCISE 3

This exercise may be used after the Latin dialogue has been presented.

In preparation for the exercise, the teacher should use one of the CPOs to put on view the following words.

quālēs (*nominative and accusative plural*)? – what sort of?

quālis (*nominative singular*)? – what sort of?

sine + *ablative* – without

unde – whence, from where

After the students have carefully read and understood the dialogue, the teacher should ask individual students the following questions. (NB: the students may look at the dialogue while they answer.) The students should be urged to use the actual words in the dialogue, changing endings and forms only where needed to fit the answer.

Teacher: Unde Christīna et parentēs in urbem revēnērunt?

Student: Christīna et parentēs ē lītore in urbem revēnērunt.

Teacher: Quālēs fēriās ēgērunt Christīna et parentēs?

Student: Fēriās bonās ēgērunt Christīna et parentēs.

Teacher: Solentne Christīna et parentēs in actā sine unguentō aprīcārī?

Student: Nōn solent Christīna et parentēs in actā sine unguentō aprīcārī.

Teacher: Quid ex harēnā aedificāvērunt Christīna et parentēs?

Student: Christīna et parentēs parva castella ex harēnā aedificāvērunt.

Chapter 16 • 347

Teacher: Quid vespere Christīna cum parentibus facere solēbat?

Student: Christīna cum parentibus cibum in crāticulā sub dīvō assāre vespere solēbat.

Teacher: Quid māne Christīna facere solēbat?

Student: Christīna māne in natātōriō natāre solēbat.

Teacher: Quid hōrīs postmerīdiānīs Christīna facere solēbat?

Student: Christīna in actā sub umbellā iacēre prope mare et librīs studēre hōrīs postmerīdiānīs solēbat.

Teacher: Quālis est Christīna?

Student: Christīna est valdē dīligēns.

PAGE 295
Standard 4.1

DERIVATIVES

avunculus – Roman terminology is very exact regarding family members. For example, *avunculus* is a mother's brother; a father's brother is a *patruus*. In English the word "uncle" applies to both.

The Latin word *avunculus* is a diminutive form of *avus* (grandfather). The derivative "avuncular" came into English in 1789 and was originally used humorously to mean "of a pawnbroker." The word "uncle" was slang for a pawnbroker during the sixteenth to nineteenth centuries. Today it describes a person who displays affection to someone as though they belonged to the same family. My father's business partner always treated us youngsters with <u>avuncular</u> affection.

caelum – Angels are considered <u>celestial</u> beings because they are thought to live in the sky.

The <u>cerulean</u> color resembles the blue of the sky (from the Latin *caeruleus* from *caeluleus* = dark blue, blue-green).

The word "ceiling" came into English during the mid-fourteenth century (spelled *celynge*) meaning "act of paneling a room" through the Middle English *ceil* (to put a cover over) and probably influenced by the Latin *caelum*. The meaning "top surface of a room" is attested by the 1530s. The figurative sense of "upper limit" dates to 1934.

causa – The word "accuse" comes through the Latin *accūsō* (*ad* = to, and *causa*; to give as a motive or reason, call to account) from *causa* (reason).

The <u>accusative</u> case functions as the direct object of a verb. It is the purpose or reason (*causa*) for the action.

The word "because" appeared in English around 1300 as *bi cause*, modeled on the French *par cause*. It became one word about a century later.

The word "excuse" (early thirteenth century) is derived from the Latin *excūsō* (*ex* = out from, away, and *causa* = law, case, suit; hence, "an attempt to clear someone from blame"). The mild apology "Excuse me" dates to 1600.

The prefix of "inexcusable" is negative.

cinis – An "incinerator" turns everything into ash (*in* = into, and *cinis*). Note the "-tor" suffix signifying the person or thing doing the action. The word appeared in American English in 1883 and by 1889 referred to "a device for waste disposal by burning." The verb "incinerate," however, dates back to the 1530s.

clādēs – None

348 • Latin for the New Millennium: Teacher's Manual, Level 1

classis – The figurative meaning of "fleet" does not carry over into English derivatives.

The word "class" appeared around 1600 meaning "a group of students," derived through the French *classe* from *classis* referring to the "six orders of citizens organized by Servius Tullius for the purpose of taxation." The school and university sense dates to the 1650s; that of natural history to 1753; and of "high quality" to 1847.

The word "classification" is derived from *classis* and *faciō* (to make).

During the 1610s the adjective "classic" appeared in English meaning "of the highest class; approved as a model." By the 1620s it also meant "belonging to standard authors of Greek and Roman antiquity." The noun came into English in 1711.

The term "classical" appeared during the 1590s meaning "of the highest rank (in literature)." In 1886 "classical" music was defined originally in opposition to romantic music. However, by the 1880s the word had come to refer to music that had stood the test of time. In the early twentieth century it was used to denote music in contrast to jazz and later (mid-twentieth century) to popular music. Today the term now refers generally to composers dating loosely from 1700 to 1830.

See also Teaching Tip 1.14.

fēmina – The word "effeminate" derives from the Latin verb *effēminō* (*ex* = out, and *fēmina*; to make a woman out of). Appearing in English during the fifteenth century, it is rarely used without reproach to this day.

fūmus – The verb "fume" appeared in English around 1400 meaning "to fumigate" from the Old French *fumer* (to smoke, steam). The figurative sense of "show anger" dates to the 1520s.

The word "fumigation," derived from *fūmus* and *agō* (to do, drive, etc.), came into English during the late fourteenth century, the verb during the 1520s. Originally it meant "to make aromatic smoke as part of a ceremony" as well as "to expose to aromated fumes" and referred to medicinal or therapeutic treatment. Today the procedure of "smoking" refers to disinfection. The pest control expert <u>fumigated</u> the house to get rid of the fleas brought in by the family cat.

A "fumarole" is a hole in or near a volcano that emits vapor.

The word "perfume" (from *per* = through, and *fūmus*) appeared in English during the 1530s meaning "fumes from a burning substance" through the Middle French *parfum* (scent). The modern meaning of "fluid containing agreeable essences of flowers" dates to the 1540s. According to the French, a woman should apply perfume by first spraying it in front of her and then walking "through the smoke."

incendium – (from *incendō* = to set fire to, burn; figuratively, "to inflame")

When an <u>incendiary</u> device bursts, it ignites a fire to cause damage. The word, which came into English around 1400, can also refer to inflammatory remarks made to fire up a crowd, and to the agitator who does it (1610s). The military use is attested from 1871.

The noun "incense" appeared in English during the late thirteenth century, derived through the Old French *encens* (sweet-smelling substance) from the fourth principal part of *incendō*. The figurative sense of "to make angry" dates to the early fifteenth century.

A "censer" is a container used for burning incense (mid-thirteenth century), not to be confused with "censor."

The word "frankincense" appeared in English during the late fourteenth century from the Old French *franc* (noble, true) and *encense* (incense), denoting "the highest quality."

Chapter 16 • 349

lītus – The word "littoral" came into English during the 1850s. My parents bought some <u>littoral</u> property on the shore of Lake Michigan.

māter – The word "matron" came into English during the late fourteenth century meaning "married woman," usually one of rank (from the Latin *mātrōna* = lady, formed from the genitive of *māter* = *mātris*). The sense of "manager of a school or hospital" dates to the 1550s.

When "matrix" (a transliteration of the Latin *mātrix* meaning a female animal kept for breeding or a parent tree) appeared in English during the late fourteenth century, it meant "womb" (the place where something is developed, as in the body of a mother). The idea of "an embedded or enclosed mass" dates to the 1640s, the logical sense to 1914.

Another meaning of the Latin *mātrix* (a list, register) led to the word "matriculate" (a diminutive of *mātrix*) which came into English during the 1570s and meant "to admit a student to a college by enrolling his name on a register." All fully <u>matriculated</u> students at the university take free classes.

A son who killed his mother after watching her suffer from dementia was convicted of <u>matricide</u> and sentenced to forty months in prison.

The word "matrimonial" is derived from the Latin *mātrimōnium* meaning "to marry" and consists of *māter* and the suffix *–mōnium* signifying an action, state, or condition.

"Matrilineal" societies reckon descent from the mother, not the father. The antonym is "patrilineal."

"Matriarchal" societies are ruled by women, not by men. The antonym is "patriarchal."

mōns – "Mountain" (ca. 1200) is derived from the Old French *montaigne* from the Vulgar Latin *montāneus* (classical Latin *montānus*), meaning "mountainous." The noun "mount" meaning "mountain" comes into use in the mid-thirteenth century from the Anglo-French *mount* and the Old French *mont*, both based on the Latin *mōns*.

The verb "to mount (a horse)" appears around 1300 while its meaning "to ascend" is from the mid-fourteenth century, derived from the Old French *monter* (from the Vulgar Latin *montāre*). By the 1530s, the verb took on the meaning "to set or place in position."

In the early 1400s, the verb "surmount" meaning "to rise above, go beyond" appears and by the end of the century adds the meaning "to overcome." The Old French *surmonter* "to rise above" is based on *sur* from the Latin *supra* (above, beyond) and *monter* noted above.

nāvis – The <u>nave</u> of a church was so called because it seemed to resemble the shape of a ship. The word came into English during the 1670s.

The "navy" bean is attested from 1856, so called because it was grown to be used by the navy. The word first appeared during the early fourteenth century meaning "a fleet of ships especially used for war purposes."

The Magellan expedition is credited with being the first to "circumnavigate" (*circum* = around, *nāvis* = ship, and *agō* = to drive) the globe although Magellan himself was killed in the Philippines in 1521 and only eighteen sailors of the original group returned to Spain in 1522.

See also 1.8 under *nāvigō*.

nūbēs – None

pars – The word "apart" appeared in English during the late fourteenth century, derived through the French *à part* (to the side) from the Latin *ad* (to) and *pars* (part, share, side, direction, etc.).

An "apartment" (1640s) is a set of rooms set aside (*ad partem*) "for the use of one person within a house." The sense of "a set of private rooms in a building entirely of these" dates to 1874 (OED).

The prefix "de" of "depart" (mid-thirteenth century) and "department" (mid-fifteenth century) means "from"; hence, "from the side of," and thus "to separate." As a euphemism for dying, "depart" is attested from around 1500. The idea of "a separate division" was borrowed (around 1735) from the French *department* meaning "a group of people" as well as "leaving."

Note the difference in the prefix "im" meanings: "Impart" means "to share, divide with another" (*in* = into), while "impartial" (1590s) means "not one-sided, not biased" (the "im" is a negative).

The word "jeopardy" came into English around 1300, derived through the Old French *jeu parti* (a divided game, a game with even chances) from the Latin *iocus* (jest) and *pars*. The sense of "danger or risk" dates to the late fourteenth century. The verb form "jeopardize" dates to the 1640s.

When the word "parcel" entered English during the late fourteenth century, it meant "a portion of something." The phrase "part and parcel" preserves the older sense; both words mean the same, the multiplicity giving emphasis. The word is derived from the Latin *particula* (a diminutive of *pars*). The meaning of "package" appeared during the 1640s from the late fourteenth century sense of "an amount or quantity of anything," a sense which was refined during the mid-fifteenth century to "the quantity of goods in a package" and thence to the package itself.

Many of the words beginning with "part" are self-explanatory, e.g., participation (to take part in from *pars* and *capio*); a participle "takes a share of both a verb and an adjective while retaining its verbal sense"; particle means "a small part" (from *particula*); a partner shares, etc.

The word "party" appeared during the late thirteenth century and meant "part, portion, side." The political sense evolved by 1300, and the reference to "a person" dates to the mid-fifteenth century. The idea of people gathering together socially is first recorded in 1716. The verb first meant "to take the side of" (1630s), but in 1922 it is also found to mean "to have a good time."

The word "repartee" is French (*repartie*), meaning "answering blow," and was originally a fencing term. The "re" prefix means "back" and *pars* here means "side"; therefore the word literally means "side back" and thus "from one side back to the other." It refers to a conversation with witty replies.

See also Teaching Tip 1.10.

fūnestus – (from *fūnus* = funeral, death, destruction, corpse). No derivatives directly from *fūnestus*.

legō – (*legere*) The words having the "lect" base, e.g., "collect" (gather together), "elect" (choose, pick out), "select" (*se* = apart; hence to single out, to choose out), and "intellect" (to read between, as in "to read between the lines" = "to understand," from the Latin *intellegō* = to understand), are based on the fourth principal part.

"Intelligence" derives from the same verb (*intellegō*) through the corresponding noun *intellegentia*.

The word "lecture" appeared during the late fourteenth century meaning "the action of reading." To read is "to pick out words (*legō*)." The meaning "to read a lesson aloud" dates to the 1520s. Ten years later it also began to mean "a discourse on a given subject to instruct an audience."

"Predilection" (1742) is derived from *prae* (before) and *dīligō* (from *dis* = apart, and *legō* = to choose; hence "to choose, to love") and means "to choose before others." Jane had a <u>predilection</u> for sweets.

A "diligent" person is attentive and conscientious because he loves or esteems highly what he is doing (from *dīligō* = prize especially through *dīligēns* = painstaking).

A "legend" is a story "which must be read" (from the gerundive *legendus*). The word appeared early in the fourteenth century and is a narrative dealing with "an unverifiable event handed down by tradition and popularly accepted as historical." The meaning "writing or inscription on a coin or medal" dates to the 1610s, on a map or illustration to 1903.

Chapter 16 • 351

The word "legion" came into English around 1200, derived from the Latin *legiō* (a body of soldiers gathered from the populace). The meaning "a large number" stems from translations of Mark 5:9. "My name is Legion . . . for we are many."

The word "lesson" (early thirteenth century) originally meant "a reading aloud from the Bible" and was derived through the Old French *leçon* from the Latin *lectiō* (selecting, reading). It also meant "something to be learned by a student." The transferred sense of "an occurrence from which something can be learned" (OED) dates to the 1580s. Let this be a <u>lesson</u> to you!

When the word "sacrilege" came into English around 1300, it meant "a crime of stealing what is consecrated to God," derived through the Latin *sacrilegium* (a stealing of sacred things) (from *sacer* = sacred, and *legō* = to pick out, select). The transferred sense of "a profanation of anything sacred" dates to the late fourteenth century.

The verb "cull" appeared around 1200 meaning "to put through a strainer" through the Old French *coillir* (to pick, choose, collect) from the Latin *colligō*. The act of "culling" involves choosing or separating the best parts from those that are inferior.

The verb "coil" appeared in the 1610s, the noun in the 1620s. It was also derived through the Old French *coillir* from the Latin *colligō* (*cum* = together, and *legō*). The meaning "to wind" may have been specialized in nautical usage, e.g., coiling a rope. The word is closely related to (or a variant spelling of) "cull" as people used it to mean "to turn, to cull, to stir, to select." The noun also came to mean "a noisy disturbance," and it is in this sense that Shakespeare used it in Hamlet's "To be or not to be" speech (Act III, Scene 1). "Mortal coil" may also be referring to "the thread of life," which was measured, wound around a spindle, and finally cut by the Fates. The meaning of "turmoil" is no longer used today.

See also *neglegō* in 1.15.

opprimō – (from *premō* = to press)

The meaning of the Latin verb (to press down, crush) comes over into the figurative sense of "to put down, subdue, pursue relentless(ly)." The heat has been <u>oppressive</u>.

studeō – A "student" (late fourteenth century) should be eager to learn (at least that is the etymological meaning of the word!).

Note the "-ous" suffix of "studious" (late fourteenth century, from the Latin *studiōsus*).

The word "studio" came into English in 1819 meaning "the workroom of a sculptor or painter." It was derived through the Italian *studio* (room for study) from the Latin noun *studium* (enthusiasm, application, inclination, study).

From the same root (*studium*) came the word "etude" in 1837, through the Old French *estudie* (to study). The word was popularized by the "Etudes" of Chopin (1810–1849). The musical meaning today is "a composition intended mainly for the practice of (the study of) technique."

The Latin word itself came over into Latin to mean "a place for enjoyment." It was a transliteration of the Greek στάδιον = *stadion* meaning a Greek measurement equaling about 1/8 of a Roman mile and thence "a racecourse."

numquam – None

igitur – None

352 • Latin for the New Millennium: Teacher's Manual, Level 1

CHAPTER 17 (PP. 297–310)

GRAMMAR IN LANGUAGE FACTS

Pluperfect Tense Active of All Conjugations; Pluperfect Tense of *Sum* and *Possum*; Fourth Declension Masculine, Feminine, and Neuter Nouns

PAGE 297

Standards 1.1, 3.2
RRA 6A

MEMORĀBILE DICTŪ VOCABULARY

sine + *ablative* – without

studium, studiī, *n*. – partisanship, zeal

TEACHER BY THE WAY

Tacitus's *Annals* are called *Annālēs* in Latin.

TEACHER BY THE WAY

A Polish painter who trained in Russia, Siemiradzki was noted for his knowledge of science and ancient history and considered an excellent colorist and draftsman. His subjects are largely historical and theological in which landscape plays the greatest role. Critics took exception to this emphasis, noting the lack of psychological analysis and deep thought under the beautiful surface. Nevertheless, the painter is considered one of the best representatives of late European neoclassicism.

TEACHER BY THE WAY

Although Tacitus describes his intent to write the *Annālēs* "*sine īrā et studiō*," the result was not unbiased. He "preferred the republic at its worst to the imperial system at its best" (*Oxford Companion to Classical Literature*, p. 549) and thus focused on the crimes, the oppression, the sycophants, and the informers far more than the occasional glimpses he gives of an efficient civil administration. He condemns Tiberius soundly and allows no such redeeming features or psychological explanations as can be found in Suetonius. Tacitus emphasizes the excesses of Claudius's wife and his freedmen instead of his learning and well-run empire; the extravagances and bloodshed of Nero's reign are far more memorable than his account of the early years of his rule.

Tacitus is certainly a captivating read, but, as Duff warns, "dispassionate history is not to be expected from a hostile judge" (J. W. Duff, *A Literary History of Rome in the Silver Age*, p. 469).

TEACHING TIP
Chapter 6 of RRA contains information on Tacitus. The teacher may wish to assign this chapter for reading or review. See p. 201.

PAGE 298
Standards 1.1, 2.1, 3.1, 3.2

TRANSLATION OF LATIN PASSAGE
About the Fire at Rome
The beginning of the great Roman fire was in the shops, in which the flames were easily nourished by the merchandise. What was the cause of this fire? Maybe the emperor Nero did it with trickery; maybe there was another cause. However, the Romans had never seen a greater disaster. The fire, carried by the force of the winds, engulfed the circus and its strength could not be suppressed. The houses did not have protections, the temples did not have walls. The streets (roads) were narrow and curved. Therefore, without obstacles, the flames were devastating everything. Flames were already burning everywhere before people tried to exstinguish them. Because of the tears and fears of the women and because of those who were running to and fro, everything was in confusion. All places were being engulfed by fire from all parts. Men and women were running on the roads and in the fields and many of them were falling on the ground. In fact, those who had lost all their things and all their (friends, family) no longer had strength because of <their> pain. Therefore the fire consumed them. However, other people were throwing torches into the fire, which they were doing perhaps at the order of the emperor.

TEACHER BY THE WAY
Tacitus's style of writing is remarkable for its terse, condensed mode of expression and epigrammatic flair. It clearly imitates that of the first century BCE historian Sallust, who also combined verbal brevity and pointed observations with a pessimistic outlook on Roman government and politics.

TEACHER BY THE WAY
After a quick review of Augustus's reign, Tacitus devotes the first six books of the *Annālēs* to Tiberius and events during his rule, including the military successes of Germanicus and his death under mysterious circumstances, the character and career of Sejanus, and the emperor's years at Capri. Books 7–10 are lost. Book 11 picks up the story during the reign of Claudius and describes the excesses of his wife Messalina. Book 12 covers Claudius's marriage to his niece Agrippina, his adoption of her son Nero, and his death by poison at the hands of his wife. Books 13–16 cover the reign of Nero to 66 CE and include a description of his early promising years, his murder of Claudius's two offspring and of Agrippina, Boudicca's unsuccessful revolt in Britain, the great fire of Rome, and the conspiracy of Piso, which resulted in the mandated suicide of Seneca. Book 16 ends with a list of Nero's extravagances and the author's lament over the unrelenting record of bloodshed. The section covering Nero's last two years is lost.

PAGE 299

ANSWERS TO COMPREHENSION QUESTIONS

1. Some say the emperor Nero started it; others mention other causes.

2. The houses had no protection; the temples did not have walls; the streets were narrow and curved.

3. People were crushed because they had lost all their possessions.

4. The reason was never discovered for certain. But Tacitus suggests they may have been doing this at the emperor's orders.

TEACHING TIP

The presence of the word *circus* in this Reading Vocabulary list may engender a classroom conversation about chariot racing in the Circus Maximus.

The only requirement for chariot races was a long and level piece of ground. Such a spot was located between the Aventine and Palatine Hills, and it was here the Circus Maximus was established during the early days of Rome. It measured 600 by 150 meters; the length of a lap was about 1,500 meters (one mile).

Speed was not the most important thing in a race because of the short stretches and sharp turns. It was the danger that fascinated the Romans; there were no rules in the circus.

Augustus segregated the seating at the Circus according to class and organization and separated the women from the men. Prior to this, both sexes sat together and Ovid, in a very humorous passage (*Ars Amātōria* 1.135–70), describes the Circus as a great place to meet a girl.

A delightful description of the spectators at a race is given by Pliny the Younger (9.6), who views them with a jaded and jaundiced eye: "I can find nothing new or different in [the races]: once seen is enough." He cannot understand the "childish passion for watching galloping horses and drivers standing in chariots" (Radice translation). The crowds are not interested in speed or skill but "it is the racing-colors they really support, and if in the middle of the race one team's colors were switched with another's, the crowd's enthusiasm and support would be switched, too, and they would abandon the drivers and horses that just before they had been cheering on" (Cobbold translation).

It is interesting to note that the famous chariot race in the 1959 movie *Ben-Hur* was staged at the Circus Maximus. It took three months to film the twenty-five-minute segment.

For more information on chariot racing, see p. 328 of this teacher's manual.

PAGE 300

Standards 3.1, 4.1

Oral Exercise 1; Workbook Exercise 3

ORAL EXERCISE 1

This exercise may be used after the pluperfect active tense has been presented.

While looking at the forms of *parō* and *capiō*, ask the students to conjugate in the pluperfect active the verbs *pōnō*, *petō*, and *maneō*.

posueram, posuerās, posuerat, posuerāmus, posuerātis, posuerant

petīveram, petīverās, petīverat, petīverāmus, petīverātis, petīverant

mānseram, mānserās, mānserat, mānserāmus, mānserātis, mānserant

Chapter 17 • 355

TEACHING TIP

Additional reproducible worksheets, morphology charts, and their associated answer keys, related to this material, are available for download at www.lnm.bolchazy.com.

- Verb Conjugations

PAGE 301

Standards 1.1, 1.2
Oral Exercise 2

▶ EXERCISE 1 ANSWERS

1. corripueram — I had seized
2. temptāveram — I had tried
3. exstīnxeram — I had extinguished
4. āmīseram — I had lost
5. cucurreram — I had run
6. lēgeram — I had read

ORAL EXERCISE 2

This exercise may be used after Exercise 1.

Use one of the CPOs to put on view the following pairs of verbs (sometimes with direct objects) and ask students to imitate the two actions. Then ask another student what the first student did (using the perfect tense), and next ask what s/he had done first (using the pluperfect tense). Also list the adverb *anteā*, "before that," for use in questions with the pluperfect tense.

ambulō
cadō
Teacher: Quid Mārcus fēcit?   **Student:** Mārcus cecidit.
Teacher: Quid Mārcus anteā fēcerat?   **Student:** Mārcus anteā ambulāverat.

stō
discēdō
Teacher: Quid Mārcus fēcit?   **Student:** Mārcus discessit.
Teacher: Quid Mārcus anteā fēcerat?   **Student:** Mārcus anteā steterat.

iaceō
saxum iaciō (a paper wad can be used in imitation of a real rock)
Teacher: Quid Mārcus fēcit?   **Student:** Mārcus saxum iēcit.
Teacher: Quid Mārcus anteā fēcerat?   **Student:** Mārcus anteā iacuerat.

librum legō
fābulam nārrō
Teacher: Quid Mārcus fēcit?   **Student:** Mārcus fābulam nārrāvit.
Teacher: Quid Mārcus anteā fēcerat?   **Student:** Mārcus anteā librum lēgerat.

epistulam parō
epistulam ostendō
Teacher: Quid Mārcus fēcit?   **Student:** Mārcus epistulam ostendit.
Teacher: Quid Mārcus anteā fēcerat?   **Student:** Mārcus anteā epistulam parāverat.

currō
flammās exstinguō (a fireman toy or a picture of flames being put out may be used in imitation of this action)
Teacher: Quid Mārcus fēcit?   **Student:** Mārcus flammās exstīnxit.
Teacher: Quid Mārcus anteā fēcerat?   **Student:** Mārcus anteā cucurrerat.

veniō
hostēs vincō (toy soldiers may be used to imitate real soldiers)
Teacher: Quid Mārcus fēcit?   **Student:** Mārcus hostēs vīcit.
Teacher: Quid Mārcus anteā fēcerat?   **Student:** Mārcus anteā vēnerat.

PAGE 302
Standards 1.1, 1.2, 4.1
Workbook Exercise 2

▶ EXERCISE 2 ANSWERS

1. attempt — temptō
2. local — locus
3. extinct — exstinguō
4. alimony — alō
5. ventilation — ventus
6. devastated — dēvastō
7. jussive — iussus
8. initial — initium
9. curriculum — currō
10. imperial — imperātor
11. murals — mūrus
12. domestic — domus
13. facilitator — facile
14. rejected — iaciō (actually reiciō)
15. tumultuous — tumultus
16. manual — manus
17. impetuous — impetus

TEACHING TIP
Although in Exercise 2 the students are directed to find only the derivatives based on the Vocabulary to Learn, they may be interested to learn that there are other derivatives in Exercise 2. The derivation of these words is provided for the teacher's convenience.

1. rescue – from *excutiō* (to shake out, drive out, banish, examine, inspect). mountaineers – from *montānus* (mountainous, highland).
3. species – from *speciēs* (appearance, form, etc.).
4. divorce – from *dīvortium* (separation, divorce [by consent]). decree – from *dēcernō* (to decide, determine). determined – from *dētermīnō* (to bound, limit, settle). spouse – from *spondeō* (to promise, pledge, vow). pay – from *pacō* (to pacify, subdue).

6. government – from *gubernō* (to steer, pilot, manage). officials – from *officium* (service, attention, duty). assessed – from *adsideō* (to sit by, attend, assist). areas – from *ārea* (vacant site, open space, playground).

7. sentence – from *sententia* (opinion, judgment, verdict, decision, etc.).

9. describe – from *dēscrībō* (to copy out, draw, sketch). me – from *mē* (accusative singular of *ego*, I).

10. in – from *in* (in, on, at). Rome – from *Rōma* (Rome). expanded – from *expandō* (to unfold) from *pandō* (to spread out, stretch, extend). Mediterranean – from *medius* (middle of, intervening) + *terra* (earth, land)

11. admired – from *admīror* (to wonder at, be surprised at). in – from *in* (in, on, at).

12. nature – from *nātūra* (birth, nature, quality, the physical world).

13. discussion – from *discutiō* (to smash, scatter, dispel [an abstract condition or situation]).

15. Roman – from *Rōmānus* (Roman). republic – from *rēs* (thing, circumstance, affair, business, etc.) + *pūblicus* (public, common, of the state).

16. people – from *populus* (people, nation, populace).

17. people – from *populus* (people, nation, populace). actions – from *agō* (to drive, do, discuss, live, spend). late – from *lassus* (tired, exhausted).

▶ EXERCISE 3 ANSWERS

1. rogāverātis   you (plural) had asked
2. discēsserant   they had left
3. aluerātis   you (plural) had nourished
4. studuerat   s/he had studied
5. fūgerās   you had fled
6. steterās   you had stood
7. habuērāmus   we had had
8. lēgeram   I had read
9. invīdērātis   you (plural) had envied
10. tetigerās   you had touched
11. scīveram   I had known

PAGE 303

Standards 1.1, 1.2, 3.1, 4.1

Oral Exercises 3, 4; Workbook Exercise 4

▶ EXERCISE 4 ANSWERS

1. Currere nōn potuerāmus.
2. In vīllā iam fueram.
3. Mātrem meam relinquere nōn potueram.
4. Fuerātisne iam in clāde?
5. Potuerāsne ambulāre ad lītus?
6. Multae fēminae iam in nāve fuerant.
7. Potuerātisne fugere?
8. Hominēs exstinguere incendium nōn potuerant.
9. Iudex stāre nōn potuerat.
10. Fūmus ubīque iam fuerat.
11. Fuerāsne ibi saepe?
12. Iam in tempestāte fuerāmus.

358 • Latin for the New Millennium: Teacher's Manual, Level 1

ORAL EXERCISE 3

This exercise may be used after the pluperfect of sum *and* possum *has been presented.*

The teacher should say each pluperfect tense form of *sum* and *possum* listed below. A different student should repeat each form, then change it orally into the corresponding pluperfect singular if it is plural and into the plural if it is singular.

Teacher: potuerāmus	**Student:** potueram
Teacher: fueram	**Student:** fuerāmus
Teacher: potuerant	**Student:** potuerat
Teacher: fuerās	**Student:** fuerātis
Teacher: potuerat	**Student:** potuerant
Teacher: fuerātis	**Student:** fuerās
Teacher: potueram	**Student:** potuerāmus
Teacher: fuerant	**Student:** fuerat
Teacher: potuerās	**Student:** potuerātis
Teacher: fuerāmus	**Student:** fueram
Teacher: potuerātis	**Student:** potuerās
Teacher: fuerat	**Student:** fuerant

ORAL EXERCISE 4

This exercise may be used after Exercise 4.

The teacher should slowly recite each sentence. A different student will in turn orally repeat each sentence. This will often require several attempts before the student can reproduce the sentence orally. When the student has done so, s/he should repeat the sentence one more time, but with all the verbs in the sentence changed to the corresponding pluperfect tense form.

Teacher: Magnum incendium fuit.	**Student:** Magnum incendium fuerat.
Teacher: Imperātor id fēcit.	**Student:** Imperātor id fēcerat.
Teacher: Templīs nōn fuērunt mūrī.	**Student:** Templīs nōn fuerant mūrī.
Teacher: Rōmānī flammās vīdērunt.	**Student:** Rōmānī flammās vīderant.
Teacher: Omnia ārsērunt.	**Student:** Omnia ārserant.
Teacher: Hominēs ignem exstinguere temptāvērunt.	**Student:** Hominēs ignem exstinguere temptāverant.

Additional sentences:

Teacher: Multī omnia sua āmīsērunt.	**Student:** Multī omnia sua āmīserant.
Teacher: Flammae domūs corripuērunt.	**Student:** Flammae domūs corripuerant.
Teacher: Multī fugere nōn potuērunt.	**Student:** Multī fugere nōn potuerant.
Teacher: Virī mulierēsque in terram cecidērunt.	**Student:** Virī mulierēsque in terram ceciderant.
Teacher: Ignis eōs cōnsūmpsit.	**Student:** Ignis eōs cōnsūmpserat.
Teacher: Aliī iussū imperātōris flammās parāvērunt.	**Student:** Aliī iussū imperātōris flammās parāverant.

Chapter 17 • 359

PAGE 304

Standards 3.1, 4.1

TEACHER BY THE WAY

At the age of sixteen, Nero (Nero Claudius Drusus Germanicus, 15–68 CE) ascended the throne upon the death of his uncle and stepfather Claudius in 54 CE. His mother Agrippina the Younger had married her uncle Claudius and convinced him to adopt her son Nero so that he might succeed his uncle as emperor. Thus, he would gain the throne and vindicate his grandfather, whose suspicious death had allowed Caligula to become emperor.

During Nero's first years in office, his advisors included his tutor, Seneca the Younger, and the prefect of the praetorian guard, Sextus Afranius Burrus. Meanwhile, Agrippina chafed as she had intended a greater role in governance than her young son allowed her. Nero proved an able administrator working with a revived Senate whose previously diminished authority was increased. Like his uncle Claudius, he is said to have taken his judicial duties seriously. In time his mother's jealousy became more than Nero could bear and Suetonius notes that he had tried four times to kill Agrippina—three times he tried to poison her and once he rigged the ceiling in her bedroom so that it would fall and crush her. Finally, he invited her to Baiae in 59 CE, contrived an accident for her galley, and replaced it with a boat that would collapse and drown her. She managed to swim to shore but Nero had her summarily killed. With Burrus's death in 62 CE, Seneca departed the capital for retirement and all constraints on Nero's behavior also departed. The young emperor who initially disliked capital punishment soon executed those he feared, those who opposed him, and even those who fell asleep during his performances.

Suetonius details Nero's exploits of debauchery and his artistic and equestrian endeavors. He fancied himself poet, playwright, actor, and singer. From his youth, he enjoyed horses and in one of his more flamboyant acts of self-indulgence, he drove a ten-horse chariot through Olympia. The fire that destroyed a full fifth of the city afforded Nero an opportunity to erect a monument to his self-indulgence. Nero appropriated a vast plot of land, some two hundred acres plus, which over the course of the years 64–68 CE became his personal gardens with a wildlife refuge, artificial pond, and a huge palace. For the vestibule he had his image cast as a golden statue whose size, one hundred twenty feet in height, was chosen so as to rival the colossal statue of Helios at Rhodes. The palace's name, *Domus Aurea*, is derived from Suetonius's description of its decoration with gold, mother of pearl, and other gems. It is estimated that the "house" itself covered some one hundred twenty-five acres.

Nero's Flavian successors readily disassociated themselves from his wanton rule by closing his palace and filling parts of it in to serve as the foundation of other buildings like the public baths of Titus. The Flavian building program, in contrast to Nero's, directly benefited the people of Rome. The Flavians drained Nero's pool and built the Colosseum. They transformed Nero's golden statue to one of the sun god set up alongside the amphitheatre. One hundred days of games and special events celebrated the opening of the amphitheatre in 80 CE.

With the reuse of Nero's palace, we are able to study and visit only a portion of it that was carved into the Esquiline Hill. This section, however, with its multiple porticoes, dining rooms, and bedrooms, evokes a rich sense of the original. Remains of stucco, fresco, and mosaic decoration dazzle and stoke the imagination. Nero's architects maximized the benefits of

Roman concrete as they were able to build quickly with sound foundations and materials. The concrete allowed them to transform the arch into the vault and to construct a revolutionary octagonal room with groin vaults.

During the Renaissance, renewed interest in things classical resulted in treasure hunts exploring Roman ruins for classical art. Thus, Raphael and other artists descended into the ruins of the *Domus Aurea* and sketched what they saw. The influence of these drawings is seen in the decorative borders of Renaissance paintings and frescoes.

PAGE 305

Workbook Exercise 1

TEACHING TIP
The teacher may wish to draw the students' attention to the macron on the masculine and feminine endings of the genitive singular, nominative plural, and accusative plural while the nominative singular does not have a macron.

TEACHING TIP
Additional reproducible worksheets, morphology charts, and their associated answer keys, related to this material, are available for download at www.lnm.bolchazy.com.

- **Noun Declensions**

PAGE 306

TEACHING TIP
The teacher may choose to discuss the names and uses of the unlabeled rooms and of the *impluvium/compluvium* on the diagram on this page. Some teachers may wish to cover the topic of rooms in a Roman house earlier in conjunction with Chapter 15 while others may choose either to initiate or to review the topic here. The unlabeled version of this diagram is available to download at www.lnm.bolchazy.com.

TEACHING TIP
Additional reproducible worksheets, morphology charts, and their associated answer keys, related to this material, are available for download at www.lnm.bolchazy.com.

- **The Roman House**

PAGE 307
Standards 1.1, 1.2

▶ EXERCISE 5 ANSWERS

Singular

Nominative	impetus	genū
Genitive	impetūs	genūs
Dative	impetuī	genū
Accusative	impetum	genū
Ablative	impetū	genū
Vocative	impetus	genū

Plural

Nominative	impetūs	genua
Genitive	impetuum	genuum
Dative	impetibus	genibus
Accusative	impetūs	genua
Ablative	impetibus	genibus
Vocative	impetūs	genua

▶ EXERCISE 6 ANSWERS

1. cornibus longīs
2. tumultuum magnōrum
3. impetuī fūnestō
4. domūs nostrae/nostrās
5. cornū pulchrum/pulchrō
6. manum armātam
7. domibus vestrīs
8. cornua omnia
9. manibus multīs

362 • Latin for the New Millennium: Teacher's Manual, Level 1

PAGE 308

Standards 1.1, 1.2, 4.1

Workbook Exercises 5, 6, 7, Content Questions

▶ EXERCISE 7 ANSWERS

Rōmānus 1: I see/am catching sight of smoke and flames. From which part of the city have they come? What is the reason for the confusion?

Rōmānus 2: Tū igitur nōn scīs Rōmam ārdēre.

Rōmānus 1: Are you telling the truth? What fire? Who did it?

Rōmānus 2: Imperātor hominēs iussit incendium facere. Nam semper cupīverat urbem in flammīs vidēre.

Rōmānus 1: I cannot believe it. Does Rome burn on the order of the emperor?

Rōmānus 2: Est tamen vērum. Ego vīdī hominēs quī facēs parāverant et eās manibus suīs in domūs et in templa iaciēbant.

Rōmānus 1: Now I think about my house. For my family is at home. Is my house also engulfed by flames? Does my family remain at home?

Rōmānus 2: Nōn sciō. Vīdī multōs virōs et mulierēs quī fugiēbant. Domūs suās et omnia sua relīquerant.

Rōmānus 1: Look! The danger is already near us. Who will extinguish these flames?

Rōmānus 2: Vīs ignis est valdē magna nec opprimī potest. Clādēs Rōmam dēlēbit.

TEACHING TIP

Students may be interested in how to say other things about their health in addition to what is presented in this chapter of the book. Here are some other phrases for the teacher to present if s/he wishes.

- *Faucēs dolent.* – I have a sore throat.
- *Faucēs sunt raucae.* – My throat is hoarse.
- *Frēgistīne os?* – Did you break a bone?
- *Frēgī* – I broke
    - *carpum* – wrist bone
    - *costam* – rib
    - *crūs* – leg
    - *digitum* – toe or finger
    - *manum* – hand
    - *patellam* – kneecap
    - *pedem* – foot
    - *scapulam* – shoulder blade
    - *tālum* – ankle.
- *Stomachus dolet.* – I have a stomach ache.
- *Tussiō.* – I am coughing.

PAGE 309

Standard 1.2
Dictation and Oral Exercise 5

TRANSLATION OF THE LATIN CONVERSATION

Teacher: Hello, everyone! I do not see Mary. Do you see Mary?

Christy: Teacher, Mary called me on the phone yesterday. She had broken her hand. You know that Mary loves fields. While she was walking in the fields, she had fallen.

Teacher: Alas, I am sorry about this disaster. What is Mary doing now?

Christy: Yesterday, at the time she was talking with me, she had already gone to the hospital and seen a doctor. The doctor had placed a cast on her hand. Because of the pain, Mary had to take medications. Perhaps now she is also taking care of her health.

Helen (*to Christy and Mark*): Will we be able to go to Mary's home after school? For I want to see her and remain with her. Perhaps Mary also wants to see friends.

Teacher: Good plan.

Mary, who is wearing a cast on her hand, enters.

Mary: Hello friends (male and female friends)!

Everyone: Hello, Mary! We are glad you are at school! How is your hand?

Mary: My hand hurts very much. So I cannot write.

Teacher: Your left hand is impaired and you cannot write with that hand. But your right hand seems to be doing fine. Therefore you'll be able to write with the right hand.

TEACHING TIP
The teacher may take the opportunity to have students research medical care in ancient Rome.

TEACHER BY THE WAY
Many of the doctors in the Roman world were Greek slaves or freedmen. Medicine was one of the few occupations open to women. When Julius Caesar granted citizenship to foreign doctors working in Rome (46 BCE), their status began to improve. Many surgical instruments, easily identifiable by comparison with modern ones, have been found in Pompeii.

DICTATION AND ORAL EXERCISE 5

This exercise may be used to conclude the chapter.

The teacher should read the following passage slowly and clearly, and the students should write it as the teacher dictates. When the students have written out the passage, the teacher should ask them orally and individually the questions following the passage (adapted from Pliny the Younger, *Letters* 9.23):

Tacitus cum amīcīs suīs comedēbat. Erat cum iīs homō Tacitō nōn nōtus. Tacitus multa dē litterīs nārrāverat, sed nōmen suum nōn dīxerat. Tunc homō nōn nōtus rogāvit: "Esne tū Tacitus an es Plīnius?"

Tacitus id Plīniō nārrāvit. Plīnius gaudēbat nōmen suum et nōmen amīcī suī Tacitī esse celebre. Dīcēbat sē ex librīs suīs magnum frūctum capere.

gaudeō, gaudēre – to rejoice (the verb has   **frūctus, frūctūs,** *m.* – gain, fruit
     gavīsus sum as perfect)   **Plīnius, Plīniī,** *m.* – Pliny
nōtus, nōta, nōtum – known   **Tacitus, Tacitī,** *m.* – Tacitus

Tacitus was eating with his friends. With them there was a man not known to Tacitus. Tacitus had told many things about literature, but had not said his name. Then the unknown man asked: "Are you Tacitus or are you Pliny?"

Tacitus told this to Pliny. Pliny was rejoicing that his name and the name of his friend Tacitus were renowned. He was saying that he gets great gain from his books.

Teacher: Quid Tacitus faciēbat?
Student: Tacitus cum amīcīs suīs comēdēbat.

Teacher: Erantne omnēs Tacitō nōtī?
Student: Nōn omnēs erant Tacitō nōtī. Cum amīcīs erat homō nōn nōtus.

Teacher: Quid Tacitus nārrāverat?
Student: Tacitus dē litterīs nārrāverat.

Teacher: Dīxeratne Tacitus nōmen suum?
Student: Tacitus nōmen suum nōn dīxerat.

Teacher: Dīxeratne Tacitus nōmen Plīniī?
Student: Tacitus nōmen Plīniī nōn dīxerat.

Teacher: Audīveratne homō nōn nōtus nōmina Tacitī et Plīniī?
Student: Homō nōn nōtus nōmina Tacitī et Plīniī audīverat.

Teacher: Fuerantne nōmina Tacitī et Plīniī eī nōta?
Student: Nōmina Tacitī et Plīniī eī fuerant nōta.

Teacher: Erantne nōmina Tacitī et Plīniī celebria?
Student: Nōmina Tacitī et Plīniī erant celebria.

Teacher: Narrāvitne Tacitus omnia Plīniō?
Student: Tacitus Plīniō omnia nārrāvit.

Teacher: Gaudetne Plīnius dē librīs suīs?
Student: Plīnius dē librīs suīs gaudet.

Teacher: Quid Plīnius ex librīs suīs capit?
Student: Plīnius magnum frūctum ex librīs suīs capit.

Chapter 17 • 365

PAGE 310
Standard 4.1

DERIVATIVES

cornū – A <u>cornucopia</u> is the "Horn of Plenty" and is associated with Thanksgiving.

The noun "corner" came into English during the late thirteenth century meaning "horn, projecting point, end." The adjective appeared during the 1530s. The verb "to corner" came from the noun and appeared during the late fourteenth century. The phrase "to turn a corner (as in a race)" dates to the 1860s. The commercial use, as in "to corner the market," dates to 1836.

A <u>unicorn</u> has one horn located in the middle of his forehead.

The word "cornet" came into English around 1400 and meant "a wind instrument made of wood and provided with six finger holes." It was derived through the Old French *cornet* (a small horn; a diminutive of *corn* = a horn) from *cornū*.

The word "cornea" (late fourteenth century) was derived from *cornea tēla* (horny web or sheath) and refers to the transparent membrane over the iris and pupil of the eye.

domus – See *domina* in 1.7 and *domī* in 1.3.

imperātor – Note the "-tor" suffix of this Latin word, which is still used in English today. For related derivatives, see Teaching Tip 1.10 and *parō* in 1.2.

impetus – See *petō* in 1.8.

initium – (from *in* and *eō* = to go; hence *initiō* = to originate)

The <u>initial</u> letter of a sentence is always capitalized in English.

"To initiate" a conversation or a project means "to begin" it. The word appeared around 1600.

The noun "initiative" is first found in 1793 in the writings of William Godwin. The phrase "take the initiative" dates to 1844.

An "initiation" ceremony marks the beginning of membership in a club or society. The word is first found in the 1580s.

See *eō* in 2.10 for related derivatives.

iussus – See *iubeō* in 1.4.

locus – The verb "couch" appeared around 1300 meaning "to overlay with gold, inlay" through the Old French *couchier* (to place, put to bed, go to bed) from the Latin *collocō* (to lay, place, arrange together). The noun came into English usage during the mid-fourteenth century through the Old French *coucher* (to lie down) from *collocō*. Traditionally a "couch" has only the head raised and only half a back; a sofa has both ends raised and a full back. The term "couch potato" was coined in 1979.

A "locomotive" moves from place to place.

The prefix of "dislocate" means "away." The verb appeared around 1600 from the earlier adjective (around 1400) "dislocate" meaning "out of joint" as in "a dislocated arm."

The word "lieu" (late thirteenth century) is an Old French word (from *locus*) meaning "place, position, rank." Today the phrase "in lieu of" is often used: The workers chose to take an extra day off at Christmas in <u>lieu</u> of a bonus.

366 • Latin for the New Millennium: Teacher's Manual, Level 1

The word "lieutenant" (late fourteenth century) literally means "one holding a place instead of another," (from *locus* and *teneō* = to hold) as in a substitute or deputy. The specific military rank dates to the 1570s.

manus – "Amanuensis" is a Latin word meaning "secretary" and came into English unchanged during the 1610s. It was formed from the phrase *servus a manū* (literally, slave from the hand). The suffix forms an ethnic adjective, as in *Athēniēnsis*.

The word "emancipation" (1620s) consists of several Latin bases: *e* (*ex* = out from), *manus*, and *capiō* (to take). Therefore, the word literally means "to take from the hand of." The figurative meaning of *manus* is "power" and in Rome referred to the power of the father, *paterfamiliās*, over his family and slaves. To "take from the hand of" thus meant "to free from the authority of" the father.

The word "maintain" came into English during the mid-thirteenth century meaning "to practice habitually" and derived through the Old French *maintenir* from the Latin *manūtenēre* (to hold by means of the hand). The meaning "to carry on" dates to the mid-fourteenth century.

The word "manumission" is a synonym of "emancipation" meaning "to let go from the hand" (*manus* and *mittō* = to send, let go; *manūmittō* = to set free).

The verb "manacle" appeared in English around 1300, the noun during the mid-fourteenth century. It was derived through the Old French *manicle* (handcuffs, bracelet) from the Latin diminutive of *manus* (*manicula*).

The word "manatee" is often associated with the Latin *manus* because the animal's flippers look like hands. The actual origin, however, comes from the Spanish *manatí* (breast).

Many derivatives beginning with forms of *manus* are self-explanatory to Latin students, e.g., "manicure" (care of the hands), "manufacture" (to make by hand), "manuscript" (written by hand), "manual" (something done by hand).

The word "manifest," as verb and adjective, came into English during the late fourteenth century derived from the Latin *manifestus* (clear, apparent, evident; the OLD states the word is based on *manus* but that the origin of *festus* is dubious, although it also appears in *infestus*).

The noun meaning "a ship's cargo" appeared in 1706, derived from the earlier idea of an "open declaration" (around 1600).

The word "manipulation" (around 1730) is derived through the French *manipule* (handful; a pharmacist's measure) from *manipulus* (from *manus*, and *pleō* = to fill; hence, "a handful, bundle"). It first referred to "a method of digging ore." The sense of "a skillful handling of objects" dates to 1826 and extended in 1828 to the "skillful handling of persons." The verb "manipulate" dates to 1827; its financial sense to 1870.

The word "manner" appeared in English around 1200, meaning "kind, sort" and derived through the Old French *maniere* (fashion, method, appearance, custom) from the Latin *manuārius* (operated by hand). The meaning "customary practice" is first attested around 1300; that of "specific nature, the way something happens" dates to the mid-fourteenth century.

The word "manage" (1560s) is derived through the Italian *maneggiare* (to handle, especially a horse) from *manus*. The prefix of "mismanage" is negative.

The word "manure" appeared in English around 1400 meaning "to cultivate land." It was derived through the Old French *manouvrer* (to work with the hands, cultivate, carry out). The idea of "working the earth" led to the meaning "to put dung on the soil" (1590s).

Chapter 17 · 367

The same French source, which was derived from *manus* and *operor* = to work, gave rise to the English noun "maneuver" in 1758 meaning "planned movement of troops or warships." The verb appeared in 1777 and was also used in a military sense. The figurative sense of "to intrigue, scheme" dates to 1801. She <u>maneuvered</u> the president of the club into agreeing with her plan.

mūrus – "Mural," a wall painting, is first used in 1921, shortened from "mural painting" (1850). The adjective "mural" (mid-fifteenth century) comes directly from the Latin *mūrālis* meaning "pertaining to a wall."

In the 1580s, "immure" appears from the Middle French *emmurer* and directly from the medieval Latin *immūrāre* meaning "to shut up within walls." Poe's "The Cask of Amontillado" describes the <u>immurement</u> of a living man in a wine vault.

tumultus – The English "tumult" derives directly from the Latin *tumultus* (commotion, disturbance), which itself is related to *tumeō* (to be swollen, be excited).

Note the "-ous" suffix of "tumultuous."

ventus – A "vent" allows air (wind) to flow into a room.

The word "ventilate" is derived through *ventilō* (to agitate, fan, set in motion) from *ventulus*, a diminutive of *ventus* meaning "breeze." In the mid-fifteenth century the verb meant "to blow something away." The meaning "to supply a room with fresh air" dates to the 1660s.

Note the suffix of "ventilator."

The prefix of "hyperventilate" is Greek in origin and means "over, above, to excess."

alō – The word "alumnus" (and "alumna," "alumni," and "alumnae") meant literally "a foster child," someone who was nourished, reared, and taught (*alō*). Medieval lords fostered each other's children. Hence the meaning of "pupil" arose (1640s).

The verb "coalesce" (1540s) comes directly from the Latin *coalescō* (an inchoative form of *cum* and *alō*) meaning "to unite."

A "coalition" (1610s) is "a growing together of parts."

The inchoative form of this verb is also seen in "adolescence," a word derived from the Latin *adolescēns* (growing, near maturity; *ad* = to, toward, and *alō*).

The word "adult" (1650s) is derived from the fourth principal part of *adolescō* (the perfect passive participle shows completed action = "having grown up").

During the 1650s the word "alimony" came into English from the Latin *alimōnium* (nourishment) meaning the same as its base but also "allowance to a wife from a husband's estate."

āmittō – None directly from *āmittō*, but see *mittō* in 1.11 for related derivatives.

corripiō – None

currō – A "cursor" runs all over the computer screen. A "courier" runs if he has important messages to deliver.

A "current" runs through electrical wires. The meaning "prevalent, generally accepted" dates to the 1560s.

The verb "concur" entered English during the early fifteenth century meaning "to collide, clash" from the Latin *concurrō* (to run together, assemble hurriedly, clash, fight). The transferred sense, "to happen at the same time," dates to the 1590s; that of "to agree in opinion" to the 1580s.

The word "concourse" (late fourteenth century) is derived from the Latin *concursus* (a running together). Originally it meant "the flowing of a crowd of people." The American sense of "open space in a built-up place" dates to 1862, e.g., a mall concourse, an airport concourse.

The word "corridor" came into English during the 1590s, derived through the Italian *corridor* (a gallery; literally, a runner) from the Latin *currō*. The meaning of "a long hallway" dates to 1814.

The word "corsair" (1540s) was derived through the Middle French *corsair* and Italian *corsaro* from *cursus* (a running, course). The meaning evolved from "course" to "journey" to "expedition" to "expedition specifically for plunder."

The sense of "currency" (1650s), which originally meant "a condition of flowing," was extended in 1699 by John Locke to "circulation of money."

The Latin word *discursus* meant "a running about in different directions" (*dis* = apart). Its derivative, "discourse" (late fourteenth century), meant "the process of reasoning" from the Latin meaning of *discursus* (conversation). The sense of "formal speech or writing" dates to the 1580s.

The Latin *excursiō* (literally, a running out) originally referred to a military expedition or raid. Its derivative (1570s) kept the military connotation but also meant "a deviation in argument." The sense of "journey" dates to the 1660s.

If Sally <u>incurs</u> any more expenses, she is going to run into heavy debt very quickly (*in* = into, and *currō*).

The word "occur" came into English during the 1530s, derived directly from *occurrō* (to run to meet, run against, present itself, from *ob* = against, toward, and *currō*). Originally the word meant "to meet in argument," but the sense gradually developed from "meet" to "present itself" to "appear" to "happen" (present itself in the course of events). The meaning "to come into one's mind" dates to the 1620s.

A "recurrent" problem occurs again and again (*re* = back, again, and *currō*).

A <u>recourse</u> to excessive force seems more and more prevalent today (from the Latin *recursus* [literally, a running back; hence, a return, retreat]).

The word "succor" (early thirteenth century) is derived from the Latin *succurrō* (*sub* = up to, and *currō*) meaning "to run to help."

dēvastō – The noun "devastation" appears in the mid-1500s coming from the Middle French *dévastation*, from the Late Latin *dēvastātiō* (from the fourth principal part of *dēvastō*). The verb "devastate" (1630s) does not become common until the nineteenth century.

exstinguō – (from *ex* = out, and *stinguō* = to put out [a fire], annihilate, destroy)

An "extinct" species no longer exists. The word is derived from the fourth principal part of *exstinguō*.

iaciō – An "adjective" is "thrown near" or "placed next to" a noun.

A "conjecture" is a conclusion reached by "throwing together facts, inferences, etc." The word appeared in English during the early fifteenth century meaning "an interpretation of signs or omens." The sense of "forming an opinion without proof" dates to the 1530s.

The word "abject" is derived from the Latin *abiciō* (to throw away, abandon, thrown down, degrade) and appeared in English during the early fifteenth century meaning "cast off, rejected." The figurative sense of "downcast, brought low" dates to the 1510s. Today it has assumed a superlative nuance, as in "abject poverty" (= the worst possible) or "abject apology" (the most humble possible).

Someone who looks "dejected" has been "cast down" by some event, e.g., losing a race, failing a math test, etc.

Chapter 17 · 369

When the politician was convicted of bribery, he was <u>ejected</u> from the party (*ex* = out, and *iaciō*; the *a* of the fourth principal part changes to an *e* in compounds, e.g., *obiciō* = *obiectus*).

The word "ejaculate," meaning "to shoot out," is derived through the Latin *iaculum* (javelin) from *iaciō* and the diminutive suffix. Its sense of "to exclaim suddenly" (to throw out [words]) dates to the 1660s.

An "injection" "throws" something "into" the body (early fifteenth century).

In "jet propulsion" air or water is "thrown" in the opposite direction to the motion. The word "jet" appeared in English during the 1690s meaning "a stream of water." The man-made *jet d'eau* (water jet) in Geneva harbor rises over 460 feet and is a spectacular sight.

A "jetty" is the projection of a building "thrown out" past what surrounds it.

The verb "to jut" (mid-fifteenth century) means "to protrude" and is a corrupted spelling of "jet" which became obsolete.

The noun "object" is derived from the Latin *obiciō* (to throw in front of). It appeared in English during the late fourteenth century and meant "a tangible thing." The sense of "not regarded as important" (as in "Money is no object") dates to 1782. The phrase "object lesson" dates to 1831. The verb "object" appeared a little later (around 1400) meaning "to bring forward in opposition" (literally, "to throw against").

The grammatical use of "objective" denotes the goal of the verb.

A "projectile" is thrown forward (*prō* = forward). A "projector" does the "throwing forth" as a movie projector throws the images forward onto a screen. Note the "-tor" suffix.

To "reject" an idea is "to throw it back."

The noun "subject" came into English during the early fourteenth century meaning "a person under the control of another" from *subiciō* (*sub* = under, and *iaciō* = to throw, lay, cast). The meaning "a person or thing to be acted upon" dates to the 1590s. The grammatical sense was first recorded in the 1630s. The verb "subject" appeared during the late fourteenth century, and the adjective "subjective" during the mid-fifteenth century when it "pertained to a political subject." The meaning "existing in the mind" dates to 1707.

The word "trajectory" is derived from the Latin *trāiciō* = "to throw across or over" (from *trāns* = over, across, and *iaciō*). The <u>trajectory</u> of a bullet is a given once a person has fired the gun.

temptō – With its "tentacle" (1762) an octopus "feels" for food (*tentō* is a variant Latin spelling for *temptō* = to feel, try, test).

The politician took a <u>tentative</u> position on the matter until he learned enough to make a definitive stand and vote.

The word "attempt" consists of the Latin *ad* (to) by assimilation and *temptō* and means, literally, "to make a test on" and thus "to make an effort." He <u>attempted</u> to run the Boston Marathon.

The <u>temptation</u> to eat more chocolate severely tested my will power.

facile – See *faciō* in 1.12 and Teaching Tip 1.11.

sine – The word "sinecure" came into English during the 1660s derived from the Medieval Latin *beneficium sine curā* and meant "the gifting of a church position that involved no duties but was remunerated." When the son of the CEO was promoted to the position of vice president without the necessary qualifications, everyone in the company labeled it a <u>sinecure</u>.

370 • Latin for the New Millennium: Teacher's Manual, Level 1

CHAPTER 18 (PP. 311–324)

GRAMMAR IN LANGUAGE FACTS

Future Perfect Tense Active of All Conjugations; Future Perfect Tense of *Sum* and *Possum*; Fifth Declension Nouns

PAGE 311

Standards 1.1, 2.1
RRA 6A

MEMORĀBILE DICTŪ VOCABULARY

fīō, fierī, factus sum (the passive of *faciō*) – to happen, to become

nēmō, nēminis, *m.* – no one

nōscō, noscere, nōvī, nōtum – to get to know (in the perfect tense, "to know")

paene (*adv.*) – almost

TEACHER BY THE WAY

Just as Ovid's *Transformations* is called the *Metamorphōsēs* in Latin, likewise Apuleius's *Transformations* is named the *Metamorphōsēs*.

TEACHING TIP

The image of Cupid and Psyche can generate a prereading discussion of what students think the Latin reading might be about. After reading the adapted Apuleius, students should return to the sculpture and discuss how it connects to what they learned from reading the Latin passage. Teachers are encouraged to have students conduct these discussions in Latin. Alternatively, students could write their responses in Latin and then share those with the class.

TEACHER BY THE WAY

The word "novel" to describe a type of literature was not used before the end of the eighteenth century and was a transliteration of the Italian *novella* (used to describe works like *The Decameron*). A novel emphasizes character rather than plot as can be seen by the titles of early English works like *Robinson Crusoe, Moll Flanders, Pamela,* and *Tom Jones*.

However, the novel was not only developed in eighteenth-century Europe, as can be attested to by *The Tale of Genji* from eleventh-century China. A thousand years earlier, Apuleius had written *The Golden Ass* which, despite its title, is a story about a man (Lucius) and his struggle to find his place in the world. Following an epic tradition, it is a story of growing up (like Achilles in the *Iliad*) and gaining wisdom (like Oedipus or Creon in Sophoclean tragedy). Despite the derivation of the word "novel" from the Latin *novus* meaning "new, strange," one could argue the genre has roots going back as far as the Sumerian Gilgamesh story and that of the Indian *Ramayana*, all of which feature character rather than plot. The primary difference lies in the type of composition: the epics are in poetic form; the novel is written in prose.

TEACHING TIP

Chapter 6A of RRA contains information on Apuleius. The teacher may wish to assign this chapter for reading or review. See p. 201.

PAGE 312
Standards 1.1, 2.1, 3.1, 3.2

TRANSLATION OF LATIN PASSAGE
About Cupid and Psyche

A king had three daughters. Two of them were beautiful, but the third sister was distinguished for beauty. She had the name Psyche. Because of (her) beauty Psyche was worshipped by many men. At last Venus thought that Psyche, who was not a goddess, should not be so keenly worshipped by others. So Venus called her son Cupid and told him: "Son, send an arrow into the heart of Psyche! The girl should be seized by love for a bad man." Cupid went to the girl, had a look at her, and immediately burned with love himself. The girl also could not now love another man. The sisters had husbands, but Psyche did not have a husband. The father felt much grief about the destiny of (his) daughter and sought the gods' advice about this matter. The gods answered to the king in this way: "If you are seeking our advice, listen! Take your daughter to the top of the mountain and leave! When you leave, a beast will come to her." The king suffered, but he took (his) daughter to the mountain. There sleep seized Psyche. After the sleep (i.e., when she woke up) Psyche saw that she was in a beautiful house and understood that she now had a very good husband, who loved her and took care of her. However, he never showed his face to (his) wife. Psyche wanted to see his face and, while the husband was sleeping, she moved a light to (his) face. A drop of oil fell onto the husband's face and awakened him from sleep. The husband was Cupid himself! "Why did you do this?" exclaimed Cupid and immediately disappeared. For a long time Psyche sought him throughout all lands. For Venus had hidden her son. Cupid also wanted to be with Psyche. At last Venus decided to give them help. So Cupid and Psyche will be able to remain together always. The power of love is great.

TEACHER BY THE WAY

This tale has been interpreted as illuminating the mystical connection between the soul and desire, since *psȳchē* means "soul" in Greek, and *cupīdō* "desire" in Latin.

TEACHER BY THE WAY

Some historians call Nerva and Trajan as well as Hadrian, Antoninus Pius, and Marcus Aurelius the "Good Emperors." Following Domitian's assassination, Nerva was acclaimed emperor by the army. His four successors were each adopted as heirs. This period of relative stability saw the addition of territories like northern Britain and Dacia (modern Romania), which extended the empire to its greatest size. These emperors exercised full authority over a centralized administration.

PAGE 313

TEACHER BY THE WAY
In Greek *psychē* means "soul." The words "psyche" and "psychology" are from the same root.

ANSWERS TO COMPREHENSION QUESTIONS
1. Because of her beauty people worshipped Psyche more than Venus.
2. Both fell in love.
3. She was in love with Cupid.
4. Cupid.
5. Psyche looked at Cupid's face after she had been forbidden to do so.
6. Venus allowed Cupid and Psyche to be together and be happy.

TEACHER BY THE WAY
Although the presence of the word *duae* in this Reading Vocabulary does not mark the first time that students have seen a form of the Latin word for "two," this might be an appropriate time to open a discussion on the Indo-European roots of words in many languages. The Latin word *duo* has its origins in the proto-Indo-European word "dwóh." The same root appears in the Sanskrit "dwi," the Urdu and Hindi "dō," and the Persian "dū" or "dō." In Greek it is also "duo." Among the Romance languages the word undergoes only slight spelling changes: in French, it is "deux"; in Spanish it is "dos"; in Italian, "due"; and in Romanian, "doi."

TEACHING TIP
While English derivatives from the asterisked words (i.e., the Vocabulary to Learn) are the topic of Exercise 2 later in this chapter, there are some interesting derivatives from the non-asterisked words. The teacher may choose to discuss these derivatives with the students.

- *cor* – core, courage, record

    Courage is often associated in English with phrases such as "stout-hearted men."

- *gutta* – gout

    The word "gout" refers to a painful inflammation of the joints, especially in the big toe. This disease at one time was attributed to <u>drops</u> of a corrupted humor (formerly considered one of the four elemental fluids in the body).

- *oleum* – found in English compounds as a prefix for substances containing oil: oleomargarine, oleograph, oleoresin

- *sagitta* – sagittal, Sagittarius, sagittate

    The adjective "sagittal" pertains to the suture between the parietal (from the Latin *pariēs*, wall) bones of the skull. Sagittarius is the archer of the Zodiac. "Sagittate" is an adjective used to describe a leaf shaped like an arrow.

Chapter 18 • 373

PAGE 314

Standards 1.1, 3.1, 4.1
Oral Exercise 1; Workbook Exercise 1

ORAL EXERCISE 1

This exercise may be used after the future perfect tense active has been presented.

While looking at the conjugation of *parō* in the future perfect, the students should conjugate the verbs *dūcō* and *dormiō* in the future perfect tense.

dūxerō, dūxeris, dūxerit, dūxerimus, dūxeritis, dūxerint

dormīverō, dormīveris, dormīverit, dormīverimus, dormīveritis, dormīverint

TEACHING TIP

Additional reproducible worksheets, morphology charts, and their associated answer keys, related to this material, are available for download at www.lnm.bolchazy.com.

- Verb Conjugations

PAGE 315

TEACHER BY THE WAY

While most bronze statues from the Roman era were melted down and used for other purposes, this equestrian statue was preserved because people incorrectly identified the rider as Constantine the Great. Because he was reputed to have been converted to Christianity and had legally protected the practice of Christianity, his statue was saved and dramatically positioned on the piazza of the Capitoline Hill.

TEACHER BY THE WAY

The triumphal visit of the Holy Roman emperor Charles V to Rome in 1536 CE was most likely the catalyst for the arrangement of the Capitolium as we now know it. Because the hill lacked proper access, his entourage was forced to proceed around it and did not ascend the hill. Thus, the following year, Pope Paul III sought to redress this and to transfer the statue of Marcus Aurelius from its position near the basilica of St. John Lateran to the Capitoline. He commissioned Michelangelo to create an overall plan for the statue's proper placement.

Michelangelo's genius was a good match for the challenge of designing an appropriate setting for the statue on this hill rich with symbolism and echoes of the triumphs of the Roman Empire. However, the hill had no formal access from the city, its plateau was uneven, and its two buildings were in need of repair. The irregular orientation of the two buildings required a creative solution, which Michelangelo found in the trapezoid. As a counterpart to the Palazzo dei Banderesi, which was renovated as the Palazzo dei Conservatori, Michelangelo proposed the Palazzo Nuovo, which together now house the Capitoline Museum, a marvelous collection of ancient and other art. The three buildings each of different size were envisioned as three walls of an open meeting space visually unified by their grand Corinthian pilasters. The double staircase placed on the facade of the renovated Palazzo Senatorio, which had been built over the ruins of the Roman Tabularium in the Middle Ages, was an architectural innovation. It complements the grand staircase designed to lead from the city to the piazza.

The oval shape of the statue base for the equestrian Marcus Aurelius reflects the oval piazza of Michelangelo's overall plan. Its marble was taken from the Temple of Castor and Pollux. The interlaced star designs of the black-and-white pavement that radiate from the statue at the piazza's center create a dynamic connection with the three buildings framing the piazza. The pavement, however, was not installed until the time of Mussolini.

PAGE 316
Standards 1.1, 1.2
Workbook Exercise 4

▶ EXERCISE 1 ANSWERS

1. lēgerimus — we will have read
2. studuerit — s/he will have studied
3. vēneritis — you (plural) will have come
4. quaesīverint — they will have looked for
5. occultāverint — they will have hidden
6. responderitis — you (plural) will have answered
7. excitāverō — I will have awakened
8. dūxeris — you will have led
9. exstīnxerimus — we will have extinguished
10. iēcerō — I will have thrown
11. corripuerint — they will have seized
12. exclāmāverō — I will have exclaimed
13. neglēxerit — s/he will have neglected
14. dēvastāveritis — you (plural) will have devastated

TEACHER BY THE WAY
The dative and ablative plural of *dea* is *deābus*, an irregular form. This form exists to distinguish it from *deīs*, the dative and ablative plural of *deus*. To distinguish *fīliīs*, the dative and ablative plural of *fīlius*, from the corresponding form of *fīlia*, likewise the form *fīliābus* exists.

PAGE 317

Standards 1.1, 1.2, 4.1
Oral Exercise 2; Workbook Exercise 2

▶ EXERCISE 2 ANSWERS

excitement	excitō	facial	faciēs
question	quaerō	fatal	fātum
occultism	occultō	marital	marītus
exclamation	exclāmō	dormitory	dormiō
cult	colō	dormant	dormiō
culture	colō	paternal	pater
ductile	dūcō		
duchess	dūcō		
duke	dūcō		

▶ EXERCISE 3 ANSWERS

1. cecidērunt — they fell
2. iēceritis — you (plural) will have thrown
3. occultāverās — you had hidden
4. temptāverit — s/he will have tried
5. lēgerāmus — we had read
6. quaesīvistī — you looked for
7. iusserō — I will have ordered
8. steterant — they had stood
9. occīderimus — we will have killed
10. responderint — they will have responded
11. vēnerō — I will have come

ORAL EXERCISE 2

This exercise may be used after Exercise 3.

The teacher should say a form in present active and the student will give the corresponding forms in imperfect and future (tenses formed with the present stem), or the teacher should say a form in perfect active and the student will give the corresponding forms in pluperfect and future perfect (tenses formed with the perfect stem). Use the first person singular only.

Teacher: quaerō   **Student:** quaerēbam, quaeram

Teacher: occultāvī   **Student:** occultāveram, occultāverō

Teacher: dormiō   **Student:** dormiēbam, dormiam

Teacher: dēlēvī   **Student:** dēlēveram, dēlēverō

Teacher: exstinguō   **Student:** exstinguēbam, exstinguam

Teacher: corripuī   **Student:** corripueram, corripuerō

Teacher: currō   **Student:** currēbam, curram

376 • Latin for the New Millennium: Teacher's Manual, Level 1

Teacher: temptāvī   **Student:** temptāveram, temptāverō
Teacher: legō   **Student:** legēbam, legam
Teacher: studuī   **Student:** studueram, studuerō

PAGE 318
Standards 1.1, 1.2, 3.1, 4.1
Oral Exercise 3

▶ EXERCISE 4 ANSWERS

1. potuerint — they were able/could — they will have been able
2. fueris — you are — you will have been
3. fuerō — I was — I will have been
4. fueritis — you (plural) will be — you (plural) will have been
5. potuerimus — we were able/could — we will have been able
6. potuerō — I had been able — I will have been able
7. fuerit — s/he/it was — s/he/it will have been
8. potueris — you were able/could — you will have been able
9. fuerō — I had been — I will have been

ORAL EXERCISE 3

This exercise may be used after the future perfect of sum *and* possum *has been presented.*

The teacher should ask the students to change the following future forms of *possum* and *sum* into future perfect tense, keeping the same person and number.

Teacher: erō   **Student:** fuerō   **Teacher:** poteritis   **Student:** potueritis
Teacher: erunt   **Student:** fuerint   **Teacher:** eritis   **Student:** fueritis
Teacher: poterō   **Student:** potuerō   **Teacher:** poterit   **Student:** potuerit
Teacher: eris   **Student:** fueris   **Teacher:** poterimus   **Student:** potuerimus

TEACHING TIP
Additional reproducible worksheets, morphology charts, and their associated answer keys, related to this material, are available for download at www.lnm.bolchazy.com.

- **Synopsis of *Sum* and *Possum***

PAGE 319

Standards 1.1, 3.1, 4.1
Oral Exercise 4; Workbook Exercises 3, 5

TEACHER BY THE WAY

There is an interesting occurrence of the use of the word *diēs* in the works of the Roman elegiac poet Tibullus. Tibullus says (3.6.32):

Vēnit post multōs ūna serēna diēs.

"After many (days) came one bright day."

In this sentence, the word *diēs* is used twice, each time with a different gender. The subject, *ūna serēna diēs*, is obviously feminine. *Multōs* is a masculine adjective: with it *diēs* is implied.

serēnus, serēna, serēnum – clear, bright

ūnus, ūna, ūnum – one

ORAL EXERCISE 4

This exercise may be used after the fifth declension has been presented.
While looking at the forms of *diēs*, ask the students to decline *faciēs*.

singular: faciēs, faciēī, faciēī, faciem, faciē, faciēs

plural: faciēs, faciērum, faciēbus, faciēs, faciēbus, faciēs

TEACHING TIP

Additional reproducible worksheets, morphology charts, and their associated answer keys, related to this material, are available for download at www.lnm.bolchazy.com.

- **Noun Declensions**

PAGE 320

Standards 1.1, 1.2, 2.1, 4.1, 5.1, 5.2

▶ EXERCISE 5 ANSWERS

1. diēī *or* diē — to/for the happy day *or* by/with the happy day
2. diērum — of long days
3. merīdiēī *or* merīdiē — to/for the wretched midday *or* by/with the wretched midday
4. faciēī *or* faciēs — of the beautiful face *or* to/for the beautiful face *or* beautiful faces
5. diēbus — to/for all days *or* by/with all days
6. diērum — of many days
7. faciem — old face
8. rēs — just things
9. rē — by/with the deadly thing

378 • Latin for the New Millennium: Teacher's Manual, Level 1

TEACHING TIP
After the students have completed Exercise 5 and the correct answers have been given, the teacher may choose to use Exercise 5 again as a review of the fourth declension, which was presented in the last chapter. Replace the words in parentheses in Exercise 5 with the following words and instruct the students to do the exercise again. This may be done in written or oral format.

- 1. (*tumultus*)
- 2. (*domus*)
- 3. (*impetus*)
- 4. (*manus*)
- 5. (*cornū*)
- 6. (*iussus*)
- 7. (*domus*)
- 8. (*manus*)
- 9. (*manus*)

PAGE 321
Standards 1.1, 1.2
Oral Exercise 5; Workbook Exercise 6

▶ EXERCISE 6 ANSWERS
1. If you greet well, you will be greeted well.
2. When she takes a look at the face of the husband, she will understand that he is Cupid.
3. If you wish to love me, I will also love you.
4. If you wake me up before midday, I will do many things.
5. If we hide her/his fates, s/he will not fear.
6. When you seek <a> place for a long time, finally you will observe it.

ORAL EXERCISE 5
This exercise may be used to conclude the chapter or anytime after the future perfect tense active has been presented.

The teacher should say the present tense form of the verb and ask the students to give the corresponding future perfect tense.

Teacher: aestimō	**Student:** aestimāverō
Teacher: conveniō	**Student:** convēnērō
Teacher: ārdeō	**Student:** ārserō
Teacher: audiō	**Student:** audīverō
Teacher: cadō	**Student:** ceciderō
Teacher: dēbeō	**Student:** dēbuerō
Teacher: cōnspiciō	**Student:** cōnspēxerō

Chapter 18 • 379

Teacher: legō	**Student:** lēgerō
Teacher: relinquō	**Student:** relīquerō
Teacher: intellegō	**Student:** intellēxerō
Teacher: dēleō	**Student:** dēlēverō
Teacher: nārrō	**Student:** nārrāverō
Teacher: dēbeō	**Student:** dēbuerō
Teacher: fugiō	**Student:** fūgerō
Teacher: cūrō	**Student:** cūrāverō

PAGE 322

Standards 1.1, 1.2, 4.1
Workbook Exercise 7, Content Questions

▶ EXERCISE 7 ANSWERS

1. Sī fāta nōn timuerimus, vincēmus.
2. Sī uxor faciem marītī cōnspicere cupīverit, eum excitābit.
3. Cum diēs fēlīx vēnerit, omnēs rēs erunt bonae.
4. Cum pater eam ad montem dūxerit, eam ibi relinquere dēbēbit.
5. Cum diū dormīveris, iam merīdiēs erit.
6. Sī dea auxilium dederit, mox marītus et uxor erimus.

TEACHER BY THE WAY

In the earliest theogonies, Eros was born at the same time as Mother Earth, directly from Chaos. He was regarded as one of the creative forces in nature and ensured the continuity of living creatures. Later Greeks associated him with sexual love as well as with devoted friendships. In later genealogies he is the youngest of the gods and his mother is Aphrodite, but the possibilities for his father are Ares, Hermes, and Zeus.

It is of interest that the statue of Augustus from Prima Porta shows a cupid on a dolphin at the emperor's feet, suggesting his descent from Venus. Eros as the baby/child with wings was a product of the art and literature of the Hellenistic era when love was rather romanticized. The beautiful, mischievous god, often looking so innocent, was both capricious and cruel, without a concern for his victim. At his mother's request, he inflamed Dido with love for Aeneas. Cupid puts off his wings and assumes the identity of Iulus, Aeneas's son. Cupid's directions are specific: while they feast, when Dido kisses Cupid, he must overcome her "with secret fire and poison." He joyfully attends to his task. Aphrodite also sent Eros to shoot Medea with an arrow. He appeared in the guise of her aunt Circe to persuade her to give in to her passion for the handsome, persuasive Jason. Helen runs away with Paris and rebukes herself at Troy for her weakness and inability to put aside her passion for Paris. Thus, when Eros prevails, the results are disastrous. Dido kills herself, Helen causes a war, and Medea betrays her father and country. Not even Cupid's own mother was beyond his reach. In a Pompeiian fresco the winged Cupid is poised with his quiver, ready to use his arrows on Mars, who hovers over Venus. In the Cupid and Psyche story he becomes a victim of the passion he inspires in others. He is sent by Venus to Psyche, a competitor in beauty, to make her fall in love with someone ugly. Instead he falls in love with her and she him, but both pay for their disobedience. Cupid abandons her and she must complete the tasks assigned by her mother-in-law. This story does have a happy ending. Zeus gives permission for the marriage and Psyche has a daughter named *Volupta* (Pleasure).

Eros has a very different representation in Roman wall paintings. Pompeiian frescoes portray the cupids as playful little gods engaged in a variety of activities. In the House of the Chaste Lovers, a group of them are recklessly racing in a cart drawn by goats. Elsewhere they are making jewelry, perfumes, and ointments. These playful, nude cupids are common in Renaissance art where they are called *putti*. Their presence usually symbolizes divine or earthly love.

PAGE 323
Standard 1.2
Dictation and Oral Exercises 6, 7

TRANSLATION OF THE LATIN CONVERSATION
Christy: Hello, Mary! How are you now? How is your hand?
Mary: My hand is already well. How are you, Helen and Christy?
Christy: I am well.
Helen: But I'm doing badly.
Christy and Mary: Why?
Helen: Today I have to go to the dentist. I fear the dentist.
Mary: We all ought to go to the dentist twice a year. For teeth should be cleaned. Don't be afraid!
Helen: But my tooth hurts. For this reason I am going to the dentist.
Christy: You, Helen, are accustomed to eat too many cookies. Therefore the doctor will put a filling in your tooth. Perhaps first he will take an X-ray of the tooth.
Helen: I'm afraid of pain.
Christy: The doctor will give you anesthesia. After he gives you anesthesia, then he will use the drill. Don't be afraid! When will you have to go?
Helen: At noon. First, I will eat lunch and cookies.

TEACHING TIP
The teacher may wish to have students research dentistry in ancient times and compare the experience then and now.

DICTATION AND ORAL EXERCISE 6
This exercise may be used to conclude the chapter.
The teacher should dictate two separate sentences in the future tense. The students will then, either orally or in writing, connect them, using the conjunctions *cum* or *sī*, and employing the future perfect tense in the subordinate clause. The adverb *posteā* will have to be omitted.

Teacher: Ad tē veniam. Posteā ūnā legēmus. (cum)
Student: Cum ad tē vēnerō, ūnā legēmus.

Teacher: Comedēs. Posteā dormiēs. (cum)
Student: Cum comēderis, dormiēs.

Teacher: Librum legēs. Posteā dē eō mihi nārrābis. (cum)
Student: Cum librum lēgeris, dē eō mihi nārrābis.

Teacher: Tē rogābō. Mihi respondēbis. (sī)
Student: Sī tē rogāverō, mihi respondēbis.

Teacher: Ad mē veniēs. Domum meam vidēbis. (sī)
Student: Sī ad mē vēneris, domum meam vidēbis.

Teacher: Praemium petent. Eīs dabimus. (sī)
Student: Sī praemium petīverint, eīs dabimus.

Teacher: Fortī animō pugnābitis. Posteā vincētis. (sī)
Student: Sī fortī animō pugnāveritis, vincētis.

Teacher: Diū dormiam. Posteā firmābor. (cum)
Student: Cum diū dormīverō, firmābor.

ORAL EXERCISE 7

This exercise may be used to conclude the chapter.

While looking at the Latin reading passage and the Vocabulary to Learn, the students should answer the following questions. You may skip some of the questions (noted with an asterisk), if you prefer.

Teacher: Erantne fīliae rēgis pulchrae?
Student: Fīliae rēgis erant pulchrae.

Teacher: Quae fīlia erat pulchritūdine praeclāra?
Student: Psȳchē erat pulchritūdine praeclāra.

***Teacher:** Colēbantne virī Psȳchēn?
Student: Virī Psȳchēn colēbant.

Teacher: Cūr virī Psȳchēn colēbant?
Student: Virī Psȳchēn propter eius pulchritūdinem colēbant.

***Teacher:** Quid Venus dē Psȳchē putābat?
Student: Venus putābat Psȳchēn nōn dēbēre tam multum colī.

Teacher: Cūr Venus putābat Psȳchēn nōn dēbēre tam multum colī?
Student: Nam Psȳchē nōn erat dea.

Teacher: Quem Venus vocāvit?
Student: Venus Cupīdinem vocāvit.

Teacher: Quid Cupīdō facere dēbēbat?
Student: Cupīdō dēbēbat sagittam in cor Psȳchēs mittere.

***Teacher:** Sī Cupīdō sagittam in cor puellae mīserit, quid puella sentiet?
Student: Puella malum virum amābit.

Teacher: Mīsitne Cupīdō sagittam in cor Psȳchēs?
Student: Cupīdō ipse amōre Psȳchēs sagittā exārsit.

Teacher: Poteratne posteā Psȳchē alium amāre?
Student: Psȳchē nōn poterat posteā alium amāre.

382 • Latin for the New Millennium: Teacher's Manual, Level 1

*Teacher: Quae fēminae marītōs habēbant?
Student: Sorōrēs Psȳchēs marītōs habēbant.

Teacher: Quid pater Psȳchēs ex deīs petīvit?
Student: Pater Psȳchēs ex deīs cōnsilia petīvit.

Teacher: Quid pater facere dēbēbat?
Student: Pater fīliam ad montem dūcere dēbēbat.

*Teacher: Cum pater fīliam ad montem dūxerit, quid ibi facere dēbēbit?
Student: Pater fīliam ibi relinquere dēbēbit.

*Teacher: Quid pater eā dē rē sentiēbat?
Student: Pater dolēbat.

Teacher: Quid Psȳchē in summō monte exspectābit?
Student: Psȳchē in summō monte beluam exspectābit.

Teacher: Vēnitne belua ad Psȳchēn?
Student: Belua ad Psȳchēn nōn vēnit.

Teacher: Quis ad Psȳchēn vēnit?
Student: Cupīdō ad Psȳchēn vēnit.

Teacher: Quid Cupīdō fēcit?
Student: Cupīdō puellam in domō pulchrā posuit.

Teacher: Amābatne Cupīdō Psȳchēn?
Student: Cupīdō Psȳchēn valdē amābat et cūrābat.

*Teacher: Quam rem uxor numquam vidēre poterat?
Student: Uxor faciem marītī numquam vidēre poterat.

Teacher: Quid Psȳchē cupiēbat?
Student: Psȳchē cupiēbat faciem marītī vidēre.

Teacher: Quid Psȳchē fēcit?
Student: Psȳchē lūmen ad faciem marītī mōvit.

Teacher: Quid intellēxit Psȳchē?
Student: Psȳchē intellēxit marītum esse Cupīdinem.

Teacher: Quid fēcit Cupīdō?
Student: Cupīdō exclāmāvit et ēvanuit.

*Teacher: Cūr Psȳchē marītum vidēre nōn poterat?
Student: Venus Cupīdinem occultābat.

*Teacher: Poteratne Cupīdō sine Psȳchē vīvere?
Student: Cupīdō sine Psȳchē vīvere nōn poterat.

*Teacher: Poteratne Psȳchē sine Cupīdine vīvere?
Student: Psȳchē sine Cupīdine vīvere nōn poterat.

Teacher: Quid tandem Venus dēcrēvit?
Student: Venus tandem dēcrēvit eīs auxilium dare.

Teacher: Erantne Cupīdō et Psȳchē fēlīcēs?
Student: Cupīdō et Psȳchē erant valdē fēlīcēs.

*Teacher: Cūr Cupīdō et Psȳchē erant fēlīcēs?
Student: Propter vim amōris erant fēlīcēs.

PAGE 324

Standard 4.1

DERIVATIVES

dea – See *deus* in 1.10 and Teaching Tips 1.1 and 1.11.

diēs – The word "diurnal" comes from the Latin *diurnālis* (daily). Its antonym is "nocturnal": Owls are <u>nocturnal</u> birds; squirrels are <u>diurnal</u> animals.

The *di* of Latin becomes a *j* in French, as in *jour* (day) and the Old French *jornel* (day's work, daily) from *diurnālis*. The word "journal" came from the French *jornel* into English during the mid-fourteenth century meaning "a book of church services." The meaning "book for inventories and daily accounts" dates to the late fifteenth century, that of "personal diary" to around 1600, that of "daily publication" to 1728.

The word "journey" entered English around 1200 meaning "a defined course of traveling; one's path in life" through the Old French *journee* (a day's work or travel) from the Latin *diurnus* (of one day). The meaning "to travel by land or sea" dates to around 1300. As recently as Johnson (1755) its primary sense was still "the travel of a day."

The word "sojourn," which came into English during the late thirteenth century and meant "to stay temporarily," was derived through the Old French *sojourner* (stay for a time) from the Latin *sub* (under, until) and *diurnus* (of a day).

The word "adjourn" came into English during the early fourteenth century, meaning "assign a day," through the Old French *ajourn* (to meet at an appointed time) from the Latin *ad* (to) and *diurnus* (daily). The literal meaning "to a day" has the sense of "setting a date for a meeting." The meaning "to close a meeting" dates to the early fifteenth century.

The word "diary" (1580s) is derived from the Latin *diāria* (daily allowance of food or pay). The earliest English sense was "a daily record of events." A written record of such events in book form is first attested in Ben Jonson's *Volpone* (1605)

The noun "dial," meaning a sundial or that of a compass, came into English during the early fifteenth century, the verb during the 1650s. It is derived from the medieval Latin *diālis*, which is based on the root *diēs*. The word was probably part of a medieval phrase such as *rota diālis* and gradually evolved to mean "any round plate over which something rotates." The telephone sense dates to 1879.

The word "dismal" (around 1400) is derived from the Latin *diēs malī* (bad days). Through the Middle Ages two days of each month were so designated. The modern sense of "gloomy, dreary" was first recorded in English during the 1590s in reference to sound.

The word "meridian" is derived directly from the Latin *merīdiānus* (midday; *medius* = middle, and *diēs*). Its use on maps is first recorded during the late fourteenth century. The Prime Meridian was assigned to the observatory at Greenwich, England, in 1884 by the International Meridian Conference held in Washington, DC. A visitor to the old observatory today will find a metal band marking that line on the ground and, by putting one foot on each side of it, can stand in both hemispheres at the same time.

For the abbreviations AM and PM, see 1.15 under *ante*.

faciēs – See *faciō* in 1.12

fātum – (from *for, fārī, fātus sum* = to speak)

384 • Latin for the New Millennium: Teacher's Manual, Level 1

The word *fātum* in Latin means "something spoken" (by the gods); hence, "a prediction, that which is ordained." This was the meaning of the derivative "fate" during the late fourteenth century. The related adjective "fatal," also appearing about the same time, came to mean "causing death" by the early fifteenth century.

The adjective "fateful" appeared during the 1710s meaning "prophetic," but around 1800 it took on the sense of "momentous consequences."

The word "fatality" is found first in English during the late fifteenth century derived from *fātālis* (destined, fatal, deadly) and meant "the quality of causing death." The modern meaning, "to denote widespread death resulting from an accident or a disaster," dates to 1840.

marītus – The verb "marry" (around 1300) is derived from the Latin *marītō* (from *marītus* which is of dubious origin [OLD]) through the Old French *marier*.

The word "marital" (from the Latin *marītālis* = of a marriage) appeared in English around 1600.

merīdiēs – See above under *diēs*.

pater – A <u>patrilineal</u> society reckons descent through the father; a <u>patriarchal</u> society is ruled by men (fathers). See 1.16 under *māter* for the antonyms.

The word "patron" (around 1300), meaning "a protector, lord-master," was derived from the Latin *patrōnus* (protector, advocate). The sense of "one who advances a cause by wealth or power" dates to the late fourteenth century, that of "a regular customer" to around 1600.

The word "patronage" (late fourteenth century), meaning "the right of presenting a church benefice to a qualified person," was also derived from *patrōnus*. The general meaning, "the power to give jobs or favors," dates to 1769, that of "regular business of customers" to 1804. The suffix "-age" comes through the French from the Latin *āticus* (or shortened to *-cus*) and means "pertaining to."

The word "patronize" came into English during the 1580s meaning simply "to act as a patron." The pejorative slant, "to treat in a condescending way," dates to 1797.

Although "patrimony" looks like an antonym of "matrimony," the sense differs. "Matrimony" means "marriage," "patrimony" (mid-fourteenth century) refers to property, an estate, or an inheritance handed down from a father. It is derived from the Latin *patrimōnium*.

The word "patrician" (mid-fourteenth century) referred originally to the members of the ancient Roman noble order. Roman senators were called *patrēs conscriptī* (originally *patrēs et conscriptī* to denote the two social classes from which the senators were drawn, i.e., nobles, and everyone else!). From this came the sense of "fatherly dignity." The word was applied to noble citizens in medieval Italy and Germany, and in England from the 1610s. From this evolved the general meaning of "nobleman, aristocrat" in the 1630s.

The name "Patrick" is derived from the Latin *patricius* and was found originally in Scotland and northern England. It became a popular name in Ireland only after 1600.

The word "paternal" (early fifteenth century) is derived from the Latin *paternus* (of a father): Sam's bachelor neighbor had <u>paternal</u> feelings toward his children and strongly encouraged them in their educational endeavors.

The word "patter" appeared in English around 1400 meaning "to talk rapidly." It was a shortened form of *pater noster* (the first words of the Lord's Prayer in Latin) and originally referred to "mumbling prayers quickly."

See also Teaching Tip 1.3.

rēs – Many of the derivatives listed come from the Latin *rēs* (which in Latin usually takes its meaning from the context and rarely means "thing") through the Late Latin *reālis* (actual, real).

The word "republic" is derived from the Latin *rēs pūblica* (the state; literally, the public business).

The word "reality" came into English during the 1540s meaning "real possession." In the 1660s it came to mean "real estate."

The word "reality" (1540s) also came to mean "sincerity" sometime during the seventeenth and eighteenth centuries.

The verb "realize" (1610s) originally meant "to bring into existence," from the French *realizer* (to make real). The sense "to understand, make real in the mind" dates to 1775, that of "to obtain" to 1753. The gambler sought to realize a fortune at the track.

See also Teaching Tip 1.3.

somnus – A "somnambulist" (*somnus*, and *ambulō* = to walk) is a "sleepwalker." The word dates to 1747.

Ambien is a "somniferous" drug (from *somnus*, and *ferō* = to bring; the Latin *somnifer* could mean "fatal"), which brings or induces sleep. A synonym is "somnific" (from *somnus*, and *faciō* = to make), which is a less common word used in referring to narcotics.

A "somniloquist" talks in her sleep (*somnus*, and *loquor* = to talk).

The boring program made me <u>somnolent</u> (from the Latin *somnolentus* = drowsy).

"Somnus" is the Roman god of sleep.

uxor – The man who killed his wife was charged with <u>uxoricide</u>.

An "uxorious" man is foolishly or excessively fond of his wife. The word can also indicate a man who is overly submissive to his wife. Note the "-ous" suffix. The word dates to the 1590s.

colō – The derivatives "colonial" and "colonize" come from *colō*; the rest of those in the list have a "cult" base and come from the fourth principal part of that verb.

The adjective "colonial" appeared in English during 1756 derived through the Latin *colonia* (settlement) from *colō* (to till, inhabit, worship). It began to mean "Americans during colonial times" in 1776. The noun meaning "inhabitant of a colony" dates to 1865. The verb "colonize" dates to the 1620s. Both derivatives are related to "colony," a word which appeared in English during the late fourteenth century meaning "an ancient Roman settlement outside Italy." (The city of Cologne in Germany derives its name from *Colōnia Agrippīna*). The modern application dates to the 1540s.

"Agriculture" (mid-fifteenth century) means "the tilling of a field."

"Horticulture" (1670s) literally means "the tilling of a garden." It is a fabricated word probably based on the model of "agriculture." (Dorothy Parker used it in a famous pun: "You can lead a horticulture, but you can't make her think.")

Notice the "-tor" suffix of "cultivator" (the person or machine who does the tilling).

The word "culture" appeared during the mid-fifteenth century meaning "the tilling of land" (from the Latin *cultūra* = agriculture) but also "care of the mind." That figurative sense of "cultivation through education" surfaced around 1500; that of "the intellectual side of civilization" dates to 1805; and that of "the collective customs and achievements of a people" to 1867.

The word "cult" (1610s) takes its meaning of "worship" directly from *colō*. It also had the sense of "a particular form of worship." The word became rare after the seventeenth century but was revived during the mid-nineteenth century with reference to "ancient or primitive rituals."

386 • Latin for the New Millennium: Teacher's Manual, Level 1

dormiō – Mt. Vesuvius may go "dormant" for many years, but it wakes up periodically to cause a lot of death and destruction, e.g., (selectively) CE 79, 203, 472, 512, etc., and in modern times 1631 (the largest since 472 and 512), 1794, 1906, 1944. In the early 1980s major land shifts occurred causing the relocation of 36,000 people, but there have been no signs of volcanic unrest since 1996 (it is "dormant").

A "dormer" is a window of "a sleeping room" (1590s). Today it refers to a vertical upstairs window (where bedrooms still are usually located) which juts out from a sloping roof.

The word "dormitory" (mid-fifteenth century) is derived from the Latin *dormītōrius* (designed or used for sleeping; the neuter noun, *dormītōrium* = a bedroom).

excitō – (from *ex* = out, and *cieō* = move, rouse)

The word "excite" (mid-fourteenth century) is derived directly from the Latin verb, which is based on the fourth principal part of *cieō* (*citus*). It meant, as in Latin, "to move, stir up, instigate." The main modern sense of "to agitate emotionally" dates to 1821.

The noun "excitement" appeared during the early fifteenth century meaning "encouragement." The meaning "condition of mental and emotional agitation" is first attested in 1846.

exclāmō – (from *ex* = out, and *clāmō* = cry, shout, call)

The verb "exclaim" dates to the 1560s; its spelling was influenced by the word "claim" (from *clāmō*). The long vowel in *clāmō* was retained in English by adding an *i* to form a diphthong.

The noun "exclamation" preceded the verb into the English language (late fourteenth century) derived from the Latin *exclāmātiō*. The punctuation symbol, now called an "exclamation point" (from 1824) or "exclamation mark" (from 1926), was also called a "shriek-mark" (1864), certainly a graphic name!

The adjective "exclamatory" dates to the 1590s.

occultō – (from *occulō*; *ob* = over, against, in front of, for the sake of [by assimilation]; and *cēlō* = to hide, keep secret; the *–to* suffix is intensive or iterative)

The word "occult" is derived directly from the fourth principal part of *occulere* and came into English during the 1530s meaning "secret, not divulged." The meaning "not apprehended by the mind, beyond the range of understanding" (OED) appears about ten years later. The association with magic, alchemy, astrology, etc., dates to the 1630s.

The word "occultation" (early fifteenth century) meant "disguise or concealment of identity." Today it is used in astronomy to describe the passing of one celestial body in front of another, thus "hiding" it, e.g., the moon coming between an observer on Earth and a star or planet.

quaerō – The word "query" is derived from *quaere*, the imperative of *quaerō*. The noun dates to the 1530s, the verb to the 1650s.

The word "inquire" is derived from the Latin *inquirō* (to search for, inquire into) through the Old French *enquerre*, which accounts for the alternate spelling (*enquire*) which still exists today. The French influence was retained during the thirteenth century, but the word was respelled during the fourteenth century on the model of the original Latin.

The word "inquest" (late thirteenth century) was originally spelled *an-queste* (through the Old French *enqueste*) and meant "legal inquiry." It was derived from *in* and the fourth principal part of *quaerō* (*quaesītum*) which means literally "having been searched for, inquired into."

Chapter 18 • 387

The noun "quest" appeared around 1300 and at first meant "an inquest," but soon (early fourteenth century) came to mean "a search for something." The romantic sense of "adventure undertaken by a knight" dates to the same time period.

The word "perquisite" is derived from the Latin *perquīrō* meaning "to inquire after, examine carefully." The prefix is an intensive meaning "thoroughly." In the mid-fifteenth century the word meant "property acquired other than by inheritance." The general meaning "fee or profit on top of general wages" dates to the 1560s. The shortened and altered form of this word, "perk," dates to 1869 (not to be confused with the verb form from "percolate"). The spelling change to an *i* from *ae* in the base occurs in Latin due to a rule involving unaccented syllables in compounds.

The word "acquisition" (late fourteenth century) from the Latin *acquīrō* (to get in addition, accumulate; from *ad*, and *quaerō*) also exemplifies this spelling rule.

The verb "acquire" appeared in English during the mid-fifteenth century spelled *acqueren* but was reborrowed in its current form from the Latin *acquīrō* around 1600.

The prefix of "conquer" is an intensive. The word came into English around 1200 and derives from the Latin *conquīrō* (to search out, hunt, collect) through the Old French *conquerre* (to defeat; a meaning which evolved from the idea that "a strong search to collect" resulted in "winning").

The noun "conquest" (early fourteenth century) is derived, with spelling alterations, from the fourth principal part of *conquīrō* (*conquisītum*) through the Old French *conquest* (acquisition).

The adjective "exquisite" (early fifteenth century) is derived from the fourth principal part of the Latin *exquīrō* (*ex* = out, and *quaerō*; to search out, investigate) which thus meant "well thought out, choice." The main modern sense of "delightful excellence" dates to 1579.

The noun "question" (early thirteenth century) derived from the noun *quaestiō* (a seeking, inquiry) and originally meant "a philosophical or theological problem." Early in the fourteenth century it came to mean "an utterance meant to elicit an answer or discussion." The punctuation term "question mark" dates to 1849. The word's use as a verb began during the late fifteenth century.

The verb "require" (late fourteenth century) meant "to ask a question" derived through the Old French *requerre* (to seek, beg, ask, demand) from the Latin *requīrō* (to search for, ask, inquire after). The prefix means "again, back" and acts as an intensive. The original meaning of this word has been taken over by "request." The sense of "demand" dates to 1751, from the fourteenth century notion of "to ask as a right."

A "prerequisite" is something "demanded or required in advance." The prefix is derived from the Latin *prae* (before).

ita – None. This word is also listed in 1.11 with another meaning.

multum – See *multus* in 1.6.

tam – None

post – See *postea* in 1.1.

cum – See *cum* in 1.3 and Teaching Tip 1.7.

sī – None

388 • Latin for the New Millennium: Teacher's Manual, Level 1

REVIEW 6: CHAPTERS 16–18
(PP. 325–340)

PAGE 325

TEACHING TIP

Another way to conduct a fun vocabulary review is to play a combination of drawing and charades with the unit vocabulary words.

- Instruct the students to review individually the words on pp. 325–326 (SE) for a short amount of time.

- Meanwhile the teacher needs to write each word in the vocabulary review on an index card or a piece of paper. The teacher may choose whether to write the first Latin word of the entry or the English meaning of the entry.

- Divide the class into two groups and instruct each group to sit together on one side of the room. It is often best to move the tables and chairs to the side of the room to make room for movement and excitement.

- Toss a coin to see which group goes first.

- One person from the first group draws a card from the deck of index cards that the teacher has written the word on. That person may draw a picture of what is written on the index card or may act out the word but is not to show the card to his group members. For some words it may be necessary for the student both to draw a picture and to act something out. If what is written on the card is shown to the group members whether on purpose or by accident, the card is put back into the deck and the other group draws a new card from the deck.

- The group has thirty seconds to guess what the word is. If the teacher wrote the word in English, the group must give the full Latin entry within thirty seconds to earn one point. If the teacher wrote the word in Latin, the group must give the remainder of the Latin entry and its English meaning.

- If the first group does not guess the right word or give the correct entry information within thirty seconds, the group gets no points but has to give the card to one person from the other group who then has thirty seconds to draw/act out the word so that his group can guess the meaning and earn the point.

- Play continues in this way until all the cards have been selected or the teacher calls time.

PAGE 326

Standards 1.1, 1.2

▶ EXERCISE 1 ANSWERS

Perfect active of *occultō:*

	Singular		**Plural**	
First person	occultāvī	I hid, did hide, have hidden	occultāvimus	we hid, did hide, have hidden
Second person	occultāvistī	you hid, did hide, have hidden	occultāvistis	you hid, did hide, have hidden
Third person	occultāvit	s/he/it hid, did hide, has hidden	occultāvērunt	they hid, did hide, have hidden

Perfect active of *studeō:*

	Singular		**Plural**	
First person	studuī	I studied, did study, have studied	studuimus	we studied, did study, have studied
Second person	studuistī	you studied, did study, have studied	studuistis	you studied, did study, have studied
Third person	studuit	s/he/it studied, did study, has studied	studuērunt	they studied, did study, have studied

Perfect active of *opprimō:*

	Singular		**Plural**	
First person	oppressī	I oppressed, did oppress, have oppressed	oppressimus	we oppressed, did oppress, have oppressed
Second person	oppressistī	you oppressed, did oppress, have oppressed	oppressistis	you oppressed, did oppress, have oppressed
Third person	oppressit	s/he/it oppressed, did oppress, has oppressed	oppressērunt	they oppressed, did oppress, have oppressed

Perfect active of *dormiō:*

	Singular		**Plural**	
First person	dormīvī	I slept, did sleep, have slept	dormīvimus	we slept, did sleep, have slept
Second person	dormīvistī	you slept, did sleep, have slept	dormīvistis	you slept, did sleep, have slept
Third person	dormīvit	s/he/it slept, did sleep, has slept	dormīvērunt	they slept, did sleep, have slept

390 • Latin for the New Millennium: Teacher's Manual, Level 1

Perfect active of *iaciō*:

	Singular		Plural	
First person	iēcī	I threw, did throw, have thrown	iēcimus	we threw, did throw, have thrown
Second person	iēcistī	you threw, did throw, have thrown	iēcistis	you threw, did throw, have thrown
Third person	iēcit	s/he/it threw, did throw, has thrown	iēcērunt	they threw, did throw, have thrown

▶ EXERCISE 2 ANSWERS

Pluperfect active of *temptō*:

	Singular		Plural	
First person	temptāveram	I had tried	temptāverāmus	we had tried
Second person	temptāverās	you had tried	temptāverātis	you (plural) had tried
Third person	temptāverat	s/he/it had tried	temptāverant	they had tried

▶ EXERCISE 3 ANSWERS

Future perfect active of *alō*:

	Singular		Plural	
First person	aluerō	I will/shall have fed	aluerimus	we will/shall have fed
Second person	alueris	you will have fed	alueritis	you (plural) will have fed
Third person	aluerit	s/he/it will have fed	aluerint	they will have fed

PAGE 327

Standards 1.1, 1.2

TEACHER BY THE WAY

Pliny the Elder was the commander of the imperial navy base at Misenum, which was stationed there to protect the Bay of Naples, an important commercial center of the Roman Empire.

In Naples the recent construction of a subway line has involved substantial excavation uncovering many Roman ruins including two Roman boats at the bed of the ancient harbor.

▶ EXERCISE 4 ANSWERS

1. corripuī, corripueram, corripuerō
2. cucurrī, cucurreram, cucurrerō
3. dūxī, dūxeram, dūxerō
4. dēvastāvī, dēvastāveram, dēvastāverō
5. excitāvī, excitāveram, excitāverō
6. exclāmāvī, exclāmāveram, exclāmāverō
7. exstīnxī, exstīnxeram, exstīnxerō
8. lēgī, lēgeram, lēgerō
9. quaesīvī, quaesīveram, quaesīverō

► EXERCISE 5 ANSWERS

	Singular	Plural
Nominative	manus longa	manūs longae
Genitive	manūs longae	manuum longārum
Dative	manuī longae	manibus longīs
Accusative	manum longam	manūs longās
Ablative	manū longā	manibus longīs
Vocative	manus longa	manūs longae

	Singular	Plural
Nominative	spēs fēlīx	spēs fēlīcēs
Genitive	speī fēlīcis	spērum fēlīcium
Dative	speī fēlīcī	spēbus fēlīcibus
Accusative	spem fēlīcem	spēs fēlīcēs
Ablative	spē fēlīcī	spēbus fēlīcibus
Vocative	spēs fēlīx	spēs fēlīcēs

EXERCISE 6 ANSWERS

1. Sī ignem cōnspexeris, fuge!
2. Incendium omnēs domūs corripuerat.
3. Sī fugere potueris, servāberis.
4. Suntne tibi vīrēs? Poterisne currere?
5. Ignis, fūmus, cinerēs ex monte vēnērunt et lītus dēvastāvērunt.
6. Multīs hominibus domūs iam nōn erant. Eī omnia āmīserant.
7. "Fāta sunt crūdēlia!" hominēs exclāmāvērunt.

PAGE 328
Standards 1.1, 1.2

► EXERCISE 7 ANSWERS

1. Avunculus causam nūbis inūsitātae intellegere cupīvit.
   The uncle wanted to understand the cause of the unusual cloud.

2. Nauta epistulam fēminae, quae prope montem Vesuvium habitābat, avunculō dedit.
   The sailor gave to the uncle a letter of a woman who lived near Mt. Vesuvius.

3. Fēmina perīculum timēbat et auxilium petēbat.
   The woman was afraid of the danger and she was seeking help.

4. Avunculus fēminam servāre nōn potuit; nam fūmus cinerēsque eam ūnā cum aliīs oppressērunt.
   The uncle could not save the woman; for smoke and ashes oppressed her together with other people.

5. Incendium ex tabernīs, in quibus erant mercimōnia, initium cēpit.
   The fire took <its> beginning from the shops, in which there was merchandise.

392 • Latin for the New Millennium: Teacher's Manual, Level 1

6. Nerō fortasse fuit causa incendiī.
   Nero perhaps was the cause of the fire.

7. Cupīdō amōre Psȳchēs ārsit.
   Cupid burned with love for Psyche.

8. Tandem Cupīdō et Psȳchē ūnā fēlīcēs esse poterant.
   At last Cupid and Psyche could be happy together.

TEACHING TIP

After Exercise 7 has been completed by the students and the correct answers have been given, the teacher may wish to extend this comprehension activity in the following manner.

- Divide the class into groups of five students.
- Assign one person in each group to be *Plīnius* (*avunculus*), one to be the *fēmina*, one to be the *nauta*, one to be Nero, and one to represent the *incendium*.
- Instruct each group to determine in what chronological order sentences 1–6 might have happened. There may be different interpretations of the order in which these events might have occurred. Then each person in the group needs to decide how to act out the sentence that belongs to him/her and to change the sentence to reflect that. When saying the sentence aloud in Latin at the same time that the acting is occurring, the first person of the verb will be used.
- Each group will perform their version of these six sentences and say the Latin aloud for the rest of the group.
- Thus the teacher might hear a group perform this order of events.

    Nerō: *Fortasse fuī causa incendiī.*

    Incendium: *Ex tabernīs, in quibus erant mercimōnia, initium cēpī.*

    Fēmina: *Perīculum timēbam et auxilium petēbam.*

    Nauta: *Epistulam fēminae, quae prope montem Vesuvium habitābat, avunculō dedī.*

    Avunculus: *Causam nūbis inūsitātae intellegere cupīvī.*

    Avunculus: *Fēminam servāre nōn potuī; nam fūmus cinerēsque eam ūnā cum aliīs oppressērunt.*

PAGE 329

TEACHER BY THE WAY

In her search for Cupid, Psyche's appeals for help were rejected by Ceres and Juno, who did not wish to offend Venus. Psyche decided to ask Venus herself for assistance. Glad for the opportunity to take revenge and humiliate Psyche, Venus imposed four impossible tasks upon her. With the help of others, she completed the tasks. They are listed below for the teacher's convenience.

- Sort an immeasurable pile of grain by nightfall: an army of ants helped her.
- Gather golden fleece from wild sheep: whispering reeds told her to wait until they sleep at night and then gather the wool caught on thorns and branches.

- Bring a flask of water from the Styx and Cocytus: an eagle helped her.
- Obtain a box of beauty ointment from Proserpina in the underworld: a tower, which she climbed in order to kill herself, gave her directions and instructions regarding how to survive a visit to the underworld. First Psyche went to the Peloponnese where a cavern was located that led to the underworld. She brought with her two obols and cakes to twice satisfy the greedy Charon and Cerberus. Upon arrival, Proserpina offered Psyche food and a chair. Forewarned, Psyche only ate some bread and sat on the floor. Mission accomplished, she departed the kingdom of the dead.

Wanting to beautify herself for Cupid, Psyche opened the box and fell into a deep sleep. Cupid healed from his wound, flew to her, awakened Psyche, put the beauty back in the box, and told her to bring it to Venus. The two lovers were reunited, reconciliation with Venus followed, and the wedding was celebrated on Mt. Olympus.

CONSIDERING THE CLASSICAL GODS

PAGE 330

Standards 2.1, 2.2, 3.1, 3.2
ODF 4.2

TEACHER BY THE WAY
Bacchus might have been called Liber because *līber* means "free" and might indicate freeing troubled human minds from their cares. Because of the orgiastic character of Bacchic rites, in 186 BCE the Roman Senate banned the celebration of the Bacchanalia.

TEACHER BY THE WAY
Minerva, coming from Jupiter's head, is goddess of intelligence and wisdom, while Bacchus comes from a lower part of the body, and he is god of emotions and feelings.

COMPREHENSION QUESTIONS AND ANSWERS FOR PAGES 330–331 (SE)
Reproducible versions of the questions alone are available at **www.lnm.bolchazy.com**.

1. How did Juno's jealousy affect Semele's relationship with Jupiter?

   Juno convinced Semele to ask Jupiter to reveal himself to her with a display of his true divine power. Jupiter complied and when he appeared with his thunderbolt and lightning, mortal Semele was consumed by fire.

2. The circumstances of Bacchus's birth are similar to those of what other god? Explain.

   Minerva shares a similar birth to that of Bacchus. In both cases, Jupiter carried and delivered the child himself. He swallowed Metis pregnant with Minerva and sewed Bacchus, whose mother Semele had been killed, into his thigh.

3. In what ways is Bacchus the antithesis of Apollo?

   Bacchus represents the irrational, immoderate, and excessive, which are the direct opposite of what Apollo represents—the rational, moderate, and harmonious.

4. Describe Bacchus's followers.

   Bacchus's followers include female worshippers called bacchants or maenads who run wild in the forest singing, dancing, and producing wine by scratching the earth in their inspired state; satyrs, little men with horns and a tail; sileni, older satyrs; and Pan, god of the woods, shepherds, and fertility.

5. Explain the origin of the English word "panic."

   "Panic" is derived from the god Pan who, as god of the woods, would surprise humans in the forest and cause terror in them.

PAGE 331

TEACHER BY THE WAY

In Christian times, the god Pan was sometimes identified with Satan.

TEACHER BY THE WAY

Dionysus and Pentheus were cousins: their mothers, Semele and Agave, were sisters. All of Dionysus's aunts spread rumors saying Semele was bedded by a mortal, not by a god, and refused to accept his divinity. Such calumny and disbelief assured their future punishment by Dionysus. After he had introduced all of Asia to his cult, alternately convincing people or punishing them for refusing to accept his worship, he decided to go to Thebes, his mother's homeland, to invite the people to join his religion. Assuming the form of a handsome young man, he visits his cousin Pentheus, the king of Thebes, who is vehemently trying to prevent the spread of the Bacchic rites. He imprisoned the maenads who had come with Dionysus, but they were miraculously freed. Warned by his grandfather Cadmus and the prophet Tiresias, who had converted to the rite, not to mock the gods or resist their will, Pentheus dismisses their advice and ignores Dionysus's attempts to persuade him otherwise. Instead, he arrogantly imprisons him. But he too miraculously escapes. The Theban women, dressed in fawn skins and wreathed in ivy with thyrsus in hand, had gone to the mountain to celebrate. Then the god convinces his cousin to witness for himself their licentiousness. Disguised as a woman, Pentheus follows the celebrants and climbs a tree to spy on their revelry. When they spot him, thinking he is a lion, the bacchants/maenads in their frenzy shake the tree and uproot it, fall upon Pentheus, and rip him to pieces. His own mother proudly puts his head on the thyrsus (a pole entwined with ivy, topped with a pine cone) and returns to the city jubilantly showing off the "lion" she has killed. Prompted by her father Cadmus, Agave gradually comes to her senses and faces the horror of her deed. Dionysus appears to pronounce that her punishment would be exile to save Thebes from pollution. Cadmus asks the god to be merciful but Dionysus reminds him that "a god insulted cannot forgive." Once his cult was established throughout Greece, he went to the underworld and brought his mother with him to Mt. Olympus, renaming her Thyone.

TEACHING TIP

For the complete story of this tragedy, the teacher might wish to encourage the students to read Euripides's *Bacchae* in English.

PAGE 332
Standards 1.1, 2.1

TEACHER BY THE WAY
Bacchus is often depicted with a tiger because one of his famous feats was the conquest of India whence the tiger came.

TRANSLATION OF READING PASSAGE
Pan was the god of fields and woods. Pan always looked for the nymph Syrinx. For from the time when he had seen Syrinx, he burned with love, but Syrinx did not love Pan. Pan used to say to Syrinx: "If you are mine, I will give you beautiful gifts." The nymph, however, did not desire to have gifts and <did not desire> to be loved by the god and fled. Pan also ran after her and tried to seize her. At last the nymph arrived at a brook and entered the brook. The gods saved Syrinx and turned her into a reed. Then Pan prepared a musical instrument from the reed with which musical instrument he afterward played.

TEACHER BY THE WAY
Pan's parentage is disputed but because he was an ancient Arcadian shepherd god, the likely father may be Hermes, who was also associated with Arcadia. His bearded face, hairy body, and cloven feet scared his mother. Hermes, on the other hand, wanted to show him off to the Olympians. Everyone was delighted with him, especially Dionysus among whose "groupies" Pan frequently appears. Pan liked to spend his time resting or playing his pipes (*sȳrinx*). Anyone who disturbed him was greeted with a frightening shout that caused sudden panic (a word derived from his name). Thus, shepherds dared not play their pipes at noon in Arcadia. Chasing nymphs was another favorite pastime. His cult reached Greece in the fifth century BCE where a cave shrine was erected to him on the Acropolis by the Athenians. He is the only god whose death was announced. A sailor en route to Italy heard a voice telling him to make it known that "the great god Pan is dead." The sailor complied and there was great mourning for the god. Though this story was told by Plutarch in the first century CE, shrines, caves, and mountains sacred to Pan were still honored a century later. The Romans identified Pan with Faunus, a god of herdsmen, and Silvanus, a god of woodlands.

CONNECTING WITH THE ANCIENT WORLD

PAGE 333
Standards 2.1, 2.2, 3.2, 4.2

TEACHING TIP
While this reading selection centers upon the topic of the gladiatorial games, the opening quote from Juvenal, "*pānem et circēnsēs*," allows the teacher to open a discussion on another game, the one held in the Circus, namely chariot racing. The teacher may also choose to ask students to find the Circus Maximus on the map on p. 233 (SE).

TEACHING TIP
The teacher may wish to point out, using the picture of the Colosseum on this page, that each level of the Colosseum featured a different type of column.

TEACHER BY THE WAY
The Colosseum covered the ornamental lake that was part of Nero's *Domus Aurea* (Golden House), which he built for himself after the 64 CE fire. At the entrance of this palace stood a colossal bronze statue of Nero, which later gave its name to the Colosseum.

Since construction was started under the emperor Vespasian and completed by his son Titus, it was then called the Flavian amphitheatre. The Flavian emperors built the amphitheatre to reward the people, and they also changed the statue of Nero to one of Apollo with the rays of the sun crowning his head.

COMPREHENSION QUESTIONS AND ANSWERS FOR PAGES 333–335 (SE)
Reproducible versions of the questions alone are available at **www.lnm.bolchazy.com**.

1. In what ways was life in imperial Rome different from life in republican times?

   Romans of the early Republic are said to have been industrious and self-disciplined. Because Romans in the imperial period did not have much of a stake in Rome's wealth and power, they craved immediate pleasures, *pānem et circēnsēs*, overeating, and the bloody spectacles of the amphitheatre.

2. Who comprised the ranks of the gladiators?

   The ranks of the gladiators contained slaves, prisoners of war, convicted criminals, and occasionally people of free birth who chose this occupation.

3. Not all gladiators fought to their death. Explain.

   After acknowledging his defeat, a gladiator might be spared death if the crowd shouted "*mitte*," set him free," and the emperor would signify his agreement by directing his thumb downward. (The emperor's "thumbs up" is thought to mean that the gladiator would be killed.)

4. Define *naumachia*.

   A *naumachia* was a mock naval battle for which an amphitheatre or area near a water supply was flooded to accommodate the ships.

398 • Latin for the New Millennium: Teacher's Manual, Level 1

PAGE 334

TEACHER BY THE WAY

The Colosseum stands as an icon immediately recognized as a Roman building. Through the centuries, it has also stood as the quintessential image of ancient Rome and her civilization. The Venerable Bede (d. 735 CE), whom students will encounter in Level 2, recognized the power of this symbol of Rome. Though he never left England, Bede proclaims, "As long as the Colosseum stands, Rome too will stand; when the Colosseum falls, Rome too will fall; when Rome falls, the world will fall as well." Pieter Bruegel's famous painting *The Tower of Babel* (1563 CE) used the Colosseum as the model for his depiction of the tower.

Over the centuries, the Colosseum has served as a quarry, a residence, a cow pasture, and more recently as a Christian shrine as well as an archaeological site. With the loss of the Roman recipe for concrete, marble taken from Roman buildings was melted to form lime, which was used as cement. After the fall of Rome, buildings fell into disuse and were often used for other purposes. According to tradition, though not fully documented, the Colosseum was believed to be the site of persecution and martyrdom. Nonetheless, this association with the early Christian martyrs saved the structure from ongoing pillage. When the Pope processes in the Stations of the Cross on Good Friday, he stops at the Colosseum.

As much as we immediately associate the amphitheatre with the Colosseum, and therefore Rome, its ancestors are structures built in the second century BCE, in Campania, south of Latium. Such examples include Cumae (first century BCE), Pompeii (ca. 80 BCE), and Capua (first century BCE) where Spartacus assembled his fellow slaves in revolt. The Campanians also developed the system of covering the open-air amphitheatre with an awning, known as a *vēlārium*. At the Colosseum, Roman sailors were assigned to control the *vēlārium*. One can still see behind the Colosseum the blocks to which the ropes for the awning were tied.

TEACHING TIP

Ask students to think of modern structures that echo the architecture of the Colosseum. Examples of sports facilities like Chicago's Soldier Field should come to mind. Have students explain how the example they have chosen is similar.

Ask students to think of modern activities that parallel the animal combats of Roman times. Some students might suggest the bearbaiting of Elizabethan England while others might cite the rodeo. Others may have experienced bullfighting in Mexico, Portugal, Spain, or Provence. Note that the Roman amphitheatres of Arles and Nimes in Provence continue to serve as performance venues for bullfighting.

PAGE 335
Standards 1.1, 1.2

TEACHER BY THE WAY
Frontier provinces supplied the demand for exotic animals used in wild beast fights in the amphitheatre. Aediles were in charge of the games and spent lavish amounts of money to entertain the populace, increase popularity, and gain votes. Julius Caesar borrowed money from the very wealthy Crassus to put on such shows frequently. Preparation and maintenance was also costly. Monies were needed for hunters and trappers, keepers, trainers, and veterinarians. Facilities for the animals were necessary. Many of the exotic animals had a short life span because of the climate differences and diseases that they caught in the new environment. From Africa and Asia came parrots, ostriches, monkeys, lynxes, tigers, leopards, elephants, giraffes, and rhinos, to name a few. The gruesome animal fights were originally performed in the morning. Bears were pitted against bulls, and elephants against rhinos. Less bloody were shows of animals performing to music. Parades of the animals preceded the beast fights.

Another form of entertainment was the *naumachia* or mock naval battle. Recently discovered water channels indicate that this event took place in the amphitheatre. Artificial lakes were also created. The best-known site was on the right bank of the Tiber. Caesar dug one in 46 BCE, and Augustus had a permanent basin built in 2 BCE. Some later emperors did the same. Historical battles, such as that at Actium, were simulated, as bloody as the real event. Prisoners of war and criminals often manned the ships.

EXPLORING ROMAN DISASTERS

PAGE 336
Standards 2.1, 3.1, 3.2

COMPREHENSION QUESTIONS AND ANSWERS FOR PAGES 336–339 (SE)
Reproducible versions of the questions alone are available at **www.lnm.bolchazy.com**.

1. Why did the Romans consider Mt. Etna the god Vulcan's home?

   Since Mt. Etna was an active volcano, the Romans considered such a location appropriate for Vulcan, god of the forge.

2. The photograph on p. 337 (SE) shows the plaster cast of one of Mt. Vesuvius's victims. Explain how the cast was made.

   In the process of excavation, when the archaeologists came upon a hollow area, they immediately injected plaster into the cavity. When the plaster hardened, they removed the surrounding ash and the plaster cast preserved the form of the humans and animals that died because of Mt. Vesuvius's eruption.

3. In studying the ancient world, scholars draw on archaeological finds as well as literary sources. What literary sources inform our understanding of Mt. Vesuvius's eruption in 79 CE?

   Pliny the Younger's letters provide an eyewitness account of the eruption and of the relief efforts of his uncle, Pliny the Elder. In addition, Suetonius speaks about the emperor Titus's relief efforts in response to the eruption.

4. How does modern technology assist scholars to interpret the remains from Mt. Vesuvius's eruption in 79 CE?

   Multispectral imaging with its infrared and ultraviolet light allows scholars to begin to read some of the almost 1,800 papyrus scrolls that were found charred in the Villa of the Papyri in Herculaneum.

5. How does Professor Thorburn account for Nero's role in the great fire of 64 CE in Rome?

   Professor Thorburn carefully cites the ancient literary sources—Dio Cassius, Suetonius, and Tacitus.

6. Why was Rome so susceptible to fire?

   The vast majority of Romans lived in multistoried apartment buildings built of wood along narrow streets.

7. The Romans had a saying, *nihil novī sub sōle*. How might this saying be relevant to the fact that police officers in New Orleans were found looting following Hurricane Katrina?

   Dio Cassius, in his account of the fire in Rome in 64 CE, notes that Roman soldiers helped spread the fire so they could continue their looting.

Review 6: Chapters 16–18 • 401

8. The Mesopotamian *Epic of Gilgamesh* contains a story of a great flood and the mortals saved by the gods. Both the Roman and Hebrew traditions have similar stories. Explain.

   In the Hebrew scriptures, the Hebrew God rewards the good man Noah by rescuing him from the flood sent to punish the wicked, and in Ovid's *Metamorphōsēs*, the story of Deucalion and Pyrrha tells of their rescue from the flood because of their virtuous behavior. The Roman tradition has Deucalion and Pyrrha after their rescue throwing stones behind their backs which turn into humans.

9. According to tradition, when is Rome's birthday?

   Rome was founded on April 21st, 753 BCE.

10. Explain how the eruption of Mt. Vesuvius in 79 CE was so fortuitous for those studying ancient Rome.

    This disaster sealed a moment in time that provides students who study ancient Rome with an astonishing snapshot of daily life.

11. Discuss how the government response to natural disaster is similar in ancient times as well as in modern times.

    Government officials in both times struggle to prevent or to cope with the suffering of their people and are sometimes faulted for contributing to or not alleviating the suffering.

PAGE 337

TEACHER BY THE WAY

The Roman writer Seneca describes the earthquake which struck Pompeii and the surrounding area in *Quaestiōnēs Nātūrālēs* 6. Scholars date this event as occurring in 62 or 63 CE, a forewarning of Vesuvius's eruption seventeen years later in 79. Recent studies by seismologists note that this earthquake was not an isolated event but was followed by others. This has in turn been confirmed by archaeological evidence in Pompeii showing several sets of structural repairs presumably necessitated by later earthquakes or aftershocks. A sculptural relief of the forum buildings in disarray attests to the power of the original earthquake. Excavations document the repairs and renovations following the earthquake. It is interesting to note that the forum repairs had not been completed by the time of the eruption but that the Temple of Isis had been fully restored. Scholars cite this as evidence for the popularity of the cult.

PAGE 338

TEACHER BY THE WAY

Titus, son of Vespasian, proved himself a worthy emperor. Suetonius, in his *Lives of the Caesars*, refers to him as "the darling of the human race." He grew into the epithet. His early years were not especially noteworthy. Titus was given the rare privilege of a court education because his father had served with distinction when Claudius invaded Britain. He remained a close friend of Claudius's son Britannicus until the young man was poisoned by Nero. When he joined his father in military campaigns, he became a very competent soldier. After a long siege, he finally captured Jerusalem (70 CE). Upon returning to Rome, Vespasian groomed him for succession. He shared the consulship with his father for an unprecedented seven times and was appointed praetorian commander without a colleague. No doubt the emperor wanted "in-house" protection, and the soldiers were devoted to his son. At this same time, according to Suetonius, he dealt with any opposition to Vespasian using cruel and barely legal methods. However, what the Roman people could not tolerate was his affair with Queen Berenice of the Judaean royal house (75 CE). Popular outrage prompted Vespasian to order Titus to send her home, which he did and refused to see her again.

When Vespasian died (79 CE), the emperor Titus underwent a dramatic change of character. His generosity and geniality became legendary. Informers were expelled and he was lenient to conspirators. The Flavian Amphitheatre was completed and elaborate baths (*thermae*) were built nearby. When fire struck Rome in 80 CE, he began rebuilding what the fire had destroyed. To cheer up the populace, he held shows and games. He was frugal in his private life and generous to the public, yet he managed financial affairs as carefully as his father. During his reign of a little over two years, he was beloved by all and universally mourned when he died. Deification promptly followed his death.

TEACHER BY THE WAY

Īnsulae (islands) or what we would call today apartment buildings or tenements were rectangular blocks of buildings, three or more stories, surrounded by streets. Heat, running water, and often toilets were not provided. The upper floors were the cheapest to rent and the most dangerous, especially in the case of fire or collapse. Windows were without glass. Light came from the central courtyard, which provided entrances to the staircases. On the ground floor were shops and businesses. The first floor had the select apartments with a series of rooms. In his early years, Caesar lived in an *īnsula* in Subura that his mother managed. Overpopulation made the *īnsulae* the best deal for poor Romans. At Ostia there are remains of better-constructed apartment buildings made of concrete and fired bricks.

TEACHING TIP

Students might enjoy reading Lindsey Davis's books about Marcus Didius Falco, who gives vivid descriptions of life in an *īnsula* as he tries to improve himself financially so he can marry his patrician lady-love.

PAGE 339

TEACHER BY THE WAY

Today, tall embankments along the Tiber protect the city from the river's periodic flooding.

TEACHER BY THE WAY

Communicating with the gods and maintaining good relationships with them was a very important part of Roman religion. Thus, the other side of the divine wrath coin was divine assistance. Attention to detail in performance of the ritual was the mantra for a positive divine response to sacrifice and for avoiding any kind of disaster. Prayers, vows, and sacrifices were the medium for connecting with the gods. To solicit the deity's favor, the wording of the person's prayer tried to cover every loophole so that the god would grant permission to do a certain activity. However, there was no assurance that the prayer would be answered. On the other hand, a vow necessitated fulfillment before a sacrifice was made to the god. Public vows on behalf of the state were frequently made in hopes of protection from an impending disaster. Pontiffs kept track of these vows in writing, and private vows were left in the temple on votive tablets. Inscriptions on altars that read *ex vōtō* (in accordance with a vow) and *vōtum solvit laetus libēns meritō* (paid his vow joyfully, freely, and deservedly) give the nature of the transaction. Sacrifices were considered gifts to the gods, and the motivation was as varied as the offering. Some were for praise, others for thanksgiving, or for expiation, or for intercession. When a god appeared in a dream and made a request, the person sacrificed accordingly. Anniversaries meant special remembrances, much as they do today. Sacrifices honored Rome's traditional birthday on April 21st. Other sacrifices were results of consulting oracles. Such was the case with M. Curtius, a young Roman, who was told to jump armed and on horseback into a chasm that suddenly appeared in the Forum to save his country.

Blood offerings were the most popular form of sacrifice. Meat was burned on an altar with wine poured into the flames. In some inscriptions mention is made that the meat can only be eaten within the sacred precinct; sometimes it was permitted to take it home. The sacrificer covered his head with his toga, and music (flute or lyre) was played. If any ill-omened sound interrupted the sacrifice, the whole ritual had to be redone. The animal had to be unblemished and appropriate, male for gods and female for goddesses. Slaughtering the animal involved a precise procedure. The entrails were roasted on the altar fire, and the important participants ate them first. The bones, fat, wine, and cakes were then burnt for the gods. Participants feasted on what was left of the animal. In Pompeii a sacrificial scene is depicted on an altar that shows a priest with head covered, accompanied by a flute player, with a bull being led to sacrifice. The column of Trajan also shows the preparation for a sacrifice as the army starts out on its campaign. By propitiating and acknowledging the divine powers, the Romans hoped for good luck and a relatively disaster-free existence.

MĪRĀBILE AUDĪTŪ

PAGE 340
Standards 1.1, 2.1

QUOTATIONS VOCABULARY

Animus meminisse horret.

horreō, horrēre, horruī, —— – to bristle, to shudder

meminī, meminisse – to remember

Citō ārēscit lacrima, praesertim in aliēnīs malīs.

aliēnus, aliēna, aliēnum – another's, foreign

ārēscō, ārēscere, ——, —— – to become dry

citō (*adv.*) – quickly

praesertim (*adv.*) – especially

Commūne naufragium omnibus est cōnsōlātiō.

commūnis, commūne – common

cōnsōlātiō, cōnsōlātiōnis, *f.* – comfort, consolation

naufragium, naufragiī, *n.* – shipwreck

Nē cēde malīs.

cēdō, cēdere, cessī, cessum – to go, to yield

nē = nōn

TEACHER BY THE WAY

The Romans (and the Greeks before them) considered Mt. Vesuvius to be sacred to the hero and demigod Hercules. The town of Herculaneum is named after him.

Large eruptions from a volcano that spew forth magma of more than 1 km are called plinian eruptions, named after Pliny the Younger, who described the 79 CE eruption of Mt. Vesuvius. Such large eruptions in general happen after the volcano has been quiet for a few thousand years. Subplinian eruptions, however, which send forth about 0.1 km of magma, happen every few hundred years. After Mt. Vesuvius erupted in 1631 CE, there were tiny eruptions about every twenty-five years until 1944 when a subplinian eruption destroyed parts of the villages of San Sebastiano al Vesuvio, Massa di Somma, Ottaviano, and San Giorgio a Cremano, as well as all eighty-eight planes in a US B-25 bomber group during World War II.

CHAPTER 19 (PP. 341–357)

GRAMMAR IN LANGUAGE FACTS

Perfect Passive Participle; Perfect Tense Passive of All Conjugations; Review of Principal Parts of Verbs; Demonstrative Pronoun and Adjective *Hic*

PAGE 341

Standards 1.1, 2.1

RRA 6B

MEMORĀBILE DICTŪ VOCABULARY

fīnis, fīnis, *m.* – boundary, limit, end

imperium, imperiī, *n.* – supreme command, territory subject to supreme command, empire

TEACHER BY THE WAY

The **Huns**, a nomadic people from the steppes of the Caucasus, were feared throughout Europe. Excellent archers and exceptional horsemanship served them well as they swept through Europe beginning with the defeat of the Visigoths living in Dacia (ca. 376 CE). The Romans employed the Huns in their struggle against the Visigoths and other Germanic tribes. Traditionally, the Huns did not have an overall ruler but by 432 CE a single ruler Rua or Rugila emerged. His nephews Bleda and Attila succeeded him upon his death two years later. When the Romans reneged on the subsidies they had pledged in a treaty, the Huns attacked the Danube border and almost made it to Constantinople in 441 CE. Attila murdered his brother in 445 CE and invaded the Balkans and Greece, then shifted westward. Attila suffered his only defeat in 451 CE at the battle of the Catalaunian Plains in Gaul at the hands of the Romans and Visigoths. His invasion of Italy was impeded by a lack of food and much sickness. Following Attila's death in 453 CE, his sons quarreled and their subjects revolted. Thereafter, the Huns disintegrated.

The **Ostrogoths**, a distinct group of the Goths, those various tribes of Teutonic origin, in the third century CE established an empire north of the Black Sea in what is today Ukraine and parts of Belarus. It is presumed that the Ostrogoths were literate but little material culture has been uncovered to date. About 370 CE, the Huns attacked and conquered the Ostrogoths. When the Hun empire dissipated following Attila's death in 453 CE, Theodoric the Great moved his peoples to Moesia and then to Italy. Probably at the invitation of Zeno, the Eastern Roman emperor, Theodoric attacked Odoacer and murdered Odoacer at a banquet. Theodoric became *Rēx Italiae* in 493 CE. Italy enjoyed stability for over thirty years until Theodoric's reign ended with his death in 526 CE.

Theodoric maintained the Roman civil service, annually appointed two consuls to govern Rome, and respected the Eastern Roman Empire. He made Ravenna capital of the Western Empire. There he built a royal palace and several ecclesiastical structures. The Ostrogoths had previously been converted to Arian Christianity. The mosaic in the dome of a baptistery in Ravenna depicts the Arian belief that Christ's nature became divine only at the time of his baptism. The depiction of Theodoric's palace in St. Apollinare Nuovo originally included his portrait and those of other officials. Under Byzantine control, these were replaced with drapes. Theodoric's monumental tomb built in 520 CE was emptied probably by the Byzantines. Instability following Theodoric's death led to the Byzantine emperor Justinian declaring war and eventually regaining control of Italy. Thus ended a distinct Ostrogoth presence.

The **Visigoths** had separated from their Ostrogoth brothers and settled in Dacia, which the Huns invaded in 376 CE. Allowed to settle there, the Visigoths soon revolted over tribute payments and killed Emperor Valens outside Adrianople in 378 CE. While in Moesia, where Emperor Theodosius settled them to protect the frontier, it is believed they converted to Arianism. By 395 CE, with Alaric as leader they moved to Greece and then Italy. They sacked Rome in 410 CE shortly after which Alaric died. His son Ataulphus led his people to southern Gaul and on to Spain. Later they settled in Gaul and fought against Attila the Hun in the Battle of the Catalaunian Plains. Their king Theodoric I died in the battle and his son Euric proclaimed himself an independent king. The Visigoths expanded their territory until they were defeated by Clovis and the Franks in 507 CE. Though they lost almost all of their territory in Gaul, the Visigoths maintained a kingdom with a capital at Toledo until its conquest by the Muslims in 711 CE.

PAGE 342

Standards 1.1, 2.1, 3.1, 3.2

TEACHING TIP
Chapter 6B of RRA contains information on Ammianus Marcellinus. The teacher may wish to assign this chapter for reading.

TRANSLATION OF LATIN PASSAGE

About the Huns

Not many things have been said about the Huns in the books of (i.e., written by) our fathers. These <people> are ferocious and wild. They want to appear terrifying and to rouse fear in other people. So their faces are wounded on purpose. After the wounds have been healed, scars remain, because of which (i.e., the scars) the beard cannot grow. The appearance of these <people> is not handsome, but terrifying!

They eat the roots of plants, which have been snatched from fields, and the meat of animals, which has not been cooked but rubbed for a little while. For the meat, before it is eaten by them, has been placed between the horse and the thighs of the person who sits on the horse, and it stays there for a little while.

They do not have houses, but they dwell and live outdoors. They wear clothes made from the skins of animals.

They always remain on <their> horses: they eat on their horses, they sleep on their horses, they fight on their horses. They swiftly launch attacks on enemies, whom they often catch in battle with lassos, and they slay the caught <enemies> with swords.

TEACHING TIP
Instruct the students to locate Antioch and Syria on the map on pp. xxxiv–xxxiv (SE) and to find Ammianus Marcellinus, Cornelius Tacitus, and Attila the Hun on the timeline on pp. 405–408 (SE).

TEACHER BY THE WAY
Julian's troops proclaimed him emperor upon the sudden death of his cousin Constantius in December 361 CE. The new emperor attended to some administrative concerns at the capital Constantinople and soon set his sights on the conquest of Sassanid Persia with whom Constantius had concluded a peace. With an army of 65,000, the largest ever assembled against the Persians, Julian began his campaign in March 362 CE. Realizing that his siege of Persian Ctesiphon, near today's Baghdad, was about to fail, Julian retreated. In a subsequent Persian guerrilla raid, Julian was mortally wounded on June 26th, 362 CE, at age thirty-one and after just twenty months in office.

PAGE 343

ANSWERS TO COMPREHENSION QUESTIONS
1. They wanted to look terrible and frighten their enemies.
2. Roots of herbs and raw meat, which had been rubbed between their thighs and the horse's back for a while.
3. They did not have houses, but were nomads. They lived mostly on their horses.
4. Animal skins.

TEACHER BY THE WAY
In addition to the word *femur* given in the vocabulary, which is the name of the thigh bone in modern medicine, there are many other human bones with names directly from the Latin with no spelling change:

- *carpus* – the wrist
- *fībula* – in the lower leg
- *umerus* – upper arm bone
- *malleus* (hammer); *incūs* (anvil); and *stāpēs* (ML, stirrup) – the three bones that make up the "ossicles" (little bones) of the ear
- *maxilla* – the upper jaw
- *os sacrum* – part of the pelvis
- *patella* – the kneecap
- *pelvis* – the cavity in the lower part of the trunk
- *radius* – located in the forearm
- *scapulae* – shoulder blades
- *tībia* – the shin bone

- *ulna* – big lower arm bone
- *vertebra* – a bone of the spine

As well as words for bones, there are other parts of the body that have Latin names, e.g., appendix, solar plexus, tendon, sinus, pulse, and tumor.

PAGE 344
Standards 3.1, 4.1

HOW TO USE THIS BOOK
In addition to the perfect passive participle, the future active participle will be taught on pp. 379–380 (SE) and the present active participle will be encountered in Level 2 of *Latin for the New Millennium*. The future passive participle, sometimes called the gerundive, will likewise be found in Level 2.

TEACHING TIP
The teacher may wish to use this simple activity in oral or written format in order to help students remember that the form of the perfect passive participle comes from the fourth principal part. Only the nominative singular masculine answer should be expected during this practice. The teacher may say, for example, "*Āmittō – Dīc mihi praeteritī temporis participium!*" Other verbs that the students have learned recently in this book are listed for the teacher's convenience with the appropriate answer.

• *Excītō – Dīc mihi praeteritī temporis participium!*	Answer: *excitātus*
• *Temptō – Dīc mihi praeteritī temporis participium!*	Answer: *temptātus*
• *Legō – Dīc mihi praeteritī temporis participium!*	Answer: *lēctus*
• *Dūcō – Dīc mihi praeteritī temporis participium!*	Answer: *ductus*
• *Corripiō – Dīc mihi praeteritī temporis participium!*	Answer: *correptus*
• *Quaerō – Dīc mihi praeteritī temporis participium!*	Answer: *quaesītus*
• *Occultō – Dīc mihi praeteritī temporis participium!*	Answer: *occultātus*
• *Exstinguō – Dīc mihi praeteritī temporis participium!*	Answer: *exstīnctus*
• *Opprimō – Dīc mihi praeteritī temporis participium!*	Answer: *oppressus*
• *Exclāmō – Dīc mihi praeteritī temporis participium!*	Answer: *exclāmātus*
• *Colō – Dīc mihi praeteritī temporis participium!*	Answer: *cultus*
• *Āmittō – Dīc mihi praeteritī temporis participium!*	Answer: *āmissus*
• *Iaciō – Dīc mihi praeteritī temporis participium!*	Answer: *iactus*
• *Dēvastō – Dīc mihi praeteritī temporis participium!*	Answer: *dēvastātus*
• *Alō – Dīc mihi praeteritī temporis participium!*	Answer: *altus/alitus*
• *Neglegō – Dīc mihi praeteritī temporis participium!*	Answer: *neglēctus*
• *Rogō – Dīc mihi praeteritī temporis participium!*	Answer: *rogātus*
• *Tangō – Dīc mihi praeteritī temporis participium!*	Answer: *tāctus*

PAGE 345
Oral Exercise 1

ORAL EXERCISE 1
This exercise may be used after the perfect passive participle has been presented.

The teacher should use one of the CPOs to put on view a perfect passive participle in the nominative masculine singular, then recite a noun in another case and number. In each case the teacher should ask a different student to make the participle agree with the noun. The student's answer should be entirely oral.

Teacher: missus (epistulae) **Student:** epistulae missae
Teacher: dictus (verba) **Student:** verba dicta
Teacher: vocātus (cīvium) **Student:** cīvium vocātōrum/vocātārum
Teacher: vīsus (urbe) **Student:** urbe vīsā
Teacher: līberātus (mātrum) **Student:** līberātārum mātrum
Teacher: neglēctus (cōnsiliō) **Student:** cōnsiliō neglēctō
Teacher: victus (mīlitis) **Student:** mīlitis victī
Teacher: servātus (animālibus) **Student:** animālibus servātīs
Teacher: petītus (praemiō) **Student:** praemiō petītō
Teacher: positus (gladiō) **Student:** gladiō positō

PAGE 346
Standards 1.1, 1.2
Workbook Exercise 4

HOW TO USE THIS BOOK
How perfect passive participles may be translated with a subordinate clause will be presented in Level 2.

TEACHING TIP
Some teachers may wish to teach their students how to translate perfect passive participles using a subordinate clause now instead of waiting until Level 2. For those who want to do this, some suggestions are given here.

- Use one of the CPOs to put on display a timeline with the following tenses marked on the timeline. Put the present tense in the center of the timeline. Use a vertical mark on the horizontal line to indicate where the present tense will be considered to be. To the left of the present tense mark, place a vertical mark and label it the perfect/imperfect tense. To the left of the perfect/imperfect tense mark, place another vertical mark and label it pluperfect. To the right of the present tense mark, place another vertical mark and label it future.

- Also put on display a few subordinating conjunctions such as the following: "when, since, after, before, while." There are many other subordinating conjunctions that may be used but generally it is best to limit which conjunctions the students may choose until this process becomes more familiar to them.

- Remind students that the action of the perfect passive participle happens before that of the main verb. Point out on the timeline that if the main verb is present, the time before is the imperfect/perfect while if the main verb is imperfect/perfect, the time before is the pluperfect.
- Use this sentence as an example:

  Vocātus ad imperātōrem ambulāvit.
- Since *ambulāvit* is perfect tense, *vocātus*, which must indicate time before, will translate like a pluperfect tense verb or its equivalent. Explain also that the student should insert one of the subordinating conjunctions before the participle and will need to give a subject to the participle from context.

  After he had been called, he walked toward the general.
- Now change the example sentence:

  Vocātus ad imperātōrem ambulat.
- Since *ambulat* is now in the present tense, show on the timeline how the time before has changed to being the perfect/imperfect tense.

  After he has been called, he walks toward the general.
- Stress to the students that, when translating a perfect passive participle in a clause, they should use a passive voice verb always.
- There are many other ways to translate participles as clauses other than the two examples given here. Once students learn the underlying principle of translating a participle with a clause, all of these many translations will come naturally to them.

▶ EXERCISE 1 ANSWERS

1. We feared the Huns <having been> seen by us.
2. The Huns devastated the city <having been> abandoned by the citizens.
3. We have to take care of the animals <having been> led to us.
4. We were able to capture the <having been> conquered enemies.
5. We now read many things about the deeds <having been> done by the Romans.
6. You have the reward <having been> owed to you.

PAGE 347
Standards 1.2, 4.1
Workbook Exercise 2

▶ EXERCISE 2 ANSWERS

1. barber — barba
2. vestments — vestīmentum
3. crescendo — crēscō
4. sanitary — sānō
5. herbal — herba
6. victuals — vīvō, victum
7. vulnerable — vulnerō
8. celerity — celeriter
9. trite — terō
10. concoction — coquō

TEACHING TIP

Although in Exercise 2 the students are directed to find only the derivatives based on the Vocabulary to Learn, they may be interested to learn that there are other derivatives in Exercise 2. The derivation of these words is provided for the teacher's convenience.

2. conspicuous – from *cum* (with, together) + *spectō* (to look at, watch); *cōnspiciō* (to observe, catch sight of). in – from *in* (in, on, at). ceremony – from *caerimōnia* (sanctity, veneration, ritual). splendid – from *splendidus* (bright, brilliant, glittering, magnificent).
3. sound – from *sonō* (to sound, make a noise).
4. restaurants – from *restaurō* (to repair, rebuild). public – from *pūblicus* (public). eating – from *edō* (to eat). places – from *platēa* (street) from the Greek *platys* (wide, broad).
5. salad – from *sāl* (salt, brine, sea).
6. army – from *armō* (to equip, arm).
7. general – from *generālis* (of the species, universal). decided – from *decīdō* (to cut off, settle, put an end to). retreat – from *retrahō* (to draw back, drag back, withdraw, remove). exposed – from *expōnō* (to set out, put out, set forth, display). position – from *pōnō* (to put, place).
8. animals – from *animal* (animal).
9. me – from *mē* (accusative singular of *ego*, I). use – from *ūtor* (to use, employ, possess, etc.).
10. interesting – from *interest* (it is of importance, it concerns). prepared – from *prae* (before); *parō* (to get ready, prepare).

PAGE 348

Standards 3.1, 4.1

TEACHING TIP
Additional reproducible worksheets, morphology charts, and their associated answer keys, related to this material, are available for download at www.lnm.bolchazy.com.
- **Verb Conjugations**

PAGE 349

Oral Exercise 2; Workbook Exercise 3

TEACHER BY THE WAY
When the auxiliary verb is a monosyllable (a monosyllable is a word of one syllable), there is a slight tendency for it to precede the participial element when the compound verb comes at the end of a sentence.

ORAL EXERCISE 2

This exercise may be used after the perfect passive indicative has been presented.

The teacher should put on view the following perfect tense verbs. Each time s/he writes another form, the teacher should ask a different student to change it orally into the perfect passive if it is active, and into the perfect active if it is passive. Note: in the case of perfect passive forms the students should supply all three nominative participial forms (masculine, feminine, and neuter) in the nominative case together with the correct form of the auxiliary verb.

Teacher: vocātī, vocātae, vocāta sunt
Student: vocāvērunt

Teacher: ostentī, ostentae, ostenta sunt
Student: ostendērunt

Teacher: vulnerātī, vulnerātae, vulnerāta sumus
Student: vulnerāvimus

Teacher: vīsī, vīsae, vīsa estis
Student: vīdistis

Teacher: nārrāvit
Student: nārrātus, nārrāta, nārrātum est

Teacher: coctus, cocta, coctum est
Student: coxit

Teacher: rogāvī
Student: rogātus, rogāta, rogātum sum

Teacher: dēlēvimus
Student: dēlētī, dēlētae, dēlēta sumus

Teacher: dedistis
Student: datī, datae, data estis

Teacher: iussimus
Student: iussī, iussae, iussa sumus

Teacher: trīvit
Student: trītus, trīta, trītum est

Teacher: relictus, relicta, relictum sum
Student: relīquī

Teacher: mīsistī
Student: missus, missa, missum es

TEACHING TIP
Remind students that in the perfect passive tense, the form of *sum* may precede or follow the fourth principal part of the verb in the sentence. Occasionally the form of *sum* may be separated from the fourth principal part by a few or more words.

TEACHING TIP
The teacher may wish to put on display these three sentences (or any three similar ones of the teacher's choosing) and ask the students to translate the three. This will help the students to see the difference between the perfect passive participle, the perfect passive tense, and the present passive tense. The teacher may want to encourage students to think up their own group of three sentences that follow the pattern below.

- *Carō cocta est.*   The meat was cooked.
- *Carō coquitur.*   The meat is cooked.
- *Carō cocta a servō datur.*   The cooked meat is given by the slave.

PAGE 350
Standards 1.1, 1.2
Workbook Exercise 6

▶ EXERCISE 3 ANSWERS

1. sunt dēvastātī

   Have your (plural) fields been ravaged by the Huns?/Were your (plural) fields ravaged by the Huns?

2. est excitātus

   Has fear been stirred up in the Romans by the Huns?/ Was fear stirred up in the Romans by the Huns?

3. sunt vulnerātae

   Have the faces of the Huns been wounded deliberately?/Were the faces of the Huns wounded deliberately?

4. sunt līberātae

   The cities of the Romans have been/were freed at last.

5. sunt facta

   Their clothes have been/were made from the skins of animals.

6. sumus captī

   We are fortunate: we have not been/were not caught by the lassos of the Huns.

7. estis captī

   I say that you (plural), who have not been/were not caught by the Huns, are fortunate.

Chapter 19 • 415

PAGE 351

Standards 1.1, 1.2, 3.1, 4.1

Oral Exercise 3

▶ EXERCISE 4 ANSWERS

1. We heard the words \<having been\> said.   perfect passive participle
2. We see the \<having been\> wounded faces of the Huns.   perfect passive participle
3. The faces of the Huns were/have been wounded on purpose.   perfect passive tense
4. The roots of plants were/have been snatched from fields.   perfect passive tense
5. We cannot eat the roots of plants \<having been\> snatched from fields.   perfect passive participle
6. We are accustomed to eat \<having been\> cooked meat.   perfect passive participle
7. The meat has not been/was not cooked.   perfect passive tense
8. The enemies have been/were captured in battle.   perfect passive tense
9. We were not able to see the enemies \<having been\> captured in battle.   perfect passive participle

ORAL EXERCISE 3

This exercise may be used after the perfect passive indicative has been presented.

The teacher should ask individual students to mimic different actions, and after that ask other students the following questions:

Example:

Teacher: Lege, Mārce, fābulam!
Teacher: Quid fēcit Mārcus?   **Student:** Mārcus fābulam lēgit.
Teacher: Quid est factum ā Mārcō?   **Student:** Fābula ā Mārcō est lēcta.

Teacher: Lege, Mārce, librum!
Teacher: Quid fēcit Mārcus?   **Student:** Mārcus librum lēgit.
Teacher: Quid ā Mārcō est factum?   **Student:** Liber ā Mārcō est lēctus.

Teacher: Comede, Mārce, carnem!
Teacher: Quid fēcit Mārcus?   **Student:** Mārcus carnem comēdit.
Teacher: Quid ā Mārcō est factum?   **Student:** Carō ā Mārcō est comēsa.

Teacher: Iace, Mārce, gladium!
Teacher: Quid fēcit Mārcus?   **Student:** Mārcus gladium iēcit.
Teacher: Quid ā Mārcō est factum?   **Student:** Gladius ā Mārcō est iactus.

Teacher: Movē, Mārce, manūs!
Teacher: Quid fēcit Mārcus?   **Student:** Mārcus manūs mōvit.
Teacher: Quid ā Mārcō est factum?   **Student:** Manūs sunt ā Mārcō mōtae.

Teacher: Nārrā, Mārce, fābulam!
Teacher: Quid fēcit Mārcus?   **Student:** Mārcus fābulam nārrāvit.
Teacher: Quid ā Mārcō est factum?   **Student:** Fābula est ā Mārcō nārrāta.

416 • Latin for the New Millennium: Teacher's Manual, Level 1

Teacher: Ostende, Mārce, vestīmentum!
Teacher: Quid fēcit Mārcus?   **Student:** Mārcus vestīmentum ostendit.
Teacher: Quid ā Mārcō est factum?   **Student:** Vestīmentum est ā Mārcō ostentum.

Teacher: Vocā, Mārce, amīcum!
Teacher: Quid fēcit Mārcus?   **Student:** Mārcus amīcum vocāvit.
Teacher: Quid ā Mārcō est factum?   **Student:** Amīcus est ā Mārcō vocātus.

PAGE 352
Standards 1.1, 1.2

▶ EXERCISE 5 ANSWERS

1. sānātī, sānātae, sānāta sunt — they were healed
2. docēbitur — s/he will be taught
3. vīxeram — I had lived
4. vulnerātī, vulnerātae, vulnerāta estis — you were wounded
5. iaciēris — you will be thrown
6. āmittēbāris — you were lost
7. coluimus — we worshipped
8. crēscent — they will increase
9. sēderis — you will have sat
10. ārserās — you had burned
11. trīverat — s/he had worn out

TEACHING TIP

The teacher may choose to ask the students in Latin the following questions about the words in parentheses in Exercise 5. Instruct the students to answer in Latin and then to give the answer originally asked for in the directions. The teacher would ask, "*Cūius persōnae et numerī et temporis est?*" Student answers are included for the teacher's convenience.

1. *tertiae persōnae, numerī plūrālis, temporis praeteritī perfectī passīvī*

    Note that the simpler phrases *praeteritī passīvī* or *temporis perfectī passīvī* may also be used.

2. *tertiae persōnae, numerī singulāris, temporis futūrī passīvī*
3. *prīmae persōnae, numerī singulāris, temporis plūsquamperfectī āctīvī*
4. *secundae persōnae, numerī plūrālis, temporis praeteritī passīvī*
5. *secundae persōnae, numerī singulāris, temporis futūrī passīvī*
6. *secundae persōnae, numerī singulāris, temporis praeteritī imperfectī passīvī*
7. *prīmae persōnae, numerī plūrālis, temporis praeteritī perfectī āctīvī*
8. *tertiae persōnae, numerī plūrālis, temporis futūrī āctīvī*
9. *secundae persōnae, numerī singulāris, temporis futūrī exāctī āctīvī*
10. *secundae persōnae, numerī singulāris, temporis plūsquamperfectī āctīvī*
11. *tertiae persōnae, numerī singulāris, temporis plūsquamperfectī āctīvī*

PAGE 353
Standards 3.1, 4.1
Workbook Exercise 1

TEACHING TIP
Instruct the student to repeat the forms of *hic* after the teacher has modeled the pronunciation of each form.

TEACHING TIP
Encourage students to create a rap, cheer, or song to help them remember the forms of *hic, haec, hoc*. Alternatively, use Bolchazy-Carducci's *Toga Beats*.

TEACHING TIP
Another activity that students enjoy is to practice saying aloud the forms of *hic* at a rapid pace. The teacher sets the pace with each three words said and the students repeat after the teacher at that pace. The teacher can gradually increase how fast the three words are being said and the students will attempt to repeat at the gradually increasing pace.

A variation of this activity is to issue a challenge to the students. Who can say all thirty forms of *hic* in the least amount of time while still pronouncing the words correctly? A watch with a second hand will be needed. One student can time how long the student undertaking the challenge takes while another student can record the student's time. Students like to compete against one another in this activity and while doing so the entire class is hearing the forms over and over again, thus cementing the declension of this demonstrative pronoun in their heads.

Still another variation is to include the thirty forms of *is, ea, id* in the challenge. Who can say the thirty forms of *is* followed by the thirty forms of *ille* the fastest?

PAGE 354
Standards 1.1, 1.2
Workbook Exercise 5

TEACHER BY THE WAY
While the cavalry played a role in Roman military maneuvers, it was not until the eleventh century CE that the stirrup was invented and gave the rider greater control of the horse in combat.

EXERCISE 6 ANSWERS
1. Saepe hīs in equīs manent.
2. Hic est gladius huius ducis.
3. Hās herbās tantum comedunt.
4. Haec sunt hominum fortium nōmina.
5. Vulnera in faciē huius mīlitis manent.
6. Multa dē hārum fēminārum fortitūdine sunt dicta.
7. Nōlīte dare haec magna praemia hīs hominibus ferōcibus.

TEACHER BY THE WAY
Though we usually associate horses with the military and chariot racing in ancient Rome, there were other domestic uses for this animal. Horses pulled beams used for turning the mill to grind the wheat. They were used on farms but not as beasts of burden; mules and oxen did that job. Good harnesses were not available and horses were costly to rear.

Reliefs portray numerous horse-drawn vehicles. Since horses were unshod, it is conjectured that they kept to a grassy dirt path at the side of the road rather than use the hard surface. The *carpentum* was a covered vehicle drawn by two horses and used exclusively by the Vestals and priests. The *raeda* was a four-wheeled, covered wagon pulled by two or four horses. The uncovered *cisium* was favored for quick trips. It was a light one-seater drawn by two to three horses. Race horses were a pampered lot. Stallions qualified, but not if less than five years old. The best breeds were the result of a cross between Libyan and European stock. Hannibal used horses from Africa effectively against the Romans in the Punic Wars. An Algerian mosaic shows doctors, trainers, and grooms all in attendance upon blanketed horses. Citizens of good standing also showed off their equestrian skills on trained horses. Reminiscent of the *Lūdī Trōiae* in the *Aeneid* Book 5, young nobles, like Ascanius and his friends, executed elaborate cavalry rotations in squadrons under a leader.

Festivals called *Equīrria* in honor of the war god Mars took place in February and March. In preparation for the campaign season, rites were performed for the benefit of the horses. On the Ides of October (15th) the Campus Martius hosted a horse race. The winning team's horse was sacrificed and the inhabitants of the *Via Sacra* and *Subura* (between the Esquiline and Qurinal Hills) vied for the head in a fierce and bloody competition. Finally, horses were used for the postal system (*cursus pūblicus*). They covered over 46 miles a day but at high speeds up to 124 miles, with replacements ready at relay stations.

PAGE 355
Standards 1.1, 2.1, 3.1
Workbook Exercise 7, Content Questions

▶ EXERCISE 7 ANSWERS
Rōmānus: Why do the Huns want to seem terrifying?
Attila: It is not difficult for us to conquer enemies who are afraid of us.
Rōmānus: Many say that for this reason the faces of the Huns are deliberately wounded. Is this true?
Attila: It is true! Do my soldiers seem to be ferocious to you?

Rōmānus: Yes! I am afraid of these people.

Attila: Therefore it will not be difficult for the Huns to conquer the Romans in battle.

Rōmānus: So we believe. I have now been sent to you by the Romans, who want to give many gifts to the Huns. If the Huns leave the Romans in peace, the Romans will give the Huns gifts, rewards, many good things.

Attila: An outstanding plan! I like this plan. But afterward we shall speak about the gifts and rewards, which the Romans will give to the Huns. Now we'll have dinner.

Rōmānus: An outstanding plan! Will you lead me to your dwelling? Where will dinner be held (had)?

Attila: We Huns are brave, wild, ferocious, not wretched, like you Romans. We don't have dwellings, but we inhabit and live outdoors. So we'll dine outdoors. You'll have good food with us.

Rōmānus: I am ready to have dinner. But what do I see? Has this meat been cooked? And what are these plants? They don't seem to be plants, but the roots of plants!

Attila: This is true, what you have said about the plants. The meat, however, hasn't been cooked, but rubbed for a little while. For meat, before it is eaten by us, has been placed between the horse and the thighs of the person who sits on the horse, and there it remains for a little while. So the meat has been well prepared for dinner. What do you say? Will you dine with us?

Rōmānus: Julius Caesar once said: "I came, I saw, I conquered." This Roman, who must dine with the Huns, says these words: "I came, I saw, I have been conquered."

TEACHING TIP
After the students have completed Exercise 7 and their translations have been checked for accuracy, a pair of students may be instructed to perform this dialogue for the class.

PAGE 356
Standards 1.2, 4.1

TEACHING TIP
The teacher may wish to have students research the furnishings in a Roman *domus*. How much was useful and how much was decorative? What items were imported? What type of lighting was available?

TEACHER BY THE WAY
Furniture of stone or metal has survived. Many pieces of furniture are described in literature or shown in wall paintings. Pouring plaster into casts in Pompeii and Herculaneum has allowed restorers to reproduce the wooden furniture that was destroyed.

TEACHING TIP

The students may be interested in knowing how to say in Latin other chores (*pēnsum, pēnsī,* n. – chore). Some are listed here.

Household Chores

- *Flōrēs adaquō, adaquāre, adaquāvī, adaquātum* – water the flowers
- *Grāmen resecō, resecāre, resecuī, resectum* – mow the lawn
- *Mēnsam appōnō, appōnere, apposuī, appositum* – set the table
- *Patinās lavō, lavāre, lavī, lautum* or *lōtum* – wash the dishes
- *Pavīmentum lavō, lavāre, lavī, lautum* or *lōtum* – wash the floor
- *Pavīmentum verrō, verrere, verrī, versum* – sweep the floor
- *Supellectilem dētergeō, dētergēre, dētersī, dētersum* – dust the furniture
- *Vāsa lavō, lavāre, lavī, lautum* or *lōtum* – wash the pots and pans
- *Vestīmenta premō, premere, pressī, pressum* – iron the clothes

Personal Chores

- *Capillōs crīspō, crīspāre, crīspāvī, crīspātum* – curl your hair
- *Capillōs pectō, pectere, pexī, pexum* – comb your hair
- *Cubiculum ordinō, ordināre, ordināvī, ordinātum* – tidy up (clean) your room
- *Dentēs purgō, purgāre, purgāvī, purgātum* – brush your teeth
- *Mē induō, induere, induī, indūtum* – get dressed
- *Mē lavō, lavāre, lavī, lautum* or *lōtum* – wash yourself, wash up

TRANSLATION OF THE LATIN CONVERSATION

Christy: Where were you yesterday? We rode on bicycles. The weather was nice.

Mary: I had to help mother. For mother decided to clean the house yesterday.

Mark: What did your father do?

Mary: Father also helped mother. Mother ordered him to sweep the floor with a broom.

Mark: Did (your) father do this?

Mary: Father did not only this, but also many other things.

Mark: What other things were done by (your) father?

Mary: Father had to shake out the bedding and all the carpets.

Helen: Your father worked with care. What were you doing, Mary?

Mary: Mother ordered me to arrange the things put in cupboards. I also had to wipe out the dust that had earlier accumulated in the cupboards. Also at mother's order(s) I quickly sucked out dust from the curtains and the floor with the vacuum cleaner.

Helen: How thoroughly you all worked! Without doubt you needed to do nothing else!

Mary: We did also other things. Both I and father made all the beds. Then we washed a lot of linen in the washing machine. Our house is now clean!

Mark: What did your mother do?

Mary: Mother ordered us to do all these things.

PAGE 357

Standards 1.2, 4.1

Oral Exercises 4, 5 and Dictation

ORAL EXERCISE 4

This exercise may be used after the Latin dialogue has been presented.

In preparation for the exercise, the following words should be put on view:

prīdiē (*adv.*) – on the previous day
quōmodo (*interrogative adv.*)? – in what way, how?

After the students have carefully read and understood the dialogue, the teacher should ask individual students the following questions. (NB: the students may look at the dialogue while they answer.) The students should be urged to use the actual words in the dialogue in their answers, changing endings and forms only where needed to fit the answer.

Teacher: Ubi prīdiē erat Marīa?
Student: Marīa domī erat.

Teacher: Quid Marīa facere dēbēbat?
Student: Marīa auxilium mātrī prīdiē dare dēbēbat.

Teacher: Quid māter Marīae facere dēcrēverat?
Student: Māter Marīae domum pūrgāre dēcrēverat.

Teacher: Quid patrem Marīae facere iusserat māter?
Student: Māter patrem iusserat pavīmentum scōpīs verrere.

Teacher: Quās aliās rēs fēcerat Marīae pater?
Student: Pater lintea lectōrum omniaque tapētia excutere dēbuerat.

Teacher: Quōmodo pater Marīae labōrāverat?
Student: Pater dīligenter labōrāverat.

Teacher: Quās rēs māter Marīam facere iusserat?
Student: Māter Marīam iusserat rēs in armāriīs positās ōrdināre, pulverem abstergēre, quī in armāriīs anteā crēverat, pulverem etiam ē vēlīs et ē pavīmentō celeriter haurītōriō exsūgere.

Teacher: Quās aliās rēs fēcerant Marīa et pater?
Student: Marīa et pater omnēs lectōs strāverant, et multa lintea in māchinā lavātōriā lāverant.

Teacher: Quid fēcerat māter Marīae?
Student: Māter Marīae et Marīam et patrem iusserat haec omnia facere.

422 • Latin for the New Millennium: Teacher's Manual, Level 1

ORAL EXERCISE 5 AND DICTATION

This exercise may be used to conclude the chapter.

Before dictating the passage, the teacher should put on view the new vocabulary listed below the passage.

The teacher should read aloud the following passage slowly and clearly, and the students should write it as the teacher dictates.

When the students have written out the passage, the teacher should ask them individually the questions listed below.

Germānī multōs gladiōs nōn habent. Hastās longās in proeliō gerunt, quās frameās vocant, quibus comminus et ēminus pugnant. Scūta habent, sed nōn multa alia arma. Mīlitum Germānōrum multī equīs vehuntur, sed equī eōrum nōn sunt pulchrī nec celeriter currunt. Sed fortitūdō Germānōrum est magna. Scūtum in proeliō relinquere flagitium esse crēdunt. Rēgēs eōrum propter nōbilitātem sunt factī, sed ducēs propter fortitūdinem creantur. Sī ad proelium parātī sunt, uxōrēs et parvulōs prope exercitum positōs habent. Ita mīlitēs intellegunt sē vincere dēbēre. Aliquid sānctum et prōvidum in fēminīs esse putant. Hārum igitur cōnsilia semper audiunt.

aliquid sānctum – something sacred
comminus (*adv.*) – hand-to-hand
creō, creāre, creāvī, creātum – to elect, create
ēminus (*adv.*) – at long range
exercitus, exercitūs, *m.* – army
flagitium, flagitiī, *n.* – disgrace
framea, frameae, *f.* – a Germanic spear or javelin
hasta, hastae, *f.* – spear

nōbilitās, nōbilitātis, *f.* – nobility
parvulī, parvulōrum, *m. pl.* – children
prōvidus, prōvida, prōvidum – endowed with foresight, prudent
scūtum, scūtī, *n.* – shield
vehō, vehere, vexī, vectum – (in the passive) to ride, to be carried on

Teacher: Quae arma in proeliō gerunt Germānī?
Student: Germānī hastās longās in proeliō gerunt.

Teacher: Quibus armīs comminus et ēminus pugnant Germānī?
Student: Germānī hastīs longīs/frameīs comminus et ēminus pugnant.

Teacher: Quae alia arma habent mīlitēs Germānī?
Student: Mīlitēs Germānī scūta habent, sed nōn multa alia arma.

Teacher: Vehunturne equīs mīlitēs Germānī?
Student: Multī mīlitum Germānōrum equīs vehuntur.

Teacher: Quid sentiunt Germānī dē mīlite cūius scūtum in proeliō est relictum?
Student: Scūtum in proeliō relinquere flagitium esse sentiunt.

Teacher: Propter quam rem rēgēs Germānōrum creantur?
Student: Rēgēs Germānōrum propter nōbilitātem creantur.

Teacher: Propter quam rem ducēs Germānōrum creantur?
Student: Ducēs Germānōrum propter fortitūdinem creantur.

Teacher: Cūr mīlitēs Germānī parātī ad proelium uxōrēs et parvulōs prope exercitum positōs habent?
Student: Ita mīlitēs intellegunt sē vincere dēbēre.

Teacher: Quid Germānī dē fēminīs crēdunt?
Student: Germānī aliquid sānctum et prōvidum in fēminīs esse crēdunt.

TEACHING TIP

The teacher may wish to explain that the verb *creō* is an exception, because it looks like a verb of the second conjugation, but is, in fact, a verb of the first conjugation.

DERIVATIVES

barba – Beards can be soft and smooth if the hair is longer, but the short ends of an unshaven face can be bristly and sharp. A good shave by a <u>barber</u> eliminates these, hence the association between "beard" and "barber."

The noun "barber" appeared in English around 1300 (although the surname is attested much earlier in the century) at which time it also referred to regular practitioners of surgery. (Medical doctors in those days treated the ill with diagnoses and medicines but were not allowed to operate.) Henry VII (reigned 1509–1547) limited barbers to haircutting and dentistry.

The word "barb" came into English during the late fourteenth century meaning "barb of an arrow," derived through the Old French *barbe* (beard, beardlike appendage) from *barba*. "Barbed" arrows could cause great damage, for the points projected backward from the heads. This prevented easy removal of the arrow from a wound unless pulled through the body to the opposite side, which could cause great damage. It was worse if the arrow had to be removed from the point of entry because it had to be either cut out or pulled out. If attempted, both techniques caused great damage to the victim.

"Barbed" wire is so called because of the small sharp pieces of wire wound around the basic strand.

carō – A "carnivorous" animal eats meat, e.g., wolves, lions, polar bears, etc. (*carō*, and *vorō* = to swallow, devour).

Many ultraconservatives today seem to look upon the Federal Government as the Devil <u>incarnate</u> (from *in* = into, and *carō*).

The city of Istanbul has undergone several <u>reincarnations</u> (*re* = back, again, *in* = into, and *carō*; hence "a rebirth").

The word "carnage" appeared in English around 1600 meaning "slaughter" and derived from *carō* through the Middle French *carnage* (from the Old Italian *carnaggio*). In English it is used more to describe the slaughter of men than of animals.

When the word "carnal" came into English around 1400, it meant "physical, human, mortal." The meaning "sensual" dates to the early fifteenth century; that of "worldly or sinful" appeared shortly thereafter.

The word "carnation" is of uncertain origin, but one of the suppositions rests on its pink color and bases the derivation on *carō* through the Middle French *carnation* (a person's color or complexion). However, as the OED points out, not all carnation flowers are pink.

The word "carnival" (1540s) originally meant "time of merrymaking before Lent" and was derived from the Latin *carō* and *levō* (to lighten, remove) through the French *carnival* and Italian *carnevale* (Shrove Tuesday). The folk etymology (popular but erroneous) was derived from the medieval Latin *carne-vale* (flesh, farewell). The meaning "a circus or fair" dates to 1931 in America.

When the word "carrion" entered English during the early thirteenth century, it was spelled *carione* through the Anglo-French *carogne* and Old North French *caroigne* from the Latin *carō*. As today, it meant "carcass, corpse; dead and putrefying flesh."

424 • Latin for the New Millennium: Teacher's Manual, Level 1

The word "charnal" (late fourteenth century) was derived through the Old French *charnal* from the Latin *carnālis* (of the flesh). A "charnal house" (1550s) was a depository for dead bodies.

herba – The word "herb" came into English around 1300, derived from the Latin but spelled *erbe* because of the French influence (*erbe*). The spelling has been refashioned according to the Latin since the fifteenth century, but the *h* remained mute until the nineteenth century. However, both pronunciations are accepted today.

A "herbivorous" animal eats plants, not meat, e.g., cows, giraffes, elephants, etc. It is an antonym of "carnivorous."

"Herbicides" (from *herba*, and *caedō* = to kill) kill plants. They are commonly known as "weed killers."

The word "arbor" came into English around 1300, spelled *herber*, through the Old French *erbier* (field, kitchen garden; later, a "shady nook") from the Latin *herba*. In the early fourteenth century it meant "a grassy plot." Although not derived from the Latin *arbor* (tree), the spelling of the word was perhaps influenced by it. The change from *er* to *ar* in Middle English reflects a pronunciation shift, which is also seen in "farm" from *ferme* and "harbor" from the Old English *hereborg*.

pellis – A "pelisse" was a fur-lined outer garment or long cloak with slits for arms and worn by women. It was fashionable during the Regency and Victorian periods. The word was derived through the French from the Latin *pellicius* (of the skin). The related Latin word *pelliō* means "furrier" or "tanner."

The word "surplice" (late thirteenth century) was derived through the Old French *surpeliz* from the Latin *super* (over, above) and *pellis*. In medieval Latin a *pellicium* was a "fur garment." A "surplice" was so called because it was a loose white robe worn over fur garments (worn by clergymen to keep warm in unheated medieval churches).

proelium – None

vestīmentum – The word "vestment" (around 1300) is derived from the Latin *vestīmentum* and refers to robes worn by the clergy and their assistants. It is a syncopated form of the Latin.

See *vestis* 2.2 for related derivatives.

vulnus – The prefix of "invulnerable" is negative. The word is derived from the Latin *invulnerābilis* (that which cannot be wounded) and is attested in English from the 1590s.

The word "vulnerable" derives from the Latin *vulnerābilis* (likely to be wounded). It appears in English around 1600.

hic, haec, hoc – None

ferōx – (from *ferus* = wild, cruel, uncivilized; the *-ōx* suffix means "denoting appearance." Therefore, a "ferocious" person is "full of" a "fierce" or wild look. It is usually pejorative today, although the word "fierce" is not.) "Fierce" came into English around 1300, keeping the meaning of *ferus* (wild, savage). By the mid-thirteenth century, however, it had acquired the meaning of "proud, noble, bold." Although the OED maintains that the later meaning died out around the sixteenth century, today it still can have the connotation of "brave, daring," e.g., a <u>fierce</u> competitor in the 100-yard dash. The spelling was influenced by its passage through the Old French *fer, fier* (strong, violent, wild, proud).

terribilis – The derivatives "terrible" and "terribly" come directly from the Latin *terribilis*, which is based on the verb *terreō* (to frighten). The suffix denotes ability; thus a "terrible" flood has the ability to frighten.

See also Teaching Tip 1.16.

coquō – The verb has several figurative meanings, e.g., to ripen, digest, plan, disturb. Several of the derivatives listed are based on these meanings rather than the basic "to cook."

The word "apricot" came into English during the 1550s, spelled *abrecock*, and was derived through the Portuguese *albricoque* (influence by the Arabic *al* = the, and *birquq* = apricot) from the Latin *praecoquum* (early-ripening; *prae* = before, and *coquō*); the sun "cooks the fruit and thus causes it to ripen." The Latin adjective was short for *persicum praecox* (early-ripening peach). The derivative is first attested as a color name in 1906.

The verb "concoct" means, literally, "to cook together." The idea of a "made-up" story dates to 1823. When the word first appeared during the 1530s, it meant "to digest," reflecting one of the meanings of the Latin *coquō*. (Digestion basically works on foods "cooked together.") During the 1670s it came to mean "to prepare an edible thing." The meaning of "concoct" expanded metaphorically beyond cooking after 1702. The thieves <u>concocted</u> a plan to hijack the plane.

The word "precocious" (1640s) is derived from *praecox* (early-ripening) and therefore refers to "someone developed before the usual time." A <u>precocious</u> child is mentally ahead of his chronological age.

The adjective "terra-cotta," literally, "cooked earth," appeared in English in 1722 and referred to hard-fired clay. After 1882 the word was also used as a color-name for "reddish-brown."

The word "cook" is derived from *coquō* through *coquus* (cook), the Vulgar Latin *cocus* (cook), and the Old English *coc*. The verb usage appeared during the late fourteenth century. The figurative sense of "to manipulate, falsify, doctor" (as in "to cook the books") dates to the 1630s.

The word "biscuit" went through several spelling changes, from *besquite* in the early fourteenth century to *bisket* in the sixteenth century, and finally to its modern form in the nineteenth century. It is derived from the Latin (*pānis*) *bis coctus* (twice-cooked bread). The American sense of "soft bun" dates to 1818.

The word "cuisine" came into English in 1786 through the French *cuisine* (style of cooking) from the Latin *coquinus* (of cooking), the adjectival form of *coquō*.

The word "kitchen" appeared in English early, around 1200, derived through the Middle English *kichene* and Old English *cycene* from the Latin *coquina* (feminine of *coquinus* = of cooking).

crēscō – A <u>crescent</u> moon is "growing" or increasing in size. This is the source for the sense of "a crescent shape" (late fourteenth century). The Latin originally applied the term only to the waxing moon (*lūna crēscēns*) but the term was subsequently used by mistake to refer to the shape, not the stage. The word "crescendo," applied to sound or music, retains the earlier Latin meaning.

The verb "accrue" (mid-fifteenth century) was derived from the Latin *accrēscō* (to increase, be added to) through the Old French *acreue* (growth; from the verb *acreistre* = to increase).

The noun "recruit" (1640s) exhibits the same type of derivation, i.e., from the Latin *recrēscō* (to grow again) through the Old French *recreistre* (to grow or increase again). The prefix of "recruit" means "back, again"; the verb root is *crēscō* (to increase). Thus the verb (1630s) means, literally, "to increase again." The military sense dates to the 1650s; to recruit student athletes is attested from 1913.

The Latin *incrēscō* (to grow in size or amount, rise, swell; literally, "to grow in or upon") is the source for "increase" and, via the Latin *incrēmentum* (growth, addition), for "increment." The meaning "amount of increase" dates to the 1630s.

The word "decrease" (late fourteenth century) is the antonym of "increase," derived from the Latin *dēcrēscō* (to wane, wear away, disappear; *dē* = down from).

The Latin *excrēscō* (to grow, rise up; *ex* = out from) gives "excrescence" (early fifteenth century) to English. The meaning "that which grows out abnormally" on a living thing dates to the 1570s. The <u>excrescence</u> on the child's face was removed by surgery.

The adjective "concrete" came into English during the late fourteenth century meaning "actual, solid." It was derived from the Latin *concrēscō* (to grow together, clot, curdle, harden; congeal). The noun sense of "building material made from mixing cement and various other materials like gravel or sand with water" dates to 1834.

The noun "crew" (mid-fifteenth century) originally meant "a group of soldiers" and was derived through the Old French *creue* (an increase, a recruit) from the Latin *crēscō*. The sense of "people working together" dates to the 1560s, that of "men on a warship" to the 1590s. The term "crew cut" is first attested in 1938, the hair cut so called because the style originated with the Harvard and Yale boat crews.

sānō – The prefix of "insane" is negative.

The euphemism for "janitor" is "sanitation engineers" (they keep a building clean and therefore healthy).

A "sanitarium" (1829) is a place "dedicated to health" and is essentially a health resort.

A "sanatorium" is a hospital for the treatment of chronic disease like tuberculosis or mental disorders.

A "sanitary" water supply is necessary for good health. The word appeared in English in 1823 derived through the French *sanitaire* from the Latin *sanitās*.

sedeō – The fourth principal part is the root for "session" (literally, "the act of sitting"). It appeared during the late fourteenth century meaning "a periodical sitting of a court" through the Old French *session* (assembly).

The word "possession" (mid-fourteenth century) is derived from the past participle of the Latin *possideō* (from *potis* = able, and *sedeō*) meaning "to hold, occupy, have" (literally, "able to sit [upon]"). The grammatical use of "possessive" dates to the 1550s.

The word "obsession" (1510s) originally meant "the action of besieging" and was derived from the Latin *obsideō* (literally, "to sit against"; besiege). The psychological sense dates to 1901.

The Latin *adsideō* (to sit by, attend, assist) is the source for the English "assess" (early fifteenth century), which meant "to fix the amount of a tax or fine." An assistant "sitting beside a judge" was responsible for this. The meaning "to estimate the value of property" for tax purposes dates to 1809; the transferred sense of "judging the value of a person or idea" dates to 1934.

The word "assizes" (around 1300), meaning "a session of a law court," is derived from *adsīdō* (the *e* of the root changes to an *i* when a prefix is added) through the Old French *asseoir* (to cause to sit).

The noun "size" appeared in English around 1300, meaning "an ordinance to fix the amount of a tax" and derived through the Old French *sise*, a shortened form of *assise* from the Latin *adsīdō*. The verb appeared around 1400. The verbal phrase "to size up" retains the original idea of "assess."

The adjective "assiduous" (1530s) meaning "attending, constantly present" and thus "busy, constant" is also derived from *adsīdō*. Note the "-ous" suffix.

The word "insidious" came into English during the 1540s meaning, literally, "to sit on, occupy" and then "deceitful, cunning" (from the Latin *insidiae* = plot, ambush).

"Preside" (1610s) derives from the Latin *praesideō* (to sit before; to stand guard) as does "president" (one who sits in front; superintends; a leader or governor).

The Latin *resideō* is the root of "reside," which came into English during the late fifteenth century and means, literally, "to sit back"; hence, "to be idle, remain behind, rest" and "residence" as well as "residue" (mid-fourteenth century) through the Old French *residu* from the Latin *residuus* (remaining, left over) and "residual" (1560s).

The word "subside" is derived from the Latin *subsīdō* (the Latin prefix means "movement down"; hence "to sit down, sink down, settle," etc.).

The Latin noun *subsidium*, related to *subsīdō* (to lie in wait for, reinforce) and meaning "help, assistance, military reserves," is the root of "subsidy" (late fourteenth century).

The word "subsidiary" is derived directly from the Latin *subsidārius* (kept in reserve, acting as support) and appeared in English during the 1540s.

The use of a computer is a "sedentary" occupation, usually pursued while sitting at a desk.

"Sediment" sinks to the bottom of a liquid and "sits there."

The Latin verb *sedō*, a causative form of *sedeō*, e.g., "causes the flames to subside," is the root for "sedate" (1660s), which means "calm, quiet."

An ill person can be <u>settled</u> down by a "sedative" (early fifteenth century).

The Latin *supersedeō* literally means "to sit on top of," then, "to refrain from, desist." Thus the English derivative "supersede" means to "sit over another law or person"; "to replace in power or authority."

The word "surcease" (early fifteenth century) is also derived from *supersedeō* through the Old French *surseoir*. The English spelling with *c* was influenced by the unrelated word "cease."

The word "besiege" (around 1300) is based on "siege" meaning "a seat" and derived from the Latin *sedeō* through the Old French *sege* (seat). The military sense of an "army sitting down before a fortress" dates to that time. The prefix is related to the Latin *ambi* (= about) and the Old English *be-* (= on all sides) and can have just about any sense required (intensive, causative, provide with, on, for, etc., e.g., to betray, besmirch, betroth, beribbon, etc.).

terō – The word "trite" (1540s) is derived from *trītus* (well-worn, commonplace), the fourth principal part of *terō*.

The adjective "contrite" (around 1300) is derived from the Latin *conterō* (to wear out, grind, crumble; the prefix *con-* is a form of *cum* and is intensive). It is used figuratively in English (crushed by a sense of guilt).

The word "detriment" (early fifteenth century) is derived from the Latin *dēterō* (*dē* = down, off, away, and *terō*) through *dētrīmentum* (a loss, harm).

The word "tribulation" (early thirteenth century) is derived through the Old French *tribulacion* and the Latin *tribūlāre* (to oppress, afflict) from *terō* (to rub) and the suffix *-bulum* denoting instrument or place.

vīvō – Many of these derivatives are clearly defined, e.g., "vivify" (to make alive, real), "vivacious" (full of life), "vivacity" (the quality of liveliness), "revive" (to live again), "vivid" (lively, animated), "viviparous" (giving birth to live young), and "convivial" (literally, "living well"; the prefix "con" is intensive): A "convivial" person is fond of good food, good drink, and good companionship.

The derivative "survive" (early fifteenth century) is formed from the Latin *super* (over, beyond) and *vīvō*, and came into English through the Old French *souvivre*.

The related Latin noun *vīta* is the base for "vital" (late fourteenth century; a body's <u>vital</u> signs indicate life), and "vitally" (referring to something almost essential to life, e.g., a <u>vitally</u> important document).

"Vitamins" are essential for life. The word was coined in 1920 by the chemist Cosimer Funk who thought these substances contained amino acids. It was originally spelled "vitamine," but the *e* was dropped "when scientists learned the true nature of the substance" (OED).

The word "viand" (early fourteenth century) means "an article of food" and was derived through the Old French *viande* (food) from the Latin *vivenda* (things needed for living). Today it usually refers to delicate or fine foods.

The word "victuals" came into English around 1300, originally spelled *vitaylle*, and was derived through the Old French *vitaille* and the Latin *victuālis* (nourishing) from *vīvō*. The spelling was altered early in the sixteenth century to conform to the Latin, but the pronunciation remains "vittles."

vulnerō – See *vulnus* above.

celeriter – When the bell rang for dismissal, all the students moved with great <u>celerity</u> to the exits.

forīs – The word "foreign" (mid-thirteenth century) was derived through the Old French *forain* (outer, strange, remote) from the Latin *forīs* (out of doors). The sense of "not in one's own land" dates to the late fourteenth century.

The word "forest" (late thirteenth century) originally meant "an extensive tree-covered district" and came from *forīs*, probably from the *forestem silvam* (outside woods) of Charlemagne's *Capitularies*, a term denoting "the royal forest." However, another theory traces it to the Latin *forum* (court, judgment); thus, "land subject to a ban."

The word "foreclose" (late thirteenth century) is derived from *forīs* (outside) and *claudō* (to shut) through the Old French *forclos* (past participle of *forclose* = to exclude).

The word "forfeit" (around 1300) is derived through the Old French *forfait* (crime) from the Latin *forīs* and *faciō* (to do) and originally meant "misdeed." The sense shifted from the deed to the penalty during the mid-fifteenth century.

See also Teaching Tip 1.10.

inter – The words "enter, entrance," and "entrée" are all derived from the Latin *intrāre* (*inter*, and *eō* = to go). "Entrée" originally (1724) meant "the opening of an opera or ballet." It began to be used in cookery from 1759 but originally referred to the dish "which was introductory to the main course." In the United States it now denotes the main course of a meal.

The "entrails" of an animal are its "inner parts" or "intestines" (Latin *interanea*).

An "intern" (from the Latin *internus*) receives his training within a hospital. The noun appeared in American English in 1879; the verb denoting this training dates to 1933. The verb meaning "to confine within set limits" dates to 1866 and is also derived from *internus* as does the adjective "internal" (early fifteenth century).

From the Latin superlative of *inter* (*intimus* = inmost) comes the adjective "intimate" (1630s) meaning "closely acquainted." The noun dates to the 1650s. The noun "intimacy" began to be used as a euphemism for sexual intercourse during the 1670s.

The Latin adverb *intrinsecus* (inwardly, on the inside) is the root for "intrinsic" (late fifteenth century). Teachers hope that their pupils will provide <u>intrinsic</u> incentives for learning and not depend solely on external stimuli.

postquam – See *posteā* in 1.1.

Chapter 19 • 429

CHAPTER 20 (PP. 359–371)

GRAMMAR IN LANGUAGE FACTS

Pluperfect Tense Passive of All Conjugations; Perfect Active and Passive Infinitives; Demonstrative Pronoun and Adjective *Ille*

PAGE 359
Standards 1.1, 2.1
RRA 6B

MEMORĀBILE DICTŪ VOCABULARY

cor, cordis, *n.* – heart

loquitur – speaks, from the verb *loquor, loquī, locūtus sum*, "to speak"

TEACHER BY THE WAY
Augustine's *Confessions* is *Cōnfessiōnēs* in Latin.

TEACHER BY THE WAY
Ary Scheffer was a nineteenth-century Dutch painter whose work is associated with "Academic Art." This movement produced painting and sculpture under the influence of the Academies in Europe and especially France. It is characterized by its polished style, its mythological or historical subjects, and its moralistic tone. This painting of Augustine and his mother is based on Book 10 of the *Cōnfessiōnēs* in which the two discuss the Kingdom of Heaven. It now hangs in the National Gallery, London.

Scheffer's painting entitled *Ecstasy at Ostia* depicts mother and son at Ostia. Following his reconversion to Christianity, which delighted his mother, Augustine and his mother were on their return to Africa. While waiting at the port in Ostia, Monica fell ill. In the *Cōnfessiōnēs* (Book 10), Augustine notes that while looking out the garden window he and his dying mother experienced a vision of "that which is."

TEACHER BY THE WAY
Augustine was a prolific writer; some 113 books and treatises, more than 500 sermons, and more than 200 letters by Augustine survive. The *Confessions* and the *City of God* are two of his longer works and have been most influential through the centuries.

The first nine books of the *Confessions* are autobiographical. The story of his pear-tree theft is an example of the lust of his adolescence. Augustine's quest for meaning sees him embrace the life of pleasure, join the Manichees (a third century CE religion from Mesopotamia that synthesized Zoroastrianism, Buddhism, Babylonian traditions, and some elements of Christianity), develop a lifelong love of philosophy from reading Cicero's *Hortēnsius*, and become a follower of the Neoplatonists. Appointed professor of rhetoric in Milan, Augustine first hears the sermons of Ambrose from the professional perspective but is gradually convinced by Ambrose's teachings and to his mother's delight converts. In Book 10 Augustine gives thanksgiving and praises God for his conversion and for the graces that help him resist temptation. The last four books provide an exegesis of Genesis including an allegorical interpretation of its first chapter.

In the *City of God*, Augustine provides a philosophy (or some would say a theology) of history in the context of the eternal city of God versus the temporal city of the world. Augustine rejects the Roman belief that polytheistic worship is critical to temporal prosperity and the Greek philosophical view that such belief is prerequisite to happiness in the afterlife. He does, however, see both Roman virtue and Greek philosophy as aids to spreading and understanding Christian revelation and man's redemption. Augustine's work was being written as the city of Rome was besieged by invaders.

TEACHING TIP
Chapter 6B of RRA contains information on Augustine. The teacher may wish to assign this chapter for reading or review.

PAGE 360
Standards 1.1, 2.1, 3.1, 3.2

TRANSLATION OF LATIN PASSAGE
About the Theft of Pears
Both human and divine laws are accustomed to punish a theft. Even a thief does not tolerate with indifference another thief. And a rich thief does not tolerate a poor thief. I also wanted to commit a theft and I did <it>. However, I did not do this because of poverty, but because of love of doing wrong/mischief. For I sought things which I had in abundance, not <those> which I lacked. In fact, I wanted to be delighted by the theft itself, not by the things that I was seeking. Near my house there was a pear tree full of fruits, which seemed very nice. A few other bad young men and I during the night (for we had played <games> during the whole day) left our houses and sought that tree. We shook off it all the fruit, and took them away with us. We ate a few of them, we threw almost all to the pigs. For we did not want to eat the fruit

that had been taken by us. In fact, all <of us> in our homes abounded with good foods. We wanted to do things against the laws and to take pleasure in mischief. The reason for this wickedness was wickedness itself. <I loved> bad things, I loved unjust things, I loved to do bad and unjust things.

Now I have grown up and my heart already understands that I loved bad things; it already understands that bad things were done by me.

TEACHER BY THE WAY
Augustine's writings synthesize Christian faith with Platonic and Neoplatonic ideas.

TEACHING TIP
Instruct the students to locate Hippo on the map on pp. xxxiv–xxxv (SE) and to find Augustine at the time of his conversion to Christianity on the timeline on pp. 405–408 (SE).

TEACHER BY THE WAY
While it is correct in Latin to say *ego et paucī aliī adulēscentēs improbī*, the corresponding English expression is "a few other bad young men and I."

PAGE 361

ANSWERS TO COMPREHENSION QUESTIONS
1. Pears from a pear tree. He ate a few of them, but gave most to the pigs.
2. He wanted to enjoy the theft.
3. It happened when Augustine was a young man, and he is writing about it many years after.

TEACHING TIP
While English derivatives from the asterisked words (i.e., the Vocabulary to Learn) are the topic of Exercise 2 later in this chapter, there are some interesting derivatives from the non-asterisked words. The teacher may choose to discuss these derivatives with the students.

- *adolēscō* – adolescent
- *ēiciō* – eject, ejection, ejector
- *improbus* – improbity
- *malitia* – malicious
- *porcus* – pork
- *tolerō* – toleration, intolerable
- *tōtus* – total, totality

TEACHER BY THE WAY

In addition to *pirus*, the pear tree, which is listed in this vocabulary, there are a number of other trees that, in Latin, are feminine in gender and are included here for the teacher's convenience.

- *castanea* – chestnut
- *fāgus* – beech
- *fīcus* – fig
- *mōrus* – mulberry
- *pīnus* – pine
- *pōpulus* – poplar
- *quercus* – oak
- *salix* – willow

It is interesting to note that *acer* (the maple tree), by contrast with the trees mentioned above, is neuter in gender.

PAGE 362

Standards 1.1, 3.1, 4.1
Workbook Exercise 1

TEACHER BY THE WAY

The way to say the "pluperfect tense" in Latin is "*tempus plūsquamperfectum.*" As with the other tenses, when responding to the question "*Cūius temporis est?*" the answer should be in the genitive case.

TEACHING TIP

Additional reproducible worksheets, morphology charts, and their associated answer keys, related to this material, are available for download at www.lnm.bolchazy.com.

- **Verb Conjugations**

PAGE 363

Standards 1.1, 1.2

Oral Exercise 1; Workbook Exercises 4, 6

▶ EXERCISE 1 ANSWERS

1. dēlectātī, dēlectātae, (dēlectāta) erāmus — we had been delighted
2. lēctī, lēctae, lēcta erant — they had been chosen
3. oppressī, oppressae, (oppressa) erātis — you (plural) had been overwhelmed
4. rogātus, rogāta, rogātum erat — s/he/it had been asked
5. līberātī, līberātae, (līberāta) erāmus — we had been freed
6. relictī, relictae, (relicta) erātis — you (plural) had been left behind
7. pūnītus, pūnīta, (pūnītum) eram — I had been punished
8. quaesītī, quaesītae, quaesīta erant — they had been looked for
9. excitātī, excitātae, (excitāta) erātis — you (plural) had been awakened

ORAL EXERCISE 1

This exercise may be used after the pluperfect tense passive has been presented.

The teacher should say the first person singular present active of the verbs below. Then, s/he should ask different students for the first person singular pluperfect passive form of each verb.

Teacher: doceō   **Student:** doctus, a, um eram

Teacher: amō   **Student:** amātus, a, um eram

Teacher: legō   **Student:** lēctus, a, um eram

Teacher: pōnō   **Student:** positus, a, um eram

Teacher: gerō   **Student:** gestus, a, um eram

Teacher: dēleō   **Student:** dēlētus, a, um eram

Teacher: faciō   **Student:** factus, a, um eram

Teacher: iaciō   **Student:** iactus, a, um eram

Teacher: intellegō   **Student:** intellēctus, a, um eram

Teacher: iubeō   **Student:** iussus, a, um eram

Teacher: cōnsūmō   **Student:** cōnsūmptus, a, um eram

Teacher: petō   **Student:** petītus, a, um eram

Chapter 20 • 435

PAGE 364

Standards 1.1, 1.2, 3.1, 4.1
Workbook Exercise 2

▶ EXERCISE 2 ANSWERS

1. cordial — cor
2. furtive — fūrtum
3. legal — lēx
4. delicious — dēlectō
5. punitive — pūniō
6. adolescent — adulēscēns
7. equal — aequus
8. divinity — dīvīnus
9. humanity — hūmānus
10. abundance — abundō

TEACHING TIP

Although in Exercise 2 the students are directed to find only the derivatives based on the Vocabulary to Learn, they may be interested to learn that there are other derivatives in Exercise 2. The derivation of these words is provided for the teacher's convenience.

1. very – from *vērus* (true, actual, real); *vērāx* (truthful). me – from *mē* (accusative singular of *ego*, I).
3. advice – from *ad* (to, toward) + *vīsus* (sight, vision) from *videō* (to see).
5. action – from *agō* (to drive, do, discuss, live, spend); *āctiō* (doing, duty, negotiation, etc.).
6. attitude – from *aptus* (attached, fitted with, suitable).
7. people – from *populus* (people, nation, populace).
8. school – from *schola* (school, sect, followers) from the Greek word *scholē* (meaning "leisure" since only the wealthy had the time for education).
9. habitat – from *habitō* (to live, dwell) from *habeō* (to have, hold).
10. trait – from *trahō* (to drag, pull out, take on, derive, get, etc.). patience – from *patientia* (endurance, stamina, forbearance) from *patior* (to suffer, allow, put up with). in – from *in* (in, on, at).

TEACHER BY THE WAY

This portrait of Augustine is one of twenty-eight portraits of outstanding men and scholars that Federico de Montefeltro, Duke of Urbino, commissioned to hang in his palace studiolo. They are attributed to the Flemish painter Joos van Wassenaer, who was working for the Duke between 1460 and 1480.

436 • Latin for the New Millennium: Teacher's Manual, Level 1

PAGE 365
Oral Exercise 2

ORAL EXERCISE 2
This exercise may be used after perfect active and passive infinitives have been presented.

The teacher should read aloud each of the following present infinitives. Then individual students should orally give the corresponding perfect active infinitive if the form is present active, and the perfect passive infinitive if the form is present passive.

Teacher: audīre   **Student:** audīvisse
Teacher: audīrī   **Student:** audītus, audīta, audītum esse
Teacher: docēre   **Student:** docuisse
Teacher: docērī   **Student:** doctus, docta, doctum esse
Teacher: lūdere   **Student:** lūsisse
Teacher: lūdī   **Student:** lūsus, lūsa, lūsum esse
Teacher: pūnīre   **Student:** pūnīvisse
Teacher: pūnīrī   **Student:** pūnītus, pūnīta, pūnītum esse
Teacher: temptāre   **Student:** temptāvisse
Teacher: temptārī   **Student:** temptātus, temptāta, temptātum esse

 TEACHING TIP
If the teacher wishes to conduct a review of present infinitives prior to introducing the perfect infinitives that are on this page, the present infinitives active and passive of the four conjugations will be be found in the student text on pp. 23, 75, 128, 142, and 170. The future active infinitive will be presented on p. 380. *Īnfīnītīvus* is the Latin word for "infinitive." Here is a quick drill that may be conducted orally.

Teacher: *Sedeō – Dīc mihi īnfīnītīvum temporis praesentis, generis/vōcis āctīvī/āctīvae!*
Answer: *Sedēre*

Teacher: *Sānō – Dīc mihi īnfīnītīvum temporis praesentis, generis/vōcis passīvī/passīvae!*
Answer: *Sānārī*

Teacher: *Terō – Dīc mihi īnfīnītīvum temporis praesentis, generis/vōcis āctīvī/āctīvae!*
Answer: *Terere*

Teacher: *Coquō – Dīc mihi īnfīnītīvum temporis praesentis, generis/vōcis passīvī/passīvae!*
Answer: *Coquī*

Teacher: *Capiō – Dīc mihi īnfīnītīvum temporis praesentis, generis/vōcis passīvī/passīvae!*
Answer: *Capī*

PAGE 366

Standards 1.1, 1.2
Workbook Exercise 5

▶ EXERCISE 3 ANSWERS

1. Augustine says that near his house there is a tree, and that this tree has many beautiful fruits.
   Augustīnus dīcit prope domum suam arborem fuisse et eam arborem multa pōma pulchra habuisse.
   Augustine says that near his house there was a tree, and that this tree had many beautiful fruits.

2. Augustine narrates that he desires bad things, and that he is pleased by the theft.
   Augustīnus nārrat sē rēs malās cupīvisse et fūrtō dēlectātum esse.
   Augustine narrates that he desired bad things, and that he was pleased by the theft.

3. Augustine says that all fruits are being shaken off the tree and taken away by the young men.
   Augustīnus dīcit omnia pōma ab adulēscentibus ex arbore esse excussa atque asportāta.
   Augustine says that all fruits were shaken off the tree and taken away by the young men.

4. Augustine says that he is eating few fruits, and he is throwing out almost all (fruits).
   Augustīnus dīcit sē pauca pōma comēdisse, et paene omnia ēiēcisse.
   Augustine says that he ate few fruits, and threw out almost all (fruits).

TEACHING TIP

The students may be interested in learning the Latin words for other pieces of fruit in addition to *pirum*, "the pear." Below is a list for the teacher's convenience. If the teacher has access to representations of fruit made of plastic or wood, then the teacher can simply hold up the object and ask the class, "*Quid est?*"

- **cerasum, cerasī,** *n.* – cherry
- **citreum, citreī,** *n.* – lemon
- **frāgum, frāgī,** *n.* – strawberry
- **mālum, mālī,** *n.* – apple
- **(ūva) passa, passae,** *f.* – raisin
- **persicum, persicī,** *n.* – peach
- **prūnum, prūnī,** *n.* – plum
- **ūva, ūvae,** *f.* – grape
- **vaccīnium, vaccīniī,** *n.* – blueberry

PAGE 367
Standards 1.1, 1.2, 3.1, 4.1
Oral Exercise 3; Workbook Exercise 3

▶ EXERCISE 4 ANSWERS
1. erant excussa

   All fruits had already been shaken off the tree by Augustine and by his friends. Then they ate a few fruits.
2. erant dēlectātī

   The young men had been pleased by only few fruits. The other fruits they threw away to the pigs.
3. esse factum

   The wicked young men thought that the theft had been done well.
4. fēcisse

   Augustine finally understood that he had not done (behaved) well.

TEACHING TIP
Instruct the students to repeat the forms of *ille, illa, illud* after the teacher has modeled the pronunciation of each form. Encourage the students to create a rap, cheer, or song to help them remember the forms of *ille*. Alternatively, use Bolchazy-Carducci's *Toga Beats*.

ORAL EXERCISE 3
This exercise may be used after the demonstrative pronoun and adjective ille, illa, illud *has been presented.*

The teacher should point out objects in the classroom, objects visible from the window, or pictures of objects put on the board that are close or far from an individual student, and then ask the student to name them using *hic* and *ille* accordingly.

Some examples:
- animal – hoc animal, illud animal
- arbor – haec arbor, illa arbor
- barba – haec barba, illa barba
- caelum – hoc caelum, illud caelum
- caput – hoc caput, illud caput
- casae – hae casae, illae casae
- cīvis – hic cīvis, ille cīvis
- corpora – haec corpora, illa corpora
- digitī – hī digitī, illī digitī
- domus – haec domus, illa domus

Teacher: Quid vidēs?
Students:
Hanc epistulam/illam epistulam videō.
Hanc fēminam/illam fēminam videō.

Chapter 20 • 439

Hōs virōs/illōs virōs videō.

Hunc hominem/illum hominem videō.

Hunc librum/illum librum videō.

Hās nūbēs/illās nūbēs videō.

Haec vestīmenta/illa vestīmenta videō.

PAGE 368
Standards 1.1, 1.2

▶ EXERCISE 5 ANSWERS

1. illās inīquitātēs — accusative plural — those injustices
2. illī fūrēs — nominative plural — those thieves
3. illīus cordis — genitive singular — of that heart
4. illīs adulēscentibus — dative or ablative plural — to/for, by/with those young men
5. illārum lēgum — genitive plural — of those laws
6. illōrum pōmōrum — genitive plural — of those fruits
7. illā causā — ablative singular — by/with that reason
8. illīs lītoribus — dative or ablative plural — to/for, by/with those shores
9. illa odia — nominative or accusative plural — those hatreds
10. illō saxō — ablative singular — by/with that rock
11. illī carnī — dative singular — to/for that meat

 TEACHING TIP
After the students have completed Exercise 5 and the correct answers have been given, as a quick review the teacher might wish to ask the students to replace the forms of *hic* in Exercise 5 with the corresponding form of *is*. The answers are provided for the teacher's convenience.

1. *eās*
2. *eī*
3. *eius*
4. *eīs*
5. *eārum*
6. *eōrum*
7. *eā*
8. *eīs*
9. *ea*
10. *eō*
11. *eī*

PAGE 369
Standards 1.1, 1.2, 3.1, 4.1
Dictation; Workbook Exercise 7, Content Questions

▶ EXERCISE 6 ANSWERS

1. erant victī — The enemies fled. They had already been overcome by us.
2. erat exstīnctum — We saw flames. The fire had not been extinguished.
3. erās occultātus — I sought you for a long time. For you had been hidden well.
4. erat pūnītus — The boy was not rejoicing. For he had been punished by <his> mother.
5. erātis vocātī — You (plural) came to us. For you had been called by us.

TEACHING TIP
The verb *sum* may either precede or follow the participles in the answers.

DICTATION

This exercise may be used to conclude the chapter.

Dictate the following sentences to the students and ask them to change each sentence from the active into the passive voice.

Teacher: Amīcōs nostrōs exspectāverāmus.
Student: Amīcī nostrī ā nōbīs erant exspectātī.

Teacher: Mīlitēs Rōmānī hostēs vīcerant.
Student: Hostēs ā mīlitibus Rōmānīs erant victī.

Teacher: Omnem pecūniam cōnsūmpserātis.
Student: Omnis pecūnia ā vōbīs erat cōnsūmpta.

Teacher: Ille liber mē dēlectāverat.
Student: Illō librō eram dēlectātus/dēlectāta.

Teacher: Dux virōs armātōs ad proelium dūxerat.
Student: Virī armātī ā duce erant ad proelium ductī.

Teacher: Verba tua nōn audīveram.
Student: Verba tua ā mē nōn erant audīta.

Teacher: Illam inīquitātem populus dēlēverat.
Student: Illa inīquitās ā populō erat dēlēta.

Teacher: Propter lēgem illum virum pūnīverant.
Student: Propter lēgem ille vir ab eīs erat pūnītus.

Chapter 20 • 441

PAGE 370
Standard 1.2
Oral Exercise 4

TRANSLATION OF THE LATIN CONVERSATION
Mary: Hello, friends! Do you want to come with me?

Helen: To which place should we come?

Mary: To the mall. For I saw a dress there which I want to buy.

Helen: What sort of dress is it?

Mary: It is a very beautiful summer dress. For a long time I had been looking for a summer dress (a summer dress had been searched for a long time by me) and finally last week I caught sight of a pretty item.

Christy: Why did you not buy (it) right away?

Mary: I did not have the money.

Helen: What now? Do you now have the money?

Mary: Father gave me a credit card.

Helen: Is this true (are you saying the truth)? How much does the dress you want to buy cost?

Mary: One hundred dollars.

Christy: I save money and I have savings in the bank. If I want to buy a dress, I withdraw money from (my) account. I do not buy things with a credit card and I do not owe money.

Mary: You are lucky/happy. The money seem to flow out of my hands.

TEACHER BY THE WAY
Exact price in Latin is expressed by the ablative.

ORAL EXERCISE 4
This exercise may be used after the Latin dialogue has been presented.
Ask the students to answer the following questions.

Teacher: Quis pecūlium habet?
Student: Christīna pecūlium habet.

Teacher: Cūr Christīna pecūlium habet?
Student: Christīna pecūniae parcit.

Teacher: Quis rēs chartulā creditōriā emit?
Student: Marīa rēs chartulā creditōriā emit.

Teacher: Emitne rēs chartulā creditōriā Christīna?
Student: Christīna rēs chartulā creditōriā nōn emit.

Teacher: Dēbetne Christīna pecūniam?
Student: Christīna pecūniam nōn dēbet.

Teacher: Quōmodo (*how*) tū solvere solēs?
Student: Solvere soleō pecūniā numerātā/chartulā creditōriā/assignātiōnibus argentāriīs.

Teacher: Solēsne pecūniae parcere?
Student: Soleō/nōn soleō pecūniae parcere.

Teacher: Solēsne multās rēs emere?
Student: Soleō/nōn soleō multās rēs emere.

PAGE 371
Standard 4.1

DERIVATIVES

adulēscēns – See *alō* in 1.17 for derivatives.

cor – When hearts are together ("con" = *cum* = together, and *cor*), there is "concord" (early fourteenth century).

The "core" of an argument is the heart of the disagreement. The nuclear reactor sense dates to 1949.

The noun "cordial" is late fourteenth century and originally meant "medicine, food, or drink that stimulates the heart" (OED). The adjective appeared about the same time meaning "of the heart," and derived through the Middle French *cordial* from the Latin *cor*. The meaning "heartfelt, from the heart" dates to the mid-fifteenth century.

The noun "discord" dates to the early thirteenth century and is derived from the Latin *discors* (*dis* = apart, and *cor*). The musical sense appeared during the late fourteenth century.

The word "courage" appeared around 1300, derived through the Old French *corage* from *cor*. The word "heart" remains today a common metaphor for "inner strength."

Note the "-ous" suffix of "courageous."

The prefix of "discourage" means "away from" or "apart from." Thus, "to discourage someone" means "to take away the heart" to do something.

The antonym of "discourage" is "encourage" meaning "to put heart into (*in* = into)" someone. Both words date to the fifteenth century.

The verb "record" came into English around 1200 meaning "to repeat, reiterate, get by heart" (*re* = again, back, and *cor*). The noun appeared about a century later. At first it meant "testimony recalled from the heart and committed to writing." The meaning "a written account of some event" is attested during the late fourteenth century. Its reference to the "best or highest achievement in sports" dates to 1883. The phrase "on the record" appears in 1900.

See also Teaching Tips 1.9 and 1.18.

fūr – The word "furtive" (late fifteenth century) is derived from the Latin adjective *furtīvus* (stolen, secret).

The noun "ferret" (late fourteenth century) is derived from *fūr* through the Old French *furet*, a diminutive of *fuirion* (weasel, ferret; literally "thief"). The related verb *ferret* (early fifteenth century) referred to "the use of half-tame ferrets to kill rats and flush out rabbits from burrows" (OED). The extended sense "to search out, discover" dates to the 1570s.

fūrtum – See *fūr* above.

inīquitās – Note the "-ous" suffix of "iniquitous" (full of injustice). The prefix "in" is negative. The word appeared in English in 1726.

Chapter 20 • 443

The noun "iniquity" came into English around 1300 from the Latin *inīquitās*. It meant "hostility, malevolence." The meaning "evil, wickedness" dates to the late fourteenth century.

See also *aequus* below for related derivatives.

lēx – (from *legō*, *legāre* = to choose, gather, read, etc.)

The verb "allege" appeared in English around 1300, derived from the Latin *allegō* (to send, commission, dispatch) and meant "to send for, name, produce in evidence" (based on the meaning of the French *alléguer*). The English form, however, is derived through the Anglo-French *alleger* and the Old French *eslegier* ("to clear at law," from the Latin *ex* = out of, and *litigō* = to bring suit). The related noun "allegation" (from the Latin *allegātiō*) dates to the early fifteenth century.

The word "colleague" (1530s) derives from the Latin *collēgium* (association in office; *cum* = with, and *legō* = to choose). Therefore it meant "one chosen with another" or "one chosen at the same time as another." The same Latin noun is the root of "college" (late fourteenth century) which literally meant "an association of colleagues." At first it referred to any corporate group, but the sense of "academic institution" (1560s) became the principal meaning during the nineteenth century via its use at Oxford and Cambridge.

The word "delegate" (late fifteenth century) is derived from the Latin *dēligō* (select, gather; *dē* = away, and *legō*) and meant "to send away as a representative." The base "legate" dates to the mid-twelfth century and originally meant "an authorized representative of the Pope." The general sense of "ambassador, delegate, messenger" appears during the late fourteenth century.

The word "legislator" came into English around 1600 derived from *lēx* and the fourth principal part of *ferō* (*lātus*). The suffix indicates the agent by whom the law was carried.

The noun "legislation" appeared during the 1650s.

The adjective "legal" (mid-fifteenth century) is derived from the Latin *legālis* (pertaining to the law). The sense of "permitted by law" dates to the 1640s.

The prefix of "illegal" and "illegitimate" is negative (from *in* by assimilation).

The noun "legacy" (late fourteenth century) at first meant "a body of persons sent on a mission." The sense of "property left by will" appeared in Scottish during the mid-fifteenth century, echoing the meaning "leave, bequeath" of *legō*.

The word "privilege" (mid-twelfth century) is derived from the Latin *prīvus* (single, own) and *lēx* through *prīvilēgium* (a law in favor of or against an individual). The meaning "advantage granted" dates to the mid-fourteenth century.

The word "loyal" dates to the 1530s when it referred to subjects of sovereigns or governments and meant "law-abiding, faithful" (in carrying out feudal obligations). The general sense, referring to lovers, dogs, etc.) appeared around 1600.

The prefix of "disloyal" means, literally, "away from" and is hence a negative.

The verb "relegate" (1590s) derives from the Latin *relegō* (to send away, reject, etc.). The meaning "to place in a position of inferiority" dates to the 1790s.

See also Teaching Tips 1.10 and 1.16.

pōmum – The word "pomegranate" came into English around 1300 derived from *pōmum* and *granātus* (containing many seeds). The classical Latin name for this fruit was *malum granātum* (seeded apple).

The rounded knob at the front of a saddle is a "pommel" (mid-fifteenth century), so called because it was shaped like an apple. Earlier (mid-thirteenth century), the word referred to the ornamental knob at the end of a sword handle.

444 • Latin for the New Millennium: Teacher's Manual, Level 1

The alteration of "pommel" to "pummel," meaning "to beat repeatedly" with fists or with the pommel of a sword (instead of using the edge or point), dates to the 1540s.

ille, illa, illud – None

aequus – The list of derivatives given is by no means exhaustive (as is the case in so many words that have multiple examples) but does demonstrate that the words are, for the most part, easily understood ("equal" and "equable"), even when they consist of a combination of *aequus* and another Latin-based word, e.g., "equidistant" (*distāre* = to stand apart), "equilibrium" (*libra* = balance), "equivalent" (*valeō* = to be worth, be well, be strong), "equipoise" (*pensum* = weight, value), and "equinox" (*nox* = night; "when the night equals the day").

The word "equanimity" (*animus* = mind, spirit) originally (around 1600) meant "fairness, impartiality." The meaning "evenness of temper" dates to the 1610s.

The verb "equivocate" (early fifteenth century) literally means "to call equally" (*vocō* = to call, name) and thus "to use ambiguous language in order not to take sides," "to mislead," "to hedge."

dīvīnus – The derivative "divine," both as an adjective and as a noun, came into English around 1300, reflecting the meaning of the Latin root (godlike, of a god, excellent). The verb usage (mid-fourteenth century), meaning "to conjure, to guess," is based on Latin verb *dīvīnō* (to prophesy) and the noun *dīvīnus* (soothsayer).

A "diviner" is thus a prophet or soothsayer. Note the suffix which, like "-tor," denotes a person.

See *deus* in 1.10 for related derivatives.

hūmānus – See *homō* in 1.8 for derivatives.

See also Teaching Tip 1.2 under *hūmānitās*.

pauper – The word "pauper" came into English during the 1510s unchanged from its Latin source. It was formed from *paucus* (little) and *pariō* (to produce); hence, "A pauper produces little."

The derivative "poor" came into English around 1200 through the Old French *povre* (modern French *pauvre*) from the Latin *pauper*.

The related Latin noun *paupertās* is the base of "poverty," which appeared in English during the late twelfth century through the Old French *poverte*.

The prefix "im-" of "impoverish" means "into"; hence the literal meaning "into poverty": The villagers were <u>impoverished</u> (by someone or something).

plēnus – Two derivatives from *plēnus*, "complementary" and "complimentary," are often confused. For example, a restaurant may list salads and vegetables as "complementary," which means they "complete" the items on the menu and are included in the stated price. This meaning of "complement" surfaced during the 1640s. Before that, it was equivalent to "compliment," both words meaning "an exchange of courtesies, an expression of civility." The two words and their meanings were differentiated by 1650. The Latin verb *compleō*, meaning "to complete," is the root of both forms and meanings, as in "forming a complement" or "completing the obligations of politeness." The Latin prefix (*com-*) acts as an intensive here; thus the word means "to fill up entirely."

A delegate with "plenipotentiary" powers is invested with full authority.

Note the "-ous" suffix of "plenteous."

Insurance policies in "compliance" with the Affordable Care Act have conformed to (fulfilled entirely) the requirements of the law.

Chapter 20 • 445

The prefix "sup-" means "up from below." The Latin verb *suppleō*, therefore, means "to make up to the full complement" and is the root of "supply" and "supplement."

The related noun *plēnitās*, meaning, literally, "fullness" and hence "abundance," is the root of "plenty" (mid-thirteenth century).

The verb "accomplish" (late fourteenth century) is derived through the Old French *accomplir* (to fill up) from the Latin *ad* and *compleō*.

The noun "depletion" (1650s) is derived from the Latin *dēpleō* (*dē* = down from, away from, and *plēnus*) meaning "to empty." The word originally referred to "blood-letting." Today it has a larger meaning, i.e., "a serious decrease or even exhaustion of an abundance or supply."

The word "expletive" dates to the 1610s and originally meant "a word or phrase used to fill out" (*ex* = out from, and *plēnus*) a sentence or metrical line. For example, we often use "there" as an expletive. There was a good reason for his action. The sense of "exclamation," often as a cuss word, was first recorded in 1815 (used by Sir Walter Scott), and in the 1970s, it was popularized by the Watergate tapes in which "expletive deleted" replaced President Nixon's more colorful remarks.

The noun "implement," derived from the Latin *impleō* (*in* = into, and *pleō*), came into English during the mid-fifteenth century and meant "a filling up" (as with provisions). The sense of "tool" dates to the 1530s from the idea that "things which do the work complete a household."

The first plenary (full) session of the Convention was held on Friday. The word appeared in English during the 1510s.

The traditional Thanksgiving dinner will be replete with all the usual dishes. The derivative came into English during the late fourteenth century, derived from the Latin *repleō* (to fill up, satiate, fill to overflowing). The prefix *re-* can mean "back, again," etc., but is often used as an intensive.

abundō – The derivatives "abound" and "abundance" both appeared in English during the fourteenth century and are derived from the Latin *abundō* (*ab* = away, from, and *unda* = wave; hence, "away from the water" as in "rise in a wave" and thus "to overflow") and the related noun *abundantia*.

dēlectō – See *delīciae* in 1.7 for derivatives.

egeō – The Latin root of "indigent" and "indigence" is *indigēns* (from *indu* = in, and *egeō* = to be in want, need). The noun appeared in English during the late fourteenth century and the adjective around 1400. These derivatives can look a bit tricky, as the prefix is not "in" and not negative.

lūdō – The word "allude" entered English during the 1530s, derived from the Latin *allūdō* (by assimilation from *ad* = toward, in relation to, and *lūdō*). Originally it meant "to mock," but it acquired the meaning "to make an indirect reference" during the 1570s.

The noun "collusion" dates to the late fourteenth century and is derived from the Latin *collūdō* (play together or with). The idea of fraud, conspiracy, or secret agreement is inherent in the word (probably based on the meaning of the Latin verb "to make sport of" and "secret understanding" from *collūsiō*). The related verb "collude" is not found in English until the 1520s.

The verb "delude" (around 1400) is derived from the Latin *dēlūdō* (to dupe; the prefix means "down"; hence, "to one's detriment").

The noun "illusion" (mid-fourteenth century) originally meant "act of deception" and was derived from the Latin *illūsiō* (ridicule, irony) from *illūdō* (by assimilation from *in* and *lūdō*; hence, "to play, jeer at, abuse, ridicule"). The sense of "deceptive appearance" developed in Church Latin and then in English.

The word "disillusion" appeared in English as a noun in 1814 and as a verb in 1855. The prefix is negative; thus, the word means "freedom from enchantment and a return to reality."

The verb "elude" (1530s) is derived from the Latin *ēlūdō* (*ex* = away, and *lūdō*), which meant "to foil, outplay, cheat, make fun of." The sense of "evade" dates to the 1610s (figurative: Contentment eluded her.) and 1630s (literal: The thief eluded the police.).

The related adjective "elusive" dates to 1719 and describes something that is hard to grasp, e.g., an elusive thief or an elusive concept.

Note the "-ous" suffix of "ludicrous."

The derivatives "interlude" (around 1300), "prelude" (1560s), and "postlude" (1821) all refer to time periods before, during, and after plays or musical compositions. For instance, between the acts of a long medieval mystery play (the "interlude") humorous episodes were performed; a "prelude" is a short composition played before the major piece; and a "postlude" is played at the end of a church service.

pūniō – (from *poena*; the verb can also be spelled *poeniō*)

The verb "punish" entered English around 1300, derived through the Old French *puniss* (participle of *punir*) from the Latin *pūniō*. The meaning "to inflict heavy damage or loss" dates to 1801.

The related noun "punishment" appeared during the late fourteenth century.

See also Teaching Tip 1.9.

noctū – See *nox* in 1.10 for derivatives.

paene – A "peninsula" (1530s) is "almost an island."

A "penult" (adjective in 1530s; noun in 1570s) is "almost the last" (*paene*, and *ultimus* = last) syllable.

An "antepenult" (1610s) is the syllable before (*ante*) the *penult*.

A "peneplain" is "almost flat," the result of prolonged erosion.

CHAPTER 21 (PP. 373–385)

GRAMMAR IN LANGUAGE FACTS

Future Perfect Tense Passive of All Conjugations; Future Active Participle; Future Active Infinitive

PAGE 373
Standards 1.1, 2.1
RRA 7

MEMORĀBILE DICTŪ VOCABULARY

The passive verbs *mūtantur* and *mūtāmur* can be expressed by the intransitive active English verb "are changing."

TEACHER BY THE WAY

Soon after their foundation beginning with Benedict of Norcia, the monasteries served as the intellectual centers of Europe. Initially, their schooling was limited to educating those who chose to become monks but with time the monks undertook the education of the local nobility's sons as well. Monasteries were run as self-sufficient communities and following the motto of the Benedictines, *Ōrā et Labōrā*, "Pray and Work," monks followed a carefully calibrated day divided between communal prayer and their work maintaining the monastery.

Monks came to specialize in a given activity. Some of them became masters in the craft of copying, illustrating, and binding books. Initially, these books were produced for use in the monastery—copies of the gospels, Gregorian chant, prayer books, and over time other works for use in their schools. Those involved in this activity worked in a large communal room called the *scrīptōrium*. This room was often located above the kitchen as the monasteries were not heated but some heat facilitated this labor-intensive, close work.

A monk first mastered how to copy the letters of the text and with time learned to create elaborate initial letters and to fill blank spaces with pen drawings. These later evolved into miniature paintings while the initial letters became highly complex in their designs. Soon, those especially adept at a given activity became specialists. Those who painted the small illuminated scenes were called miniators while those who excelled at initial letters were rubricators.

These illuminated manuscripts, especially the prayer books and books of hours, sometimes especially commissioned by a noble, are a treasure trove of images from the medieval world. The images of the manuscripts also came to serve as models for the frescoes, narrative sculpture, and stained glass windows of medieval churches.

As a market developed for these manuscripts, professional artists with apprentices undertook this activity.

• 449 •

TEACHING TIP
Chapter 7 of RRA contains information on Boethius. The teacher may wish to assign this chapter for reading.

PAGE 374
Standards 1.1, 2.1, 3.1, 3.2

TRANSLATION OF LATIN PASSAGE
About the Wheel of Fortune

You have received many things from me. I nourished you for a long time. You had riches and honors. You made a mistake. You thought you would always have those things given to you for the time being. But constancy is foreign to me. Always being about to go away, I gave you nothing. Eventually you were abandoned by me. Riches and honors departed together with me. Why do you rebuke me? I snatched from you nothing that was yours. You will not be able to accuse me of theft!

People have many things, but they possess nothing. I, Fortune, possess everything. If things will have been given to people by me/if things are given to people by me, I will take those things back afterward. For all those things are mine, not people's. If a person will have been abandoned by me/If a person is abandoned by me, all things given to him will go away <from him> with me. I am the owner/mistress of all riches and all the external things that people have. I never stay always with any person, but all wealth and external things always remain with me.

Everything in the life of man/humans is always changing. People live as if on a huge wheel, which is always being turned around <its> axle. This wheel is mine! A person who will have been lifted up/is lifted up in my wheel will afterward descend and fall for certain. Therefore a person who has wealth and honors ought to know for certain that he will finally leave those things.

TEACHER BY THE WAY
During the Middle Ages Boethius's translations of Aristotle's writings on logic were widely studied. Interpretations of his *Cōnsōlātiō Philosophiae* vary, but all agree that it represents the author's personal vision, expressed with great spiritual conviction, of the immortality of the human soul.

TEACHING TIP
Instruct the students to find Boethius and Theodoric the Great on the timeline on pp. 405–408 (SE).

PAGE 375

ANSWERS TO COMPREHENSION QUESTIONS
1. Boethius is accusing Fortune that she has abandoned him.
2. Fortune has not taken away from Boethius anything that was not hers.
3. All relationships she has with men are temporary.
4. Man can rise and fall in accord with the turning of the wheel.

TEACHER BY THE WAY

The name of the Roman goddess *Fortūna*, a word derived from the Latin *ferre* "to bear, bring," means "that which has been brought." In that sense, she was associated with fertility, prosperity, and abundance, as the source of goods. This aspect of the goddess was represented visually with the cornucopia. Another aspect visualized in the prow or rudder of a ship presented her as directing the course of one's life and as the source of safe, steady passage. A third aspect of *Fortūna*, that of the ball or the wheel, spoke to the capricious nature of fortune. Romans initially understood fortune as inconstancy, that which comes and goes as a matter of life. To counter its effects, Romans cultivated *virtūs*. By the time of the later empire, *Fortūna* became more focused on the pejorative aspect of the wheel of fortune as laying mortals low.

Many aspects of *Fortūna* were worshipped in the Roman world. Her role as protector of grain and a good harvest, *Fortūna Annōnāria*, is seen in a garden statue of her in a home at Ostia named for the presence of the statue. The massive temple complex built by Sulla in the first century CE at Praeneste, one of the largest in the Roman world, is dedicated to *Fortūna Prīmigenia*. In this capacity, *Fortūna* is worshipped as the goddess who attends her favorite from birth. In addition, the sanctuary at Praeneste included an oracle site related to the worship of *Fortūna*.

The wheel that can turn readily served as a symbol of the vagaries of fortune. It is regularly depicted in medieval art, as in the illustration of p. 373 (SE), with four figures depicting four stages of life. Two figures at nine o'clock and noon are positive and the other two at three o'clock and six o'clock respectively are negative. The figure on the top of the wheel is usually crowned. The crowned female figure in blue behind the wheel in this illustration represents *Fortūna*. Note that, like Justice, she is blindfolded. In other representations, Latin captions accompany each figure. Again, following clockwise from nine o'clock: *rēgnābō*, "I shall reign"; *rēgnō*, "I reign"; *rēgnāvī*, "I have reigned"; and *sum sine rēgnō*, "I am without reign, without a kingdom, or, I do not reign."

The first page of the illuminated manuscript of the *Carmina Burāna*, Codex 4660 in the Bayerische Staatsbibliothek in Munich, includes an illustration of the *Rota Fortūnae* with the Latin captions and the text of a Latin song about the fickleness of fortune. Students will read a selection from the *Carmina Burāna* in Level 2. American students will immediately think of the popular television show "Wheel of Fortune." Contestants spin a brilliantly colored wheel of fortune in the game show.

PAGE 376

Standards 3.1, 4.1

TEACHING TIP

Now that the students have read a selection from every author in the chapters of this book, the reproducible activity sheet noted below may be used.

TEACHING TIP

Additional reproducible worksheets, morphology charts, and their associated answer keys, related to this material, are available for download at www.lnm.bolchazy.com.

- **Author, Author!**

PAGE 377

Workbook Exercise 1

TEACHING TIP

Now that the students have learned all six tenses in Latin, this might be an appropriate time to review how to answer the question "*Cūius temporis est?*" for each tense. The answers are summarized here for the teacher's convenience.

Answers:

- *temporis praesentis*
- *temporis imperfectī*
- *temporis futūrī*
- *temporis praeteritī perfectī*
- *temporis plūsquamperfectī*
- *temporis futūrī exāctī*

TEACHING TIP

Additional reproducible worksheets, morphology charts, and their associated answer keys, related to this material, are available for download at www.lnm.bolchazy.com.

- **Verb Synopsis**

PAGE 378

Standards 1.1, 1.2

Oral Exercise 1; Workbook Exercise 4

▶ EXERCISE 1 ANSWERS

1. I (f.) was/have been changed   mūtāta erō   I (f.) will have been changed
2. you (m.) had been received   acceptus eris   you (m.) will have been received
3. you (f. plural) were/have been blamed   reprehēnsae eritis   you (f. plural) will have been blamed
4. they were/have been accused   accūsātī erunt   they will have been accused
5. we were/have been turned   versātī erimus   we will have been turned
6. I (m.) had been neglected   neglēctus erō   I (m.) will have been neglected
7. it was/has been taken away   sublātum erit   it will have been taken away

ORAL EXERCISE 1

This exercise may be used after the future perfect tense passive has been presented.

The following forms are either in the future active or in the future passive. The teacher should read each form aloud, then ask individual students to change each form orally into the corresponding forms of the future perfect active or passive.

Teacher: relinquēris   **Student:** relictus, relicta, (relictum) eris

Teacher: petentur   **Student:** petītī, petītae, petīta erunt

Teacher: servābiminī   **Student:** servātī, servātae, (servāta) eritis

Teacher: iubēbis   **Student:** iusseris

Teacher: cūrāberis   **Student:** cūrātus, cūrāta, (cūrātum) eris

Teacher: intellegam   **Student:** intellēxerō

Teacher: cōgitābimus   **Student:** cōgitāverimus

Teacher: cōnspiciēmur   **Student:** cōnspectī, cōnspectae, (cōnspecta) erimus

Teacher: pugnābit   **Student:** pugnāverit

Chapter 21 • 453

PAGE 379

Standards 1.2, 3.1, 4.1
Workbook Exercise 2

▶ EXERCISE 2 ANSWERS

1. rotary — rota
2. alien — aliēnus
3. descendants — dēscendō
4. accusatory — accūsō
5. erratic — errō
6. honorary — honor
7. receipt — recipiō
8. mutations — mūtō
9. possessive — possideō
10. reprehensible — reprehendō

TEACHING TIP

The teacher may wish to share some additional translations of the future active participle with the students. Two examples follow.

audītūrus, audītūra, audītūrum – being ready to hear/on the point of hearing/intending to hear

cōnspectūrus, cōnspectūra, cōnspectūrum – being ready to observe/on the point of observing/intending to observe

TEACHING TIP

Although in Exercise 2 the students are directed to find only the derivatives based on the Vocabulary to Learn, they may be interested to learn that there are other derivatives in Exercise 2. The derivation of these words is provided for the teacher's convenience.

1. motion – from *moveō* (to move). add – from *addō* (to bring to, increase, add). force – from *fortis* (strong, brave). violent – from *violentus* (impetuous, boisterous, violent).
2. reject – from *rēiciō* (to throw back, throw off, repel). simply – from *simplex* (single, simple, natural, straightforward).
3. inherit – from *hērēditārius* (inherited) from *hērēs* (successor, heir, heiress). safer – from *salvus* (alive, intact, safe).
5. motion – from *moveō* (to move). quite – from *quiēscō* (to rest, cease); adverbial form of "quit" which comes from "quiet."
6. distinguished – from *distinguō* (to divide, distinguish, discriminate, set off). degrees – from *dē* (down from, about, in accordance with) + *gradus* (step, stage, standing, rank, etc.). completed – from *compleō* (to fill, fulfill, finish). curriculum – from *curriculum* (race, running, course, lap) from *currō* (to run).
7. visitors – from *vīsitō* (to see often) from *vīsō* (to look at, see, visit). please – from *placeō* (to please, satisfy). sure – from *sēcūrus* (untroubled, unconcerned, carefree).

454 • Latin for the New Millennium: Teacher's Manual, Level 1

8. scientists – from *scientia* (knowledge) from *sciō* (to know). genetic – from *genus* (birth, descent, race, kind, class).
9. parents – from *pariō* (to give birth to, produce, create).
10. behavior – from *habeō* (to have, hold). especially – from *speciēs* (appearance, sight, idea, vision, beauty) from *speciō* (to observe, consider, regard). in – from *in* (in, on, at). public – from *pūblicus* (public). official – from *officium* (service, attention, duty).

PAGE 380
Standards 1.1, 1.2, 3.1, 4.1
Workbook Exercise 3

▶ EXERCISE 3 ANSWERS

1. lēctūrus, -a, -um — about to read, going to read
2. mūtātūrus, -a, -um — about to change, going to change
3. respōnsūrus, -a, -um — about to reply, going to reply
4. temptātūrus, -a, -um — about to try, going to try
5. cursūrus, -a, -um — about to run, going to run
6. cāsūrus, -a, -um — about to fall, going to fall
7. dormītūrus, -a, -um — about to sleep, going to sleep
8. pugnātūrus, -a, -um — about to fight, going to fight
9. cupītūrus, -a, -um — about to want, going to want
10. gestūrus, -a, -um — about to carry, going to carry
11. statūrus, -a, -um — about to stand, going to stand
12. possessūrus, -a, -um — about to possess, going to possess
13. āctūrus, -a, -um — about to drive, going to drive
14. dēlētūrus, -a, -um — about to destroy, going to destroy

TEACHING TIP
After the students have completed Exercise 3 and the correct answers have been given, the teacher might wish to ask the students to change the nominative singular form of the future participle with which they answered the questions to a different case. Suggestions for this type of practice and answers are provided for the teacher's convenience.

1. nominative masculine plural – *lēctūrī*
2. ablative singular neuter – *mūtātūrō*
3. dative plural feminine – *respōnsūrīs*
4. accusative singular neuter – *temptātūrum*
5. dative singular masculine – *cursūrō*
6. genitive plural feminine – *cāsūrārum*
7. genitive singular masculine – *dormītūrī*
8. nominative plural feminine – *pugnātūrae*
9. ablative singular feminine – *cupītūrā*

10. dative plural masculine – *gestūrīs*

11. accusative singular feminine – *statūram*

12. dative singular feminine – *possessūrae*

13. genitive plural neuter – *āctūrōrum*

14. genitive singular feminine – *dēlētūrae*

PAGE 381
Oral Exercise 2

ORAL EXERCISE 2

This exercise may be used after future infinitives in indirect statements have been presented.

In each of the following indirect statements there is a present infinitive. The teacher should recite a sentence slowly and clearly. Students should be allowed to ask the teacher to repeat the sentence any number of times until they can reproduce it from oral memory. When the student can repeat the sentence, then s/he should repeat it once more, but this time changing the infinitive of the indirect statement to the correct form of the future infinitive. No writing is needed for this exercise.

Teacher: Boēthius sē multās rēs ā Fortūnā accipere putābat.
Student: Boēthius sē multās rēs ā Fortūnā acceptūrum esse putābat.

Teacher: Hominēs sē multās rēs ā Fortūnā accipere putābant.
Student: Hominēs sē multās rēs ā Fortūnā acceptūrōs esse putābant.

Teacher: Fortūna sē nihil Boēthiō dare sciēbat.
Student: Fortūna sē nihil Boēthiō datūram esse sciēbat.

Teacher: Fortūna Boēthium nihil ā sē accipere sciēbat.
Student: Fortūna Boēthium nihil ā sē acceptūrum esse sciēbat.

Teacher: Fortūna hominēs nihil ā sē accipere sciēbat.
Student: Fortūna hominēs nihil ā sē acceptūrōs esse sciēbat.

Teacher: Fortūna sē omnia possidēre crēdit.
Student: Fortūna sē omnia possessūram esse crēdit.

Teacher: Boēthius sē omnia possidēre crēdit.
Student: Boēthius sē omnia possessūrum esse crēdit.

Teacher: Hominēs sē omnia possidēre crēdunt.
Student: Hominēs sē omnia possessūrōs esse crēdunt.

Teacher: Fortūna sē numquam manēre dīxit.
Student: Fortūna sē numquam mānsūram esse dīxit.

Teacher: Fortūna omnia ab homine discēdere dīxit.
Student: Fortūna omnia ab homine discessūra esse dīxit.

Teacher: Fortūna sē ab homine semper discēdere dīxit.
Student: Fortūna sē ab homine semper discessūram esse dīxit.

456 • Latin for the New Millennium: Teacher's Manual, Level 1

PAGE 382
Standards 1.1, 1.2
Workbook Exercise 5

▶ EXERCISE 4 ANSWERS
1. (future active infinitive)   I believe that Fortune is going to snatch away riches and honors.
2. (future active infinitive)   Fortune seems to be about to snatch away riches and honors.
3. (future active participle)   Fortune, ready to give gifts and rewards, is loved by men.
4. (future active infinitive)   Fortune seems to be on the point of giving gifts and rewards.
5. (future active infinitive)   We do not believe that Fortune is going to give gifts and rewards.

TEACHING TIP
If additional practice on future participles and infinitives is needed, here are a few supplemental sentences of the same type as in Exercise 4.

6. Nihil ā mē in rotā Fortūnae dēscēnsūrō tenērī potest.   (future active participle)
   Nothing can be held by me being about to go down (descend) on the wheel of Fortune.
7. Mē in rotā Fortūnae mox dēscēnsūrum esse sciō.   (future active infinitive)
   I know that I am soon on the point of going down (descending) on the wheel of Fortune.
8. In rotā Fortūnae mox dēscēnsūrus esse videor.   (future active infinitive)
   I seem to be about to descend soon on the wheel of Fortune.

▶ EXERCISE 5 ANSWERS
1. Fortūna nihil mihi datūra esse vidētur.
2. Fortūnam numquam discessūram esse crēdimus.
3. Dīvitiās meās relictūrus/a sum.
4. Crēditis Fortūnam omnēs rēs externās semper possessūram esse.
5. Vidēorne tibi mox in rotā Fortūnae dēscēnsūrus/a esse?

TEACHING TIP
If additional practice is needed, here are a few more sentences for translation.

6. I do not think that those men will have many things.
   Illōs hominēs multās rēs habitūrōs esse nōn putō.
7. I know for sure that Fortune will afterward take back those things given to you.
   Fortūnam illās rēs tibi datās posteā receptūram esse prō certō sciō.
8. Fortune said that constancy would always be foreign to her.
   Fortūna cōnstantiam semper ā sē aliēnam futūram esse dīxit.

Chapter 21 • 457

PAGE 383

Standards 1.1, 1.2

Workbook Exercises 6, 7, Content Questions

▶ EXERCISE 6 ANSWERS

1. Why does Boethius says that he has made a mistake?
   Putābat sē dīvitiās et honōrēs semper habitūrum esse.
   He used to think that he would always have riches and honors.

2. Why does Fortune say that she cannot be accused of theft?
   Fortūna nihil, quod erat Boēthiī, ex eō ēripuit.
   Fortune snatched nothing, which belonged to Boethius, from him.

3. Why is constancy said to be alien to Fortune?
   Fortūna numquam cum ūllō homine semper manet.
   Fortune never always remains with any person.

4. Why are all riches and external things said to belong to Fortune, not to people?
   Dīvitiae rēsque externae cum homine manent dum Fortūna cum eō manet, sed semper cum Fortūnā manent.
   Wealth and external things remain with a person as long as Fortune remains with him, but they always remain with Fortune.

5. Why are people said to live as if on a great wheel?
   Omnia in vītā hominum semper mūtantur.
   Everything in the life of humans is always changing.

6. Why should a person, who has riches and honors, know for certain that he at last will leave those things?
   Homō, quī in rotā Fortūnae sublātus erit, posteā prō certō dēscendet et cadet.
   A person who is raised up on the wheel of Fortune will afterward descend and sink for certain.

PAGE 384

Standards 1.2, 4.1

TEACHING TIP

After the students have looked at the Talking Vocabulary on this page, the teacher may wish to use one of the CPOs to put on view the month names and the numbers from eleven to twenty in Latin.

Months
- *Iānuārius*
- *Februārius*
- *Mārtius*

- *Aprīlis*
- *Māius*
- *Iūnius*
- *Iūlius*
- *Augustus*
- *September*
- *Octōber*
- *November*
- *December*

Numbers 11–20 (The numbers 1–10 are on p. 236 [SE])

- *ūndecim*
- *duodecim*
- *tredecim*
- *quattuordecim*
- *quīndecim*
- *sēdecim*
- *septendecim*
- *duodēvīgintī*
- *ūndēvīgintī*
- *vīgintī*

In either oral or written format, the teacher may ask individual students one or both of the following questions. Some correct answers are provided.

Quot annōs nāta/us es? – How old are you?	*Quīndecim annōs nātus/a sum* or *quīndecim annōs*
	Sēdecim annōs nātus/a sum or *sēdecim annōs*
Quō mēnse nāta/us es? – In what month were you born?	*Mēnse Iānuāriō nātus/a sum* or *Mēnse Iānuāriō*
	Mēnse Septembrī nātus/a sum or *Mēnse Septembrī*

The teacher may also have one student ask another in Latin how old s/he is. After the student replies, s/he then asks another student how old s/he is, and this continues until all students have asked another student the question and each student has given an answer.

Chapter 21 • 459

PAGE 385

Standards 1.2, 4.1
Oral Exercises 3, 4, Dictation

 TEACHER BY THE WAY
Exspectāte in this dialogue means "Wait a minute!"

TRANSLATION OF THE LATIN CONVERSATION

Mary, Mark, Christy (*in unison*): Greetings, Helen! May fortune be kind to you not only on this birthday, but also (your) whole life!

Helen: Welcome to you all! My birthday will be very happy, because you all came! It is good to celebrate (one's) birthday with friends.

Mark: We want to have a birthday party with you. We have many birthday gifts.

Helen: If so many and such great gifts are given to me, I will have great riches.

Christy: We also have a cake.

Helen: We will eat soon. However, first I want to open those beautiful packages.

Christy: How old are you today, Helen?

Helen: Today I am seventeen years old.

Christy: And so we need to put seventeen candles on the cake.

Mark: Who will light the candles?

Helen: I!

Mark: Fine. Then you ought to blow out strongly and extinguish all candles simultaneously. Then we will eat the cake—but not the candles.

Helen: Wait you all! First I will open those packages, then we will light the candles and eat the cake!

ORAL EXERCISE 3

This exercise may be used after the Latin dialogue has been presented.

In preparation for the exercise, the teacher should use one of the CPOs to put on view the following words:

ubi? (*interrogative adv.*) – where
quōmodo? (*interrogative adv.*) – in what way, how?

After the students have carefully read and understood the dialogue, the teacher should ask individual students the following questions. (NB: The students may look at the dialogue while they answer.) The students should be urged to use the actual words in the dialogue in their answers, changing endings and forms only where needed to fit the answer. They should be encouraged to use the new words and phrases introduced in this dialogue.

Teacher: Cūr putat Helena nātālem diem sibi futūrum esse fēlīcissimum?
Student: Quia vēnērunt Marīa, Mārcus, Christīna, et bonum est nātālem diem cum amīcīs celebrāre.
Teacher: Ubi nātāliciam Helenae agitāre cupiunt Marīa, Mārcus, Christīna?
Student: Marīa, Mārcus, Christīna nātāliciam Helenae apud Helenam agitāre cupiunt.

460 • Latin for the New Millennium: Teacher's Manual, Level 1

Teacher: Quās rēs habent Marīa, Mārcus, Christīna, quās Helenae dare cupiunt?
Student: Marīa, Mārcus, Christīna multa dōna nātālicia et lībum habent, quae omnia Helenae dare cupiunt.

Teacher: Quid prīmum facere cupit Helena?
Student: Helena prīmum fasciculōs pulchrōs aperīre cupit.

Teacher: Quot annōs nāta est Helena?
Student: Helena septendecim annōs nāta est.

Teacher: Ubi Christīna putat sē et amīcōs septendecim candēlās pōnere dēbēre?
Student: Christīna putat sē et amīcōs septendecim candēlās in lībō pōnere dēbēre.

Teacher: Quis candēlās accendere cupit?
Student: Helena candēlās accendere cupit.

Teacher: Quōmodo Helena omnēs candēlās simul exstinguere dēbēbit?
Student: Helena vehementer efflāre (in candēlās) dēbēbit.

ORAL EXERCISE 4

This exercise may be used to conclude the chapter.

The teacher should make a simple statement, and then ask a student *Quid dīxī?* ("What did I say?"). Each student should respond *Dīxistī, magister/magistra, . . .* ("You said, teacher . . .") with the correct version of the teacher's original statement in indirect speech. The original statement will have to be changed into the accusative and infinitive and sometimes the person of pronouns will have to be changed to reflect the perspective of the person answering. Don't forget that the accusative subject in indirect discourse should always be expressed, whereas it is often, indeed usually, omitted in direct speech (because of the endings of verbs). Remind the students to take special care with the tense of the infinitive! The students may ask the teacher to repeat the original direct statement any number of times, to make sure they can recall it before converting it to indirect speech. No writing is needed for this exercise, but the teacher should provide an example before starting this activity.

   Example:
   Teacher: Verba mea audiēs.   **Teacher:** Quid dīxī?
   Student: Dīxistī, magister/magistra, mē verba tua audītūrum/am esse.

Teacher: Boēthius dīvitiās habuit.   **Teacher:** Quid dīxī?
Student: Dīxistī, magister/magistra, Boēthium dīvitiās habuisse.

Teacher: Boēthius dīvitiās habet.   **Teacher:** Quid dīxī?
Student: Dīxistī, magister/magistra, Boēthium dīvitiās habēre.

Teacher: Boēthius dīvitiās habēbit.   **Teacher:** Quid dīxī?
Student: Dīxistī, magister/magistra, Boēthium dīvitiās habitūrum esse.

Teacher: Dīvitiās habeō.   **Teacher:** Quid dīxī?
Student: Dīxistī, magister/magistra, tē dīvitiās habēre.

Teacher: Dīvitiās habuī.   **Teacher:** Quid dīxī?
Student: Dīxistī, magister/magistra, tē dīvitiās habuisse.

Teacher: Dīvitiās habēbō.   **Teacher:** Quid dīxī?
Student: Dīxistī, magister/magistra, tē dīvitiās habitūrum/am esse.

Chapter 21 • 461

Teacher: Dīvitiae apud mē nōn sunt.
Student: Dīxistī, magister/magistra, dīvitiās apud tē nōn esse.

Teacher: Quid dīxī?

Teacher: Dīvitiae apud mē nōn erant.
Student: Dīxistī, magister/magistra, dīvitiās apud tē nōn fuisse.

Teacher: Quid dīxī?

Teacher: Dīvitiae apud mē nōn erunt.
Student: Dīxistī, magister/magistra, dīvitiās apud tē nōn futūrās esse.

Teacher: Quid dīxī?

Teacher: Multī hominēs Fortūnam nōn intellegunt.
Student: Dīxistī, magister/magistra, multōs hominēs Fortūnam nōn intellegere.

Teacher: Quid dīxī?

Teacher: Multī hominēs Fortūnam nōn intellegent.
Student: Dīxistī, magister/magistra, multōs hominēs Fortūnam nōn intellēctūrōs esse.

Teacher: Quid dīxī?

Teacher: Multī hominēs Fortūnam nōn intellēxērunt.
Student: Dīxistī, magister/magistra, multōs hominēs Fortūnam nōn intellēxisse.

Teacher: Quid dīxī?

Teacher: Multa dōna accipiēs.
Student: Dīxistī, magister/magistra, mē multa dōna acceptūrum/am esse.

Teacher: Quid dīxī?

Teacher: Multa dōna accēpistī.
Student: Dīxistī, magister/magistra, mē multa dōna accēpisse.

Teacher: Quid dīxī?

DICTATION

This exercise may be used to conclude the chapter.

Dictate the following sentences to the students, and ask them to change each sentence from the active into the passive voice.

Teacher: Multās rēs accēperis.
Student: Multae rēs ā tē acceptae erunt.

Teacher: Dīvitiās et honōrēs habuerō.
Student: Dīvitiae et honōrēs ā mē habita/ī erunt.

Teacher: Sī tē relīquerō, nihil habēbis.
Student: Sī ā mē relictus/a eris, nihil ā tē habēbitur.

Teacher: Dīvitiae et honōrēs mēcum discēdent, sed nihil āmittēs.
Student: Dīvitiae et honōrēs mēcum discēdent, sed nihil ā tē āmittētur.

Teacher: Sī rēs externās habuerimus, illās rēs posteā recipiet Fortūna.
Student: Sī rēs externae ā nōbīs habitae erunt, illae rēs ā Fortūnā posteā recipientur.

Teacher: Sī Fortūna tē amāverit, tēcum tamen nōn manēbit.
Student: Sī ā Fortūnā amātus/a eris, tēcum tamen nōn manēbit.

Teacher: Sī rēs externās amāveris, Fortūna vītam tuam mūtābit.
Student: Sī rēs externae ā tē amātae erunt, vīta tua ā Fortūnā mūtābitur.

Teacher: Sī cōnstantiam amāverō, Fortūnae rotam nōn petam.
Student: Sī cōnstantia ā mē amāta erit, Fortūnae rota ā mē nōn petētur.

462 • Latin for the New Millennium: Teacher's Manual, Level 1

DERIVATIVES

axis – The word "axis" came into English unchanged from the Latin during the 1540s, meaning "an imaginary straight line around which a body (like the Earth) rotates." The figurative sense in world history meant the German-Italy alliance (1936), originally referred to as the "Rome-Berlin axis."

The term "axial skeleton" refers to the head and trunk of the human body.

cōnstantia – See *stō* in 1.15 for derivatives.

dīvitiae – None. The word derives from *dīves* (rich) which is a cognate of *dīvus* (deified) from *deus* (god). One can thus presume that the early Romans considered those who possessed wealth (*dīvitiae*) to be favored by the gods! That connection holds true for many today as well!

fortūna – The word "fortune" appeared in English around 1300 meaning "chance, luck as a force in human affairs" (OED). The Latin is derived from *fors* (chance, luck).

The word "fortunate" dates to the late fourteenth century and meant "prosperous, lucky," and hence, "happy."

The prefixes of "misfortune" and "unfortunately" are of course both negative.

honor – The noun "honor" came into English unchanged from the Latin around 1200; the verb during the mid-thirteenth century.

The term "honors" for "distinction in scholarship" is attested by 1782. The scholastic sense of "honor roll" dates to 1872.

The word "honorary" appeared during the early seventeenth century.

The adjective "honest" came into English around 1300 from the Latin *honestus* (honorable, respected), which itself is derived from *honor* (gen. *honōris*), the base of *honor*.

In "dishonest," the "dis" prefix means "away" and is therefore a negative.

rota – The adjective "rotary" appeared in English in 1731 through the medieval Latin *rotārius* (pertaining to wheels) from *rota*. The international service club, founded in 1905, was so called from the practice of clubs entertaining in "rotation" (1550s; from *rotātiō* = turning about in a circle).

The adjective "rotund" dates to 1705, although it is found earlier but spelled differently (*rotounde* = early fifteenth century; *rotound* = 1610s).

A "rotunda" (1680s) originally meant "a round building," e.g., the Pantheon. The meaning "a circular hall or room within a building" dates to 1780.

The word "roulette," meaning "a small wheel," was derived (1734) through the French *roulette* (a gambling game played with a revolving wheel) from the Old French *roelete*, which was formed like the diminutive of *rota* (*rotella*).

The word "role," meaning "the part or character one takes," appeared around 1600, derived from the French *role* (literally, "a roll of paper on which an actor's part is written"). The phrase "role model" dates to 1957.

The noun "roll" (early thirteenth century) meant "a rolled-up piece of parchment paper" (especially one with an official record). The verb "roll" appeared around 1300 meaning "to turn over and over." The noun "roller" dates to the late thirteenth century. It is an agent noun of "roll."

To "enroll" in a college means to be entered into the register of students there ("en" = *in*, and *rotula* = diminutive of *rota*).

Chapter 21 • 463

The word "control" (early fourteenth century) is derived from *contrā* (against) and *rotula* and meant "to check accounts against a register." The sense of "to dominate, direct" dates to the mid-fifteenth century.

The word "comptroller" (around 1500) is a variant of "controller" (late fourteenth century). Its bad spelling is due to the influence of the unrelated French *compte* (an account), which is derived from the Latin *computō*.

The word "around" came into English around 1300 (but found rarely before 1600) meaning "in circumference." The sense of "here and there with no fixed direction" dates to 1776 and is an American English usage. The time reference dates to 1888. The prefix "a" is an alpha privative (from the Greek meaning "not"). The spelling of "round" was affected by its passage from *rota* through the Old French *rond* and *ront* and the Anglo-French *rounde*.

A "rondo" (1797) is a "musical composition containing one principal theme which is repeated at least once." It is derived through the Old French *rondel* (a little round) from *rota*.

A "rowel" is the pointed wheel on a spur (mid-fourteenth century from the Old French *roelle* = small wheel).

The word "roundabout" appeared in English during the mid-fourteenth century meaning "by a circuitous route." The noun sense of "traffic circle" dates to 1927.

aliēnus – See *alius* in 1.13 for derivatives.

externus – (from *ex* = out of, and *extrā* = beyond, outside)

The word "external" came into English during the early fifteenth century: Although the <u>external</u> walls of the house were covered with snow, the internal walls stayed warm.

Note the antonym "internal" (see *inter* in 1.19).

futūrus – Both the noun and the adjective "future" entered English during the late fourteenth century. The plural noun "futures," meaning "goods sold on agreement for future delivery," dates to the 1880s.

The adjective "futuristic" entered English in 1915 meaning "avant-garde, ahead of the times." The meaning "pertaining to the future" dates to 1958.

See *sum* in 1.2 and 1.6 for related derivatives.

ūllus – None

accipiō – See *recipiō* below and *capiō* in 1.10 for related derivatives.

accūsō – See *causa* in 1.16 and Teaching Tips 1.11 and 1.13 for derivatives.

dēscendō – The verb "descend" appeared in English around 1300, derived from the Latin *dēscendō* (*dē* = down, and *scandō* = to climb). The sense of "originate" dates to the late fourteenth century and is the source for the noun "descendant" (mid-fifteenth century). Before 1900 there was a tendency to spell the adjective as "descendent" and the noun as "descendant," but since then the latter spelling is found "five times more often than its rival" (OED).

The noun "descent" also came into English around 1300. The evolutionary sense dates to 1859 and Charles Darwin although there are uses that suggest essentially the same thing dating back to the 1630s.

The word "condescend" dates to the mid-fourteenth century and originally meant "to yield deferentially, agree, consent" (from the Latin *cum* = together, and *dēscendō* = to climb down). The idea "to sink willingly to equal terms with inferiors" came into vogue a century later. The corresponding adjective "condescending" retained the positive sense until the late eighteenth century. Today these words have a pejorative nuance, i.e., the idea of someone behaving as if conscious of descending from a superior rank or position.

ēripiō – None

errō – The word "aberration" (1590s), derived from the Latin *aberrō* (*ab* = away, and *errō*), originally meant "a wandering, straying." The sense of "deviation from the norm" dates to 1846.

Note the "-ous" suffix of "erroneous."

A page with a list of the *errāta* found in a book is sometimes inserted in front of the volume after it has been printed (a custom dating to the 1580s).

The adjective "errant" appeared in English during the mid-fourteenth century from the verb "err" (around 1300), which reflected the meanings of the Latin verb. Originally the word just meant "traveling," as in "a knight errant searching for adventure." It later came to emphasize the "aimless" or "highly changing" manner of the wandering, as in "an errant breeze." The meaning of "mistake" is also seen today, as in, "The government is bringing errant Wall Street executives to justice."

The derivative "arrant" (late fourteenth century) at first was merely derogatory, meaning "wandering, vagrant," but during the 1540s it acquired the meaning of "thoroughgoing, downright, notorious," as in "arrant stupidity," or "an arrant coward." The spelling is a variant of "errant."

The adjective "erratic" dates to the late fourteenth century and simply meant "wandering, roving," but by 1841 it had come to mean "irregular, eccentric" also.

mūtō – The prefix of "immutable" is negative.

The related Latin word *mūtābilis*, meaning "changeable, fickle," is the source for "mutable" (late fourteenth century).

The noun "mutation" dates to the same period and meant "an alteration." The genetic sense arose in 1894.

The verb "molt" dates to the mid-fourteenth century and was derived from the verb *mouten* (of feathers, to be shed) from the Latin *mūtō*. The transitive sense, of "birds shedding feathers," dates to the 1520s. The word is also spelled "moult," chiefly in Britain.

The verb "commute" (mid-fifteenth century) is derived from the Latin *commūtō* (to change, exchange, interchange). The prefix is intensive. The sense of "to make less severe" (e.g., the prisoner's sentence was commuted from life imprisonment to 15 years), appeared during the 1630s. The meaning "to go back and forth to work" dates to 1889. The noun "commuter" appeared in American English in 1865.

The word "mutual" dates to the fifteenth century and originally referred to feelings "exchanged with others." The term "mutual fund" is first recorded in 1950. The Cold War's "mutual assured destruction" dates to 1966.

The word "transmutation" came into English during the late fourteenth century, derived from the Latin *transmūtō* meaning "to shift" (*trāns* = across, over, and *mūtō*). It was used in alchemy to describe the change of one mineral into another, e.g., the transmutation of lead into gold.

possideō – See *sedeō* in 1.19 for derivatives.

recipiō – See *capiō* in 1.10 for related derivatives and *accipiō* above.

See also Teaching Tips 1.9, 1.10, and 1.15.

reprehendō – The verb "reprehend" appeared in English during the mid-fourteenth century derived from *reprehendō* (*re* = back, and *prehendō* = to grasp, seize). The Latin verb also means, figuratively, "to blame, rebuke, censure."

Chapter 21 • 465

The adjective "reprehensible" came into English a little later (late fourteenth century), derived from the Latin *reprehensibilis* (open to censure), and means "blameworthy."

The noun "reprisal" appeared in English during the early fifteenth century, meaning "seizing property or citizens of another nation in retaliation for loss inflicted on one's own" (OED), and derived through the Old French *reprisailee* and the early Italian *ripresaglia* (from *riprendere* = to take back) from the Latin *reprehendō*. The general sense of "retaliation" dates to 1710.

tollō – The word "extol" came into English around 1400, derived from the Latin *ex* ("out from" but also "upward") and *tollō*. It meant "to lift up." The figurative sense of "praise highly" is attested about a century later.

The other three derivatives come more properly from *tolerō* (formed from *tollō* by adding -*erō* as in *vulnerō*, *onerō*, etc.) meaning "to support" (from "to lift, raise" of *tollō*) but also, figuratively, "to bear, endure."

The word "tolerance" appeared in English during the early fifteenth century meaning "endurance, fortitude." The sense of "free from bigotry or severity" dates to 1765. The meaning "allowable amount of variation" is found in 1865; the "ability to take large doses" in 1865.

Note the negative prefix of "intolerable."

versō – (formed from *vertō* and -*tō*, making it an iterative = to keep turning, twist; ponder, consider [in the mind]). For derivatives, see *versor* 2.13.

circum – (preposition and adverbial form from the accusative of *circus* = circle)

This word acts as a prefix for many words, among them "circumnavigate" (to sail around), circumference (carrying around; a loan translation from the Greek περιφέρεια *periphereia* = the line "carried around" a circular body), "circumcision" (cutting around, from *caedō*), "circumlocution" (talking around a topic), "circumscribe" (to draw a line around), "circumspect" (to look around with caution; cf. the word describing Sinon in Vergil's *Aeneid*, 2.68), "circumvent" (to go around, from *circumveniō*, which also means, figuratively, "to oppress, cheat"), and "circumstance" (standing around). This word originally (early thirteenth century) meant "conditions surrounding an event." During the mid-fourteenth century it came to mean "a person's surroundings, environment." The sense of "that which is nonessential" dates to the 1590s. The obsolete sense of "formality about an important event" (late fourteenth century) lingers on in Shakespeare's line "pomp and circumstance" (*Othello* 3.3) and in the music played at graduations ("Pomp and Circumstance" by Edward Elgar), still largely a formal affair.

The term "circumstantial evidence" dates to 1691 and refers to "a proof of facts from which inferences are to be drawn," e.g., from a glove found at a crime scene it is inferred that its owner was present. As in this example, the inferences may not always be valid. Further proof is then required.

REVIEW 7: CHAPTERS 19–21
(PP. 387–400)

PAGE 387

TEACHING TIP

Another way to conduct a fun vocabulary review is to play a written vocabulary race.

- Instruct the students to review individually the words on pp. 387–388 (SE) the night before this activity.

- Before the students enter the room, the teacher should decide how many rows to divide the students into and should write the first Latin word of each vocabulary entry in the same number of rows that the students will sit/stand in. There should also be as many Latin words in each row as there will be students in that row. The teacher may choose whether to substitute the English meaning of the entry for the Latin word.

- When the students enter the room, the words should be on display using one of the CPOs. Instruct the students not to talk to any other student about the words on display and not to open their books.

- Divide the class into the number of rows decided upon and instruct them to sit/stand in the order in which they will play.

- Give the first person in each row a piece of chalk or marker, depending on what display option the teacher is using.

- On a signal given by the teacher, the first person in each row runs to the row of words for his/her group and finishes the information for the first word. S/he then runs back and hands the chalk/marker to the second person in the row who in turn runs up and finishes the information for the second word in the row. Play continues in this way until the first team to finish all the words on display in their row is done.

- NB: If any person in a row writes incorrect or misspelled information for his/her word, either the next player or any player after that may make whatever correction is needed. The team that finishes first does NOT win if any word in their row is incorrect. In this case, play begins again until there is a row that finishes with all the information correct.

PAGE 388

Standards 1.1, 1.2

▶ EXERCISE 1 ANSWERS

Perfect passive indicative of *vulnerō*:

	Singular		Plural	
First person	vulnerātus, vulnerāta, (vulnerātum) sum	I was wounded	vulnerātī, vulnerātae, (vulnerāta) sumus	we were wounded
Second person	vulnerātus, vulnerāta, (vulnerātum) es	you were wounded	vulnerātī, vulnerātae, (vulnerāta) estis	you were wounded
Third person	vulnerātus, vulnerāta, vulnerātum est	s/he/it was wounded	vulnerātī, vulnerātae, vulnerāta sunt	they were wounded

Pluperfect passive indicative of *mūtō*:

	Singular		Plural	
First person	mūtātus, mūtāta, (mūtātum) eram	I had been changed	mūtātī, mūtātae, (mūtāta) erāmus	we had been changed
Second person	mūtātus, mūtāta, (mūtātum) erās	you had been changed	mūtātī, mūtātae, (mūtāta) erātis	you had been changed
Third person	mūtātus, mūtāta, mūtātum erat	s/he/it had been changed	mūtātī, mūtātae, mūtāta erant	they had been changed

Future perfect passive indicative of *ēripiō*:

	Singular		Plural	
First person	ēreptus, ērepta, (ēreptum) erō	I will have been snatched away	ēreptī, ēreptae, (ērepta) erimus	we will have been snatched away
Second person	ēreptus, ērepta, (ēreptum) eris	you will have been snatched away	ēreptī, ēreptae, (ērepta) eritis	you will have been snatched away
Third person	ēreptus, ērepta, ēreptum erit	s/he/it will have been snatched away	ēreptī, ēreptae, ērepta erunt	they will have been snatched away

468 • Latin for the New Millennium: Teacher's Manual, Level 1

▶ EXERCISE 2 ANSWERS

1. coctus, cocta, coctum — cooked *or* having been cooked
   coctūrus, coctūra, coctūrum — about to cook *or* going to cook
2. dēlectātus, dēlectāta, dēlectātum — pleased *or* having been pleased
   dēlectātūrus, dēlectātūra, dēlectātūrum — about to please *or* going to please
3. sānātus, sānāta, sānātum — healed *or* having been healed
   sānātūrus, sānātūra, sānātūrum — about to heal *or* going to heal
4. trītus, trīta, trītum — rubbed *or* having been rubbed
   trītūrus, trītūra, trītūrum — about to rub *or* going to rub
5. versātus, versāta, versātum — turned *or* having been turned
   versātūrus, versātūra, versātūrum — about to turn *or* going to turn

PAGE 389
Standards 1.1, 1.2

▶ EXERCISE 3 ANSWERS

	Singular	**Plural**
Nominative	hoc pōmum	haec pōma
Genitive	huius pōmī	hōrum pōmōrum
Dative	huic pōmō	hīs pōmīs
Accusative	hoc pōmum	haec pōma
Ablative	hōc pōmō	hīs pōmīs

	Singular	**Plural**
Nominative	illa inīquitās	illae inīquitātēs
Genitive	illīus inīquitātis	illārum inīquitātum
Dative	illī inīquitātī	illīs inīquitātibus
Accusative	illam inīquitātem	illās inīquitātēs
Ablative	illā inīquitāte	illīs inīquitātibus

▶ EXERCISE 4 ANSWERS

1. Poēta dīcit sē esse ā fortūnā relictum et omnia bona esse ab eā ērepta.

   The poet says that he has been abandoned by Fortune and all good things have been snatched away by her.
2. Poēta dīcit sē Fortūnam fūrtī esse accūsātūrum.

   The poet says that he will accuse Fortune of theft.
3. Nam poēta dīcit sē omnēs rēs prō certō possēdisse.

   For the poet is saying that he owned everything for sure.
4. Fortūna dīcit omnia in vītā hominum semper mūtārī.

   Fortune says that everything in the life of people is always being changed.
5. Fortūna quoque dīcit hominēs vīvere sīcut in magnā rotā.

   Fortune also says that people live as if on a big wheel.

Review 7: Chapters 19–21 • 469

▶ EXERCISE 5 ANSWERS

1. pugnātūrī   The Huns, about to fight/going to fight, want to look/seem terrible.
2. facta   The Huns wear clothes made of animals' hides.
3. coctam, trītam The Huns are accustomed to eat not cooked, but rubbed meat.
4. ēreptās   They take not only meat, but also herbs snatched away from the earth.
5. dormītūrī   The Huns, about to sleep/going to sleep, sit on their horses.

PAGE 390
Standards 1.1, 1.2

▶ EXERCISE 6 ANSWERS

1. Augustīnus est reprehēnsus. Nam multae malae rēs ab eō erant factae.
2. Arbor ab Augustīnō et ab eius amīcīs est petīta. Cōnsilia capta erant ab eīs dē fūrtō.
3. Omnia pōma ex arbore erant capta. Nōn multa tamen eōrum sunt ā fūribus comēsa.
4. Cum Augustīnus fūrtī erit accūsātus, dolēbit.
5. Sī inīquitās ab Augustīnō erit intellēcta, is pūnīrī cupiet.

TEACHER BY THE WAY

This portrait of Augustine like that on p. 364 (SE) depicts him as the Bishop of Hippo. However, his garb is not necessarily that worn by bishops in the fifth century but that which became canonical dress in the Middle Ages.

The headdress known as a miter (*mitra*) is the sign of episcopal office, which the bishop accepts during his ordination as a bishop. It consists of two triangular pieces of stiff cloth that are joined by two *infulae* or strips of cloth from behind. While the tradition of such a headdress dates back to that worn by the Jewish high priest, it is only in the eleventh century that we have written documentation of its use by bishops. The miter's embellishment shifted through the centuries following contemporary decorative taste.

On the third finger of his right hand, Augustine wears his ring signifying his being wedded to his diocese. Such rings usually depicted the bishop's coat of arms and the ring would have been used to seal official documents and correspondence. The insignia on Augustine's ring is echoed on the glove covering his left hand.

The crozier, *baculus pastōrālis* in ecclesiastical Latin, is similar to a walking stick or shepherd's crook. The latter evokes the bishop's role as shepherd of his flock, like Christ the Good Shepherd. Some believe the crozier may also hearken back to the Roman *lituus*, a rod used by an augur.

The cope from the Latin *cappa* is a vestment worn by the ordinary priest or the bishop in processions and for special liturgical occasions. Beneath his cope, Augustine wears a surplice, from the Latin *super* "above" and *pelliceus* "made of skins, leather," which was introduced in northern Europe. The Augustinian Canons, a group of religious men founded in the eleventh century who followed the religious rule established by St. Augustine, wore a surplice as part of their regular dress, known as a habit. The artist may have been thinking of this. Beneath the surplice is the alb, "*alba*," a white robe more closely fitting than a surplice. These latter were ordinary liturgical dress for priests and bishops.

In his left hand in both paintings, Augustine has a book, which would refer both to his episcopal authority as teacher and to his own scholarly writings.

Beginning in the seventeenth century, it became common for bishops to wear a *crux pectorālis*, a pectoral cross. Placed near the heart, the cross, which initially contained the relic of a saint or of the "True Cross," served as a reminder of Christ's suffering. In the painting on p. 390 (SE), Augustine wears a pendant around his neck, which probably contains a relic.

The term "bishop" is derived from the Late Latin *epīscopus*. The bishop governs a diocese (from the Greek *diokesis*, meaning "management of the household"). For many centuries, in each city, the Roman *cīvitās*, was a diocese with its own bishop. When Diocletian reorganized the empire, he divided it into twelve dioceses, each governed by a *vicārius*. In the Church of England, a vicar receives a stipend for serving a parish. In the Episcopalian Church, a vicar is in charge of a chapel or a mission.

CONSIDERING THE CLASSICAL GODS

PAGE 391

Standards 2.1, 2.2, 3.1, 3.2

ODF 3.12

TEACHER BY THE WAY

Reproduction without the participation of a male is called parthenogenesis.

TEACHING TIP

Ask students to explain the etymology of "parthenogenesis."

TEACHING TIP

The teacher may wish to have students read Ovid's story about how Vulcan traps Mars and his wife Venus who are having an affair. Alternatively, have half of the class read Ovid's version and the other half read the version in the *Odyssey* when the bard Demodocus is entertaining at the banquet in Phaeacia.

COMPREHENSION QUESTIONS AND ANSWERS FOR PAGES 391–392 (SE)

Reproducible versions of the questions alone are available at **www.lnm.bolchazy.com**.

1. The story of Vulcan provides evidence for the oral tradition in mythology. Cite that evidence.

   The two different explanations for Vulcan's physical challenge—the result of Vulcan's interference in a quarrel between Jupiter and Juno and Vulcan's being flung down to earth by Jupiter in a fit of rage, and Vulcan being cast out of heaven by Juno who was ashamed of his deformity—attest to the oral tradition.

2. Recount from earlier in the text (p. 274 [SE]) how Vulcan used his metallurgical skills to trap his wife and her lover.

   According to tradition, Vulcan set a trap with invisible chains in his bed, which ensnared his wife Venus and her lover Mars as they were about to commit adultery again.

TEACHER BY THE WAY

Vulcan was associated with destructive fire in early times and was also perhaps a smithy god. He is thus the antithesis of Vesta, the goddess of the sacred beneficent flame that represents the stability of the state. In Book 8 of the *Aeneid*, Vergil tells the story of Cacus, a fire-breathing monster who is the son of Vulcan. Cacus was a seer in Etruscan mythology, suggesting that Vulcan also had Etruscan connections of some sort. A festival for Vulcan was celebrated in August and live fish from the Tiber were thrown into the fire—a hard rite to explain! His shrine was outside the Servian wall, though a new one was built in the Campus Martius, both locations suggesting fear of fire within the city itself. Vulcan had an important cult in Ostia where

472 • Latin for the New Millennium: Teacher's Manual, Level 1

he was the patron god of the city. In classical times he was identified with Hephaestus and became the divine craftsman and god of forges, which relate to another Roman attribute, *Mulciber*, smelter of metals. His workshops were in the hollows of the volcanoes under Mt. Aetna with the skilled and powerful Cyclopes as his assistants, according to Hesiod, author of the *Theogony*.

PAGE 392

TEACHING TIP
The teacher may choose to use the picture of the Doric temple of Hephaestus to open a discussion on the types of columns used in Greek and Roman architecture.

TEACHER BY THE WAY
Like the Parthenon, the Temple of Hephaestus is an excellent example of the classical Greek sense of proportion and symmetry. The columns follow the formula for a classical temple, L = 2W + 1 (the corner columns are counted twice).

TEACHER BY THE WAY
This view of the Pantheon shows how its porch, built in the form of a classical temple facade, masks the round interior crowned by the dome. The pediment, the triangular space above the inscription on the facade, would have held a set of statues of the Olympian pantheon. The unabbreviated inscription reads as follows: M[ARCUS].AGRIPPA.L[UCI].F[ILIUS].CO[N]S[UL].TERTIUM.FECIT

This inscription translates as "Marcus Agrippa, son of Lucius, consul for the third time, built this."

TEACHING TIP
Instruct the students to find Agrippa and Hadrian on the timeline on pp. 405–408 (SE).

PAGE 393
Standards 1.1, 2.1

TEACHING TIP
The teacher may wish to have the students research the specifically Roman features of the Pantheon's architecture and to discuss its use in ancient and later times and how much of the original structure is extant.

TEACHER BY THE WAY
This photograph demonstrates how the sunlight coming through the *oculus* (which is ca. thirty feet in diameter) shone in the course of the day on each of the gods' shrines. The dome is a testament to Roman engineering.

PASSAGE TRANSLATION

Aeneas had wandered with great constancy for a long time through many lands and had sailed through many seas. Many things had been seen and done by him. Foreign lands full of dangers had been sought by him. The queen Dido had been loved and afterward abandoned by him. At last Aeneas was in Italy near his future fatherland. There terrible enemies were expecting him. Being about to fight with them Aeneas needed weapons. His mother Venus went to Vulcan and asked: "Will you be able to prepare a shield for my son?" Venus said that Aeneas would conquer the enemies and that after Aeneas the Romans would have great glory. <She> said that Vulcan had to engrave all these things on the shield. Vulcan forged the new shield, armed with which Aeneas entered the battle and defeated the enemies.

TEACHING TIP

The teacher may want the students to review the story of Aeneas in Chapter 2 of RRA.

CONNECTING WITH THE ANCIENT WORLD

PAGE 394

Standards 2.1, 3.2, 4.2

COMPREHENSION QUESTIONS AND ANSWERS FOR PAGES 394–395 (SE)

Reproducible versions of the questions alone are available at **www.lnm.bolchazy.com**.

1. Provide the various Latin terms for schools and teachers and their English meanings.
   paedagōgoi, "leaders of the children"
   lūdus litterārius, primary school
   schola grammaticī, middle school
   grammaticus, the middle school teacher
   schola rhētoris, upper school
   rhētor, the upper school teacher

2. Teachers in today's high school English or language arts class require students to make frequent revisions to their compositions. What parallel do you find in Roman schooling?
   The Roman parallel is found in the practice which gave rise to the Roman proverb *Saepe stilum vertās*, "Turn the pen often," an admonition to revise one's writings frequently.

3. List the Latin and their English meanings for the six parts of a public speech.
   exordium, the beginning
   nārrātiō, the statement of facts
   partītiō, the outline
   cōnfirmātiō, the proof
   refūtātiō, the refutation
   perōrātiō, the summing up, or conclusion

4. Why did Roman upper school education devote so much time to public speaking?
   Excellent public speaking skills would serve Romans well in public life where oratory played a key role.

PAGE 395

TEACHER BY THE WAY

Educated Romans could both read and speak Greek. Tradition has it that as he lay dying Julius Caesar addressed his assassin and former friend Brutus in Greek "*kai su teknon*?" In English this means "And you, child?"

Review 7: Chapters 19–21 • 475

TEACHER BY THE WAY

According to tradition, Ephesus was founded by Greeks in the eleventh century BCE. Lydians, Persians, and the Syrian successors of Alexander the Great controlled the city. It became part of the kingdom of Pergamum in 199 BCE and when Pergamum was bequeathed to the Roman people in 133 BCE, Ephesus was included. In the first century BCE, Ephesus figured prominently in two massacres, one of which was initiated by King Mithridates of Pontus who signed the decree ordering all Romans in Asia to be put to death. Some 100,000 Romans thus met their deaths; the massacre continued for four years until the Roman leader Sulla executed the leaders of the rebellion. Augustus established Ephesus as the capital of the proconsular province of Asia, which was governed through the Senate. Ephesus enjoyed great commercial prosperity as a port.

Ephesus was renowned throughout the ancient world for its temple to Artemis, hailed as one of the seven wonders of the ancient world. In its last restoration, the temple with its intricately carved column capitals measured four hundred feet in length by two hundred in width. The Goths destroyed it in 262 CE. According to the Acts of the Apostles, the goldsmith Demetrius and others fomented a riot against St. Paul, who had lived and preached in Ephesus for three years. Paul's disciple Timothy was a native of Ephesus. Next to Antioch, Ephesus was the second most important Christian community in Asia Minor.

Today, tourists flock from Mediterranean cruise ships to visit Ephesus, whose Roman remains include a well-preserved theatre, the largest in Anatolia, with a capacity of 25,000. It was here that Demetrius and his followers launched their rebellion. An undocumented but much-revered tradition that Mary, the mother of Jesus, died in Ephesus also attracts pilgrims to the "House of Mary."

EXPLORING ROMAN LIBRARIES

PAGE 396

Standards 2.1, 2.2, 3.1, 3.2, 4.2

TEACHER BY THE WAY

Trajan's ashes were contained in a golden urn at the base of the column, and on its summit was a golden statue of the emperor. A spiral staircase runs inside the column, lit by narrow slits in the wall. In the sixteenth century the statue was replaced with the figure of St. Peter.

COMPREHENSION QUESTIONS AND ANSWERS FOR PAGES 396–399 (SE)

Reproducible versions of the questions alone are available at **www.lnm.bolchazy.com**.

1. How did the emperor Trajan's forum reflect his respect for learning?

   One of the key features of Trajan's forum was a set of paired libraries, one for Latin texts and one for Greek texts, that flanked the Column of Trajan.

2. Many of the first public libraries in the United States were built with funds offered by the nineteenth century millionaire industrialist Andrew Carnegie. Cite a comparable development in ancient Rome.

   Roman aristocrats like Pliny the Younger and the consul Tiberius Julius Celsus dedicated libraries for public use, the former in Comum in northern Italy and the latter in Ephesus in the province of Asia.

3. How does the modern book differ from the "book" of ancient Rome?

   While the modern book may be an audio edition, a book on tape, a printed and bound version either hardcover or paperback, or an internet edition, Roman books were actually rolls made of sheets either of papyrus or of animal skin.

PAGE 397

TEACHER BY THE WAY

During the imperial period, the emperors regularly renovated and redecorated various buildings throughout Rome. In addition, they built new buildings and monuments. Alongside the Roman Forum, five imperial fora were constructed. The following brief descriptions follow chronologically.

- The **Forum of Julius Caesar,** completed by his heir Octavian Augustus, is aligned with the Curia where the Roman Senate met. In the center of a large colonnaded square stood an equestrian statue of Caesar. Directly opposite the Curia which Caesar had rebuilt, he erected the Temple of Venus Genetrix, mother of Aeneas, the mythical founder of Rome. The alignment of Caesar's forum with the Curia, his own statue, and the temple set the dictator up as an equal to the Senate.

Review 7: Chapters 19–21 • 477

- The **Forum of Augustus** is wedged into an odd-shaped piece of land he was able to purchase from the landowners. The back of the forum consists of a thick, somewhat irregular ninety-plus-foot wall that served as a firewall protecting the forum from the densely residential Subura area behind it. Built to serve as additional space for legal and commercial meetings, the forum like Caesar's delivered a powerful message. The forum centers on a Temple to Mars Ultor, which Augustus had vowed to build in thanksgiving for his victory at Philippi over Brutus and Cassius. Mars, according to one of Rome's foundation myths, impregnated the Vestal Virgin Rhea Silvia, who bore the twins Romulus and Remus. The two porticoes flanking the temple contained statues of Aeneas with Anchises and Aeneas and the ancestors of the Julian clan on one side and those of Romulus and distinguished figures of the Roman Republic on the other. The forum also featured a statue of Augustus on his triumphal chariot. The message is clear—Augustus is the culmination of this Roman history. Thus, the forum serves as a visual complement to Vergil's *Aeneid*.
- The **Forum of Vespasian,** also known as the Forum of Peace, consisted of a large open space surrounded by a portico with four exedra. The complex contained two libraries and the Temple of Peace, which Vespasian built to commemorate his victory over the Jews. The menorah and other treasures taken from the Temple of Solomon in Jerusalem and depicted in the reliefs on the Arch of Titus were probably housed here.
- The **Forum of Nerva,** also called the *Forum Transitōrium*, served as a passageway between the Forum of Peace and the Forum of Augustus. A narrow elongated area, the forum's chief feature was a Temple to Minerva as patron of handicrafts. Little of the temple remains today but a relief sculpture shows scenes of handicraft production.
- The **Forum of Trajan** is a singularly spectacular construction and one of the few public buildings in Rome whose architect is known—Apollodorus of Damascus. According to tradition, Pope Gregory the Great was so impressed with Apollodorus's architectural achievement that he prayed for the salvation of the "pagan's" soul. The forum consisted of four major spaces: a large open square surrounded by a colonnade with an equestrian statue of the emperor Trajan at its center; the Basilica Ulpia (Trajan's family name) with semicircular halls at either end; the Column of Trajan, some ninety feet tall, which housed Trajan's ashes, flanked by two libraries; and the Temple of the Divine Trajan.

PAGE 398

TEACHER BY THE WAY

From early times Romans washed for health and cleanliness. By the late Republic bathing had become as important as dinner in the daily routine. Some houses still had private bathrooms, but most Romans preferred the public baths, first heard of after the Second Punic War. At least 170 were operating in Rome in 33 BCE, a number that eventually rose to over 800 during the empire. The best examples of the imperial *thermae* are those of Trajan, Caracalla, and Diocletian.

The Baths of Trajan were built (104–109 CE) on and near the *Domus Aurea* of Nero. The overall dimensions, including the grounds, measured 1,072 x 1,023 feet; the building itself was 517 feet wide by 689 feet long. The complex as usual was axially symmetrical and included the usual rooms plus a swimming pool, palaestras for exercise, and exedras for philosophical discussions or athletic contests.

The best preserved and surely the most magnificent of the *thermae* are the Baths of Caracalla, still a setting for summer outdoor opera performances. The whole exterior was a mile in circumference, and as many as 1,600 bathers could be accommodated at one time in the complex. They could be bathing, walking casually with friends while "conversing idly or on philosophical subjects; thronging the lecture rooms; running, jumping, racing, playing ball, or watching spectator sports in the stadium at the back" (P. L. MacKendrick, *The Mute Stones Speak* [New York, 1983], p. 400). Some say the second floor housed picture galleries and libraries, also open to the visitors, although there is no direct evidence for this.

If Caracalla built the most magnificent baths, Diocletian surely built the largest (dedicated in 305 CE). Situated in the northeastern part of Rome, it measured 1,235 x 1,202 feet (about 1½ million square feet!); the central building, 812 x 585 feet. Three thousand people could use this complex at one time. In addition to the usual amenities, the Greek and Latin libraries of Trajan's Forum were transferred here.

When Michelangelo designed the church of Santa Maria degli Angeli, he incorporated a part of Diocletian's Baths. It is in the nave of this church that the towering granite columns and the arched roof far above give some idea of the breathtaking grandeur that characterized the imperial *thermae*.

Information about the rooms in a bath complex can be found on p. 5 of this teacher's manual.

PAGE 399

TEACHER BY THE WAY

This tradition of calling the sides of the twice-used Greco-Roman papyrus sheets the *rectō* and the *versō* continued during the era of the writing of manuscript codices. One leaf or page of a manuscript on the front is called the *rectō* and on the back the *versō*. So, for example, F36ʳ means the *rectō* to folio 36, or in modern book terminology, this is page 71. When you turn F36ʳ over, you are looking at F36ᵛ which is the *versō* and which again, in modern book terminology, is page 72. The words *rectō* and *versō* live on in modern publishing houses where the recto is still the front of the page and the verso is the back of the page.

MĪRĀBILE AUDĪTŪ

PAGE 400
Standards 1.1, 4.1

PHRASES AND QUOTATIONS VOCABULARY

Alma māter.
almus, alma, almum – nurturing

Alumnus/Alumna.
alumnus, alumnī, *m.* – student

Floruit.
flōreō, flōrēre, flōruī, —— – to blossom, flourish

Vādemēcum.
vādō, vādere, ——, —— – to go

Verbātim.
verbātim (*adv.*) – literally, word by word

Annō Dominī.
annus, annī, *m.* – year
dominus, dominī, *m.* – master, lord

Exemplī grātiā.
grātiā + *genitive* – for the sake of

TEACHING TIP
Additional reproducible worksheets, morphology charts, and their associated answer keys, related to this material, are available for download at www.lnm.bolchazy.com.
- **Famous Words**